PSYCHOLOGY AND THE TEACHER

Other titles in the Cassell Education series:

Psychology and the Teacher

Fifth Edition

Dennis Child
Professor of Educational Psychology (Emeritus)
University of Leeds

CASSELL

Cassell
Wellington House
125 Strand
London WC2 0BB

387 Park Avenue South
New York
NY 10016–8810

First published by Holt, Rinehart & Winston in 1973
Fifth edition first published 1993
Reprinted 1995

British Library Cataloguing-in-Publication Data
A catalogue record for this book is available from the British Library.

ISBN 0–304–32651–8 (hardback)
   0–304–32649–6 (paperback)

Typeset by Colset Private Limited, Singapore
Printed and bound in Great Britain by
Redwood Books, Trowbridge, Wiltshire

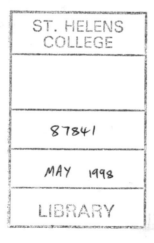

Contents

Preface to Fifth Edition

This book has now been in regular use by students and teachers for twenty years. During that time many readers have made useful comments and criticisms and they have informed the revisions. *Applications of Psychology for the Teacher*, written to accompany this general text, has found favour with students and continues to be used as a companion volume. *Readings in Psychology for the Teacher*, a Reader that accompanied earlier editions, is now out of print, but reference copies can be found in college, university and local libraries. Therefore, I have retained the references to that book (marked **R**). Those who have difficulty getting hold of the relevant journals should find the Reader helpful.

The last ten years have seen rapid and appreciable changes in the education system, some of which are rooted in psychological principles. The introduction of the National Curriculum and the attendant changes in curriculum emphasis, statements of attainment, standard assessment tasks (SATs) and profiles and records of achievement have given rise to many new and demanding activities for teachers. The basic subjects in primary school have been revisited and, amongst other things, new schemes for reading, speaking, listening, mathematics and science have been generated. The Reading Recovery scheme in particular has attracted a lot of attention. The Warnock Report continues to have an influence on the education of children with special needs and new procedures for identification (called 'statementing') have come into prominence with the introduction of the 1981 and 1988 Education Acts.

Career education and guidance is a buzz phrase at present with unemployment and shifting emphasis in the kind of work available to school-leavers. The use of computer aids in career guidance has blossomed in recent years. Changes in school life have led to increased stressfulness in the job of teaching. All these matters have received attention in the revision.

Mention is also made of new findings in brain localization. Within the province of learning, several interesting ideas about 'learning to learn' (metacognition), short- and long-term memory, how children probably construe their surroundings in forming scientific hypotheses and the increasing use of computer-assisted instruction are mentioned. Intelligence, as ever, attracts the eye of researchers and new ideas about its malleability, effects of diet, influence of coaching and practice in tests of all kinds and the information processing approach to intelligent behaviour are included. In the personality field, a little is added about adaptors and innovators and the ideas about the stressed personality type known as Type A.

Every effort has been made to update the references where the older texts are no longer relevant.

University of Leeds   *Dennis Child*
February 1993

Preface to First Edition

This book was written as an introductory text for students in colleges and departments of education. It should also serve those who are embarking on advanced courses in education and who wish to renew their acquaintance with basic concepts in the psychology of education.

The central aim of the book is to introduce teachers to elementary ideas in psychology which have some relevance for their work with young people. In addition to drawing on my own experience in teaching and teacher-training, I have benefited greatly from the publisher's findings in making contact with education lecturers in a number of colleges and departments of education and sounding out their opinions about the most important elements in a course involving educational psychology. From their comments, it has been possible to build up a picture of current curriculum content and aspirations. The text aims to include those topics which are representative of this picture.

Growth in the application of psychological principles to educational problems has become rapid and diverse in recent years. New and illuminating lines of approach are born out of, or become grafted on to, old ones. Occupational development and choice, creativity and curriculum development and design are but a few which have established such a firm place in educational psychology that they merit inclusion in a basic text.

The book has several special features which I hope will appeal to lecturers and students. I have deliberately started with a chapter introducing the meaning of psychology in educational settings in order to put the book in context. The choice of further topics has been governed by my conception of the role of the teacher. The better-established work of biologists on the biological bases of behaviour forms the foundation for a study of the less certain factors in educational practice. Chapters on motivation, perception and attention then lead into the core of the text which examines theories of learning and concept formation and shows how the effects of individual differences in intelligence and personality can be assessed and taken into account. With this knowledge the teacher should be in the position to create a stimulating learning environment in the classroom. He will then be called upon to evaluate the results of his efforts using standardized tests and examinations, and to give guidance in occupational and curriculum choice. The last chapter on psychological research in education is intended to act as a bridge between this introductory text and the more advanced and more recent approaches which the reader will meet during his studies.

By using the traditional topic approach of child psychology I have made it possible for students to dip in at a particular point to supplement lecture material or to find guidance for further study and reading. But the reader will soon become aware, from the extensive notes and cross-references, that the topics are interdependent. It could not be otherwise because human attributes are also interdependent.

A textbook is not the last word, but the beginning of several additional activities. With this in mind I have concluded each chapter with references and notes, further reading and points for enquiry and discussion. Experience with college and post-graduate students convinces me that they are not in possession of the statistical and methodological sophistication which would enable them to read, evaluate and use the information contained in research papers at the time when they need a basic text in educational psychology. I have therefore tried to select the less onerous examples which will aid students who wish to study a topic in greater detail.

The enquiry and discussion sections are intended to stimulate the investigation of important questions such as reward and punishment, incentives, self-fulfilling prophecies and streaming. These can be pursued in seminars and tutorial groups and particularly during teaching practice or on school observation. Several questions relate to the work of students in colleges in the belief that it is important to examine our own assumptions and arrangements with the same fervour as we would examine any other sector of education.

I also hope that the student will get personal satisfaction from a knowledge of psychology both as a discipline and as a means of exploring his own qualities as a person as well as a potential teacher.

No book of this kind could possibly be written without the help and encouragement of others. Among these I particularly want to thank Mick Adams of Endsleigh College of Education for reading the first draft and making many significant suggestions. To students and colleagues past and present I owe a debt of gratitude for their participation in sharpening my thinking in psychology. Michele Benjamin deserves a special word of thanks for her part in collecting opinions and information about curriculum content in a sample of colleges of education and in making smooth the tricky operation of compiling the finished article. Being a two-fingered and sluggish typist, I simply could not have coped without the help of Joyce McGregor who typed the whole manuscript. I am greatly indebted to her.

Acknowledgements relating to references, quotations and examinations material will be found at the appropriate point in the text.

University of Bradford   *Dennis Child*
January 1972

Chapter 1

Psychology and Education

No one today can afford not to know psychology; it touches virtually every aspect of your life.

(R. L. Atkinson *et al.*, *Introduction to Psychology*[1])

THE STUDY OF PSYCHOLOGY

Understanding ourselves and others has probably always been a human preoccupation. Certainly from the time when the first written record appeared it showed that we have a deep interest in human and animal behaviour. Yet our ideas have been almost entirely unsystematic and unrepresentative. Even now we casually watch others or listen with prejudiced ears to conversation and from this evidence build up distorted rules of thumb about human nature. In this way, the earliest explorers of human nature[2] produced a number of 'armchair' theories which became established as a branch of philosophy. Although this kind of theory is still in evidence and still finds a place in contemporary theorizing, it has been replaced gradually from the last century onwards by a serious attempt to adopt the methods of the natural sciences in order to make the study of behaviour more systematic. Outstanding examples of founder members of this movement are Wundt, in experimental psychology, Galton, in devising and applying statistical procedures to the study of genius, and Freud, who in his own way tried to build a model of the causes and cures of mental illness from careful observations of his patients.[3] But it is to the present century that we must turn to see a marked and rapid growth in the application of scientific methods to behavioural problems.

Psychology is concerned with a wide area of interest. It has been defined as the systematic study of animal and human behaviour (observable and mental processes) and covers all kinds of pursuits from making dogs salivate at the sound of a bell to a study of the growth of intelligent behaviour in humans. The term 'behaviour' includes all those aspects of human activity which we can observe: in effect it represents the outward life of individuals which is public knowledge and which can be noted dispassionately. But behaviour also involves personal experience, which can be studied only by asking individuals to express their feelings and thoughts. For example, frequently we sit motionless while watching television or solving a problem 'in our heads'. Yet our senses and brains are operating or 'behaving'. To discover anything about this internal action we would have to seek out some physiological method of 'tapping' the nervous system, and also would have to ask the individual about his or her experiences. This method of *introspection*, attempting to expose the private knowledge of persons by asking them to recount their conscious experiences, attitudes, opinions or values, is regarded with suspicion by some (for example the *behaviourists*), but it does constitute a widely used technique in some fields of psychology (**R**).[4]

APPROACHES TO PSYCHOLOGY

Contemporary textbooks[1] identify five perspectives in the study of psychology. Only brief mention will be made here of the approaches, but all of them appear regularly in this textbook.

The *biological* perspective places emphasis on the central fact that the human body is composed of chemicals. The chemicals associated with the brain and central nervous system are especially responsible for influencing behaviour not just of humans but all animals. One example of the work in this field is that of neurobiologists exploring the link between the brain and intellectual or speech functioning.

Behaviourism is well known these days and its impact is still with us. Observable behaviour is central to the behaviourist's concerns. The activities of 'out-of-sight' nervous systems or feelings are not of much direct interest to the behaviourist.

Cognitive perspectives, almost as a reaction to behaviourism, are especially directed to the internal processes assumed to accompany observable human behaviour such as thinking, remembering, decision-making, and so on.

Most readers must have heard of Freud. His views and those of his successors (neo-Freudians) are called *psychoanalytic* and concentrate on the possible roots of human behaviour in subconscious or unconscious motives. These motives were assumed to have their origins in the interaction between inborn instincts and child-rearing practices.

Finally, *phenomenological* approaches emphasize the here and now subjective experiences of humans, in stark contrast to the mechanistic beliefs of the other four approaches outlined above. Humans have centre stage as the 'actors' rather than the 'acted upon'.

The following branches of psychology, in general, call upon most of the approaches mentioned.

BRANCHES OF PSYCHOLOGY

The study of animal or human behaviour can take many forms. Some psychologists are concerned with general principles about *normal* or *animal* psychology without particular regard for the application of these principles. As the physicist attempts to discover the laws which govern planetary motion, so the psychologist might try to discover the laws which govern learning in organisms. At this broad level, the psychologist concentrates on *animal* behaviour either for its own sake or in the belief that, if humans have emerged from the animal kingdom as part of the evolutionary process, we will have brought with us some of the characteristics of animals. Therefore a study of animals might give a clue, at a rudimentary level, to human nature.

Some psychologists prefer to look at the *physiological psychology* of animals and humans, to study body structures and their bearing on behaviour. In our study of the brain and the central nervous system we shall find many examples of physiology being used to discern body–behaviour connections. *Social psychology*, the study of social institutions and their impact on the behaviour of individuals, concentrates on the external agencies that influence people, while physiological psychologists are more interested in the internal agencies. Social psychologists would be interested in, for example, the psychological characteristics of people in particular social settings such as the family or a village, the role of the head teacher in a school or the effect of family background on achievement at school. *Developmental psychology* is yet another example of a broad field of interest in which the physical, emotional and intellectual characteristics and development of children, from the prenatal stage onwards, are studied. Clearly, educational specialists draw extensively on this knowledge for its possible relevance to teaching. All these branches have their interconnections and it would be futile to attempt to devise a classification without recognizing this.

There have developed a number of applied fields which draw on the findings of general, physiological, social and developmental psychology. Thus, *clinical psychology* is the study of abnormal mental life and is of interest to psychiatrists and clinical psychologists. It has not only used the findings of other branches of psychology but has offered useful criteria for defining the attributes of normal mental life.[5] *Occupational psychology*, the study of such problems as vocational development and job satisfaction, has grown rapidly into a prominent applied field and a chapter of this book has been devoted to the problem of vocational development and guidance in schools. Other examples of applied branches are *industrial psychology* and *cybernetics*, which is the study of machine simulation of human functions, e.g. in the automaton or 'George', the automatic pilot in aircraft. For the purposes of student teachers and others engaged in work involving young people, an important applied field is *educational psychology*.

EDUCATIONAL PSYCHOLOGY

Traditionally, educational psychology has endeavoured to apply the findings of general, social and child psychology to assist in a better understanding of learning processes. (The term 'learning processes' includes social and moral as well as academic learning.) It seeks to discover, by studying the mental, physical, social and emotional behaviour of children and adults, the factors which influence the quality and quantity of learning; ideally it offers to replace 'common sense' or trial-and-error notions of learning and teaching with a variety of hypotheses regarding learning environments derived from systematic studies of individuals in those environments. The application of psychology in education, therefore, gives us a means of appraising individual children's similarities and differences and thus enables us to create more efficient learning environments for them. It provides us with a means of making evaluations of our own strengths and weaknesses as learners and teachers[6] (**R**) and is a useful background for anyone concerned with the young. It might also help us as parents or in the context of our daily lives and dealing with others.

It is important to remember that most of the concepts used in psychology and conse-quently applied in education are *invented* and not *discovered*. Theories, rationalizations and generalizations are concocted from observations. The concept of intelligence is a good example. Psychologists invented it in the nineteenth century. They defined what they meant by it and proceeded to seek out measures which would suit the definition. We define what we mean by a particular invention and then shape our researches to see how close our invention comes to the findings.

In this book an attempt is made to define and elaborate those aspects of psychology which would seem to illuminate the work of those dealing with young people. Psy-chology teaches us about people – how they think, respond and feel, why they behave as they do and what initiates and sustains their actions. Such fundamental processes are so central to our understanding of children's learning that they cannot help but form a substantial part of a course in teacher-training. We cannot rely on our independent observations alone. When we observe children in class or at play, it is deceptively easy to draw conclusions based on isolated incidents and to make generalizations about all children from these incidents. This is called *anecdotal evidence*. It is sometimes helpful as a starting point for more systematic observations or as confirmation of a general principle, but anecdotes cannot serve as the sole criterion for making decisions about children's education. Instead, psychologists try to formulate generalizations based on representative groups of people, ideally *in situ*, or on animals, where they think the findings can be transferred validly to human situations. Here the problem is to convert a generalization into a form which makes it useful in individual cases. However, these tightly controlled experiments have disadvantages, and we shall return to a considera-tion of these in Chapter 17 and in the Reader.

In attempting to write a comprehensive book suitable for students in training and for teachers who wish to refresh their background knowledge in educational psychology, there is the danger of covering too much in one volume. This is particularly evident when considering the basic, practical applications of educational psychology familiar to experienced teachers but not to the student. Obtaining a balance between theoretical and practical aspects under one cover and for such a wide readership, without producing an unwieldy volume and possibly losing the wood in the trees, was very difficult. I have therefore written a separate text, *Applications of Psychology for the Teacher*, which concentrates on the immediately practical contributions of psychology to learning and teaching. The two books should be used in conjunction with one another in order to achieve a coherent picture of the theoretical and practical issues involved. Cross-references are made in the *Applications* text wherever more detail is available in this textbook.

There are so many questions of common concern to psychologists, teachers, and social, youth and community workers that a single book could not possibly touch on them all. Therefore value judgements have to be made about the most important con-tributions. The first chapters deal with physical, emotional and cognitive growth in children and adults, on which subjects there is extensive literature. By starting with a consideration of the brain and the central nervous system, we are recognizing that the physical and mental lives of children have their origins in biological mechanisms. The fascinating story of brain function and its possible connection with day-to-day learning skills and problems has only just begun to unfold. We know in a general way that the nervous system is closely related to mental functioning, memory, emotional development and behaviour, and this has been a source of feverish research activity. Although at present the findings offer teachers no direct help in dealing with children, knowledge of the biological mechanisms provides a background context in which they can consider the behaviour processes of their charges.

It is a platitude to say that people must be motivated before they will learn, and psychologists have progressed beyond this point. For example, we are beginning to specify some of the conditions which give variations in levels of motivation both in terms of individual differences and in the environmental settings of the child. Other important questions connected with this are related to the effects of attention and perception in learning. There are also chapters in this book which look at the development of thinking skills in children and the influence of home and school on language acquisition – important in an essentially verbal world.

What have theorists to say about the processes of learning? So far, they have not been too revealing. The basic data on which they are working are the same, but the theoretical explanations are confusingly disparate. Nevertheless, the student who understands the origins of the present position concerning learning theories is more able to make decisions and to evaluate the innovations suggested in contemporary research than a student who is ignorant of them. Innovation and speculation in learning and teaching, as in any other field, are more likely to succeed when they are informed by sound theoretical frameworks.

Exciting new developments in the study of individual differences of intelligence and personality continue to shed light for everyone whose work entails communicating with children. Most frequently one deals with individuals, each of whom possesses a unique blend of mental, emotional, physical and social attributes. An awareness of the possible differences, even in cases where no precise measure is available, is an important asset in determining the motives and achievement of children and in making decisions about how to handle learning and behaviour problems. Intellectual, behavioural and emotional variability is the order of the day for all teachers, especially in these days of unstreamed classes. The teacher, therefore, must know what to look for and what action to take.

There comes a time when teachers have to take stock, when they have to determine whether their ambitions of encouraging and developing children's learning have been realized. For this, a knowledge of the art and science of assessment and evaluation is necessary. Examining the work of children is a skilled task if it is to be reliable and valid.

Recent experimental areas in psychology with obvious application in schools are vocational development and guidance, and curriculum planning. The former is, perhaps, of more concern to those in secondary and higher education, but the latter is of crucial concern to everyone in education. In one sense, it might have figured at the beginning rather than at the end of the book, but the technicalities of the subject are better considered after a grounding in other, more fundamental, topics in the psychology of education.

In the future

The most successful techniques in education seem to be those involving one-to-one methods between teacher and pupil. Programmes for children with special needs

(Chapter 12), teaching exceptional children (Chapters 9 and 12), methods used for teaching musical instruments or practical work or the New Zealand Reading Recovery scheme (Clay's work, discussed in Chapter 6) are largely dependent on individual teaching schemes. Were it not for the economic prohibitions which face education at present, there could well have been more facilities for individual tuition. As computers, word processors and their successors become cheaper, we shall see more of them in our classrooms (*electronic learning*).[7]

Most theories applied to educational problems tend to *describe* rather than *assist* learning and intellectual development. The reason is that the former is much easier than the latter; also, description is easier to live with than prescription especially when one is dealing with the future of someone else's child. Nevertheless, this is the direction in which the subject is heading. Teaching is becoming more diagnostic. Learning is becoming more clearly directed towards greater self-sufficiency in the learner. The history of the learner, such as home influences, early schooling, life experiences, is more and more the subject of intense inspection by researchers for its impact on later learning. Syllabuses and subjects are being dismantled and scrutinized for improved methods and sequences of presentation. A number of these advances are mentioned in subsequent chapters.

READING THE RESEARCH LITERATURE

Keeping up to date in a rapidly expanding market of research literature associated with the psychology of education is difficult for professional researchers, let alone teachers in training. Libraries are splitting at the seams with the onslaught of new periodicals and books reporting research, which, if nothing else, is a testimony to the increasing vitality and enthusiasm for pursuing answers to our many questions. Therefore it might be of help to the student to say a few words about reading research papers.

Much of what follows in the book is based on research findings reported in either learned journals or books. Some of these references appear at the end of each chapter. Those marked (**R**) also appear in the Reader. Quite understandably, the student will find a few of the technical papers almost unreadable. Children become 'subjects'; classes of children become 'biased samples' of size 'N'; 'variables' are manipulated using 't-tests', 'chi-square' or 'correlation coefficients', and so on. Fortunately, most journals use a similar format of which the summary, consisting of a few hundred words at the beginning or the end of an article and intended to give a brief impression of the major findings, should prove to be the most readable part. Also towards the end of a paper will be found a discussion section which endeavours to summarize the findings and make suggestions about their implications. Summary and discussion sections do not normally contain too much statistical terminology, and provided students can pick their way through the technical jargon of the subject matter of the paper, they should gain something from their reading.

The list of educational research journals is very long indeed. To get some idea of the British journals, the student should look at the *British Education Index*,[8] where a list of periodicals appears on the first page. This Index is also a most useful starting point for a project which requires recent research references. The Index and most of the major journals to which it refers are usually available in college and university libraries. To mention just a few of the most significant ones: *Educational Research* (and the leaflet *Educational Research News*) is produced by the National Foundation for Educational Research as a review of research for the benefit of teachers. This organization also publishes research reports in book form.[9] The *British Journal of Educational Psychology*, published for the British Psychological Society, contains many useful papers, although the statistical sophistication will probably limit the student to summaries and discussion sections in the absence of a college or university course on research methods and statistics.

Other British journals of psychological interest are *Educational Psychology*, *Educational Review*, *Durham and Newcastle Research Review*, *Research in Education*, *British Educational Research Journal*, and *Educational Studies*. At a more popular level, *Forum* sometimes contains useful papers of psychological significance and, in any case, it contains many relevant articles on the contemporary educational scene. The American research literature is vast and no attempt will be made here to select journals. Students are advised to browse in the library to discover for themselves the range and scope of this literature.

SUMMARY

Psychology is the study of overt and covert behaviour in humans and animals and therefore has an obvious contribution to make to our understanding of education problems relating to the learner, the processes of learning and the conditions of learning. Much of the information in educational psychology has been applied from specialist branches such as developmental, social, physiological and clinical psychology. As a scientific enterprise, the psychology of educational matters still has a long way to go (see Chapter 17 and Readings), and consequently the message of this chapter has been one of cautious optimism for the application of psychology to the daily routines of the teacher. While it cannot provide unequivocal or black and white answers to the teacher's problems, nevertheless it provides an essential ingredient in the diagnoses and decisions of classroom practice.

ENQUIRY AND DISCUSSION

(a) First impressions often become a means of deciding the nature of others. Consider the dangers of this approach, particularly when faced with a group of children with differing intellectual skills, personalities and social experiences.

(b) What do you think will be the difficulties in building up a profile of individual pupils?

(c) How do teachers actually keep up to date in the psychology of education? Ask them when you are out on school observation or practice.

(d) Discuss the educational psychology syllabus with your tutor in terms of: (1) the significance of the content for teachers; (2) why particular aspects are chosen in preference to others; and (3) how the course will unfold and its rationale.

(e) Next time you visit the library, look out for the research journals in education. Select one or two psychological journals to get some idea of the format. At this stage you may find that only the summaries are readable.

(f)   As a group discussion with a tutor, examine some of the most influential educational experiences which you had as pupils. As the course unfolds, it is hoped that many of these experiences will be explored for their psychological significance.

NOTES AND REFERENCES

1.   R. L. Atkinson, R. C. Atkinson, E. E. Smith and D. J. Bem, *Introduction to Psychology*, Harcourt Brace Jovanovich, New York, 1992 (11th edn).

2.   Educational theory prior to the nineteenth century was conducted largely from the comfort of the theorist's armchair. Jean-Jacques Rousseau, in his *Émile*, theorizes on the subject of child development, and Hippocrates and Galen many centuries ago speculated about personality typologies (Chapter 11) without the advantages of experimental evidence. Ancient Greece is regarded as the source of these methods of deductive reasoning. Aristotle's name, for instance, is usually associated with the technique of using syllogisms as a means of arguing a case. For a definition of these earlier methods, read K. Lovell and K. S. Lawson, *Understanding Research in Education*, University of London Press, London, 1970.

3.   Sir Francis Galton is recognized as the founder of psychological studies of individual differences. In 1869 his book, *Hereditary Genius*, marked the beginning of a movement applying scientific and mathematical methods to the study of human capacity. Wilhelm Wundt, a German physiologist, turned his scientific training to the study of psychology and established the first experimental laboratory in 1879. At the turn of the century, Sigmund Freud founded the school of psychoanalysis. As a qualified doctor and neurologist interested in the mentally ill, Freud was prompted to direct his energies to curing the mentally disordered.

4.   (R) J. Richer, 'Two types of agreement – two types of psychology', *British Psychological Society Bulletin*, **28**, 342–345 (1975). This paper raises a central issue in psychology: the place of introspection in a behavioural science. Much has been written on the subject because it constitutes a widely used source of information. Some, like Hebb in the paper 'What psychology is about' in the Reader, are decidedly against the method, and this could fruitfully be read alongside Richer's.

5.   We shall see in the chapter on personality that Eysenck used the symptoms of the mentally ill, particularly neurotics and psychotics, for defining the dimensions of personality believed to be common to us all. His claim is that the mentally ill are simply extreme examples in a continuum of personality qualities which are approximately normally distributed in the population. It is interesting to note how frequently extreme conditions are used as the basis for defining a dimension of behaviour.

6.   (R) R. Glaser, 'Educational psychology and education', *American Journal of Psychology*, **28**, 557–566 (1973). See also the first entry in Further Reading.

7.   A recent scheme initiated in America by C. Whittle, an industrialist, seeks to replace teachers with an 'electronic learning system'. Every student will have a computer/word processor which will be on line to a library of disks carrying a detailed breakdown of all the subjects in the curriculum. Mass communication is proposed, bringing well-developed lectures (not unlike the Open University system in the UK) to large numbers of pupils who would have their own monitors.

8.   The *British Education Index* is published three times a year by the University of Leeds. It contains a catalogue of references to research in Great Britain which might be of interest to educationists.

9.   Three recent examples of books produced by NFER-Nelson are: D. Vincent with J. Powney, L. Green and J. Francis, *A Review of Reading Tests*, 1983; B. Goacher and M. I. Reid, *School Reports to Parents*, 1984; and E. E. Clough and P. Davis with R. Sumner, *Assessing Pupils: A Study of Policy and Practice*, 1984.

FURTHER READING

The paper in Notes and References by R. Glaser[6] gives an interesting argument for an 'interactive mode of operation between application, technology and basic science' using four central areas of: subject-matter learning, basic aptitudes and abilities, individual differences, and testing and measurement. Chapter 17 and the Reader provide further reading on the question of new approaches.

L. Cohen, J. Thomas and L.Manion (eds), *Educational Research and Development in Britain 1970–80*, NFER–Nelson, Windsor, 1982; N. Entwistle (ed.), *New Directions in Educational Psychology I. Learning and Teaching*, Falmer, London, 1985.

E. G. S. Evans, *Modern Educational Psychology: An Historical Introduction*, Routledge and Kegan Paul, London, 1969. The writer gives a historical perspective to our present educational psychology scene. This is the kind of book the student can return to as the course proceeds. For an introduction to approaches to psychology, dip into the book by J. Medcof and J. Roth (eds), *Approaches to Psychology*, Open University, Milton Keynes, 1979.

R. L. Atkinson, R. C. Atkinson, E. E. Smith and D. J. Bem, *Introduction to Psychology*, Harcourt Brace Jovanovich, New York, 1992 (11th edn) is among the most comprehensive and readable general textbooks in psychology. E. R. Hilgard was the original author.

Chapter 2

The Nervous System

The most important scientific enterprise of all time is now well under way: the search for human nature within the living tissues of the brain. The machinery inside our heads does not yield its intricate secrets easily but new discoveries and ideas about how it works are already displacing the simple-minded psychological theories of past decades.

(Nigel Calder in *The Mind of Man* [1])

Human nature is an extremely complex affair. The variety of possible human experiences and their impact on our development is in itself a vastly intricate subject, the surface of which we are only just beginning to scratch. At the core of the problem is an organism whose biological equipment sets the scene for the immense potentialities of each person's lifestyle. The statement by Calder with which the chapter began is, however, an overstatement. It is important to reflect on the argument [Joynson[2] **(R)** and Hebb[2] **(R)**] that if human behaviour is ultimately capable of being explained in terms of the physiology of the nervous system, then there will no longer be an independent science we can call psychology! With this teasing philosophical problem, let us take a cautious look at some of the biological equipment of human beings.

It is now firmly established that certain body structures are closely linked to the behaviour we can observe in animals and humans. The central nervous system, in particular the brain, is undoubtedly the most important structure in this respect. Injuries to specific parts of the brain, as we shall see presently, cause specific behaviour changes and disorders; severing nerve fibres in the front part of the brain can bring about obvious and sometimes radical changes in the personality of individuals; abnormalities in brain or nerve structures at birth bring with them a corresponding variation in, or absence of, behaviour consistent with normal brains. But our knowledge of the precise causal connections between behaviour and body mechanisms is far from complete. For instance, we have only a gross and sketchy notion of the part played by the brain in emotional activity, perceiving and memory. Nevertheless, what little we do know is important for any student of human behaviour.

ORGANIZATION OF THE NERVOUS SYSTEM

The two bodily control systems of particular interest are the nervous and endocrine systems.[30] At present we will look at the reception, transmission and control mechanisms of the nervous system. For a detailed but readable description of the structure and functioning of these systems the student is recommended to read a basic text in biology or psychology.[3]

The nervous system has been classified in several ways, the classifications depending on the location or function of the various portions of the system. Common to all these classifications is the *central nervous system* (often abbreviated to CNS), comprising the brain, brain stem and spinal cord, and the *peripheral nervous system*. The CNS is a central mass of nerve cells which integrates messages received from *receptors* and sends out responses to the *effectors*. These messages are sent through the nerve fibre system of the peripheral nervous system.

The peripheral nervous system is composed of two functional parts called the *somatic* (or *voluntary*) nervous system and the *autonomic* (or *involuntary*) nervous system. The somatic nervous system supplies, as indicated in the last paragraph, the sense organs with nerve fibres to the CNS (*receptor fibres*) and from the CNS to the muscles (*effector fibres*). It is responsible for: (a) transmitting impulses set up in the sense organs by external or internal stimuli (sights, sounds, source of pain, etc.) to the brain (interpreting and responding to these receptor impulses is done within the brain) and (b) transmitting the effector impulses from the brain through the spinal cord to muscles which then contract if required. The final phase represents a response to the stimulus.

The somatic nervous system can be brought under the direct control of an individual. When a hungry child sees an inviting apple he or she might reach out, pick it up and eat it. The stimulus through the sense of sight has set up impulses transmitted through the optic nerve fibres to the brain, from which the effector impulses are transmitted to bring about an appropriate response pattern of muscular movements necessary for grasping and lifting the apple. Conduction paths from sense organs in other parts of the body, e.g. pain, temperature and kinaesthetic sensory regions (the *periphery*), pass through the spinal cord to the brain and back to the musculature by the same nerve but different fibres.

This, of course, is an over-simplified version of what goes on inside our bodies. The effects of socialization, to mention just one complication, may prevent the child from taking the apple if it belongs to someone else. Something intervenes between the stimulus and the response to inhibit the child from taking the apple. What precisely goes on in the brain in this case is still a mystery. In our discussion on motives we shall raise the matter again.

There is a way in which the receptor and effector organs are connected directly without necessarily involving interpretive functioning of the brain. This is called the *reflex arc*. Humans and certain higher animals are born with certain reflexes such as swallowing, eye blinking, sneezing, coughing and knee jerking in response to the presence of threatening stimuli. A puff of wind directed at the eye will cause the lids to close automatically to protect the delicate surface of the eye. Swallowing prevents unwanted particles from passing into the air passages leading to the lungs.

The other important system, the *autonomic nervous system* (ANS), supplies the glands and various organs of the body. As the term implies, the autonomic, self-controlling, involuntary system operates without a conscious effort on the part of the individual. Organs such as the heart, lungs, stomach, intestines, bladder and glands (tear and salivary) continue to throb, expand, contract, open, close and secrete quite independently of our conscious control. Routine operations that are managed by the system have their origins in the hypothalamus (see pp. 19–20) and pass from there to the organs via the spinal cord. Two divisions known as the *sympathetic* and the *parasympathetic* have been identified. The sympathetic portion innervates and stimulates organs which enable the organism to respond rapidly, especially in circumstances which spell danger or create fear. A frightening experience, as readers will know, causes increased and irregular breathing and heartbeat, sweating, pallor and the hair to stand on end. The extra supply of oxygen and release of energy-giving chemicals (glucose from liver glycogen, for instance) provide the excess energy which enables the organism to escape or fight. The parasympathetic section also innervates the same organs, but has the opposite effect on them, by acting as a braking system to the sympathetic nerves and slowing down the body mechanisms.

Implicit in all we said in the previous paragraph is the assumption that the organs regulated by the autonomic nervous system may not be brought under the control of the will. This, however, is not the case. At a simple level, it is possible to arrest lung action and bring about a change in heartbeat. More sophisticated control is achieved by those on the stage, who can think themselves into emotive states (weeping, anger) without really 'feeling like it'. Devotees of yoga are able to control their metabolic rates so as to reduce the amount of oxygen needed for body functioning. Several yogis[1] have been known to survive in confined spaces for much longer than would be possible in normal circumstances. Controlled experiments in the United States by Miller[4] support the view that autonomic functions are susceptible to conscious control. By a system of rewards in the form of a pleasant buzzer sound, he encouraged high-blood-pressure patients to think about reducing their heart rate. When the heart rate had reached a predetermined lower level, the buzzer sounded. In this way the patients were able to lower the rate to quite a marked extent. This process, by which a person regulates a normally involuntary body function (heartbeat, brainwaves, blood pressure, breathing, certain muscles) by the use of information from internal organs is known as *biofeedback*. It is rapidly becoming a most important development in medical science. Further uses to which biofeedback has been put are in the control of breathing during bronchitic or asthmatic attacks, by regulating air-passage sizes, and in the relief of tension headaches by controlling a forehead muscle which tightens during certain kinds of stress along with scalp and neck muscles.

This model has also been used to explain some psychophysiological disorders. One example, familiar to parents and teachers, is the child who because of fear (an exam, a distressing episode with a teacher) may claim to feel sick. The fear causes physical changes, some of which involve paleness and stomach contraction (even sickness). These symptoms are read by the parents as illness and the child is kept at home. This successful event may reinforce subsequent similar fearful occasions when the child begins to develop more chronic symptoms. These are often inadvertently learned responses to fear.[4]

RECEPTORS

Our lives are filled with testing the environment with our senses. In fact, our continued existence depends on our sensitivity to the environment and the appropriateness of our responses. To receive this information from the surroundings, there are groups of cells which are receptive to light, sound, touch, taste, smell, movement, heat and the like. The cells are known as *receptors*, and some groups of cells form the sense organs, such as the eyes, ears, taste buds on the tongue and 'olfactory' areas in the nose; less obvious receptors of pain, temperature change and movement (kinaesthetic sense) are widely distributed both outside and inside the body. The complex structure of these organs is a subject which need not detain us here.[5]

In general terms, a receptor cell will operate when there is a change or difference in the environment. The change is known as a *stimulus*. The difference in light intensity between the dark letters and the white background of this page enables you to observe the stimulus of the letters. When an object vibrates sufficiently it sets up a disturbance in the surrounding air. The disturbance spreads out in all directions from the source and, on striking the ear-drum, sets it in sympathetic motion. In turn this is transmitted to the sound-sensitive receptors in the inner ear. A change in pressure or temperature on the body surface is soon detected. Where a change does not reach a perceivable *threshold*, obviously it will not be detected. By 'threshold' we mean a level of stimulation below or above which we are not aware of the stimulus, and this constitutes the first clear source of individual differences. Regular background stimulation, e.g. the ticking of a clock or the pressure of clothes on the body, often goes unnoticed. This provides a sound reason why teachers should vary their voices and take note of the colours used on blackboards or visual aids. There are also variations in the threshold levels from one person to the next. It is thought that some people have low pain thresholds and soon succumb by showing marked anxiety symptoms. Some children are more upset by pain than others, although the differences probably arise from the experiential as much as from constitutional sources.

Vision

It has been shown that vision in the newborn is very rudimentary. Its eyes are sensitive to light and they can adapt to darkness. Colour discrimination may also develop very quickly in the first few months. But the eye lenses cannot alter (accommodate) readily to focus on objects at different distances. The eye movements are not co-ordinated. In fact, each eye can move independently at first in a fashion disturbing to unsuspecting mothers and fathers. They need not worry, because it is not an abnormality and eye movements ultimately become co-ordinated.

Colour blindness is the inability of some people to distinguish particular colours, chiefly red and green, which look greyish. Four in every hundred people are colour blind, so on average there will be one pupil in every class you might take who is unable to distinguish some portions of those colourful visual aids, colour reading or colour-factor apparatus so lovingly prepared.

There are several ways in which the eyes move according to their usage. *Pursuit movements* occur when we watch a moving object such as a car. *Compensatory movements* happen when we fix our attention on an object and move our heads from side to side. A third kind of movement is *convergence* or *divergence*, when an object travels towards or away from an observer. Finally, and most significant for the teacher of reading, is *saccadic movement*, which occurs when the eye moves along a line of print, and *fixation* when it pauses. The present sentence might require, on average, eight to ten eye movements, one every two words. But the length and difficulty of the words, coupled with the reading speed of a person, will govern the number of eye movements required by each person. The following sentences demonstrate the possible positions at which the eyes fixate as they jump along the line of words. The fixation points are shown as black dots.

The 'visual span' (the number of words taken in at each fixation point) of a slow reader is small, and the movements would look something like this:

The eye only sees when it is stationary.

For a fast reader, the following might apply:

Therefore the more you take in at each jump the bigger can be the jumps.

Reading efficiency, among other things, is related to saccadic movement because the distance between each fixation of the eye will govern the pace of reading – but *not* necessarily the understanding of the reading material. Pace is also affected by other mechanical aspects such as fixing for long periods at each point, using too many jerky forward and backward movements over the words already viewed, or by the arrangement of the print. Courses for improving reading speed concentrate some of their time on these factors.[6]

Hearing

Research with babies as the subjects is plainly a precarious business. Because they cannot communicate verbally and since their motor skills are still rudimentary, it is not always possible to plot the progress in some aspects of their development. Response to sounds seems to be fairly general, in that babies do not appear to discriminate readily between types of sound. Of course they react to sounds of varying intensity. Loud sounds may produce a startle reaction, although there could be dissimilar reactions to the same loud sound. But we have to wait until babies are several months old before they begin to respond to their mothers' voices in a way that differs from their responses to other similar sounds.

Hearing and sight are the two important communication senses for the teacher. Faulty hearing or eyesight in children can, and often does, go unnoticed by parents and teachers. The effect of these deficiencies on learning is obvious. The teacher can do much to improve the situation by judiciously placing children who have partial hearing or seeing defects in suitable positions in the classroom.

Touch

The sense of touch in infancy is our first hard evidence of reality. We probably underrate the importance of tactile experience for our children. Our preoccupation with the written and spoken word has led to our neglecting the sense of touch, which includes the detection of pressure, pain and temperature. Many primary school teachers now give their children opportunities to manipulate various materials or identify objects hidden from view using only the sense of touch, as in the 'feeling' boxes or bags used in primary schools. Some regions of the body are devoid of pain; some areas are more sensitive to pressure than others. The fingertips are particularly sensitive, whilst the sole of the foot is comparatively less discriminating.[7]

For further discussion of sensation and perception, see the beginning of Chapter 4.

TRANSMISSION

Reception of stimuli from outside or inside the body is only the beginning. Impulses set up by the receptors need to be conveyed to the brain for interpretation and possible response.

The impulses are the result of electrical and chemical changes passing along the length of the nerve fibres with great rapidity. The slowest is around one metre per second and the fastest approaches 100 metres per second. Witness the speed with which a pinprick which excites the pain receptors on the body will give rise to withdrawal of that area from the painful stimulus.

The tissues making up the nervous system are living cells of various shapes and sizes, depending on the work they do. Our bodies contain roughly 30 000 000 000 of these cells. Scientists are now able to study their structure using the powerful magnifying properties of the electron microscope.

Figure 2.1 gives an indication of a nerve fibre magnified many times. The whole nerve cell, or *neuron*, consists of the *cell body* with fine hair-like processes called *dendrites*

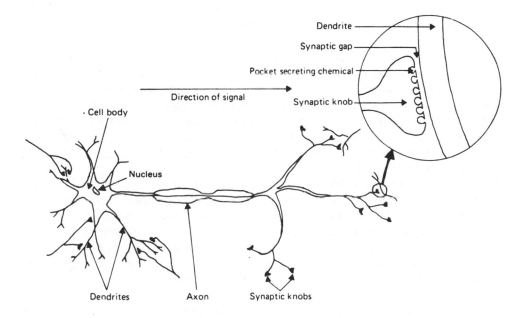

Figure 2.1 *A simplified diagram of a neuron or nerve cell.*

and a drawn-out portion which is the nerve fibre or *axon*, ending in similar processes to the dendrites. The tips of the processes end in knobs referred to as *synaptic knobs*. They form connections with the next neuron or with muscle fibres (end plates). The dendrites from one cell interlace with the synaptic knobs from an adjacent cell. Note from the diagram that they do not actually touch the dendrites. The minute gap (roughly a millionth of an inch) is known as the *synaptic gap* or *cleft* and the surrounding area as the *synapse*. Electrical impulses are conveyed along the neurons by means of electrical potential differences between the inside and the outside of the neuron membrane.

On reaching the synaptic gap the signal does not pass across in electrical form but by chemical means. On arriving at the gap (see Figure 2.1) the electrical impulse encourages the release of a transmitter chemical from the synaptic knob pockets into the synaptic material which either excites or inhibits the dendrite processes of the next neuron. The sum total of those excitatory or inhibitory impulses governs whether the impulses will or will not pass along the next neuron, and this is known as *facilitation* or *inhibition*. There appear to be no half measures. The neuron either fires or it does not fire, a phenomenon known as the 'all or nothing' principle. The chances of an impulse reaching the brain depend on the strength of the incoming signals, so the stronger the signal the more rapid is the impulse rate. The presence of inhibitory processes enables many possible courses of action (or simple inaction). It also helps to deal with all the extraneous perceptions in the field of view or hearing by eliminating them and preventing the brain from having to cope with an excess of information from the senses.[8]

THE STRUCTURE OF THE BRAIN

The brain is a massive concentration of nerve cells representing about a third of all the nerve cells in the body. The outer layer, or *cortex*, consists of many folds (*convolutions*) so as to confine a large surface area into a small volume. The finished article looks like a walnut. Brain tissue has one of two shades depending on its composition. Where there is an abundance of nerve cells the resulting tissue is called *grey matter*. The outer cortex consists of grey matter. Where there are many nerve fibres, which are normally surrounded by a white sheath, the tissue is called *white matter*. The cells require a constant and rich supply of oxygen, otherwise they develop serious and permanent malfunction within one or two minutes. In instances where oxygen supply is limited, as when the windpipe is blocked or, more directly, in stroke conditions, serious and permanent mental impairment can result. Well-ventilated classroom conditions are an obvious necessity to enable normal oxygen supply and the reduction of carbon dioxide for efficient brain activity.

Viewed from the side, as shown in Figure 2.2(a), there are two conspicuous folds which act as convenient boundary lines for the division of the brain. Bear in mind that we are looking only at one side. The other side, because of the approximate bilateral symmetry of the body, looks very much the same. The fold running across the top and a little way down the sides is the *central fissure*. The second, at the sides, is the *lateral fissure* (or fissure of Sylvius). Figure 2.2(a) also gives an idea of the positions of these fissures. Viewed from above, the brain appears to be divided into two equal parts by a deep groove, the *median fissure*, running the length of the brain with a connecting band of fibres, called the *corpus callosum*. Using these fissures as boundary lines,

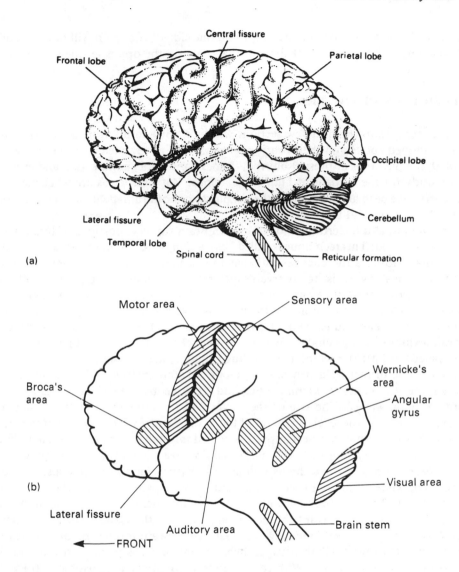

Figure 2.2 *Structure–function relationships of the brain (left side).*

Figure 2.2(a) shows how the surface cortex has been divided into *frontal*, *parietal*, *temporal* and *occipital* regions, or lobes. These lobes have corresponding partners on the other side of the brain. It is worth noting that these are only broad divisions partly reminiscent of the functional aspects of the brain.

If the brain is divided down the median fissure to expose the central organs, we find the termination of the spinal cord forming the *brain stem* and at the rear we find the *cerebellum*. The cortical region normally enveloping the brain stem (sometimes referred to as the *cerebrum*) can be seen as a thick and extensive covering of nerve cells. A curious crossover of nerve fibres occurs between each side of the brain so that the left-hand side supplies the right-hand side of the body and vice versa for the other side. Consequently, damage to the motor region (Figure 2.2(b)) on one side of the brain will bring about a corresponding malfunctioning of the motor activity on the opposite side of the body.

BEHAVIOUR AND THE BRAIN

Our chief concern in the next few sections will be a consideration of the parts of the brain mentioned above and their bearing on behaviour as revealed by recent research. Although the picture is at present blurred, it does constitute an important and exciting area of study for the student of human behaviour. But first let us see what methods researchers have been able to apply in their explorations of brain–behaviour connections using both humans and animals as subjects.

With animals, and in certain kinds of human brain surgery, portions of brain tissue have been removed. This technique is called *extirpation* or *ablation*. Observations could then be made to note the changes in behaviour accompanying extirpation. Severing nerve tracts can also give rise to observable differences in behaviour. Later we shall look at the effects of cutting the connections between the frontal lobes (leucotomy).

Electrical activity in the brain is also used. As we saw above, the impulses in the nervous system are the outcome of electrical and chemical changes, and the surface of the brain exhibits voltage changes which can be picked up using small plate-like electrodes placed against the scalp. These voltage changes are translated and recorded as a wavy ink-line drawn by a pen moving along a rotating drum. The instrument[9] is known as the *electroencephalogram* (EEG) and is erroneously regarded as a lie-detector recording 'brain waves'. The size of the waves and the number per unit of time are employed to estimate the level of arousal of the brain. *Electrical stimulation of the brain* (ESB), when an external electrical impulse is passed through electrodes which have been implanted in specific regions of the brain, has been most successful in identifying functions of deep regions of the brain as well as in studying emotion in animals.[10] Probes can be used, while an animal is conscious and without pain, to detect the activity of individual cells. This has been accomplished using microelectrodes[11] small enough to penetrate single cells and capable of movements of a few thousandths of a millimetre.

Post-mortem operations following the death of a brain-injured or brain-diseased patient can often reveal a link between behavioural patterns prior to death and the damaged portion of the brain. With conspicuous nerve tracts it is possible to trace the paths using careful dissection techniques. Hebb's work, to be mentioned in the section on intelligence,[12] was amongst the first to show that substantial proportions of the frontal regions of the brain in adults could be removed without seriously diminishing intellectual performance, although the same is *not* true of children.

A relatively new line of attack has been the study of *brain chemicals*, and we shall say more of this in the discussion of memory and the brain at the end of this chapter.

The brain stem

In Figure 2.2(b) the brain stem is shown as a deep-seated portion of the brain and in an evolutionary sense it is the oldest part of the brain. Crudely, it is a hollow tube of nerve tissue at the top of the spinal cord through which all impulses from the cord must pass *en route* to the brain. It consists of two areas, the *medulla* on the outside, surrounding the inner core or *reticular formation* which lines the hollow tube and runs through to connect with the hypothalamus and thalamus. The reticular formation has two systems, the *descending reticular system* for motor functions and the *ascending reticular activating system* (ARAS) for sensory functions. This latter system is of particular importance. In broad terms its function is to monitor the impulses coming from the senses. Stimuli are selected or ignored so as to prevent overloading the brain with too much incoming information. Selective attention, therefore, is accomplished by the ARAS. Interestingly, the receipt of sensory information is necessary for normal functioning of the brain. If sensory cues are eliminated, as in many experiments where the subject's arms are encased in tubes and the eyes and ears are shut off from the surrounding stimuli, the subject becomes disorientated and distressed. Students at McGill University[13] have been bribed with money to undergo this kind of experiment only to abandon it after a day because of intense frustration. It seems, then, that we must have sensory stimulation or spontaneous body activity. Humans and animals must satisfy what appears to be their basic need to explore, driven by curiosity. This fact has obvious implications for the teacher, who must take advantage of the ready-made inquisitive nature of children.

The brain stem is also related to the cycle of sleep and wakefulness. Different areas of the stem appear to be responsible for the states of waking, sleeping and dreaming. Operations on the brains of rats[14] have enabled the identification of specific regions relating to arousal (reticular formation), and sleep promotion (raphe nuclei). If the raphe nuclei are destroyed by operation or accidental brain damage in animals or humans, the victims are unable ever to sleep normally. In the normal mechanism of sleep and waking there appears to be a built-in *biological clock*, known as the *circadian rhythm*, which has its first settings laid down both by the control of the individual and by unconscious habits formed in childhood and the daily light and dark cycle, although scientists have shown that we have a natural cycle of 24.9 hours. Babies spend a fair proportion of their lives snoozing or sleeping during the day, and the habit carries over to reception classes, where the teachers are well acquainted with their children's dropping off during the afternoon.

Hypothalamus

Near the top of the brain stem and close to the pituitary gland we find the hypothalamus. This organ contributes to starting, maintaining and stopping behaviour associated with satisfying the basic body needs such as food, water intake and temperature control. The balance between need and satisfaction is called *homeostasis*. When 'fuel' is running low in our bodies, the homeostatic balance is said to be disturbed. Sensations of hunger leading to food-seeking activity will occur until the balance is restored by eating. The hypothalamus also exerts some control over the activities of the pituitary gland, which is an endocrine gland controlling the hormone-producing glands of the body.

There is good reason for believing that the hypothalamus acts like a thermostat in controlling appetites by switching the controls of hunger, thirst, temperature, etc. on and off in response to body chemistry. This control is sometimes referred to as the *appestat*. Much research using electrode stimulation of the brain (ESB) has enabled us to pinpoint the sites in the hypothalamus that are responsible for excitation accompanying hunger, thirst, temperature variation, sex, pleasure and aggression. In the next chapter, on human motivation, we shall often refer to these basic physiological needs of the body and our striving for their satisfaction. There are sites which inhibit excitation once the organism is satisfied. Anand and Brobeck[15] are largely responsible for this research and the theory of centres in the hypothalamus. In a hungry animal the 'eating' site brings about excitation which initiates eating. A corresponding satisfaction site begins to inhibit eating as the animal becomes satisfied. ESB of the hunger excitation site will, in fact, elicit eating long after the animal would normally be satisfied. Delgado[16] also used ESB techniques to control the aggressive behaviour and movement of animals – including bulls!

One alarming point about ESB is its immediate effect on specific behaviour patterns to which the recipient has little resistance. Movements and feelings can be affected and consequently a detailed study of emotions and abnormal mental life has been made. Already epileptics and those suffering from narcolepsy (irresistible feelings of drowsiness) have been helped.

Thalamus

The thalamus surrounds the top of the brain stem and has nerve connections from its position deep in the brain cortex in the roof of the brain. Fibres from all sense organs except the olfactory organs (the nose in humans) pass through this region. It provides a centre for sorting and directing information from sensory organs to specific sensory and motor regions in the roof of the brain (Figure 2.2(b)).

The limbic system

The limbic system appears as a lining to the roof of the brain and surrounds the top of the brain stem. The important functional units are the hippocampus, amygdala, the septal area and cingulate gyrus. Damage or stimulation to these units gives rise to perceptual changes and disorders such as an inability to distinguish visual cues (caused when the cortex in contact with these units is removed), impairment of recent memory (hippocampus) and the disappearance of avoidance behaviour, as when a person no longer appears to be afraid of painful stimuli (amygdala). Broadly speaking, the limbic system exercises some control over motivational and emotional behaviour.

Cerebral hemispheres

In this brief, whistle-stop tour of the brain we have now reached the extensive outer cover, described above as a highly convoluted grey mass of nerve cells. The outer layer is called the *cerebral cortex*, and has a conspicuous median fold that appears to divide the brain into two *cerebral hemispheres*. We also note four regions which will help us in defining some of the functions associated with the cortex (see Figure 2.2(b)).

First notice the *primary motor* and *sensory* areas bordering the central fissure. The motor strip, of all brain regions, has been explored in great detail by such men as Wilder Penfield.[17] Motor control of the left toe can be located at the top of the strip in the median fissure in the *right* hemisphere and, as we work down the strip, motor-control regions progress from the lower to the upper parts of the left-hand side of the body. The sensory strip on the other side of the central fissure is responsible for the senses of touch, pain and kinaesthesia. Note the separate regions for sight and hearing. A knock on the back of the head will make one 'see stars', because the visual area impinges on the rear of the skull.

Regions outside these areas are known as the association areas. They are divided into the *frontal association area*, sited in the frontal lobes, and the *PTO association area*, made up from portions of the *P*arietal, *T*emporal and *O*ccipital lobes.

The frontal association area has eluded the efforts of scientists to determine with any precision the purposes of the tissues. In adult humans, extensive damage to frontal tissue seems in most cases to have had little effect on performance in conventional intelligence tests. Hebb,[18] on the other hand, has noted that similar kinds of damage in children appear to have a lasting effect. It may be that frontal tissue is particularly relevant in establishing, in a diffuse manner, intellectual schemas in children. Damage at this stage will have a more potent, lasting effect on intelligent behaviour than when the schemas are well established and dependent on a wide distribution in the brain tissues. Psychologists seem agreed that the frontal lobes are connected with the processes involved in problem-solving. Certainly the size of the frontal lobes seems to be proportional to the intellectual complexity of animals. But this by itself does not tell us much about the workings of the lobes.

Teuber[19] supposes that the frontal lobes have something to do with willed or purposeful aspects of activity. If the side of the frontal lobe is stimulated the head moves sideways, leaving the eyes looking in the same direction. The conclusion from the experiment is that the eyes must have compensated, that is, they have rotated in their sockets in order to maintain their original position. Luria[20] has supported this point of view in his work on brain-damaged patients. Damage to certain areas of the frontal association region gives rise to incongruous behaviour and loss of power to control behaviour in some circumstances. These symptoms are known as the 'silliness syndrome'.

Deep in the frontal region we find areas which have a direct bearing on personality. *Frontal leucotomy*, or severing certain connections between the frontal lobes, has been used in the past to alleviate patients suffering from morbid conditions such as acute depressive states. The method is rarely used now because the damage to other surrounding tissues which accompanied the operation gave rise to complications which became manifest in such behaviour as carefreeness to the point of inconsequentiality. Several patients were not cured at all and some suffered post-operational epileptic fits. In the 1960s, Knight[21] replaced the surgeon's knife with radioactive 'seeds' planted in specific locations in the brain and the radiation from the seeds is just sufficient to destroy surrounding tissue in minute quantities with which it would be impossible to deal using surgery. Clearly, this reduced damage to surrounding tissue has proved extremely effective in curing suicidal and psychoneurotic conditions; but surgery is no longer used.

The PTO association area governed by the thalamus covers those remaining portions of the brain, chiefly the parietal, temporal and occipital lobes not already mentioned. Damage to the cognitive association cortex results in speech and language deficiencies known collectively as *aphasias*. Sensory and motor aphasias are possible. On the sensory side we find *auditory aphasia*, an inability to understand speech, and *visual aphasia* (alexia), an inability to read or understand the written language. This does not mean that all children who cannot read suffer from brain damage in this region. Far from it, for there may be many other causes. Motor aphasia appears in three forms: *verbal* (cannot pronounce words), *manual* (cannot write) and *nominal* (cannot name objects).

The impression so far has probably been one of a symmetrical brain with the right and left sides mirroring each other. But this is not correct. Figure 2.2 is a view of the brain from the left side. Three areas have been identified *on this side only* which are related to the aphasic conditions mentioned previously. These are Broca's and Wernicke's areas and the angular gyrus. The top view in Figure 2.3, left side, gives the corresponding language functions associated with these areas, which are speech, writing and language usage. The same locations on the right side have different functions in spatial and pattern arrangements.

These lateral differences first came to light in the last century when the French physician Paul Broca in the 1860s noted that damage to a particular point on the left frontal lobe was accompanied by a speech disorder where people had great difficulty saying words. They tended to speak in a slow and tortuous way. Some words were omitted and others, like nouns, had plurals removed. But they could understand what others were saying. The disorder is sometimes referred to as *expressive aphasia*.

Carl Wernicke in Germany in the mid-1870s found that those who had damage to a spot in the left temporal lobe could not understand words they had previously been able to before damage. Hearing words was not a problem, but understanding them and producing correct word order was difficult. This disorder is known as *receptive aphasia*.

He went on to produce a model of language functioning which was only slightly modified by Geschwind[22] to become the Wernicke–Geschwind model of language expression and understanding. The three areas of Broca, Wernicke and the angular gyrus are connected. There is also a connection between these and the motor, auditory and visual areas, depending on whether the language is being spoken, heard or seen. Broca's area stores the 'know-how' for articulating words and sends messages to that part of the motor region responsible for articulation (muscles of the lips, tongue and voice-box). Hence, any defect of the Broca area prevents proper expression of words. Wernicke's area stores auditory codes and word meanings. When someone else speaks, the auditory area is stimulated and the results sent to Wernicke's area for interpretation.

The two operations just described can be linked together. If someone heard a spoken word and was asked to repeat it, the sequence would be: ear (to hear the word) → auditory area → Wernicke's area (interpretation code) → Broca's area (articulation code) → motor area → speech organs (to say the word). The angular gyrus helps in the process of linking the written word (transmitted from the visual area) with the sound of the word stored in Wernicke's area. If someone is shown a written word and asked to repeat it, the sequence would be: eye (to see the word) → visual area → Wernicke's area (interpretation) → and so on through the same process as with the spoken word.

So far we have possibly given the impression that both sides of the brain are identical apart from the reference above to the cross-over effect where the right side of the brain controls the sensory and motor functions on the left side of the body, and vice versa for the left side of the brain and right side of the body. There is evidence for further differentiation of the right and left sides of the brain. Figure 2.3 is a diagrammatic view of the brain from above showing the main areas located so far. The pioneer in this area

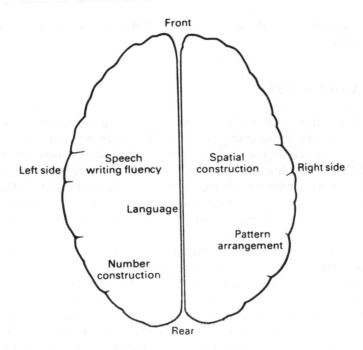

Figure 2.3 *Top view of brain showing lateral specialization.*

of split-brain research is Sperry (Nobel prize winner in 1981).[23] Studies with brain-damaged patients, for example those in whom the corpus callosum had been severed, show important lateral differentiation. The left side controls written and spoken language, spelling, reading and calculation, the right side controls spatial perceptual functions (patterns and geometric constructions).

Penfield has used ESB methods to tap the temporal lobes. From his work, patients have claimed to experience vivid 'flashbacks' to their past. He supposes this to be evidence that the brain retains in the interpretive cortex a record of conscious experience which can be revived randomly with electrical stimulation. Removal of the temporal cortex impairs visual learning where discrimination is required, for instance where coloured or shaped objects have become linked with food rewards in animal experiments. Symptoms similar to those described for a malfunctioning limbic system are also in evidence.

Cerebellum (or little brain)

The conspicuous lump of tissue at the rear of the brain and under the occipital lobes (see Figure 2.2(a)) is known as the *cerebellum*. ESB studies by Eccles,[11] using micro-electrodes, have attempted a minute exploration of this part of the cat brain. His conclusion is that it is responsible for the control of movement in routine activities such as walking and balancing. Damage to this region leads to coarse, clumsy and inaccurate movements. Eccles has refined his method to such a point that he can now detect information from a particular part of the body through the nerves to a specific cell in the cerebellum.

MEMORY AND THE BRAIN

Memory is one of those eye-catching subjects of interest to most of us and its study has been the centre of considerable research effort over the years. At a simple, but inaccurate level, the workings of the brain in the recall of information have been likened to a computer's storage banks. The analogy breaks down when we realize that information stored in a computer has a precise location and is retrieved in exactly the same form each time. 'Information' storage in the brain seems to be much more diffuse and can be of different natures, as in short-term or long-term memory (see also Broadbent's filter theory in Chapter 4).

Questions such as how and where memories are stored, or what part the brain plays in thinking and reasoning, remain unanswered, although several intriguing leads have come to light in recent years. Earlier experiments by Lashley[24] were unsuccessful in finding specific locations for these activities. However, we now know that if the hippocampus (part of the limbic system) is destroyed, individuals can no longer lay down long-term memories. Memories previous to damage are preserved and short-term memories such as recalling a telephone number for a few minutes are still possible, but no lasting learning is possible without the agency of the hippocampus. We have also seen various aphasic conditions when the PTO association area is damaged and the impairment of visual learning when the temporal cortex is removed.

Perhaps the most exciting advance in the last few years is the prospect of a chemical explanation of learning and memory. The electrical activity in the brain can be detected using the EEG, and there is no doubt about chemical processes occurring in the synaptic clefts. Further, when animals are taught to run a maze and the animals' temperatures are lowered to halt the electrical activity, the animals can still remember how to complete the maze task. This has forced scientists to conclude that memory storage is more likely to depend on chemical than on electrical factors. Baldwin, at Cambridge, has injected into the brains of goats drugs contrived to have a disruptive effect on electrical activity; yet this has no effect on short-term memory, and thus strengthens the case for a chemical theory of learning. Also, Brown *et al.*[25] (1988) have reported the importance of a chemical (NMDA) in the process of storing memories in new neuron connections.

But the evidence which has caused most concern among brain scientists emerges from the work of McConnell.[26] In 1966 he reported that if flatworms (not related to ordinary worms and much simpler in body design) were taught to turn in a given direction, and then were killed and their tissues injected into another, untutored flatworm, the latter was able to learn the task much more quickly than could non-injected animals. The theory behind this extraordinary result is that learning has been accompanied by a chemical change which has been transmitted with the cells into the host flatworm. More recently, hamsters were taught to enter a feeding box at the sight of a flashing light. RNA (short for a chemical found in all cells, ribonucleic acid) was then extracted from the brain tissue and injected into rats. The rats apparently turned toward the boxes when the light was flashed. Many explanations are possible, and the conclusion that there has been some chemical transfer of the stored information which, by injection, has found its way into the brain of the host is only one. Replications of this research afford little support for the original findings.

A stimulating report of possible chemical–long-term memory connections came from Hydén[27] in Sweden, who was able to show differences in the RNA content of cells before and after a learning task. An ingenious method was devised to contrast the left and right sides of the hippocampus part of the brain. By teaching normally 'right-handed' rats to carry out tasks with their left paws and comparing the chemical nature of the RNA content of the cells on the left and right sides of the brains of control and experimental groups, they were able to show that RNA was being manufactured more profusely on the relevant side for the paw in use. This research has been extended to demonstrate that a special protein molecule (S 100) suddenly appears in the cells extracted from the 'active' side of the brain. Though some scientists are sceptical about the connection between specific chemicals and learning, research continues in this field.[28] These researches, if nothing else, indicate how important chemical activity and protein manufacture are to the normal functioning of brain tissue. But we have a long way to go before the problem is resolved.

EMOTION AND THE BRAIN

You have just settled down in the carriage of a train. The train begins to move off and suddenly you notice your suitcase standing on the platform. Intense feelings quickly take over, along with a sudden burst of action or frozen dread. Our language is rich with expressions one might use to describe your state of mind and body - astonishment, alarm, panic, despair and many others. In cases of this kind we are said to be experiencing emotions. Disgust, joy, hopefulness, pity and a whole range of experiences from highly pleasant to deeply unpleasant sensations are described, although the hard evidence from physiology or psychology for the separate existence of these supposed emotional states is not yet available. One simple classification by Watson embraced fear, rage (anger) and love. More recently, some have postulated[29] that, as neonates, we experience only excitement, which becomes differentiated as we grow older into positive emotions (such as happiness, surprise, disgust) and negative emotions (such as anger, fear and sadness).

All these reactions, whether we attempt to distinguish different patterns of response for dissimilar circumstances or not, have their beginnings in internal physiological changes assisted by the sympathetic nervous system and the endocrine secretions.[30] A general definition of emotion would be 'physiological and psychological responses that influence perception, learning and performance'.[31]

The classical interpretation of emotive activity and responses was that, after a stimulus which is interpreted as threatening or pleasing has been received, the body reacts via the nervous and endocrine systems and these give rise to feelings of emotion. Fear, anger, joy and tenderness were said to be the outcome of body secretions and nerve action. Fear was then made manifest by increased breathing and heartbeat, drying of the mouth, hair on end, and so forth. Lange and James[32] contested this hypothesis independently and suggested quite the reverse. They maintained that the outward reaction of the body to an emotive stimulus - running, crying, fighting - gave rise to sensations of fear, anger, etc., expressed in the well-known James-Lange theory of emotion. James, summarizing his views, says 'we are afraid because we run, we do not run because we are afraid'.

Cannon[32] provided evidence to confound the James–Lange theory. When the nerve connections between the organs influenced by the autonomic system and brain are severed, organisms still show fear, rage, affection and other emotional states. The Cannon–Bard theory (again, independent investigators coming to much the same conclusions from their researches) was proposed. According to this the impulses from incoming stimuli pass through the thalamus, sensitizing it and passing the impulses to the cortex, organs and muscles. The cortex input represents conscious knowledge of an emotive state and the feelings which accompany emotions. The organs and muscles would be responding at the same time.

A more recent theory has been proposed by Schachter,[33] who believes that emotion results from the interaction of cognitive factors and physiological arousal. Feedback to the brain from physiological activity sets up an undifferentiated state of arousal. The emotion felt by the person depends on the circumstances existing at the time and the source which the person believes to be the cause of the activity. Past experience is thought to play a part in 'labelling' the source. Thus if a person insults you, you become aroused and from previous experience you associate anger (or embarrassment) with the feeling of arousal. However, this view has its critics. Unfortunately, no one theory answers all the questions and the subject remains one of intense interest for those psychologists in this field.[33]

From our viewpoint, it is probably more helpful to think of emotional behaviour in terms of three dimensions in preference to numerous specific states which are loosely tied in our minds to ill-defined terms which exist in our language to describe our feelings. The three dimensions proposed by Murray[31] are intensity, pleasantness–unpleasantness and approach–avoidance. Intensity is related to the level of arousal and is widely recognized by psychologists (see the section on drive and performance in Chapter 3). The second dimension helps to remind us of the infinite variety of experiences from complete ecstasy to utter terror (while being vaguely reminiscent of the hedonistic theory of man as a pleasure-seeking, pain-avoiding animal). The third dimension concerns the feelings of attraction towards, or repulsion from, emotively charged objects or situations. Fear arising from unpleasant experience may give rise to either fight or flight.

Returning to the place of the brain in emotional response, we know that two systems are involved. One is the limbic system, including parts of the thalamus and hypothalamus, and the inner portion of the cortex (old cortex or paleocortex). Stimulation of this system, as we have observed, is associated with fear, anger, aggression and many other reactions. The other is the ascending reticular activating system (ARAS) in the brain stem, already identified earlier in the chapter as responsible for arousing the cortex and moderating messages from the sensory systems. Its function is not directive, but energizing.

The sequence of events might be easier to follow by looking at Figure 2.4. A sensory stimulus is received by receptor organs and transmitted to the brain via the ARAS. Arousal of the latter is noted by the cortex and also by the hypothalamus in the limbic system. As the hypothalamus transmits to the ANS and pituitary gland, the sympathetic and endocrine systems are alerted. Organs which might aid in escape by providing additional sources of energy are activated, and this is recorded by internal sensory systems. Thus we are made aware not only of the external stimulus, but also of our

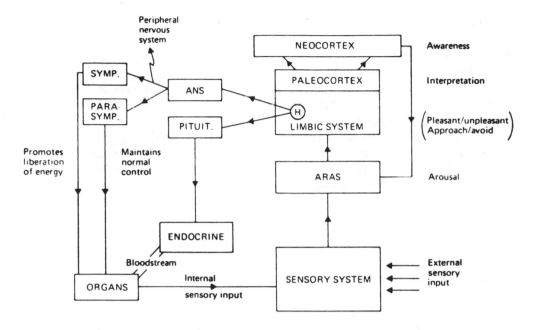

Figure 2.4 *Representational diagram of emotional arousal sequence (H = hypothalamus).*

internal body reactions. The exact point at which the body as a whole responds by approaching or avoiding the stimulus is not fully understood, but it may take place when the ARAS is arousing the cortex along with internal emotional reactions subsequent to ANS and pituitary stimulation.

The utility of emotional states is clear. In a stressful situation – taking a driving test or going into one's first classroom full of children to be taught – increased supplies of blood sugar are released from the liver to provide extra fuel for physical and mental activity. Hormones are also released to convert fats and proteins into sugar. Typical reactions to threatening stimuli begin to appear, such as increased heartbeat and breathing (to supply the muscles with energy-giving oxygen). Other activities, such as digestion, decline. The mouth dries up to increase the capacity of both the mouth and air tubes. Capillaries in the skin contract to lessen blood loss if injury occurs.

All these reactions have survival value by aiding the 'emergency reaction'.[32] They provide the extra resources to fight or flee. Many stressful experiences cannot be reacted to physically and prolonged stress of this kind can lead to serious physical and psychological disturbances (ulcers, cognitive impairment, lack of confidence). But not all stressful experiences end up as harmful. Apart from providing useful supplies of energy, stress in small, intermittent doses can be of benefit in producing, over time, *stress tolerance*, a 'hardening' process which enables a person to become toughened to further stresses of the same or similar kind.[34]

A discussion of stress in teaching will be taken up in Chapter 3.

HEREDITY

An important biological fact is that the human race has a vast pool of characteristics, which can be transmitted from generation to generation during the process of reproducing its kind. In our discussions of such complex human qualities as intelligence and personality we will frequently have cause to wonder to what extent the potential for individual characteristics is inherited and to what extent the life experiences of individuals shape the outcome of these inherited properties. At this stage it is necessary to give readers a brief idea of the biological mechanisms of inheritance.[35]

It is common knowledge that the basic structures for reproducing human characteristics are the germ cells (female ovum, or egg, and male sperm). Within each is found a nucleus which contains the *chromosome* material – long, thread-like structures now known to be made up of chains of chemicals. The basic unit for the transmission of characteristics from parent to offspring is the *gene*. Using powerful chemical and electron-microscopic techniques, biologists have found that each gene is a specific area along the chromosome with a unique chemical composition. The mechanism of gene reproduction and interaction is a rather detailed biological phenomenon which need not concern us here, but we do need to discuss the broad ideas underlying the transmission of physical and mental qualities.

One way of regarding the process of evolution and inheritance is to think of the genes, with their enormous potential for variety, as a *population*. Within this population we would find a pool of characteristics for a given trait ranging from one extreme, let us say intense blue eyes, to the other, deep brown eyes, and in the middle of the range would be found hazel eyes. Each new generation brings with it a selection from this pool which depends on the particular genes carried by the parents. Strains which are beneficial to survival will continue, while other strains which are maladaptive will die out. This is, crudely, the Darwinian theory of the survival of the fittest, by which the natural environment will support only those who are best suited to that environment. This reshuffling of gene content is one way of producing variety in a species. There is a second method called *mutation*, which arises from sudden, often accidental, alterations in the gene structure and gives rise to unique characteristics. Mutations are known to be caused by exposure to radioactive fall-out, and many examples have been reported from the A-bomb aftermath in Japan. Fortunately, in well-established species, many mutations do not survive.

An intriguing example of positive adaptation by a mutant is provided by the resistance of certain strains of bacteria to streptomycin. Normally, a population of a bacterium called *E. coli* can be destroyed when exposed to streptomycin. However, very occasionally a mutant appears which is quite resistant. The fact that it is a mutant strain and not a question of the bacteria becoming resistant has been shown quite conclusively.

Note that the offspring do not exhibit a mixture of the parents' gene contributions. In other words, if dad has brown eyes and mum has blue eyes, the sons and daughters will *not* inherit hazel eyes. Each parent carries in the germ cells certain possibilities for a given characteristic which he or she, in turn, has inherited from parents. So there is some element of luck attached to the specific characteristic which has been 'drawn' from the parents' pool. Should the contributions from the parents be in conflict (father brown, mother blue), then one gene will be dominant in its influence. At the same time, the child now possesses the dominant gene from the father's side *and* the recessive gene from the mother. When the child is about to pass on the characteristics, once more there will be two possibilities.

There are now numbers of well-established anomalies in both physical and mental characteristics arising from faulty chromosomal and gene structure. *Down's syndrome* is well known and exhibits several distinct facial and body features, such as upward-slanting eyelids, conspicuous tongue and unusual fingerprints, as well as a mental defect which in some cases is quite severe. This connection between chromosomal defect and mental ability is used as evidence in support of the argument that the gene pool contains a factor (or factors) relating to human intelligence. (For further discussion of the problems associated with physical disability see note (36).)

The genotype and phenotype

Two commonly used biological terms will be introduced. These are *genotype* and *phenotype*. The genotype refers to the genetic characteristics of individuals transferred in the genes of the parents at fertilization. We have already seen in this chapter that many human characteristics are transferred from generation to generation by the genes, which are the biological blueprints of physical and mental features found in the germ cells of the parents. Hair and eye colour, potential for height and body dimensions are examples of features carried through from previous generations into the embryo. But inherited characteristics, especially mental skills, cannot be observed and measured directly because external influences are at work from the moment of conception. The intellectual similarities of identical twins and the variations in development which frequently occur in environments which are similar and fairly constant are just two indirect sources of evidence for believing in the inheritance of intellectual characteristics. We shall return to this point later in the chapter.

The phenotype results from the interaction of genetic potential and environmental effects from the moment of conception onwards. Thus, by the time the child is born, he or she has already begun phenotypic development. The concept of the phenotype is frequently misused, and confused with *acquired* characteristics. It is important to remember we are talking about the extent to which environmental circumstances will *allow* inborn potential to materialize, and not about acquired characteristics. A young plant which is undernourished or short of light or water does not grow into a healthy plant, so the genotypic potential has been distorted to give a phenotype. The essential features of the genotype are still there, however, and an undernourished cabbage can still be distinguished from an undernourished oak. In the same way, undernourished children, in both physically and mentally impoverished circumstances, do not realize their full potential. On the other hand, we can acquire certain habits or physical injuries during life which are unique to us and die with us. If we cut off the tails of successive generations of mice we would *not* in time produce a tailless generation. This can happen only by mutation (that is, distortion of the genetic material). Similarly, families with a boxing tradition do not ultimately give birth to a child with a boxer's nose. In short, we do not inherit acquired characteristics.

Later in the book we shall refer to heredity and intelligence. There we will deal with a very complex genetic make-up; in fact, intelligence is most likely partly dependent on several interrelated genes (*polygenic* condition) and not just one gene. Therefore the inheritance of intelligence is far more subtle than that of some physical characteristics. The environment also plays a significant part in permitting intellectual potential to be realized, and this point will be taken up in Chapter 9.

MATURATION

Behaviour changes in mankind are brought about by the interaction of both external and internal agencies which we bring to each situation. For convenience, the origins of these changes are separated into *learning* and *maturation*. Learning is due to environmental influences, that is, influences external to us which can affect development. The teacher's job is plainly an instance of environmental influence intended to bring about learning. Maturation, on the other hand, is a built-in tendency in all members of a species to grow and age in an ordered sequence of events. The changes should occur in the absence of experience, although an adverse environment can affect the maturational process.

The physical growth pattern of children is a clear example of maturation. However, there are other kinds of development said to be maturational. Skill in locomotion, which starts with crawling and ends in walking, is one. Gesell studied the motor development of children and postulated several landmarks of motor competence in normal development. More recently, norms of physical development have been published,[37] along with information about differences occurring between children from dissimilar socio-economic backgrounds. As we shall see in the course of this book, there are several maturational theories relating to speech development, cognitive development, vocational development, and so on. We will notice that in all cases there is said to be a systematic unfolding of competence which follows a predictable path, which varies from one individual to another in quality and quantity but is, nevertheless, always present in some degree.

SUMMARY

The mind of mankind has puzzled philosophers and psychologists for many years. Study of the functioning of the central nervous system implies an assumption that we may discover some biological explanations for our behaviour, although this idea should be tempered with the possibility that our behaviour is more than the sum of the actions of our physiological parts, and that conscious life is more than an epiphenomenon arising from body functioning.

Certainly the important body mechanisms which bring us into sensory contact with, and help us to respond to, our surroundings are located in the central nervous system. A brief description of the structure of the CNS was given to illustrate the nature of the systems. In this description we looked at the receptor, transmission and brain processes, relating them to activities of general interest to teachers.

Several sections were concerned with behaviour and the most significant parts of the brain. Whilst this has no direct bearing on the day-to-day workings of an educational system, nevertheless it provides a background of factual information which fits the physical body into a behavioural context. Some of this may be quite difficult for the non-biologist, though an attempt should be made to understand the functioning of the brain stem, homeostasis and the hypothalamus, the higher regions of the brain including aphasic conditions and the lack of bilaterality in the cerebral hemispheres.

Memory and brain action involved a somewhat speculative look at current theories intended to give the reader a glimpse into the research of the near future. The subject of memory comes up again in Chapter 4. Emotion and the brain was dealt with from the point of view of the arousal sequence involving hypothalamus action and the organization of the sympathetic and parasympathetic nervous systems.

The final two sections, on heredity and maturation, were included in this 'biological' chapter as a basis for later elaboration of such important considerations as intelligence, personality, cognitive and language development and the earlier theories of vocational development.

ENQUIRY AND DISCUSSION

(a) Read the relevant parts of R. Davie, N. Butler and H. Goldstein, *From Birth to Seven*, Longman, London, 1972, and use this as a starting point to consider the physical growth, sensory development and the use made of medical services in relation to socioeconomic background.

(b) Discuss in seminar the distinction between maturation and learning. Of what significance is this distinction to the teacher?

(c) Review the literature and draw up a list of the major sensory defects which are likely to affect the work of schoolchildren. How might the teacher discover these abnormalities? Discuss with tutors the action which must be taken when a teacher finds children in the classroom who suffer from sensory and related defects.

(d) Discuss the place of biological knowledge such as brain structure, heredity and physiological needs to an understanding of human behaviour. What use can a teacher make of this knowledge?

NOTES AND REFERENCES

1. This BBC publication, the outcome of a programme on the mind of man, was compiled by Nigel Calder. For beginners it should prove to be a most stimulating and readable book which attempts to introduce the lay person to some of the numerous and intricate researches relating to the workings of our minds. N. Calder, *The Mind of Man*, BBC Publications, London, 1970.
2. (R) For both sides of the dispute about physiology and psychology see R. B. Joynson, 'The return of mind', *Bull. Br. Psychol. Soc.*, **25**, 1–10 (1972) and D. O. Hebb, 'What psychology is about', *Am. Psychol.*, **29**, 71–79 (1974), in the Reader.
3. A particularly helpful chapter on the biological bases of psychology for the beginner has been written by R. L. Atkinson, R. C. Atkinson, E. E. Smith and D. J. Bem, *Introduction to Psychology*, Chapter 2, Harcourt Brace Jovanovich, New York, 11th edn, 1992. Several other specific and technical books are given in the further reading list.
4. N. E. Miller, 'Biofeedback and visceral learning', *Annual Review of Psychology*, **29**, 373–404 (1978). For an introduction to biofeedback see D. Carroll, *Biofeedback in Practice*, Longman, London, 1984.
5. A simple, interesting introduction to the structure and function of the important sense

organs is given in R. L. Atkinson, R. C. Atkinson, E. E. Smith and D. J. Bem, *op cit.*

6. Several books have been written on the subject of improving reading efficiency for adults. For those interested, have a look at S. Harri-Augstein, M. Smith and L. Thomas, *Reading to Learn*, Methuen, London, 1982.

7. A measure of contact sensory discrimination is accomplished by touching various places on the body with a pair of dividers and measuring the distance between the points at which the subject can identify the separate points of contact without seeing the dividers. For example, compare the fingertip with the sole of the foot.

8. For an excellent, simplified version of neuronal action, see the reference given in note (1) above.

9. For a recent application of electroencephalographic method – specialization of the left and right sides of the brain – see S. P. Springer and G. Deutsch, *Left Side, Right Side*, 3rd edn, Freeman, San Francisco, 1989.

10. A recent example of brain stimulation research is offered by K. D. Carr and E. E. Coons, 'Rats self-administered nonrewarding brain stimulation to ameliorate aversion', *Science*, **215**, 1516–1517 (1982).

11. Sir John Eccles, probably the world's most renowned neurophysiologist, established a large research team in Australia. His book, *The Neurophysiological Basis of Mind*, Oxford University Press, London, 1953, is a standard work in this field. See also J. C. Eccles, *The Understanding of the Brain*, McGraw-Hill, New York, 1978 (2nd edn).

12. D. O. Hebb, 'The effect of early and later brain injury upon test scores, and the nature of normal adult intelligence', *Proc. Am. Philos. Soc.*, **85**, 275–292 (1942).

13. W. H. Bexton, W. Heron and T. H. Scott, 'Effect of decreased variation in the sensory environment', *Canad. J. Psychol.*, **8**, 70–76 (1954). Also J. C. Lilly, 'Mental effects of reduction of ordinary levels of physical stimuli on intact, healthy persons', *Psychiat. Res. Rep.*, **5**, 1–9 (1956).

14. M. Jouvet, 'The states of sleep', *Scientific American*, **216**, 2, 62–72 (1967).

15. B. D. Anand and J. R. Brobeck, 'Hypothalamic control of food intake', *Yale J. Biol. Med.*, **24**, 123–140 (1951).

16. Some ESB research is quite spectacular and is a common topic for popularization. The work of José Delgado is particularly remarkable. His book *Physical Control of the Mind*, Harper and Row, New York, 1970, contains a summary of his findings.

17. W. Penfield and T. Rasmussen, *The Cerebral Cortex of Man*, Macmillan, New York, 1950.

18. D. O. Hebb, *The Organization of Behavior*, Wiley, New York, 1973, 9th impression.

19. H.-L. Teuber, 'The riddle of frontal lobe function in man', in J. M. Warren and K. Akert (eds), *The Frontal Granular Cortex and Behavior*, McGraw-Hill, New York, 1964.

20. A. Luria, *Higher Cortical Functions in Man* (translated by Haigh), Tavistock, London, 1966. *Traumatic Aphasia* (translated by Critchley), Macdonald, London, 1970.

21. G. Knight, 'Stereotactic surgery for the relief of suicidal and severe depression and intractable psychoneurosis', *Postgraduate Med, J.*, **44**, 1–13 (1969). The operation using radioactive seeds goes by the unrepeatable title of 'bi-frontal stereotactic tractotomy'.

22. N. Geschwind and A. M. Galaburda, *Cerebral Lateralization*, MIT, Cambridge, MA, 1987.

23. See the Springer and Deutsch reference in note (9) above. This book gives an interesting account of split-brain research.

24. K. Lashley, one of the first in this field of brain surgery and memory, carried out numerous extirpations to discover the precise location in the brain of memory storage. He was entirely unsuccessful in this venture and concluded that learning ought to be impossible! A summary of his early work appears in *Brain Mechanisms and Intelligence*, University of Chicago Press, Chicago, 1929.

25. T. H. Brown, P. F. Chapman, E. W. Kairiss and C. L. Keenan, 'Long-term synaptic potentiation', *Science*, **242**, 724–727 (1988).

26. J. V. McConnell, *New Evidence for the Transfer of Training Effect on Planarians*, 18th International Congress of Psychology, Moscow, 1966, Symposium on Biological Basis of Memory Traces.

27. H. Hydén, 'The question of a molecular basis for the memory trace', in K. H. Pribram and D. E. Broadbent (eds), *Biology of Memory*, Academic Press, New York, 1970.

28. J. A. Deutsch, *The Psychological Basis of Memory*, Academic Press, London, 1973, contains a collection of researches which those interested in the biological science of memory and learning would find fascinating. A paper by R. M. Best, 'Encoding of memory in the neuron', *Psychol. Rep.*, **22**, 107–115 (1968), gives an idea of some recent formulations. For a summary see Chapter 12 in R. A. Levitt, *Physiological Psychology*, Holt, Rinehart and Winston, 1981.

29. P. Ekman, R. W. Levenson and W. V. Frieson, 'Autonomic nervous system activity distinguishes among emotions', *Science*, **221**, 1208–1210 (1983).

30. The endocrine glands secrete special chemicals called *hormones* into the bloodstream. The glands are ductless; in other words, they pass their secretions directly into the bloodstream without the aid of tubular ducts (in contrast, say, to the salivary glands, which secrete through ducts into the mouth). The important glands, their position and the function of their hormones are:

    pituitary – suspended beneath the hypothalamus – controls the action of the endocrine system;

    thyroid – in the front of the neck – secretes thyroxine, which aids in growth and metabolic control;

    adrenals – near each kidney – continuously secrete adrenaline and noradrenaline to mobilize various organs already mentioned in connection with the ANS; also exude excessive quantities of the hormones in emergency and emotive states;

    pancreas – level with kidneys – secretes insulin, which is responsible for sugar control in the body; the well-known disease of diabetes occurs when insufficient insulin is secreted, therefore, the body must be supplied artificially by injecting insulin into the bloodstream;

    gonads – testes or ovaries – the sex glands which control the appearance and maintenance of secondary sexual characteristics such as face, chest and pubic hair, voice breaking and body stature in men and the menstrual cycle and breast formation in women.

    Deficiencies or excesses of the hormonal secretions give rise to various diseases, the nature of which can be read about in any standard biology textbook containing human physiology.

31. E. J. Murray, *Motivation and Emotion*, Prentice-Hall, Englewood Cliffs, NJ, 1964.

32. C. Lange and W. James, *The Emotions*, Williams and Wilkins, Baltimore, 1922; W. B. Cannon, *Bodily Changes in Pain, Hunger, Fear and Rage*, Appleton-Century-Crofts, New York, 1929.

33. S. Schachter, *Emotion, Obesity and Crime*, Academic Press, New York, 1971. For a recent appraisal, see R. Reisenzein, 'The Schachter theory of emotion: two decades later', *Psychol. Bull.*, **94**, 239–264 (1983).

34. See R. A. Dienstbier, 'Arousal and physiological toughness: implications for mental and physical health', *Psychological Review*, **96**, 84–100 (1989).

35. R. Plomin, J. C. DeFries and G. E. McClearn, *Behavioral Genetics: A Primer*, Freeman, New York, 1989 (2nd edn); A. Milunsky, *Know Your Genes*, Pelican, London, 1980; L. Gonick and M. Wheelis, *The Cartoon Guide to Genetics*, Barnes and Noble, New York, 1983.

36. E. Anderson, *The Disabled School Child*, Methuen, London, 1973.

37. J. M. Tanner, *Education and Physical Growth*, Hodder and Stoughton, London, 1978 (2nd edn), and a most important report of development in early childhood by R. Davie, N. Butler and H. Goldstein, *From Birth to Seven*, Longman, London, 1972. One important conclusion reached by this report is that 'equality' of educational opportunity cannot be achieved solely by improving our educational institutions. The child is often handicapped both physically and mentally before he reaches school as a result of deficits in opportunities at home.'

FURTHER READING

R. L. Atkinson, R. C. Atkinson, E. E. Smith and D. J. Bem, *Introduction to Psychology*, Harcourt Brace Jovanovich, New York, 1992 (11th edn).

A. Gale and J. A. Edwards (eds), *Physiological Correlates of Human Behaviour*, Vol. 1: *Basic Issues*, Academic Press, London, 1983. Two other volumes in this series, Vol. 2: *Attention and Performance*, and Vol. 3: *Individual Differences and Psychopathology*, are also very useful for other chapters in this book.

J. G. Nicholls, A. R. Martin and B. G. Wallace, *From Neuron to Brain*, Sinauer Associates, distributed by Freeman, Oxford, 1990 (3rd edn).

R. Plomin, J. C. DeFries and G. E. McClearn, *Behavioral Genetics: A Primer*, Freeman, New York, 1989 (2nd edn).

Chapter 3

Human Motivation

INTRODUCTION

The increased complexity of living in our society has made it necessary to cultivate in the young the will to acquire many varied cognitive as well as physical skills. In fact, schools are created as artificial arrangements in which we require our children to carry out all kinds of activities which, for many of them, would not have been a significant part of their young lives and which would certainly not have occurred to them spontaneously. Left to themselves, the majority of children would not learn to read or pore over arithmetic problems without prompting from adults. Those teachers who have taken a bewildered group of little ones in reception class fresh from the security of home to the uncertainty and properness of the school setting, or have taught a class of school-leavers, with their minds on worldly things, will know all about the problems of prompting the young.

A study of motivation, therefore, is crucial for a teacher. Without a knowledge of the ways and means of encouraging children's learning, knowing about their 'appetites' in the widest sense of the word, being sensitive to their interests, the teacher's task would be impossible. For this purpose, most teachers would place an understanding of motivation very high on their list of priorities.

A working definition of motivation would be that it consists of internal processes which spur us on to satisfy some need. We shall return to examine some of these 'processes' and 'needs' shortly, but first it is necessary to look at some of the broader issues. In some cases we may be fully aware of a particular need and our actions will be quite deliberate in attempting to satisfy it. Hunger has fairly obvious symptoms and well-tried cures. A hungry child eats food in the full knowledge that this will relieve the feeling of hunger. On the other hand, we may be oblivious of the underlying motives when we, say, undertake a course of training to enter the teaching profession. The analysis of those motives which drive us to engage in such complicated activities embodied in a course of training is very difficult. Simpler creatures with a limited span of behaviour for detecting and imbibing food or reproducing their own kind have fairly inflexible and obviously essential mechanisms for their survival. As we pass through the animal kingdom to *Homo sapiens* we find that the origins of our motives become obscured by layers of cultural influences on our behaviour. Satisfaction of basic body requirements such as food, air and water is still essential, but it gives way to, or is possibly built into, an intricate network of other activities designed to satisfy acquired needs within the 'rules' laid down by a society.

The internal processes cannot be observed directly. Therefore, we guess or *infer* that they must exist from the behaviour we observe or experience. What people do can be observed; why they do it is still a matter for speculation.

MOTIVATION THEORIES

Theorists in the study of motivation have generally concerned themselves with four basic questions representing stages in the processes assumed to be present in motivated behaviour. They are: what initiates action, what direction does such action take and why, how 'strong' is the action, and why does action terminate? By 'action' is meant not only obvious movement, but also mental action: you can solve a problem in your head without appearing to do so. Detailed discussion of the speculations each major theorist has made in an attempt to answer these questions would not be profitable. Instead, we shall select from them those aspects which seem to hold out most hope and worth for the teacher. However, to place the development of these theories in perspective, it is worth while to spend a few lines indicating the most prominent views which have survived.

In trying to answer the questions posed above, several themes, which reappear throughout psychology, are in evidence. Is the *source* of action inborn (*biogenic* – having origins in inherent biological processes[1]), acquired (*sociogenic* – having origins in social processes), a mixture of both, or irrelevant (Skinner[2])? Is the stimulus which 'taps' the source internal (*intrinsic*) and/or external (*extrinsic*)? Is all human behaviour motivated by a stimulus (humans are seen as passive agents responding to biological or social stimulation) or are some actions performed for their own sake (exploration or play, in which humans are active agents spontaneously sampling the environment)?

There have been three broad lines of development during this century: *instinct*, *drive and need*, and *cognitive* theories.

Instinct theories

Prior to the eighteenth century it was generally held that humans exercised complete control over their actions. As rational creatures they had the power to direct, redirect or inhibit their passions at will. These ideas were bound up with the early philosophies relating to religion and morals. Humans were seen as pleasure-seeking, pain-avoiding creatures (*hedonistic* outlook). Animals, on the contrary, were activated by instinctive mechanisms which gave rise to fixed ways of satisfying animal needs. Darwin's *Origin of Species* (1859) thus came as a nasty shock to those who thought that humans and animals were completely unalike in their motives.

McDougall[3] in 1908 saw the arguments of Darwin as confirmation of his 'hormic' or *instinct theory*, which postulated that the actions of humans, as well as those of the animals to which humans are related, were the outcome of inborn *instincts* – innate, unlearned tendencies 'which are essential springs or motive power of all thought and action'. According to this theory, instincts have survival value for both the individual and the race: for example, gregariousness leads us to want to be with our own species and aggression drives us to preserve ourselves.[4] The idea that humans, like animals, were born to fixed patterns of behaviour was widely attacked and McDougall modified his view by suggesting that humans were endowed with *propensities* rather than with animal instincts. Burt[5] defined a propensity as a

> complex inherited tendency, common to all members of a species, impelling each individual: (a) to perceive and pay attention to certain objects and situations; (b) to become pleasurably or unpleasurably excited about those objects whenever they are perceived; (c) thereupon to act in a way likely in the long run to preserve the individual by so acting.

The theory in its original form has very little support nowadays. Only the simplest reflexes of humans appear to be invariable in nature. Vernon[6] was amongst many who had harsh things to say about human behaviour having its beginnings in inborn rituals of survival value. The main argument against the instinct theory was that human beings do not display stereotyped patterns of unlearned behaviour. One need only contrast the rigid antics apparent when a baby bird is being fed by its mother, or the courtship rites of many species of birds and animals, with similar events in humans to realize how unlike an instinctual drive our behaviour is. Support for this stems from the work of social anthropologists,[7] who claim that the supposed instincts of aggression, acquisition and sex vary considerably from tribe to tribe. Again, our motives become so overlaid with secondary and acquired desires that it makes the theory of inherited tendencies impossible to validate. Allport[8] recognized this and coined the phrase 'functional autonomy' to describe the acquisition of new motives derived from more fundamental motives which ultimately become independent of the latter. Drug-taking, smoking or developing professional attitudes (high standards of craftsmanship) are examples of activities which continue to give satisfaction long after they have become divorced from the initial starting motive.

A revival of the concept of instinct as applied to humans has been brought about by the work of Lorenz and Tinbergen,[9] two famous ethologists (students of animal behaviour in natural surroundings). Their main contention is that humans, being biological organisms and subject to evolutionary development like the rest of the animal kingdom, are possessed of instinctive urges which, if studied, would give a sound scientific basis to human behaviour. They would argue that certain crimes, for example, are the result of individuals trying to satisfy basic needs in ways not accepted by the society in which the crimes were committed.

Two concepts central to their work are the *sign* or *environment stimulus* and the *innate release mechanism* (IRM). Largely by analogy from animal studies, Lorenz considers that humans have a parental instinct which can be released by various cues. The sight of a doll (environmental sign stimulus) elicits parental behaviour in female children (innate release mechanism). The pattern of stimulation which brings about the release of instinctive parental responses is thought by Lorenz to consist of the doll's short face, large forehead, chubby cheeks and disjunctive limb movements. This is reminiscent of Burt's definition of innate propensities mentioned earlier in the chapter. Tinbergen thinks that, at the very least, patterns of locomotion, sexual behaviour, sleep, food-seeking, care of the body surface and parenthood are instinctive in humans. Lorenz would add social and aggressive drives to this list. The IRM is seen as an innate tendency to carry through a sequence of actions triggered off by some external or internal stimulus.

The key to a creature's springs of action, according to ethologists, relates to these IRMs. The mating habits of animals have frequently been studied as illustrating IRM. Male sticklebacks have a regular cycle of behaviour consisting of territory isolation, building a nest, seeking out a mate by courting rituals, mating, fanning fresh water over the fertilized eggs in the nest and keeping watch over the territory. The satisfactory completion of one stage in the cycle seems to herald the start of the next stage and we have a hierarchy of behaviour organization in which progress through the sequence depends on ordered emergence and completion of each stage. Sticklebacks and gulls seem a far cry from human learning, but human ethologists suggest that we too have IRMs from birth. However, they differ in their greater susceptibility to change.

One further idea which may have some application in human learning is animal *imprinting and critical periods* (see p. 40). It would seem that many animals become attached to objects other than parents soon after birth, if those objects are seen first. Birds have become attached to humans who were the only living things present at hatching. This special social attachment is termed imprinting, and the time at which imprinting is keenest is known as the critical period. Imprinting occurs in many species of bird and animal, including monkeys.

The notion of critical periods is still around today. For example, Dame Marie Clay in her work on reading recovery believes that early detection and cure (about six years of age) of reading difficulties are essential for any lasting effects to take place (see note (32) in Chapter 6 for references).

Two useful concepts expounded by Tinbergen arise from his distinction between *appetitive* and *consummatory activity*. The former involves all those activities which take place in the search for a goal (food, mate) and the latter takes place when the goal is reached (eating, courting or mating).

A recent 'popularizer' of the ethological approach is Desmond Morris,[9] who in a series of very readable books makes a strong case for developing our knowledge of instinctive behaviour in humans. In a book published in 1977, *Manwatching*, he makes a powerful case for thinking that many non-verbal actions are inborn and that much information can be read into these actions. For the teacher, non-verbal cues in the classroom are an important source of ideas about children and it should pay to do further reading. The topic of non-verbal communication is mentioned again in Chapter 8.

The theory of personality expounded by Freud[10] (further discussed in Chapter 11), referred to as *psychoanalytical* (*depth psychology* or *psychodynamic*) theory, also contains references to instinctual drives. Indeed, Freud's theory is as much a theory of motivation (what drives us to behave as we do) as of personality. In Freud's later theorizing (1920 reference in note (10)) he gave these drives the striking Greek titles of Eros and Thanatos, or the *life* and *death* instincts. The life instincts include sexual instincts (*libido* instincts), required for reproducing the species, and self-preservation instincts, relating to hunger and thirst, which are required for life preservation and maintenance (*ego* instincts). Of the death instincts, only one was defined specifically by Freud – the aggressive, destructive instinct. He believed these instincts to be there at birth, a 'cauldron' of instinctual energy referred to as the *id*. The constraints placed on the expression of these basic desires by conscious effort on the part of individuals or as a result of social pressures, chiefly parental influences, lead to repression of the desires. The 'taming of the passions' of the id is made possible by the ego, such that many *defence mechanisms* replace the immediate gratification of basic desires and the motive energy is used in more socially acceptable ways. Exclusion from the conscious mind of less desirable solutions to instinctive cravings does not mean that they have disappeared altogether. Freud creates the *unconscious* mind, which contains the traces of unpleasant and repressed memories. Later behaviour is influenced whenever circumstances similar to the original experiences occur, but the individual is not aware of the source of his or her behaviour. The root causes of motives will break through only in special circumstances such as hypnosis, dreams, drugs or in a psychotherapeutic session when the defences are down. For a fuller discussion of Freudian and similar views, the student should read the relevant part of Chapter 11 where a number of criticisms are also considered. For the moment, it is sufficient to note how Freud accounts for the source and direction of our motivation.

Drive and need theories

The problem with instinct theory was that the arguments became circular and tied to inherited qualities. Anything humans did routinely was seen as a possible instinct, and the list grew to 6000 in the 1920s. By concentrating on the innateness of instincts, psychologists created a problem when it came to connecting them with physiological functions of the body.

In the 1930s, Cannon[11] introduced the concept of *homeostasis* (mentioned in the last chapter) to represent the process by which the body attempts to regulate and protect the balance of physiochemistry in the tissues (food, water, oxygen, temperature of the body). Thus the body is 'driven' into action to correct any imbalance between the internal and external environment. The *drive* is seen as the source of motivation resulting from homeostatic disequilibrium. Hull[12] in the 1940s developed the notion of psychological drives arising from basic physiological needs and equated these by the process of homeostasis. The drives are classified as *primary* and *secondary*. Primary drives are those immediately necessary for bodily survival (e.g. hunger, thirst, sexual behaviour). Secondary (or acquired) drives appear as by-products of the satisfaction of primary needs.[13] Drive stimuli such as fear, money or tokens (cf. token economies in behaviour modification, pp. 109–10) are examples of secondary drives. Hull also suggested that, as drives are reduced when a goal is reached, the consequent drive reduction is said to be 'rewarding' and habits are established.

The appeal of drive theory is its obvious correlation with physiological functions of the body. In Chapter 2 we showed some recent research which strongly suggests that parts of the hypothalamus are localized into 'appestat' centres, i.e. control of the body's appetitive needs within survival limits. Centres discovered so far are hunger, thirst, sex, temperature, aggression and a 'pleasure' site.

Since these early researches much time and effort has been expended in both speculating about and deriving primary and secondary drives. Murray and Cattell are amongst the most prominent to have derived models of motivational structure and deserve particular mention because their views have had some influence on psycho-logical thinking in education.

Murray[14] speculated about two broad groups of human needs, *viscerogenic* and *psychogenic*. The viscerogenic are the physiological survival needs mentioned pre-viously. But the importance of Murray's contribution lies in the psychogenic needs (or social motives), which, as we shall see, have had a marked influence on contemporary thinking. Twenty psychogenic needs were postulated,[14] of which the need for achieve-ment (n Ach), the need for affiliation (n Aff), the need for aggression (n Agg) and the needs for dominance (n Dom), play and understanding are, perhaps, the most widely used. These needs are said to be learned and culture-specific. The term *'need'* is used by Murray in a particular way, meaning a tension or force that affects perception and action in such a way as to try to alter an existing unsatisfactory or unsatisfied situation. We are reminded here of Cannon's homeostatic imbalance.

Needs can be activated either by internal or, most commonly, by external stimuli. Arousal resulting from disequilibrium exerts a stimulating force referred to as 'press'. Thus, seeing another person being bullied is a press which brings out the need for aggression (or harm-avoidance). An attractive career may be a press for n Ach.

The notion of social motives is still widely accepted. Some of the *culture-pattern* and *field* theories which have sprung into being in the past 70 years emphasize the influences of social pressures and patterns of culture on the developing child. Social anthropologists have already been mentioned.[7] Their concern is the effect that culture patterns might have on the rearing of children and the subsequent behaviour patterns which arise from these motivational precursors.

The research of Harlow and Zimmerman[15] is important in this context, as well as in illustrating the social development of young monkeys and the theory of *critical periods* – that is, periods during which particular aspects of growth to maturation are most effectively and permanently developed.[9] In these investigations newly born monkeys were placed with two substitute (or 'surrogate') mothers. They were not live mothers but were made of wire and cloth. One was kept as a plain wire shape with a feeding bottle protruding at the front, whilst the other was surrounded by a soft material, though without a feeder. The young ones always preferred cloth surrogate mothers and would even cling to the cloth while reaching across to the wire model for milk. When frightened, the babies would leap onto the cloth rather than the wire surrogate. This response is said to give 'contact comfort', which Harlow and his co-workers believe to be an essential basic need of young animals, including human babies. There was some evidence of a *critical period*[9] between roughly the 30th and 90th days after birth, when attachment became strong and security firm. Another important observation was the distorted emotional development of monkeys raised in wire cages or with wire mothers. The monkeys tended to be: (a) lacking in affection; (b) lacking a will to co-operate; (c) aggressive; and (d) deficient in sexual responses to other monkeys.

Cattell,[16] in his seminal *dynamic trait theory of motivation*, postulated a frame-work of interdependent factors called the dynamic lattice, using a technique known as factor analysis. Starting from a large number of measures by which human attitudes could be assessed (*devices*), he produced two basic motivational influences. One he called *ergs* – innate sources of reactivity to human needs such as food-seeking, mating, gregariousness, fear, self-assertion, narcissism (self-care), pugnacity and acquisitiveness. Note that the needs included in this list are both viscerogenic and psychogenic in Murray's terms: they go well beyond the physiological needs. The other influence he termed *sentiments* – acquired sources of reactivity to persons, objects and social institutions. Examples of sentiments already discussed are self-sentiment (the desire to maintain a favourable image in the eyes of oneself and significant others, and comparable with the 'self' concept), superego (rule-abiding and maintaining a 'moral' reputation), career, boy- or girl-friend/spouse, parental home, religion and sport. Recent developments and applications to education indicate that self-sentiment, superego and a high, positive sentiment (attitude) to school correlate with achievement in school subjects (Child[16]).

Cognitive theories

The two previous groups of theories, instinct and need-drive, place considerable emphasis on human beings as passive agents, pawns in nature's grand plan for the survival of the fittest. While some theorists acknowledge the role of secondary needs, which to some extent are under the control of the individual, essentially they are regarded as linked to the primary needs, which are rarely in one's consciousness (e.g. we don't sit down to a meal concentrating on the need to nourish the body tissues).

Cognitive theorists hold that the intervention of human thinking has a substantial influence on our motivations (hence *cognitive* theories). A person's awareness of what is happening to him or her has an important effect on future behaviour in similar situations. Perceiving, interpreting, selecting, storing and using information from the environment are crucial processes which affect our present and future motivation. In fact, this view has a lot in common with the field of information processing.[17] Thus environmental information is perceived and processed in such a way as to have an impact on future parallel events.

As an illustration of the way our reaction to an event could be tempered by previous experience and our present perceptions, take a question-and-answer session in class. A particular child's willingness to respond (stressing that humans have a choice and do not simply react mechanically) will depend on many experiential and circumstantial factors, e.g. what has happened previously when answering a particular teacher, how difficult the questions are, how other children view those who are willing to answer questions, and so on. It will be observed that the influences quoted here are environmental/social.

One advanced cognitive theory was expounded by Rotter.[18] Three basic concepts are *behaviour potential*, *expectancy* and *reinforcement value*. Behaviour potential is the likelihood that a person will respond in a given situation in order to receive reinforcement. This likelihood of a person reacting in a given setting will depend on that person's expectation of a reward, i.e. reinforcement, and the value that person places on the reward. The expectations are that certain kinds of action (*behaviours*) will give rise to corresponding outcomes which will reward (or punish). The likelihood of a pupil completing homework set in a lesson will depend, in part, on how much the pupil values the rewards which accrue from completing it, e.g. mastering the work, praise from the teacher, achieving a good grade, learning for some future important exam, pleasing parents who value work at home, etc.

Another concept of *locus of control* by Rotter[18] has been developed in recent years. A person grows to believe that his or her own actions will bring about reinforcements he or she values most. This is referred to as *internal control*. Examples of internally controlling factors are personal competence and effort. The logic of this statement is self-evident: a person who is competent at something (e.g. mathematics) and likes doing it is most likely to succeed by his or her own efforts and be reinforced – and knows it! *External control*, that is, reinforcement which is beyond the control of an individual, is exemplified by luck or by the difficulty of the task. These are not within the control of an individual. We shall see later an illustration of how locus of control has been developed into a systematic motivational view which can be applied to educational settings.[19]

This approach must not be confused with Skinner's behaviourist view, which also highlights the influence of the environment as a source of stimulation and reinforcement. Although Rotter uses terms familiar to behaviourists (extinction, reinforcement), the fundamental distinction between Rotter and Skinner lies in Rotter's emphasis on a situation having *meaning* for a person in order to initiate and guide subsequent behaviour, that is, he introduces elements of conscious control (see also reference to Brewer, note (7) in Chapter 5). For Skinner this excursion into consciousness is irrelevant.

A line of argument presented by some cognitive psychologists suggests that activity by humans need not be the result of a stimulus (homeostatic need, pain, external incentive, etc.). Berlyne[20] refers to *ludic* behaviour (actively seeking out particular kinds of external stimulation or images and thoughts without first having received a stimulus). Curiosity, exploratory behaviour and play have been used synonymously with the term. McV. Hunt[21] also rejects the idea that 'all behaviour is motivated and organisms become inactive unless stimulated by homeostatic need or painful stimulation or conditional stimuli'. He prefers to think of organisms as 'open systems of energy exchange which exhibit activity intrinsically and upon which stimuli have a modulating effect, but not an initiating effect'. The evidence for this is quite convincing, and it has led several psychologists to the conclusion that, even when a person is entirely satisfied (in terms of primary and secondary needs), there is still a desire to be active and explore. Knowledge of one's environment is sought for its own sake.

One further concept espoused by cognitive theorists is the notion of *cognitive imbalance* or *dissonance*. In fact, this idea of imbalance runs throughout psychology in one form or another. Earlier we discussed homeostasis (physiochemical imbalance); Piaget uses the term 'equilibration'; Bruner speaks of 'mismatch'. Cognitive dissonance, a theory developed by Festinger,[22] involves the creation of tension when we have two or more psychologically incongruous events (beliefs, attitudes, etc.). Festinger's basic theme is concerned with the motivational value of tension which accompanies 'dissonance'. Dissonance, according to Festinger, occurs when we are aware of differences between the related 'elements' in a situation. If a child who regularly does well in the school football team has a bad day, dissonance arises because of the incongruity between previous experience and present performance. The tension arising from the dissonance may be dissipated in a number of ways. If the footballer has an injury, is feeling ill or has another problem on his mind, these may be used to disperse the tension. Festinger's central hypotheses are (i) that dissonance is psychologically uncomfortable and therefore will motivate individuals to reduce the dissonance, and (ii) when dissonance is in evidence, individuals will do all they can to avoid meeting information which is likely to increase the dissonance.

Common ground between theories

Whilst there is controversy between psychologists who have made a study of motivation, it is possible to see some common elements in their theories.[23] As a background to our understanding of a possible sequence of events which might occur when a person is motivated to action, the following simple diagram is offered which attempts to draw together the less controversial aspects of the theories:

$$
\left.\begin{array}{l} \text{instinct} \\ \text{need} \\ \text{dissonance} \end{array}\right\} \rightarrow \text{drive} \rightarrow \text{activity} \rightarrow \begin{array}{c} \text{satisfaction} \\ \text{(or conflict)} \end{array} \rightarrow \text{drive reduction}
$$

$$
\longleftarrow \text{learning occurs} \longrightarrow
$$

The source, whether it be called an instinct, need or whatever, is assumed to give rise to tension, which drives an organism to action in an attempt to reduce the tension. Successful tension-reduction is clearly an event which is likely to be remembered, and so learning takes place.

To illustrate a successful sequence, take an example of modelling in the classroom. We all *need* to explore and manipulate our environment whether for curiosity or to satisfy some other need. Few but the senile and ill can sit motionless and uninterested for long. If you distribute modelling clay to a class of seven-year-olds there will be few who do not take up the challenge to shape the clay. Most children enjoy this kind of manipulation (for many reasons) and feel a *drive* to construction, destruction or ludic (i.e. play) *activity* with the material. *Satisfactions* appear when a recognizable shape emerges, when the teacher shows approval or just from the feel of the material. The challenge does not last indefinitely. The initial desire to model wanes (again for many reasons) and we might conclude that the *drive* has been *reduced*.

The likelihood of the cycle of events being repeated is high when there is success and satisfaction. Where drive is not reduced we frequently have conflict. Where a child has produced a useful, attractive or personally satisfying object, *reinforcement* of the sequence is possible, for example when the child's need for social approval is fulfilled when the teacher or the other children praise the finished article.

Successful sequences lead to learning. Manipulative and perceptual skills in this case are encouraged. But learning also occurs from unsuccessful sequences, even if one learns not to repeat the task because it gives little satisfaction. Children soon learn that some kinds of activity also lead directly to disapproval. In this event the sequence will be inhibited, a process known as *extinction*. The teacher's task is to find alternative sequences to arrive at satisfying and educative ends. Whatever the teacher's objective might be, whether it is the improvement of manipulative, perceptual or learning skills, routes must be found which offer the chance of satisfaction and need reduction in order to facilitate positive learning. Punishment, while necessary in certain circumstances, often has the effect of cutting short a sequence without replacing it with an alternative, acceptable sequence.

Activity, satisfaction and drive reduction are treated together because they are important to learning. When a sufficient level of arousal is reached, mobilization of the body or mind takes place. The resulting activity is referred to by some as *goal-seeking behaviour*. Thus the internal demands of drive states impel the individual to seek a means of gratification. The body need not move, since the arousal might be connected with the solution of a mathematical problem requiring no more than an alert mind. Reading a book to acquire knowledge is another case of covert activity. 'Goal-seeking' assumes that a direction is clearly defined by the teacher and clearly under-stood by the pupils. The teacher's function is to provide the direction, and much of his or her scheming in lesson preparation hinges on devising ways in which children will acquire knowledge. Badly organized goal-seeking and goal-planning might have disastrous effects on children's morale. 'Discovery' techniques, if poorly devised, can produce frustrated children with no idea of what they are intended to discover, busy pooling their combined ignorance (class participation in which the teacher plays no part) and often feeling needlessly insecure on such open-ended paths to the acquisition of knowledge. Drive reduction may, unfortunately, be attained by alternative and less acceptable forms of activity where children become desperate.

MOTIVATION APPLIED IN EDUCATION

The relevance of most theories of motivation, especially those involving complex inherited instincts and needs, is so obscured by the detailed realities of life that it is impossible to apply them directly. A knowledge of the idea of primary needs is background, rather than foreground, information. Students of motivation have tried, with little success, to derive links between the fundamental postulated requirements necessary for survival and the day-to-day behaviour of, say, a pupil in a classroom. Therefore the trend in recent years has been to build up models of motivation which are situation-specific. Thus we now find a greater insistence on patently obvious concerns such as the prepotency of needs in creating conducive classroom learning environments, the need for achievement and affiliation among schoolchildren, success and failure and their causes as sources of motivation, and academic motivation measures.

In trying to apply the foregoing we must be careful to distinguish between those aspects of theory which provide coherent background, and within which one might try to place broader observations about human behaviour, and those other aspects of theory which start with a pupil, classroom or school as a particular case having particular motivational problems (see Chapter 17 and (R) papers 54 and 55). Sufficient has been said about theories and models of motivation to convince the reader that many assumptions have to be made in attempting to give meaning to our observations in both the description and the explanation. Peters,[24] a philosopher, has little to say in favour of all-inclusive theories. Like many teachers, he feels that we should classify the *goals* of human beings if we want to make their actions intelligible. For the teacher, the external, situational and easily manipulated factors of human motivation are of primary concern. In the following pages we will explore some of the topics found to be of significance in classroom practice from the point of view of *outcomes* rather than their *origins*. In two practically oriented books on motivation by Ball and Kolesnik[25] a number of the following topics are dealt with in greater depth.

A pragmatic view of needs: Maslow's hierarchy

A model which appeals to teachers because of its common sense is that expounded by Maslow.[26] His description of human motivation derives from his own psychoanalytic research and that of others. He postulates certain *basic* human needs and arranges them in an order, a hierarchy, the needs becoming more 'human' as one proceeds through them. The hierarchy is shown in Figure 3.1 as a pyramid. Maslow distinguishes the basic needs in order of their importance and therefore prepotence, so physiological deficiencies must be satisfied before we attend to safety needs. The pyramid shape is used not only to demonstrate the hierarchical arrangement but also to show the broad base of physiological and safety factors necessary before other possible needs are likely to be considered. Progress through the hierarchy is more likely as more important needs are satisfied. Obviously, these levels are not exclusive. Food-seeking in primitive tribes when food is scarce would be accompanied by some regard for body safety, although probably greater risks would be taken when physiological drives were strong.

Sexual behaviour – courtship, mating, parenthood – is not classified as a physiological need because the urges do not arise from homeostatic imbalance in the same way as food or oxygen deficiency. The behaviour has more to do with species survival than with personal survival. A corollary of this is that humans in extreme hardship, e.g. in prisoner-of-war camps during the Second World War, experience atrophy of the sex organs and consequently have no desire for sexual or social behaviour.[27] Hungry humans think of little else but food: all the human capacities, such as intelligence, memory and dreams, are put to work in trying to seek psychological as well as physiological comfort (Minnesota Starvation Studies).[28]

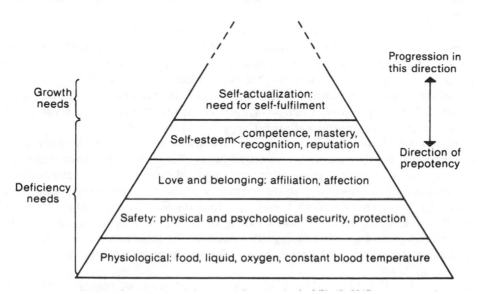

Figure 3.1 *A hierarchy of basic needs. Based on A. H. Maslow,* Motivation and Personality, *Harper and Row, New York, 1970 (2nd edn).*

Once the organic needs are satisfied, 'higher' needs emerge to be satisfied. The safety needs, that is, protection from potentially threatening objects, situations or illness, come to the fore. Children are especially susceptible to unfamiliar surroundings. They seek refuge in routines because too much open-ended and ambiguous experience may constitute a threat to their safety. Maslow suggests that one indication of children's need for safety is their preference for some kind of undisrupted routine or rhythm in life. Tolerance to ambiguity may be an acquired characteristic depending for its quality and extent on child-rearing and childhood encounters. Inconsistency in the expectations and demands of parents and teachers can give rise to disturbing and insecure feelings among children.

The 'love needs' assert themselves when physiological and safety needs are reasonably well gratified. Most humans appear to need to give and receive affection. They need the feeling of belonging, which has nothing to do with sexual desire. To some extent the feeling of belonging adds to our safety needs. Parents and teachers, inadvertently, can bring powerful pressure to bear on children who feel insecure because of lack of affection. On a wider front, 'society' can exact high levels of social control and conformity by the implicit threat of social isolation (prison, borstal, secret societies, religious sects). In the United States, those who do not successfully move to higher education are described as 'drop-outs'. Psychotherapy places great faith in the influence of thwarted love needs on the conscious life.

Maslow sees two sets of 'esteem' needs. First there is the desire for *competence*, achievement, adequacy, confidence in front of one's fellows, independence and freedom. Second, he posits the desire for *recognition*, reputation and prestige, attention, importance and appreciation by others. The first is the desire for confidence in oneself; the other is a wish for prestige and respect from others. Thwarting of opportunities for these desires to be realized is said to produce feelings of inferiority, weakness or helplessness.

The next step in the pyramid, self-actualization, refers to the desire to fulfil one's potential. Maslow declares, 'What a man *can* be, he *must* be.' Self-actualization is also dependent on self-realization. We have to know what we can do before we know we are doing it efficiently. 'Self-actualization is growth-motivated rather than deficiency-motivated', and takes many forms, which depend upon an individual's perceived beliefs about his or her competences. Pupils will want to express themselves in a variety of ways – artistic, musical, mathematical, athletic.

Connected with basic needs, but forming their own hierarchy, are the desires for knowledge and understanding: the *cognitive* needs. The search for knowledge (cf. attention needs of curiosity, exploration and manipulation and ludic behaviour) is evident in much of the searching, active behaviour of children. But the accumulation of knowledge is not enough. With knowledge, humans tend to systematize, organize and analyse in a search for order and meaning in the world: they possess a desire to understand. The relevance of these cognitive needs to the basic needs is obvious when one considers the necessity of possessing the former in order actively to seek satisfaction of the latter.

As indicated earlier, Maslow's is a descriptive model based on observational data. Those who have applied it claim that it has face validity. Cautious analyses of its applications may prove of value. For example, is there any justification in believing that hungry or frightened children are less likely to fulfil the requirements of school than well-fed and secure children, or are children starved of affection at home less likely to cope than those from emotionally well-balanced home backgrounds?

Parents and teachers have a major stake in discovering, encouraging and advertising each child's capabilities for the enhancement of self-esteem and self-actualization. Teachers, too, will possess the needs speculated in Maslow's scheme. The educational system within a school, the interactions with staff and pupils, the subject(s) of interest and the status afforded by the role of teacher are vital aspects in the satisfaction of basic and cognitive needs. These are just as likely to affect work at school as unsatisfied needs of children.

Extrinsic and intrinsic motivation

A teacher, in trying to adapt the subject and the classroom setting to appeal to a child, relies broadly on two sources of satisfaction, *extrinsic* motivation and *intrinsic* motivation. No clear distinction can be made between incentives (objects external to ourselves which act as a 'pull' from without) and internal drive states (the 'push' from within, which is self-generated). The place of rewards in school – praise, grades, recognitions of progress – is crucial, and clearly they are used as incentives to encourage learning. There is no set way in which a reward is linked to the activity performed in order to obtain it (e.g. successful performance in a physical education exercise and a house point). On the other hand, as we mentioned previously in discussing the ideas of Berlyne and McV. Hunt, there is a good case for thinking that some activities, e.g. exploration and play, are rewarded not by tangible things, but simply by the pleasure they give. This is regarded as intrinsic motivation. The fact that the body needs to be active and receive cues is well established (see sensory deprivation researches in Chapter 2, note (13)). The step from these built-in intrinsic urges to their utilization in the classroom is a necessary one.

Extrinsic motivators: incentives

Whilst accepting the value of intrinsic motivation for long-term rewards, all teachers are obliged to press into service extrinsic motivating systems of immediate rewards or incentives. The knowledge that children delight in exploratory or manipulative activities and that they have a need to achieve and set themselves goals must act as a potent starting point for a teacher. Sometimes the inherent interest in some aspects of school work is sufficient to arouse the children to cognitive activity, but often it will be necessary to apply external stimuli.

Work in the field of extrinsic motivation owes much to endeavours in reinforcement theory, which is one of the most researched areas of psychology. In its simplest form, the theory follows from Thorndike's 'law of effect' (see Chapter 5), which tells us that, if our efforts are rewarded with something we like to receive (positive reinforcement), we are more likely to repeat our efforts, and thus habits are born. It is not invariable (Ferster[29]), but it is a most useful, common-sense guideline.

Knowledge of results. Obtaining information about how successfully one is performing (feedback), as we have seen, has high motivational value, especially when the news is good. Skinner,[29] as we shall see in Chapter 5, makes much of the idea that pupils should have *immediate* knowledge of their performance for the knowledge to have any value. The longer the time between completing work and being told the verdict, particularly if it is favourable, the less chance there is of the results having a motivational impact on the pupil. This applies equally well to essays at any level of education. Skinner applied the idea in constructing the linear teaching programme (see Chapter 5), where the response given by a pupil is evaluated immediately. As we have seen, knowledge of failure, particularly if it is frequent, can be equally devastating, hence Skinner suggests that the steps taken in the programme should be short and give a slow build-up in level of difficulty to ensure a high level of success (see later under attribution theory).

Reward and punishment. In a classic experiment by Hurlock[30] in 1925, ten-year-olds were given practice in a series of addition tests, all of equal difficulty. Four groups were formed: (a) a *control* group given no special motivation and kept separate from the other groups; (b) a *praised* group who were complimented on the preceding day's work irrespective of the level of performance; (c) a *reproved* group who were chided for poor work, careless mistakes or lack of improvement – in fact, any pretext by which to chastise individuals; and (d) an *ignored* group who were neither praised nor reproved but were present in the same room with the praised and reproved groups so that they could hear comments made to other children. Figure 3.2 displays some clear differences in the performances of the groups over the five days of the research.

The conclusion is that, while the performances of the pupils on the first day were

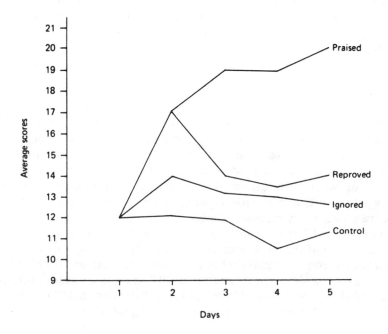

Figure 3.2 *Effects of praise and reproof as incentives. Adapted from E. B. Hurlock, 'An evaluation of certain incentives used in school work', J. Educ. Psychol., 16, 145–159 (1925).*

the same, the praised group outstripped all the others in subsequent performance. The reproved group improved in the short term, but continued harassing tended to have a deleterious influence. It may be that where standards are too exacting, where teachers are perfectionists, study and performance suffer because the pupils, unable to live up to the impossibly high standards, just capitulate. The complacency of the ignored and control groups is worth noting. This research was repeated by Schmidt[31] with rather less success, because the variations in settings in which praise or reproof can occur also have a marked effect on the extent to which they influence performance as well as on the level of anxiety experienced by the pupil (see later section on drive and performance).

The misfortune is that we tend to dichotomize reward and punishment. There is doubtless a continuum of feedback mechanisms employed between teacher and taught (from high praise through mild words of caution to much more serious rebuking on the punishment side) which induces a whole spectrum of pupil reaction.[32] Also, what is rewarding for some may be punishment for others (and vice versa). Given the limitation of Hurlock's work, it does support the contention that both praise and reproof are more effective in their different ways than is a neutral setting. Operational conclusions also arising from this work are that the balance along the continuum of reward and punishment should be tipped in favour of reward. The problem with punishment is in its effects, which tend to be less predictable than those of rewards. Some punishments are actually enjoyed by pupils and therefore are more likely to reinforce than extinguish misbehaviour. Temporary suspension from school may be welcomed by a pupil, and staying on after school may free a pupil from household chores. Punishment tends to indicate what *not* to do: some idea of what ought to be done does not always accompany punishment. Unfortunately, some teachers treat necessary day-to-day class activities as if they were punishments: doing extra mathematics or essays as a punishment could turn some children off these activities. A summary of the effects of physical punishment can be found in Walters and Grusec,[33] who, in general, conclude that there is a place for punishment in the socialization process, given careful consideration of the intensity, duration and timing (the punishment should not take place too long after the misdemeanour).

Errors need to be pointed out, and misbehaviour which is antisocial should be corrected, but the teacher should always attempt to ascertain the reasons for failure or blatant misconduct before applying punitive methods. Personal problems, home circumstances, misjudgements in the standard of work being given to a child (either too hard or too easy) and many other causes may be at the roots of underachievement (performance below that expected from previous performance or standardized tests). Therefore, one should not be too hasty in applying pressure until valid and reasonable causes have been eliminated.

Co-operation and competition. Research into the relative merits of co-operative and competitive methods in class has not been particularly illuminating. To begin with, we have the dilemma of encouraging both co-operation and competition within the same teaching systems. The only generalization which emerges from a mass of research is that in none of the studies does competition yield more effective learning than co-operation.[34] Nevertheless, the one thing that seems certain is that both devices are valid motivators.[35] Provided the level of competitive antagonism is not too high, performance appears to be improved.[34] Where the stakes are very high, children opt out or resort to cheating. Self-competition has already been alluded to as an effective means in our discussion of n Ach and levels of aspiration. The matter of social motives[14, 22] such as dependence, affiliation and desire for approval also have a great deal to do with encouraging children to participate in co-operative ventures.

Intrinsic motivators: curiosity, exploration and manipulation

We started the chapter by suggesting that the classroom was a far from natural setting. Teachers have to sell their wares and to depend upon *cognitive drive* (to adopt a term from Ausubel and Robinson[36]). We are very much dependent on children's will to know and understand, and on their manipulative and physical awareness (modelling, crafts, physical exercise, games). Often the teacher will appeal to needs lower in Maslow's scheme. Illustrations are the children's intrinsic desire for self-esteem, confidence in the presence of others or in themselves, the need to satisfy curiosity,[37] the need for approval and social needs.

Collectively the activities of exploration, manipulation and curiosity[20, 21] are known as *attention needs*. They depend for detection or satisfaction on the senses and the extent to which we pay attention to our surroundings. The McGill experiment referred to in Chapter 2, note (13), indicated that almost total inaction has serious disorientating effects on the mind. Even before this stage is reached, people subjected to prolonged inaction become extremely frustrated. Belief in these as components of human behaviour reflects an active rather than a passive view of life, with humans as goal-orientated animals actively engaged in exploring their environment. Children, once they can move, do not lie or sit around waiting for information to wash over them: they actively seek out and manipulate. Mothers and teachers in primary schools are fully alive to this. The idea of an active, experience-seeking child is prominent in Piaget's theory of cognitive growth (see Chapter 7).

Play is regarded by some psychologists as a manifestation of the attention needs. It is a universally spontaneous activity, especially among the young of most higher animals. Many theories have arisen to explain the purposes it serves,[38] but we are still not really certain. Regardless of theory, it is plain that play can be of significance in the intellectual, physical, social and moral development of children and can be converted to therapeutic and educational ends. Body tone (muscles, organs, circulation) is kept in trim by the exercise afforded in play. Co-operation and competition provide an opportunity for social development. Initially, children appear to prefer solitary play or, at the most, playing side by side without mixing (parallel play). Later they engage in associative and co-operative play in which the rules of procedure and coexistence with others are gradually observed or taken into account. Thus play also gives children the chance to develop moral judgements, as Piaget has shown (see the Kay and the Kohlberg references, note (20), Chapter 7). Play also opens up the opportunity for children to manipulate the materials of their environment, to discern shape, texture, size, weight, etc., and assists them in differentiating the real from the imaginary.

Among the theories we find the 'surplus energy' theory, which regards play as the inevitable outlet for the abundant energy of youth made available for the survival of the species. Once the business of survival has been catered for, the surplus is used in exploratory activities. 'Recreative' theories emphasize the therapeutic, hedonistic aspects of play. We play for pure joy, pleasure and relaxation. Play has also been thought of as a rehearsal for adult roles in which life is played out in miniature. These views are sometimes referred to as 'instinct' or 'preparatory' theories. 'Achievement-mastery' and a desire to have physical mastery over the environment have also been seen as having some bearing on the motivation to play. Finally, a view which now has few supporters is the 'recapitulation' theory, which supposes that play follows a series of stages similar to the evolution of the species; thus the behaviour of young children is reminiscent of the early stages in human development.

The use of play in education, the *playway* in its most extreme form, has its origins in the belief that all children want to play and that learning will occur at the same time, as a bonus in a sense. By suitably shaping the order and nature of the materials and devising situations in which children can both play and learn, as well as having a keen sense of the things which children enjoy doing, play can be pressed into productive service in the process of learning. However, long periods of unstructured, unguided, 'accidental' practice in the classroom are wasteful, frustrating and unnecessary. The gravest disservice to our young would be to transmit, by default, the idea that learning does not require personal effort and sacrifice. As students know, learning has its enjoyment, but it also involves hard work.

Achievement motivation

Need to achieve

The motive to achieve, whilst having no well-established origins in primary needs, is nevertheless a useful concept which has some face validity in the classroom. Ausubel[36] perceives at least three components in achievement motivation. They are: (a) *cognitive drive*, which is *task-oriented* in the sense that the enquirer is attempting to satisfy the need to know and understand (see Maslow), and the reward of discovering new knowledge resides in the carrying out of the task; (b) *self-enhancement*, which is *ego-oriented* or *self-oriented* and represents a desire for increased prestige and status gained by doing well scholastically, and which leads to feelings of adequacy and self-esteem; and (c) a broader motive of *affiliation*, which is a dependence on others for approval. Satisfaction comes from such approval irrespective of the cause, so the individual uses academic success simply as a means of recognition by those on whom he or she depends for assurances. Parents play an active part in the young child's affiliation needs. Later the teacher often becomes another source of affiliation satisfaction.

Earlier we mentioned the views of Murray, who postulated a number of needs.[14] McClelland,[39] greatly influenced by Murray, developed the need for achievement aspect (n Ach). The persistence of both children and adults to master objects and ideas suggests that they have a strong desire to achieve. Whatever the cause, its presence is a constant source of hope and encouragement to teachers. McClelland adopted 'projection' techniques (see reference at the end of note (38) and Chapter 11) to differentiate the levels of need to achieve following a variety of experimental conditions. In one research there were two stages to the experiment: the first stage consisted of seven pencil-and-paper verbal and motor tests; the second stage followed with a test of 'creative imagination', in which the subjects had to write stories about several pictures (projecting their achievement motive) from which a measure of achievement motivation was taken. Six experimental conditions were chosen:

(a) Relaxed: the students were told that the research had been devised to improve the quality of the tests; in other words, the tests and not the students were being tested.

(b) Neutral: again, the tasks were oriented towards the tests rather than the students, but in this instance they were asked to take the tests seriously and to do their best.

(c) Success: the first of the seven tests was first completed and scored as a carefully timed exercise. Students were then asked about their individual class marks and positions, IQ and a personal estimate of their ability. They were also told that the present series of tests were measures of intelligence in which students at a rival institution had excelled. After these false statements the students were given some invented 'norms' for the first test, making it look as though most had done well. Similarly, results of the next six tests were announced to maintain the impression that the group had been successful.

(d) Achievement oriented: instructions were the same for this group as for the 'success' group, except that no norms were given.

(e) Failure: similar instructions to those given to the 'success' group were used, except that the invented norms after the first and the next six tests were so high as to make it appear as though most of the group had failed.

(f) Success–failure: the norms announced after the first test were low, so that almost everyone was successful, while very high norms followed the six tests.

The results are expressed diagrammatically in Figure 3.3. The order in which the conditions appear bears some profitable information for the teacher. Note the relative position of 'relaxed' and the other forms of motivation. The results seem to show that the difference between the 'success' and the 'success–failure' groups is statistically significant.

A direct outcome of McClelland's work is the development of training programmes aimed at encouraging achievement motivation in students of all ages. The argument used is that if we can specify the characteristics of the high achiever, some of these might be stimulated in less achievement-oriented individuals, using tailor-made programmes of training. The ultimate aim would be to improve the performance of students. The findings so far summarized by McClelland[40] (R) are encouraging, in showing that some students display significant improvement. Just how permanent the improvement is has still to be discovered.

Atkinson,[41] using n Ach concepts, has developed McClelland's ideas into a theory of behaviour which has some relevance to teaching. For him, three factors were important in determining the level of arousal and likelihood of actually carrying out a task. These were the particular level of n Ach in the task, the person's expectations of success, and the strength of the incentive following a successful outcome on completion of the task. These are all positive factors – the higher each one is, the greater is the possibility of action to achieve the task. But Atkinson introduced another element which was in a sense negative – a disincentive or need to avoid the task. This he called *fear of failure* (FF). FF also has the same three factors of the motive to avoid

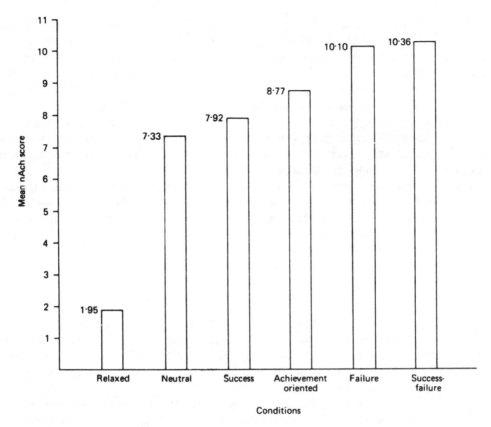

Figure 3.3 *Need achievement in different circumstances. From the work of D. C. McClelland* et al., The Achievement Motive, *Irvington Publishers, New York, 1976.*

failure, the likelihood of failure and the strength of the incentive for failure. If the product of the positive factors is greater than that of the negative factors, there is an overall positive achievement motivation – the stronger, the better. The reverse applies if the negative factors are greater.

There are some interesting implications of use to teachers in this theory. Research comparing those high on n Ach and low on FF with those low on n Ach and high on FF have shown the former to be more realistic in decision-making which involves achievement (Atkinson and Litwin[41]). With high motivation to achieve, the former do not take the risk of choosing very difficult tasks, nor are they interested in easy tasks because the incentive will be too small. With those having high FF, moderately difficult tasks create the greatest anxiety. With easy tasks there would be no problem; with difficult tasks there are similarly no perceived problems because the *negative* incentive of failing is small. Mahone[41] has found that those higher on n Ach are more realistic in career choices than those high on FF.

Birney[41] has also looked at fear of failure. He points to the paradox in our society, with its overriding respect for those who strive and succeed, that an advance towards achievement is also a retreat from the fear of failure.[42] Notice that in McClelland's work the highest levels of n Ach are obtained by those who think they have failed, especially those who have tasted success. As Birney observes, 'success and failure can best be understood *only in an interpersonal context. . . .* In an achieving society, success is highly instrumental in gathering esteem and respect, while failure is a standard way of losing esteem.' Fear of failure may have many causes, but three important ones are lessening of self-esteem, lowering of public image, and the loss of rewards accompanying poor attainment. Where self-ratings on a questionnaire are used[43] to show differences in expressed attitudes towards achievement motivation and actual performance, those with high achievement professed to be self-confident, diligent, serious, single-minded and conformist.

Children need to succeed. In catering for this we have to keep a close watch on their abilities and potential when devising their classroom work. Herein lies one of the important reasons for individual attention of children: that we can set goals for each child in accordance with what the teacher sees as being within the capabilities of that child, thus ensuring that the child tastes success in preference to failure.

Level of aspiration

In the light of experience and advice, we all set ourselves standards of achievement. These can be referred to as *levels of aspiration.* Plainly the level at which we set our sights has an important bearing on our levels of performance. Children without a challenge are less likely to improve their skills than those who are encouraged to strive for better performance.

In a well-known study by Sears,[44] fourth-grade, fifth-grade and sixth-grade children (ten- to twelve-year-olds) were divided into three groups of those who had been successful, unsuccessful and 'differentially' successful in school subjects, including arithmetic and reading. The differential group had succeeded in reading, but had done badly in arithmetic. Under familiar, normal classroom conditions the children were given several tasks in arithmetic and reading. After a task each child was asked to give an estimate of how long it would take to carry out the next task; this was taken as a measure of the level of aspiration. Discrepancies between actual time taken and estimated time needed were used to compare groups. Three particularly interesting findings were: (a) children with a background of success set themselves realistic levels of aspiration; (b) those with a background of failure tended to set unrealistic levels of either overestimates or underestimates; (c) the differential group was realistic in reading, i.e. its normally successful subject. In a continuation experiment in which each group was divided randomly into two, one half was told falsely that it had done well. Self-estimates of the time needed to complete the tasks were again requested of the pupils. In this case, Sears was interested in the short-term effects of success and failure for those who usually experience long-term effects. The results showed that (a) the short-term success group tended to set realistic levels of aspiration; and (b) short-term failure had little effect, particularly for those in the group normally experiencing long-term success.

Several helpful pointers can be gleaned from this and other evidence:

(a) Repeated failure does not enable children to make a reasonable estimate of their capabilities; naturally, if children have no idea what they can do successfully they cannot possibly be in a position to set themselves realistic goals.

(b)   The effects of intermittent failure are more varied than those of success.

(c)   Unexpected failure gives lowered levels of aspiration.

(d)   Continued failure produces a decline in levels of aspiration; nothing enhances failure better than failure.

(e)   A combination of failure and success (see McClelland's work, referred to earlier in the chapter) raises levels of aspiration and the need to achieve.

(f)   Where there is knowledge that a goal has been achieved, children will often be inspired to set their sights higher on the next occasion; their levels of aspiration are raised.

(g)   The greater the success of a child, the stronger is the tendency to raise levels of aspiration.

(h)   Where success comes too easily, levels are frequently lowered.

(i)   Highly cherished goals may be reflected in lowered levels of aspiration to ensure some success.

(j)   Unexpected success often leads to raised levels of aspiration.

In conclusion, the judicious use of success and, to a limited extent, failure must form an important element in classroom practice. Children need help in discovering their capacities and setting realistic goals for themselves.

Attribution theory and expectation

The *expectancy process* has become a most important development in social psychology applied to education. Rogers[45] identifies four factors whereby teachers' expectations might influence pupils' performance: (a) teachers form impressions of pupils, and on the basis of these they derive expectations of the pupils' performance; (b) consciously or otherwise the behaviour of teachers must be affected by these expectations; (c) the pupils must, whether they are consciously aware of it or not, recognize the teacher's expectations through the latter's behaviour; (d) the pupils respond to the teacher's behaviour in a manner which more closely matches the teacher's expectations. Before discussing teacher expectation it is first necessary to look at two related concepts of attribution and self-concept.

Above was mentioned Rotter's idea of locus of control. Some events were regarded as being within the control of an individual (internal), while others were not (external). Weiner[19, 46] developed this further by suggesting that individuals tend to *attribute* their success or failure to either internal or external causes, and this in turn affects their perception of a similar task undertaken in the future. The causes of success and failure are classified by Weiner in two ways: the *locus of control* mentioned above, and *stability*. Four main locus-of-control attributions are *ability* and *effort* (internal, because a person already possesses ability and can be personally responsible for the amount of effort), and *task difficulty* and *luck* (external, because a person does not feel responsible for either task difficulty or unpredictability, e.g. unlucky in the questions revised for an exam). On the other hand, ability and task difficulty are reasonably stable, in that they do not vary all that much from occasion to occasion when the same task is undertaken. Effort and luck, however, are unstable, because they can vary from one time to the next. Table 3.1 should help to illustrate this.

Table 3.1. *To what do we attribute success and failure?*

| | Locus of control | |
	External	Internal
Stable	Task difficulty	Ability
Unstable	Luck	Effort

In turn, a person reacts with pride or shame depending upon his or her perceived source of success and failure. This also affects future attempts. For internal locus of control, there is a maximum pride with success and maximum shame with failure. There are also greater expectations of success with stable than with unstable causes.

The crux of attribution theory is the *causal perception*, to what an individual attributes the cause of his or her success or failure, and the influence this has on perceptions of future performance. Pupils who attribute their failure to stable causes (lack of ability) generally do not persist when they fail ('if ability is fixed there's not much I can do about it'). Pupils who believe their failure is brought about by unstable or internal causes, e.g. lack of effort, tend to persist in the face of failure ('I'm just not trying hard enough').

The link between this and McClelland's n Ach is most instructive (Weiner, 1974).[46] It seems that pupils with a high need to achieve attribute their success to internal causes of ability and effort and their failure to lack of effort, while low need achievers attribute their failure to external factors (and in some cases to lack of ability). This knowledge, alongside the training programmes developed by McClelland and his associates, has been used with some success (**R**).[40]

A word of caution about the findings from attribution research is needed. From a review of the research, Rogers[45] concludes that

> teacher expectancy effects are more likely to occur (but certainly not exclusively so) when younger pupils are involved, when teachers have formed social expectations for their pupils under conditions likely to lead to the establishment of relatively distant teacher–pupil relationships and under conditions (as yet largely unspecified) where the actions and expressed attitudes of the teacher are most likely to affect pupils' level of tuition and self-concepts.

Self-concept and achievement: expectations of pupils

A theme running through the researches mentioned in the last few pages is the importance attached to how we rate our competence in a particular task. The image we create of ourselves and the self-value or esteem generated from this image are going to affect our approach and level of performance in solving life's problems. These conceptions which we hold of ourselves as a result of interaction with significant others and which influence our behaviour are known collectively as the *self-concept*. The topic will be considered in Chapter 11 and in the Reader,[47] but the motivational aspects are of interest here.

In Maslow's theory, a prominent position was given to self-esteem and self-actualization in the hierarchy of human needs. Confidence in oneself and the need for respect from others were felt to be crucial in providing a base for intellectual pursuits.

Ausubel suggested the importance of self-enhancement and affiliation, that is, the prestige we gain by doing well in school or college and the dependence we have on others' recognition and approval of our academic prowess. McClelland's n Ach researches clearly highlight the importance of differing effects of failure-oriented and success-oriented feedback in the enhancement of achievement motivation. Fear of failure, says Birney,[41] drives the student towards trying to be successful because to be a failure is a damaging image (failure repels, success attracts). Of course, persistent failure, or continually telling a child he or she is stupid, is like the Chinese water torture: one ultimately capitulates to the belief that one is a failure or stupid, and a depressing self-concept is formed. As Rosenthal and Jacobson found, children fulfil the prophecy they think others expect of them. In the work of Cattell (above and in the Reader), well-designed motivation tests used with both adult and school samples gave support to the high position of self-concept in relation to achievement. The picture emerging with high and low achievers is consistent[48] (**R**) and underlines the importance to high achievement of the esteem one has been led to have of oneself (self-sentiment), of a sense of duty, conscientiousness and acceptance of authority (superego), of curiosity, of fear of insecurity (cf. Birney), and of positive attitudes to school.

A useful point is made by Brookover *et al.*,[49] who distinguish *self-concept of academic ability* as one of a number of possible self-concepts. This distinction has enabled him to concentrate on those aspects of school life which impinge directly on self-concept and academic achievement. The results from his and similar studies[50] show a positive relationship over time: the better the self-concept of academic ability, the higher achievement, and changes in self-concept correspond with changes in achievement. The relationships are not strong but are sufficient to suggest that teachers have an important part to play in establishing positive but realistic self-concepts in their children. In another study, of the evidence so far collected, Bloom[51] concluded that 'academic self-concept is the strongest of the affect measures in predicting school achievement'.

The self-fulfilling prophecy: expectations of teachers

Once we have made up our minds about the capabilities of each child, to what extent does this decision adversely influence our treatment of the child? Do children perform in the way we expect them to perform? In a survey of the literature and research by Rosenthal and Jacobson[52] (**R**), it appears that performance and attainment in school subjects were significantly improved where improvement was anticipated. They go on to speculate that:

> by what she said, by how and when she said it, by her facial expressions, postures, and perhaps by her touch, the teacher may have communicated to the children of the experimental group that she expected improved intellectual performance. Such communications together with possible changes in teaching techniques may have helped the child learn by changing his self-concept, his expectations of his own behaviour, and his motivation, as well as his cognitive style and skills.

The opportunities for these unintentional influences abound in every classroom. Presumably the reverse effect of inadvertently depressing a child's performance by setting goals which are too low is yet another possibility. In many ways, the self-fulfilling prophecy can be used to advantage by adopting an optimistic attitude towards the performance of children in the hope that they will learn more than was deemed possible at first sight. But it must be said that several pointed criticisms of this and similar research have been made and should be consulted.[53] One obvious criticism has been that these researchers used intelligence tests and not school achievement tests.

DRIVE AND PERFORMANCE

Throughout this chapter several terms have been used which suggest that motivation involves some kind of tension state. We talk of 'fear of failure', anxiety and drive states, conflict, frustration or emotional tension, all implying some kind of disturbance or dissonance. What we have not discussed is the connection between the 'amount' of drive present and the nature and extent of the ensuing activity. Is there a straightforward link between drive and performance such that an increase in one gives rise to a corresponding increase in the other? Or are there times when a maximum level of performance is reached beyond which no amount of drive will increase output? Will highly motivated (or highly anxious) performers invariably do better than moderately motivated ones? The answers to these questions are not simple. The factors involved are many and of devious influence. But two factors of primary importance which have been examined are the *level of motivation* or *arousal* and the *difficulty*, of the task. As long ago as 1908, Yerkes and Dodson[54] found from their work with rats that, as the level of motivation is increased for a given task, an optimum is reached beyond which performance increasingly deteriorates. Figure 3.4 is a theoretical graph of this statement. As we pass from one kind of task to another, the difficulty of each task also affects the optimum level of arousal at which learning and performance are adversely influenced. A general statement of this finding is that, as the difficulty of tasks increases, the optimum motivation for learning or performance decreases. This became known as the Yerkes–Dodson law. The law is beautifully demonstrated by Broadhurst,[55] (**R**) using three levels of difficulty for tasks performed by rats as shown in Figure 3.5.

Everyday examples of achievement being influenced by the level of difficulty are not hard to find. Very simple tasks (shelling peas) are not likely to cause us concern even under stressful circumstances, whereas highly provoking tasks where emotional arousal is in evidence (e.g. sitting an examination or taking a driving test) do not need to become too complex before we begin to make silly mistakes. However, there are dangers in drawing direct analogies between the moderately simple activities required of rats in maze-running or food-seeking problems and the highly intricate tasks required of children or students. The relationship could not be as clean-cut as the Yerkes–Dodson effect. The curvilinearity (the inverted U-shape of Figure 3.4) applies to rat performance. What little evidence we have for complicated tasks will be considered in more detail in Chapter 11, but we have cause to believe that those in highly provoking situations, or high-anxiety-prone people as measured in tests of neuroticism, may experience disruptive influences from the very outset of task performance. In other words, as the stress in a situation mounts, our performance

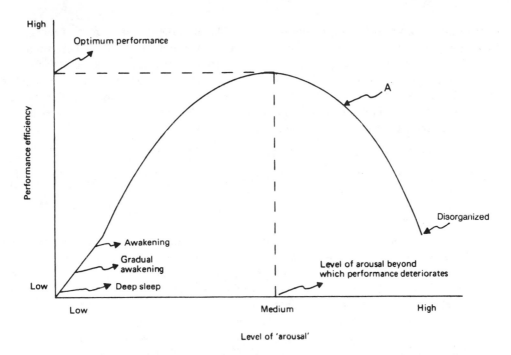

Figure 3.4 *Hypothetical relationship between arousal and performance efficiency (after Hebb).*

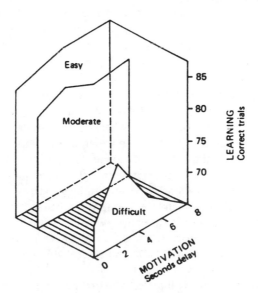

Figure 3.5 *A three-dimensional graph of the Yerkes–Dodson law. Reprinted from P. L. Broadhurst, 'Emotionality and the Yerkes–Dodson Law', J. Exp. Psychol., **54**, 348 (1957) with the permission of the American Psychological Association.*

deteriorates immediately. Representing this graphically, the starting point of our graph in Figure 3.4 would be around point A, which is beyond the peak of performance.

It would be premature to draw generalizations about class practices from the evidence presented above. A little tension or 'dissonance' might well be essential for arousal and learning. What we do not know is the limit of the tension which can be tolerated by individuals in given circumstances. The main point is to be wary of creating a classroom atmosphere which is too stressful.[56]

STRESS

Definition

Much of this book is devoted to children and their problems. But teachers too have problems, not least of which is the growing volume of demands which have been placed on their shoulders by changes in the education system. Teaching has always presented stresses and strains, but there can be little doubt that today's teachers are high amongst over-stressed professionals.[57] The introduction of so many innovations into school life, such as the National Curriculum, more detailed and time-consuming methods of assessment, more administration and committee meetings within the school, fewer sanctions which teachers can apply for misbehaviour, changing attitudes of children to schoolwork, etc., have all conspired to increase the tension in teaching. The topic straddles a number of chapters in this book, but there is logic in including stress in a chapter on motivation since this is one of the first things to be affected by stress.

How is stress defined? We saw in Chapter 2 that threatening stimulation can provoke emotional states and chemical changes in our bodies, giving rise to emotional responses. The 'drive' harnessed from these emotional states affects performance, as indicated in the previous section. The scientists amongst readers will recognize that stress and strain are physical terms and the analogy is useful. Stress, for the physicist, is the external pressure (force) applied to an object such as a length of wire. Strain is the result of applying that pressure. A weight hung on the end of a dangling wire could cause it to stretch. The weight is the stress. The greater it is, the more likely that stretching will take place. With lower weights, the wire returns to its original length when the weight is removed. With heavier weights, the lengthening (deformation) is permanent. With even greater pressure, the wire snaps. Different materials have different flexibilities and strengths. With humans, stress can be regarded as the pressures in an environment which are brought to bear on an individual. Strains are the outcome of how these pressures are perceived by the individual. Textbooks sometimes use stress to cover both terms (i.e. the whole process) or just strain (i.e. the effects of stress). In what follows, we shall use the 'whole process' definition. Figure 3.6 illustrates one interpretation of this process.

Demands are made of an individual from his or her environment. At best, if these demands are perceived as manageable, even exciting, performance is enhanced. If the demands are perceived as threatening or intolerable, then we are likely to exhibit symptoms of strain. These cover a range of physical, behavioural, mental and emotional reactions.[58] Under all these headings there are many manifestations, not all of which appear in one person at the same time or to the same degree. Physical signs

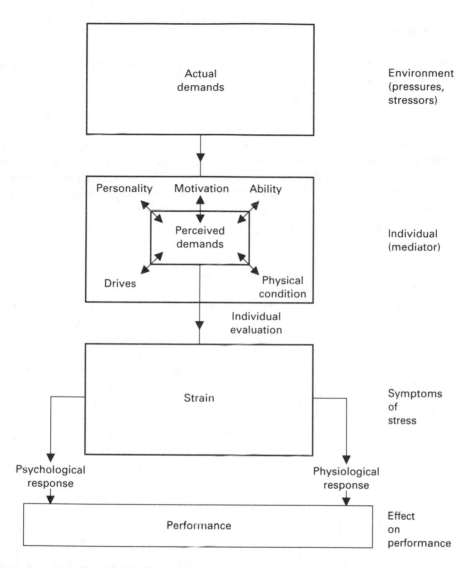

Figure 3.6 *Simplified model of stress process.*

include heart beat and breathing rates (usually increased), digestion problems, skin irritations and sweating, sleep disturbances and excesses of drink and drugs, etc. Behavioural problems might appear as self-neglect (body cleanliness, food), work does not get done, forgetfulness, disorganization. Mental effects, at the simplest level, involve confusion, feelings of being trapped, and at their worst become *psychosomatic* – that is, the physical symptoms described previously which have their origins in distressed mental states. They are just as real and potent as conditions and complaints arising from physical causes. Emotional effects involve coming to the aggressive boil rather quickly, 'touchiness', intolerance to noise and anxiety, appearing as feelings of fear at having to face similar demands (such as having to face a class and of losing control).

Stress in teachers

The general process outlined in Figure 3.6 will now be applied to the specific case of problems encountered by teachers. Some expansion of the sources (stressors), individual characteristics, symptoms and diseases, effects on performance and some suggestions for managing stress are outlined below. Several good textbooks on stress in teachers have appeared in the last decade.[59]

External sources of stress are numerous. But there are some basic ingredients which many researchers have identified in the workplace. Cooper[60] gives a useful summary of occupational stressors such as (a) those *intrinsic to the job* (poor physical conditions, work overload, time pressures); (b) one's *role in the organization* (role ambiguity and conflict, self-image in the job); (c) *career development* (over- or under-promotion, lack of job security); (d) *relationships at work* (with headteacher, head of department, colleagues, pupils); (e) *organizational structure and modus operandi* (little participation, rule bound, poor channels for consultation).

Of these sources, research[61] has shown that poor motivation, attitudes and behaviour of the pupils, poor working conditions (including resources such as equipment), time pressures, low status, and conflict with colleagues are rated the highest causes of stress in roughly the order presented here. It is important to reiterate that individuals react to different stressors to different extents. For some, the cut and thrust of classroom life is exciting. For others, it proceeds to cumulative despair.

A teacher has responsibilities laid down in the job description. These duties interact with the occupational expectations, desires, abilities and personality of the individual. To some extent there is an interaction between these two. Conflict comes when the perceived demands of the workplace, that is, demands by the regime (resources, local rules), and the pupils (unwilling workers, indiscipline) are not matched by the competences *as perceived by the individual.* If the duties, desires and capabilities required of the task of teaching are greater than the demands, the energies of stress can be used to advantage. If the demands created by the above sources are greater than the duties, expectations and capacities required of the job, as anticipated by the teacher, then we have the potential for overload and stress.

The characteristics of the teacher which are invoked by stressors will be the subject of later chapters in the book. Motivation and emotional reaction have been dealt with already, and here it was argued that individual differences occur in levels of physiological reaction, aggression or fear. Ability to cope with the school subjects being taught and with the relationships in the classroom are significant. Personality, particularly *Type A,*[62] is important. Type A behaviour is exhibited by people who are driven, impatient, over-workers, overactive, ambitious, impatient with those who get left behind, and so on. Type A teachers tend to be early victims of strain. Anxiety, neuroticism and difficulty in coping with ambiguity can also heighten strain. (See Chapter 11 on Personality for more detail of Type A characteristics.)

The symptoms exhibited by stressed people vary enormously. Broadly, the reactions can be divided into physical and psychological (mental, emotional, behavioural).

The physical reactions of the body help to mobilize energy used to support body functions, concentrate effort and increase the defensive functions. When present in temperate quantities all are advantageous, but excesses can lead to abnormal functioning. For example, the release of chemicals into the bloodstream (e.g. hormones, see Chapter 2) increases heart rate, sugar production and metabolic rate. An excess and prolonged secretion of these chemicals can lead to heart attack, strokes, high blood pressure, kidney damage, exhaustion, weight loss, ulcers, slowing down of mental and sensory functioning, and sexual impotence.

Psychological reactions can take many forms. Cognitive problems include decline in memory and attention, errors increase and delusions are possible in extreme cases. Emotional reactions involve increased tension (can't relax), personality changes or exaggerations (tidy people become sloppy, anxious people get progressively worse), depression sets in and feelings of worthlessness appear. Also psychosomatic disorders appear, such as asthma, high blood pressure, colitis or ulcers, and are caused by emotional rather than physical damage.

Uncharacteristic behaviour intrudes. Leisure pursuits are dropped ('can't be bothered doing anything these days') and absenteeism appears. Escapist drinking and drug-taking might start. Sleep patterns are affected. Job dissatisfaction and exhaustion is expressed in several ways such as doing the absolute minimum, passing the buck to others, adopting a laid-back and negligent style and losing the ambition to progress. In extreme cases, there may be suicide threats.

A prolonged period of stress with its progression of physical and mental ill-health culminates in *teacher burn-out*. This is a collective term for those symptoms appearing in an overstretched individual which affect his or her performance as a classroom teacher. Burn-out is most often associated with the behavioural attitudes described in the previous paragraph.

What can be done to avoid or handle stress? A helpful book on managing stress by Fontana[63] suggests three steps. These are *mobilization, knowledge* and *action*. Mobilization is the conscious process of persuading oneself that something must be done. It must be recognised that something is wrong and that it can be corrected. The next stage is to discover what the stressors are, what needs to be done and what is stopping the individual from doing it. Once the problems are identified, decisions about suitable courses of action are possible. Some stressors are beyond our control and we may have to learn how to adapt to them; others are in our control and a plan of action has to be carried out.

Stress in pupils

Young people in educational settings have their problems too, sometimes of sufficient intensity for them to end up in serious physical or mental states. Extreme cases, fortunately few in number, reach suicidal proportions and there are also on record students who have developed ME (myalgic encephalomyelitis). The causes are varied and range from parental pressure to do well at school or university, feelings of inadequacy (often ill-founded), to bullying. Broadly, these reasons group into *academic* and *interpersonal* pressures.

Most schools, universities and colleges have counselling and personal tutorial systems designed to give students a contact who might act as a mentor in academic work or in a pastoral role. This is more characteristic of further and higher education, but it has been introduced in recent years in some secondary schools. This topic is dealt with later in Chapter 15. In this section we shall concentrate on the topic of bullying in school children.

Bullying has been variously defined,[64] but for our purposes it can be said to happen when a person is persecuted or oppressed by physical or mental threat by another person or group. Bullying takes the form of physical violence, threats of violence, persistent and nasty teasing, extortion for money or goods, and deliberate isolation of a person by excluding that person from the group.

Bullying can be very hurtful to the recipient and the degree of hurt often not realized by those doing the bullying. The systematic study of bullying by psychologists has intensified in recent years and some good schemes have been created. One such, devised by Maines and Robinson, is known as the 'no blame approach'.[65] Central to their argument is that punishment is not the most effective way of stopping the bully. With the most persistent offender, punishment may have to be the last resort, but in the general run of things the following strategies are effective. Maines and Robinson offer a seven-step plan:

1. interview the person being bullied. The emphasis of the interview is on the feelings of the victim rather than who did it, when and how;
2. bring together the people responsible. This group could include bystanders. A group of six to eight is found to be a good number;
3. explain the problem by telling the group of the feeling experienced by the victim using any verbal, written or drawn material. No specific blame is directed at anyone in the group;
4. share the attribution of blame by saying that they are all responsible in some way;
5. get each member of the group to suggest ways in which the victim could be helped to feel happier. The teacher might contribute some positive ideas, but no 'contract' is drawn up. The ideas need to be listed and agreed by those present;
6. leave it to the group to solve the problem and arrange to meet the group at some later date for a progress report;
7. meet the victim and individual members of the group about a week after the first meeting to see how things have progressed.

The full scheme from which the outline above was taken is available as a training pack of written and videoed materials.[65]

SUMMARY

Children abound with vitality and an urge to satisfy many kinds of human needs. Armed with this knowledge, teachers are able to make the formal setting of school into an environment in which children can learn and develop efficiently. The process of motivation sees the release of energy which can be utilized for, and directed towards, educational objectives. Where children are physiologically satisfied, where they feel secure and wanted, and where they have the opportunity to grow in confidence, independence and self-esteem through achievement, there is every likelihood that they will go on to seek the intellectual satisfactions provided at school.

For our purposes, the important emphasis is in the testable outcomes of our methods in the classroom, rather than in seeking the elusive origins of human needs. For example, we know that young children become puzzled by their surroundings; they poke around, question, and show inquisitiveness; they manipulate and inspect most things that come within reach. The classroom, therefore, should be designed to take advantage of these ready-made characteristics. Children also strive to succeed or achieve in their attempt to master environmental obstacles (material, social or intellectual). We would not have survived if this had not been so. Of course, the conditions for achievement are varied, and research shows that a skilful combination of success and failure is more favourable for stimulating positive achievement than a distant or 'neutral' atmosphere. Children tasting success and failure – in that order – are most likely to continue the struggle to achieve. They also set themselves goals, and teachers must ensure that these goals are adequate and realistic for each child. The teacher must beware, however, of prejudging the capabilities of a child to the point where the teacher consistently underestimates or overestimates them. It is so easy to 'give a dog a bad name'.

Extrinsic motivators in the form of incentives are a very necessary part of a teacher's life. Children, like adults, want to know how they are faring in relation to their own previous performance and the performance of others. Research tells us that the sooner people know the outcome of their work the more likely it is that they will be reinforced to continue learning – always provided they meet with sufficient success, because knowledge of repeated failure is not likely to stimulate further activity. As we observed above, positive achievement must be part of the teacher's design. Praise and reproof from a respected teacher are powerful incentives. Children delight in approval in the presence of their peers.

A knowledge of childhood motives is one of the essentials of teaching skill. When children are pursuing purposeful activities in class because they feel the need and want to learn, their teacher is clearly well on the way to an understanding of these motives.

Stress in the workplace, arising from increasing demands made on an individual's physical and mental resources, has become a real problem for the teaching profession. Performance in various aspects of a teacher's life suffers as a consequence. Awareness of what the stressors are and what might be done to overcome them goes some way towards alleviating the stressful symptoms.

ENQUIRY AND DISCUSSION

(a) Examine Maslow's theory for its possible applications in education. Using the theory as a possible framework, consider the varied conditions of home and school likely to affect the highest desire of humans to satisfy their need for knowledge and understanding.

(b) On school observation, carefully note those activities which children in particular age groups most enjoy. Can these be turned to good effect in class? What criteria have you used for detecting interest and enthusiasm amongst children? Discuss with your tutors whether these are valid criteria.

(c) Observe children at play and note the differences according to age. Is play a 'natural' educator? Some believe that play (in both children and adults) is a way of acting out fantasies where one has power without restraint. What do you think? How can it be canalized to good effect in school work? Where should teachers draw the line between 'play' and 'work'?

(d) In the text we talked about 'a continuum of feedback mechanisms' running from high praise to severe punishment. Explore this continuum of possible 'rewards' and 'punishments' using your knowledge of schooldays, school observation and parental control. Which do you think are effective at particular ages and why? Discuss this matter with children.

(e)   Read *Pygmalion in the Classroom*[52] (**R**) and the criticisms of this work.[53] Discuss the possibility that the performance of girls in science and maths, or French in primary schools, is partly a product of self-fulfilling prophecies. What can a teacher do to avoid the self-fulfilment of adverse prophecies?

(f)   Note the use made by teachers of incentives. Compare the relative merits of incentives in particular age groups and, where possible, with different ability ranges.

(g)   The previous suggestions for enquiries could be pooled for group discussions with your tutor. At the same time, discuss the extent to which your findings fit in with previous work.

(h)   Explore the ways in which personal factors (pupils and teachers) affect the effectiveness of internal and external motivators.

(i)   How can the teacher of disadvantaged or deprived children compensate for their inadequate motivational systems (see the work on 'Head Start' and EPA (Educational Priority Area) projects and the Warnock Report)? References under 'Compensatory programmes' in Chapter 12 will be helpful.

(j)   After reading the recommended literature on stress, discuss the issues with teachers on teaching practice which they believe to be the important stressors. How do they cope with stress?

NOTES AND REFERENCES

1.   D. O. Hebb, 'The role of neurological ideas in psychology', *J. Personality*, **20**, 29–55 (1951).
2.   B. F. Skinner, *Science and Human Behavior*, Macmillan, New York, 1953, and *Beyond Freedom and Dignity*, Knopf, New York, 1971.
3.   W. McDougall, *An Introduction to Social Psychology*, Barnes and Noble, New York, 1960 (original: Methuen, London, 1908).
4.   McDougall posited 14 such human instincts, some with a corresponding 'sentiment', which was the emotional disposition characteristic of individuals arising from their particular experience and training in coping with each instinct. Those instincts such as food-seeking and gregariousness have no obvious corresponding sentiments. Here are some:

Instinct	Sentiment
Food Water } seeking	?
Gregariousness	?
Acquisitiveness	?
Constructive	?
Aggression	Anger
Mating	Sexual desire
Curiosity	Wonder
Self-assertion	Elation
Maternal	Tenderness
Repulsion	Disgust
Escape	Fear
Self-abasement	Submission

5. C. Burt, 'Is the doctrine of instincts dead?', A symposium. I – The case for human instincts. *Br. J. Educ. Psychol.*, **11**, 155–172 (1941).

6. P. E. Vernon, 'Is the doctrine of instincts dead?', A symposium. II. *Br. J. Educ. Psychol.*, **12**, 1–10 (1942).

7. The much quoted work of M. Mead, *Sex and Temperament*, Routledge, London, 1935, showed major differences in child-rearing practices which led to obvious differences in the characteristics of the tribes. The Arapesh of New Guinea, we are told, were peace-loving and not particularly interested in taking on the roles of leadership. Children were reared with great tenderness, given every attention and suckled at the breast for as long as the mother could hold out. The Mundugumour were aggressive, warlike and ruthless, and their babyhood likewise was made into a struggle between parent and child. Babies had to fight for the breasts for the short time they were available, and were starved of affection and handled roughly, if rarely. One is left wondering how much of the adult characteristics are the outcome of direct teaching from the parents, not so much as a baby, but later when the child could begin to understand the language and learn the tribal mores. Again, the fertility or hostility of the environment, which was easy for the Arapesh and harsh for the Mundugumour, may have determined the particular traits which would assist the tribes to survive. Thus, the question of whether we are dealing here with inherited or acquired characteristics is wide open. See also R. Benedict, *Patterns of Culture*, Routledge, London, 1935.

8. G. W. Allport, *Personality*, Holt, New York, 1937.

9. An elaboration of the ethologists' work can be found in N. Tinbergen, *A Study of Instinct*, Oxford University Press, Oxford, 1951. W. H. Thorpe also has a readable summary in *Learning and Instinct in Animals*, Methuen, London, 1956.

   E. H. Hess, in a chapter in *New Directions in Psychology*, Holt, Rinehart and Winston, New York, 1962, suggests that orphans who grow to be incurably unsocialized do so because they have missed out on social contact during an early critical period. See W. Sluckin, *Imprinting and Early Learning*, Methuen, London, 1964.

   For a statement showing Lorenz's adaptation of animal instincts to human behaviour see K. Lorenz, *On Aggression*, Methuen, London, 1966, and *The Foundations of Ethology*, Springer-Verlag, New York, 1981. J. Archer, *Ethology and Human Development*, Harvester Wheatsheaf (Simon & Schuster), Hemel Hempstead, 1992.

   Xenophobia, or the hatred existing between human races, has been described by Robert Ardrey, in *The Territorial Imperative*, Collins, London, 1967, as an example of an inborn biological tendency akin to the animal's desire to protect its territory against predators. We are said to dislike foreigners because they constitute a threat to survival or to our way of life.

   See also D. Morris, *The Naked Ape* (1968), *The Human Zoo* (1971), Corgi, London, and *Manwatching*, Cape, London, 1977.

10. Sigmund Freud (1856–1939) was a prolific writer and thinker. His gift to psychology and in turn to education is not so much a theory of motivation or personality, but a way of thinking about the mental life of human beings. His postulates, in the main, have been criticized because their circularity makes verification difficult; his theories are an act of faith. Attempts have been made to put his point of view on a firm scientific footing and these are summarized by Kline and challenged by Eysenck and Wilson (see note (14) in Chapter 11). For Freud's views on instincts see 'Instincts and their vicissitudes' (1915) in *A Collection of Papers of Sigmund Freud*, vol. I (translated by Riviere), Hogarth, London, 1949, and 'Beyond the pleasure principle' (1920) in J. Strachey (ed.), *The Standard Edition of the Complete Psychological Works of Sigmund Freud*, vol. 22, Hogarth, London, 1955.

11. W. B. Cannon, *The Wisdom of the Body*, Norton, London, 1932.

12. C. L. Hull, *Principles of Behavior*, Appleton-Century-Crofts, New York, 1943.

13. For a clear summary see W. F. Hill, *Learning: A Survey of Psychological Interpretations*, Methuen, London, 1980 (3rd edn).

14. H. A. Murray, *Explorations in Personality*, Oxford University Press, Oxford, 1938. The needs postulated by Murray in this book are listed below:

Abasement: the need to submit.
Achievement: master, accomplish.
Affiliation: form friends and be with people.
Aggression: forceful opposition.
Autonomy: overcome coercion.
Counteraction: refuse defeat.
Defendance: defend oneself.
Deference: admire another.
Dominance: control human environment.
Exhibition: attract attention.
Harmavoidance: avoid pain.
Infavoidance: avoid failure.
Nurturance: aid the helpless.
Order: to organize.
Play: relax, seek fun.
Rejection: ignore another.
Sentience: search for and enjoy sensuous things.
Sex: form erotic relationships.
Succorance: to seek help.
Understanding: to theorize and analyse.

15. H. F. Harlow and R. R. Zimmerman, 'Affectional responses in the infant monkey', *Science*, **130**, 421 (1959). Also see the work of the field theorist, K. Lewin, *Principles of Topological Psychology*, McGraw-Hill, New York, 1936.
16. R. B. Cattell and D. Child, *Motivation and Dynamic Structure*, Holt, Rinehart and Winston, London, 1975. To get an idea of Cattell's theory of motivation, Chapters 1 and 2 should prove sufficient. See also Chapter 8 for applications to education. For a recent assessment of the applications of Cattell's work in education, see D. Child, 'Recent developments of MAT and SMAT', in K. M. Miller (ed.), *The Analysis of Personality in Research and Assessment*, Independent Assessment and Research Centre, London, 1988, pp. 81–92. Also see D. Child, 'Motivation and the Dynamic Calculus – a teacher's view', in *Multivariate Behav. Res.*, **19**(2-3), 288–298 (1984).
17. P. N. Johnson-Laird, *The Computer and the Mind*, Fontana, London, 1988.
18. J. B. Rotter, *Social Learning and Clinical Psychology*, Prentice-Hall, Englewood Cliffs, NJ, 1954, and 'Generalized expectancies of internal versus external control of reinforcement', *Psychol. Monogr.*, **80**, 1 (1966).
19. B. Weiner, 'An attributional approach for educational psychology', in L. Shulman (ed.), *Review of Research in Education*, Peacock, Itasca, IL, 1977.
20. D. E. Berlyne, *Conflict, Arousal and Curiosity*, McGraw-Hill, New York, 1960.
21. J. McV. Hunt, 'Experience and the development of motivation: some reinterpretations', *Child Dev.*, **31**, 489–504 (1960).
22. L. Festinger, *A Theory of Cognitive Dissonance*, Row Peterson, Evanston, IL, 1957.
23. P. Evans, *Motivation and Emotion*, Routledge, London, 1989.
24. R. S. Peters, *The Concept of Motivation*, Routledge and Kegan Paul, London, 1958. Although he lays emphasis on providing for an examination of human motivation by starting with the classification of people's observable goals and, as it were, working back, Peters does see a place for causal theories, particularly in looking at devious cases.
25. S. Ball (ed.), *Motivation in Education*, Academic Press, New York, 1977; W. B. Kolesnik, *Motivation: Understanding and Influencing Human Behaviour*, Allyn and Bacon, Boston, 1978.
26. A. H. Maslow, *Motivation and Personality*, Harper and Row, New York, 1970 (2nd edn).
27. Planarians, small, simple creatures very low in the animal kingdom, absorb their reproductive organs back into the body tissue when there is no food. It almost seems as though reproduction is taken as being pointless when basic body needs cannot be satisfied. There is no purpose in bringing young into the world if they cannot be fed. But this would endow the planarian with the ability for conscious control, where in fact the absorption of the reproductive organs is entirely physiological.

28. In the Minnesota Starvation Studies, 26 normal men were put on a six-month semi-starvation diet. In all other respects, such as living quarters, social life and exercise, their provisions were normal. All were soon preoccupied with food. A few extreme cases displayed serious mental disorders. A. Keys, 'Experimental introduction of psychoneuroses by starvation', *The Biology of Mental Health and Disease*, 27th Annual Conference: Millbank Memorial Fund, Harper and Row, New York, 1952.

29. C. B. Ferster, *Schedules of Reinforcement*, Appleton, New York, 1957; B. F. Skinner, *The Science of Human Behavior*, Macmillan, New York, 1963.

30. E. B. Hurlock, 'An evaluation of certain incentives used in school work', *J. Educ. Psychol.*, **16**, 145–159 (1925).

31. H. O. Schmidt, 'The effect of praise and blame on incentives to learning', *Psychol. Monogr.*, **53**, 240 (1941).

32. I. Johannesson, 'Effects of praise and blame upon achievement and attitudes in school children', *Child and Education*, Munksgaard, Copenhagen, 1962.

33. G. C. Walters and J. E. Grusec, *Punishment*, Freeman, San Francisco, 1977.

34. C. B. Stendler, D. Damrin and A. C. Haines, 'Studies in cooperation and competition: I: the effects of working for group and individual rewards on the social climate of children's groups', *J. Genet. Psychol.*, **79**, 173–197 (1951).

35. There is a long literature on this subject, stretching back to J. C. Chapman and R. B. Feder, 'The effect of external incentives on improvement', *J. Educ. Psychol.*, **8**, 469–474 (1917). See also J. Vaughn and C. M. Diserens, 'The experimental psychology of competition', *J. Exp. Educ.*, **7**, 76–97 (1938). For a more recent overview see D. W. Johnson and R. T. Johnson, *Learning Together and Alone*, Prentice-Hall, Englewood Cliffs, NJ, 1975.

36. D. P. Ausubel and F. G. Robinson, *School Learning*, Holt, Rinehart and Winston, New York, 1969.

37. J. S. Bruner, *Toward a Theory of Instruction*, Chapter 6, Norton, New York, 1968.

38. For a comprehensive summary of the role of play in development see J. S. Bruner, A. Jolly and K. Sylva, *Play: Its Role in Development and Evolution*, Pelican Books, London, 1976. For background reading which attempts to analyse the research literature see S. Millar, *The Psychology of Play*, Penguin, Harmondsworth, 1968, or M. J. Ellis, *Why People Play*, Prentice-Hall, Englewood Cliffs, NJ, 1973. Recent texts include J. R. Moyles, *Just Playing? The Role and Status of Play in Early Childhood*, Open University Press, Buckingham, 1989.

39. An enormous volume of research has sprung from D. C. McClelland's concept of n Ach. Some of this is summarized in his books *Studies in Motivation*, Appleton-Century-Crofts, New York, 1955, and *Motives, Personality and Society*, Centennial, 1984, but the most detailed statement of his view is to be found in D. C. McClelland, J. W. Atkinson, R. A. Clark and E. L. Lowell, *The Achievement Motive*, Irvington Publishers, New York, 1976. See also J. W. Atkinson and J. O. Raynor, *Motivation and Achievement*, Winston & Sons, Washington, DC, 1974. For more information about McClelland's use of TAT (Thematic Apperception Test), see note (40**R**).

40. (**R**) D. C. McClelland, 'What is the effect of achievement motivation training in the schools?', *Teachers College Record*, **74**, 129–145 (1972). For advice to teachers see 'Towards a theory of motivation acquisition', *American Psychologist*, **20**, 321–333 (1965).

41. J. W. Atkinson, *An Introduction to Motivation*, Van Nostrand, Princeton, NJ, 1964. J. W. Atkinson and G. H. Litwin, 'Achievement motive and test anxiety as motives to approach success and avoid failure', *Journal of Abnormal and Social Psychology*, **60**, 52–63. (1960). C. Mahone, 'Fear of failure in unrealistic vocational aspirations', *Journal of Abnormal and Social Psychology*, **60**, 253–261 (1960). R. C. Birney, H. Burdick and R. I. Teevan, *Fear of Failure*, Van Nostrand, Princeton, NJ, 1969.

42. T. Gjesme, 'Motive to achieve success and motive to avoid failure in relation to school performance for pupils of different ability levels', *Scand. J. Educ. Res.*, **15**, 81–99 (1971).

43. H. G. Gough, 'What determines academic achievement of high school students?', *J. Educ. Res.*, **46**, 321–331 (1953).

44. P. S. Sears, 'Levels of aspiration in academically successful and unsuccessful children', *J. Abnorm. Soc. Psychol.*, **35**, 498–536 (1940).

45. C. Rogers, *A Social Psychology of Schooling: The Expectancy Process*, Routledge and Kegan Paul, London, 1982. See also R. Burns, *Self-Concept Development and Education*, Holt, Rinehart and Winston, Eastbourne, 1982. Rogers's book contains some useful cautious comments. See also D. Satterly and J. Hill, 'Personality differences and the effects of success and failure on causal attributions and expectancies of primary school children', *Educational Psychology*, **3**, 245–258 (1983).

46. Weiner's theory of 1974 is restated in a later book; see B. J. Weiner, *An Attributional Theory of Motivation and Emotion*, Springer-Verlag, New York, 1986. Also 'A theory of motivation for some classroom experiences', *Journal of Educational Psychology*, **71**, 3–25 (1979).

47. (R) R. B. Burns, 'The self-concept and its relevance to academic achievement', in D. Child (ed.), *Readings in Psychology for the Teacher*, Holt, Rinehart and Winston, London, 1976.

48. (R) D. Child, 'Recent developments of MAT and SMAT', in K. M. Miller (ed.), *The Analysis of Personality in Research and Assessment*, Independent Assessment and Research Centre, London, 1988, pp. 81–92, and 'Motivation and the Dynamic Calculus – a teacher's view', in *Multivariate Beh. Res.*, **19**, 2–3, 288–298 (1984).

49. W. B. Brookover, E. L. Erikson and L. M. Joiner, *Self-concept of Ability and School Achievement* III, Final report on Cooperative Research Project No. 2831, East Lansing, Michigan State University, 1967.

50. J. C. Barker Lunn, *Streaming in the Primary School*, NFER, Slough, 1970.

51. B. S. Bloom, *Human Characteristics and School Learning*, McGraw-Hill, New York, 1976.

52. (R) R. Rosenthal and L. Jacobson, *Pygmalion in the Classroom*, Holt, Rinehart and Winston, New York, 1968. See also D. A. Pidgeon, *Expectation and Pupil Performance*, NFER, Slough, 1970. See R. Rosenthal and L. Jacobson, 'Teachers' expectancies: determinants of pupils' IQ gains', *Psychol. Rep.*, **19**, 115–118 (1966) in the Reader.

53. *Pygmalion Reconsidered*, published by C. A. Jones, Worthington, OH, 1971. There is also a summary of the main criticisms under the same heading by J. D. Elashoff and R. E. Snow in *Psychology of Education: New Looks*, edited by G. A. Davies and T. F. Warren, Heath, New York, 1973. There is an excellent summary of the research on self-fulfilling prophecy by C. Braun, 'Teacher expectation: sociopsychological dynamics', *Rev. Educ. Res.*, **46**, 185–213 (1976). In this he gives a most useful table on pp. 201–202 of how expectation cues might be transmitted from teacher to learner. For instance, teachers form opinions about the different levels of performance of pupils and this leads to their treating pupils differently; then pupils respond differently, and so on. See Rogers's book in note (45) for a good summary of this process.

54. R. M. Yerkes and J. D. Dodson, 'The relation of strength of stimulus to rapidity of habit-formation', *J. Comp. Neurol. Psychol.*, **18**, 459–482 (1908).

55. (R) P. L. Broadhurst, 'Emotionality and the Yerkes–Dodson Law', *J. Exp. Psychol.*, **54**, 345–352 (1957).

56. It has been claimed by Biggs, in research on the teaching of mathematics in primary schools, that very high levels of anxiety are created regularly by inadequate teaching of the subject (partly because the teachers are not themselves numerate). The outcome is a widespread dislike of the subject because pupils associate high tension with it. See J. B. Biggs, 'The psychological relationships between cognitive and affective factors in arithmetic performance', Ph.D. thesis, London University.

57. B. Fletcher, 'The epidemiology of occupational stress', in C. L. Cooper and R. Payne (eds), *Causes, Coping and Consequences of Stress at Work*, pp. 3–50, Wiley, Chichester, 1988.

58. R. L. Atkinson, R. C. Atkinson, E. E. Smith and D. J. Bem, *Introduction to Psychology*, Harcourt Brace Jovanovich, New York, 1992 (11th edn).

59. C. Kyriacou, 'Teacher stress and burnout: an international review', *Educ. Res.*, **29**(2), 146–152 (1987). M. Cole and S. Walker (eds), *Teaching and Stress*, Open University Press, Milton Keynes, 1989, gives a good introduction to the subject. G. Claxton, *Being a Teacher: A Positive Approach to Change and Stress*, Cassell, London, gives a readable and not too technical account of stress in teachers from within the classroom.

60. C. L. Cooper, 'Job distress: recent research and the emerging role of the clinical psychologist', *Bull. Br. Psychol. Soc.*, **399**, 325–331 (1986).
61. C. Kyriacou, 'The nature and prevalence of teacher stress', pp. 27–34, in M. Cole and S. Walker, op. cit., note (59) above.
62. Type A behaviour was first identified and defined by Friedman and Rosenman, two heart specialists in the USA who started their studies in the late 1950s. Since then, much research has been done with varying degrees of success in verifying their original speculations. A book edited by M. J. Strube, entitled *Type A Behavior*, Sage, Beverly Hills, CA, 1991, contains many reports of recent research including one using meta-analysis – that is, combining the results of several similar researches into one statistically acceptable single data set. These are in general supportive. Type A behaviour is characterized by ambitiousness, aggressiveness, competitiveness, impatience. The overt signs are often muscle tenseness, quick-fire speaking style, abruptness and alertness, irritation, hostility and a penchant for anger.
63. D. Fontana, *Managing Stress*, British Psychological Society (Leicester) and Routledge (London), 1989.
64. V. E. Besag, *Bullies and Victims in Schools*, Open University Press, Milton Keynes, 1989.
65. Barbara Maines and George Robinson have produced a number of publications and schemes for dealing with bullying in schools. For a general reference see B. Maines and G. Robinson, *Stamp Out Bullying*, Lame Duck Publishing, 71 South Street, Portishead, Avon, 1991. Packs containing information about the schemes can be obtained from this address.

FURTHER READING

S. Ball (ed.), *Motivation in Education*, Academic Press, New York, 1977. A sound text with a readable selection of articles.

P. Evans, *Motivation*, Essential Psychology Series, Methuen, London, 1975.

W. B. Kolesnik, *Motivation: Understanding and Influencing Human Behavior*, Allyn and Bacon, Boston, 1978.

E. J. Murray, *Motivation and Emotion*, Prentice-Hall, Englewood Cliffs, NJ, 1964. Concise and well written.

M. D. Vernon, *Human Motivation*, Cambridge University Press, London, 1969. A detailed, well-balanced book with plenty of value for a teacher.

W. D. Wall, 'The wish to learn: research into motivation', *Educ. Res.*, **1**, 23–37 (1958). Extremely readable introduction to the subject.

Chapter 4

Attention and Perception

The ceaseless, simultaneous bombardment of stimuli on the sense organs and their subsequent treatment in the nervous system and brain were mentioned in a previous chapter without considering the prevention of overloading (see, for example, the section on the brain stem in Chapter 2). Clearly we could not possibly cope with every stimulus that falls on the eyes in a given instant, let alone those falling on all the other senses at the same time. Just consider for a moment some aspects of what is happening around you at this very instant. Your eyes are taking in the print impressions (and I hope the brain is *encoding* and translating them into meaningful patterns!), as well as the peripheral images of other nearby objects on the table or of your hand gripping the book. You may be the victim of audible noises from other students, vehicles, building in progress, and so on. There may be perfume or other chemicals in the air. Your body is experiencing pressure from contact with clothes, and objects such as this book, the chair and the table. Along with many other sensory possibilities, the brain would have to deal with a phenomenal number of sensations. The study of attention is concerned with finding an answer to the question of how the body manages so many signals and why an individual selects certain stimuli for attention and ignores others.

Again, having selected stimuli for attention, what do we make of them? If, for example, we looked at the same object or listened to the same piece of music, would we interpret the sensory stimuli in precisely the same way? It is more than likely that we would not. There may be cultural differences in the way we perceive objects because of differences in our sensory experience (see the section on illusions later in the chapter), or the combinations of notes in the music may be recognized as a tune by some and simply seem an indescribable, formless noise to others. Most important is the fact that the interpretation of present sensory information is dependent on our past experiences. As Kant once said, 'we see things not as they are but as we are'. A consideration of sensory interpretation, or perception, will be the second major concern in this chapter.

THE MEANING OF SENSATION, ATTENTION AND PERCEPTION

First let us distinguish between three terms, sometimes confused, which frequently recur in this chapter. They are sensation, attention and perception. *Sensation* is said to occur when any sense organ (eye, ear, nose) receives a stimulus from the external or internal environment. This can, and frequently does, occur without our knowledge. Sound waves, for instance, are impinging on the ear-drum and causing disturbances which we do not register. If you listen attentively for a moment you will soon discover many sounds which would have passed you by had you not made a search for them.

With so many senses being activated at the same time, how is it that we are aware of only one stimulus at a time? One possible explanation is that a selection mechanism operates which is either voluntary (where we make a deliberate effort and search for a particular kind of stimulus) or involuntary (where some peculiar quality of the stimulus arrests our attention). The ability of human beings to process some part of the incoming sensations to the sense organs and to ignore everything else is referred to as *attention*[1] (some psychologists use the term *orientation reaction*).

Receiving and attending to a noise or the touch of a material is only part of the story, because we need to interpret the selected sensations in the light of the present context and our past experience. This internal analysis and integration of sensations by the brain is termed *perception*. Although these three terms are defined separately, it is clear from the definitions that they are closely connected and constitute an integral part of human information-processing.

A common and inaccurate belief is that the sensations picked up from our surroundings are selected, received, interpreted and reproduced by the brain like a photograph or gramophone record of sights and sounds – as if there were a little man sitting in the recesses of the brain making exact reproductions of incoming signals. This is not the case. The physical images received by the sense organs must first be translated (*encoded* – see the next section on Broadbent's filter theory) into a form compatible with nerve impulses previously received and stored so that the incoming impulses can be matched with past experience. Consider how many ways you have experienced the concept 'rose' – spoken word, written word, touch, smell, sight, etc. In the spoken word alone you will have heard many accents, voice pitches and intensities, but all have been transformed to a common code. So there is a wide latitude within which sensory experience is given a common meaning (*perceptual constancy*). Therefore the nervous system must carry out appreciable transformations of the input of physical images in order for perception to take place.

ATTENTION

At the beginning of the present century, James[2] generated considerable interest among psychologists in the topic of attention. Experimentation was not his strong point, but his insights into the processes of attention and perception served until the early 1950s, when Broadbent[3] revitalized interest with his seminal researches and speculations.

Above we defined attention in a rather specific fashion. It refers chiefly to *selective* or *voluntary* attention, when the individual is actively seeking some signals and ignoring others. Sometimes the term is used to describe search behaviour, as in vigilance tasks where the individual is required to identify specified signals on a screen or clock. Sometimes our attention is demanded rather than controlled (*involuntary* attention), as when we hear an unusual sound, see contrasting colours on a blackboard or sense a harsh smell. Factors influencing attention are discussed later in the chapter. The work we shall describe below deals essentially with purposeful attention.

Broadbent's filter theory

Broadbent's work on selective attention has been a productive model (**R**).[4] Basically, the filter model (see Figure 4.1) is taken from communication theory, including much of the jargon, and attempts an explanation of how selective attention is managed. The sense organs and nervous system receiving and transmitting impulses are referred to as the *input channels*. Several input channels are operating simultaneously in parallel. However, the amount of information passing along the channels is far too much for the brain to cope with at any one time because overloading would occur if all the information was assimilated. Thus, to regulate the intake Broadbent supposes that there is a filter followed by a bottleneck (*limited-capacity channel*) which selects some of the incoming impulses for processing in the brain. The input not selected may be held in a *short-term storage* system and can be taken out of store provided this is done within a very short time (a few seconds at the most). However, the stored input signals grow weaker with time and when 'a line becomes available' for one impulse through the limited capacity channel, the remaining stored impulses suffer a further weakening effect. The phenomenon of short-term memory accounts for both our ability to recall a very recent incident and the deficit in information when it has been stored for a short time compared with the moment of reception. In other words, we have a temporary and limited capacity for remembering events which the sense organs have received but to which we have not given our immediate attention.

Transmissions through the limited capacity channel are said to be processed by a perceptual system possessing at least the *long-term memory* store and a *decision-making system*. The latter is subsequently responsible for *effector* activity and *output*.

Several modifications have been recommended to accommodate subsequent research findings. For example, the model assumes that selection of input takes place *before* the interpretation of its meaning, which confines the selection to the physical sensory characteristics of the input. Treisman[5] questions this stage at which Broadbent places selection and argues from her researches that a more complex analytical mechanism operates to filter out levels of increasing complexity. Thus, starting with physical characteristics, let us say of spoken sentences, one voice sound is chosen from all others. Then comes a test of that sound for syllables, words, grammatical structure and finally meaning. Therefore the sentence input is progressively attended to and defined. Peripheral input is stored temporarily in the short-term memory and *attenuated* ('subdued' or 'reduced' in value).

More recently, Craik and Lockhart[6] proposed three levels into which information might be translated (*encoded*) in readiness for storage in the long-term memory. (This subject is developed further in Chapter 6.) These are *visual/auditory*, *syntactic* and *semantic* levels, forming a hierarchy. At the simplest level a visual or auditory stimulus is received and processed for storage. If we give a young person an unfamiliar word,

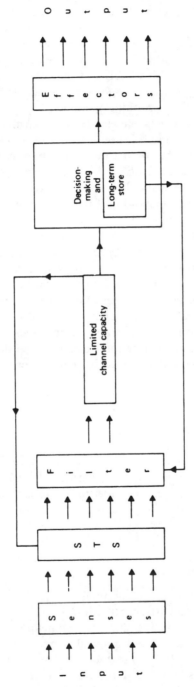

Figure 4.1 Adapted from D. E. Broadbent, Perception and Communication, Oxford University Press, London, 1987. (STS = short-term store.)

e.g. 'braise', the pattern of letters or the sound of the word could be stored, but without meaning. However, if we placed the word correctly in a phrase, additional meaning could be given to it. For example, 'you can braise meat' tells the child that the word is a verb – something can be done when you braise – but it does not convey a definition of the word. To do this would require a definitive statement making semantic-level processing possible, e.g. 'you can braise meat by frying it quickly and then stewing it in water'. This information will probably not be stored in isolation from previous knowledge: it will most likely be *accommodated* (cf. Piaget in Chapter 7) into previous similar kinds of knowledge about cooking methods.

All three levels of process occur in the classroom. Learning without understanding of isolated visual and auditory stimuli is not uncommon. For example, in learning the shapes and sounds of the alphabet or the numbers, there is no inherent logic in the link between the sight and sound of the symbols. Teachers would be wise to consider the level in the hierarchy of the work they are giving to pupils in order to assess the steps needed to arrive at an understanding of the material being taught.

And how is the information encoded for storage in the long-term memory? A contemporary view of Paivio[7] has found support from physiological and psychological sources. His dual system suggests a *non-verbal imagery* process and a *verbal symbolic* process. The first process involves storage of information as a non-verbal representation – sight, sound, touch; the second involves the storage of word meanings. The first line of the poem 'The boy stood on the burning deck' may be stored and retrieved either as a visual image or as a verbal statement. One source of supporting evidence for the dual-encoding idea comes from the split-brain research mentioned in the last chapter, where it was indicated that a differentiation exists between the left and right sides of the brain: the right hemisphere is involved in imagery processes, the left in verbal symbolic processes.

The factors which influence attention

Workers in this field are agreed that both the observer and the stimulus possess characteristics which are likely to influence attention. The following are of particular relevance for the teacher. For convenience let us divide them into external and internal factors.

External factors

The most important are as follows:

(a) Selection of information does not occur in a random fashion. The *intensity* of a stimulus, for instance, can attract attention. Loud noises, bright colours, strong odours and high pressure on the skin are compelling stimuli.
(b) *Novel* stimuli attract attention. Any unusual or irregular event is liable to distract us. The reason for using italics in a textbook or colour on a blackboard is to draw your eye to key concepts by printing the words in an irregular form. Ringing the changes of methods of presenting subject matter in school has obvious possibilities of catching children's attention.

(c)   A *variable* or *changing stimulus* demands our attention. Animals stalking their prey (cats for instance) move as little as possible so as not to attract attention. Teachers quickly discover how to use their voices by changing the intonation frequently. Wall charts and aids should be changed regularly, otherwise they no longer attract the children's interest: the children become *adapted* to the aids in the same way as happens with the ticking of a clock to which one becomes accustomed and takes for granted.

(d)   *Regularity* of stimuli presented in space (spatial) or time (temporal) has an effect on attention. Distributed presentations, again to avoid becoming adapted, have a better chance of becoming noticed than rapid, regular presentations.

(e)   Certain *colours* are more attractive than others. Infants are much more interested in coloured than in grey backgrounds, and both children and adults pay more attention to red and white designs than to black and white ones.

(f)   *High sounds* are more likely to be listened to than low sounds when the two are presented simultaneously.

(g)   *Conditioned* and habitual stimuli are likely to be picked out from other stimuli. When your name is announced in the midst of other names or conversation, you will pick it out. This is called the 'cocktail party' effect because it is often possible to hear a familiar phrase or name over and above the chatter of conversation at a party.

(h)   *Cueing* involves the deliberate use of clues or hints which direct attention to a stimulus. Teachers frequently use cues to orientate pupils. For example, verbal cues such as 'watch this' and 'note that' or physical cues such as pointing or demonstrating are employed.

Internal factors

Physical and mental dispositions are necessarily important influences on attentiveness. The fact that people in identical or very similar physical circumstances display striking differences in the degree to which they attend to stimuli is partly a matter of internal dispositions. The following are among the most important:

(a)   *Interest* and the lack of it, as in boredom, are clearly factors likely to cause differential attention. Events in which a child has already gained an interest are more likely to attract attention than events which have not previously been of interest. Attitudes and prejudices also affect the extent to which we are drawn to pay heed to events or ideas.

(b)   Physical or social *deprivations* pertaining to basic human needs (see Chapter 3) have a marked effect on the direction and intensity of attention. Sensory deprivation for any length of time can have a disorientating effect. It affects both physical and mental capacities. Feelings of being off balance, hallucinations, irritability and being unable to concentrate or solve problems are some of the effects. Those subjected to experiments (frequently university students) in which they wear translucent goggles, gloves, long cardboard cuffs on the arms and are asked to sit still in one position find the sensory deprivation unbearable after a time. Some students, despite a handsome financial inducement, had to abandon the experiment.[8] Recent work by Suedfeld and Coren[8] has shown that reduced stimulation under controlled conditions can help to reduce sleeplessness and tension headaches.

Extreme deprivation frequently leads to excessive orientation of all the senses towards the satisfaction of the deprived need. Excessive starvation ultimately gives rise to all manner of unusual manifestations where the individual dreams of, fights for, has hallucinations about, and directs all physical and mental energies towards food (see the Minnesota Starvation Studies, Chapter 3, note (28)).

(c) *Fatigue* has a detrimental effect on attentiveness. It stands to reason that, as our physical reserves become depleted, our vigilance in any sense modality will be correspondingly reduced. Fatigue can occur in a general way where the whole body is affected, or it can occur in one or some of the senses which have been over-used. A child who is short of sleep or exhausted from strenuous physical or mental activity is unlikely to attend in class. This can be related to *span of attention* (see also Chapters 6 and 11), in which it can be shown that we differ in the extent to which we can concentrate on or cope with sheer quantity of information. One wonders how many children become swamped with information, thus lessening their capacity for attention.

(d) In the chapter on motivation (and subsequently in our discussions of personality) we met with a theory of drive which states that performance improves with increased *arousal* up to a point. Beyond this point, performance begins to deteriorate until, at high levels of arousal, the quality of performance is extremely poor. A graph of this relationship (Figure 3.4) approximates to an inverted U-shape. Attention is also thought to be affected in a similar way as the arousal level increases. A basic level is needed in the first place for attention to be attracted (a threshold of arousal) and once this level has been passed the individual's attention increases usefully. Beyond an optimum level, which varies with the sense in use and the intensity of the external and internal factors mentioned above, attention becomes adversely affected.

(e) The *attention needs* mentioned in Chapter 3 – curiosity, exploration and manipulation – are clearly influential in directing attention.

(f) Our attention is most frequently drawn to those activities or ideas which we least expect. *Expectation* is an important factor in directing attention (see Chapter 3). This is also related to several external factors mentioned above.

(g) *Personality characteristics* have a differential influence. Students will be introduced later to a theory of personality structure involving several personality types, and one type, defined by the dimension of extraversion and introversion, will be considered in more detail then. For the present, it is enough to point out that many behavioural distinctions exist between extraverts and introverts. Extraverts need more *involuntary rest pauses* while performing tasks requiring concentration. Consequently their vigilance suffers in comparison with introverts, who do not require so many pauses. Extraverts also accumulate inhibition to the continuation of a repetitive task and therefore cannot attend as consistently as introverts.[9] The sensory thresholds (levels of stimulation required for us to be aware of the stimulus, mentioned in Chapter 2) tend to be lower for introverts than for extraverts. The implications for the class teacher are that children with extravert qualities are more likely to wilt and become distracted during long periods of attentive activity and to work at a lower level of sensory susceptibility than introverts.

The notion of *set induction* is a useful one in the context of attention-seeking applied by teachers in their work.[10] *Set* is a term used by some psychologists to describe the state of readiness to receive a stimulus. *Induction* relates to the process of trying to encourage set. Teachers are obviously in the business of inducing various kinds of readiness in the classroom. We have already had an example of one kind of set inducer in cueing (a behaviourist term originally) which is a direct call for attention ('Watch', 'Pay attention, John'). Another example is Ausubel's *advance organizers*. These are ideas fed to learners at the beginning of a lesson in order to give structure to what is to follow and to help the learner in organizing the material.

Several kinds of set have been defined (Hargie *et al.*[10]). There are *motivational*, *perceptual*, *social*, *cognitive* and *educational*. Hargie *et al.* give a fuller indication of the intentions of set induction in all these forms:

(a) to induce in participants a state of readiness appropriate to the task which is to follow, through establishing rapport, gaining attention and arousing motivation;

(b) to ascertain the expectations of the participants and the extent of their knowledge about the topic to be considered;

(c) to indicate to participants what might be reasonable objectives for the task to follow;

(d) to explain to participants what one's functions are, and what limitations may accompany these functions;

(e) to establish links with previous encounters (during follow-up sessions);

(f) to ascertain the extent of the participants' knowledge of the topic to be discussed.

Motivational set refers to those aspects of, in this case, the learning environments which are used to gain the attention of learners. The list of external factors above indicates some of the more important stimulants. Perceptual set has to do with how a person perceives the personal attributes of others and how this might influence performance. The teacher has an important role to play in making sure that the setting is conducive to learning. Impressions of the teacher, other children, the school organization have, in some cases, had an effect on the performance of children. Social set refers to the interrelations which set the scene for learning, for example the social rituals (or graces) such as welcoming, smiling, using voice or eye contact. Cognitive set relates to mental preparedness – creating a comprehensive framework for the lesson to follow (cf. Ausubel's advance organizers). Finally, educational set concerns the learning style preferences contrasting 'factual set' learners and 'conceptual set' learners (Siegel and Siegel[11]). These style preferences will influence the readiness of children to participate in different lesson methods (rote learning, theoretical or analytical sessions).

PERCEPTION

We cannot help making sense of our world. How this might be done varies from one person to another. The basic sensory signals from objects are the same, but the way we apprehend them differs because of the circumstances in which similar sensory experiences have occurred. The newborn child with crude sensory equipment and next to no backlog of experience against which to evaluate incoming signals builds up, from recurring stimulus patterns presented in a multitude of sizes, shapes, colours, distance from the eye, etc., a perception of its surroundings.

In effect we impose structure on our environment by building models from our sensory experience. In doing this we scan a scene or listen to sounds and pick out particular features which become *the figure*. The background against which the figure is observed is known as *the ground*. Thus, in identifying a shape, the contour outline is most important. It is probably aspects of the figure which pass through the filter to the brain and the immediate ground which is stored temporarily in the short-term memory. Figure–ground discrimination applies in all the sense modalities. For example, music can be picked out and understood against a background of other moderate sounds. Tomato sauce is identified against a background of other foods in one's mouth. When one tries to discriminate one taste from another, they successively take on figure and ground by conscious selection.

Attempts to find a figure against a background are usually not difficult, but occasionally we can be deceived. Figure 4.2(a) in one instant is seen as a candlestick, and in the next as the side view of two faces looking at each other. Note the decisiveness with which the figure is *either* a candlestick *or* faces, and not a mixture of both. We automatically select a figure. Moreover, when it is a candlestick the brain fills in the lines at the top and bottom. You may even get the impression that the candlestick is of a brighter nature than the surrounding white page, so strong is the tendency to distinguish figure from ground in terms of previous models (in this case a candlestick).

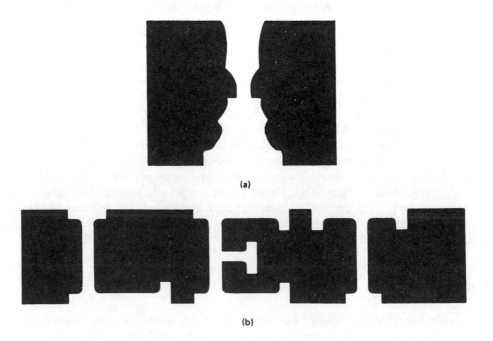

(a)

(b)

Figure 4.2   *Figure–ground reversal.*

Figure 4.2(b) has a similar effect. You may at first notice only meaningless shapes like a plan of a housing estate, but it should transpose into a word which will suddenly leap out of the page when you realize what it is.

The nature of perception

Theories of how we establish perceptions and how things appear to us are of two basic kinds. At one extreme it is commonly believed that, apart from in-built tendencies to distinguish figure and ground, we gradually learn to identify and interpret objects or arrangements of objects. Hebb[12] proposes that sensory experience is registered in the brain cortex in the form of 'cell assemblies' – groups of neurons which become associated with particular sensory events and which change structurally as a result. As sensory patterns become more complex and stable, whole sequences of cells 'fire' in conjunction in response to stimulation. These larger sequences are known as 'phase sequences'. Thus Hebb sees perception as an acquired characteristic.

A second and more widely used view was founded in Germany earlier this century, and held that perceptual organization is inborn. Psychologists such as Wertheimer, Koffka and Köhler created a school of thinking known as the *Gestalt School* of psychology. The word 'Gestalt' is German for 'pattern' or 'form' and the theory emphasizes our ability to perceive patterns as *wholes*. The motto for this movement could well be that 'the whole is more than the sum of the parts'. In other words, we perceive and give meaning to objects by their characteristics *in toto* and not by considering a jumble of the parts which go to make up the total figure.

Several criteria affect the meaning we ascribe to objects. Four arrangements seem to be of primary assistance in recognizing and determining the dominant pattern of the figure in order to form a 'good' pattern, or gestalt. The formation of 'good' perceptual patterns is referred to as the *Law of Prägnanz*. They are similarity, proximity, continuity and closure.

Similarity

Where a figure consists of similar elements we tend to group them to form a pattern. Details such as similar shape, size and colour tend to be grouped. In Figure 4.3(a) we are more likely to see four columns of Xs or Os than rows of XOXO, even though we normally read horizontally. We prefer to order and arrange similar objects in rows rather than at random to avoid the uncomfortable sensation which randomness creates. Instruments, e.g. violins in an orchestra, are heard as an entity and not as separate instruments.

Proximity

Proximity applies where similar objects appear close together. In Figure 4.3(b) the pattern would most probably be described as three groups containing three, two and one Xs respectively, and not as six crosses. The Morse code relies on the differential

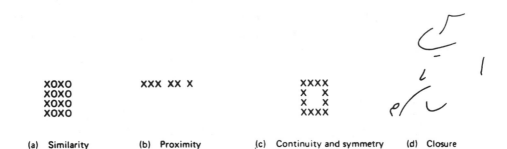

```
XOXO        XXX XX X          XXXX
XOXO                          X    X
XOXO                          X    X
XOXO                          XXXX
```

(a) Similarity   (b) Proximity   (c) Continuity and symmetry   (d) Closure

Figure 4.3 *Patterns which assist in forming* gestalten.

proximity of dots and dashes. However, note the importance of context in the interpretation of perceptions. Once the idea of a code is given, the penny drops.

Continuity and symmetry

Similar parts of a figure which appear in lines (straight or curved) tend to stand out. When they make recognizable shapes such as circles or squares they become conspicuous. The illustration given in Figure 4.3(c) will be seen as a square not as twelve Xs. We spontaneously join up the Xs to make lines. Music is perceived as a continuous rather than a separate system of sounds.

Closure

Closed or partially closed figures are more readily perceived than open figures, except when the open figure has an acquired meaning such as the letters of the alphabet (for example, letter C is open but is recognized a letter). Figure 4.3(d) is incomplete, but doubtless it will be recognized from previous models as a man's face. In this recognizable instance we have closed the figure in order to give it a familiar meaning.

Visual illusions and perceptual constancy

Evidence that we tend to perceive in 'gestalten' rather than by building up the separate elements of an object is provided from the study of *visual illusions*. They are false perceptions of reality. The three illusions of Figure 4.4 are well known. If the book is held so that you are looking along the vertical lines of (A) from the bottom edge of the page they will be seen to be straight and parallel. (B) is the Müller–Lyer illusion, with (a) and (b) exactly the same length. In the third illustration (C), it looks as though the lines are curved. But if you look along them from the direction of the arrow they will be seen to be parallel and straight. Even when we know the details it will still be impossible to compensate. One explanation for the illusion[13] is that we are compensating for perspective. Take the Müller–Lyer illusion (B). The outward-pointing arrows

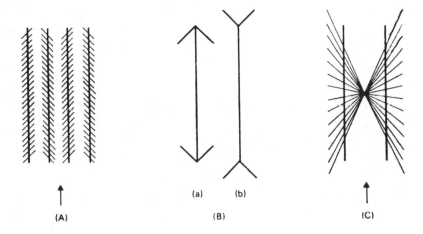

Figure 4.4   *Three common illusions: (A) Zöllner illusion; (B) Müller–Lyer illusion; (C) Hering illusion.*

(a) could be taken as a near corner jutting out, and (b) could be taken as a far corner. Consequently we compensate for this possible perspective by perceiving the drawing (b) as larger than it is. *Perceptual constancy* is another case of compensation where we allow for the distance of an object from our sense organs when judging its magnitude. A man seen at a distance may look as if he is 200 mm high, but we allow for the distance.

Actually, the more experience we have of perspective in our daily routines, the more we are taken in by illusions. African tribesmen who live in round huts are apparently less prone to the Müller–Lyer effect. The essential point about illusions is that, no matter how hard we try, it is impossible to separate out the parts of the figures. Invariably we perceive the figure as a whole.

Bruner and Goodman[14] found that young children from poor socioeconomic conditions tended to underestimate the size of coins, whilst children from favourable conditions were accurate in their judgements. This was regarded by Bruner and Goodman as evidence for cultural experience being a significant influence on perception. Selective attention as an outcome of a particular upbringing (e.g. parents who encourage their children to observe the behaviour of animals) is similarly thought to be a factor in perceptual development.

Perceptual style

Later, in Chapter 10, we shall discuss in some detail the notion of style – characteristic ways in which intellectual, motivational and temperamental factors influence a person's problem-solving techniques. Witkin[15] has shown that people also vary in their perceptual styles, i.e. their characteristic patterns of perceiving in the process of problem-solving. Two famous experiments, the rod and frame and the Embedded Figures tests, were used to detect differences between individuals. The rod and frame consists of an illuminated rod placed inside an illuminated frame in a dark room (Figure 4.5(a)). Both can be adjusted independently and they are set at different angles from which an individual is required to adjust the rod until he or she believes the rod

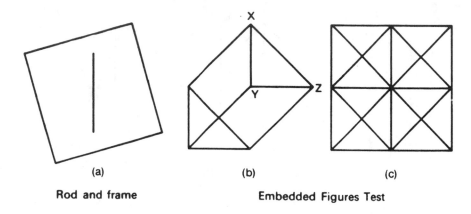

(a)   (b)   (c)

Rod and frame   Embedded Figures Test

Figure 4.5 *Witkin's tests.*

to be vertical. Some people are sufficiently influenced by the frame as to be thrown off the vertical. Others seem, however, to be able to ignore the frame. The former are referred to by Witkin as *field-dependent* and the latter as *field-independent*. In other words, some people are more affected in their perceptual judgements of a figure (the rod) by the ground (the frame) than others are. Another method used by Witkin was the Embedded Figures Test, which consists of several shapes similar to Figure 4.5(b) and (c) from which an individual is asked to trace the shape in (b) by drawing over the corresponding lines in (c).

Researches of Witkin and his associates[16] show that there are other differences between field-dependent and field-independent children. Field-dependent children tend to be better at cognitive tasks which are spatial, and in temperament they tend to be more assertive and independent. There is further discussion of these differences in Chapter 10.

The search for meaning

One dominant conclusion from the research is that human beings are not passive receptor organisms of incoming stimuli. We try to make sense of the stimuli in terms of the context and our previous experience. At a simple level, this is shown by the examples given above in defining the Law of Prägnanz. A few dotted lines or marks are transformed into recognizable shapes, faces, etc. There is yet another example of how we, according to gestalt psychologists, set up hypotheses from the sensory information received. In Figure 4.5(b), is the face XYZ of the triangular prism the front face or the rear face? (This effect is sometimes illustrated with a cube – Necker's cube.) You will find that in one instant the face XYZ is at the front, the next instant it is at the back of the prism. You are trying out hypotheses about a three-dimensional problem drawn in two dimensions – and there is no solution. Therefore, you are switching from one possible solution to the other.

Our perceptions are influenced not only by the immediate sensory data, but by the context and our previous experience. If you were given several sounds (either aurally or visually) such as 'dit dit dit dah dah dah dit dit dit' you would probably say first that they were groups of three sounds, the first three and last three being identical. If it was a lesson on Morse code, you would be searching for some further interpretation of the letters represented by the code (the context has been defined). If you have sufficient experience with the code you would probably conclude that it spells out 'SOS' – the distress signal.

A theory by Neisser[17] summarizes the way in which the stimulus, context and past experience combine to give a perceived 'best guess' at the 'meaning' of a stimulus. He refers to this as *analysis-by-synthesis*. The stimulus input, say the sight of an object, is received and a guess – a hypothesis – is made about the identity of the object from the context, previous experience and expectations. The main features of the object are then compared with the information retrieved from memory and a decision made as to whether the object is familiar or not. If not, a fresh guess and search is made of previous memories until recognition or abandonment. The meaning associated with the input from the object is provided by the person observing and not from the object itself.

Perception and the teacher

We have still much to learn about perception in human beings, but what we do know of value to a teacher will now be summarized.

(a)   The idea of the Law of Prägnanz in perceptual matters is thought to apply equally well to mental activity. Having clear organization and classification of intellectual experience therefore would obey the same rules as perceptual phenomena; therefore the field of learning should have structure.

(b)   Pupils should be given opportunities to use closure. This amounts to leaving something for pupils actively to complete for themselves. Attempting to give meaningful structure to concepts helps to implant them in long-term memory (see the work of Piaget, as discussed in Chapter 7).

(c)   Perception always depends on previous experience. Therefore, it is essential to start from a point in the presentation of material which enables the pupil to call on previous experience (advance organizers). Understanding rather than rote learning is important in the formation of clear perceptions and is more likely to assist in long-term memory. However, 'understanding' is not always possible as, for instance, when learning letters of the alphabet or numbers. The teacher should emphasize that the learning process consists of discovering meanings, building up patterns of knowledge and meaningful relations (**R**).[18]

(d)   Some have argued that learning by getting the total picture rather than learning material piecemeal is more efficient. Methods of learning a poem by re-reading it through until it is learned, or the 'look and say' (and not the 'phonic') method of reading, are based on 'whole' rather than 'part' learning. However, the generalization is questionable. A lot would depend on the type and extent of material to be assimilated. As we shall see from Miller's work (see Chapter 6), 'chunking' does have its place in learning, and even then there are limitations to the amount of channel capacity.

(e) The extent to which young children perceive their surroundings and themselves is subject to developmental limitations. Piaget has proposed that the child *centres* on a particular dimension of the sensory field to the exclusion of all others. In two-dimensional or three-dimensional problems the young child is not able to escape from the single dimension to make judgements about changes or constancies in such matters as volume and area (see Chapter 7).

(f) There are individual differences in the way pupils perceive the process of problem-solving. 'Perceptual styles' is a developing area which could have an influence on the teaching styles adopted.

(g) False perceptions can arise because:

   (1) Sensory information is inadequate or inaccurate. Auditory, visual or tactile materials should be plentiful, appropriate and unambiguous.

   (2) Attention is not full or the direction is misguided: we have already given several reasons why attention might stray. Another cause may be that too much latitude is provided in the perceptual field, so models cannot begin to be formulated.

   (3) The existing percepts are inadequate for incoming sensory experience. This should soon be evident to the teacher who is evaluating his or her work as an ongoing process.

   (4) The wrong 'set' is present; that is, the pupil is looking out for, or picking up, the wrong cues.

As an illustration of the role played by visual perception in school, we might consider some of the concepts dealt with in geography and geology. In both these subjects there is a need to imagine shapes in three dimensions, usually from two-dimensional information. For example, the interpretation of a contour map requires some effort to convert the contour lines into an elevation. Equally, the orientation of a map for direction finding, or the transfer of information from an aerial photograph to a map (or vice versa), requires spatial visualization skills. The term *graphicacy* has been used to describe communication of spatial information that cannot be conveyed adequately by verbal and numerical means. Thus, map and photograph readings would be regarded as forms of graphicacy.[19]

SUMMARY

Sensory reception, attention and analysis have an important place in the work of teachers. Needless to say, without the pupils' attention the teacher might as well retire. But gaining their attention is not just a question of insisting on their looking at and listening to what is going on. There are many factors conspiring to distract or fatigue the child at a more subtle level than this. We have noted that external factors such as intense, novel, changeable, colourful, high-pitched and conditioned stimuli can operate to assist or defeat the teacher's intentions. Internal variables of interest, fatigue, need deprivation, arousal state and personality qualities are likewise of relevance.

   Memory was considered in Chapter 2 from the viewpoint of physiological functioning. We explored the subject using a speculative model derived from Broadbent's filter theory of attention. A development of this by Craik and Lockhart proposes three levels of translation of incoming information for storage in long-term memory – visual/ auditory, syntactic and semantic. The forms most likely to prevail in the encoding of the information are non-verbal and verbal symbolic images. In considering the use of this in the classroom, teachers might give thought to the non-verbal material used for illustration and the level of verbal communication most appropriate to the lesson content in terms of past work done and new content to be taught.

Of the theories of perception, the most influential to date has been that proposed by the Gestalt School. Perceptual discrimination is seen to be more than just the sum of sensory experiences. Questions of interpretation are often distorted by the acquired perceptual characteristics of one's culture or sub-culture (i.e. we learn *how* to look at things and *what* to look at as an outcome of cultural inheritance). The deceptions of illusions are partly a question of cultural experience. It is also believed that social-class background can affect the perceptions of children.[14]

Finally, we gave several suggestions from research on perception which should be of assistance to the teacher. These included: set induction; the importance of structure in the presentation of material; the need to leave children to complete some part of their learning, provided they are in possession of sufficient knowledge to do this (closure); the importance of starting with familiar perceptual experience from which to derive the unfamiliar; 'whole' learning, in some cases, as more valuable then learning 'in bits'; a consideration of the developmental level of the child; and some common sources of false perceptions.

ENQUIRY AND DISCUSSION

(a) Read through the suggestions given under the heading of 'Perception and the teacher' and use these in your observations at school. Analyse the content and presentation of lessons or class activities with these in mind. Try to seek out examples for each suggestion.

(b) With the help of your tutors see if you can devise a series of experiments to show that the intensity, novelty, variability, distributed regularity, colour and conditioned stimuli are variables in arresting our attention. In what ways can this information be used in the classroom?

(c) Examine the literature to discover whether there are any important differences in the extent to which we use our senses (e.g. whether we tend to use our eyes more than our ears). Do we tend to learn through one sense more than another? How do your findings help in deciding on the arrangement and emphases of lesson presentation? Are there differences according to the age of pupils?

(d) Explore the work of C. Stern, Z. P. Dienes and C. Gattengo (Cuisenaire rods) on the use of structured apparatus for the teaching of mathematics.

(e) Read Chapter 6 on set induction in Hargie *et al.* (note (10) below). Look at and discuss the different kinds of set defined above. There is further elaboration in *Applications of Psychology for the Teacher*.

NOTES AND REFERENCES

1. A good general text in E. B. Goldstein, *Sensation and Perception*, Wadsworth, Belmont, CA, 1989 (3rd edn). See also R. Lynn, *Attention, Arousal and the Orientation Reaction*, Pergamon, Oxford, 1966.
2. W. James, *The Principles of Psychology*, vol. 1, Holt, New York, 1890. The reference is given for those interested in early ideas in modern experimental psychology. This man made some remarkable introspections, some of which have only recently been put to the test.
3. D. E. Broadbent, *Perception and Communication*, Oxford University Press, London, 1987. The book gives a detailed review of research prior to the 1980s and evidence from his own researches which has provided innumerable lines of exploration in attention and perception.
   Much recent experimentation in perception has involved the technique of *shadowing*. This means presenting, usually aurally through headphones, a message which the listener has to repeat while some other distraction (often another message) is given in the same ear, in both ears, or in the opposite ear to the shadowed message. N. Moray, *Listening and Attention*, Penguin, London, 1969, describes several shadowing experiments.
4. (R) For an appraisal of the application of perception to education see D. E. Broadbent, 'Cognitive psychology and education', *Br. J. Educ. Psychol.*, **45**, 162–176 (1975) in the Reader.
5. A. M. Treisman, 'Verbal cues, language and meaning in selective attention', *Am. J. Psychol.*, **77**, 215–216 (1964).
6. F. I. M. Craik and R. S. Lockhart, 'Levels of processing: a framework for memory research', *J Verb. Learning and Verb. Behav.*, **11**, 671–684 (1972).
7. A. Paivio, *Imagery and Verbal Processes*, Holt, Rinehart and Winston, New York, 1971, and 'Imagery and long-term memory', in A. Kennedy and A. L. Wilkes (eds), *Studies in Long-term Memory*, Wiley, London, 1975.
8. J. P. Zubek, *Sensory Deprivation: Fifteen Years of Research*, Appleton-Century-Crofts, New York, 1969. For a specific experiment see W. Heron, B. K. Doane and T. H. Scott, 'Visual disturbances after prolonged perceptual isolation' *Canadian Journal of Psychology*, **10**, 13–16 (1956). P. Suedfeld and S. Coren, 'Perceptual isolation, sensory deprivation and rest', *Canadian Psychol.*, **30**, 17–29 (1989).
9. H. J. Eysenck, *The Biological Basis of Personality*, Thomas, Springfield, IL, 1967. See also A. Gale and J. A. Edwards (eds), *Physiological Correlates of Human Behaviour*, vols 2 and 3, Academic Press, London, 1983, and A. Gale and M. W. Eysenck (eds), *Handbook of Individual Differences: A Biological Perspective*, Wiley, London, 1992.
10. R. S. Woodworth and D. G. Marquis, *Psychology*, Methuen, London, 1949. O. Hargie, C. Saunders and D. Dickson, *Social Skills in Interpersonal Communication*, Brookline Books, London, 1987 (2nd edn).
11. L. Siegel and L. C. Siegel, 'Educational set: a determinant of acquisition', *Journal of Educational Psychology*, **56**, 1–12 (1965).
12. D. O. Hebb, *The Organization of Behavior*, Wiley, New York, 1966 (8th impression).
13. R. Gregory, *Eye and Brain: The Psychology of Seeing*, Weidenfeld and Nicolson, London, 1966.
14. J. S. Bruner and C. C. Goodman, 'Value and need as organizing factors in perception', *J. Abnorm. Soc. Psychol.*, **42**, 33–44 (1947).
15. H. A. Witkin, *Psychological Differentiation: Studies of Development*, Wiley, New York, 1962.
16. The work is summarized in P. E. Vernon, *Intelligence and Cultural Environment*, Methuen, London, 1969.
17. U. Neisser, *Cognition and Reality: Principles and Implications of Cognitive Psychology*, Freeman, San Francisco, 1976. See also *Memory Observed*, Freeman, San Francisco, 1982, by the same author.
18. (R) J. Morton, 'A singular lack of incidental learning', *Nature*, **215**, 203–204 (1967).
19. P. Chadwick, 'Some aspects of the development of geological thinking', *Geology Teaching*, **3**, 142–148 (1978).

FURTHER READING

N. Calder, *The Mind of Man*, BBC Publications, London, 1970. Gives several of the more spectacular findings in perception.

S. Coren and L. M. Ward, *Sensation and Perception*, Harcourt Brace Jovanovich, San Diego, 1989.

M. W. Eysenck, *A Student Handbook of Cognitive Psychology*, Erlbaum, London, 1990 (2nd edn).

R. Lynn, *Attention, Arousal and the Orientation Reaction*, International Series of Monographs in Experimental Psychology, Pergamon, Oxford, 1966. Very technical and only for those who need depth in this field.

N. Moray, *Listening and Attention*, Penguin, London, 1969.

D. A. Norman, *Memory and Attention*, Wiley, New York, 1976 (2nd edn). A very clearly written book combining previous research with present speculations.

R. J. Riding, *School Learning: Mechanisms and Processes*, Open Books, London, 1977.

J. M. Wilding, *Perception: From Sense to Object*, Hutchinson, London, 1982.

Chapter 5

Learning Theory and Practice

Previous chapters have made it abundantly clear that learning is a very necessary activity for living things. Their survival depends on it. For humans, the versatility of their adaptation to diverse environments and the joys of abstraction in art and science are founded on their phenomenal learning capacity. Whilst there is no complete agreement amongst psychologists about the details of learning processes, they do accept the basic premise that learning occurs whenever one adopts new, or modifies existing, behaviour patterns in a way which has some influence on future performance or attitudes. Unless there were in fact some influence, we would not be able to detect that learning had taken place. This reasonably permanent change in behaviour must grow out of past experience and is distinguished from behaviour which results from maturation or physical deformity. This view of learning therefore excludes certain kinds of reactions which are thought to be inborn, such as reflex action or innate release mechanisms (mentioned in Chapter 3) where these have not undergone modification in the course of growth. But the definition includes learning which occurs without deliberate or conscious awareness, bad as well as good behaviour and covert attitudes as well as overt performance. The importance of studying learning processes is self-evident, since one of the central purposes of the teacher's task in formal educational settings is to provide well-organized experiences so as to speed up the process of learning, thus enabling pupils to make reasoned choices in solving life's problems.

Whether we recognize it or not, every parent and teacher has a personal theory or theories about how learning best takes place. In the home, the nature and severity of punishments or rewards tell us something about parental theories of learning. In the use of corporal punishment, some believe that actions almost invariably speak louder than words, whilst others never beat their children because they believe that to apply corporal punishment to children would be to show them that violence is an acceptable way of solving problems. Most people manage to strike a balance between these extreme views of the place of physical punishment in teaching children to behave, although even here the particular occasions chosen to apply punishment reveal something of a parent's philosophy of learning.

In the classroom we constantly observe methods which depend on assumptions about the process of learning. What assumptions are made by teachers who use question-and-answer techniques, rewards (sweets, marks, class positions, etc.), i.t.a. or traditional orthography, 'look and say', 'phonic' or 'alphabetic' methods of teaching reading, 'Nuffield' or traditional methods of science teaching, learning tables or the alphabet to *exercise* the memory, deductive or inductive methods of teaching, the direct method of teaching in modern languages, and teaching social sciences to increase social awareness (transfer of training)?

As with so many complex issues in psychology, no one theory has provided all the answers to the kinds of questions of concern to teachers. Some theorists, as we shall see, have cornered the market in particular aspects of learning (Skinner and pro-grammed learning, for example), but no single theory has yet been formulated which satisfactorily accounts for all the facts. Nevertheless, it is worth while looking at the main tenets of some theories because we must have a background against which to examine our own suppositions about learning in the light of existing experimental evidence, and to illuminate the origins and development of commonly held views about learning amongst professionals. For an excellent summary of the major theories, readers should look at W. F. Hill's book entitled *Learning*.[1]

THE TASK OF LEARNING THEORISTS

Let us attempt to summarize the major problems of importance to teachers which any comprehensive theory of learning should be capable of answering.[2]

(a) How can we determine the limits and influence the capacity of learning in the individual? In this respect, what is the influence of inheritance, age, intelligence, maturational level, environmental opportunities, aptitudes, personality, motivation or practice? (See the relevant chapters.)
(b) What is the influence of experience, that is, the effect of early learning on later learning? How are cognitive strategies and habits assimilated and how are they affected by future experience?
(c) There should be a place for an explanation of the complexities of symbolic learning in man (see Chapter 8).
(d) What is the connection between animal and human learning, and is a compromise between them possible without investing animals with human qualities, or vice versa (*anthropomorphism*)? As we shall see, Skinner has managed to build a most elaborate theory of human learning using the findings from research on animals such as rats and pigeons.
(e) Because learning takes place as part and parcel of body mechanisms, any theory should be capable of incorporating physiological and ethological findings (see Chapter 2).
(f) Practice has a central function in learning, but we still need to know far more about the conditions which favour or adversely affect achievements after practice. Is there a threshold of practice beyond which one cannot improve? Under what circumstances is massed or distributed practice most effective?
(g) What is the place of drives, incentives, rewards and punishments in learning pro-grammes (see Chapter 3)?

(h)   Is it possible to transfer learned skills from one activity to another (transfer of training)? In other words, to what extent can our learning in specific situations be generalized to similar, but not identical, situations?

(i)   What happens when we retain or forget information (see Chapter 6)? What part does attention or perception play in the processes of remembering and forgetting (see Chapters 4 and 6)?

(j)   What is the importance of 'understanding' in attempting to learn? Some things we seem able to do without any apparent 'understanding', such as physical movements of muscles in writing, and eye movements in reading, whilst to understand poetry or differential calculus requires long, sometimes arduous, mental effort involving the accumulation of simpler concepts.

Most of the salient questions posed in the above list are elaborated in other chapters. In this chapter we shall deal with the rudimentary propositions of the major theories of learning. *What* happens is there for all to see; the divergence between the theories occurs in the interpretation of the causal processes which give rise to that behaviour i.e. *why* it happens. Of the many theories of learning extant, we have chosen the following because between them they form the foundation stones on which several views of teaching and learning in schools have been built. But we must hasten to add that the contribution of learning theories up to now has been only marginal to the successful formulation of educational programmes, and the questions posed above have not been satisfactorily answered by any one theory.

TWO APPROACHES TO LEARNING

The present stances in the study of learning have their origins in the different opinions held by psychologists about how human behaviour should be studied. There are several such stances[3] of which two have been particularly influential. These are referred to as *behaviourist* (or *connectionist*) and *cognitivist*.

These broad traditions arise from differences in philosophical views about the way humans function and how these functions can be observed to derive generalizations about behaviour. Behaviourists have something in common with Hobbes, a seventeenth-century philosopher, who assumed that a human being can only be a material system. Therefore the task of psychology would be to discover the laws which govern the relationships between *externally* observable input and output without bothering about such inventions as 'the mind', 'purpose', 'free will', 'ability', and so on. The behaviourist similarly is chiefly concerned with stimulus (S) and response (R) connections (hence the alternative term 'connectionist'). These S–R links are of importance only when they can be manipulated and the results observed. The individual develops certain responses to given stimuli, and inferences are made by direct observation of manipulations of these in human and animal behaviour.

Most other approaches in psychology are based on the belief that inner functions of humans are also worthy of study. The brain, perception, memory, personality, motivation are but a few 'internal' structures and processes which affect human behaviour. The philosopher Kant, for example, regarded humans as free agents faced with choices and having the capacity to formulate plans of action. Therefore, to *understand* human behaviour it is necessary to know how people acquire conceptions and how these influence subsequent behaviour. The formula of S–R would need to include the organism (O) to give S–O–R, thus recognizing the importance of the organism as an interpreter of stimuli and as a wilful responder. To explore the 'O' in the above simple formula it is necessary to use *introspection* – that is, an attempt to get a person to describe internal events from which an observer would try to discover the processes of S–O–R. More will be said in Chapter 17 about introspective methods. The cognitive school has contributed to our knowledge of learning, and subsequent sections will deal with this work.

THE BEHAVIOURISTS (OR CONNECTIONISTS)

J. B. Watson (1878–1958)

Before the last century, humans had never really been the subject of scientific experiment. The establishment by Wundt of a psychological laboratory in Germany in 1879 saw the beginning of a more objective attack on the study of animal and human behaviour, and the impetus thus given soon created a firmer foundation for psychology. At the turn of the century, Pavlov in Russia and Watson and Thorndike in the USA directed their attention to detailed study of *how* animals and humans *behaved* in given laboratory circumstances rather than relying on introspective beliefs or feelings. The earliest and most ardent of behaviourists was Watson.[1, 3] His fundamental conclusion from many experimental observations of animal and childhood learning was that stimulus–response (S–R) connections are more likely to be established the more *frequently* or *recently* an S–R bond occurs. A child solving a number problem might have to make many unsuccessful trials before arriving at the correct solution. Of the many responses he or she can possibly make in an effort to solve the problem, the unsuccessful ones will tend not to be repeated; thus there will be an increase in both the frequency and recency of successful responses until a correct S–R pattern appears. Trying alternative paths in the solution of problems of any kind is known as *trial and error* learning.

E. L. Thorndike (1874–1949)

Thorndike, working about the same time, similarly held that we *stamp in* effective S–R connections and *stamp out* those responses which are useless. Using cats, dogs and chickens, he devised experiments in which an animal was placed in a cage from which it could escape to reach food. The food was visible but not accessible from the cage, and the hungry animals soon began to seek the lure. The door of the cage could be opened only by pulling a cord hanging within reach outside the cage. In an endeavour to reach the food the animal clawed, banged and prowled around the cage, occasionally touching the release cord. In this 'trial and error' fashion some animals hit on the solution to their problem. Successive attempts by the same successful animals took shorter periods of time by cutting out the useless activities. From this work Thorndike derived several 'laws' of learning which he believed applied equally well to man as to animals.

Whereas for Watson the important thing was the simultaneous presence of stimulus and response (*contiguity* theory), Thorndike gave more weight to the end effects of the response. Satisfying and gratifying outcomes from a response are more likely to lead to that response reappearing; in other words, the S–R connection is *reinforced* whenever satisfying results are apparent. The statement that satisfaction serves to strengthen or reinforce S–R bonds is known as Thorndike's *Law of Effect*. Note also in this connection that dissatisfaction does not necessarily extinguish responses: rather, it causes the respondent to look for alternatives and seek out satisfactory solutions by trial and error. Of course, Thorndike accepted Watson's position, and it appears in the *Law of Exercise*, which states that bonds are strengthened simply by the same stimulus and response repeatedly occurring together, while a reduction in a response weakens the S–R bond to the point where it finally becomes redundant. The relevant point here is that exercise or practice alone is not enough. Knowledge of results must follow for reinforcement to take place, so the Law of Exercise is a corollary or consequence of the Law of Effect.

The particular contribution of Thorndike to learning theory and to teaching is his insistence on the use of scientific measurement as a means of examining learning skills among children and his belief in motivation through the agency of rewards rather than punishment as an efficient means of establishing good learning habits. However, punishment may have an indirect influence for the better by redirecting the attention of pupils from their existing ineffective S–R bonds to more suitable ones, and this is where the teacher can assist by providing appropriate alternative S–R routes. While the laws are somewhat rudimentary and limited in their usefulness to teachers, nevertheless they contain the germs of reinforcement theory prevalent in the work of later connectionists such as Skinner and Hull.

I. P. Pavlov (1849–1936)

Though his major findings are of limited pragmatic value in the classroom, it would be difficult to put the present behaviourist position into perspective without reference to the physiological work of Ivan Pavlov.[4] Like Thorndike and Watson, he viewed behaviour as responses initiated by stimuli – a reactivist. But, unlike them, his interests were strictly to do with physiological reflex actions, in particular the salivation reflex in dogs. Quite by accident he discovered (*circa* 1880) that dogs would salivate when some other previously neutral stimulus, besides food, was present, provided that on some previous occasions the stimulus had appeared at or just before the presentation of food. From this finding he set about intentionally teaching dogs to associate salivation with neutral stimuli, a process known as *classical conditioning*. In one such experiment, a hungry dog was placed in a harness in a sound-proof room and a tuning fork was sounded. Very soon after, meat powder was presented, causing the dog to salivate. Observe that learning has already taken place, because the reflex action of salivation normally occurs initially in response to food in the mouth and not from the sight of food. However, the dog soon learns to anticipate food in its mouth and experiences anticipatory salivation from the signs (sight, smell) of the food. Pairings of the tuning fork and the presentation of meat powder ultimately led to the dog salivating at the sound of the tuning fork in the absence of the meat powder. The time lapse between the tuning fork and meat powder stimuli is critical, because the greater the time gap between the stimuli the less likely it is that the dog will connect the two events. The salivation is an *unconditioned response* (UR) innately governed and available when food, in this case meat powder, is presented as an *unconditioned stimulus* (US). The tuning fork acts as a *conditioned stimulus* (CS) giving rise to salivation as a *conditioned response* (CR). The relationship is sometimes shown diagrammatically as:

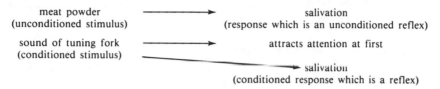

meat powder   ⟶   salivation
(unconditioned stimulus)   (response which is an unconditioned reflex)

sound of tuning fork   ⟶   attracts attention at first
(conditioned stimulus)
                               salivation
                          (conditioned response which is a reflex)

Whenever the tuning fork is sounded along with food, *reinforcement* takes place. But several abortive soundings of the tuning fork will lead to a lessening of the quantity of saliva and ultimately *extinction* of the conditioned S–R link.

A human condition which displays classical conditioning is a child's visit to the doctor for an injection (or to the dentist). The unconditioned situation is:

pain   ⟶   'activation syndrome' (heart increases in beat along with other
(US)   autonomic reactions, UR)

If the child experiences pain when he or she is injected by doctors, the waiting room may act as a conditioned stimulus for the activation of autonomic reactions. Where the child continues to experience pain on each visit, the conditioning is reinforced, otherwise the absence of pain will bring extinction of the fear.

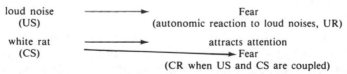

doctor's surgery   ⟶   general interest
(CS)   activation syndrome

Classical conditioning is rooted in the reactions of involuntary systems in the body such as the organs, emotional reactions controlled by the autonomic nervous system (see Chapter 2), and reflex actions such as salivation, eye blinking, knee-jerks and pupillary constriction in response to light intensity changes. Learning takes place by acquiring responses through conditioned ties to these reflexes. Fear has been a popular experimental condition. In the 1920s, Watson made successful attempts to condition or extinguish children's responses to fear-provoking events. By pairing pleasant and feared objects with each other or with a neutral stimulus, Watson was able to condition children. 'Little Albert'[5] was conditioned to fear a white rat. Whenever the eleven-month-old Albert reached out to touch the rat a loud bang was created behind the child. In time, Albert was petrified by the sight of the white rat.

loud noise   ⟶   Fear
(US)   (autonomic reaction to loud noises, UR)

white rat   ⟶   attracts attention
(CS)   Fear
                 (CR when US and CS are coupled)

Extinction of a fear or phobia can sometimes be accomplished by pairing the conditioned stimulus with a pleasurable stimulus. Albert's white rat might have been gradually introduced and brought progressively nearer at meal times. Bribes to persuade children who have built up a conditioned fear of school to go to school can be of a similar nature. The special variety of extinction is called *reciprocal inhibition*. In Chapter 2 we discussed the relationship between the sympathetic and parasympathetic parts of the autonomic system and it is believed that reciprocal inhibition results from the parasympathetic system (responsible for putting a brake on the energy-producing mechanisms of the body) overriding the sympathetic system (activates and excites body mechanisms which produce the symptoms of fear) and encouraging deconditioning. Sometimes a supposed extinguished conditioned response suddenly reappears after a lapse of time in which the US has not been in evidence. This is called *spontaneous recovery*.

How exact must the conditioning stimulus be each time it is presented? In fact some stimuli can have pretty wide limits within which a response is instigated and we call this *stimulus generalization*. The frequency of the tuning fork in the experiment described above does not have to be exactly the same each time; there is usually a range of effective frequencies. The animals used in the reciprocal inhibition experiments with children can vary in size and shape and still produce the desired effect. Children who fear starting school are not particular about which school. In Chapter 7 we shall note that the definition of a particular concept is not easy because our generalizations require a knowledge of the limits within which a classification is possible. Poodles and Irish wolf-hounds can elicit the same response 'dog' even though there are staggering differences in size, shape, colour and habits. We also met with generalization at the beginning of Chapter 4 in the discussion of encoding. In some way our reception system seems to have a built-in tolerance to divergence in percepts presented either through the various sense modalities or, as mentioned above, in the written and spoken word. There are, of course, limits to stimulus generalization and it becomes necessary to draw distinctions between similar, but non-identical, stimuli, especially when the discrimination of response is a matter of adaptive survival. This is known as *stimulus discrimination*. For a rat running a maze in order to obtain food or a child classifying the attributes of the concept of colour (see Chapter 7), there has to be differentiation of superficially similar stimuli before satisfactory responses materialize.

Extinction, spontaneous recovery, stimulus discrimination and generalization emphasize the complexity of S–R connections. However, classical conditioning is limited to reflex mechanisms and in turn emotional reactions. Unfortunately the effect of, say, reward and punishment is complicated by learning processes of a higher order than a reflex. Although fear of failure and pleasure from praise might be regarded as potent unconditioned responses, they are probably the result of much more complex acquired reactions than can be explained by Pavlovian conditioning.

C. L. Hull (1884–1952)

Clark Hull was another influential American theorist who created a complex hypothetical model of learning which, as yet, has found little or no outlet in the day-to-day work of the teacher. Like other behaviourists (except Skinner) Hull believed that S–R bonds depended on elicited responses and not on emitted responses to stimuli. But his major theme involved the inner states in people, for he set great store by the *intervening variables*[6] occurring in the formation of S–R bonds in an effort to predict responses from given stimuli. Symbolically, his view is expressed as S–O–R to signify the importance of the intervening happenings in the organism O. Like Freud, he has provided a theoretical conceptual framework the terms of which, for want of better, have become an inescapable part of psychology. We have already met his theory of primary and secondary drives in Chapter 3 and we shall refer to the intervening variables of *excitatory potential* (the tendency to make a response to a stimulus) and *reactive inhibition* (the tendency not to repeat a response which has just been made) in Chapter 11. The only other term we need to mention is his theory of *need reduction*. When there is a deprivation such as food or water, or a secondary need derived from primary needs as indicated in Chapter 3, responses which lead to a reduction of the need are likely to produce an S-O-R connection. The need reduction provides the reinforcement for the connection. Learning, then, takes place as part and parcel of the process during which animal or human needs are being satisfied, which, even if we argue with the details, is not an unreasonable generalization.

B. F. Skinner (1904–1990)

Amongst recent behaviourists, the American psychologist B. F. Skinner was undoubtedly the best known. His contributions to programmed learning and behaviour therapy have been widely publicized. His main interest, like Pavlov's, was conditioning, but his special brand is termed *operant conditioning*. Initial laboratory experiments involved hungry rats placed in 'Skinner boxes', consisting of levers which, when pressed, would cause the release of food pellets. Exploratory activity of the rat in a confined space would usually end up in a chance contact with a lever. After two or three accidental lever contacts the rat would display a dramatic change in behaviour by intentionally pressing the lever, often very quickly, to obtain food. We have here another example of trial and error learning. More important is the rat's instrumental or 'operant' behaviour by which it produces its own reward or *reinforcement* by converting a productive accident into an intentional behaviour pattern. When the rat obtains a pellet of food every time it presses the bar Skinner referred to it as *continuous reinforcement*. When the rat is sometimes rewarded and sometimes not it is known as *intermittent reinforcement*. In the early stages of conditioning continuous reinforcement is needed to establish the S-R link. However, perseverance wanes when hunger is satisfied and intermittent reinforcement can then be introduced with gradually increasing intervals between each reward. In TV advertising of popular goods (soap powders, etc.), in gambling where the winnings are intermittent, and in the judicious use of praise in the classroom we have examples of the powerful effects of intermittent reinforcement.

A second important series of experiments, using pigeons, will help to elucidate some of the basic principles of learning derived by Skinner. A hungry pigeon was to be taught to walk in a figure of eight. At first sight this is a difficult task because the bird must walk first in one direction and then the opposite direction in order to complete the figure. A pellet of food was given immediately the bird began to move in a clockwise direction. Once the movement was initiated, intermittent reinforcement was used to reward extensive clockwise movements until the bird walked or ran in a clockwise circle. By carefully planning the reinforcement it was possible to introduce rewards for anticlockwise movements because on those occasions when the pigeon was not given a food pellet for a clockwise motion it would tend to explore other kinds of movement, including anticlockwise motion. Apparently it takes a surprisingly short period of time to encourage the pigeon to walk in a figure of eight, provided the pellet rewards are carefully planned; this planning of rewards by the experimenter is known as a *schedule of reinforcement*.

From many similar animal and human experiments, Skinner drew several valuable conclusions about learning:

(a) Each step in the learning process should be short and should grow out of previously learned behaviour.

(b) In the early stages, learning should be regularly rewarded and at all stages carefully controlled by a schedule of continuous and/or intermittent reinforcement.

(c) Reward should follow quickly when the correct response appears. This is referred to as *feedback* and is based on the principle that motivation is enhanced when we are informed of our progress. This is allied to (a) since to ensure a high success rate the steps in the learning process must be sufficiently small and within the capacities of the learner.

(d) The learner should be given an opportunity to discover stimulus discriminations for the most likely path to success. In the pigeon experiment the bird has to perceive the difference between clockwise and anticlockwise motion.

Two distinctions exist between classical and operant conditioning, hinging upon the nature of the response and the source of reinforcement. In Pavlovian conditioning the response is controlled by the experimenter because he or she determines what the stimulus is and when to present it. Thus the response is *elicited* using existing reflex action either inborn or acquired. In a sense the individual's role is passive, since the response must await a particular stimulus to appear – *respondent behaviour*. On the other hand, in Skinnerian conditioning, we must wait for the desired response to appear before learning can proceed. Only when this response is *emitted* can reinforcement occur. Therefore the individual must act or operate on the environment in order to be rewarded – *operant behaviour*. The second difference is in the action of the reinforcement. In classical conditioning the unconditioned stimulus is correlated with reinforcement, so that the meat powder in Pavlov's work acts as an encourager for the repetition of behaviour. In operant conditioning the response acts as the source of reinforcement: when a reward follows a response (lever pressing in rats, or pigeon movements), the response is more likely to be repeated.

We can identify at least two kinds of reinforcement. *Differential reinforcement* occurs when only responses satisfying some specific criterion are recognized for reward. A certain pressure might have to be applied to a bar lever in the Skinner box before a food pellet is expelled. Children might have to reach a given mark in school subjects before a teacher gives praise (see mastery learning later in the chapter). Alternatively, we can condition by reinforcing each bit of behaviour which approximates to that required, a technique known as learning by *successive approximation*. The method used for teaching the pigeon to walk in a figure of eight demonstrates this technique.

Operant conditioning is far more prevalent in both animal and human learning than Pavlovian conditioning, and examples applicable in education will be discussed later in the chapter. One commonplace example is animal training in circuses. Note that

Skinner was not unduly concerned about knowing what happens 'inside' an organism when learning proceeds. Such intermediate or intervening variables involved in physiological or cognitive processes which might affect the nature and direction of learning are not subject to direct observation and do not figure in Skinner's psychology. For him observable and modifiable stimuli and responses for the control and delineation of behaviour were the key variables. The stimulus may be an accident, but the overt response constitutes the means by which the organism *operates on its environment*. We see now the reason for regarding Skinner as a 'structuralist' or 'activist' rather than a 'reactivist' psychologist.

THE COGNITIVE APPROACH

One of the cardinal problems raised by the behaviourist approach is whether it is possible to evaluate total human or animal response by teasing out, observing and analysing bits and pieces of the behaviour. To what extent is it necessary to account for an organism's perception of a situation as a basis for responding to stimulation? Many have argued that human behaviour is too complex and exhibits such original pathways to the solution of problems that a simple S-R theory could not possibly explain all of it.

Wertheimer, the earliest worker to attempt a cognitive interpretation, thought that breaking down behaviour into constituent parts obscured or possibly obliterated the full meaning of that behaviour. Along with Köhler and Koffka he founded the school known as *gestalt psychology* which concentrates on a study of perception for a better understanding of learning. Some of the basic principles of this school have already been dealt with in the section on perception in Chapter 4.

In Chapter 4 (see also Chapter 7) we met with theories using information-processing models which base their views clearly on the belief that activities do occur in an organism between stimulus and response and that these activities are crucial to an understanding of behaviour. Words such as 'understanding', 'thinking', 'memory', 'cognitive structures' and 'cognitive processes' are characteristic of cognitive theorists. The possibility of stored information in the memory which can be retrieved and used – not just in an identical way to the initial experience, but originally – is of interest to the cognitivist.

One contribution of gestalt psychologists to learning is their study of *insight*, a term now popularly used to mean 'intuitive'. But to gestalt psychologists insightful learning is more than this. It occurs as a sudden solution to a problem in a way which can readily be repeated during a similar event in the future and which has some transfer to new situations. Köhler's first demonstrations of insightful learning took place when he was a First World War internee on the Canary Islands. Using chimpanzees as subjects he arranged a number of problems in which bananas were placed out of arm's reach outside the cages. The chimpanzees were provided with short sticks which, whilst not long enough to reach the bananas singly, could be made to do so when slotted together. Sometimes bananas were hung from the roof of the cage and were obtainable by piling up boxes that were strewn about the cage. In both instances *some* animals, after unproductive exploratory activity, suddenly got the 'idea' of how to solve the problem. This sudden, immediate, repeatable and transposable behaviour he called *insight*. Trial and error might be evident in the early stages of animal exploration, but once the animal had seen the task as a whole it seemed able to restructure or reorganize the perceptual field in ways which afforded solutions to the problem.

Apart from the differences in interpretation of learning which exist between connectionist and cognitive theorists referred to above, there is a very fundamental distinction in the experimental organization. As Köhler points out, if you cage a starved rat in a puzzle box with levers, or press buttons of which it has no knowledge whatever, it is clear you will evoke trial and error learning. In other words, the structuring of the problem situation dictates the nature of the problem-solving. The puzzle box is so difficult for a rat that it can do little else but learn by trial and error. This is an important point in gestalt psychology, and one which is significant for teachers. In effect, Köhler is telling us that insight, problem-solving and trial-and-error learning all depend upon the context in which a problem is being solved. The stimulus for the problem-solver is not just the problem, but also its context. Illusions afford a good example of the subjectivity of perception. Also, a child presented with a problem for which it is possible to form a mental image may find a solution more readily, provided mental manipulation can be achieved. The emphasis in gestalt psychology, then, is on adaptability in the use of existing knowledge to form new insights rather than the mechanical repetition of stimulus–response bonds.

Brewer[7] makes the further point that human conditioning may also be a measure of how much the individual being conditioned understands what is required and to what extent that individual is prepared to co-operate. In other words, conditioning makes too little of a person as a rational creature trying to discover what the experimenter is up to and, possibly, attempting to comply with (or sabotage) the proceedings of the experiment. This point of Brewer's highlights one difference between some of the classical reflexological research (eye blinking, knee jerking) in which the individual knows nothing, and the operant conditioning over which the *reasoning* individual has some control.

In this book we refer several times to the work of Piaget, in particular his theories of cognitive development (Chapter 7) and the place of language in the intellectual growth of children (Chapter 8). While his observations may not be recognized as a theory of learning, nevertheless he has quite a lot to say about the steps which lead to the acquisition of knowledge. The primary, secondary and tertiary circular reactions built on to reflex activity of babies, the role of imitation, the internalization of actions to become thought, and the place of language as a mediator in intellectual growth and learning skills are but a few of his most important suggestions which are pointers to learning processes.

One further name of note is that of Tolman. His major work[8] attempts to marry the objectivity of behaviourism to a cognition theory. For him, behaviour is purposive, that is, most of our behaviour is a striving towards a particular goal. Organisms learn to recognize *cues* or *signs* and the relationship of these cues to the satisfaction of specific goals. Rats solving a maze to reach food, or Köhler's chimpanzees, are not just connecting or associating particular responses with particular stimuli: they are assimilating signs which will lead most effectively to solving a problem (reaching a goal, in Tolman's words). These assimilated signs are known as *cognitive maps* of meanings (not movements) by which we acquire whole patterns of behaviour (*sign-gestalts*). In simple language, organisms learn from experience that purposeful behaviour based on cues and previously learned plans of action will lead to the attainment of goals. The creature acquires expectations of its environment (intervening variables again, as in Hull's case) from present and previous perceptions and learning consists essentially of modifying these expectations in the light of new experience.

Later in this chapter we shall deal with the application to learning and teaching of the behaviourist and cognitivist schools.

LEARNING THEORIES AND TEACHING CHILDREN

We have made the point that no one learning theory provides us with all the answers. Furthermore, all the theories put together do not provide us with all the answers. The only course we can justifiably take is a pragmatic one, choosing from among the experimental findings the points of clear relevance to our task. In most cases, psychologists are not really arguing about the findings so much as the interpretations of those findings.

Motivation

It would be safe to say that all theorists in the field of learning either explicitly or by implication argue that a motivated creature is more likely to learn than one which is not. The matter is so important that we have already devoted a whole chapter to it. Pavlov had to starve his dogs and Skinner his rats and pigeons to ensure they would learn. Children need to satisfy their desire to explore and manipulate their surroundings; they need the approval of others (affiliation) and to achieve; they pursue success and eschew failure. Incentives in the form of rewards (words of praise, encouragement, recognition), immediate knowledge of satisfying results (not always possible of course), co-operation and self-competition or competition with others are potent sources of motivation for learning. As we have seen elsewhere (Chapter 3), motivation, particularly achievement- and fear-generated, must not be too intense or performance suffers as a result of distracting emotional conditions such as pain, fear or anxiety. Controlled reward also appears to be a more profitable motivator than failure or punishment. Bower and Hilgard[2] conclude from their analysis of learning theories that tolerance of failure is best realized after a history of success because it helps to compensate for the failure.

Optimum interest can be gained where information is unambiguous and the curriculum designed to engage children in pursuits that have everyday relevance. Misgivings about the raising of the school-leaving age are partly caused by our inability to motivate young people who would rather be earning than learning. 'Everyday relevance' for them is highly instrumental in terms of work when they leave school, preparation for adulthood and leisure. Whatever designs we might have about higher-order educational objectives – enhancing intellectual skills, encouraging social awareness, preserving our habitat, using leisure time, etc. – they must be superimposed on the down-to-earth, 'bread-and-butter', outlook of our young adults.

Habits and learning sets[9]

A term in common usage is *habit*. We talk about forming bad or good habits in many everyday activities in both social and educational contexts. We behave, by and large, in characteristic ways because we have discovered through experience that some responses are (in the short or long term) more effective than others. Therefore, we are *conditioned* to respond in these particular ways. Habits are automatic response patterns elicited by particular stimuli and are generally acquired by repeating a sequence of activities (the Law of Exercise) until the sequence is spontaneous. Many of our daily practical routines such as dressing and eating are carried out in a regular pattern without any apparent conscious effort. Parents and teachers inevitably are concerned with encouraging children in the formation of habits – habits relating to common courtesies, habits of cleanliness and survival, habits of number and letter recognition, and so on. As Thorndike has shown, the more frequently a pattern of activity is completed successfully, the more likely it is to be repeated. Repetition to the point of overlearning, that is, rehearsing a task beyond the point of successful accomplishment, as in the case of concert pianists who continue to practise familiar pieces or actors who continue to recall their lines long after they know them, not only helps to substantiate the material, but enables the performer to concentrate on the refinements of presentation.

Apart from habits of doing things, we also develop habits of thinking and characteristic ways of tackling problems (see Chapter 10). Studies with human and animal subjects have revealed that an ability to learn how to solve problems of a given kind can be developed with sufficient practice on tasks of a similar nature. This ability is known as *learning set* or *learning to learn*. There is another, more limited sense in which we use the concept of transfer, known as 'transfer of training', which we shall deal with later. But this wider, more general application in the formation of learning sets is the outcome of Harlow's work[9] with monkeys and young children. He found that routines formed in the solution of certain tasks were readily adapted for use in the solution of other, similar tasks. Teaching children sets and matrices in modern mathematics syllabuses is rooted in the notion that, by establishing routines about the fundamental understanding of the nature of number, children will have a better chance of coping with more complex mathematics. Learning how to learn a subject (raised again in Chapter 6), as well as acquiring the rules to be applied to the subject matter, is a crucial classroom activity. Children's whole approach to problem-solving depends on the learning sets they bring to the solution. Their experiences at home and school, their attitudes and values all predetermine how they will characteristically organize their responses. As we saw in Chapter 4 there are also predispositions among learners for factual or conceptual styles of learning (Siegel and Siegel[9]).

Knowledge of results

Most theorists and practitioners are agreed that favourable feedback about performance has a positive effect on subsequent performance. Skinner called it reinforcement; Thorndike called it the Law of Effect. In human terms, there must be some reassurances about levels of success and to be a really effective reinforcer in educational achievement, knowledge of results must follow quickly upon completion of a task for it to have maximum influence on future performance. School work should be dealt with and commented on as soon as possible after children have completed work; children's progress should be up to date and fed back to them while the work is still fresh in their minds and still likely to have a reinforcing effect. Skinner claimed that the steps taken in a learning programme should be sufficiently small to ensure high success rates among children (nothing succeeds like success). Knowledge of poor results for some children could be devastating, and this is why Skinner suggested that we should try to strike at the right level with each child to ensure high success rates. Nevertheless, we should avoid the fallacy of trying to pretend that a child's performance is good when it is not. This only leads to low personal standards being set and maintained. By insisting on realistic goals, and thus ensuring some measure of success for each child, we are increasing the likelihood of reinforcement.

Whole or part learning

A theoretical debate surrounds the subject of whether it is better to learn by small steps (Skinner) or large chunks (Gestalt psychologists). For the teacher, there is clearly a time and a place for both approaches. Later (in Chapter 6) we shall see that programmes of learning can be constructed using either technique. With some children, especially the mentally dull, small steps are useful because with a limited 'channel capacity' there is more chance that the information will be held in mind. Part learning by small steps, however, might be a disadvantage where the material is connected in some way. Poetry, theories and laws of science, for example, really need to be presented in their entirety, otherwise the relationship between the parts is lost. Learning a poem line by line was a popular compulsory pastime for schoolchildren not so long ago, and it is surprising how difficult it was to put the whole poem together without a conscious effort to establish connections between the end of one line and the beginning of the next in order to preserve the continuity. Where total context is important, 'whole' learning is an advantage because taking parts of the content out of context may lead to the material being meaningless. When to use whole or part learning is a matter which the teacher must judge from his or her experience of the content.

Schematic v. rote learning

Schematic learning (using organizations of past actions which become the seed bed for interpretation and development in future learning) is thought by Skemp (**R**)[10] to be underrated in importance. In an intriguing experiment using a set of symbols he had invented to represent attributes capable of being combined to give more complex forms (for example, O = container, → = moves, therefore ⟶O = vehicle), he showed that schemata were absolutely essential, even in relatively straightforward learning tasks, because of the meaning they gave to the learning in hand. In any new field the schemata first formulated have a lasting consequence on future learning in that field (see learning sets, above). Therefore the first and most important task for any teacher is to discover and carefully define the elementary schemata required to enable the most productive assimilation. He or she should proceed from a familiar framework to unfamiliar knowledge. Overlapping lesson content and teaching by analogy, that is, using familiar instances to exemplify unfamiliar ones, have much to commend them. A second conclusion of Skemp's was that schematic learning can be more efficient than rote learning, in which one builds systematically on previously acquired knowledge. Rote learning in the absence of understanding precludes the logical acquisition of further meaningful knowledge.

However, this is not to imply that there is no place for rote learning. Some of the demands we make of children require rote learning. Any symbolic form new to the child will require rote memorization. For example, the letters of the alphabet, numbers, musical notation and chemical symbols (although there is a logic behind these once you know the chemical names) have to be learned 'by heart'. Basic mathematical or physical equations, causes and outcomes in history, structure and functions in biology, etc., require a combination of straight memorization and logical build-up from previous knowledge. Two obvious examples are provided by the illustrations in the last paragraph and in a child's first attempts at learning a language. In Skemp's experiment with the symbols, the first task in building up coherent and understood schemata was to *learn* the basic symbols. The first stages in language acquisition (see Chapter 8) involve some very straightforward stimulus–response experiences for the child, such as when a parent touches an object and says 'table'. These *tact* responses (see the section 'Language learning and operant conditioning' in Chapter 8, which also discusses echoic and mand response learning) are good examples of operant conditioning. Where the cognitivists part company is in speculating about the next stages of learning. Does a person go through life accumulating and reproducing the conditioned material, or does the person become inventive and original? (See Chomsky's work as discussed in Chapter 8.) Is the meaning behind a newly devised sentence that has never been heard or spoken by an individual before created from more than the sum of its parts (i.e. the words)? The sentence you have just read and the one being created now are probably unique. How can this creative capacity in the use of a symbol system be explained only in terms of a stimulus–response model? 'Symbol system' is used intentionally here because it could apply to number, music, mime in drama or dance as well as to written and spoken language.

Active v. passive learning and learning by discovery

The role of pupil participation in the learning process and the place of the teacher in this process has been a recurring issue in this book. There are times when children want and need to sit back and listen; there are times when they need actively to be engaged in work. Piaget has suggested that active involvement helps to lay down schemata. Model making, visits and well-organized project work plainly encourage the child to participate in learning.

The place of direct instruction and learning by discovery, either in a 'pure' form where children are left to find out things either for themselves (a very rare method, one would imagine) or in a partially structured and guided setting, have been hot potatoes in educational psychology, particularly since the Second World War. For example, discovery methods, or their variants, have been adopted by some teachers as an alternative to verbal instruction and ready-made learning schemes (learning-by-rote approaches). The processes of learning by discovery have been interpreted and applied in many ways and research findings are still the centre of controversy **(R)**.[11] For an excellent discussion of the dilemmas thrown up by this subject, students should read *Learning by Discovery: A Critical Appraisal*, edited by Schulman and Keislar,[12] in which several famous American psychologists conferred and debated the numerous issues involved. The process of learning by discovery involves (a) *induction* (taking particular instances and using them to devise a general case) with the minimum of instruction; and (b) *'errorful' learning* employing trial-and-error strategies in which there is a high probability of errors and mistakes before an acceptable generalization is possible.

Bruner cites some useful illustrations[13] which demonstrate both these activities. One describes a class of fifth-graders (ten to twelve years of age) who were handed charts of north Central America containing nothing but the major rivers, lakes and natural resources. The pupils were asked to indicate where they thought we might find the principal cities, the railways and the major roads. The children were not allowed to use other maps or source books. Naturally, the children were not starting from scratch because they would have some prior knowledge of geography, but this knowledge now had to be pooled in an effort to find the answer to the question. In the discussion which followed, the children had to justify their choices. By piecing together the particulars they had accumulated from previous geography lessons, the children formed for themselves generalizations from which to locate the positions (both induction and deduction). When the actual chart was exposed at the end of the exercise, the children discovered their mistakes, and in so doing they learned, by induction, that cities arise where there are water and other natural resources, where materials can be shipped, and where climatic conditions and land shape are congenial.

The argument continues to rage. The research findings of Bennett and the ORACLE project fuelled the fires, and a paper by Branwhite comes out strongly in favour of direct instruction in boosting reading skills (see also the references given in his paper).[14] Later we shall say more about the contrasting views of Bruner and Ausubel on this issue. The latter psychologist is much more favourable to direct instructional methods than the former.

One of the confusions presented by the term 'learning by discovery' is whether it is intended to imply the means – to give practice at discovery in order to acquire knowledge – or to imply the end product – to develop the ability to discover. Indeed, the programmes of 'free' or 'guided' discovery embarked on in schools produce an *ability to learn in particular ways* as well as enabling an accumulation of knowledge (quality of learning as well as quantity of learning)? One needs to discern what a teacher can do to encourage the process, what the pupil must do in discovery learning and what is achieved by the procedures encouraged and adopted. These variables are still the focus of research work. In research by Rowell *et al.* **(R)**[11] the relative effectiveness of discovery and verbal reception programmes was tested using the kind of material adopted by Skemp, mentioned in the previous section.

In common with several other researchers, Rowell and his associates found that verbal instruction had significant merit, more so than is often given credit for by those who take up an extreme 'discovery method' position. Further, the verbal reception technique produced relatively superior results, both in the short term and in the long term, to the discovery approach when used with students who had reached the formal operational stage of Piaget's theory of mental growth. One possible explanation offered was that

> 'discovery learning, even guided discovery, requires that the student first discover and organize any new subject matter before internalisation in schematic form is possible. For verbal reception learning, however, the student has only a minimum of reorganization of the material before he can internalise the schema, provided that the material has been carefully structured to meet his requirements.'
>
> (p. 242)

The findings, of course, are limited to particular forms of schemata with students who have reached mental maturity in an educational system which is essentially oriented to verbal reception techniques. The students, in effect, are more familiar with, and probably better at, verbal reception than any other strategy of learning.

Ideally, teachers who favour learning by discovery hope to produce problem-solving skills, especially those involving inductive reasoning; they assume that discovery learning is intrinsically more satisfying and therefore of greater motivational value than rote learning; they hope that pupils will learn the art of modifying generalizations in the light of new evidence, i.e. that pupils will not accept propositions without examining them; they expect that their pupils will become more self-sufficient and resourceful and will not have to rely too much on the transfer of ready-made solutions from others; they anticipate that discovery learning helps in rule-finding at a time when knowledge is expanding at a phenomenal rate, and thus, by learning the rationale of a subject, knowledge acquisition is made easier. But these aspirations remain as intuitions and speculations in need of investigation using meaningful material from current curricula.

The debate about declining standards and their causes has occupied government publications in recent years. For a summary of the arguments about and references to curriculum organization and classroom practices, particularly in the primary school, see a recent discussion paper produced by Alexander *et al.*[15]

'Insightful' learning

The special contribution of gestalt psychology to education is in emphasizing that we should structure our learning. Learning must involve organization of the material. The Law of Prägnanz (Chapter 4), which states that we try to impose the best possible pattern on a new perceptual experience, should be a constant source of consolation to teachers. The insightful 'penny-dropping' experience is quite common in perceptual events and has a remarkable effect in discovering meaning. An experience common to the author illustrating the sudden appearance of a solution to a perceptual problem may be familiar to other readers. The 'instant artist' in programmes such as *Vision On* (BBC TV) had an uncanny knack of being able to reach an advanced stage in a painting before it suddenly dawned on the viewer what the painting was about. When this happens, the lines, blotches and smudges miraculously become railway lines, signal boxes, signals, trains, platforms, etc. The transformation from confusion to almost complete recognition is quite startling. Structure has given meaning to parts previously incomprehensible. Those interested in the experimental work surrounding insightful learning in children should read Wertheimer's book *Productive Thinking*.[16]

BEHAVIOUR MODIFICATION: SOCIAL AND ACADEMIC LEARNING

The term *behaviour modification* involves the systematic application of learning theories (particularly those of Skinner and his operant conditioning) to bring about a desired change in patterns of behaviour. Its relevance to the classroom is obvious, because the major function of any teacher is to change 'for the better' the academic, social and moral behaviour of children. The technique of reinforcement, already mentioned above, is used. Positive reinforcers are intended to maintain or increase the observed behaviour. Encouraging comments about work, and rewards of various kinds, are examples. A negative reinforcer is intended to reduce and even eliminate an observed behaviour. Shouting for silence, punishments, etc. are negative reinforcers. Unfortunately, some of these reinforcement schedules have a nasty habit of working in unforeseen directions. Attention-seeking children are often prepared to put up with the milder negative reinforcers because of the attention which they receive as a result of trying to apply the schedule. These and other strategic ploys are described in readable detail in Poteet.[17]

One of the first direct applications of laboratory psychology has come largely from the work of Skinner,[17] using his techniques of operant conditioning schedules of reinforcement for controlling and shaping human behaviour. The system has been used to reshape the behaviour of children and adults who are autistic, criminal, delinquent, grossly misbehaving in class or in need of some special educational programme, using such methods as rewarding and/or ignoring behaviour, modelling, shaping, token economies and programmed instruction. A further example, which demonstrates self-education, is provided by the biofeedback technique mentioned in Chapter 2, by which an individual is helped, usually, by conditioned responses to information about some autonomic function (muscle, heart, respiration, etc.).

Rewarding and/or ignoring behaviour

The rewarding of appropriate behaviour is bread and butter to the teacher. But often we can be oblivious to the differential effects of reward, especially when disruptive behaviour is also present. Take the case of a young child who is attracting attention by making loud, banging noises with wooden objects during a class activity. It could well be that making 'an example' of the child by pointing him or her out provides the very reinforcement of that behaviour which the teacher does not want. Therefore in this case one would need to combine carefully selected behaviours for reinforcement and for extinction. Whenever the child moves the objects quietly under similar circumstances, praise follows immediately: this should reinforce the desired behaviour. Banging, if ignored, might become extinguished (although so might the teacher's patience!), assuming that attention from the teacher was the object of the child's banging in the first place. In summary, rewarding desired behaviour will tend to reinforce that behaviour, and ignoring disruptive behaviour will tend to lead to its extinction. The evidence so far suggests that ignoring disruptive behaviour without accompanying rewards for acceptable behaviour is not very effective. (For an interesting research using this technique of combining praise and other forms of teacher attention as reinforcers, see note (18).) Another application of reinforcement theory is referred to as the 'Premack Principle' – a rewarding activity can be used as 'bait' to undertake a less rewarding activity, e.g. 'If you eat your food now I will let you go out to play.'

Modelling

As the term implies, *modelling* depends upon one person setting a pattern of behaviour which is copied by another. Children frequently try to imitate adults or the peer group. There is much discussion, and little convincing evidence, about the effects of television as a source of models for children's behaviour, although many people believe that violence and aggression on television affect the child's behaviour.[19]

The study of learning as a consequence of social interaction and imitation has become a primary contribution of Bandura and his co-workers,[20] who have postulated that we all, especially children acquire large units of behaviour through watching and imitating others. There are, according to Bandura, at least three effects of exposure to *models* (parents, teachers, friends, famous people) which give rise to behavioural change. First, children may copy an entirely new response pattern not in their behaviour repertoire. This is called the 'modelling effect'. The unit of behaviour is frequently complete at an early stage of imitation and seems to bear little resemblance to the trial and error or successive approximations of stimulus–response theory. A now famous piece of research by Bandura *et al.*[20] presented several children with a film showing aggressive adults. Without prompting or reinforcement of any kind, the children quickly began to display similar aggressive behaviour. Second, observation of behaviour of a model may lead children to alter their own established responses by strengthening or inhibiting the responses. In this way children adjust the 'limits' of their behaviour as they discover, through watching others, the tolerance levels in particular situations. For example, if children see a certain kind of behaviour go unpunished which they previously regarded as punishable, they are less likely to inhibit their behaviour on subsequent similar occasions. These are called 'inhibitory' or 'disinhibitory' effects.

The third behavioural change arises from what Bandura calls the 'response facilitation effect' (sometimes known as the 'eliciting effect'). Behaviour is sometimes initiated in an observer by the cues given to that person from a model. The process has much in common with the ethologists' explanation of innate release mechanisms (see Chapter 3) except that the patterns of social behaviour are not regarded by Bandura as inborn. The child matches the behaviour observed in others with behaviour already in the repertoire. It appears as if the behaviour of the model acts as a releaser for parallel behaviour in the observer.

The distinctive styles of the teacher as a model of social behaviour, that is, his or her aggressiveness, friendliness, aloofness, co-operativeness, calmness, etc., will act as the initiators of novel behaviour changes in the child or will modify or trigger off existing patterns. The teacher is clearly a potent figure in the social behaviour modifications of children. Once language has been acquired, the models need not be actual but can be pictorial or verbal. The acquisition of certain kinds of language usage and meaning are thought by Bandura to be partly the result of modelling from adult conversation (see the work of Bernstein in Chapter 8). Some children from working-class backgrounds have difficulty in compromising between their home models and those of their middle-class teachers. Another point worth considering is the extent to which the student-teacher's style is modelled on others she or he has seen as teachers.

The holistic rather than the 'bit-by-bit' approach to social learning is emphasized by Bandura, who concludes:

> It is evident from informal observation that vicarious learning experience and response guidance procedures involving both symbolic and live models are utilized extensively in social learning to short-circuit the acquisition process. Indeed, it would be difficult to imagine a culture in which the language, mores, vocational and avocational patterns, familial customs, and educational, social, and political practices were shaped in each new member through the gradual process of differential reinforcement without the response guidance of models who exemplify the accumulated cultural repertoires in their own behaviour. In social learning under naturalistic conditions responses are typically acquired through modelling in large segments or *in toto* rather than in a piecemeal, trial-and-error fashion.
>
> (Bandura, 1970)[20]

Shaping methods in classrooms

Shaping is the technique of reinforcing successive bits of desired behaviour in order to build up an acceptable pattern of action. This is a very familiar procedure in many behaviour-therapy schedules. Autism, for instance, is an apparent inability on the part of the child to communicate with others. An autistic child even finds looking at another person very difficult. To improve this condition, Lovaas[21] used a schedule involving food and drink as a reward. A therapist is seated opposite the autistic child, who is rewarded with a spoonful of food or a drink each time he or she attempts to look in the direction of the therapist. Next, the therapist concentrates on rewarding sounds or lip movements, then words and finally sentences. The technique has much in common with the experiment described earlier, where a pigeon was taught to walk in a figure of eight. Note the need in both schedules to use a step-wise reward system until the total behaviour required has been pieced together. The method works, although its critics feel it to be an inhuman way of dealing with children, particularly when the long-term effects are not completely known, even if it does work better in many cases than other methods.

Token economies

The use of tangible reinforcers such as stars, prizes, money or gifts is not new, but the systematic application of a reinforcement schedule of tokens is quite recent. In fact, the rapid growth of *token economy* methods with humans has taken place over the past ten years or so, from the earlier work of such people as Tyler and Brown (academic performance of delinquent boys)[22] to the original and stimulating work of Hoghughi (token treatment methods for gravely disturbed adolescents in residential care).[23] In normal classrooms the idea of using extrinsic rewards which might be expensive is prohibitive. Therefore several programmes[18] have been devised which start with external rewards of one kind or another (prizes, etc.) and become transferred to inexpensive reinforcers (free time, enjoyed activities).

Work with a group of delinquents in a Washington reform school provides an example. Forty young criminals, including murderers, rapists and other serious offenders, were submitted to a schedule involving their living conditions. Leisure activities, food and living quarters were used as incentives for improving their behaviour and learning a trade. At worst, the offender could sit around doing little of interest, live on a boring frugal diet and sleep in a dormitory. Good behaviour and learning using teaching machines, however, were rewarded by better food, private quarters, colour television and a free day out. By the time they were due out, many had learned useful skills from the programmed learning texts – a feat they had abandoned at school. Normally, most delinquents are in trouble within three years of leaving a reform school in America. In Skinner's sample only 45 per cent were in trouble within three years.

Applied behavioural methods in classroom management

Behaviour modification programmes applied in normal school settings to change disruptive and antisocial behaviour have been especially prominent in some American schools (**R**).[24] In Britain there is still a reluctance to apply what appear to some to be mechanical strategies in such an essentially varied habitat as the classroom. However, there has been a recent upsurge of interest arising from the work of Wheldall and associates at Birmingham.[25] As the term 'behaviour modification' has had some unfortunate associations, they prefer to use the expression 'applied behavioural analysis' to the techniques used.

The behavioural approach to teaching is based on conventional Skinnerian traditions:

(a) the concern of the psychology of teaching is with the observable, i.e. what a child actually does rather than speculations about the underlying processes;

(b) for all practical purposes behaviour can be regarded as learned, i.e. what a person does depends on his or her learning from interaction with the environment and is not innate;

(c) learning means change of observable behaviour, i.e. the only way one can know that learning has taken place is by a change in behaviour;

(d) learning is governed principally by the 'law of effect', i.e. behaviour which has led to a desirable or rewarding outcome tends to be repeated, whereas aversive or punishing outcomes of behaviour tend not to be repeated;

(e) learning is also governed by the context in which it occurs, i.e. certain kinds of behaviour are more appropriate in some situations than others and we quickly learn to recognize this and act accordingly.

A useful table summarizing a pattern of teacher behaviour designed to change, appropriately, learner behaviour is adapted from Skinner:

Table 5.1 *Techniques for changing behaviour (after Skinner)*

	To increase behaviour(s)	To decrease behaviour(s)
Delivery of	'Good things', i.e. rewarding with smiles, sweets, toys, praise, etc.	'Bad things', i.e. punishing with smacks, frowns, reprimands, etc.
	Technical term: **Positive Reinforcement**	Technical term: **Punishment**
Removal of	'Bad things', i.e. allowing escape from pain, noise, nagging, threats, etc.	'Good things', i.e. losing privileges, house points, money, opportunities to earn 'good things', etc.
	Technical term: **Negative Reinforcement**	Technical term: **Response Cost**

With these lines established, Wheldall and Merrett have designed a behavioural approach to classroom management for the in-service training of teachers called the BATPACK (Behavioural Approach to Teaching Package).[26] The idea is to provide a method for training primary and middle school teachers in some key behavioural skills. It is skill-based and aims to change teachers' methods towards more positive teaching, e.g. effective use of praise, positive rule-setting, pinpointing behaviours. It is carried out in groups rather than by individuals and is therefore of more value in a school setting where several teachers are working on the BATPACK together. It is run after school, on school premises if possible, by a tutor who is trained in its use.

The BATPACK course consists of six one-hour sessions taught weekly. The units are:

Unit 1: Identifying troublesome behaviour.
Take-home 1: The five principles of the behavioural approach to teaching.
Unit 2: Focusing on desirable behaviour.
Take-home 2: The behavioural teacher's ABC.
Unit 3: Eliminating (or, at least, reducing) the negative.
Take-home 3: Negative consequences.
Unit 4: Accentuating the positive.
Take-home 4: Using positive reinforcement effectively.
Unit 5: Getting the classroom setting right.
Take-home 5: Antecedents – settings for behaviour.
Unit 6: Where do we go from here?
Take-home 6: Behavioural charter and evaluation.

The take-home material is more theoretical and intended to reinforce the sessions.

The method concentrates on improving the teacher's ability to manage the classroom situation as a whole rather than the behavioural/learning problems of particular children. It attempts to do this by helping teachers to define clearly the commonest classroom behaviour problems and to observe them carefully, whilst concentrating upon positive measures to bring about change. . . . The contingent use of praise is particularly emphasized. Teachers are taught praising skills alongside related skills such as 'rule setting' and deliberate 'ignoring'.[26]

Wheldall is now able to claim that it is possible to modify teacher behaviour to benefit classroom behaviour.

Programmed instruction using teaching machines[27]

Skinner's best-known contribution was in the realm of teaching machines and programmed learning, although he was not the only contributor. In 1926, Pressey produced the first recognizable teaching machine involving multiple-choice answers to each item of information. It was not until 1954 that Skinner applied his findings from animal conditioning to the production of the first *linear* teaching programme. However, before we discuss the kinds of programmes available let us define some important concepts.

Where a machine is used there are two main constituents, the *hardware* and the *software*. Hardware is the mechanical device designed to provide a means of controlling the presentation of information and checking the responses of the pupil. These now appear in various shapes and sizes, from small cardboard or wooden boxes to television-type machines.

The really important part in the whole process is the software, which is the programme containing the subject matter organized in a carefully arranged progression of information, questions and answers. Each unit of information appearing before the pupil is called a *frame*. Machines are not the only presentation device. It is possible nowadays to use *scrambled textbooks*, each page being a frame of information or an answer, and these are scattered throughout the book rather than in page order to discourage cheating.

At least six components are needed for an efficient mechanical teaching device. These are (a) a subject-matter store; (b) a display system; (c) a response system for the pupil; (d) a marking or evaluation system; (e) a response store; and (f) a control for the presentation of information which governs the rate of progress of the pupil.

If we add to the above components the essential requirements of an operant conditioning schedule we have the makings of a *linear programming* system. The requirements are:

(a)   Small pieces of subject matter presented in a logical sequence at such a pace as to pretty well guarantee success on the part of the pupil.

(b)   Active responses on the part of the learner. This, called 'constructed response', usually entails writing a word or phrase in answer to a question.

(c)   Immediate knowledge of the accuracy of the response, which is usually correct if (a) is followed.

(d)   The pupils can work at their own pace. Often, in formal settings, bright children can be bored and dull children left behind.

The linear programme, therefore, consists of a series of frames, each containing a small item of information to which the pupil must respond. Frames also contain the answer to the problem set on the preceding frame. There will be overlap of information from one frame to the next and revision from time to time. Diagrammatically the system can be represented as in Figure 5.1, where capital letters represent information frames and small letters the answers. Extracts from linear and branching programmes are to be found in the Reader (**R**).[28] A linear system might look like this:

1. If learning is defined as a change in behaviour, teaching is   (Frame)
   an *interaction* with the student that effects this _____   (response)
   _____   (end of frame)
   change in behaviour   (answer)
2. Teaching generally entails an _____
   with the student.

   _____

interaction

(From J. L. Becker, *A Programed Guide to Writing Auto-instructional Programs*, RCA Service Co., NJ, 1963, p. 49.)

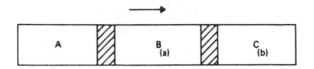

Figure 5.1

Branching programmes are an alternative to the linear type and differ in several important respects. Crowder's name is linked with this kind of programming because he developed the first *branching* (or *intrinsic*) system for use in the United States Air Force in 1955. In these programmes the frames of information are larger and are followed by questions offering several answers of which only one is correct; that is, multiple-choice responses (see Chapter 13). The alternative answers are chosen either because they are plausible (though inaccurate) or because they represent common errors. A student choosing the right answer will be passed on to the next frame of information. Inaccurate answers lead to a detour, a remedial loop, intended to show the pupil the source of the error. The pupil is then returned to the original frame to give another opportunity to respond. This use of remedial loops is called *wash back*. A diagram of the system might be as shown in Figure 5.2.

There are, however, many ways in which branching can take place involving the remedial sub-sequences of differing length and difficulty. The following is an example of a branching system.

1. Branching can be considered a separate idiom of programing or merely a technique. This branching idiom, called intrinsic programing by Dr Norman Crowder, differs radically from linear programing. It is based on the belief that a person can learn effectively even from his mistakes provided they are quickly followed up by proper guidance. A high error rate is unhealthy in a linear program but not necessarily unhealthy in an intrinsic program.

   In intrinsic programing much emphasis is placed on the student's covert reorganization of material. Thus, it is important to point out why the student is right and why he is wrong. To a linear programer, however, branching is not so much a way of teaching as it is a means of providing for individual differences.

   The linear idiom considers branching as:
   (a) an opportunity for guidance (see frame 7);
   (b) a method of teaching (see frame 3);
   (c) a means of providing for individual differences (see frame 5).

   (From J. L. Becker, *A Programed Guide to Writing Auto-instructional Programs*, RCA Service Co., NJ, 1963, p. 149.)

Apart from the obvious differences in the arrangement of frames between linear and branching techniques and the point made in the programme above, there are three

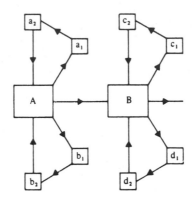

Figure 5.2 *Branching programme with three alternative answers, two leading to remedial loops, the third to the next frame.*

other distinctive features which rest on different psychological beliefs. Skinner believed that knowledge of results is central, while Crowder gave students knowledge of results incidentally. The important part for Crowder was information – information about incorrect responses as well as new matter. So there is regard for the reinforcement except that it includes information about errors as well as successes. Second, Skinner avoided error as much as possible. He made the steps small, with a gradual increase in difficulty to minimize errors. Crowder used errors as the starting point of information to the student and as an opportunity to revise the subject matter of the frame. The third distinction is the size of the information given. Skinner used small amounts of information, while Crowder programmes appear to favour the gestalt view that one must see the whole context to make the parts more meaningful; therefore the frames contain much more information.

The multiple-choice branching method has probably been the most popular. It has the advantage of enabling the student to adapt knowledge because there are several alternative routes, each attempting to account for different levels of understanding. Nevertheless, constructing programmes, especially those containing plausible alternatives, is an extremely arduous task. One has to specify characteristics of the *target population* (the pupils who are going to use the programme) with some precision in terms of age, ability and previous experience, so as to design the subject matter around this information. As we shall see in Chapter 13, finding alternative solutions to a multiple-choice question which are not distracters is not easy. Detailed breakdown of the syllabus is required, and this constitutes a very salutary exercise for anyone who has not tried it. Certainly a good programme requires a very sound knowledge, not only of the subject matter but of the difficulties encountered by pupils and the many pitfalls to which they are prone. It is always wise to try out the programme on a *pilot sample* which is representative of the target population.

The place of programmed instruction in schools

In a comparatively short period of time, programmed learning techniques and teaching machinery have spread from the psychologist's laboratory through the business world into education. Circulars and periodicals with information relating to software and hardware now abound. In all, a formidable campaign has been launched to convince teachers that programmed teaching aids can play a major part in improving our standards of education and serve as a remedial device, while also providing the teacher with a bonus of free time for more creative activity.

But there lurks in the minds of some teachers the feeling that a price may have to be paid (literally and metaphorically) for introducing too much inanimate machinery into the classroom. They have asked whether programmed learning is the antipathy of creative thinking in not allowing the pupil sufficient opportunity for self-expression. In turn, does this mean that programming is more appropriate for subjects which are more factual in content (science, mathematics) than for subjects which are more evaluative (English literature)? The less practical teachers may not like the thought of having to watch over the machinery. Again, is the time made available for 'creative activity' going to be spent in proliferating time-consuming programmes? Motivation of pupils is another source of concern, for it seems that once the novelty of the method has worn off some pupils express a feeling of boredom and monotony, especially those using linear programmes. Again, when pupils can work at their own pace there is no guarantee that they are working to the best of their ability. It might be seen as an opportunity for slacking.

We have already pointed out some good features such as immediate knowledge of results and pupils working at their own pace and by themselves, thus avoiding the embarrassment and humiliation of displaying ignorance in front of the class. A good programme becomes widely available for all to use (but so does a bad one!). In addition, the protagonists of programmed instruction claim that programmed learning is as effective as teaching by conventional methods, is usually faster, and usually achieves better results. In a system which espouses discovery methods and encourages strategies which must meet the needs of individual children, one requires an army of teachers far in excess of the number likely to be appointed. Therefore we must find and exploit additional modes of communication with the children. This is particularly clear with bright pupils who outstrip their classmates and need to be given a chance of progressing faster than the rest, as well as with children in need of remedial help, where a programme (provided they can read) would serve to reduce the repetitive work of the teacher. Wisely used, programmed instruction should make a valuable contribution in our schools.

Computer-assisted instruction (CAI) (or *computer-based learning* (CBL), which is sometimes used as an alternative term) is a noteworthy development from programmed learning. It has become well established both in Britain and in the USA. CAI is defined by Steinberg[29] as computer-presented instruction that is individualized, interactive and guided. By individualized is meant the presentation of learning material by a computer which is acting as a tutor to one person. It is possible to arrange for more than one person to receive from a computer, but by far the commonest use is for individuals. The instructional programmes are written in such a way as to require the learner to respond. The response is analysed by the computer program and fed to the learner, to which another learner response might be requested. In this way an interactive relationship can be established between the learner and the instructional material. Guidance occurs because programmes are written in such a way as to set up a response pattern between learner and program depending on the learner's responses.

There is little doubt that CAI or CBL is going to become a crucial, widespread method of instruction in our schools. It should be remembered that computers are the *means* whereby instruction is presented and not the instructional material itself. The latter is prepared by teachers who decide on the method of teaching.

MODELS OF INSTRUCTION

One outcome of developments in cognitive psychology has been the elaboration of instructional methods. We shall turn in a moment to pick out some useful aspects of instructional suggestions from the views of Bruner and Ausubel, but before doing so it would be of help to define the main characteristics of a model of instruction[30] (see the four titles in Further Reading on the nature and role of instruction at school).

There are six major specifications necessary to any theory of instruction, all of which are sensitive to individual differences. The six specifications are:

(1) the cognitive predispositions of the learner – that is, the knowledge, skills and abilities which a learner brings to a task and which would influence performance;
(2) the affective predispositions of the learner – that is, the interests, attitudes and self-concept brought to a task;
(3) how a body of knowledge needs to be structured in order for efficient and effective learning by individuals to take place;
(4) the sequencing and best methods of presenting that body of knowledge;
(5) the reinforcement mechanisms necessary to ensure continued interest such as rewards, incentives, feedback; and
(6) evaluation of pupil performance and of the system used.

To help in summarizing the advances which might be generated from these specifications, Figure 5.3 is a cannibalized diagram from Bloom (see Further Reading).

Entry predispositions

The first two represent what are called 'student entry characteristics' or 'predispositions'. In plain language they are about the history of the learner prior to the task in hand, which will be of relevance to that task. The third, fourth and fifth are about structuring of knowledge, sequencing of presentation and reinforcement mechanisms, and are incorporated into the central part of the diagram under 'instruction'. Learning outcomes are about the effects of learning and must involve evaluation of some kind. Note also that the outcomes become part of the history of the learner and that is why the model is cyclical.

Entry variables such as general intelligence and personality, whilst they give useful background knowledge, are fairly stable and we should concentrate on the other predispositions which can be modified for the benefit of the learner. The numerical, verbal, reading, writing, and communication skills of the young are inescapable and profoundly affected by child-rearing practices. We have a lot to learn about early home and school influences, and about discovering ways of improving these skills by capitalizing on this critical early period. Studies in paediatrics and the

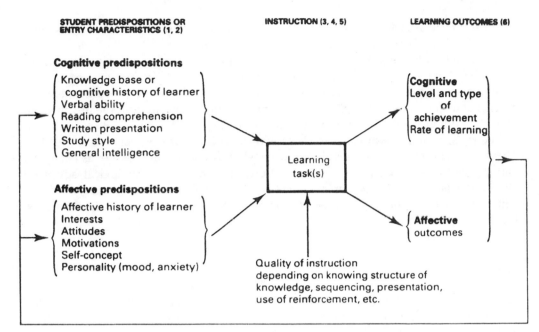

STUDENT PREDISPOSITIONS OR
ENTRY CHARACTERISTICS (1, 2)

INSTRUCTION (3, 4, 5)

LEARNING OUTCOMES (6)

Cognitive predispositions

Knowledge base or
 cognitive history of learner
Verbal ability
Reading comprehension
Written presentation
Study style
General intelligence

Affective predispositions

Affective history of learner
Interests
Attitudes
Motivations
Self-concept
Personality (mood, anxiety)

Learning
task(s)

Quality of instruction
depending on knowing structure of
knowledge, sequencing, presentation,
use of reinforcement, etc.

Cognitive
Level and type
of
achievement
Rate of learning

Affective
outcomes

Figure 5.3   *The Instructional Process (adapted from B. S. Bloom,* Human Characteristics and School Learning, *McGraw-Hill, New York, 1976).*

physiology of early child development will make significant contributions to educational psychology.

We have only a hazy idea of how a child assimilates and organizes knowledge and how this process in turn will affect decision-making and problem-solving. How do previous experiences, and the generalizations formulated from them, impinge upon new experience? Driver[31] is looking at the ways in which children develop specific ideas and concepts in science and how these compete with accepted scientific generalizations. Whether we like it or not, children, it seems, formulate their own laws of nature from their experiences and these may be in conflict with those presented by the science teacher. This illustrates very clearly the importance of studying the entry characteristics of pupils from their learning history and of finding ways of unravelling false notions and replacing them with methods for finding those which are more acceptable.

'Study style' is listed on the diagram. By this is meant the characteristics and unique ways in which an individual tries to cope with the learning process. We all have our own favoured tactics and strategies which we bring to study. How efficient are they? Could they be improved? Is the teaching we receive compatible with our favoured strategies? Most of the research in this field has been concerned with secondary and higher education (see the next chapter) giving useful descriptive glimpses of student methods or characteristics. Unfortunately, the study methods of students in higher education are probably already so well ossified that there is little chance of encouraging modifications for improved performance. Yet at the other important end of the system, in junior schools, we almost completely ignore training in study methods. We wrongly assume that effective methods of study are automatically picked up as children progress through the system. We need detailed researches of how study skills grow and how to teach them to the individual's best advantage.

One need hardly remind the reader of the central importance of interest and motivation to pupil or student performance. Yet we have a long way to go in trying to comprehend and do something about the credibility gap which exists between pupils, teachers, parents and society as to the place of a formal system of education in the life-chances of an individual. Selling the system gets harder as one reaches the final two years of secondary school life, especially to those with little hope of obtaining good GCSEs. There will have to be a considerable shift in syllabus content and design as changing patterns of work and leisure, individuals' expectations and technological advances bite deeper and deeper into our present way of life. Unfortunately, society inadvertently generates in the young expectations which the educational system can rarely fulfil.

Instruction

The central portion of Figure 5.3, 'Instruction', places great demands on the teacher as a manager of learning. The aspiration of teachers should be to lead learners to a point where they, the pupils, can help themselves. This is becoming increasingly more important as our knowledge base rapidly increases. Information retrieval and self-help are growing in significance. The cheap miniaturization of equipment suitable in educational settings will have a marked effect on educational provision in both the curriculum and teaching arrangements in some subjects. The design of software requires a deep knowledge of the structure of a subject, and teachers will need to know more about how to unwrap their areas of knowledge for presentation in a variety of ways.

The simulation of human thinking and action in the form of artificially intelligent systems may have something to offer to teachers. Our inventions are often extensions of ourselves. Telescopes and microscopes are extensions of our eyes, amplifiers of our ears, tools and vehicles of our limbs. Robotics combines some of these senses and is taking the routine out of some manufacturing industries. Apart from the obvious impact this will have on our work and leisure activities in the future, the study of artificial intelligence must in time have some bearing on the analysis and presentation of subject matter, and knowledge about the human being as a learner.

To enhance the quality of instruction a number of innovations are finding their way into the system. A few examples are (a) flexi-programmes and adaptive tutoring which are designed to be adjusted to the needs of particular children by using either reproduced materials, video or microprocessors; (b) courses for students on instructional craft knowledge; (c) the use of simulation exercises using closed-circuit or recorded television programmes; (d) the more extensive use of recorded teaching episodes – sometimes called micro-teaching; or (e) courses in diagnostic techniques and social skills.

Learning outcomes

In a sense, learning outcomes need to be considered alongside entry predispositions, because one needs to know the destination before being able to choose an appropriate route.

Evaluation is an essential part of the process of learning. Indeed, that is life! The development of skills and tools which enable teachers to make accurate diagnoses and to treat individual children's problems competently is crucial, and is badly in need of research.

Two particularly significant contributors to instructional ideas are Bruner and Ausubel.[32] They are similar in many of their views, both having a cognitive outlook and rejecting behaviourism. Bruner emphasizes active restructuring of knowledge through experience with the environment. Learners should organize knowledge for themselves, for example by using discovery methods, rather than having material pre-packaged by the teacher. He has been a most prolific writer; in this book we refer to him several times on concept development, perception, the origins of speech, play and symbol systems. Unfortunately Bruner has not yet brought his many ideas together in a coherent overview. Nevertheless, he does believe that learning is most effectively achieved when children are encouraged to engage in guided discovery (see the example from geography in this chapter under 'Active v. passive learning').

His train of thought for the purposes of deriving a method or methods of instruction runs like this: starting with the categorization of our environment (see Chapter 7), in an attempt to reduce its complexity, we develop coding systems which are hierarchies of categories. To assist this process, education should be concerned with the analysis of areas of knowledge so as to ensure that the most fundamental aspects are presented first, i.e. there is an ordering in the exposure we give an area of knowledge based on the levels of complexity of the categories involved. To ensure that children 'crack' the codes, they should be encouraged to explore for themselves at an appropriate level of presentation (see symbolic systems in Chapter 7) using a *spiral curriculum*. This latter involves the exposure of children to subject matter in such a way as to ensure both overlap with previous material (repetition and revision) and a steady progression in the complexity of the material – hence a spiral effect.

Ausubel emphasizes the role of *expository* or *reception learning* and is quite critical of some aspects of discovery learning. At the heart of Ausubel's ideas are the concepts of *meaningful verbal learning* and *advance organizers*. To be meaningful, new material must be related to existing knowledge. The teacher therefore has to find ways of associating the new material with ideas or objects with which the pupils are familiar. This, according to Ausubel, is most efficiently done by straightforward explanation and exposition rather than by time-consuming pupil-generated discovery methods. To help in this process, Ausubel recommends the use of *advance organizers*, which he defines in two forms – *expository* and *comparative organizers*. An advance organizer is introductory subject matter presented before a lesson begins in order to put it into the context of the pupil's existing knowledge. With completely new material expository organizers are used. They present a simplified outline of ideas and/or concepts of the new learning. Where the material overlaps with the previous knowledge of the pupils, comparative organizers can be employed. As the term implies, comparisons are drawn between the existing and the new subject matter.

One further concept, *mastery learning*, needs to be mentioned here. The concept was first elaborated by Carroll[33] and its effectiveness discussed by Bloom.[33] An argument within education which is fundamental to the instructional procedures used relates to whether anything could be taught to anyone, given the right approach and plenty of time. Bloom summarizes the 'mastery learning' position by claiming that 'what any person in the world can learn, almost all persons can learn if provided with appropriate prior and current conditions of learning'. The essential characteristics of mastery learning are that the appropriate method of presentation has to be carefully worked out to meet the abilities and needs of a child; as much time as is necessary must be provided for the child to achieve a predetermined level of accomplishment (or mastery) – this is often in the region of 80 per cent correct response rate along with ample cues, pupil participation, feedback (reinforcement) and the tactful correction of errors.

SUMMARY

In this chapter we have looked briefly at some of the major theories of learning and tried to extract from them some common ground and guidelines which might be of service to teachers. The next chapter on learning and memory continues the discussion. When we face a classroom full of children, what important matters do we need to consider in order to effect behavioural changes in directions which we might prescribe? In other words, how do we encourage children to learn? In other chapters throughout the text we have considered the influence of body mechanisms such as the brain and central nervous system, motivation, language, cognitive development, intelligence and personality on the learning process. Here we have tried to provide a framework of theory as a background to these other influences.

The connectionists, or behaviourists, led by Watson and Thorndike, are predominantly concerned with the relationship between stimulus (S) and response (R). Behaviour, according to them, is acquired or changed when the organism, be it a hungry rat or a child in school, builds up connections between S and R. The connections may arise because of the closeness of S and R (contiguity theory favoured by Watson), or by satisfaction which comes from giving a correct R to a given S (reinforcement theory favoured by Thorndike). Of the other behaviourists, the work of Pavlov and Skinner is outstanding. Pavlov's contribution was to show that animals and humans can be taught to respond to a stimulus, chosen by the experimenter, which may not have any apparent resemblance to the response. The well-known salivation response of dogs to the sound of a bell or tuning fork is an illustration. This is known as classical conditioning. In operant conditioning, enunciated by Skinner, a response sometimes arises spontaneously and the subsequent satisfaction will strengthen the bond between stimulus and fortuitous response. If a hungry rat accidentally touches a lever and receives a pellet of food, a connection between lever-pressing and good reception is very soon established. This latter kind of learning has been used extensively in therapy for autism and criminal deviance. Programmed learning using linear techniques also owes a lot to Skinnerian theories of operant conditioning.

As connections between S and R can be forged, so can they be extinguished by removing the reward which accompanies the response. Introducing an unpleasant or a neutral response as an alternative to the rewarding response is the most common way.

Of the cognition theories, the best known and most useful for the teacher belong to the Gestalt School. Insightful learning occurs with a sudden, immediate, repeatable and transposable flash of inspiration. Tolman, whose stance was midway between gestalt and behaviourism, developed this view by showing that animals quickly learn to recognize cues and the link between these cues, thus giving rise to cognitive maps which assist in the solution of problems. A hungry rat running through a maze for food is thought, by Tolman, to form a pattern of clues, each one leading to the initiation of the next stage in the solution of the maze.

Summarizing some of the main conclusions arising from these theories, we find that they agree on several vital issues. Children can be encouraged to learn using intrinsic (affiliation, exploration, manipulation, achievement) and extrinsic (incentives, praise and reproof) rewards. Immediate relevance and importance have high motivational value. Habits of thinking, that is, personal and unique ways of tackling problems, are laid down in early life as learning sets (Harlow). These apply not only to cognitive habits, but also to social behaviour (Bandura), by imitating models of behaviour. Knowledge of results too – particularly successful results – has reinforcement value.

Whether to learn in moderate chunks or by successive, small portions depends upon the kind of material being learned. But there is support for both whole and part methods of learning. Starting from familiar, basic schemata and using analogy as a means of proceeding to the unfamiliar has much to commend it. There is also something to be said for both guided discovery and verbal reception techniques of teaching, depending on the subject matter, the previous experience of the pupils, their intelligence and the cognitive stage they have reached. This was linked with the views of Bruner and Ausubel.

A section on programmed learning includes a detailed discussion of programmed instruction using teaching machines. Consideration is given to the design of linear and branching programmes and their place in the growing technology of education. Recent applied behavioural approaches for disruptive behaviour in normal classrooms are examined.

A final section looks at the contribution of models of instruction.

ENQUIRY AND DISCUSSION

(a) On teaching practice or observation, draw up a list of the factors which you consider would influence the learning habits and skills of pupils. These observations should be pooled and discussed in tutorials. To what extent have learning theories contributed to evaluating these factors?

(b) Look round for examples of operant conditioning in the classroom. Is language acquisition partly dependent on operant conditioning? Examine the steps and methods which lead to teaching a child its first word.

(c) Try to get hold of the BATPACK and explore with tutors the value of this procedure in classroom management. Try to observe it in action in a school.

(d) Read up and write about the schedules of reinforcement used by Skinner in his work with autistic children, delinquents and criminals.

(e) Take a very small topic in your main subject of study suitable for a given age and ability group. Try to draw up a short linear programme covering the topic. You will soon discover what a difficult task this can be and how much it calls on a detailed and well-informed knowledge of the subject.

(f) Look for examples of 'modelling' among children, i.e. the imitation of novel chunks of behaviour *in toto*. Compare and contrast the technique needed for teaching behaviours using modelling or operant conditioning.

(g) Look at the work of Bruner, Ausubel, Bloom and Gagné (references at the end of this chapter). Examine their contributions in the light of the model of instruction, Figure 5.3. How firm is the evidence for the comparable effects of discovery learning and expository learning? Are there situations when one method is more suitable than the other?

NOTES AND REFERENCES

1. W. F. Hill, *Learning: A Survey of Psychological Interpretations*, Harper and Row, London, 1990 (5th edn).
2. Some of the problems raised are discussed in some detail by G. H. Bower and E. R. Hilgard in *Theories of Learning*, Prentice-Hall, Englewood Cliffs, NJ, 1981 (5th edn).
3. For a more detailed text on different traditions in psychology see J. Medcof and J. Roth (eds), *Approaches to Psychology*, Open University Press, Milton Keynes, 1988. A reference is also given in Chapter 1 to an interesting theoretical paper about observation by J. Richer – see note 3(**R**) in Chapter 1.
4. For an interesting, readable account of behaviourism see R. L. Atkinson, R. C. Atkinson and E. E. Smith and D. J. Bem, *Introduction to Psychology*, Harcourt Brace Jovanovich, New York, 1992 (11th edn), Chapter 7. For a recent educational reference see D. Fontana (ed.), *Behaviourism and Learning Theory in Education*, Scottish Academic Press, Edinburgh, *British Journal of Educational Psychology* Monograph 1, 1984.
5. The story of 'little Albert' and other children who were 'conned' in the interests of science can be found in J. B. Watson, *Behaviourism*, Routledge and Kegan Paul, London, 1931.
6. The details of Hull's intervening variables are not too important because there is no way, at present, of verifying the details of their existence. In general, however, he postulates physiological internal needs which create *drives* (hunger, thirst) and provide activation for the satisfaction of these body needs. Another intervening variable is *incentive*, that is, the strength of the reward on previous, recent occasions is likely to intensify goal-seeking activity. *Habit strength*, the strength of the bond created between S and R, is also said to be involved.
7. W. F. Brewer, 'There is no convincing evidence for conditioning in adult human beings', Paper read to the Conference on Cognition and the Symbolic Processes, Pennsylvania State University, October 1972.
8. E. C. Tolman, *Purposive Behavior in Animals and Men*, Appleton-Cenury-Crofts, New York, 1949 (recent edition).
9. J. M. Thyne, *The Psychology of Learning and Techniques of Teaching*, University of London Press, London, 1963. Thyne defines a habit as 'an instance of learning in which a relatively simple response is made, automatically and fairly frequently, to a relatively simple kind of situation'; H. F. Harlow, 'The formation of learning sets', *Psychol. Rev.*, **56**, 51–65 (1949); L. Siegel and L. C. Siegel, 'Educational set – a determinant of acquisition,' *J. Educ. Psychol.*, **56**, 1–12 (1965).
10. (**R**) R. R. Skemp, 'The need for schematic learning theory', *Br. J. Educ. Psychol.*, **32**, 133–142 (1962), and *The Psychology of Learning Mathematics*, Penguin, Harmondsworth, 1986 (2nd edn).
11. (**R**) J. A. Rowell, J. Simon and R. Wiseman, 'Verbal reception, guided discovery and the learning of schemata', *Br. J. Educ. Psychol.*, **39**, 235–244 (1969). This paper contains a useful collection of researches in this field.
12. L. S. Schulman and E. R. Keislar (eds), *Learning by Discovery: A Critical Appraisal*, Rand McNally, Chicago, 1965.
13. J. S. Bruner, 'The act of discovery', *Harvard Educ. Rev.*, **31**, 21–32 (1961), and *The Process of Education*, Cambridge, Harvard University Press, 1977.
14. The findings of Bennett and the ORACLE team at Leicester University are discussed in Chapter 11 under 'Learning and teaching styles'. We also look at some of the criticisms levelled at this research. N. Bennett, *Teaching Styles and Pupil Progress*, Open Books,

London, 1976; M. Galton, B. Simon and P. Croll, *Inside the Primary Classroom*, Routledge and Kegan Paul, London, 1980; M. Galton and B. Simon (eds), *Progress and Performance in the Primary Classroom*, Routledge and Kegan Paul, London, 1980. A. B. Branwhite, 'Boosting reading skills by direct instruction', *Br. J. Educ. Psychol.*, **53**, 291–298 (1983).

15. R. Alexander, J. Rose and C. Woodhead, *Curriculum Organisation and Classroom Practice in Primary Schools: A Discussion Paper*, DES, London, 1992. See also N. Bennett, 'Changing perspectives on teaching–learning processes in the post-Plowden era', *Oxford Rev. Educ.*, **13**(1), 67–79 (1987).
16. M. Wertheimer, *Productive Thinking*, Tavistock Publications, London, 1961 (enlarged edition edited by M. Wertheimer).
17. J. A. Poteet, *Behaviour Modification: A Practical Guide for Teachers*, 'Unibooks', University of London, 1973. For the original sources of the behaviourist movement, see B. F. Skinner, *Science and Human Behavior*, Macmillan, New York, 1953.
18. K. D. O'Leary and S. G. O'Leary, *Classroom Management: The Successful Use of Behavior Modification*, Pergamon Press, New York, 1971 (2nd edn).
19. Note (18), particularly Chapter 3 in the O'Learys' book.
20. A. Bandura and R. H. Walters, *Social Learning and Personality Development*, Holt, Rinehart and Winston, London, 1963; A. Bandura, *Principles of Behavior Modification*, Holt, Rinehart and Winston, London, 1970; A. Bandura, D. Ross and S. A. Ross, 'Imitation of film-mediated aggressive models', *J. Abnorm. Soc. Psychol.*, **66**, 3–11 (1963).
21. O. I. Lovaas, 'A behavior therapy approach to the treatment of childhood schizophrenia', in J. P. Hill (ed.), *Minnesota Symposium on Child Psychology*, University of Minnesota Press, Minneapolis, 1967.
22. V. O. Tyler (Jr) and G. D. Brown, 'Token reinforcement of academic performance with institutionalized delinquent boys', *J. Educ. Psychol.*, **59**, 164–168 (1968). See also notes (18) and (24) for further work on token economy research.
23. M. Hoghughi, 'The Aycliffe token economy', *Br. J. Crim.*, 384–399 (1979). See also A. Kazdin, *The Token Economy*, Plenum, New York, 1977. Also have a look at M. Hoghughi, *Treating Problem Children: Issues, Methods and Practice*, Sage, London, 1988.
24. (R) M. Whitman and J. Whitman, 'Behaviour modification in the classroom', *Psychology in the Schools*, **8**, 176–186 (1971); J. A. Poteet, *Changing Behavior: A Practical Guide for Teachers and Parents*, Phi Delta Kappa, 1985; also F. J. Sparzo and J. A. Poteet, *Classroom Behavior: Detecting and Correcting Special Problems*, Allyn and Bacon, Newton, MA, 1989.
25. A great deal of research and development occurred in Birmingham in the 1980s which is summarized in K. Wheldall and T. Glynn, *Effective Classroom Teaching*, Blackwell, Oxford, 1989. For other commentaries on the applications of behavioural methods in education, see 'The behavioural approach to classroom management', in D. Fontana (ed.), *Behaviourism and Learning*, Monograph No. 1 of the *British Journal of Educational Psychology*, Scottish Academic Press, Edinburgh, 1984, and 'Training teachers to be more positive: a behavioural approach', in S. N. Bennett and C. W. Desforges (eds), *Recent Advances in Classroom Research*, Monograph No. 2 of the *British Journal of Educational Psychology*, Scottish Academic Press, Edinburgh, 1985.
26. K. Wheldall and F. Merrett, *The Behavioural Approach to Teaching Package*, Positive Products, Birmingham, 1985; see also K. Wheldall and F. Merrett, 'BATPACK: Evolution and Evaluation', *Behaviour Change*, **2**, 21–32 (1985).
27. J. Leedham and D. Unwin, *Programmed Learning in Schools*, Longman, London, 1965.
28. (R) J. L. Becker, *A Programed Guide to Writing Auto-instructional Programs*, RCA Service Co., NJ, 1963.
29. For a clear, well-written introduction to CAI, see E. R. Steinberg, *Computer-Assisted Instruction: A Synthesis of Theory, Practice and Technology*, Erlbaum, Hillsdale, NJ, 1991.
30. D. Child, 'Psychology in the service of education: a review', in *The University of Leeds Review*, **27**, 1984–85.
31. R. Driver, *The Pupil as Scientist?*, Open University, Milton Keynes, 1983.

32.   G. R. Lefrancois, *Psychology for Teaching*, Wadsworth, Belmont, CA, 1988 (4th edn) presents a particularly helpful and detailed analysis of Bruner's and Ausubel's contributions, including a comparison of the two positions.

33.   J. B. Carroll, 'A model of school learning', *Teachers College Record*, **64**, 723–33 (1963); B. S. Bloom, *Human Characteristics and School Learning*, McGraw-Hill, New York, 1976.

FURTHER READING

M. L. Bigge, *Learning Theories for Teachers*, Harper and Row, London, 1982 (4th edn).

W. F. Hill, *Learning: A Survey of Psychological Interpretations*, Harper and Row, London, 1990 (5th edn). A sound basic text.

W. F. Hill, *Principles of Learning: A Handbook of Applications*, Alfred Publishers, Sherman Oaks, California, 1981.

K. Wheldall and T. Glynn, *Effective Classroom Learning: A Behavioural Interactionist Approach to Teaching*, in the series Theory and Practice in Education, D. Child (ed.), Blackwell, Oxford, 1989.

Four books containing independent views about the nature and role of instruction at school which should be of interest are:

D. P. Ausubel and F. G. Robinson, *School Learning: An Introduction to Educational Psychology*, Holt, Rinehart and Winston, New York, 1969.

B. S. Bloom, *Human Characteristics and School Learning*, McGraw-Hill, New York, 1976.

J. S. Bruner, *Towards a Theory of Instruction*, Norton, New York, 1966.

R. M. Gagné and M. P. Driscoll, *Essentials of Learning for Instruction*, Prentice-Hall, Englewood Cliffs, NJ, 1988 (2nd edn).

Chapter 6

Learning and Memory

The blanket term 'memory'[1] has often been used to describe the activities of acquiring, retaining and recalling, and at one time it was thought to be a faculty capable of being exercised, like a muscle, in order to improve the quality and quantity of what we learn. The use of mechanical memorization in, for example, Latin, mathematics and history was, and probably still is, held by some teachers to be a good means by which pupils can flex their memories by sheer, dogged effort. The present view is that we are endowed with a capacity for memorization and, although we can improve on our methods of assimilating information, it is possible that we have limits to our capacities. Since we probably never reach the full extent of our capacities, it should certainly be possible to improve the amount we memorize by correspondingly improving the acquisition techniques (see Gagné later). Furthermore, there may be a case for believing that several kinds of memory exist. Some people have better rote memories than others; visual, auditory and kinaesthetic memory (that is, movement memory, which is helpful in touch typing, sport, or any other activity requiring muscle co-ordination) also vary from one person to another.

The physiological mechanisms which accompany memorization are not really understood. We have seen in Chapters 2 and 4 some postulates about the biological, chemical and perceptual nature of memory, and although we can be fairly certain of a chemical explanation of memory storage, there is still a long way to go in our understanding of the exact processes involved.

How is it possible to show that learning has taken place? We have to rely on a person's ability to remember something by either mental or physical means. We refer to a hypothetical possession – the memory – which is regarded almost as a place, located in the head, where recoverable experience and knowledge are housed. When we call upon the memory, the process of recovery is called *remembering*. But this crude picture, rather like a computer bank system, is not sufficient to explain the many complex activities of which humans are capable. This chapter attempts to look at some of those complexities and the most recent, coherent models used to describe them.

INFORMATION-PROCESSING MODEL OF MEMORY

The information-processing model of memory postulates two aspects. One relates to internal structures (mainly in the brain) and the other to the processes related to these structures.[2] The processes hypothesized in contemporary views about memory are *encoding, storage* and *retrieval*. Encoding is the process whereby information is thought to be put into the memory; storage relates to the methods assumed to be involved in the retention of information; and retrieval relates to the processes of recovery of stored information from memory. Encoding has already been referred to in Chapter 4. Retrieval will be dealt with later in this chapter.

The short- and long-term memory appear to depend on different functional locations in the brain as can be deduced from the effects on memory of brain damage.

STORAGE

Figure 6.1 gives a rough idea of the storage structures hypothesized.

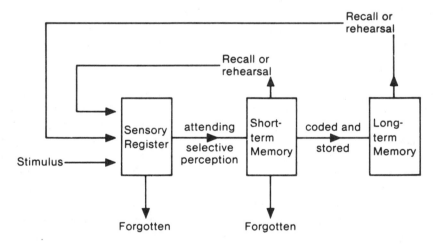

Figure 6.1 *Hypothetical structures of the information-processing model of memory.*

Sensory register

When our sense organs pick up a signal from the environment there is a momentary image registered (Sperling describes research into visual registry and decay[3]). The corresponding process of attention and selective perception ensures that only particular stimulation is conveyed to the next structure, the short-term memory. The remaining patterns of stimulation are thought to die away from the register. The period over which the image is registered is very short (a few hundred milliseconds) before complete decay. The after-image in the eye, experienced when we look at a bright light and can detect the image for some time afterwards, is an example, although in this case the image, being so potent, tends to remain longer than a few hundred milliseconds. Three hypothesized registers are *iconic* or *visual memory*, *echoic* or *auditory* (or verbal) and *semantic memory*.

Short-term or 'working' memory (STM)

Information entering the short-term memory also decays rapidly, but in seconds rather than in milliseconds as with the sensory register. If information is not selectively attended to and encoded so as to pass to the long-term store it decays. The STM is seen as a temporary store of a limited amount of information. Unattended information occurring simultaneously with that to which we are attending can be retrieved with diminishing accuracy as time goes by. Close your eyes and try to recall the objects on your desk. You should have some success in recalling peripheral images of surrounding objects which have impinged on the senses without your consciously having recorded them. Of course, the act of recalling one aspect of an event in STM interferes with the recall of remaining events.

A number of studies have suggested that the STM has a limited capacity. For example, these are exemplified in studies of 'span of attention' or 'apprehension' where a person is required to recall a stimulus (objects on a table, dots on a sheet of paper) exposed for a brief interval. On average, people can recall between six and ten objects, numbers or letters arranged at random. So a telephone number heard or seen for a short time would be within the competence of most people. Where learning is required, teachers are well advised to note the limitations of immediate memory span.

In an amusing discussion by Miller[4] it is suggested that our *span of absolute judgement*, which is about seven objects at once, can be improved radically by a process known as *chunking*. This consists of grouping items into chunks numbering about seven. The technique is widely used in learning subjects like morse, typing and chemistry, where items (dots and dashes, letters or chemical symbols) are brought together and learned as groups.

Recent thinking about the working memory by Baddeley[5] suggests that the short-term memory, like the long-term memory, is context- and subject-specific. Also, there are sub-systems which cope, for example, with short-term retention of verbal or visual–spatial material. This whole question of context and subject specificity is crucial to our purpose in teaching. Later in the chapter we shall discuss the question of study and some implications of the influence which this specificity might have on performance.

As mentioned previously in this chapter, memory skills appear to be task-specific. The generalizations from early research, which tended to use laboratory settings with nonsense syllables, should be regarded with some suspicion. The current view is that to discover useful and transferable information about memory, one has to get as close to the actual conditions of the situation as possible. Variations in the material, the processes and strategies used for memorizing and the skills which the person brings to the learning all play some part. Consequently, it would be very difficult to see how knowledge from learning nonsense material could be generalized to learning meaningful material in the classroom. Such factors as prior knowledge, how understandable the information being learned is to the person and the time allowed for memorization are also crucial.

Recall or rehearsal of information in the short-term store is thought to occur by passing the information through the limited-capacity channel and re-entering it in the short-term store. In other words, rehearsal is closely related to rote learning, as when we repeat a telephone number, a shopping list or historical details. The more this cycle is repeated, the more likely it is that information will pass into the long-term store. There are probably telephone numbers, car registrations and childhood incidents lurking in our long-term memory from years ago because of repeated recall.

Craik and Watkins[6] have put forward a theory that rehearsal takes two forms – *maintenance* and *elaborative rehearsal*. The former is like the empty repeating of information in order to retain it in the short-term memory for sufficient time to be of use. How many times have you chanted a number (car registration, telephone number) until it is needed, only to forget it immediately afterwards? Elaborative rehearsal should not only maintain information in the STM; it is also intended to assist in placing it in the LTM.

Long-term memory (LTM)

The information entering the long-term store, unlike that in previous stores, does not decay but seems to be permanent in most circumstances. Information flow between the three hypothetical structures is believed to be under the control of the individual.

The prospect of information 'reaching' the long-term memory store depends on several factors relating to the information. Four of these are the length, the content, the opportunity for initial learning and the activity taking place between successive units of information (R).[7]

As every student knows, long messages are less likely to be remembered than short ones. Technical messages, the level of familiarity, the particular sense or language of a message are all significant for long-term storage. Clearly revision is going to assist pupils in transferring information from the STM to the LTM. Multiple ways of presenting the same material, permitting active recall between each unit of information and reducing the speed of presentation will help in this respect. The effect of introducing a distraction at the outset of a revision session, or producing interference (proactive and retroactive, see later) before, during or after a learning session can have a devastating effect on the amount recalled. Vocalization as a means of revision helps in the short term. Dale (R)[7] concludes that:

> for material to enter long-term storage it has to survive an initial period during which retention loss can be extremely rapid. In order to survive, the amount of material should be small; it should be as free as possible from inter-item acoustic confusions; it should be varied so that interference between successive messages is minimised; also an opportunity for a brief period of silent rehearsal should be provided after each component message is presented.

The storage capacity must be enormous when one considers the amount of information we use each day. Memories from long ago can be recalled, in some cases in great detail, probably through constant repetition. Whether we ever completely forget anything once it has been transferred satisfactorily to the LTM is an unanswered question. Later we shall look at some of the reasons why we forget information.

The theory of a two-part (or stage) memory system, sometimes called the *duplex theory*, has much to commend it. There is a degree of common sense about it and teachers will readily see from the above how it can be applied to their day-to-day classroom activities. The differences between the STM and LTM are worthy of note (see Table 6.1).

Table 6.1 *Differences between the STM and LTM*

Type of memory	Capacity	Persistence	Retrieval	Input
Short-term	Limited	Very brief	Immediate	Very fast
Long-term	Practically unlimited	Practically unlimited	Depends on organization	Relatively slow

(Adapted from F. Smith, *Comprehension and Learning: A Conceptual Framework*, Holt, Rinehart and Winston, Eastbourne, 1975).[8]

One of the problems associated with the information-processing model is the implicit assumption that the human being is essentially a passive recipient of stimulation and that processing takes place in an ordered sequence and not in any parallel sense.

Some models, including psychoanalysis, behaviourism and psychometrics, tend to forget the role of that most human of activities – thinking. This, along with the influence of specific aspects of each feat of memory, has caused Morris[9] to claim:

> the evidence suggests that there is so much variability in the type of material, the types of processes, the strategies and the processing skills upon which people can draw when they tackle memorising in different situations that the way in which information is entered into the memory will often be very different from one situation to another.

Neisser[10] suggests that there is concurrent and interactive processing between what is referred to as 'bottom-up' and 'top-down' processes. 'Bottom-up' (or stimulus-driven) processing is said to be directly influenced by the stimulus. The stimulus is analysed into specific features, like building blocks, and assembled into a pattern which has meaning for the receiver. The written word PEAR, made up from various straight and curved lines, will stimulate the reader to interpret the information to mean a familiar fruit.

Top-down (or conceptually-driven) processing does *not* require the detailed analysis of all the data in order to make sense of it. We can use the situation to help in the interpretation of meaning. If I *said* 'which $\frac{pear}{pair}$ would you like?' and pointed to a set of stockings, the context would quickly indicate that 'pair' was the intended meaning.

Meaning is most important in ensuring long-term memory. Whilst most people may find it difficult to give the precise details of an event or give the exact words in sentences they have read, they will often be able to recall the general meaning of the event or sentence. In the main, the preferred code for long-term memory is verbal, but sensory codes such as visual scenes, smells, tastes also exist.

RETRIEVAL (RECALL, REMEMBERING)

Retrieval is the process of recovering information from the memory. The term is used synonymously with recall and remembering. It is applied to either the short- or long-term memory. Retrieval from the LTM consists of returning information to the STM from the LTM store, i.e. into the working memory. To initiate retrieval a cue is needed, either from an external stimulus or by a person's conscious effort to 'search' through the memory store for a link with material already in the working memory.

Three ways in which we can recover information have been described and they are *recall*, *recognition* and *relearning*.

Recall depends upon the active remembering of performances learned previously. Some examples are repeating a poem, a dance routine, mathematical equations and how to drive a car. We have to dig into our memories for an answer to a problem and rely entirely on our ability to recapture the relevant information. Examples of simple recall are given as part of the examination exercises mentioned in Chapter 13. This is the most difficult method of retrieving information.

In the case of recognition, we are given a clue or shown the information from which we can remember something learned on a previous occasion. To some extent multiple-choice questions, where alternative answers to a question are offered and the individual is required to select one answer, rely on recognition. However, in many instances the solution has first to be worked out and tallied with those provided, and this involves a high level of recall. We have all experienced the occasion when we see a face in the newspaper or on television and cannot put a name to it. Someone suggests a few names and the moment the correct name is mentioned we recognize it. The method is easier than recall, as can be concluded from Figure 6.2, which illustrates an experiment comparing retrieval by recognition, recall and *relearning*. In the latter case a pupil is

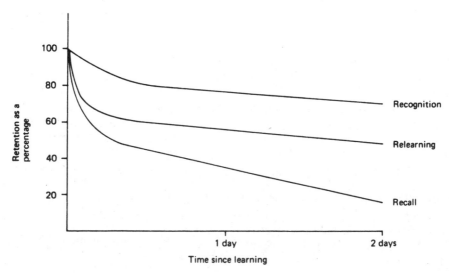

Figure 6.2 *Efficiency of three methods of retrieval. After C. W. Luh, 'The conditions of retention', Psychol. Monogr., 31 (1922).*

asked to relearn something after a lapse of time and his or her efficiency in recall is measured by finding the time taken to relearn the task. We have all experienced the greater ease of revising something already learned.

The marked contrast between recall and recognition is worth bearing in mind, not only in the design of multiple-choice examination questions but in the prevalent method of question-and-answer teaching. Using only recall methods is exacting and fatiguing for children and should be interspersed with recognition tasks. Translation from French to English is easier for us than is translating from English to French because we can recognize the English equivalents of French words much more readily than in the reverse case. Note finally that relearning something which has been forgotten gets easier on each successive occasion, and this is why regular revision is a vital aspect of studying. Retrieval is aided where the original learning has been systematic, thorough and understood by the learner. Thus trying to recall material memorized by rote methods is more difficult than when the material is meaningful.

FORGETTING

Forgetting is the loss of ability to retrieve from either the STM or the LTM. 'Forgotten' does not necessarily mean 'gone for ever'. We have all experienced the situation where we cannot retrieve a particular memory, but it returns to us some time later. There are various theories as to why we forget and they depend on whether we are dealing with short- or long-term memory.

With the STM, three sources of forgetting have been postulated. They are *overload*, *decay* (or *atrophy*) and *displacement*. We have already referred to the capacity limitations of STM (seven plus or minus two) and it appears that beyond a certain number of units, which varies from one person to another, we can overload. How many people have tried to carry, say, a nine-digit telephone number from one place to another only to arrive at the telephone unsure of its correctness? Teachers should bear this overload possibility in mind when covering extensive topics. The careful use of chunking is important here.

Decay theory means what it says, that memories gradually disappear with time. Some physiological psychologists believe the cause is chemical. Some chemicals cause a metabolic change in the storage system bringing with it the decay and, finally, disappearance of memory traces in the nervous system.

Displacement theory assumes that if limited capacity prevails, there is a case for some information in the STM being pushed out – displaced – to make room for new inputs.

For the LTM, causes of forgetting are thought to be *interference, destruction of brain tissue* and *motivated forgetting*.

Interference is thought to be the most problematic of all sources of memory loss. It arises when materials being retrieved from memory have similar, but not identical, features. For example, trying to recall names or numbers which are similar can give rise to interplay and confusion both when trying to retain or recall. Some memories may not actually disappear altogether, but become obscured and overlaid with more recent memories. The sudden reappearance of long-lost memories either normally or under hypnosis is offered as evidence of interference theory.

In the short term, the recall of information can be inhibited in two ways. If we learn two lots of work, X and Y, in that order, the nature of X might influence the recall of Y, and this we call *proactive inhibition*. Underwood[11] cites an example, well known amongst teachers, in which several lists of similar material are given to a group of subjects who are required to memorize them on successive days. Performance in terms of amount recalled deteriorates progressively from the first to the last list. The correct responses remembered from the preceding lists interfere with the recall of the one being learned.

When Y, the second task, inhibits the recall of X we call it *retroactive inhibition*. If the second learning task, Y, is repeated several times, each occasion makes the recall of X that much more difficult. The proactive effect of task X on Y is gradually eliminated by repeated trials of task Y, but in so doing the extinction of task X is taking place.[12]

Experiment reveals that interference is a function of the similarity of tasks X and Y and their closeness in time. In both proactive and retroactive inhibition the subject matter is similar. Even when a task of a different nature is interposed between X and Y, recall is worse than when a complete rest is taken. Sleep between learning and recall helps retention for this very reason (also see the section on reminiscence below). In view of these findings, lessons should be interspersed with short intervals of relaxation, and the subject matter of adjoining lessons should not be similar. Learning just prior to bedtime (if one is not too tired), followed by a revision period first thing in the morning, is effective for some.

Some very helpful information about the sites in the brain responsible for memory function has been obtained from brain-damaged patients. It would appear that STM and LTM depend on several different parts of the brain. Indeed, there are cases in which damage has affected one but not the other, an observation often quoted as evidence for the dual theory of short- and long-term memory.

Motivated forgetting is familiar to those in psychoanalysis as *repression* (see Chapter 11) or the inaccessibility of some memories because of the (usually) unpleasant origins associated with them. Amnesia is a striking illustration in some psychopathological cases.

Reminiscence

Ballard[13] found a curious phenomenon in 1913. Some children who had partially learned a poem were able to recall better after a period of time than immediately after the learning session. This is known as *reminiscence*. One explanation is that inhibition builds up during the task, but once the task is abandoned, dissipation of inhibition sets in and enables a better recall performance. Thus, for a short time after the learning, the dissipation might proceed at such a rate as to enable the individual to improve performance. In a research with schoolchildren the author[14] was able to show that neurotic extraverts display significantly higher reminiscence effects than stable introverts, using the inverted alphabet test. The direction of this finding is in keeping with the postulates of Eysenck regarding the levels and dissipation of inhibition in different personality types (see Chapter 11). As extraverts develop higher levels of inhibition than introverts, their performance will be poorer, relatively speaking, as the task proceeds. Consequently, after a break in which inhibition has dissipated, the performance of extraverts will appear as temporarily superior to that of introverts. Once again we see a possible connection between personality characteristics and performance which one would hope might become a valid source of information in class teaching.

Massed and distributed practice

Massed practice occurs when little or no rest is permitted during a task or between tasks. When intervals during the task are allowed we have *distributed* practice. In general, massed conditions of learning are less productive than distributed conditions. A possible reason has already been broached in the discussion of interference and reminiscence, where we proposed that retention is inhibited as a task proceeds and, until there is some rest, the inhibition continues to affect performance. A rest pause enables the inhibition to dissipate. If you have ever tried 'press-ups', you will recall that a point is reached when it seems absolutely impossible to raise the body one more time. In a way, this illustrates the effects of mental inhibition, when the mind is pushed to a point where it cannot function adequately, although we rarely reach the kind of dramatic standstill experienced in physical exercise.

No satisfactory solution has been found to the questions of how long the rests should be, or how long is a reasonable stint of work in particular school subjects. The periods normally used in school are based on a rule-of-thumb and not on scientific analysis. Choosing periods of 35 minutes in primary schools, for example, is mostly experience and intuition. The idea that young children can only take about 20 minutes of narration from a teacher has very little experimental support. Nevertheless, teachers have doubtless arrived at a knowledge of timing lessons from observation and experience of handling children. The signs of fatigue or work decrement are plain to see, and inexperienced teachers would be wise to keep a wary eye open for such signs of inhibition.

A curve of forgetting

Ebbinghaus[15] and his associates were amongst the first to study remembering and forgetting. His famous experiments related chiefly to the rate of forgetting with the passage of time. We are well aware that most learned material gradually fades away, and Ebbinghaus devised experiments to see if there was any pattern to the nature of forgetting. His subjects were required to learn a list of *nonsense syllables* until they could repeat the list perfectly. A nonsense syllable consists of a three-letter arrangement of two consonants with a vowel as the centre letter. The resulting combination must not be a word in the language. Syllables such as BOL, QIS and WEJ are examples. Nonsense syllables are chosen to make sure that the learners have no prior knowledge of the task: everyone starts from scratch. The criterion of learning is the ability of the subject to repeat the list of, say, ten syllables once through completely while the task is being timed. At various intervals of time after learning, the subject endeavours to repeat the list, and if (as is usually the case) unable to repeat it he or she is timed in the relearning of the list.

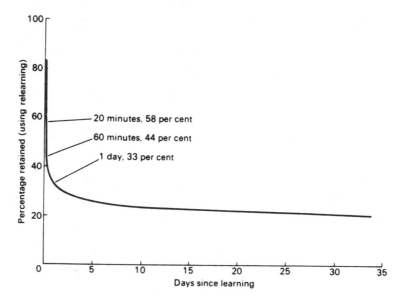

Figure 6.3   *A curve of forgetting (after Ebbinghaus).*

The usual formula for deriving the time needed for recall is:

$$\frac{\text{original learning} - \text{relearning time}}{\text{original learning time}} \times 100$$

This gives a ratio of time saved in relearning expressed as a percentage. A typical curve of retention (or conversely forgetting) using several time intervals is shown in Figure 6.3. The higher the percentage, the more efficient recall has been. Note the rapid fall in the amount remembered and the levelling out of the curve after about five days to something like 22 per cent of the original amount retained. Later, in Figure 6.5, we shall see some marked differences in this quantity, which varies according to the kind of material being learned.

In a moment, we shall discuss how applicable Ebbinghaus's work is to learning in classrooms.

Serial learning

In a particular learning programme, the position of the material as it is presented can have a marked influence on the prospects of retention. Again, using lists of nonsense syllables which it is assumed can be generalized to meaningful material, it has been shown that the first and last few syllables are usually learned and remembered first and the central syllables last. If we plot the number of trials required to learn a syllable against its position in the list we generate a *serial position* curve (see Figure 6.4). One explanation of this phenomenon is the *primacy* and *recency* effects. The primacy effect is said to occur because we tend to remember best the first information we receive because it has the greatest effect on us. We also tend to remember better, information we have received most recently. Hence the research shows better performance at the

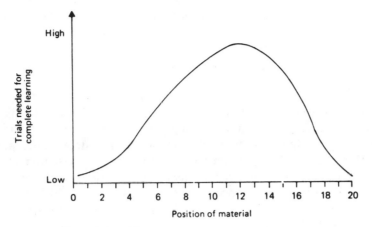

Figure 6.4 *A representative serial position curve.*

beginning and the end. This is very useful information for the class teacher: in devising lessons some thought should be given to the order of presentation in terms of difficulty and length, and in re-ordering for revision purposes.

In a study by Murdock[16] using English words a similar marked serial position effect was noted. Figure 6.5 illustrates the findings. These fit in remarkably well with the duplex theory of STM and LTM. The first words to be memorized probably 'entered' a comparatively free short-term memory store and were rehearsed more frequently than the middle words. These would therefore stand a better chance of being committed to the LTM store. The middle words were entering an already 'occupied' STM store. The last words on the list would still be in the LTM when recall was required. In fact, many people give the last words first 'before I forget them'. In other

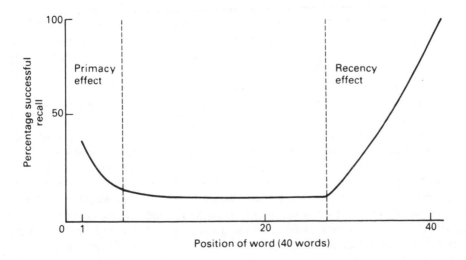

Figure 6.5 *Serial position curve for 40 words.*

words they would suffer the transient fate of STM unless they were repeated soon after being learned.

AIDS TO LEARNING

Our main concern here will be to discuss the factors which are thought to affect the efficiency of learning for retention and recall. It is taken as self-evident that the study habits, as well as the abilities, of individuals are important in determining performance in all forms of recall, including conventional examinations. Yet research into the effect of different study habits has not given us any clear indications of the precise patterns best suited to individuals. This is not surprising when one considers the complexity of the studying task itself, quite apart from cognitive and personality factors contributing to performance.

Many factors appear to impinge on study effectiveness, most are mentioned in other chapters (motivation, intelligence, personality, knowledge of results, etc.). Texts for students have been written on the subject of study since the turn of the twentieth century.[17] Many of the suggestions, such as ensuring that a suitable location or the material needed are available, are common sense and will be referred to later in this section. But most of these texts have tended to give a set of techniques and skills to be mastered without concern for individual differences or the contexts within which learning is taking place. In recent years greater emphasis has been given to the role of students in self-awareness about their learning methods and this issue will be dealt with first.

Learning to learn (metacognition)

During the past twenty or so years, research has focused on the idea that students ought to have greater awareness of their thinking strategies. Individual students, by understanding the processes of study, their own characteristics, work conditions and subject contexts, are thought to have a better chance of improving the effectiveness of study sessions. This concept of a person self-consciously examining his or her mental processes, becoming aware of problems and adjusting accordingly in order to improve effectiveness is known as *metacognition*[18] – learning how to learn.

The study methods movement was clearly an attempt to provide a framework which students could use to examine their own methods. Unfortunately, it has not been as useful as was hoped. One serious flaw is that the recommended techniques are not always transferable from one context to another. For example, many texts on study methods[17] give strategies for remembering lists of words, usually unconnected words. Would these strategies easily transfer to remembering laws in physics, chemical equations, poetry or music? These texts also quickly get into discussions of thinking styles. How does a teacher organize material and presentation to account for the variety of styles in a class? – a daunting task for, say, a secondary teacher of science who might see as many as 300 pupils in the course of a week. From the individual pupil's point of view, someone good at languages and poor at mathematics is not likely to adopt the same learning style in these subjects.

Providing for individual variability is a very complex problem. But some attempts have been made. The Instrumental Enrichment intervention programme devised and used by Feuerstein[19] for children with special needs and John Biggs's[20] SOLO taxonomy scheme (Structure of the Observed Learning Outcome) for evaluating the quality of learning in school and higher education are two examples. They are both orientated towards individual analysis.

The question of transferability of skills from one learning situation to another has been examined by Howe and others in a series of articles.[21] His conclusions are helpful. For transfer to be possible between two learning tasks there ought to be four different kinds of identical elements. They are (a) knowledge common to both; (b) common skills or sub-skills; (c) habits of learning (some of these are discussed below); and (d) characteristics of the learner which would generally help study (such as persistence, competitiveness, enjoyment of learning from textbooks). The first two relate to the contexts and the second two to personal differences of learners.

The following have been shown to affect the way we learn and how much knowledge we acquire (**R**).[22] Some of the issues apply to students in higher education as well as to those in primary and secondary schooling, and a short but useful paper is included in the Reader for your benefit (**R**).[23] The important thing to remember is that efficient study is an individual activity and one must work out the best methods for oneself.

Organization

There is nothing more soul-destroying than to be groping from one topic to another without any clear plan of action: it is uneconomic in terms of both time and effort. Gestalt psychologists have pointed out the need for an understanding of the context within which to work and for this we need to organize and order our subject matter and methods both as students and as teachers. Children quickly become confused and intolerant of situations which are unstructured and undisciplined. As students it is worth while forming some simple study routines which become habits, otherwise the many attractions of the non-academic life of a student can take over completely.

Place to study

For concentration and learning it is necessary to have peace and quiet. A noisy classroom, television or radio in the background at home, roadworks or building noises, or even the voice of others, constitute a distraction for most people. Some claim that a background of music is not a hindrance, but it does constitute a source of competition for one's attention. Technically speaking, the level of extraneous sound should not reach a level which is likely to break through the threshold of one's attention. In private study, body comfort is essential, although one must avoid sleep-inducing conditions such as easy chairs or beds or smoky atmospheres in students' rooms.

Time of day and length of study

No hard-and-fast rule applies about the best time of day or for how long one should study at a given session. Variations between individuals make it necessary for each person to discover his or her own optimum conditions. Some individuals like to rise early in the morning and work 'whilst the mind is fresh', but few students find themselves able to take advantage of this suggestion (Child (**R**)).[22] But there is reason to believe that personality is a significant variable contributing towards differential performance according to the time of day, and whether people work best individually or in a group. Using a task in which subjects were required to cancel the letter 'e' on a sheet of print, Colquhoun and Corcoran (**R**)[22] showed that in the morning or working by themselves, introverts perform better than extraverts. However, in the afternoon, or when working in a group, the performance of introverts is the same as (or even worse than) that of extraverts.

The span of attention (the length of time one can concentrate before distraction sets in) clearly is relevant here and probably is related to personality differences. This point will be elaborated in Chapter 11, where there is some discussion of Eysenck's theory that extraverts normally require more involuntary rest pauses than introverts in tasks requiring concentration. Some people might be unshaken by a two-hour stint of work, whilst others need more frequent rests. The build-up of inhibition to studying can be dissipated by distributing the rest and work periods. But we are not yet in a position to say with conviction how long the work or rest period should be for a given person or, for that matter, how best to use the work time. A few short breaks of about five minutes during a long study session (of about two hours) are essential, and a longer break should be taken between tasks (see proactive and retroactive inhibition in the earlier section 'Forgetting'.) One thing is certain – very few children are taught how to study or how to make a self-evaluation of their study strategies to obtain maximum efficiency. In a study by the author (**R**),[22] 72 per cent of a sample of university, college of education and sixth-form students claimed to have taught themselves how to study by the process of trial and error while at secondary school. Even obvious points about organization and work conditions, timetabling or avoiding fatigue are rarely mentioned by teachers.

Personal problems

Many students are adversely affected in their work by the existence of personal problems arising from emotional, social, academic and, for older students on grants, financial difficulties (see Chapter 12). Learning becomes more tedious as these influences intrude on the concentration of the learner. In both young and older pupils alike, the emotional and social 'cut and thrust' of home life and friendships probably play a significant part in learning efficiency, although the strongest evidence so far on this point comes from American research.[24] Feelings of inadequacy are another source of trouble (see the sections on need to achieve, level of aspiration and self-fulfilling prophecy in Chapter 3). The relationship between teacher and taught is frequently held to influence the latter's attitude to learning. Where there is some good-natured friendliness with authority, derived not so much from his or her position as a teacher as from knowledge of the subject, then an atmosphere more conducive to learning seems to prevail.

One aspect of pupil–teacher relationships which has not yet been researched is the influence of characteristic teaching styles on the study habits and learning skills of children – in other words, the problem of compatibility of teaching and learning styles.[25]

The peer group

Teachers probably underrate the extent to which study strategies are influenced by one's friends. The Americans[24] have gone some way in exploring the nature of agreements and understandings among secondary education and higher education students about their roles as students, but there is insufficient evidence for similar conclusions in Britain. The topic is concerned partly with competition and co-operation between pupils in comparing work by discussing standards, requirements and lesson content. However, it is also concerned with the motivation generated by rivalry between peers to obtain a teacher's attention, and understandings between children about what is a 'group norm' of work (and play).

Meaningfulness of task

Grasping the meaning of a task is essential for efficient learning (also see Bruner and Ausubel in Chapter 5). Most of what we learn requires an understanding of the gist of an argument and not a follow-my-leader repetition of the argument. To see the logic of what is being learned greatly assists in its memorization.

It is nevertheless true that some things have to be learned by heart. There is no inherent logic in the letters of the alphabet or the actual symbols for the numbers 0 to 9. Formulae, scientific principles and laws, passages of prose or dates, zoological systems such as the cranial nerves often have to be learned by heart, even when one understands the meaning of the facts. Some people use props such as rhymes and mnemonics; that is, taking the initial letters of a sequence of facts and using these initial letters to make up an amusing or memorably pornographic sentence. Most students have come across these, especially in science. For example, the colours of the rainbow can be memorized using: Richard Of York Gave Battle In Vain, the initial letters of which make Red, Orange, Yellow, Green, Blue, Indigo, Violet. The rules for finding sines, cosines and tangents of angles are sometimes remembered using SOH CAH TOA (S = sine, C = cosine, T = tangent, O = opposite side, A = adjacent side, H = hypotenuse), from which we get *S*ine equals *O*pposite over *H*ypotenuse, and so on. Remembering the jingles is only half the battle because then we have to recall the facts they represent. However, their main function is to produce a link between unrelated things. Rhymes such as 'Thirty days hath September . . .' or 'Willie, Willie, Harry, Ste . . .', for the kings of England from William the Conqueror onwards, and 'i before e except after c' are also commonplace aids.

The rapidity with which we forget different kinds of material is illustrated in Figure 6.6. Note that the more meaningful topics, such as laws and concepts, are by far the best retained, whilst nonsense syllables are quickly forgotten.

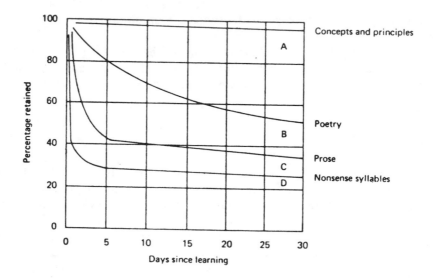

Figure 6.6 *Curves of forgetting for different types of material. From H. Maddox,* How to Study, *Pan, London, 1963.*

Revision

This is important because memories begin to fade with the passage of time unless we actively recall them periodically. While learning a subject it is a useful idea to set aside some time both during and after the learning session for sitting back and actively recalling or committing to paper the work covered. It is believed by some psychologists[25] that we should spend at least half the study time trying to recall the work we are learning. Often the time is totally taken up in reading, without necessarily absorbing the work. Apart from anything else, it helps to vary the learning task and reduce the influence of reactive inhibition (the tendency not to repeat a response which has just been made). Active reconstruction and organization of learned material helps to fix it in one's mind.

Various suggestions have been made to help students remember material. Some have already been mentioned, such as *chunking* and the use of mnemonics or acronyms (initial letters which spell out memorable words, e.g. ASH = Action on Smoking and Health). If you are not convinced of the effectiveness of chunking, compare the difficulty you have in remembering:

EVLEWTSIEMITEHT

with the ease of remembering:

THETIMEISTWELVE

This is particularly so when you realize that the last set of letters consists of four familiar words – 'the time is twelve'. How much more quickly would you have remembered the first set of letters if you had realized they were 'the time is twelve' in reverse order?

Peg-type mnemonics are sometimes used by those who make a living from remembering vast lists of objects. The peg-word method is first to memorize a code such as one is gun, two is shoe, three is tree, four is door and so forth, then to number the objects and associate each with the peg-word; for example, if the first object is a glass, picture it stuck on the barrel end of the gun.

Linking systems are quite common. The most famous is 'Thirty days hath September, April, June and November'.

Another system is the 'keyword' method, often used in learning foreign languages. A word in the foreign language is linked with a familiar object in one's own language. When at school I remembered words relating to silver – argentum, l'argent – by using the country name of Argentina.

'Whole' and 'part' learning

Given a learning task requiring the assimilation of large slices of information, we may read through the information several times to get an overall picture of the content and to try to memorize it. On the other hand, we may break the information down into parts and learn each part first before drawing it together again. This crudely distinguishes 'whole' and 'part' learning. The pros and cons of the two approaches have been researched and debated for several years without any resulting clear-cut advice about which is the superior method. The compromise conclusion is that the nature of the material and the condition of the learner dictate the most suitable method. The holistic approach is useful where the amount of information is sufficiently small to be absorbed at one time. Also it is said to provide a better grasp of meaning and continuity between the elements of the material once the overall pattern of knowledge is understood. It is not always possible to treat chunks of information in this way, particularly if the material is difficult and unfamiliar; consequently we must resort to breaking it down into manageable portions. The central issue is understanding: provided the total context is understood, 'part' learning can be effective.

Reading

One application of the 'whole' or 'part' approach to learning is found in the teaching of reading. No attempt will be made here to advise students on the teaching of reading because it is not possible to do justice to the findings and arguments surrounding the subject in a few paragraphs of a basic general textbook. Reading, quite rightly, takes pride of place in junior schools, and the subject deserves detailed and careful scrutiny[26] for which specific references are more appropriate.

Loosely speaking, the *decoding* methods of teaching reading, as they are called, are based on the 'part' approach and have the support of many behaviourists. The *reading for meaning* (see Goodacre[27]) methods are holistic approaches typified by gestalt psychology.

Decoding methods include the *alphabet* and *phonic* approaches. Alphabetic teaching is carried out by first naming the letters of the alphabet and using these names to build up words. Thus the word 'pod' would first be introduced as 'pee-oh-de gives pod'.

Phonic systems use the sounds of letters in the words, so 'pod' would be 'puh-o-duh', 'puh-od' or 'po-duh' ('o' is the phonetic symbol as in rock). The words are gradually pieced together from the basic names or sounds of letters. Letter recognition and the relationship between letters and their sounds in particular word contexts lie at the root of the phonic method. Its special advantage is that it can be taught systematically, starting with synthetic word building. Transferring the pronunciation of combinations of letters to similar groupings of letters (cow, now, sow) is sometimes possible, but we have so many exceptions in our language (tow, row, low) that the task is made tedious.

In 'reading for meaning' methods we find *look-and-say, whole word, whole sentence* and *whole language*. The principle is that children will remember the configuration or 'shape' of the whole word and associate it with a meaning – where possible, a pictorial representation. The whole-word method is frequently accompanied by pictorial aids in the first stages, while look-and-say can be applied to non-pictorial words as well. So the word 'log', probably already in the oral vocabulary of the child, would be presented along with a picture of the object. This is good psychological thinking because we are moving from the familiar (sight of, and sound of, a familiar object) to the unfamiliar (sight of the whole word). Decoding methods, on the other hand, are said to be boring and sometimes meaningless, because the phonic-taught child can piece together long words without any idea of what the words mean. However, the 'look-and-say' child does have to wait until his or her knowledge of words is sufficient to enable unfamiliar-looking words to be deciphered. Again, the teacher's help is sought more frequently (with the consequent disadvantage of long queues waiting to be told the meanings of words). The starting vocabulary also tends to be limited because of the amount of learning required of the child. Each word is learned as an entity, although some transfer might be possible, as with phonic methods. The whole-sentence method is an extension of the look-and-say method, using sentences as the unit to be learned. Small groups of short words giving a meaningful sentence are taught along with visual props.

It is probably the case that look-and-say methods predominate in British schools, moderated in some cases by phonic teaching. At the earliest stage of reading, children need to appreciate the shapes of letters and what they represent. Therefore, to assist in establishing recognition of these shapes for their ultimate usage in meaningful words, some combination of the two approaches seems to be a sensible way of tackling the early stages.

The Initial Teaching Alphabet (i.t.a.) was launched by Sir James Pitman[28] as an alternative and more logical aid to reading. The idiosyncrasies of our language are well known to readers. You only need to think of the different ways in which 'ough' can be pronounced to realize how much of a barrier our *traditional orthography* (conventional spelling) is to the development of reading skills. Pitman suggested replacing traditional orthography with a consistent system of spelling derived from 44 basic characters covering the whole of our language pronunciation. For a thorough introduction to i.t.a. see John Downing's *The Initial Teaching Alphabet*, 1965 (5th edn, revised). There are at least six ways of representing the simple word 'and' in traditional print:

And ɑnd AND ɑND and ɑnd

because the letter 'a' can occur in lower case as 'a' or 'ɑ' and in capitals as 'A' or 'ɑ', 'n' appears as 'n' or 'N' and 'd' as 'd' or 'D'. Try the word 'nag' to see how many combinations are possible, remembering that we can have 'g', 'g', 'G' or 'ɡ'. With the i.t.a. system, capitals are enlarged lower-case letters, thus 'and' appears as 'and' (capitals) 'and' (capital a) or 'and' (lower case).

By reducing the appearance of letters to one system and making each sound appear as the same combination of symbols, there are 44 characters to cover the English language. Similar sounding words with different spelling in traditional orthography such as 'eat', 'feet', 'key' and 'pier' become 'ɛɛt', 'fɛɛt', 'kɛɛ' and 'pɛɛr' in i.t.a. Similar combinations of letters, such as 'ough' in 'rough', 'ought', 'bough' and 'trough', which give different sounds become 'ruf', 'aut', 'bau' and 'trof'.

The advantages and limitations of i.t.a. as a medium to aid reading are still the subject of an active research programme. Protagonists amongst teachers are convinced that it does help some young children with reading difficulties towards efficient reading more than traditional orthography does. Warburton and Southgate,[28] in an extensive comparison of i.t.a. and traditional orthography, concluded that i.t.a. was a superior medium for teaching young children to read. Apparently, infants learn to read earlier, more easily and at a faster rate with i.t.a. However, the advantages gained by using i.t.a. frequently were lost after transition to traditional orthography. Those not so keen on i.t.a. have reservations about the need for such an elaborate detour when ultimately the children are going to have to learn the vagaries of our language in any case. Still to be established is the value of i.t.a. in remedial cases, its long-term influence upon mature reading skills, and especially the extent to which conversion to traditional orthography, particularly in writing down words from memory as in essay writing, will cause problems.

The Bullock Report[29] contains much of interest to the student of psychology and the teacher of reading, writing, speech and language skills (**R**).[30] The arguments are based on theoretical considerations leading to practical guides for teachers. The Report was inevitable following, as it did, the publication of a study by Start and Wells[31] on the trends in reading standards in Britain. One implication of the latter report was that reading standards appear to be declining. But the debate is a contentious one and students should consult the references given for the details.

Publicity has recently been given to a reading scheme devised by Marie Clay in New Zealand entitled Reading Recovery.[32] The main purpose of the scheme, which is gaining support in the UK, is to help six-year-old children who, after one year in school, are behind in reading and writing. A diagnostic test is used by a trained teacher to detect the sources of difficulty. The sources are used as the starting point for a concentrated diet of learning sessions at the rate of one 30-minute period a day for 12 to 20 weeks. The sessions are undertaken with a one-way screen behind which is a second teacher who also helps in the analysis.

The key features of the programme are that the child's existing competence is carefully analysed and used as the starting point for a concentrated remedial scheme. There is a one-to-one setting with each child having individual attention appropriate to the child's particular problems and in daily doses for several weeks with a second teacher in attendance. The teaching focuses on comprehension in reading and writing relevant messages.

With such concentrated effort, there is little wonder that the statistics of performance are impressive. Of 20 needy cases taken from every 100 pupils in school at age six, 19 will reach average reading performance in the 20-week period of the programme. What is even more significant is the follow-up three years later when these children are still performing as well as their own age group of nine years.

Trials are taking place in the UK, organized by the Institute of Education, London University. The scheme has been in use in Surrey for some time.[33]

Transfer of training

At one time the Royal Air Force had a battery of aptitude tests for those hoping to enter as aircrew. One test presented the candidate with a board full of pegs placed in square holes. One half of the top of each peg was painted white, the other black. The candidate was told to reverse as many pegs as possible with the non-preferred hand in a given time. Some had what seemed to be a natural skill at the game, but there were also those who had had previous experience as packers in industry (such as chocolate, biscuit or component packing) whose skill enabled them to perform this task with outstanding dexterity. Some of the skills they had learned in one situation were now being applied in a similar situation. This we call *transfer of training*. It is particularly apparent in physical skills and to some extent it is applicable in mental activity. Around the turn of the century there was a belief amongst psychologists and teachers that some school subjects acted as a training ground for exercising mental skills. This became known as 'the doctrine of formal training'. Mathematics was thought to develop children's powers of logic, science was seen as training children to be observant, and learning Latin and historical or geographical facts was thought to exercise the memory.

These views are no longer held by the majority of psychologists and teachers. However, there is a case for believing that some skills can be transferred and that the curriculum can play a part in this. We have seen from the researches of behaviourists that stimulus generalization occurs where animals and humans are disposed to recognize a stimulus within fairly wide limits. The dogs in Pavlov's work, whilst presumably realizing that there was a difference, were prepared to respond to a range of tuning forks or bells of slightly differing frequencies as if they were all from an identical stimulus. We also saw in concept formation that we formulate our concepts flexibly within wide limits: cats come in a variety of shapes and sizes, yet we generalize our perceptions to constitute the single concept 'cat'.

A lot of research has been directed towards finding the factors most necessary for transfer.[37] The most significant finding is that where there are common factors in the content or in the procedures adopted in carrying out two tasks, transfer is possible. The content of mathematics is useful in the solution of problems in physics and chemistry. Some of the procedures of mathematics are helpful in statistics. Physical skills involving similar procedures, as in the illustration at the beginning of this section, encourage transfer. Length of training also has a long-term effect, as when a person who has concentrated his or her efforts on science subjects at A level and at university may find that objectivity and conciseness begin to permeate into other aspects of life requiring the assembly and dissemination of knowledge.

Three other factors which affect transfer should be mentioned. There is a better chance of transfer, assuming similarity of content and procedure, where the learner is made aware of the possibility of transfer. It was pointed out earlier in this section that transfer of training had much in common with the behaviourists' concept of stimulus generalization. Having made the point, I hoped that what the reader had gleaned about stimulus generalization would be transferred to the subject of 'transfer of training' because of content similarity. This brings us to the second influence. The more thoroughly the first task is learned, the more likely it is that transfer will occur, given the conditions in the previous paragraph. This is tantamount to saying that if one task is not learned properly it is hardly likely to have a positive influence on the performance of a similar task. Intelligence also affects transfer, because more intelligent children and adults are more likely to spot the relationship between tasks.

The instances cited above have been examples of positive transfer, but it is quite possible to have negative transfer. Where the second task possesses content or requires procedures in conflict with the first task, then negative transfer is likely. An example from sport is the hindrance experienced in trying to learn a second style of swimming after mastering one style. Negative transfer is also apparent in learning foreign languages, where the rules of grammar (adjective position, masculine–feminine rules, etc.) differ to a point which impedes transfer (see also proactive and retroactive inhibition in the section headed 'Forgetting', above).

AN OVERVIEW: GAGNÉ'S CONDITIONS OF LEARNING

So much has been contributed to learning and memory that an overview which attempts to incorporate the most applicable parts is worth mentioning. Such an eclectic overview, has been proposed by Gagné.[35] He draws upon the major theories of learning mentioned in the last chapter – the fields of perception, selective attention, information-processing models of memory, concept formation and language skills – all of which are discussed in this book.

He believes that our knowledge of learning and the influence we might have upon learners is helped by identifying and elaborating three aspects of learning. These are the *conditions of learning*, the *events* or *processes of learning* and the *types of outcomes* or *capabilities displayed after learning*.

The conditions of learning are divided conveniently into *internal* and *external*. The internal conditions for learning to take place consist of the previous learning which relates to the skill and the processes which are used in order to inform the performer of the skill. External conditions include a variety of factors such as stimulation by others to recall, inform and guide the learner. A number of these factors, such as making sure the task has meaning, rehearsal techniques, transfer and motivation, are discussed earlier in this chapter.

The events or processes-of-learning model most favoured by Gagné is information-processing, discussed in this and the previous chapter. It is, of course, a postulate and not a fact, although the processes and structures are inferred from the behaviour of people as well as reflecting what we know of the action of the nervous system. Further, Gagné tries to link these processes to the outcomes of learning in the hope of providing indicators for adjusting the conditions of learning.

The outcomes of learning or the types of human capabilities learned have been

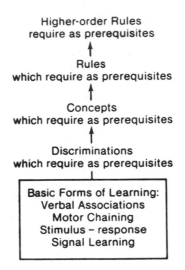

Higher-order Rules
require as prerequisites
↑
Rules
which require as prerequisites
↑
Concepts
which require as prerequisites
↑
Discriminations
which require as prerequisites

Basic Forms of Learning:
Verbal Associations
Motor Chaining
Stimulus – response
Signal Learning

Figure 6.7   *Adapted from Gagné.*[35]

classified by Gagné. To some extent this classification tries to answer some of the questions posed at the start of Chapter 5: what are the important issues which have to be explored by a learning theorist for the theory to have an impact on the work of teachers? It also draws on the work mentioned in Chapters 7 and 8. In answer to the question of what is learned, Gagné gives five categories: *intellectual skills*, *cognitive strategies*, *verbal information*, *motor skills* and *attitudes*.[35] As intellectual skills are central to the present topic more will be said about them.

A significant characteristic of intellectual skill is the dependence on previous knowledge, usually of simpler skills. This interdependence is illustrated in Figure 6.7.

Figure 6.7 reads from bottom to top in order of complexity and dependence. *Signal learning* is exemplified by Pavlov's classical conditioning, where a signal initiates a general *involuntary* response. An example was given in Chapter 5, with the child visiting the doctor for an injection and experiencing a fear response on hearing about the visit or on sitting in the surgery. The diffuse emotion of fear is aroused by the conditional signal (sounds of words relating to visit).

Stimulus–response learning has also been illustrated in the work of Thorndike and Skinner, in which a particular stimulus becomes associated with a particular *voluntary* response. Examples are found most frequently in young children when they first learn words (e.g. 'echoic', 'mand' and 'tact' responses) or body responses (e.g. smiling in response to a smile).

As sensory motor behaviour and development precede verbal behaviour, the logic of Gagné's hierarchy is self-evident. An illustration of *motor chaining* is seen in the 'circular reactions' of Piaget (see Chapter 7). At a more complex level, the sequence of motor responses accompanying the throwing of a ball or using a pen demonstrates chaining. As one S–R bond is completed (reaching out) the next is set in motion (grasping the ball), and so on through the sequence.

Verbal chaining (or *association*) occurs when two or more established verbal S–R links are put together. Gagné uses several examples from the learning of a foreign language. For instance, we frequently use intermediate clues in translating words as in the sequence 'roi' – image of king – 'king', or 'dent' – dentist – 'tooth'. The possibility of limits to chaining are expressed in Miller's paper[4] on the span of absolute judgement in which he regards 7 ± 2 as the optimum number of elements (digits, words, chemical formulae, etc.) capable of being chained and recalled comfortably for immediate memory span.

Discrimination learning means exactly what it says, that an individual can make different and appropriate responses to different members of a particular collection of stimuli. The process of identifying critical attributes of an object, dealt with in more detail in Chapter 7 under 'Concepts', is an illustration of discrimination learning. When a child can distinguish between numbers, objects and phonemes, he or she has accomplished the first step in concept formation. The next step, *concept learning*, requires the individual to respond to groups of objects or events. In discrimination learning the individual would respond to each object or event and distinguish it from a similar one, but to achieve concept learning, Gagné suggests, the individual must also be capable of placing an object or event into a group. He requires the skills not only of discrimination but of identifying attributes of a single example of a concept sufficiently to be able to classify it. It is one thing to distinguish between three similar trees, but yet another to have sufficient knowledge of the concept 'tree' to be capable of deciding whether to include or exclude an object from the concept 'tree'.

Rule learning consists of chaining two or more concepts. Mathematical rules, for example, enable the individual to respond to a whole range of stimuli with corresponding appropriate responses: $(a + b)^2 = a^2 + 2ab + b^2$ leads to many responses, depending on the values of a and b. What is more, several mathematical concepts are required to understand the equation.

Finally, at the pinnacle of mental activity we have *problem-solving*, which involves higher-order rules. According to Gagné, two or more rules are combined and applied to give 'higher-order' solutions, or rules. This process still requires learning. By the selective process of setting up and testing hypotheses using various strategies (see the 'formal operations' of Piaget, or Bruner's 'strategies') and different rules known to the individual, problems are attempted and sometimes solved.

Gagné concludes,

> There are several varieties of performance types that imply different categories of learned capabilities. These varieties of performance may also be differentiated in terms of the conditions for their learning. In searching for and identifying these conditions, one must look, first, at the capabilities internal to the learner and, second, at the stimulus situation outside the learner. The learning of each type of new capability starts from a different 'point' of prior learning, and is likely also to demand a different external situation.

The educational implications, provided the models are acceptable and can be shown to have practical outcomes, centre on those issues which can be manipulated by the teacher. Thus the conditions of learning, particularly the external ones, can to some extent be controlled by teachers. Planning of learning and management of the learning sessions, from both the learner's and the teacher's points of view, are central to the learning of intellectual, motor, verbal and attitudinal characteristics.

SUMMARY

The early part of the chapter was taken up with a theoretical discussion of the recent information-processing model of memory. Other considerations included useful information on remembering and forgetting.

For the purposes of description, the overall process of remembering is divided into three stages. These are: (a) the acquisition stage, in which we deliberately try to memorize material; (b) retention, which is a storage stage inferred from the fact that we can reproduce information by conscious effort; and (c) the act of recalling information. Emphasis was also given to the context- and subject-specific nature of memory.

Effective acquisition of knowledge is aided in a number of ways. Organization of the material to be learned, careful control of working conditions, the absence of distractions (whether physical, emotional, social or academic), dealing with meaningful rather than nonsense material, and frequent revision interspersed in the learning session are all of benefit to the learner. The most significant point arising from the discussion is that there is no *one* best method of study. Each person has to discover his or her optimum conditions for effective learning. The upsurge of texts on study methods and 'learning to learn' has given new impetus to guiding students in their efforts to improve study effectiveness.

The debate surrounding 'whole' and 'part' learning was related to the teaching of reading in which decoding methods (alphabetic and phonic) were compared and contrasted with 'reading for meaning' methods (look-and-say, whole-word and whole-sentence). Mention was made of recent developments in reading schemes, particularly those trialled in New Zealand as 'Reading Recovery'. I.t.a. and traditional orthography were also discussed briefly.

Transfer of training was seen to be possible when the tasks involved have similarities of content or procedures of learning, where the elements to be transferred are pointed out, when the first task is thoroughly mastered and when the ability of the learner is sufficient to enable him or her to see the transferable elements.

Retention has been studied using rates of forgetting of both nonsense and meaningful material. Studies have concluded that with most topics there are marked differences in the prospects of retention, which depend on the temporal position in learning of the material. Material at the start or finish of a learning session is more likely to be retained than material learned in mid-session. But this generalization applies particularly where tasks are extensive or difficult. The manner of interspersing the learning sessions and the kind of activity which precedes or follows a learning task have a significant effect on the chances of retention and retrieval. Reminiscence effects and the phenomenon of massed and distributed practice were also discussed.

Reproducing what we have retained in our memories can be achieved in at least two ways: either by recall, in which we are required to drag information from our minds without being prompted, or by recognition, in which we are presented with clues or information from which previously learned material can be recognized. One difference between unseen written examination papers and multiple-choice items is that recall is most often employed in the former and recognition in the latter.

Some aspects of the theories expanded in the last few chapters are summarized using Gagné's 'conditions of learning' theories.

ENQUIRY AND DISCUSSION

(a) In the Reader there is a paper entitled 'Some aspects of study habits in higher education'. A list of questions appears relating to general study, study prior to examinations, the influence of the peer group and the effect of attitudes and anxiety on study. Read through this list, see how you compare with the students reported in the research and note the pattern of study habits revealed in this research. Use the most relevant questions in the list to ask children how they study.

(b) If you were helping children of a given age and ability to develop the art and science of study, what would be the main points you would stress? How do these points differ with age and ability? You will find the basic texts on study habits suggested in Further Reading of help.

(c) Whilst on teaching practice, discover the importance attached to, and the opportunities given for, the following as aids to learning: (1) revision; (2) 'whole' or 'part' learning; (3) 'massed' and 'distributed' practice; (4) different methods in the teaching of reading or numbers; (5) transfer of training.

(d) Read the chapter in Gagné's book, note (35), on intellectual skills (Chapter 5). Analyse it in terms of your own subjects.

(e) Primary specialists should read and follow up the references in the books given in note (29) particularly those edited by D. Fontana and by N. Bennett and C. Desforges.

(f) Primary specialists involved in teaching reading should obtain the new material relating to 'Reading Recovery' and explore the diagnostic instruments used. References in note (32) should be a helpful start.

NOTES AND REFERENCES

1. A standard work on memory is I. M. L. Hunter, *Memory: Facts and Fallacies*, Penguin, London, 1964 (2nd edn). See also A. D. Baddeley, *Human Memory: Theory and Practice*, Erlbaum, London, 1990; U. Neisser, *Memory Observed*, Freeman, San Francisco, 1982.

2. R. L. Klatzky, *Human Memory: Structures and Processes*, Freeman, San Francisco, 1980 (2nd edn). Also R. C. Atkinson and R. M. Shiffrin, 'The control of short-term memory', *Scientific American*, **224**, 82–90 (1971) or 'Human memory: a proposed system and its control processes', *Psychol. Learning Mot.*, **2**, 89–195 (1968).

3. G. Sperling, 'The information available in brief visual presentations', *Psychol. Monogr.*, **498** (1960). See also Klatzky in note (2) above.

4. G. A. Miller, 'The magical number seven, plus or minus two: some limits in our capacity for processing information', *Psychol. Rev.*, **63**, 81–97 (1956) (or 'the 7 ± 2 paper').

5. A. D. Baddeley, *Working Memory*, Clarendon Press, Oxford, 1986. Also, for a summary, see M. S. Halliday and G. J. Hitch, 'Developmental applications of working memory', in G. Claxton (ed.), *Growth Points in Cognition*, pp. 193–222, Routledge, London, 1988.

6. F. I. M. Craik and M. J. Watkins, 'The role of rehearsal in short-term memory', *J. Verbal Learning and Verbal Behavior*, **12**, 599–607 (1973).

7. (R) H. C. A. Dale, 'Memory and effective instruction', *Aspects of Education*, **7**, 8–21 (1968). For a useful summary with educational applications see also R. J. Riding, *School Learning: Mechanisms and Processes*, Open Books, London, 1977.

8. F. Smith, *Comprehension and Learning: A Conceptual Framework*, Holt, Rinehart and Winston, Eastbourne, 1975.

9. P. Morris, 'Memory research: past mistakes and future prospects', in G. Claxton (ed.), *Growth Points in Cognition*, pp. 91–110, Routledge, London, 1988.
10. U. Neisser, *Cognition and Reality*, Freeman, San Francisco, 1976.
11. B. J. Underwood, *Forgetting*, reprint from *Scientific American*, March 1964.
12. Meaningful as well as nonsense material has been used in researches on retention. See J. Deese and S. H. Hulse, *The Psychology of Learning*, McGraw-Hill, New York, 1967, for some examples.
13. P. B. Ballard, 'Oblivescence and reminiscence', *Br. J. Psychol. Monogr.* (1913).
14. D. Child, 'Reminiscence and personality – a note on the effect of different test instructions', *Br. J. Soc. Clin. Psychol.*, **5**, 92–94 (1966). The inverted alphabet test requires the subject to print the letters of the alphabet upside-down from left to right as quickly as possible in a given time.
15. H. Ebbinghaus, *Memory* (translated by Ruger and Bussenius), Dover, New York, 1966.
16. B. B. Murdock, 'The serial position effect of free recall', *J. Exp. Psychol.*, **64**, 482–488 (1962).
17. The subject of study and study habits has quite a useful literature for our present purposes. Of recent vintage there is D. Rowntree, *Learn How to Study*, Macdonald and Jane's, London, 1976 (2nd edn); C. Parsons, *How to Study Effectively*, Arrow Books, London, 1976. For students see G. Gibbs, *Teaching Students to Learn*, Open University, Milton Keynes, 1981; L. A. Marshall and F. Rowland, *A Guide to Learning Independently*, Open University, Milton Keynes, 1983; R. M. Smith, *Learning How to Learn*, Open University, Milton Keynes, 1983; L. J. Haynes, P. D. Groves, P. J. Hills and R. B. Moyes, *Effective Learning*, Tetradon Publications, Guildford, 1977. An illustration of a book from the turn of the century is Hinsdale's text, *The Art of Study*, published in 1900.
18. The term *metacognition* was first introduced by J. H. Flavell in his article 'Metacognitive aspects of problem solving', in L. B. Resnick (ed.), *The Nature of Intelligence*, Erlbaum Hillsdale, NJ, 1976. For a résumé of the field and some useful references, see J. Nisbet and J. Shucksmith, *Learning Strategies*, Routledge and Kegan Paul, London, 1986.
19. R. Feuerstein in collaboration with Ya'acov Rand, M. B. Hoffman and R. Miller, *Instructional Enrichment: An Intervention Program for Cognitive Modifiability*, University Park Press, Baltimore, 1980.
20. J. B. Biggs and K. F. Collis, *Evaluating the Quality of Learning: The SOLO taxonomy*, Academic Press, New York, 1982.
21. M. J. A. Howe, 'A fine idea but does it work?', *Educ. Section Rev.*, **15**(2), 43–46 and 54–57 (1991). There are other useful papers on the same subject by N. Entwistle, G. Gibbs, P. E. Morris, J. Nisbet and M. Shayer in the same volume.
22. (R) For your benefit, some research into study habits in higher education: see D. Thoday, 'How undergraduates work', *Universities Q.*, **11**, 172–181 (1957); B. Cooper and J. M. Foy, 'Students' study habits, attitudes and academic attainment', *Universities Q.*, **23**, 203–212 (1969); D. Child, 'Some aspects of study habits in higher education', *Int. J. Educ. Sci.*, **4**, 11–20 (1970); W. P. Colquhoun and D. W. J. Corcoran, 'The effects of time of day and social isolation on the relationship between temperament and performance', *Br. J. Soc. Clin. Psychol.*, **3**, 226–231 (1964).
23. (R) M. Bassey, 'Learning methods in tertiary education', unpublished paper, Trent Polytechnic, 1968.
24. J. S. Coleman, *The Adolescent Society*, The Free Press, New York, 1961; N. Sanford (ed.), *The American College*, Wiley, New York, 1962.
25. C. R. B. Joyce and L. Hudson conducted one of the few researches into this realm of student/teacher styles in a medical school, but their findings are somewhat limited and could not be applied to school-based learning. The research was 'Student style: an experimental study', *Br. J. Med. Educ.*, **2**, 28–32 (1968).
26. R. Beard, *Developing Reading 3–13*, Hodder and Stoughton, Sevenoaks, 1987.
27. An exceptionally good book for those needing an introduction has been written by E. J. Goodacre, *Children and Learning to Read*, Routledge and Kegan Paul, London, 1971.
28. For a primer on i.t.a., see J. Downing, *The Initial Teaching Alphabet* and *Evaluating the Initial Teaching Alphabet*, Cassell, London, 1965 and 1967. O. M. Gayford has produced a clear beginners' text entitled *I.t.a. in Primary School*, Initial Teaching Publishing, London, 1970. Research into the effectiveness of i.t.a. is reported in F. W. Warburton and

V. Southgate, *I.t.a. An Independent Evaluation*, Murray and Chambers for the Schools Council, London, 1969. A very handy non-technical version of this report was written by V. Southgate, *I.t.a.: What Is the Evidence?*, published for the Schools Council by Murray and Chambers, London, 1970. A detailed overview of reading difficulties is given in M. D. Vernon, *Reading and Its Difficulties*, Cambridge University Press, Cambridge, 1971.

29. The literature on reading is becoming extensive. But the Bullock Report, *A Language for Life*, HMSO, London, 1975, is important. Other recent useful commentaries which give some good references for students wishing to explore more deeply are P. Horner, 'Learning and teaching reading skills', in D. Fontana (ed.), *The Education of the Young Child*, Blackwell, Oxford, 1984 (2nd edn), and H. Francis, 'Reading development in school', in N. Bennett and C. Desforges (eds), *Recent Advances in Classroom Research*, Monograph No. 2 of the *British Journal of Educational Psychology*, Scottish Academic Press, Edinburgh, 1985.

30. (R) J. Downing, 'Psychology and the Bullock Report', opening address for the Annual Conference of the British Psychological Society Education Section, University of Sheffield, 1975.

31. K. B. Start and B. K. Wells, *The Trends in Reading Standards: 1970-71*. NFER, Slough, 1972.

32. M. M. Clay, *The Early Detection of Reading Difficulties*, Heinemann, 1985 (3rd edn). For a recent comment, see M. M. Clay, 'The Reading Recovery programme: coverage, outcomes and Educational Board District figures 1984-1988', *New Zealand J. Educ. Stud.*, 61-70 (1990).

33. As recently as 1992, the Runnymede Centre, Chertsey Road, Addlestone, Surrey, was running a Reading Recovery programme.

34. The first nails in the coffin of 'formal learning' were hammered home by E. L. Thorndike and R. S. Woodworth, 'The influence of improvement in one mental function upon the efficiency of other functions', *Psychol. Rev.* (1901), and since then research has concentrated on isolating the particular factors concerned in transfer. For a summary see the chapter on transfer in K. O'Connor's book, *Learning: An Introduction*, Macmillan, London, 1968.

35. R. M. Gagné, *The Conditions of Learning*, Holt, Rinehart and Winston, New York, 1985 (4th edn).

FURTHER READING

A Baddeley, *Your Memory: A User's Guide*, Pelican, Harmondsworth, 1982. This is really an excellent, readable book.

R. Beard, *Developing Reading 3-13*, Hodder and Stoughton, London, 1987.

T. Buzan, *Use Your Head*, BBC, London, revised edition 1989. A guide for students.

M. M. Clay, *The Early Detection of Reading Difficulties*, Heinemann, 1985 (3rd edn).

M. J. A. Howe, *Introduction to the Psychology of Memory*, Harper and Row, London, 1983. Apart from being a helpful study guide, it also summarizes some of the evidence relating to learning and memory.

H. Maddox, *How to Study*, Pan, London, 1963. Extremely useful introduction to learning, retention and recall.

J. Nisbet and J. Shucksmith, *Learning Strategies*, Routledge and Kegan Paul, London, 1986.

R. M. Smith, *Learning How to Learn*, Open University, Milton Keynes, 1983.

J. M. Thyne, *The Psychology of Learning and the Techniques of Teaching*, University of London Press, London, 1963. The relevant chapters make very good reading.

Chapter 7

Concept Formation and Cognitive Development

In the chapter on perception, we assumed the existence of internal mental processes as a necessary step in the analysis of sensory experiences. One simplified interpretation suggested was a long-term store of past experiences which are made available when we need to appraise incoming signals, the outcome of which is to regulate our behaviour. The mental activity which we assume is taking place is defined by the familiar term *thinking*. Vinacke[1] suggests that thinking involves 'internal processes which bring the organization laid down in past learning to bear upon responses to current situations, and which shape these responses in keeping with inner needs'. The existence of these inner processes is supported from observations we make of our own thought processes (introspection) and from the simple fact that our responses to problem situations have much more in them than the original information with which we are provided. In this chapter we shall concentrate on the building-blocks of thought, the 'organization laid down in past learning', to use Vinacke's phrase.

Unfortunately, 'thinking' has become a confused and multipurpose term; it has even come to mean different things to different psychologists. However, one broad distinction which we can draw is between *perceptual* and *ideational* thinking. Perceptual thinking is the term we apply to the mental activity occurring during problem-solving which relies on the presence of the object or objects involved in the problem. Much of Piaget's work with very young children, for example, calls for an understanding of perceptual thinking (see later in the chapter). Ideational thinking, on the other hand, is much more complex and relies on the existence of a symbolic form such as a language or number system, and does not necessarily rely on the presence of cues from the environment. We shall meet both these types of thinking in our discussion of concept formation later in the chapter. Other uses of the term are mentioned in note (1) at the end of the chapter. But first we must turn to a consideration of the means whereby thinking is made possible.

CONCEPTS

If we were not able to classify the things and events around us we would find it impossible to carry out the simplest task let alone the highly complicated mental operations of which we are capable. To attempt to treat all objects or events as unique would lead to an unmanageable task when it came to trying to comprehend and represent our environment. Instead we categorize objects and events. From accumulated experience we learn to group characteristics which are common to particular objects or events, even though these characteristics are only roughly similar; for example, 'chairs' come in various shapes and sizes, colours, numbers of legs, but they are given the name 'chair'. The end product is a concept – an idea consisting of attributes that are sufficiently similar as to be grouped together. For example, flowers (like the chairs above) come in many forms, but they have properties in common: they all serve the same purpose in providing for the production of seeds; they have, by and large, similar structures such as petals, stamen and pollen grains. These *critical attributes* which connect one flower with the next enable the category 'flower' to be formed.

The clarity with which a concept can be defined ranges from near certainty to hazy probability. An example of a 'certain' (sometimes called a classical) concept is 'virgin' or 'earth's moon'. The defining attributes of both these concepts are clear and referred to as *core* properties. However, most concepts are probabilistic. For each attribute there is a range of acceptable criteria. Take the concept 'table'. There are many objects we call a table. The predominant characteristic is a flat surface with some means of support. But the range of variations – in the shape and size of the surface, its colour, height from the ground, material from which it is made and the kind of support – is tremendous. The permutations and combinations of characteristics at first seem to defy generalization, yet we are able to apply the concept 'table'. These vaguer properties are called *prototypes* (see Smith and Medin in note (2)).

In addition to accumulating characteristics of particular concepts from observation, other people, reading, etc., we also establish relationships between them. Several theories have developed amongst which the *hierarchical* (and more recently the *spreading activation*) theory has common currency.[2] For instance, a 'goldfish' is a sub-set of 'fish', which is a sub-set of 'animal'. These networks of concepts can be arranged hierarchically and consist of *nodes* which represent key concepts. The information 'stored' at these nodes (this is clearly an information-processing model) is illustrated in Figure 7.1.

The characteristics common to the vast majority of fish would be stored only at the 'fish' node. Attributes which distinguish one variety of fish from another would be stored at the lowest node. Exceptions to the generality of fish would have to be learned as a technical distinction.

A recent modified view by Collins and Loftus,[3] which tries to meet a number of weaknesses in the hierarchical theory, is called the *spreading activation* theory. This relies on semantic relatedness and distance. Nodes are used as described above but in a network rather than a hierarchy. The theory is quite complex, but put in its crudest form it depends on the strength of links between nodes for the process of concept characterization. When a concept is presented a node is activated and this activity spreads out to neighbouring nodes. By a process of 'true'/'false' decisions at the nearby nodes, evidence is accumulated to define the presented concept.

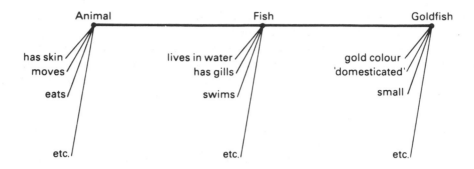

Figure 7.1   Hierarchical theory of concepts – an illustration.

This process has been used to explain the acquisition of concepts as a form of hypothesis-testing (Bourne *et al.*)[3] But there are many unresolved problems as to the 'how' of concept formation. Young children, for instance, are particularly prone to over-generalization and this is assumed to be the result of not having learned the criteria for the limits to be imposed in forming a classification. Any part of a plant, be it a leaf, root, stem or whatever, is likely to be labelled as a flower. By the same token, all men *may* be 'daddies' to a young child because the critical attributes of fatherhood have not yet been established in the child's mind. The two-year-old daughter of a friend of mine saw, on different occasions, mothers breastfeeding their babies. Shortly afterwards the youngster was seen trying to put her nipple in her doll's mouth, and enquired of mother why the doll wasn't feeding, and where was her milk? At a more advanced level, refined distinctions will be necessary before a child can discriminate between different kinds of flowers and between 'daddies'. The argument surrounding this point is whether the child has not assimilated the criteria because he or she lacks the necessary level of mental maturity or because *we* have not discovered how to put it over to young children in a manner which they can understand.

The speed and inevitability of concept attainment in the young, despite varied child-rearing practices and in some cases alarming cultural disadvantages, have led many to believe that we are born with a predisposition to order our perceptions into concepts. However, though the *act* of concept formation might be inborn, the substance of the concepts is acquired from experience and it is this vital point which is of concern to teachers. Both parents and teachers constitute reference groups for assisting children in establishing concept attributes.

It is believed that in the early stages, some concepts become established as images. *Imagery* is the term we use to describe calling up a mental replica (using any sense modality) of an object or event which we have previously experienced. If I said 'call up the image of a bell ringing', you would imagine the sound of an actual bell which you had heard sometime in the past. Bruner (see Chapter 8) supposes that we actually recall a composite sound by combining previous similar experiences. He calls this *iconic* representation. Piaget (later in this chapter) refers to imagery as *internalized imitation*; in other words, we take in the actual sensory events and reproduce some aspects of them on request. *Eidetic imagery* is an extreme case of the ability to recall a sensory event in great detail. This is done by casting an actual image of what is seen on to a surface and using it to identify parts of the total scene. Children are especially gifted (about 6 per cent) in exhibiting the skill. Probably the talent becomes redundant because it is not put to use. The phenomenon is sometimes known as 'photographic memory', although it seems unlikely that the images are as perfect as a photograph.

Images can be used as the basis for simple reasoning. For example, the simpler scientific and geometrical concepts involving apparatus and figural arrangements can occasionally be manipulated as an image in our minds. It is also possible that animals use imagery as an aid in their responses. They also try out their reactions to the environment physically rather than by manipulating mental concepts because, it is believed, animals have more highly developed and organized sensory organs than humans.

But many concepts cannot even be imagined because they are far too complex or abstract. We cannot imagine 'energy' or 'honesty'. We might be able to conjure up an image of a body moving and therefore possessing energy, or perhaps the picture of someone stealing (and by implication what an honest person should not do), but these are only instances (*exemplars*) of some aspect of the concepts. People's ability to deal with problems in the absence of material evidence or mental images and to reach higher levels of complexity in appreciation of and response to the environment (in contrast to animals) is due entirely to the use of *symbolic languages*. These include number systems, musical notation, etc., as well as the spoken and written word. By classifying and labelling with words and phrases, humans can represent the world economically while at the same time freeing ourselves from the need for material evidence in our reasoning. Through the acquisition of concepts, from the simplest discrimination and classification of objects to the complex moral, mathematical or scientific concepts, we order our experiences. In the process, language plays a vital role, and we shall devote the next chapter to a consideration of this aspect. For the time being it is important to remember that words are not concepts: they only stand for concepts. In the case of class concepts a word is a label which represents, symbolically, a class of objects or events.

Some characteristics of concepts[1]

To help us in our understanding of the development of thinking in children, let us first take a closer look at some of the more important characteristics of concepts.

(a) They are not the actual sensory events, but representations of some aspects of these events. With most concepts there are wide margins of attribute acceptability, e.g. a leaf can be small, glossy, dark green and prickly like a holly leaf or large, dull, light green and harmless like a chestnut leaf. In some cases the boundaries which distinguish concepts are hazy and ill defined (some of the abstract concepts we have to deal with in the study of human behaviour are of this nature), but generally speaking there is a large measure of agreement in the definition of most class concepts within a given culture (see Mervis and Rosch[4]).

(b) Concepts are dependent upon previous experience. We have noted that home background and educational opportunity are possible variables in the formation of concepts. Likewise there are emotional as well as perceptual connections associated with concept formation (see (e) (2) on the intentional use of concepts).

(c) Concepts are symbolic in human beings. The concept 'bee' can be called to mind from numerous stimulus sources. The sight of the insect or the word 'bee', a relentless droning sound, honey, a piece of music ('The Flight of the Bumble Bee') can all trigger off the concept 'bee'. Words, numbers, chemical symbols or physical formulae have symbolic significance beyond the simple meaning normally associated with the actual symbol. For the chemist, the symbol 'O' is not just a circle: it represents the element oxygen. Sometimes objects have complex symbolic meaning, e.g. the crucifix, a V sign, or road signs.

(d)   Concepts can form 'horizontal' or 'vertical' organizations. An example of a horizontal classification would be if we were to give children some examples of reptiles – snakes, lizards, crocodiles and dinosaurs. They all belong to the same major group of animals because they possess certain attributes in common. However, they also differ in several other respects, thus permitting us to classify them into separate groups *within* the same level in the animal kingdom.

Vertical classification results from the presence of hierarchies, that is, categories which increase in complexity as we proceed through the classification. A dog belongs to the family of animals called *canis*, which is subordinate to the order of animals called *carnivora* (along with cats, bears, otters and seals), which is subordinate to the class of animals called *mammals*, which in turn are *vertebrates* (with backbones), which are *animals*. You will notice the increasing inclusiveness of the groups as we pass up the hierarchy of the animal kingdom (see Figure 7.1).

Some higher-order concepts are very complicated. Try working out the number of subordinate concepts required to understand the concept of 'force', the theorem of Pythagoras, the Ten Commandments or the causes which led to the fall of the Roman Empire.

(e)   Concepts function in at least two ways: extentionally and intentionally.

  (1)   The *extentional* use of concepts applies where the meaning given is the widely acknowledged one defined in terms which are patently clear to anyone observing the object or event. Concept usage arises from common agreement and acceptance of the objective attributes of the object. A particular variety of plant or animal, let us say a lupin or a giraffe, has a 'public' meaning which we all accept.

  (2)   The *intentional* use of concepts can vary considerably from one person to another. In this case the concept is defined as a result of personal, subjective experiences accompanying the formation of the concept. A rose might arouse pleasant associations or unpleasant ones if one has suffered the thorns during pruning. A botanist might view the plant from a technical standpoint, an artist from a creative, aesthetic angle, and a cricket fan in Yorkshire as an emblem of the county in the 'Roses match'. In all these cases, special significance which has no universal acceptance has become attached to the object.

(f)   Some concepts can be irrational. Superstitions (black cats, ladders, opening an umbrella indoors, lucky numbers and colours) provide many illustrations of irrational concepts. Their origins are obscure.

(g)   Many concepts are formed without our conscious awareness. Values established by our culture and which regulate our daily conduct have often been formed as habits in our childhood without our realizing it. Aversions and prejudices frequently are stamped into our repertoire of responses in this way. Dislike of animals, racial prejudice and attitudes towards religion or politics are planted imperceptibly during a lifetime.

In our discussion of concepts it has been argued that concept formation is dependent upon several psychological processes. First, a young child, by whatever means, has to be able to *differentiate* the attributes of the environment. By this we mean that the child must have sufficient perceptual skills to distinguish the characteristics observed in order even to begin the formation of categories, As we observed before, there will be a time when a child may refer to all men as 'daddy' or all four-legged creatures as 'doggy', possibly because of the child's inability to limit the scope of generalizations, because he or she has not yet learned the rules of differentiation, or because the concepts are formed but the child has not yet learned how to use the words.

Second, having consolidated an ability to differentiate features, children have to perceive *grouping*, that is, they need to recognize structural or functional similarities. Finally, they have to *categorize* the groupings into hierarchies, thus devising classes of experience with increasing levels of complexity and abstractness.

PIAGET'S THEORY OF COGNITIVE DEVELOPMENT

Contemporary views on the nature of cognitive development have been vastly influenced by the work of one man. This was Jean Piaget (1896–1980), once a biologist, who turned his energies to a study of the evolution of children's thinking. His impetus from the Universities of Paris and Geneva has led to a world-wide search for important factors in concept development. His particular line of thinking and the abundant research it has generated is sometimes known as the *Geneva School* of thought to distinguish it from the *Harvard School* in the United States typified by the work of Bruner, the *Russian School*, founded by Vygotsky and Luria, and the *Anglo-Saxon School* in Britain. His findings[5] probably have done more to influence educational practices in Britain than most theories (see the first reference to Piaget in note (5)). He would have claimed that *epistemology*, that is, the study of how we know what we know and the extent of this knowledge, was his primary interest.

His method of investigation was the clinical approach: detailed face-to-face discussion and questioning of individual children in many problem situations (he used his own children in the first experiments in the 1920s). It aims to discover, by analysing performance and verbal introspections, the quality and nature of children's concept attainment at a particular time in their lives. The work has led to a descriptive analysis of development of basic physical, logical, mathematical and moral concepts from birth to adolescence (concept growth in such things as number, time, space, velocity, geometry, chance and morality). At heart, his theory is:

(a)   a genetic one, in that higher processes are seen to evolve from biological mechanisms which are rooted in the development of an individual's nervous system (compare this view with Hebb's[6]);

(b)   a maturational one, because he believes that the processes of concept formation follow an invariant pattern through several clearly definable stages which emerge during specific age ranges;

(c)   a hierarchical one, in that the stages he proposes *must* be experienced and passed through in a given order before any subsequent stages of development are possible.

Piaget also maintained that three factors are of special importance in ensuring the appearance of the stages of cognitive development. These are: (a) biological factors, which account for the regularity and inevitability of the stages he postulates in much the same way as we see the appearance of sexual characteristics during a given period in the development of boys and girls before we are justified in saying they are mature adults; (b) educational and cultural transmission, which, according to Piaget, account for the discrepancies in the chronological ages at which his stages appear as we pass from one individual to another; and (c) the activities in which children engage. Piaget took an 'active' rather than a 'passive' view of the part played by children in their own development. The child's self-directed motor activity is seen as a necessity in cognitive development.

His earlier preoccupation with biology and logic was reflected in the widespread use he made of the technical language used in these subjects. It will be necessary, therefore, to sort out some of these terms before we describe his developmental theory.

In the first days of life, a baby responds to the surroundings by reflex activity which, as we know, is *not* acquired. Very soon, the baby develops beyond reflex action and begins to react to the surroundings in a way which leads us to suspect purposeful behaviour. The baby seeks the mother's nipple, grasps objects in contact with the palm of its hands; general body movement begins to show signs of co-ordination. These actions, which become organized into distinct patterns of behaviour, Piaget referred to as *schemata* ('schema' is the singular, 'schemata' or 'schemas' the plural). Note that the key to the formation of schemata is *action* on the part of the baby in attempting to *adapt* to the demands of the environment. Once a schema has appeared, it becomes directed to similar, parallel situations, rather like transfer of training (see Chapter 6). For example, arm movement, grasping, then lifting towards the mouth is a cycle of activity which is likely to happen to any object which comes within the child's range.

The process described in the last paragraph, of incorporating new perceptions either to form new schemata or integrating them into existing schemata, was termed *assimilation* by Piaget (analogous to humans taking in a variety of foods which the body uses to build into existing tissue). When the child is capable of modifying existing schemata to meet new environmental demands, it is said to experience *accommodation*. (Using the biological analogy again, the infant being weaned from milk to solids will have to accommodate to the change in the nature of the food in order to assimilate the food for use by the body.)

In summary, Piaget considered that conceptual growth occurs because the child, while actively attempting to adapt to the environment, organizes actions into schemata through the processes of assimilation and accommodation.

The schema is an important element in Piaget's theory. Bartlett[6] coined the expression to describe 'an active organization of past actions'. Hebb[6] uses 'cell assemblies' as the counterpart of Piaget's schemata. In effect, the mental framework of past experiences is the substance of Broadbent's long-term memory store (see Chapters 4 and 6). When the actions become replaced by symbols (words, numbers, etc.), they become known as *representational schemata*. When a child is able to represent the world mentally, by means of memory, imagery or symbolic language, it is said to have *internalized* these experiences.

Thought or thinking, according to Piaget, has its origins in actions physically performed and then internalized. Bluntly then, thought is internalized actions. The starting point of cognitive development, therefore, must be activity on the part of the neonate, not passive reception of sensory data. The child's striving to adapt and structure experiences enables patterns of actions to be formed. At a primitive level, the patterns may be simple perceptual patterns which become internalized. When these are recalled, they reappear as images of the original experience. We have already mentioned this phenomenon as imagery (internalized imitation).

Once symbolic language frees children from the need to manipulate raw reality in order to form schemata, they can begin to develop logical thinking and are able to reason using representations of facts. The ability to carry out activities in one's imagination is known as an *operation* and, as we shall see presently, a child's growth to intellectual maturity depends on its capacity to carry out these mental operations.

In the developmental description which follows, we shall see how Piaget accounts for the gradual unfolding of thinking skills, starting with simple sensory and motor activities in babyhood and gradually being superseded by internal representation of actions carried out by the child; then, through the agency of language, reaching the highest form of logical thinking, at first in the presence of objective evidence and finally by mental reasoning.

Piaget's stages of development[7]

We argued above that Piaget's theory was genetic, maturational and hierarchical. Adaptation takes place in a set sequence of stages associated with successive mental (not chronological) ages. Several schemes representing the stages exist. The outlines in Table 7.1 are the two most popular.

Table 7.1 *Outline of Piaget's stages of development*

Period	Stage	Mental age range in years
Sensori-motor	I Sensori-motor	0–2
Preparation for, and use of, concrete operations (or latency)	II Pre-operational	
	(A) Pre-conceptual	2–4
	(B) Intuitive	4–7
	III Concrete operations	7–11
Formal operations	IV Formal operations	11 onwards

I: The sensori-motor stage (mental age approximately 0–2 years)

Developmentally, the first two years of life are very important and full. So much is achieved in motor and mental skills by way of walking, talking, playing and establishing a self-identity. Yet, at birth, actions are severely limited to reflex grasping, sucking and general body movement. Within the first months, the reflexes become adapted to very simple tasks. The first schemata involve grasping or sucking anything which comes in contact with hand or mouth.

As the senses and limb movements rapidly improve and co-ordinate, cycles of activity are discovered and repeated by the infant. For example, the baby may combine an arm movement with placing thumb in mouth and sucking it. These cycles of action Piaget calls *primary circular reactions*. They are significant because their appearance gives the first clues to the existence of a primitive memory. Note, however, that the voluntary motions of the infant are extensions of reflex action and not purposive movements. Equally, the movements are directed towards the baby's own body rather than objects outside it. These rudimentary habitual schemata are called 'primary' because they are at first built into the baby's inherent reflex systems.

Soon new activities appear, with less and less apparent connection with reflexes. Around four to eight months the baby begins to direct its activities towards objects outside the body, and this enlarges the range of actions. Increasing visual–motor co-ordination enables the child to carry out these tasks. With each new object, the baby carries out party pieces with schemata already assimilated. These are called *secondary circular reactions*, where patterns of action become generalized to any object within reach. Up to one year of age the secondary circular reactions are co-ordinated and applied to new situations. There is every sign of purposeful behaviour as sequences of movements seem to be directed toward the attainment of goals. For example, the infant will move objects out of the way to obtain a desired toy, which implies that schemata are being assimilated and co-ordinated by combining secondary circular reactions.

Accommodation has played a minor role up to this point. The child has been preoccupied with the assimilation of schemata. Initially, when an object is hidden, even in the presence of the child, it will not be pursued – out of sight, out of mind! There is no suggestion of reasoning as we know it. Life is all go!

From 12 to 18 months, however, the child becomes capable of inventing new ways of attaining ends. Circular reactions may be repeated with several variations. In other words the child is beginning to accommodate to new situations by modifying and experimenting with existing schemata. These are called *tertiary circular reactions*.

Towards the end of the sensori-motor stage, the child is beginning to represent the world in mental images and symbols. The onset of language enables the child to represent objects in their absence. Playing bricks become cars or real building bricks in the child's imagination. Play becomes very important. For Piaget, play enables the child to assimilate. Imitation, on the other hand, is an example of accommodation, because the child is attempting to modify behaviour to become someone or something else. *Deferred imitation* is the ability to copy someone else in their absence and represents a great advance, because it shows that the child is now able to form images of events which can be recalled for future reference.

II A: Pre-conceptual stage (mental age approximately 2–4 years)

The direct link between sensory experiences and motor activity, so apparent in the first of Piaget's stages, gradually becomes obscured by the intermediate process of mental activity. This occurs largely because the child is internalizing imitations and actions.

As the term 'pre-conceptual' implies, children are not yet able to formulate concepts in the same way as older children and adults. Concept formation which relies on abstracting and discriminating the characteristics of objects or situations in order to form generalizations is known as *inductive* reasoning. Where generalizations are used to describe particular instances, we call the process *deductive* reasoning. Children at this stage tend neither to induction nor to deduction. Instead, they use *transductive* reasoning. By this Piaget means that children reason by going from one particular instance to another particular instance in order to form *pre-concepts*.

One or two illustrations of transductive reasoning should help to show how pre-concepts are formed. My daughter, Louise, at 3 years 6 months saw her mother combing her hair. She said, 'Mummy is combing her hair. She is going shopping.' I asked her why mummy was going shopping and apparently she had noticed that on the previous day the two events had been linked. Louise had reasoned transductively by going from the particular to the particular. Mummy combs her hair on many occasions for many reasons – similarly she goes out on some occasions without combing her hair – but the coincidence of these two events had created a pre-concept. In summary, A occurs with B once, therefore A occurs with B always. The pre-concept 'all men are daddies' has been formed by the child who has used only one characteristic (voice, clothing or features) which all men have in common. We tend to play on this fact in the Father Christmas confidence trick. Young children are not sophisticated enough to distinguish between the men dressed up and appearing in different places. For children, they are all one man. Piaget thus claims that the child cannot successfully form classes of objects.

The period is also progressively dominated by symbolic play – dolls become babies, flowers become rows of children. Similarly, imitation of what other people are doing is in evidence. *Egocentricism* predominates because the child is unable to view things from another person's point of view. The child does not appreciate that if he or she and another person were looking at an object from different angles, the two views would be different. We shall see the importance of egocentric speech (rehearsing with oneself) in the next chapter.

Recent research (**R**)[8] has cast some doubt on the inevitability of pre-concepts. Piaget's theory, being essentially maturational and hierarchical, assumes a systematic unfolding of ability. But the central role of language, very much a social activity, may have been undervalued by Piaget and his followers, not only as a source of variation between children's concept development but also as the vehicle by which children convey their ability to form concepts. This point will arise again under 'Some criticisms of Piaget's theory', later in the chapter.

II B: Intuitive stage (mental age approximately 4–7 years)

The child begins this period of intellectual development very much dependent upon superficial perceptions of the environment. Ideas are formed impressionistically – hence the name 'intuitive' stage. This arises because the child appears to be unable to account for all aspects of a situation simultaneously. Also, the outlook is dominated by the perceptual field, in that the youngster fixates on one dimension of an object or event to the exclusion of all others. Piaget calls this phenomenon *centring*. The child grasps only one relationship at a time.

A simple experiment described by Piaget will demonstrate the notion of centring. Two Plasticine balls are rolled until the child agrees that they are the same size. One ball is then chosen and rolled into a sausage shape, as in Figure 7.2, and put alongside

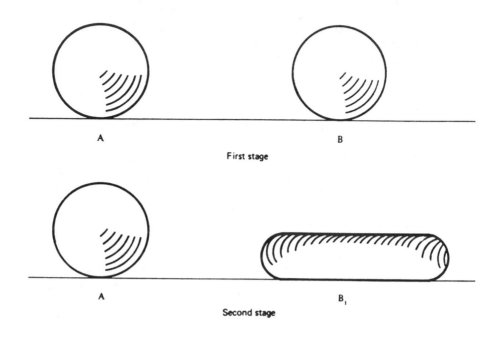

A   B

First stage

A   B₁

Second stage

Figure 7.2   *To demonstrate conservation using balls of Plasticine. First stage: balls appear equal in quantity. Second stage: to conservers, balls are still accepted as equal in quantity; to non-conservers, B₁ is more or less than A.*

the other ball. If a five-year-old is asked if they are the same size (or whether one ball has more Plasticine in it than the other), the child will most frequently say that the sausage is bigger. If asked why, the child usually says, 'because it is longer'. Occasionally a long, narrow shape is taken as being smaller because it is narrower. In the first case the child has 'centred' on the length dimension of the sausage shape and has compared it with the width of the ball to arrive at the conclusion that the former is more. In the second case, where there are claims that the sausage is smaller, the child has centred on the width.

To explain this, Piaget says that children, by centring on a single aspect of a problem and ignoring all others, lack the ability for *conservation of quantity* (Plasticine or water would be described as a 'continuous' quantity, beads as a 'discontinuous' quantity). An inability to conserve arises because at this stage of their development children seem unable to reverse the situations they are observing. While watching a ball being rolled into a sausage shape, they 'centre' on one dimension changing in length without being capable of reversing the process back to the point of origin and realizing that the actual quantity of material is unchanged.

Another example of irreversibility in a conservation experiment is afforded by filling two identical vessels with water to the same level. They must be accepted as similar in level by the child. One vessel is taken and the contents poured into a vessel of a different shape – tall and thin or small and squat, as in Figure 7.3(a). Children who cannot reverse and therefore conserve would claim that there was more liquid in vessel C than in A (or less in D than in A). When asked why, the children soon display that they have centred on length or width without compensating for changes in the other dimensions.

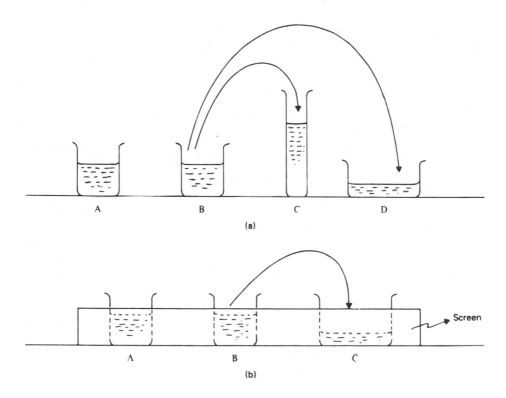

Figure 7.3 *Conservation of continuous quantities using vessels of water.*
(a) The conserver appreciates that the quantities in C and D are the same as in A. The non-conserver says
there is more in C and less in D when they are compared with A.
(b) Bruner's experiment.

An interesting modification reported by Bruner **(R)**[9] is shown in Figure 7.3(b). The third vessel, C, was chosen to be the same height as the other two and all but the tops of the vessels hidden from view using a screen. When asked which vessel, A or C, had the most drink in it, younger children (four- to five-year-olds) did no better than chance (half were correct), 90 per cent of the five- to six-year-olds got the correct answer, while 100 per cent of six- to seven-year-olds came up with the answer. It would seem that the younger children who can see what is going on are overwhelmingly influenced by the perceptual field and, when this is partly removed, they resort to intuitive guesswork.

According to Piaget, the act of repeating the sequence of activities performed in these experiments in one direction makes it very difficult for the child to reverse the process. Therefore, reversibility is a central skill which frees the child from intuitive impressions, enabling an appreciation of the *invariance* of materials undergoing a change in physical dimensions without changes in total quantity.

Another interpretation of Piaget's findings has been made by Bryant **(R)**.[10] He has questioned the basic assumptions of conservation and has offered alternative explanations which have far-reaching implications for education if they are correct. The central issue is the question of invariance. Piaget, as we have seen, claimed that children who cannot conserve have not yet learned the invariance principle. Bryant challenges this position in the following way. In all the conservation experiments there are usually three steps. First, the child establishes a hypothesis about the equality of the Plasticine balls or amounts of liquid as in our particular examples. In other words, the child appreciates that $A = B$ (for Plasticine in Figure 7.2 and for the vessels of water in Figure 7.3(a)). Furthermore, there is consistency in the appraisal of equality which shows success in making a definite hypothesis. At the next step, the child applies the invariance principle such that the child sees $B = B_1$ (Plasticine) or $B = C$ or D (water). Finally, to solve the problem correctly, the child co-ordinates these first two stages to establish a final hypothesis that $A = B_1$ (Plasticine) or $A = C$ or D (water). Unfortunately young children without knowledge of counting, weighing or measuring must rely on some other criterion, possibly estimates of length or width in the case of the experiments above. Therefore there is a conflict of hypotheses between the first ($A = B$, using length) and the last (A is not equal to B, C or D, again using length). Faced with this conflict, the child chooses the most recent deduction and says that A is not equal to B, C or D. Bryant goes on to substantiate his conflict-hypothesis theory by experiment (**R**).[10] His major conclusion is an optimistic one for education because, unlike Piaget, he believes that teaching hypothesis-testing and memory-training would serve a useful purpose. 'Piaget's experiments effectively demonstrate that young children find transitivity problems difficult, but these difficulties are simply the result of *inadequate strategies of recall*' (emphasis added). In effect, we must teach children how 'to distinguish correct hypotheses about quantities and numbers from incorrect ones' and thus avoid failures of memory (not to be confused with failures in logical thinking).

III: Concrete operations (mental age approximately 7–11 years)

As we have seen, an operation for Piaget is internalized action. At first children's reasoning is tied almost exclusively to concrete experience. They may be able to formulate in the mind a hypothesis which takes them one step beyond the concrete evidence available to them, but they are largely dependent on the perceptual facts before them. The child at this stage *describes* the environment; at the highest levels of abstract reasoning he or she tries to *explain* it. This distinction will be clarified later in the section describing the pendulum experiment.

Conservation, irrespective of number, shape or quantity transformations, is crucial for reasoning at the concrete stage of operations. For example, children would have to be aware that no matter how one presented the problem $2 + 4 + 3$ ($4 + 2 + 3$, etc.) it would still add up to the same quantity. Similarly, they would need to achieve reversal of number to solve any combination of the problem $2 \times 6 = 12$ or $12/6 = 2$ or $12/2 = 6$, all of which require a knowledge of reversal. There are numerous properties capable of being conserved and these, according to Piaget, appear in a particular sequence. Conservation of substance, for instance, occurs around the age of seven to eight years and precedes the conservation of weight (around 9 to 11 years), which in turn precedes the conservation of volume (at about 12 years of age). Number conservation appears before area. Another essential process mentioned previously is that of *decentring*. This involves the realization that the same fundamental quantity, be it number, volume, area, weight or whatever, exists no matter how the dimensions might be altered; the child's attention is no longer fixed on one dimension.

A second important operation in the development of concepts is the formation of consistent *classifications*. Previously we saw how the child tended to form pre-concepts by passing from the particular to the particular (transductive reasoning). Now, the formation of valid concepts depends on accurate sorting out of similar and irrelevant properties.

Allied to classification is another process known as *seriation*; that is, the ability to cope with the ordering of similar objects according to, say, size or position. A child who can count (cardination) may not be capable of appreciating the ordering of objects (ordination). Given six sweets arranged in a row, the pre-conceptual mind may not be able to select the fourth from a specified end. Classification and ordination are plainly interdependent, so much so that a child is not able to operate at the concrete level until able to cope with both these processes. Seeing relationships between groups and understanding similarity and subordination of classes are essential skills[11] in concrete operational thinking.

There is still a failure to distinguish between hypothesis and reality. At a more advanced stage of cognitive development, a person will test a hypothesis against evidence, whereas in the latency period of concrete operations the person will often adjust the facts to meet the hypothesis. This kind of operation is known as making *assumptive realities*.

One particular assumptive reality is described by Elkind,[12] who observes an interesting egocentric characteristic which he refers to as *cognitive conceit*. Up to this time children have tended to take the wisdom of adults on trust. However, during the period of concrete operations they come to recognize that adults are not infallible. They are sometimes wrong and the child is sometimes right. But this becomes distorted: if adults are wrong in one or two things they are wrong in most things, while if children at this stage are correct in one thing they think they will be correct in almost everything – hence cognitive conceit. In support of his contention, Elkind points to children's literature and cartoons, which are replete with examples of children outwitting adults (*Peter Pan*, *Emile and the Detectives*, *Tom Sawyer*, *Alice in Wonderland*, *Winnie the Pooh* (with the numbskull bear as adult and the cool, clever Christopher Robin as the child), *Tom* (adult) and *Jerry* (child)). The kind of verse which tickles children's fancy often pokes fun at what many adults take to be serious, e.g. the Church, Royalty, and Elkind cites several examples, including one from the short reign of the Duke of Windsor:

> Hark the herald angels sing,
> Mrs Simpson's swiped our King.

Another which springs to mind and is calculated to arouse adults of even mild religious conviction is 'While shepherds wash their socks by night', etc. As with other Piagetian stages, it is held that the characteristics may continue to reappear later, and examples of 'assumptive realities' therefore can be found in adult behaviour.

IV: Formal operations (mental age approximately 11 onwards)

Nine- and ten-year-olds are quite capable of dealing with concepts involving such things as weight, number, area, distance or temperature provided they can operate in the presence of concrete referents. Concepts involving an understanding of, for instance, volume, density, justice or cruelty are not well formed. These require more subtle levels of reasoning which we call *formal operations*. These highest levels of thinking of which individuals are capable develop once they can follow the *form* of an argument without needing the concrete materials making up the substance of the argument.

At the formal level of operations, individuals can reason hypothetically and in the absence of material evidence. They set up hypotheses and test these to determine real solutions to problems amongst a number of possible solutions. This is known as *hypothetico-deductive reasoning*.

To illustrate the difficulties in hypothesis-testing experienced by children at the concrete stage as contrasted with those at the formal level, let us take an actual illustration. My son, Paul, at 9 years 6 months was given the pendulum problem originally used by Inhelder and Piaget.[13] With one or two minor modifications from the original experiment this consisted of a length of string with a lump of Plasticine on the end. The string could be changed in length and more Plasticine made available for adding to, or removal from, the existing lump. Paul was required to discover the factor or factors which governed the time of swing of the pendulum we had made.

His first reaction was to say that the further one pulls the lump to one side before release the longer it takes to slow down because gravity (a concept vaguely mentioned at home and school) gradually pulls it 'slower and slower towards the middle' (of the swing). After a good deal of somewhat random exploration with the length, amount of Plasticine and method of release (either pushing with different forces or releasing freely) and with little regard for accurate measurement, he concluded that altering the length, weight on the end, force of release and 'gravity' would change the time of swing. I then put it to him that of the possible variables he had suggested, only one made much difference to the time of swing; how, then, would he set about discovering which of the four variables he had suggested was the important one?

His first proposition was to alter the length while varying the 'push'. What happens to the other variables? He would include those as well. After some trials and tribulations trying to arrange an experiment involving all the variables at once, he concluded, 'I'm completely lost. There are too many, what do you call them, variables.'

Paul's responses were typical of concrete operational thinking. He was capable of sorting out the factors which might vary by making direct observations of the apparatus. He pinpointed length, weight, gravity and method of release. He could also carry out seriation: as the string gets longer and longer, the pendulum swings slower and slower. But he could not at this stage manage to *test hypotheses* which were unambiguous by considering only one variable while holding the others constant. In fact, his mind boggled at the prospect of having to change the variables simultaneously. For formal operations he would need not only to theorize about the *possible* influences of all factors, but then to design an experiment to test the influence of each one in a systematic way while keeping the others invariant.

There is a second characteristic of formal reasoning, not too well illustrated by the pendulum experiment; that is, the *setting up of hypotheses*.[14] We saw how hypotheses were tested in the experiment, but the relevant variables were fairly obvious and the child has no need to go much beyond the raw materials in front of him or her to discover the attributes necessary for hypothesis-testing. Length, weight or 'push' are self-evident. Frequently, formal reasoning requires more subtle processes of abstracting the important criteria from the objective evidence. Moreover, the reasoning must go beyond the tangible and perceivable to the construction of propositions about objects and events from the attributes extracted. Piaget calls these 'second-order operations' to distinguish them from the 'first-order operations' of the concrete stage. Second-order operations, then, are operations on first-order operations. Problems involving proportion require second-order operations because we must first establish the relationship from the information given (first-order), and use this to discover a second relationship.

Some extremely interesting research by Driver[15] suggests that

> by the time children are taught science in school, their expectations or beliefs about natural phenomena may be well developed. In some cases these intuitions are in keeping with the ideas pupils will meet in their science lessons. They may be poorly articulated but they provide a base on which formal learning can build. However, in other cases the accepted theory may be counter-intuitive with pupils' own beliefs and expectations differing in significant ways from those to be taught.

These beliefs Driver refers to as *alternative frameworks*. One important aspect of this is that as children begin to test hypotheses and attempt to explain what they are observing, the alternative frameworks may well, if they are inaccurate, be counter-productive in a child's formulation of scientific principles.

The view underpinning the findings of Driver and others is referred to as *constructivism*. This means that the learner actively constructs both the knowledge acquired and the strategies used to acquire it. The illustration above of Paul trying to handle the pendulum problem is a good example of a learner bringing his previous experiences and inventions to the present situation. Paul's own previous observation, deduction and other people's ideas are all brought to bear. The constructivist view is in stark contrast to the *transmission* view of learning where it is assumed that a person's knowledge is assimilated from the words and actions of others in demonstrating a point. If a classroom of children are shown the pendulum experiment, transmissionists would assume that the children will take up some or all the points as delivered by the teacher. According to the constructivist view, there would be as many interpretations of what is happening as there are children in the classroom.

Constructivism has been particularly prevalent in science and mathematics. Cobb[16] rightly reminds us that not only the pupils but the teachers bring to their task a lifetime of their own internal structures and experiences. Consequently, he believes:

> the teacher who points to mathematical structures is consciously reflecting on mathematical objects that he or she has previously constructed. Because teachers and students each construct their own meanings for words and events in the context of the ongoing interaction it is readily apparent why communication often breaks down, why teachers and students frequently talk past each other. The constructivist's problem is to account for successful communication.

Some criticisms of Piaget's theory

Like so many theories in psychology, Piaget's has not been without its critics. Before pointing to the implications of his work, we must first consider the most common objections raised by psychologists.[17]

(a) Some American psychologists have been very sceptical of the clinical methods he adopted to establish his views. They are said to depend too much on the verbal introspections of immature minds. Behaviourists much prefer evidence to be independent of attitudes and self-reports. Nevertheless, replications using representative samples and all kinds of adaptations to overcome the shortcomings of introspection have yielded results which are very similar and coherent. Children from very different social and ethnic backgrounds with varying degrees of verbal talent still appear to give the developmental pattern described by Piaget.

(b) Inevitably, the haste to formulate a neat and tidy unfolding of events at prescribed 'ages and stages' in the child's development overlooked the part played by differences in mental and environmental factors, but the stages propounded are not so rigidly coupled with age.[18] The conservation of substance, for instance, appears at different ages in children. Moreover, appearance of the ability to conserve in a child is not sudden or all-embracing. There is a gradual emergence of the ability to conserve which varies from one property to the next. This point has considerable value for teachers. Individual differences in children's conceptual development will greatly influence the design of the curriculum by the teacher who is aware of the criteria for determining when certain conceptual possibilities can be entertained.

(c) Some (Bruner[19] and Bryant (**R**)[10]) place greater emphasis on the part played by experience than Piaget. It is argued that the consistency of the stages is a function of the regularity of a culture's child-rearing patterns rather than of some in-built and inevitable sequence of development. Also an inability to carry out the kinds of tasks set by Piaget and his followers may arise from insufficient information rather than from lack of ability as a function of maturation. However, 'training programmes' designed to ring the changes of these patterns and accelerate development have not, as yet, produced more than minor deviations in Piaget's developmental sequence.

(d) The role of language has been paramount in the process of trying to discover from children the course of their cognitive functioning and growth. In fact, some of Piaget's original experiments are almost entirely dependent on the child's understanding of the verbal instructions. For example, questions such as 'are all the primroses some of the flowers?' or 'are all the ladies some of the people?' are quite semantic tongue-twisters for a child of four years. Povey and Hill (**R**),[8] for example, using children in the age range two to four years, found with pictorial material that the children had acquired some specific and generic concepts. The term 'pre-conceptual' stage, according to them, implies, wrongly, that children cannot form concepts. Whilst they may make errors in conceptual judgements (decentring, transductive reasoning), nevertheless they do form correct concepts and apply them (see also the discussion of 'virtuous errors', mentioned by Herriot in Chapter 8, in which children have established rules of language for plurals or past tenses).

(e) The bulk of Piaget's theorizing has been applied to mathematics and science, with much less regard for other school subjects. Naturally, concept formation extends far beyond the bounds of maths and science, and this has to some extent been rectified over the past few years by an increase in research and curriculum development in other areas of interest to schools (**R**).[20]

(f)　Piaget offers no adequate explanation of cognitive development. A descriptive structure is given, but no satisfactory means of making predictions from it of structural change.

IMPLICATIONS OF PIAGET'S WORK FOR THE TEACHER

Whilst bearing in mind these limitations of Piaget's work, we can still learn much which is of service in teaching. Some of the more relevant aspects are discussed below.

(a)　The existence of a maturational unfolding of conceptual skills being linked with certain periods in the lives of children has an obvious bearing on curriculum planning.[21] Piaget is quite clear in his belief that neurological development and a progression of concept-forming skills must appear before full intellectual maturation is possible. The theory implies that certain periods are critical in mental growth. Teachers should, therefore, have some awareness of the range of possibilities in the concept formation of their children. As contemporary research shows, this does not mean that we must stick rigidly to a programme of teaching based exclusively on Piaget's sequence of concept development. Such a philosophy is too pessimistic if it leads us to sit back and wait for the next stage to appear. We should continue to explore teaching environments crucial to concept formation and hypothesis testing.[19] (R)[8, 10] In this respect, mental age is a more valid concept than chronological age because we are concerned here with intellectual and not physical development.

(b)　Teaching at middle and upper school level should begin from concrete considerations, building up, where applicable, to more abstract reasoning. This is reflected in many teaching programmes in mathematics and science which begin with experimental, practical aspects before attempting deductive work. (Recommendations of the Mathematical Association and Nuffield Science are very much concerned with this approach.)

(c)　The idea of active participation is in keeping with Piaget's view that concept formation arises from the internalization of actions. Building up schemata requires practical experience of concrete situations, as far as possible, to encourage active assimilation and accommodation.

(d)　Research[19] also suggests that explanation should accompany experience. Children should be helped to realize how hypotheses are reached.

(e)　It is probably true to say that most of us, for most of the time, are operating at the concrete level. Less able secondary-school children may rarely, if ever, reach the heights of abstract thinking.[22] Even university students have their problems.[23] Discretion must be exercised in the presentation of abstract concepts, particularly where they are of such an order of abstraction as to require an understanding of several subordinate concepts.

(f)　With primary school children and less able secondary school children, be on the lookout for intuitive, pre-operational thinking. Again, practical as well as verbal experience must assist the formation of concepts. Note also that operational thinking in some aspects of school work is by no means an indication of similar competence in other related aspects. Remember that research has shown marked irregularities for individuals in both the character and the level of concept attainment.

(g)   Cognitive development is a cumulative process. The hierarchical nature requires the formation of lower-order schemata on which more advanced work can be built. If, therefore, cognitive frameworks depend on what has preceded, it is important to regulate the difficulty level and order of presentation of material. To apply an ordered sequence of work is to admit that we can monitor children's progress. Therefore we can use the pattern of development in each child as a means of assessing attainment both in respect of the child's own progress and in relation to the expectations of his or her mental age group.

(h)   Verbalization is very important. Language aids internalization and consequently the formation of concepts. Verbal interchange between teacher and child or parent and child constitutes an important communication channel by which the world is defined. More will be said about its role in the next chapter.

INFORMATION-PROCESSING APPROACH TO COGNITIVE DEVELOPMENT

An alternative approach to cognitive development has been presented by Klahr and Wallace[24] which uses the theory of information processes as the model. Children are assumed to be born with processes enabling them to 'construct' their world as a result of experience and interaction with the environment. One major difference between this approach and Piaget's is that the former attempts to cast light on the *process* of mental activity.

Using the model described in Chapter 6, memory is one of the key concepts. It would seem reasonable to assume that in order to handle the variety and quantity of incoming stimuli, the human being must possess innate processes which enable a search for consistency and structure in the information received by the senses. This makes the process of coping with large quantities of information easier because it can be 'chunked' (see Chapter 6). These innate capacities are believed by Wallace to be *discrimination processes* activated by the flow of stimuli from the environment, processes for the *detection of regularities in structures* and, thirdly, *problem-solving processes*. The information built up in the memory in this way then acts as a guide to coding of further input.

Wallace[24] summarizes his views by reference to the development of quantification. The three innate processes mentioned above

first use the common consistent sequences to predict the effect of transformations on the relationship between the initial and resultant collections. The relationship is simply read off the sequence without carrying out quantification after the transformation. The predictions are verified by quantitative comparison with the initial collection. Success in this predictive phase results in confirmation that quantification of the collection after the transformation and the subsequent quantitative comparison constitute unnecessary processing and may be eliminated. The redundant processing is eliminated from each of the common consistent sequences to yield three rules governing the effect of addition, subtraction, and perceptual transformations on discrete quantity. These rules endow the child with the ability to discriminate quantity-preserving transformations from quantity-modifying transformations.

CONCEPT ATTAINMENT

Vygotsky (1896–1934)

Piaget is by no means the only person to attempt an analysis of concept formation, but there are differences in emphasis which distinguish the researchers in this field. Piaget was interested in the structural side of concept growth, but other psychologists, notably Vygotsky and Bruner, have concentrated more on function than structure.

Another difference between Piaget and Vygotsky is the greater stress placed by the former on biological factors which account for the systematic unfolding of development, whereas Vygotsky placed emphasis on social influences. This is not to deny Piaget's belief in the importance of educational and cultural transmission which he thought would partially account for some of the discrepances in development, but this theory was genetic and maturational, both depending largely on physiological properties.

Vygotsky,[25] in his short life of 37 years, was a most prolific researcher living in Russia early in the twentieth century. He postulated that human mental activity was the result of cultural learning using social signs. The culture into which a child was born was the source of concepts to be internalized and this affected the physiological functioning of the brain. Tools such as language, number, art were seen as the means by which a culture would conceptualize, organize and transmit thinking. Therefore, our thinking processes are a product of the culture in which we happen to be born.

He[26] carried out several ingenious investigations into concept formation using a method which did not depend on language skills already acquired by the child. His main purpose was to show a relationship between language and thought across widely differing cultures, and recent revitalization of interest in his work originates from his views about the link between language and thought.

Briefly, his materials consisted of 22 wooden blocks varying in colour, shape, height and size. These *attributes*, as they are called, occurred in a variety of combinations derived from five colours, six shapes (square, triangle, circle, semi-circle, six-sided figure and trapezium), two heights (tall or flat) and two sizes of horizontal surface (large or small). Each block had a nonsense syllable written on the underside so that the subject could not see it. Only four syllables were used, LAG, BIK, MUR and CEV, representing specific combinations of attributes (e.g. LAG is written on all tall, large blocks). Colour is not used as an attribute but is included as a distraction. The experimenter thinks of a concept and exposes a syllable on the underside of one block (called the *sample*) and asks the subject to pick out all the other blocks having the same syllable on them – that is, the subject must deduce the critical attributes of the block which make up the concept (in this case tallness and largeness). When a wrong choice is made the experimenter shows the subject an inaccurate block and the game proceeds until the subject tracks down the concept.

In the course of this research Vygotsky and his co-workers arrived at conclusions about concept formation in close agreement with those of Piaget. Three stages were isolated: first, there is the *vague syncretic* ('syncretic' in this context means random rather than reasoned groupings of blocks), in which the child at an early stage of development piles the blocks into heaps without any recognizable order. The groupings result from trial and error, random arrangement or from the nearness of the blocks.

The second stage is called thinking in *complexes*. These are a kind of primitive concept in which the child groups attributes by criteria which are not the recognized properties which could be used for the classification of the concepts. Five sub-stages were identified. Classification of the blocks was drawn up: (a) according to one common characteristic – *associative complexes*; (b) in collections like a square, a circle and a semi-circle (similar to the idea of having a knife, fork and spoon); (c) as *chain complexes*, where the child first picks out some triangles and notices that the last one chosen was, say, green and this in turn makes the child's next series of selections green, etc.; (d) *diffuse complexes*, consisting of chains which are unrelated, such as green–blue–black, and so forth; and (e) *pseudo-concepts*, which arise when the child perceives superficial similarities based on the physical properties of objects without having grasped the full significance of a concept. The formation of pseudo-concepts is not spontaneous, but is determined by the meaning given to a word by adults. In effect, the pseudo-concept is the product of mechanical and rote learning without an understanding of the underlying attributes, and led Vygotsky to place more weight on the role of cultural experience in concept formation than Piaget.

The third stage identified by Vygotsky is called the *potential concept stage*, in which the child can cope with one attribute at a time but is not yet able to manipulate all the attributes at once. Maturity in concept attainment is reached when the child can do this.

The description of how children progressed from haphazard grouping through pseudo-concept to full concept formation is illuminating. One can spot the grave difficulties presented to the infant and primary school child when faced with classification problems. We must be wary of creating too many pseudo-concepts using drill methods without first providing a rationale. Verbal labels are too readily acquired from adults with insufficient exemplars to aid in the construction of class concepts. Children often use terms which give the appearance of understanding, yet on closer inspection it becomes obvious that they do not really know the concepts involved. The shift in emphasis from traditional to modern mathematics and the use of structured apparatus (Cuisenaire rods, Dienes apparatus, colour factor) is a recognition of the need to establish an understanding of number operations as well as manipulative skills with numbers.

Bruner's strategies

We have dealt in some detail with concept development from birth to mid-adolescence. We shall now look briefly at some work which attempts to answer the question of how adolescents and adults, who already have well-formed concepts, expand on these in order to acquire more elaborate concepts. Bruner and his colleagues[27] devised a method seeking to discover the routes used by people who are attempting to expand, modify and adapt existing concepts to meet new demands.

To do this, Bruner, like Vygotsky, used objects with several attributes; using well-defined attributes such as colour, shape, size or number which can have different *values* and combining these to create concepts which were drawn on cards, Bruner asked subjects to deduce the concept which he had chosen. Peel[1] provides a reduced version of the task in his book *The Pupil's Thinking*. Using verbal reports from

B oy		B oy		B oy		B oy
T all		T all		S hort		S hort
F air		D ark		D ark		F air

G irl		G irl		G irl		G irl
T all		T all		S hort		S hort
F air		D ark		D ark		F air

Figure 7.4 *Sample cards containing the attributes of sex, size and hair shade.*

subjects and by watching the direction taken by them in trying to arrive at a solution, Bruner distinguished two broad strategies or plans of action. These are *scanning* and *focusing* strategies.

To elucidate their meaning, let us take a simple illustration. We shall use three attributes of human beings, each with two values. These are sex (boy (B) and girl (G)), size (tall (T) and short (S)) and hair colour (fair (F) and dark (D)). To simplify the presentation, each attribute value will be given a letter of the alphabet; these are shown after each value. Cards containing these attributes are then presented to someone as displayed in Figure 7.4. We have used words instead of a card carrying a picture of the attributes. The cards contain all the possible combinations of the three attributes. Given the values, we can arrange them to form concepts containing three, two or one attribute values. Thus with the values:

$$B \quad oy \qquad G \quad irl$$
$$T \quad all \qquad S \quad hort$$
$$F \quad air \qquad D \quad ark$$

we can get the following combinations:

eight 3-attribute concepts by combining (see Figure 7.4)

$$BTF, \quad BTD, \quad BSD, \quad BSF$$
$$GTF, \quad GTD, \quad GSD, \quad GSF$$

twelve 2-attribute concepts by combining

$$BT, \; BF, \; BS, \; BD, \; GT, \; GF, \; GS, \; GD, \; TF, \; TD, \; SF, \; SD$$

six 1-attribute concepts from

$$B, \; G, \; T, \; S, \; F, \; D$$

making 26 concepts in all.

The tester now thinks of one of the concepts (let us say the 2-attribute concept of *fair girl*, GF) without telling the subject. The former then selects one of the eight cards (the sample card) which includes the concept (let us say card GSF). The subject tries to deduce the concept by pointing to another card which is thought to be another instance of the concept. The tester answers 'yes' or 'no' to the selections until the subject is able to specify the precise combination of attributes making up the concept.

Returning now to the strategies observed by Bruner, in the scanning strategies a boy, say, works out hypotheses from the information given. In the case above, he has been shown GSF and he can now assess the combinations of attributes still open to him. Of the concepts, there are seven remaining possibilities: GSF, GS, GF, SF, G, S, F. With these in mind, he can adopt a completely logical approach known as *simultaneous scanning* by holding in mind all the combinations while setting up further hypotheses. To cut down the range of options still further, let us say the subject now chooses GTF, to which the experimenter says 'yes' because it contains GF. The number of alternatives is now reduced, since the only common values in the two selections GSF and GTF are G and F. This, therefore, leaves three concepts, namely girls (G), fair girls (GF) and fairness (F). By a process of elimination, it would not take long to track down the correct concept. However, simultaneous scanning can be a tedious and uneconomic procedure putting a premium on having a good memory, especially when there are a lot of attributes. A less exacting variation is *successive scanning*, by which a person takes one step at a time. In our example, at the stage where GTF is picked, the subject would then go on to look at each attribute in turn, noting the positive instances only (in simultaneous scanning, negative instances are also taken into account). Guesswork and anticipation (two popular ploys with us all) are used in the early stages of this method.

Focusing does not involve hypothesis-testing. The individual proceeds by altering one attribute value at a time (*conservative focusing*, which can be a long-winded affair) or more than one attribute at a time (*focus gambling*). The safest, or most conservative, method is to change and test the attribute values one at a time. In our example using GSF as the sample card, if one wished to test the presence of *girl* in a concept one might point to the card containing BSF. By this means one is holding SF constant. Building up to two and three values, if necessary, will finally enable the concept to be specified. The focus gambler, as the term implies, chances an arm by varying two attributes at each choice to test, in the first place, for single attribute concepts. One might, in our example, offer BSD as the first choice to test the significance of the size attribute. Lack of success would lead one to test double and ultimately treble attribute concepts.

Teachers will soon recognize the tactics employed by pupils (and themselves) in trying to solve problems involving attribute discrimination. The more concrete methods of successive scanning, particularly the focusing methods, are the commonest. Note the rapid increase in task difficulty as one increases the number of attributes. At any level of mental operations it is important to avoid unduly overloading the problems with variables where simultaneous scanning is important (many physics problems, for example, can be approached in this way, e.g. the pendulum experiment mentioned earlier). There is also a suggestion (**R**)[28] that strategies adopted by individuals are a function of the conditions in which they work. As a laboratory exercise, the games, mentioned above are more likely to induce focusing techniques, while everyday problems appear to encourage scanning. As yet, research has not been able to provide any precise information about the appropriateness of strategies for particular kinds of problem.

SUMMARY

Much of our experience is assimilated in the form of concepts and expressed in a symbolic form, as in verbal and mathematical modes. Thus, by the processes of forming categories and discriminating between the critical attributes of objects and events, we can organize our percepts and employ symbol forms to represent these experiences. Concepts have several distinctive characteristics, of which the following are among the most important. Concepts are: (a) representations with wide margins in defining the critical attributes of objects and events; (b) subject to experiential influences; (c) symbolic; (d) they can be used either in a way which is widely accepted by everyone (extentionally), or in a highly personal way (intentionally); (e) they form hierarchies of increasing complexity (think of the classification of animals as an illustration of hierarchical structure); (f) they can be irrational, as in superstitions and phobias; (g) they may be formed without the conscious knowledge of an individual.

Concept formation has been one of the special provinces of the Swiss psychologist, Jean Piaget. His researches led him to postulate a theory of qualitative changes during cognitive development from birth to adolescence which take place in a definite, inevitable sequence of maturational steps starting with biological mechanisms and culminating in a highly developed system of abstract operations. The child, while striving to come to terms with the surroundings, organizes activities into schemata by the processes of assimilation and accommodation. Piaget suggested four stages from birth to maturity, consisting of the sensori-motor, pre-operational (composed of pre-conceptual and intuitive sub-stages), concrete operations and formal operations.

A particular contribution of Piaget's theory to the educational scene is in drawing attention to the child as an active participant in concept-learning processes. Moreover, curriculum planning needs to be informed by the stages he postulated, but without being too rigid and ignoring either the variations in individual concept growth or the potential of children for concept formation. With new topics at any stage, one should proceed from the concrete and practical to the more difficult abstract. With younger children there may be little success in going beyond the concrete aspects of a topic. Where concepts are cumulative, the order of presentation must be worked out carefully so as to build up schemata in a logical and orderly sequence.

Language is most important for the internalization of concepts. The work of Vygotsky pays attention to the build-up of concepts alongside the acquisition of verbal symbols representing the concepts. His developmental theory was similar in many respects to that of Piaget, but see Chapter 8 for a discussion of the function of language in concept growth. Bruner's main interest was to elucidate the thinking strategies of adults who already had a grasp of concepts. He concluded that there are four basic ways of attaining concepts, in the form of simultaneous scanning, successive scanning, conservative focusing and focus gambling.

ENQUIRY AND DISCUSSION

(a)   It is very important for student teachers to meet children of all ages. With care, several of Piaget's original experiments can be repeated with the children (not particularly at school, but whenever or wherever the occasion presents itself). The materials are usually inexpensive and readily available. Try to choose a range of ages likely to include children from each stage of cognitive development. As a guide to materials, procedures and characteristic findings see K. R. Fogelman's book, *Piagetian Tests for the Primary School*, NFER, Slough, 1970, and Furth and Wachs's book.[21]

Do not forget to let the children know where they have gone wrong once the experimentation has been completed. You will find this a particularly exacting task, especially where the developmental stage of the child clearly falls short of that required for an understanding of the problem.

(Much very pointed criticism has been levelled at Piaget's work. The references in note (17) should be read and a careful analysis made of these criticisms *before* trying out any experiments.)

(b)   Explore Bruner's strategies using materials indicated in *The Pupil's Thinking*.[27]

(c)   Using as a starting point the references in note (20), read up and examine in terms of learning and teaching techniques the theories of concept growth associated with those of the following which are of particular interest to you: science; mathematics; history; geography; moral judgement; religion.

NOTES AND REFERENCES

1.   W. E. Vinacke, *The Psychology of Thinking*, McGraw-Hill, New York, 1952. This book gives a thorough discussion of concept characteristics. R. J. Sternberg and E. E. Smith (eds), *The Psychology of Human Thought*, Cambridge University Press, Cambridge, 1988, and J. Baron, *Thinking and Deciding*, Cambridge University Press, Cambridge, 1988, also provide summaries. E. A. Peel, in *The Pupil's Thinking*, Oldbourne, London, 1960, presents a number of different ways in which the term 'thinking' has been used. He classifies them under four headings: *thematic* (imaginative thinking in creative writing, painting or music, where one is not bound by a given problem), *explanatory* (describing and explaining events and things), *productive* (applying knowledge in new situations, giving rise to new inventions or products) and *co-ordinating* or *integrative* thinking (seen in the discovery of new theories and systems of thought). The work of Sperry mentioned in Chapter 2 also points to a distinction between *spatial* and *verbal* thinking which may even be specific to a certain hemisphere of the brain.

2.   A. M. Collins and M. R. Quillian, 'Retrieval time from semantic memory', *J. Verbal Learning and Verbal Behaviour*, **8**, 240–248 (1969), and 'Does category size affect categorisation time?', *J. Verbal Learning and Verbal Behaviour,* **9**, 432–438 (1970). See also E. E. Smith and D. L. Medin, *Categories and Concepts*, Harvard University Press, MA, 1981.

3.   A. M. Collins and E. F. Loftus, 'A spreading activation theory of semantic processing', *Psychological Review*, **82**, 407–428 (1975), L. E. Bourne, R. L. Dominowsky and E. F. Loftus, *Cognitive Processes*, Prentice-Hall, Englewood Cliffs, NJ, 1979.

4.   R. H. Forgus, *Perception: The Basic Process of Cognitive Development*, McGraw-Hill, New York, 1966. He classifies four schools of thinking about how these generalizations might arise. There are those psychologists who believe that concepts are formed by choosing *identical* elements. Others believe that *common relationships* define a concept. For example, apple, pear, banana, orange and plum all share the relationship of 'fruitiness'. A third basis for concept formation is *similarity of function*. The example listing fruits also serves to illustrate a functional concept. Finally, we have what Osgood refers to as the *common mediation process*, with which we shall deal in Chapter 8. See also C. B. Mervis and E. Rosch, 'Categorisations of natural objects', *Annual Review of Psychology*, **32**, 89–115 (1981).

5. J. Piaget's books are generally very difficult to understand. One of his most recent and relevant books entitled *Science of Education and the Psychology of the Child*, Longman, 1970, is amongst the easiest to understand. Readers who would like to sample his other writing should consult *The Child's Conception of Number*, Routledge, London, 1952, or B. Inhelder and J. Piaget, *The Growth of Logical Thinking from Childhood to Adolescence*, Routledge, London, 1958. There are now many introductory texts interpreting Piaget for the benefit of students, and some of these are given in the Further Reading list.

6. D. O. Hebb, *The Organization of Behavior*, Wiley, New York, 1973; F. C. Bartlett, *Remembering*, Cambridge University Press, London, 1932.

7. A straightforward summary of his theory can be found in 'The stages of the intellectual development of the child'. *Bull. Menninger Clinic*, **26**, 120–128, (1962) reproduced in P. Barnes, J. Oates, J. Chapman, V. Lee and P. Czerniewska, *Personality, Development and Learning*, Hodder and Stoughton, Sevenoaks, 1984.

8. (**R**) R. Povey and E. Hill, 'Can pre-school children form concepts?', *Educ. Res.*, **17**, 180–192 (1975). See also M. Donaldson, *Children's Minds*, Fontana/Croom Helm, London, 1978; P. E. Bryant (ed.) *Piaget: Issues and Experiments*, British Psychological Society, 1982.

9. (**R**) J. S. Bruner, 'The course of cognitive growth', *Am. Psychol.*, **19**, 1-15 (1964). This paper is in the Reader under Part 8, 'Language and thought'.

10. (**R**) Some of these experiments look so simple to the adult, and the child's errors so incredibly naïve. In an experiment of Piaget's, several sweets or counters are arranged in equal rows, some for the child, and an opposite row for another person.

child

· · · · · ·

· · · · · ·

other person

When the child's row is spread out,

· · · · · ·

· · · · · ·

the child will say, if at the intuitive level of development, that he or she has more than the other person. A contracted row is said to be smaller and contain less. We again meet up with a transitivity problem involving invariance similar to those described in the body of the textbook. The child uses length as the criterion of quantity and is immediately faced with a conflict of hypotheses.

Bryant attempted to remove the conflict in a research reported in the following: P. E. Bryant, 'Cognitive development', *Br. Med. Bull.*, **27**, 200-205 (1971), and (**R**) P. E. Bryant and T. Trabasso, 'Transitive inferences and memory in young children', *Nature*, **232**, 456-458 (1971) (see the Reader). If the arrangement of counters is such that the child has more, as indicated in the illustration beneath:

· · · · · · · ·

· · · · · ·

the child will, even at the intuitive level, set up the correct hypothesis by saying he or she has more than the other person (by, as yet, some unsubstantiated method). If the second state is now made indeterminate by placing the counters in two identical glass containers such that they appear the same height (in other words, two counters have not made an appreciable difference to the height), the child, according to Bryant, still says that he or she has more than the other person, regardless of the fact that it can be seen that the heights are equal. Why? Because, says Bryant, the child has been able to establish a 'definite hypothesis' at the first stage, can appreciate the invariance principle in the transformation to the second stage and is not so perceptually dominated at this second stage as to say that the quantities are equal when the heights are equal. When equal numbers of counters are used in the same experiment but are arranged to give unequal lengths in the rows, as in the second part of the illustration at the beginning of this note, the child sets up the incorrect, but definite, hypothesis of a difference in the quantities and maintains it throughout even though, as in the first case, the heights in the glass vessels look equal. Bryant's conclusion is that we ought to concentrate on how children arrive at definite hypotheses rather than debate the invariance issue.

11.   The grouping of operations is carefully defined by Piaget. For a summary, the reader might like to refer to R. M. Beard, *An Outline of Piaget's Developmental Psychology*, Routledge and Kegan Paul, London, 1969, pp. 81–83, or J. L. Phillips, Jr, *The Origins of Intellect: Piaget's Theory*, Freeman, San Francisco, 1969, pp. 69–75, These groupings are seen by Piaget as an essential prerequisite to concrete operations.

12.   D. Elkind, 'Cognitive structure in latency behavior', in J. C. Westman (ed.), *Individual Differences in Children*, Wiley, New York, 1973.

13.   B. Inhelder and J. Piaget, *The Growth of Logical Thinking from Childhood to Adolescence*, Routledge and Kegan Paul, London, 1958.

14.   A chapter on 'Formal reasoning' by E. A. Lunzer, in E. A. Lunzer and J. F. Morris (eds), *Development in Human Learning*, vol. 2, Staples, London, 1968, gives a clear analysis of hypothesis construction and hypothesis testing by children at the concrete and formal stages of development.

15.   R. Driver, *The Pupil as Scientist?*, Open University, Milton Keynes, 1983; also R. Driver, E. Guesne and A. Tiberghien (eds), *Children's Ideas in Science*, Open University, Milton Keynes, 1985.

16.   P. Cobb, 'The tension between theories of learning and instruction in mathematics education', *Educ. Psychol.*, **23**, 87–103 (1988). Also see V. Lee (ed.), *Children's Learning in School*, Hodder and Stoughton, Sevenoaks, 1990.

17.   Recent publications about Piaget's work have generally contained a section which is cautious towards and critical of the Piagetian position. In the main, the criticisms are about the interpretations, which Piaget placed on his findings more than the findings themselves. Critical books include the Bryant references in notes (8), (10), and his book *Perception and Understanding in Young Children*, Methuen, Andover, 1975; M. Donaldson, *Children's Minds*, Fontana, Glasgow, 1978; S. Modgil and C. Modgil, *Jean Piaget: Consensus Controversy*, Praeger, New York, 1982; G. Brown and C. Desforges, *Piaget's Theory: A Psychological Critique*, Routledge and Kegan Paul, London, 1979. To get a recent, balanced overview, see P. Sutherland, *Cognitive Development Today: Piaget and His Critics*, Chapman, London, 1992.

18.   For example, see the work of K. Lovell and E. Ogilvie, 'A study of the conservation of substance in the junior school child', *Br. J. Educ. Psychol.*, **30**, 109–118 (1960), and 'A study of the conservation of weight in the junior school child', *Br. J. Educ. Psychol.*, **31**, 138–144 (1961)

19.   J. S. Bruner believes that children are remarkably flexible in their ability to acquire concepts. He places instruction and experience at a higher level of priority as potent influences in concept development than would Piaget. See his book, *Toward a Theory of Instruction*, Norton, New York, 1966.

20.   (R) Over the last 20 years, several workers have looked at concept growth in particular subject areas. For a summary up to the mid-60s have a look at J. G. Wallace, *Concept Growth and the Education of the Child*, NFER, Slough, 1965. The growth of religious concepts has been examined by R. Goldman, *Religious Thinking from Childhood to Adolescence*, Routledge and Kegan Paul, London, 1964. J. H. Peatling, 'On beyond Goldman: religious thinking in the 1970s', in J. M. Hull (ed.), *New Directions in Religious Education*, Falmer Press, London, 1982. Also look at G. Jahoda, 'Children's concepts of time and history', *Educ. Rev.*, **15**, 87–104 (1963); K. Lovell, *The Growth of Basic Mathematical and Scientific Concepts in Children*, University of London Press, London, 1968; M. Shayer, 'The need for a science of science teaching', *Educ. in Chem.*, **15**, 150–151 (1978); W. B. Sloan, 'The child's conception of musical scales: a study based on the developmental theory of Piaget', M.Sc. dissertation (unpublished), University of Bradford, 1969; G. Jahoda, 'The development of children's ideas about country and

nationality', *Br. J. Educ. Psychol.*, **33**, 47–60, 143–153 (1969); R. Hallam, 'Piaget and the teaching of history', *Educ. Res.*, **12**, 3–12 (1969) in the Reader; W. Kay, *Moral Development: A Psychological Study of Moral Growth from Childhood to Adolescence*, Allen and Unwin, London, 1968; L. Kohlberg and T. Lickona, *The Stages of Ethical Development: From Childhood through Old Age*, Harper and Row, New York, 1986.

21. H. G. Furth and H. Wachs, *Thinking Goes to School*, Oxford University Press, New York, 1974.
22. K. Lovell, 'A follow-up study of Inhelder and Piaget's *The Growth of Logical Thinking*', *Br. J. Psychol.*, **52**, 143–154 (1961).
23. M. L. J. Abercrombie, *The Anatomy of Judgement*, paperback, Columbia University Press, New York, 1990.
24. D. Klahr and J. G. Wallace, *Cognitive Development: An Information Processing View*, Lawrence Erlbaum, New Jersey, 1976. See also J. G. Wallace, 'Cognitive development', in D. Fontana (ed.), *The Education of the Young Child*, Open Books, London, 1978.
25. A recent book which gives a thorough, but technical, summary of Vygotsky's work is L. C. Moll (ed.), *Vygotsky and Education: Instructional Implications and Applications of Sociohistorical Psychology*, Cambridge University Press, Cambridge, 1990. For recent trends, see N. Mercer, 'Accounting for what goes on in classrooms: what have neo-Vygotskians got to offer?', *Educ. Sect. Rev.*, **15**(2), 61–67 (1991).
26. L. S. Vygotsky, *Thought and Language*, MIT Press, Cambridge, MA, 1962, gives a detailed examination of the impact of language on concept formation.
27. J. S. Bruner, J. J. Goodnow and i. A. Austin, *A Study of Thinking*, Wiley, New York, 1965. For a simplified version of the research see E. A. Peel, *The Pupil's Thinking*, Oldbourne, London, 1960, or R. Thomson, *The Psychology of Thinking*, Penguin, London, 1959.
28. (R) N. E. Wetherick, 'Bruner's concept of strategy: an experiment and a critique', *J. Gen. Psychol.*, **81**, 53–58 (1969).

FURTHER READING

G. Brown and C. Desforges, *Piaget's Theory: A Psychological Critique*, Routledge and Kegan Paul, London, 1979.

R. W. Bybee and R. B. Sund, *Piaget for Educators*, Charles Merrill, Columbus, OH, 1982 (2nd edn).

D. Cohen, *Piaget: Critique and Reassessment*, Croom Helm, London, 1983.

M. Donaldson, *Children's Minds*, Fontana, London, 1978.

M. Donaldson, *Human Minds: An Exploration*, Viking Penguin, New York, 1992.

S. Meadows, *Developing Thinking*, Methuen, London, 1983.

E. A. Peel, *The Pupil's Thinking*, Oldbourne, London, 1960. A thorough and technical text with several detailed descriptions of experimental work.

J. L. Phillips, Jr, *The Origins of Intellect: Piaget's Theory*, Freeman, San Francisco, 1969. One of the best introductory texts available.

P. Sutherland, *Cognitive Development Today: Piaget and his Critics*, Chapman, London, 1992. This is a contemporary text attempting to give an even-handed view of Piaget's contribution.

B. J. Wadsworth, *Piaget's Theory of Cognitive Development*, Longman, New York, 1989 (4th edn).

Chapter 8

Language and Thought

Language is a human being's finest asset. Many essentially human activities spring from this unique characteristic by which we become detached from our physical world. As far as we can tell, animals normally go into action because they are prompted by physical stimuli (internal as well as external). A cat stalks a bird which has attracted attention; a dog begs for food when it can smell or see it, when feeding rituals are set in motion or as a result of 'feeling' hungry. In contrast, humans can indulge in reveries which take them well beyond the present reality into the realms of abstract thought. They communicate to themselves in some symbolic form. Moreover, they can communicate their ideas to others by using these symbolic forms. These two uses of language, personal and social communication, are very important for teachers because their work is built around the efficient communication of ideas. The importance of language competence and the role of teachers in making sure that such competence is relentlessly encouraged in schools are the concern of both the teaching profession and the Department for Education (DfE). The appearance of the Bullock Report (briefly mentioned in Chapter 7) is evidence of the growing concern about standards of literacy.

How far is language solely a human activity? Animals can, of course, communicate – ants, bees and primates afford well-known examples of animal contact – but the level is primitive. It is habitual, situation-specific and initiated by internal or external physical cues which are not symbolic. Primates have systems of sounds for survival and emotional needs (grunts, howls) which are *not* symbolic. But the vocalizing apparatus of the primates does not seem to be able to produce the vast range of meaningful characteristic vocalizations of human beings. Viki, a chimpanzee belonging to the American psychologists C. and K. Hayes, took six years of hard work to learn four rather imperfectly spoken words. (See also the work of the Gardners.[1]) With human beings, competence to assimilate a spoken language is universal and comparatively rapid. In addition, human communication has the potential for creating new meanings and having duality of meaning for similar sounds.

CHARACTERISTICS OF SPOKEN LANGUAGE

Language has been defined as the term denoting '*the psychological processes which regulate speech*'.[2] Speech is language behaviour by the articulation of sound patterns. Talk involves using speech to communicate experience and convey meanings. The two basic requirements of a language are that it is symbolic and systematic. We tend to regard language in a somewhat atomistic fashion by looking upon it as a collection of words strung together in sentences, each word having a separate identity and meaning. This is a false way of looking at language. In fact, the words are brought together in special ways to give a highly systematic order from which we get a meaning. Similarly, there is no one meaning for each word in a sentence. The meaning we ascribe to a sentence can change from one context to another. For example, 'What on earth are you doing for Heaven's sake!' could be taken in two ways, depending on whether it is a show of annoyance or a priest after souls. Altering the position of words in a sentence alters the sense of the sentence, even though the same words are there. 'The sun is shining' is not the same as 'Is the sun shining?' Language, then, is not random behaviour, but is systematic, where certain orderings are accepted as having prescribed meanings.

The raw materials of each language are the basic sounds. These give the character of the language and form one method of distinguishing different languages. The *phoneme*[3] is the term we use for the perceived basic speech sounds of a language – 'perceived' because the latitude in pronunciation within a culture may vary (compare the Scot, the Londoner and the Lancastrian), but all have the same interpretation. Certain phonemes are specific to a language. 'Th' (as in 'the') in the English language has no equivalent phoneme in French. The French pronounce it as 'z', to begin with, because, as one *au pair* girl from France put it, 'I say "z" instead of "th" so zat I don't bite ze tongue.'

Phonemic utterances are put together to form *morphemes*, which are the smallest units of a language with a grammatical purpose. They are not necessarily words as we know them. In the word 'plans' there are two morphemes: 'plan' and 's'. 'Plan' is a word, but 's', which serves the useful grammatical function of converting plan into the plural, is not a word as such. Prefixes, suffixes and word endings which change singular to plural or alter the tense are therefore morphemes. Linguists find morphemes much more useful than words for defining language content. Broken into morphemes, the sentence 'The girl liked to dress her dolls' would be 'The + girl + like + ed + to + dress + her + doll + s'.

The systematics of a language involve more complex combinations of symbols. Each morpheme has a particular function, and the formation of sentences by combining these morphemes so that they obey rules requires a knowledge of *grammar* (some call this *syntax*). Most, if not all, readers will recall having to discover the parts of speech represented by words in a sentence and making sure that they are presented in a certain order for a particular meaning. But combining morphemes in a specified order does not necessarily mean that the resulting sentence makes sense. Combining morphemes to make words and arranging them together to give meaning in a particular tongue is called *semantics*. In the sentence 'the green toes fought on the apple', the grammatical structure is correct, but the sentence is meaningless in our culture. The study of semantics involves the resolution of the meaning we ascribe to systems of morphemes.

THE FUNCTIONS OF SPOKEN LANGUAGE

At the beginning of the chapter it was suggested that speech served two broad purposes, personal and social communication. These two functions are referred to as *egocentric* and *socialized* speech. Egocentric speech is characterized by the child who behaves and talks as if all points of view were his or her own. He or she seems unable to appreciate another's point of view, to conceive things from another position. The egocentric monologue is a running commentary on the child's present situation and frequently acts as a means of self-regulation and direction. At three years of age about half a child's utterances are egocentric (the rest are socialized), and this rapidly reduces to a quarter at age seven. Socialized speech has such functions as requests, persuading, providing information, and so forth. Several classifications of the functions of speech have been attempted[4] (see also the work of Tough, mentioned later in the chapter), but for our present purposes it is sufficient to note the broad self and social functions. The child progressively recognizes the listener and tries to adapt his or her language in order to convey information which has meaning for the listener.

Jane was two-and-a-half and lived next door to the author. An extract from a tape-recording of her chatter while she was alone in a bedroom illustrates some features of a little one's language. She is looking out of a window and has seen a neighbour's dog, Rajah. After a lot of chatter about visiting Rajah's house, she continues the conversation, we think, with a teddy bear, or on some occasions hoping that her mother can hear. 'Look, what's that man doing? You can see. Look, he's digging the soil up. Can you see him? We have to ask mummy if we can go to Rajah's mummy's house (Rajah's mummy is the owner of the dog). We can if mummy says "yes". Can't undo this lock. Better ask mummy if we can have the paddling pool out at Rajah's mummy (thought to be the bath in which Rajah is rubbed down). Have to try and open it. Can we go to Rajah's mummy's house?'

'No. Get into bed,' says Jane's mother.

'Jane get into bed. No, I'm bright and chirpy now (a little family saying). Mummy, I'm bright and chirpy now. That sock doesn't fit me. Better see if it fits Teddy.'

The first snatch of conversation seems to be socialized speech, where Jane is trying to encourage someone else (probably her mother, who, although not there, may be thought to be within earshot) to repeat what she is doing. But then she appears to direct her conversation to something else (most likely Teddy) because she talks about her mummy as a third person. There is also evidence of monologue intended largely for self-direction. On several occasions she rehearses what she is going to say or do. 'We have to ask mummy if we can go to Rajah's mummy's house', 'I'm bright and chirpy now' and 'Better see if it fits Teddy' are three examples. Egocentric speech is not necessarily indicated by the recurrence of 'I' or 'me'. The question is for whom the speech is intended. Is it intended for self-direction or is it an attempt to communicate with others?

The relative development of egocentric and socialized speech and the functions they serve was a bone of contention between Piaget and Vygotsky. The latter's position has now been accepted by most (including Piaget). Vygotsky (also see Chapter 7) supposed that all speech is social by implication, although it may not always be used as a means of communicating with others. One source of evidence for Vygotsky's belief in speech as being social in origin is that if one put normal children with deaf or foreign children, egocentric speech disappears.[5] When the potential listener cannot understand, speech is no longer overt. Egocentric speech was crucial as a directive for the child's actions. It was not, as Piaget once held, a simple accompaniment to the actions with no other purpose: rather it was used by the child for laying down plans of action. Further, for Vygotsky, egocentric speech was a transitional step from outward vocal socialized speech to inner speech. Interiorization of speech means that thought processes are facilitated and self-direction follows without the attendant overt speech. (It is, none the less, difficult to determine which comes first, a thought or the speech. When Jane talks about an action she might be reminding herself of a thought.) In short, we see a change in the regulating function of speech from external sources (like mother), through egocentric speech for everyone (including self) to hear, and ultimately to speech for communication and 'internalized speech' for the regulation of behaviour and logical thinking.

LANGUAGE ACQUISITION

How does a verbally helpless infant develop into an articulate adult? A widely held belief is that we are born with vocal equipment and a neural system which gives us the capacity to verbalize. It does not take a child very long to discover and utilize a vast range of phonemic utterances no matter which culture he or she happens to be born into. Equally, the speed with which these utterances are converted into meaningful (to both child and parent) and reproducible sounds during the first few years of life is convincing testimony to an inborn capacity. Contrast this with the slavish way in which Viki, the chimpanzee, was taught to say only four utterances in six years. Even then, there is very little evidence to lead us to suppose that the 'words' are any more than the result of conditioning. Two further capacities essential to communication are the ability to reproduce utterances *at will* when required, and the realization that one is being understood.

The onset of language

The origins and influence of sounds heard and rehearsed by a baby and their place in language acquisition are still matters of dispute. A central point separating workers in this field is whether the baby is a passive or an active agent in the process of developing language. The acquisitive view is represented essentially by the behaviourist school of psychology; the active, but 'hereditary', view has a wide range of adherents, including linguists and cognitivists. Do babies start with a clean slate and build up language by imitation and reinforcement, or do they have certain inherent facilities which are activated by them or in response to stimulation?

Babies make sounds from the moment of birth. These sounds accompany discomfort (cries) and pleasure (chuckles, cooing), although little is known about whether the sounds can be further differentiated in the very young baby. Between 6 and 12 months the *babbling stage* is reached; this stage is thought to be inherent in human beings, because deaf children also babble. Ricks[6] has attempted to differentiate these sounds into requests, frustration, greeting and pleased surprise.

Language learning and operant conditioning

The behaviourist position suggested by B. F. Skinner[7] is that the babbling sounds are one starting point for conditioning the child to associate particular objects or events with particular sounds. For him, language is a skill fabricated by trial and error and reinforced by reward (or extinguished by non-reward). The reappearance of a verbal response is conditional on the receipt of a reward. Bluntly, if there is no reward when you do something, you are less likely to repeat the activity on a future occasion. In the case of language usage, the reward could be one of many possibilities. Social approval from parents or others when a child makes an utterance is probably the most potent in the early stage of development.

Skinner distinguishes three ways in which the repetition of speech responses may be encouraged. First, the child may use *echoic* responses. In this case, he or she imitates a sound made by others, who immediately display approval. These sounds need to be made in the presence of an object to which they may be linked. Second, we have the *mand*, a response which begins as a random sound but ends up by having meaning attached to it by others. Echoic response frequently follows a mand expression where a parent on hearing 'mama' or 'baba' uses it to form a word and encourages the child to repeat the utterance. Once the sound is firmly implanted, it gradually becomes associated with an object. Finally, there is the *tact* response (a contraction of the word contact). Where an acceptable verbal response is made, usually by imitation, in the presence of the object and the child is rewarded by approval, there is every likelihood that the response will appear again (see the Helen Keller story later).[8] Clearly, these types of responses are closely related in the early stages of children's language formation. Note how imperative the presence of other people is. With no one around to show approval or test the accuracy of verbal utterance, they would soon be discarded.

Not all psychologists are satisfied with this paradigm of Skinner's. To begin with, verbal responses quickly take on much wider meaning, as indicated by the range of usage, than can be explained by operant conditioning. Again, there are many words which do not 'name' objects (they have no *referents*). Learning articles such as 'the' or 'a' is difficult to explain in Skinnerian terms. Add to this the phenomenal vocabulary count of young children, accumulated in a comparatively short spell, and Skinner's theory does not appear to provide the whole explanation. Noam Chomsky[9] takes up a completely different position in asserting that there are common structural factors in all languages, from the simplest native tongues to the most complex in the world. Although his interests lie in theories of grammar and linguistics, he has something to say about language acquisition.

The inheritance of linguistic competence

Chomsky could not hold with the mechanistic view of man as a computer – being fed with words (input) and reproducing them (output) in the required order from suitable programmes laid down in childhood. Apart from anything else, the actual process is far too elaborate: not even a computer could cope with a fraction of the language capacity of humans. But his theory is a difficult one and only the bare essentials are given here.

By mastering the rules governing the structure of language (syntax), a child is able to generate utterances and understand the utterances of others, even when they are completely original to the child. Language is 'open-ended', and those who can use it fluently can produce and understand sentences which they have never used or heard before. According to Chomsky, stimulus–response theories are not sufficient to account for this creative capacity in language usage or the child's ability to understand novel sentences. Further, it is assumed that children have a potential for linguistic skill which is inborn. The built-in facility is called the *language acquisition device* (LAD) – a hypothetical inner mechanism. It enables children to process incoming signals, make sense of them and produce a response. The rules of language seem to come to children quite naturally even when they are of widely differing intelligence and cultural background. The rules are obeyed (within limits) without apparent understanding. Chomsky also supports the theory that humans are unique in possessing linguistic aptitudes and can in no way be studied, by implication, using animal comparisons. Humans are qualitatively different from other animals. This view is a far cry from the developmental view of Skinner's behaviouristic outlook described above.

Note that we are back in the arena of dispute between behaviourists and cognitivists (Chapter 5). In the previous section, we observed how Skinner developed a theory of verbal behaviour without necessarily referring to any internal operations of the organism. The nearest approach to a consideration of internal processes by the behaviourists is in the mediation theory of Osgood (a 'neo-behaviourist'), whose work is considered later in the chapter. Even here, the emphasis is still on stimulus–response connections, but they have been transferred to the interior of the individual. On the other hand, the language of the cognitivists is replete with terms like 'schemata', 'styles' and 'images', and concentrates on the mental state of individuals (at a given time) in order to capture the essence of what is taking place between a human being 'receiving' and 'transmitting' information.

The evidence for the child making up his or her own rules is not hard to find. Listen to any child as he or she makes what Herriot[10] calls 'virtuous errors' by applying standard rules to irregular cases. 'Mouses' instead of 'mice' and 'sheeps' instead of 'sheep' are common errors. Tense errors are also frequent – 'catched' rather than 'caught' and 'teached' instead of 'taught'. These errors still arise after many learning occasions in which the correct usage has been instilled. The reason is probably that the child is still trying to apply the 'correct' rule (hence 'virtuous' error) and has not had sufficient experience to remember the irregular morphemes.

Teachers must handle these errors with care. Herriot, like many others, puts in a plea for tactful handling of mistakes in language usage arising from innocent breaking of the rules through inadequate knowledge of the exceptions. This can generally be done by repeating a *correct* version in a reply to the child without making it too obvious that you are correcting a mistake, i.e. no punishments or ridicule in front of others. Some mistakes are quite hilarious, but it is often insensitive and unproductive with young children to poke fun at their language errors. Note that structure is the all-important thing in language usage (using the system with meaning), and not individual words or phrases. New concepts represented by single words or phrases must ultimately be set in a language context for an improvement in language skills.

For a summary of the debate between Chomsky and Skinner, see the paper by McLeish and Martin in the Reader (**R**).[11]

On the question of imitation, an extreme view is held by Jakobson,[12] who does not accept that children begin their language acquisition by imitation. Babies, he believes, have a facility for differentiating sounds which are phonological contrasts (for example, voiced/voiceless, e.g. 'd' and 't' as in 'dig' and 'tig' or 'p' and 'b' as in 'pig' and 'big'; nasal/oral, e.g, 'n' and 'l' as in 'not' and 'lot' or 'm' and 'b' as in 'man' and 'ban'). At first the differentiation is simple dichotomous contrast of all sounds. New sounds of contrast are added to the repertoire until those in a particular language are mastered. Dodd[13] studied vocalization at the height of the babbling stage and found there was indeed no imitation of sounds after a period of stimulation from an adult. Further, there was no increase in the types of sounds produced, although the amount of babbling increased.

A middle way in language acquisition

Probably an answer lies somewhere between these extremes. It is hard to believe that babies do not imitate some sounds, and equally hard to believe they do not have *some* in-built facility for language acquisition. It is most likely that they combine imitation with phonological rules, take into their systems sounds made by adults and assimilate utterances which are both phonemes and morphemes. It is at this stage that the foundations of pseudo-concepts are laid down (see Vygotsky's work in Chapter 7).

Later, children begin to accumulate more rules by which the system works. They learn plural endings or other morpheme combinations. Grammatical skills appear when they can put two words together (sometimes known as *telegraphic* use of words), e.g. 'cat gone', 'mamma give', and this occurs between 24 and 30 months. Herriot[10] summarizes one point of view so:

> Children notice certain features of language behaviour, and use these features to form their own individual system of combination. However, the needs of communication, the requirement for more words and more complex ways of combining them, force them to approximate more and more to adult systems. So, of course, does the need to be understood by a variety of other people. When his only communicant is his mother or his twin, the child may be held back by baby language. But as soon as he needs to speak to other members of the community, the rules of the conventional code of language become more necessary.

It is not necessarily assumed that children are born with linguistic potential already laid down in the brain, but rather that, as the brain develops, more elaborate regulation of language behaviour becomes possible.

Vocabulary growth

The earliest clues to the child's ability to comprehend his or her surroundings come from the use made of *signs*, *signals* and *symbols*. The newborn relies on reflex action and soon comes to depend on direct evidence which can be assimilated from his or her senses. Oral contact with objects such as a milk bottle or the mother's nipple will soon initiate sucking. Quickly the child begins to associate one aspect of the feeding ritual with the whole process. The sight of milk in the bottle or the sound of the bottle being prepared is often sufficient to set in motion anticipatory behaviour in advance of the actual feeding process.

Perception of some piece of the action, then, gives the cue for the whole action. The cue which represents part of the real thing (sight of nipple or milk, smell of milk, clank of bottle) is called a *sign*. Babies become quiet when their nappies are being removed; to a dog a lead can be a sign of the prospect of a walk; tears are a sign of joy or sorrow.

In the discussion of intuitive thinking in children, we showed how children are often deceived by signs. By over-generalizing they take the same sign to mean that the same event is going to take place. When mother puts her coat on it may be taken erroneously to represent a sign that she is going shopping. The important thing about a sign is that it produces behaviour characteristic of the whole response to a situation.

Certain signs become significant in the absence of the real thing. When a sign is given this special meaning in the absence of the object and it gives rise to behaviour *as if* the object were there, we call it a *signal*. Signals are often the outcome of conditioning. The hand movements, whistles and calls which send a sheep dog cavorting round a flock of sheep are signals. Likewise words take on the function of signals. To a dog the word 'sit' is a signal which has become part of the act of sitting down. Experiments with chimpanzees have shown that words are little more than signals. As we supposed above, the first childlike utterances such as 'dada' are signals acquired, possibly, through repeated association and conditioning connecting word sounds with physical objects.

When signals become endowed with meaning which bears no resemblance to the original object we call them *symbols*. Words in our language are obvious examples. The symbols actually represent things without looking or sounding at all like them. A symbol is sometimes referred to as a secondary signal because it is once removed from the real thing. Unlike commands to a dog or the first words of a child, the symbol becomes detached from physical events. Mead[14] says that 'The vocal gesture becomes a significant symbol ... when it has the same effect on the individual making it that it has on the individual to whom it is addressed.' 'The same effect' is used with the reservation that no two people respond in precisely the same way.

Many stimuli not normally brought together can be represented by symbols and juxtaposed within a short time. Language results when these verbal symbols are brought together and organized into systems of meaningful patterns.

An unusual example of a transition from sign and signal to symbol systems is brilliantly illustrated by Helen Keller in *The Story of My Life*.[8] Deaf and blind from infancy, she had made little progress until, at the age of seven years, she was given a tutor, Miss Annie Sullivan. In their first days together the tutor got Helen to feel objects while they were being spelt out into the palm of her hand. But there was little realization that the shapes drawn out on her palm were labels for the objects she was touching. Helen, in fact, was not even detached from the signs around her. The moment of truth came when:

> We walked down the path to the well-house, attracted by the fragrance of the honeysuckle with which it was covered. Someone was drawing water and my teacher placed my hand under the spout. As the cool stream gushed over one hand she spelled into the other the word *water*, first slowly, then rapidly. I stood still, my whole attention fixed upon the motions of her fingers. Suddenly I felt a misty consciousness as of something forgotten – a

thrill of returning thought, and somehow the mystery of language was revealed to me. I knew then that 'w–a–t–e–r' meant the wonderful cool something that was flowing over my hand . . .

I left the well-house eager to learn. Everything had a name, and each name gave birth to a new thought.

The rate at which the child is able to use and understand words is quite slow in the early stages of language development. Note that there is a difference between the numbers of words we actually use (*active vocabulary*) and the larger number we are able to understand (*passive vocabulary*). Of course children vary enormously in their vocabulary size and usage, depending largely on intellect and linguistic opportunities. But a general picture of the average rate of vocabulary growth we can expect is shown in Figure 8.1. At one year of age the average word count is three or four. At one-and-a-half years the count is around 20 and at two years this figure rises sharply to about 200. Note how, in the Piagetian sensori-motor stage of cognitive development, progress is slow, and it is not until the transition into the stage of pre-operational thought that the child really begins to amass words. Assessing an average count is quite difficult with young children, because one is never quite sure whether all the possible utterances of which a person is capable have been spoken, or indeed if the utterances are understood. Morpheme counts are popularly used and an estimate of between 4000 and 7000 is thought to be the case for children just entering school,[15] rising to 10 000 at 14 years of age.

Growth in the acquisition of elementary meaningful forms of our language, as in the formation of plurals and tenses (morphology), has been extensively studied. Berko,[16] for example, has shown, using nonsense syllables, that at seven most children can cope with a plural formed by adding 's', but experience greater difficulty when 'es' is required. Likewise, in the formation of the past tense, 'ed' is not found to be too difficult to apply, but where a change such as 'ring–rung' is required, only a third of the seven-year-olds could manage. Grammatical skill, which is said to occur when a child can put two words together to form a meaningful expression, generally appears around two years of age.

The important, detailed work of Templin[17] set out to investigate four aspects of language amongst children of three to eight years of age. These were articulation of speech sounds, speech sound discrimination, sentence structure and vocabulary size. Of the many conclusions reached in this valuable work, perhaps the following are of particular note. In articulation skills, the three-year-old is still making, on average, 50 per cent errors, whilst at eight years he or she is accurate 90 per cent of the time. In five years the child reaches close to articulatory maturity. Boys usually take about a year longer than girls, and children from working-class homes about a year longer than those from middle-class homes. In speech sound discrimination, that is, the ability to recognize auditory differences among speech sounds, there is a consistent increase in the ability, with a gradual deceleration beyond five years of age. At the lower ages there does not appear to be any significant difference in the ability between boys and girls, but at eight years of age girls are better than boys. Sentence length and structure now appear to be longer and more complex than in previous studies (25 years earlier). No differences were detected for the boys and girls, but children from middle-class homes made longer and more complex remarks than working-class children. About half the remarks made by three-year-olds are grammatically accurate, and this

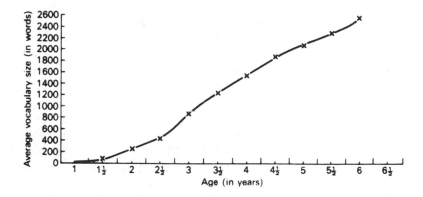

Figure 8.1 *Active vocabulary size and age. Adapted from E. H. Lenneberg in 'The natural history of language' (a chapter in* The Genesis of Language, *edited by F. Smith and G. A. Miller).*[15]

improves to about three-quarters at age eight. The vocabulary count presented a lot of problems, and there seems to be little agreement between researchers about methods of finding the recognition or recall vocabulary of young children. The estimates of basic vocabulary for the six- to eight-year-olds ranged from 13 000 to 23 000 in Templin's work, although these figures seem rather high when compared with the work of Lenneberg (see Figure 8.1). The *total* vocabulary, Templin suggests, is even higher at eight, and could be as high as 28 000.

LANGUAGE AND THOUGHT

It would be impossible to speak of language development without considering the possibility that it is related in some way to thinking skills. Do we need to have language in order to think, or does our cognitive equipment enable us to indulge in the use of a sophisticated language? Do language and thinking skills grow as separate entities or are they interconnected from the outset? These and many other questions continue to tax the minds of psycholinguists.

Origins of language and thought

There is, as yet, no single, widely accepted, comprehensive account of the relationship between language and thought. In a most readable summary of work in this field, Cromer[18] presents a spectrum of speculations based on research evidence. These range through: (a) language determines thought (strong form of linguistic-relativity hypothesis); (b) language does not determine thought but only predisposes people to think in particular ways (weak form of linguistic-relativity hypothesis); (c) cognition determines language acquisition (strong form of cognitive hypothesis); and (d) cognitive abilities enable us to understand and use creatively the linguistic structures *only* when abilities are adequate (weak form of cognitive hypothesis).

(a)   For some of the earliest investigators there appeared to be no problem. Watson, an American psychologist in the behaviourist tradition, concluded that thought *was* language. Accordingly, thinking is manipulating words in the mind. These word-thoughts were regarded as internal speech which showed up in sub-vocal movements of the speech organs. Elaborate experiments aimed at detecting these movements while subjects were thinking out the solution to a problem were not entirely convincing. The present moderate view emphasizes the role of the CNS rather than the peripheral motor system, of which the speech organs form a part. The child quickly learns to suppress the peripheral nervous system, therefore motor action accompanying reading or thinking gradually (but not entirely) declines. The more difficult the verbal task, the more likely is sub-vocal movement. Drugs used to paralyse the larynx show that its movement is not necessary for thinking to occur. Again, the example of deaf people who can think without vocalizing at all is evidence that thought can occur without the agency of a verbal language system such as that used by hearing people. The outline of the Skinnerian hypothesis of language acquisition clearly demonstrates yet another linguistic-relativity perspective. Children accumulate language by imitation and reinforcement which, in turn, enables them to think.

Whorf and Sapir[19] are most widely known for their strong contention that 'thought is relative to the language in which it is conducted'. This viewpoint is known either as the *Sapir–Whorf hypothesis* or *linguistic-relativity hypothesis*. According to Whorf,[20] 'We can cut up and organize the spread and flow of events as we do largely because, through our mother tongue, we are parties to an agreement to do so, not because nature itself is segmented in exactly that way for all to see.' Further, he believed that languages differ in the way in which they break down nature in order to make words and sentences. Thus the way we think is dependent upon the language we are using; that is, the agreed ways in which a culture has carved up its view of the world and represented it in the language. In a review of this extreme position using comparisons in concept formation between native tribes, eastern cultures and western cultures, Carroll[3] concludes that the hypothesis has not received much convincing support: 'Our best guess at present is that the effects of language structure will be found to be *limited* and *localized*' (emphasis added).

(b)   The weak form of the Sapir–Whorf hypothesis, elaborated by Brown,[21] supposes that, rather than determining our thinking, language predisposes us to think along particular lines. This leaves open the door to an explanation of how it is that an individual can cope in several languages and also explains some notable differences in concepts between different cultures. Idiosyncrasies in languages in terms of idioms for which no translation is available in other languages will be familiar to anyone who has studied a foreign language. The term 'gestalten' in Chapter 4 really has no precise translation into English. Similarly, many of Piaget's terms in French have no equivalent translation, and interpreters have had to resort to literal translation. Another much-quoted example comes from the work of Lenneberg and Roberts[22] on Zuni-speaking people compared with English speakers. The Zuni speakers do not differentiate yellow and orange colours and therefore make far more mistakes when asked to distinguish between them. The Zuni/English bilinguals have less difficulty, whilst English-speaking people have none at all.

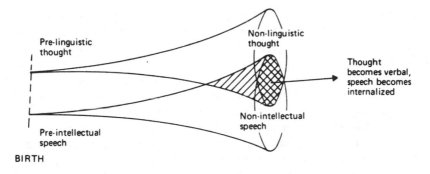

Figure 8.2 *Representative model of theory relating thought and language (after Vygotsky).*

(c)   The 'strong cognitive hypothesis' approach is lucidly summarized by Cromer,[18] who defines it in this way: 'We are able to use the linguistic structures that we do largely because through our cognitive abilities we are enabled to do so, not because language itself exists for all merely to imitate.' The evidence presented is of two kinds. First, Cromer attempts to show that cognition precedes language by quoting the work of, among others, Jakobson[12] and Ricks[6] on phonological rules as precursors of language acquisition rather than imitation methods (see earlier). He also examines the link between cognition and language acquisition at later ages, and he refers to Piagetian workers who maintain that language is not the origin of thinking operations. Second, Cromer emphasizes the independent development of language[18] (see also the following paragraph on Vygotsky).

(d)   Possibly the most popular current position is the 'weak cognitive hypothesis' first formalized by Vygotsky.[23] He considers language and thought as originating from different roots. At first, there is what might be described as pre-linguistic thought and pre-intellectual speech, which gradually merge together as the child approaches the pre-operational stage. The 'fusion' of thought and speech, however, is not total, and Figure 8.2 shows a continuing independence of some aspects of language and thought. Pre-linguistic thought is very much in evidence, as we have seen, in the sensori-motor activity of infants. Beyond this stage we still employ imagery and motor skills in practical pursuits. Learning by heart without any grasp of meaning may lead to pre-intellectual speech. Jane's phrase 'bright and chirpy' (see previous section) is probably used with little idea of what it means. Verbal strings implanted in the memory without any logical reasoning behind the content can produce non-intellectual speech.

Cognitive growth and representation

Another approach to the study of language in the development of thinking comes from Bruner (**R**).[24] His concern is for discovering the functions of language in concept formation – the how and why of language and concepts. Piaget, as we have observed, concentrates on the description and structure of cognitive growth – the 'what happens in concept formation' approach.

How do we fix in our minds the repeated regularities of our observations? How, in other words, do we represent our experiences to ourselves? Humans, in the course of evolution, have developed systems by which they can implement their actions with increasing efficiency. First, they develop the use of tools as an extension of their *motor capacities*. A spade, for example, becomes the extension of a man's (or a woman's) hand. He makes instruments to replace his less efficient body structures. Next, he extends his *sensory capacities* by, for example, the use of signal systems. In order to enlarge on his sensory experience he builds telescopes and microscopes or uses radio to transmit sound over great distances. At the pinnacle of representational skills we find *symbol systems* for conveying experience of real (or imaginary) things in their absence. These three evolutionary changes coincide with the course of language development through *enactive*, *iconic* and *symbolic* representation as postulated by Bruner, and they compare closely with Piaget's theorizing.

Enactive representation, the earliest stage of development, enables us to internalize repeated motor responses so that in time they become habitual. Numerous physical activities carried out in life are habitual. Opening a familiar door, driving a cricket ball, writing, walking, etc. do not always require conscious effort in terms of directing one's muscles to do certain things. The muscles seem to behave as if the memory of familiar events had been imprinted on them without the aid of mental images. The circular reactions suggested by Piaget are the beginnings of enactive representation.

When mental images enable us to build up a picture of the environment, iconic representation is possible. We amplify sensory experiences and combine these percepts to construct images. These 'internalized imitations', as Piaget calls them, are thought by Bruner to be a composite representation of several similar events. (Calling up the sound of a bell would produce a combination of bell sounds heard in the past. See Chapter 7.) An exception occurs in eidetic imagery, where a vivid image of a single event is recalled in great detail.

The transition from iconic to symbolic representation occurs around the age of four years, although the child begins to symbolize at about the age of two. Symbolic representation sees the use of language systems which bear no resemblance to actual objects. Symbols do more than represent reality: they enable us to transform it. This transition from iconic to symbolic representation and the central position of language are well demonstrated by an experiment of Bruner's. Children between five and seven were shown nine glasses of different sizes arranged in a pattern as shown as in Figure 8.3.

The children were asked to describe the arrangement, pointing out how the glasses were similar or different. The glasses were then dispersed and the children asked to rearrange them as nearly as possible to the original. Most children succeeded in this task. The glasses were dispersed again except that the glass marked A was placed in another position at X and the children asked to reconstruct the pattern with A at X. The younger children did not succeed while the seven-year-olds accomplished the task.

This and other research points to valuable conclusions for the teacher. Children who still depend on iconic representation are dominated by the images they perceive. This is in agreement with Piaget's notions of 'centring' and 'decentring' alluded to in Chapter 7. We ought, according to Bruner, to give children every opportunity to describe events in order to encourage symbolic rather than iconic representation. This is just a high-powered way of saying that we should get our children to talk or write about experiences, to express themselves in language, as well as to do things. Frank's work,

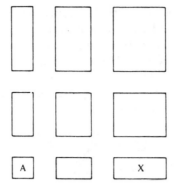

Figure 8.3 *Matrix of glasses in Bruner's transposition task. Modified from Bruner by D. G. Boyle,* A Student's Guide to Piaget, *Pergamon, London, 1969.*

reported by Bruner (**R**)[24] (see also the Reader, Part 8), with the well-known Piagetian experiment, in which glass vessels containing water were hidden from view (apart from the tops of the vessels) and children were asked the typical conservation questions, demonstrates the importance of diverting the child from visual to symbolic modes of representation and testifies convincingly to the improvement in the performance of young children when we deliberately activate symbolic reasoning. Language, then, is to be encouraged as an essential accompaniment to perceptual experience.

LANGUAGE AND MEANING

We are all familiar with the feelings and characteristic reactions which can be evoked when particular signs are used. Some people recoil in horror at the word 'snake' or 'spider'. Some visibly change at the sight of a baby's photograph or even the word 'baby'. Children and adults often display inappropriate or prejudiced behaviour at the sound or sight of particular words. Occasionally one meets a reception class child or first-form secondary school pupil who has developed a distorted reaction to school (especially if the parents have said 'you wait until you get to school. They'll sort you out'). But how does meaning become attached to signs?

Of the many theories extant, Osgood's[25] has received the widest currency. In a nutshell, he supposes that, in addition to receiving the direct stimulation from an adult, we regularly experience other kinds of stimulus which, by conditioning, become associated with the stimulus-object and become part of our response to the stimulus. Osgood gives an example of the spider. The hairy, long-legged body and quick movements representing the visual pattern received by our eyes may be encountered at the same time as a frightening description of its habits or when someone is leaping about in dread of the creature. With sufficient repetition of these extraneous reactions alongside the stimulus-object a complex behaviour response is established. As there are many and varied encounters with the stimulus-object, the total response pattern becomes very complicated. When the spoken word 'spider' occurs on some of these occasions, part of the total response pattern becomes linked with the word so that the sight or sound of the word 'spider' will provoke that part (or 'fraction' as it is sometimes known) of the total response. This system by which a previously neutral stimulus (a sign) involves a response (or mediates between stimulus and response) is known as a *representational mediation process*. The term 'representational' is used because the mediating response produced by the sign is only a representative portion of the whole response which would usually appear in the presence of the stimulus-object. A diagram should help to summarize the process.

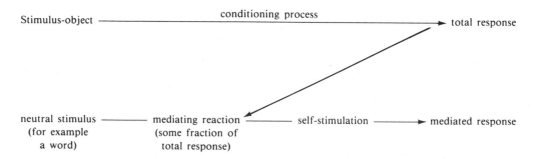

Stimulus-object ————————— conditioning process —————————▶ total response

neutral stimulus ——————— mediating reaction ◀——— self-stimulation ———▶ mediated response
(for example   (some fraction of
a word)   total response)

To quote from Osgood, 'Stimulus-objects elicit a complex pattern of reactions from the organism' and 'when stimuli other than the stimulus-object, but previously associated with it, are later presented without its support, they tend to elicit some reduced portion of the total behaviour elicited by the stimulus-object'.

It does not follow that direct association with the stimulus-object is necessary for mediating processes to arise. In fact we may never see an actual snake or giraffe, and yet we develop characteristic responses to signs of these animals. Photographs or verbal descriptions of the animals are sufficient to enable a response to be formulated. Where mediation responses arise from other signs rather than from the actual object we call them *assigns*, meaning assigned by association with other signs rather than the real thing.

The leap between the theoretical model of Osgood and the practical problem of how we can actually measure the meaning ascribed to a concept has been attempted in Osgood's semantic differential. In this, he tries to tap the universe of meaning built up from previous experience (as outlined above) which surrounds a given concept. This is done using a large number of rating scales consisting of bipolar adjectives (good–bad, fast–slow, active–passive). In so doing, he hopes to define the cognitive and affective meaning which the individual has grown to associate with the concept. Each scale is divided into a number of points expressing degrees of favourable or unfavourable attitude as expressed in the adjectives at each end of the scale. 'Neutral' attitude would occur at the centre of each scale. This tendency towards one end or the other is regarded as an expression of 'meaning', thus:

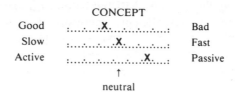

CONCEPT

Good :....:....**X**....:....:....:....: Bad
Slow :....:....:....**X**....:....:....: Fast
Active :....:....:....:....:....**X**....: Passive

↑
neutral

By using several of these adjectival bipolar scales with each concept, it is hoped to define the semantic space, and thus to measure the 'meaning' the individual attaches to the concept. To quote from Osgood *et al.*:[25]

> By semantic differentiation, then, we mean the successive allocation of a concept to a point in the multidimensional semantic space by selection from among a set of given, scaled semantic alternatives. Differences in the meaning between two concepts is then merely a function of the differences in their respective allocations within the same space . . .

A paper (**R**)[26] is included in the Reader which illustrates research into self-concepts as well as the use of Osgood's semantic differential.

In summarizing this sensitive area of the relationship between language and thought, it seems clear that there is no shortage of theory, but an embarrassing scarcity of well-founded information which can be employed by the teacher. The topic is well summarized by Greene.[27]

NON-VERBAL COMMUNICATION

It is surprising how much information is conveyed by non-verbal means. Mime is a very common example. Friends can often carry on a wordless dialogue of meaningful nods and facial expressions. Stress, unhappiness or joy are frequently seen in certain faces without a word being spoken. While speaking, people use facial and body movements which become clues to the meaning of the spoken words.

Gesture is the commonest form of non-verbal contact. It is not just hand movements, but involves facial and body movement. A clenched fist, bared teeth, frown, tongue out, stamping feet in a tantrum, voice intonation, all assist in revealing the mood of a person. Sometimes gestures accompany and interplay with verbal communication, adding emphasis or purpose to what is being said. Hand movements are said to portray something of the speaker.[28] It has been argued that gestures are much more revealing in their psychological meaning than the speech which goes with them. Conversation is too obvious, laying bare our thoughts and feelings, and we therefore tend to be guarded in what we say by the social conventions of our culture. At the same time the significance of gestures is less well understood and therefore we do not disguise them with the same subtlety as in vocalizing. You may have noticed on occasions that the implicit meanings of gestures are in conflict with the explicit message of a verbal communication, e.g. when a person is telling a lie and you can read it in his or her face and voice.

The skilful use and observation of gesture and expressive movement are assets in teaching. Well-coordinated intonation and facial expressions should add to what is being said. Rather obvious movements such as prowling back and forth in front of a class can be off-putting and reminiscent of a tennis match. Also watch children's facial and body movements. These often reflect the mood and understanding of a class.

Argyle[29] and Morris[29] have some useful and interesting points to make about the role of non-verbal cues for interpersonal relationships. Argyle refers, for example, to various social behaviour styles such as 'affiliative' and 'dominant' styles. Both are commonplace in the classroom. The former is exemplified by closeness, body contact, eye contact, friendly tone of voice, etc., and the latter by 'talking loud, fast and most of the time, in a confident tone of voice, interrupting others, controlling the topic of conversation, giving orders or using other kinds of influence, ignoring attempts at influence by others, adopting an attentive but unsmiling facial expression, and an erect posture with the head tilted back'. Rewards and punishments based on gestures are also common. The need for affiliation makes a reward out of smiling, agreeing, head-nodding and so on, whilst punishment is related to frowning, looking away or looking bored, disagreeing and looking impatiently at one's watch.

A particularly important application of non-verbal communication is the use made of sign language by deaf people. Many countries have developed their own sign languages. In this country, the British Sign Language (BSL) is regarded as the native language of deaf people[30] with its own grammar, syntax, and its own social and cultural implications. There are other signing systems such as signed English, which uses roughly the word order of the English language and the signs of BSL. Since about 1970,[31] a philosophy has developed which encourages the use of all relevant and available means of communication. It has become known as *total communication*.[32] An appropriate combination of speech, lip speaking and reading, signing, finger-spelling, gestures, etc. form the basis of this approach, which has taken a firm hold in many countries.

On teaching practice, students will very quickly notice the reaction of a class to a lesson by watching the children's faces and interpreting the silences either as a sign that they are spellbound or, conceivably, that they have not a clue as to what the student is talking about.

TEACHING LANGUAGE SKILLS

There is far more to language usage than an ability to read well. Naturally, a good reader is more likely to develop the broader language skills of communication and comprehension, but many teachers have become aware of the need for a systematic attack on basic language usage amongst children which has more to it than just reading. Most programme designers are generally agreed that at least three overlapping stages are required in order to assist language development. These are *reception* (listening with understanding), *internal symbolization* (interpreting, reasoning and concept-building) and *expression* (communicating by speaking or by writing). As we have suggested elsewhere, between reception and internal symbolization we require a process of *decoding* the incoming signals into a form which is readily interpreted in terms of previous traces in the brain. Similarly, the outcome of reasoning is thought to be converted or *encoded* into a form which enables individuals to communicate to their fellows.

In the home

Children can learn the language in the early stages of their development only if, and when, they hear the language spoken. Different linguistic environments have a start-lingly variable effect on language usage, not just as a regional accent or dialect, but in the systematics of the language. The mother is a particularly important figure in the early language development of her children. The frequency and content of her conversation with her babies and toddlers significantly affect their progress. Mothers who provide simple explanations in answer to the many questions which children pose, lead a dialogue or describe the host of objects surrounding the child, play games involving language usage, read stories, and buy toys which develop language skills are more likely to raise the linguistic standards of their children.

There may still be controversy about whether or not some linguistic structures are innate, but there is no doubt that different home environments give rise to different uses being made of language. What has given rise to disagreement is whether the distinctions observed between, for example, the language of a child from a working-class home and that of a child from a middle-class home are the result of *language deficits* or *language differences* in usage.

Of recent theories on the study of language and home background (chiefly in social-class terms), that of Bernstein[33] emphasizes the deficit model: conditions are such as to impair the progress of language growth. Bernstein's interests are essentially socio-logical, but his findings point to several possible implications for students of language and cognition. He believes that language is 'one of the most important means of initiating, synthesizing and *reinforcing* ways of thinking, feeling and behaviour which are functionally related to the social group'. Children from more articulate back-grounds, generally found in middle-class homes, not only display marked differences in the vocabulary they use as contrasted with children from working-class homes, but also organize and respond to experience in more sensitive ways.

Different use of language forms does seem to relate to social class. These forms have been described by Bernstein as the *restricted code* (at one time he used the term 'public language') and the *elaborated code* (formal language). The restricted code is used by both working-class and middle-class people. The elaborated code is mostly limited to middle-class usage.

A tentative catalogue of ten basic differences between the language codes appears in a research paper by Bernstein.[34] To illustrate some of these, the restricted-code user has short, grammatically simple, unfinished sentences with poor syntactical struc-ture. Simple conjunctions (so, then, and) are used repeatedly. Short commands and questions are frequently used. Impersonal pronouns (one, it) are rarely in evidence. Term's of *sympathetic circularity* such as 'like', 'you know', 'isn't it' are often used. On the other hand, the elaborated-code user has accurate grammatical and syntactical structure, uses complex sentences containing conjunctions and relative clauses and makes discriminative use of adjectives and adverbs.

The restricted code also possesses implicit understanding through grammatically incomplete expressions (or even non-verbal communication) as well as the sympathetic circular terms and widely understood clichés. Whenever people know each other well (husband and wife, brother and sister), contracted verbal and non-verbal codes exist. An eye movement might be sufficient to replace a sentence! Note, however, the ability of those from middle-class backgrounds to use either code. Most mothers (and teachers for that matter), whether working-class or middle-class, have been heard to say 'sit down and wrap up' (restricted) as an alternative to 'do sit down and make a little less noise please, darling' (elaborated).

Labov[35] does not accept the language-deficit explanation of language differences.

He declares that there is no linguistic deprivation and no lack of intelligence or linguistic thinking amongst non-standard English users. He believes that the main reason for the distinction in usage is related more to the influence of the peer group than the home for setting language-usage norms. Note how quickly the young develop and use the catch-phrases of their generation. Each generation seems to create its own collection of clichés, often leaving the older generations in comparative ignorance of their meaning.

The work of Tough,[36] for the Schools Council's Communication Skills in Early Childhood Project, provides some interesting evidence of home influences on language. Tough argues that the range of language acquired is largely a function of the range of experiences enabling language usage in the home. This is very much a 'difference' rather than a 'deficit' viewpoint, and is in the Vygotsky/Piaget tradition (see earlier in the chapter). The conclusion from the research was not that disadvantaged children had an inadequate knowledge of language (although for some this may be the case), but that they had had insufficient experiences of language being used in particular ways in the home. Her study led to several conclusions about the functions of children's use of language (see earlier section on functions). These are worth noting:

(a) Self-maintaining: maintaining the rights and property of the self.
(b) Directing: the child's activity and that of others (cf. egocentric speech).
(c) Reporting on present and past experience.
(d) Logical reasoning.
(e) Predicting and anticipating possibilities.
(f) Projecting with the experiences of others.
(g) Building up an imaginative scene for play through talk.
(Extract from reference (37).)

Using these criteria, distinctions were apparent between children from educationally advantaged homes (higher education and professional occupations) and those from disadvantaged homes (minimum period of education and unskilled or semi-skilled manual occupations), yet all the children had comparable measured intelligence. All the children used self-maintaining and reporting of present experiences; however, disadvantaged children were less likely to use language for the other purposes indicated above.[36, 37] The disadvantaged child tends not to be as explicit as the advantaged child, and also tends not to be in tune with the 'communication needs' of the listener in terms of thinking about the spoken messages so as to give a clear indication of the meaning behind them.

This greater emphasis on the communication aspects of language and its impact on later language skills is of value to the teacher. By 'communication' is meant transmitting meanings so that the meaning intended by the sender is the one interpreted by the receiver.

The role of the family, particularly the mother, in exposing children to language usage is clear. The language skills of parents and the purposes for which language is used are dominant influences. Elaboration of the language is more likely to evolve where two-way conversation takes place, as in question-and-answer exploration, rather than one-way communication consisting essentially of instructions. Equally, opportunities for and encouragement in language usage in the home in the form of books, newspapers, games involving words ('I spy') and bedtime stories are important language contacts.

Not all language deficits originate from environmental disadvantages. Several physiological conditions exist. Stammering is a case in point. It often arises from poor co-ordination of breathing and articulation of words. The precise cause has not been substantiated, but it may start as a mild physical deformity which, when aggravated by careless handling, produces emotional tension. Adult intervention (constant prompting) or ridicule does seem to make the complaint worse. It could, therefore, be a case of a mild defect being caught up in a cycle of tension and self-consciousness which becomes magnified beyond proportion. Other physical defects of voice and articulation organs (voice box, tongue, palate) are possible. They originate from damage to the organ, the brain or the sense of hearing. Injuries to the speech regions of the brain, producing aphasia, have already been mentioned in Chapter 2. Be on the lookout for the 'late developer' in speech. The reasons are obscure, but we do know that some children, without any apparent evidence of physical or mental defect, are very slow off the mark, only to improve quite rapidly later in their school lives. However, when the teacher spots a linguistic defect, it is wise to seek professional advice in the first place to eliminate the possibilities of physical or mental abnormality.

At school

Of all the areas in the school curriculum, English has produced the most imposing avalanche of books for teachers and children. The National Curriculum (see Chapter 16) will undoubtedly create yet another growth point for texts. It is therefore a task for the specialist tutor in this area to provide the student with suitable detailed reading lists. In this text it is sufficient to indicate a general series which students will find helpful.[38]

The National Curriculum Council[39] has emphasized the importance of speaking and listening, reading, writing, spelling and handwriting and has made them the five attainment targets to be measured.

Speaking and listening

There are now many programmes (**R**)[40] which set out to encourage the three skills of reception, symbolization and expression. Their purpose is 'the development of the pupils' understanding of the spoken word and the capacity to express themselves effectively in a variety of speaking and listening activities, matching style and response to audience and purpose'.[39] The psychological research in, for instance, spoken language in nursery and infant schools[41] is well documented.

It is essential to distinguish between those programmes designed for the disadvantaged – the deficit model (e.g. *Head Start* in the USA and *Talk Reform*)[42] – and those designed or adapted for normal use (e.g. *Listening to Children Talking*,[37] for use in primary schools, and *Language in Use*[43] in secondary schools). Tough[37] has developed a teaching scheme in the use of language with the emphasis on function rather than structure of spoken language. The scheme is designed to encourage a child to 'formulate ideas, examine relationships, reflect and reason about what he experiences, and consider the viewpoint of other people'.

For a useful commentary on talking, see Bruner's book *Child's Talk*.[44]

Reading

Something is said in Chapter 6 about the teaching of reading. The National Curriculum attainment target hopes to promote 'the ability to read, understand and respond to all types of writing' and 'the development of information-retrieval strategies for the purposes of study' (note (39)). Here, it ought to be mentioned that the focus of attention has been on *when* and *how* to start the teaching of reading to children (excluding the somewhat specialist work of the Adult Literacy movement). Some parents (we don't know the proportion) take delight in trying to encourage children in the art of reading, but one question of interest to psychologists has been whether there is an age below which it would be a waste of time to attempt to teach reading. The concept of critical times is referred to as 'reading readiness', and is a matter of dispute.[45]

The literature on the subject of teaching reading is becoming quite extensive. For critical comment and summary refer to the references in note (46).

Writing

Just as important as reading is writing. There can be very few days in the lives of secondary-school pupils which do not contain some kind of writing commitment. The National Curriculum target here is 'to promote a growing ability to construct and convey meaning in written language matching style to audience and purpose' (note (39)). The ability to spell and write clearly are also expected.

One particularly thorough piece of research into writing (not without its critics[47]) has been conducted by the Writing Research Unit, in which Britton is a key figure. In an effort to help teachers to decide on the form and functions of writing, Britton *et al.*[48] define two sets of categories, one relating to the *audience* for which the writing is undertaken and the second relating to the *functions* of written language. Any writer, whether child or mature author, tries to adjust what is being written according to the audience likely to read it. A sense of audience 'is revealed by the manner in which the *writer* expresses a *relationship with the reader* in respect to the former's *undertaking*'.[48] Britton *et al.* see five categories of audience for the child at school. These are self, teacher, wider audiences such as parents and other children, unknown audience and additional categories not accounted for above, such as 'pretend' audiences which might result when a teacher asks the child to write a letter to a fictitious person.

A second classification was carried out using 'functions' as the basis. In answer to the question 'What is the purpose of the content of the written work?' Britton *et al.* defined three purposes: *transactional, expressive* and *poetic*. The central expressive mode is essentially a means of establishing contact with readers to 'explore togetherness'. It consists of the 'personal everyday undifferentiated language in which we exchange opinions, attitudes, beliefs and immediate preoccupations'. The transactional category, as the term implies, is concerned with participation between the writer and others through the written word. This is the language of informing, advising, persuading and instructing others. The poetic category is used for self-presentation, in which the writer's feelings are expressed in poetic patterns. A Schools Council project, Writing Across the Curriculum,[49] uses the findings of the study conducted by Britton *et al.* for the work in writing, particularly in the 11 to 18 years age range. For the primary school, Beard[50] has produced a useful text.

SUMMARY

Readers do not have to be convinced that language is a most important skill for human learning and communication. There are two basic requirements of a language, namely that it should be symbolic and systematic. The symbolic aspects were discussed in the form of phonemes and morphemes and the systematics in relation to grammar and semantics.

Templin's work on establishing norms of articulation, speech–sound discrimination, sentence structure and vocabulary size among children from three to eight years of age was followed by a brief introduction to some contemporary views of language acquisition. At one extreme we find the behaviourist position, illustrated from the theories of Skinner, in which language is said to be acquired largely by the processes of imitation and reinforcement of acceptable sounds. On the other hand, Chomsky, whilst not rejecting the possibility of stimulus–response learning of phonemes and morphemes, nevertheless cannot accept that the highly creative nature of language is derived largely from the Skinnerian type of language conditioning. Those with some degree of fluency are well able to create and understand entirely original sentences. Human language is far more open-ended than that of other species. Although bees can communicate and even vary the intensity of their messages to give shades of meaning (variable activity amongst bees is commensurate with the distance from the hive of a supply of pollen), they cannot recombine their code to give original messages. The potency of humans' communication lies in the infinite combinations possible. New rules of language can develop, or recognized rules can be broken, especially by young children who are still in the process of learning the rules.

Efficient language acquisition is very much dependent on the linguistic environment to which children are exposed. Bernstein has shown some marked differences in the language patterns and skills deriving from different home backgrounds, and he named these patterns 'restricted' and 'elaborate' codes.

The function of speech was the centre of controversy some years ago when Piaget and Vygotsky disagreed about the purposes served by the early speech of children. Now it is widely accepted that egocentric speech (speech intended essentially for one's own benefit) and socialized speech (for the benefit of others) are the two major functions. Egocentric speech is most often used as a self-directive – giving instructions to oneself. Once this speech becomes internalized, it can regulate behaviour for both personal and social motives.

The connection between language and thought is yet another source of disagreement among psychologists. A range of speculations is presented, from strong linguistic-relativity (Whorf and Sapir), in which it is speculated that language determines thought, to strong forms of cognitive hypotheses (see Cromer[18]), in which it is held that we can use linguistic structures largely because of our cognitive abilities. A weak form of this latter hypothesis is proposed by Vygotsky, namely, that language and thought start from different origins at birth and gradually, but only partially, merge in the early years of life. Figure 8.2 summarizes the possibilities of pre-linguistic thought and pre-intellectual speech either fusing to become interdependent or remaining throughout life as non-linguistic thought and non-intellectual speech.

We then dealt with Bruner's work on the place of language in concept formation and the theory of Osgood, which proposes that 'meaning' is ascribed to stimuli in accordance with the actual sensations experienced at the time the stimulus is presented. The representational mediation processes suggested by Osgood are responsible for the patterns of reaction (either physical or verbal) which occur on the next presentation of a stimulus.

Non-verbal communication was also held to be important to the teacher and for the deaf community. We communicate with our fellow human beings not only in words, but in all our actions.

A final section on teaching language skills developed the impact of the home and school. The work of Tough on early childhood experiences and the role of the family, particularly the mother, were discussed. A look at the place of talking, reading and writing at school in terms of the new arrangements of the National Curriculum concluded the chapter.

ENQUIRY AND DISCUSSION

(a)   Take tape-recordings of both monologue and dialogue of children at several ages (including pre-school children). Note:
(1) egocentric and socialized speech;
(2) virtuous errors;
(3) restricted and elaborate code and whether they are related to social class.
(b)   Examine the methods of language teaching in schools that you visit. Try to familiarize yourself with some of the modern programmes in action, if possible.
(c)   Discover what you can about non-verbal communication. Observe the non-verbal behaviour of children in the classroom and their reaction to different kinds of non-verbal activities of the teacher.
(d)   Read your tutor's recommended texts with an eye towards the problems facing teachers who are in schools where the catchment area is largely from ethnic minorities. What problems face the teacher of immigrant children?
(e)   There is now a hefty body of literature commenting on the teaching of reading, writing, communication and the place of talk in the learning process. Using the references in the relevant notes at the end of the chapter, analyse the practical advice given on talking, reading and writing at (i) pre-school or (ii) primary or (iii) secondary level depending on your chosen school age.
(f)   It is necessary for students going out on school practice in a junior school to ascertain the levels of competence in reading and writing of those in their class. How is this achieved?

NOTES AND REFERENCES

1.   R. A. Gardner and B. T. Gardner, 'Teaching sign language to a chimpanzee', *Science*, **165**, 664–672 (1969). The Gardners have had a little more success in teaching chimpanzees a

hand sign language, whilst D. Premack, University of California, has managed to teach a chimp a simple communication device using shapes which act as symbolic characters. These results can be found in N. Calder, *The Mind of Man*, BBC Publications, London, 1970. Note that in both cases the chimp must operate the system manually and not vocally.

2. P. Herriot, *An Introduction to the Psychology of Language*, Methuen, London, 1976.
3. A clear analysis of language structure can be found in J. B. Carroll, *Language and Thought*, Prentice Hall, Englewood Cliffs, NJ, 1964.
4. D. H. Hymes, 'The functions of speech', in J. P. De Cecco (ed.), *The Psychology of Language, Thought and Instruction*, Holt, Rinehart and Winston, New York, 1967.
5. An upsurge of interest in Vygotsky's ideas on the role of speech in the development of thinking is summarized in L. C. Moll (ed.), *Vygotsky and Education: Instructional Implications and Applications of Sociohistorical Psychology*, Cambridge University Press, Cambridge, 1990. Also see J. V. Wertsch (ed.), *Culture, Communication and Cognition: Vygotskian Perspectives*, Cambridge University Press, Cambridge, 1985.
6. D. M. Ricks, 'The beginnings of vocal communication in infants and autistic children', unpublished Ph.D. thesis, University of London.
7. B. F. Skinner, *Verbal Behavior*, Appleton-Century-Crofts, New York, 1957.
8. H. Keller, *The Story of My Life*, Doubleday, New York, 1917.
9. J. Lyons, *Chomsky*, Fontana Modern Masters, London, 1970, and J. Aitchison, *The Articulate Mammal: An Introduction to Psycholinguistics*, Hutchinson, London, 1976.
10. P. Herriot, *Language and Teaching: A Psychological View*, Methuen, London, 1971.
11. (R) J. McLeish and J. Martin, 'Verbal behavior: a review and experimental analysis', *J. Gen. Psychol.*, **93**, 3–66 (1975).
12. R. Jakobson, *Child Language, Aphasia and Phonological Universals*, Mouton, The Hague, first published 1941, translated 1968.
13. B. Dodd, 'Effects of social and vocal stimulation on infant babbling', *Dev. Psychol.*, **7**, 8–83 (1972).
14. M. Mead, *Mind, Self and Society*, University of Chicago Press, Chicago, 1934.
15. A. F. Watts, *The Language and Mental Development of Children*, Harrap, London, 1955 (reprint); E. H. Lenneberg also gives an account of word counts in a chapter in F. Smith and G. A. Miller (eds), *The Genesis of Language*, MIT Press, Cambridge, MA, 1966. For recent research, see G. A. Miller and P. M. Gildea, 'How children learn words', *Scientific American*, **257**, 94–99 (1987).
16. J. Berko, 'The child's learning of English morphology', *Word*, **14**, 150–177 (1958).
17. M. C. Templin, *Certain Language Skills in Children*, Minnesota University Press, Minneapolis, 1957.
18. R. F. Cromer, 'The development of language and cognition: the cognition hypothesis', in B. Foss (ed.), *New Perspectives in Child Development*, Penguin, Harmondsworth, 1974.
19. For a summary of the Sapir–Whorf hypothesis consult D. I. Slobin, *Psycholinguistics*, Scott, Foresman, Glenview, IL, 1971.
20. B. L. Whorf, *Collected Papers in Metalinguistics*, Department of State, Washington, DC, 1952.
21. R. Brown, *A First Language*, Harvard University Press, 1973. See also H. Sinclair-de-Zwart, 'Developmental linguistics', in D. Elkind and J. H. Flavell (eds), *Studies in Cognitive Development*, Oxford University Press, London, 1969.
22. E. H. Lenneberg and J. M. Roberts's work is discussed in G. A. Miller and D. McNeill, 'Psycholinguistics', in G. Lindsey and E. Aronson (eds), *The Handbook of Social Psychology*, vol. 3, Addison-Wesley, New York, 1969 (2nd edn).
23. L. S. Vygotsky, *Thought and Language*, translated by E. Haufmann and C. Vakar, MIT Press, Cambridge, MA, 1962.
24. (R) J. S. Bruner, 'The course of cognitive growth', *Am. Psychol.*, **19**, 1–15 (1964).
25. C. E. Osgood, G. J. Suci and P. Tannenbaum, *The Measurement of Meaning*, University of Illinois Press, Urbana, 1957.
26. (R) B. Thompson, 'Self-concepts among secondary school pupils', *Educ. Res.*, **17**, 41–47 (1974).

27.   J. Greene, *Memory, Thinking and Language. Topics in Cognitive Psychology*, Methuen, London, 1987.

28.   P. E. Vernon, 'Expressive movements', in *Personality Tests and Assessments*, Methuen, London, 1953, Chapter 4.

29.   M. Argyle, *The Psychology of Interpersonal Behaviour*, Penguin, Harmondsworth, 1978 (3rd edn); M. Argyle and P. Trower, *Person to Person: Ways of Communicating*, Harper and Row, London, 1979; D. Morris, *Manwatching*, Cape, London, 1977.

30.   Several books are now appearing about BSL. For an introduction to the subject see M. Deuchar, *British Sign Language*, Routledge and Kegan Paul, London, 1984, or J. G. Kyle and B. Woll, *Sign Language: The Study of Deaf People and Their Language*, Cambridge University Press, Cambridge, 1985. Books and dictionaries of signs are now being published – see the *Sign and Say* series published by the Royal National Institute for the Deaf (RNID); C. Smith, *Communication Link*, Beverley School for the Deaf, Middlesbrough, or E. Scott-Gibson, *The Dictionary of British Sign Language*, Faber and Faber, London, 1992.

31.   D. M. Denton, 'The philosophy of Total Communication', *Br. Deaf News*, August 1976.

32.   L. Evans, *Total Communication: Structure and Strategy*, Gallaudet College Press, Washington, DC, 1982.

33.   Summarized in M. Stubbs and H. Hillier (eds), *Readings on Language, Schools and Classrooms*, Routledge, Chapman and Hall, London, 1983. See also D. Lawton, *Social Class, Language and Education*, Routledge and Kegan Paul, London, 1968.

34.   Described in B. Bernstein, *Class, Codes and Control*, vol. 1 (1971) and vol. 2 (1973), Routledge and Kegan Paul, London.

35.   For a discussion by W. Labov see 'The logic of non-standard English', in A. Cashdan and E. Grugeon (eds), *Language in Education*, Routledge and Kegan Paul, London, 1970.

36.   J. Tough, *The Development of Meaning: A Study of Children's Use of Language*, Allen and Unwin, London, 1976.

37.   J. Tough, *Listening to Children Talking*, Schools Council Communication Skills in Early Childhood Project, Ward Lock, London, 1976.

38.   The Open University has produced a series under the heading of English, Language and Education. Examples are, M. MacLure, T. Phillips and A. Wilkinson, *Oracy Matters*, 1988; C. Sarland, *Young People Reading: Culture and Response*, 1991; J. Nicholls, A. Bauers, D. Pettitt, V. Redgwell, E. Seaman and G. Watson, *Beginning Writing*, 1989. But many other useful titles appear in the series.

39.   National Curriculum Council, *National Curriculum English: The Case for Revising the Order*, 1992, and *Aspects of English: English in the National Curriculum in Key Stages 1 to 4* – teachers' notes, 1991.

40.   (R) *Concept 7-9*, Arnold, Leeds, 1972, was an early example of a Schools Council programme (produced by staff at Birmingham University).

41.   A readable summary of the earlier work appears in 'Children and programmes: how shall we educate the young child?', in A. Davies (ed.), *Language and Learning in Early Childhood*, Heinemann, London, in association with the SSRC and SCRE, 1977. See also C. Criper and A. Davies, 'Research on spoken language in primary school', in the above book; J. Tough, *Talking and Learning: A Guide to Fostering Communication Skills in the Nursery and Infant School*, Ward Lock, London, 1977.

42.   *Head Start* – an attempt to 'improve' intellectual skills of socially and culturally deprived children using enrichment programmes at pre-school ages. For an introduction see M. Pines, *Revolution in Learning. The Years from Birth to Six*, Harper and Row, New York, 1966; D. M. Gahagan and G. A. Gahagan, *Talk Reform: Explorations in Language for Infant School Children*, Routledge and Kegan Paul, London, 1970.

43.   P. S. Doughty, J. J. Pearce and G. M. Thornton, *Language in Use*, Arnold, London, 1971. For recent evidence in support of pre-school provision see K. Sylva, 'Some lasting effects of pre-school provision – or the Emperor wore clothes after all', *Education Section Review*, British Psychological Society, 7, 10–16 (1983); L. J. Schweinhart and D. P. Weikart, 'Young children grow up: the effects of the Perry Preschool Program on youths through age 15', Ypsilanti, MI, *Monographs of the High Scope Educational Research*

Foundation no. 27 (1980); I. Lazar and R. Darlington, *Lasting Effects of Early Education: A Report from the Consortium for Longitudinal Studies*, Monographs of the Society for Research in Child Development, no. 195 (1982).

44. J. Bruner, *Child's Talk: Learning to Use Language*, Oxford University Press, Oxford, 1983.
45. M. M. Clark, 'Language and reading: research trends', in A. Davies (ed.), *Problems of Language and Learning*, Heinemann, in association with the SSRC and SCRE, London, 1975. See also the discussant's comments (J. E. Merritt) following Clark's paper.
46. H. Francis, 'Reading development in school', in N. Bennett and C. Desforges (eds), *Recent Advances in Classroom Research*, Monograph No. 2 of the *British Journal of Educational Psychology*, Scottish Academic Press, Edinburgh, 1985. P. Horner, 'Learning and teaching reading skills', in D. Fontana (ed.), *The Education of the Young Child*, Blackwell, Oxford, 1984 (2nd edn). Also see a recent paper linking Piaget's work to reading by T. Roberts, 'Piagetian theory and the teaching of reading', *Educ. Res.*, 26, 77–81 (1984).
47. J. T. Williams, *Learning to Write, or Writing to Learn?*, NFER, London, 1977.
48. J. Britton, T. Burgess, N. Martin, A. McCleod and H. Rosen, *The Development of Writing Abilities (11–18)*, Macmillan Education, London, 1975.
49. Writing Across the Curriculum Project, Schools Council, discussion pamphlets for teachers 1973–75.
50. R. Beard, *Children's Writing in the Primary School*, Hodder and Stoughton, Sevenoaks, 1984.

FURTHER READING

D. Barnes, J. Britton and H. Rosen, *Language, the Learner and the School*, Penguin, Harmondsworth, 1971 (revision).

A. Ellis and G. Beattie, *The Psychology of Language and Communication*, Erlbaum, Hove, 1992.

J. Greene, *Memory, Thinking and Language: Topics in Cognitive Psychology*, Methuen, London, 1987.

P. Herriot, *Language and Teaching, A Psychological View*, Methuen, London, 1971. This is a basic text intended for students and teachers.

M. Stubbs, *Language, Schools and Classrooms*, Methuen, London, 1976.

J. Tough, 'The development and use of language', in D. Fontana (ed.), *The Education of the Young Child*, Blackwell, Oxford, 1984.

Chapter 9

Human Intelligence

Few topics in psychology can have attracted more widespread attention than intelligence. The reasons are not hard to find. Up to quite recently, everyone's educational and career prospects hung almost entirely on standardized tests of number, verbal and general ability and subjective assessments by teachers; the confirmation of educationally subnormal children (ESN) for purposes of providing special educational facilities has been based on IQ tests; the civil service, armed forces, some professions such as nursing and even some universities of late include an IQ test in their selection procedures. The subject is also a tender spot for many social scientists, who see it as having a divisive effect in social and ethnic matters, and it must be admitted that intelligence measurement has had a decisive influence on the educational and occupational lifestyles of many people. However, the exploration of human ability is inevitable. It is almost a platitude to say that an intelligent creature will question the nature of its intelligence.

The existence of differences in the distribution of human abilities is self-evident. Heim[1] defines intelligent activity as consisting of 'grasping the essentials in a given situation and responding appropriately to them' and we are all well aware that some can cope with certain situations better than others. Thus the detection and measurement of differences are important for the teacher. It would be disastrous for children if we did not quickly recognize their cognitive strengths and weaknesses, because the intellectually dull cannot, in general, cope with the same cognitive tasks as the intellectually bright of the same age, although they may possess special skills in particular abilities. In some cases it is difficult to discover the scholastic potential of a child by observing school work and we need to resort to standardized tests of intelligence. This chapter, therefore, will be concerned with a discussion of how far we have got in defining the nature of intelligence, in assessing intelligent behaviour and in elaborating models of the intellect.

THE NATURE OF INTELLIGENT BEHAVIOUR

The word 'intelligence' has developed some unfortunate implicit meanings over the years. In common parlance it has erroneously come to mean a possession, something one has in a fixed quantity, and probably located in one's head! The concept of the intelligence quotient (IQ) is probably responsible for conveying the impression of intelligence as a quantity: 'She's a bright young thing – her intelligence is 140!'

The habit of looking on intelligence as a possession of precise dimensions (known as *reification*) has been discussed by Miles (**R**).[2] He recommends that we abandon the term 'intelligence' and replace it with the less ambiguous term 'intelligent behaviour'. In so doing we lay stress on the activity of a person exposed to certain kinds of experience and how he or she would respond. We can then define this behaviour as more or less intelligent. Of course, this still leaves undefined the vital question of *what* intelligent behaviour is. Nevertheless, having noted Miles's cautionary comments and the dangers of misusing the term 'intelligence', we shall continue to apply it in the text synonymously with intelligent behaviour.

Vernon,[3] in an address to the British Psychological Society, perceived three broad categories for defining intelligence. These were biological, psychological and operational. Biological definitions emphasize the individual's capacity to adjust or adapt to environmental stimuli. 'Adaptation' here refers to modifying behaviour either overtly or covertly as a result of experience. There is something of this definition in the work of Piaget. Hebb has also maintained that adaptation depends on the quality of neurological connections in the brain and CNS: high intelligence for him is founded on having a 'good' brain and CNS. Humans have certainly outstripped the animals in their gift as adaptors of, and to, environments, essentially by virtue of their more advanced neural endowment in the form of a large neocortex (see Chapter 2). But it still remains patently clear that many people are irreconcilably ill-adapted in particular situations. A popular, but overrated, example is that of some famous scholars, politicians and creative artists who have the utmost difficulty in catering for themselves in the mundane things of life. Another problem in studying biological adaptation as a definition of intelligence is the masking effect of our self-made systems which have overgrown and obscured our adaptive qualities from the hard biological facts of life.

Psychological definitions stress *mental efficiency* and the capacity for abstract reasoning which requires the use of symbolic language. Spearman's famous formulation of intelligent behaviour as 'the eduction of relations and correlates' is an example of a psychological definition. This approach accounts much more for the higher abstract conceptualization prevalent in humans. There is more recognition of verbal, numerical and spatial skills. Taking a common example from an intelligence test to illustrate Spearman's definition, find the missing word:

Hand is to arm as foot is to . . .

There are two statements here:

hand is to arm (A)
foot is to   (B)

The relationship we *educe* (infer) from statement (A) is based on our knowledge of limb attachments. Using this fact, we attempt to *correlate* the first part of the statement (B) with the second part, in this case 'leg'.

Operational definitions involve making detailed specifications of intelligent behaviour and then finding measures of these specifications. Intelligent behaviour thus becomes expressed in terms of these measures. As Miles **(R)**[2] so aptly puts it:

> psychologists have desired standardized tests – it is the items in these tests which are regarded as exemplars of the word intelligent (exemplars = actual or possible manifestations of behaviour which are claimed to be intelligent). Correct responses to these items shall be deemed to constitute acts of intelligent behaviour.

As the definition offered by Heim – intelligent activity consists of grasping the essentials in a given situation and responding appropriately to them – goes a long way towards embracing the biological and psychological views of intelligence in the design of intelligence tests while at the same time satisfying the common-sense view of intelligence, it has generally been adopted in designing tests. The expression 'intelligence is what intelligence tests measure' is often used to describe the operational definition, although, as we shall see, it is not really as superficial as this statement would suggest.

Intelligence A, B and C

A prevailing view of intelligent behaviour brings out the dynamic interplay between inborn potential and circumstances **(R)**.[4] One particularly instructive approach was elaborated by Hebb.[5] He distinguishes between *Intelligence A* and *Intelligence B*, which we can identify with the genotype and phenotype, respectively, of intelligence. For Hebb, Intelligence A represents an innate potential which depends entirely on neurological facilities and signifies the capacity of an individual to develop intelligent responses. Whether the individual realizes this capacity or not depends on his or her life-chances. Thus, Intelligence B represents a hypothetical level of development which has resulted from the interaction of Intelligence A and environmental influences.

Neither Intelligence A nor Intelligence B can be measured directly. As we have suggested above, Intelligence A is masked by the immediate impact of experience. In the case of Intelligence B, we would have to devise a vast array of measures in order to sample the numerous aspects of human ability. Note that we would be *sampling* intelligence, not measuring it directly. Intelligence B is not fixed because changes of environment produce variations during its emergence particularly in childhood and adolescence. Consequently we must expect to find anomalies in the sampling of Intelligence B between cultures or sub-cultures arising partly from major differences in child-rearing habits which encourage or inhibit mental development, partly because there will be natural variation in the genotypic distribution of intelligence between cultures (as one finds giants and pygmies), and partly because the sampling measures may favour some cultures more than others (verbal skills are often at a premium in some cultures).

Vernon[3] introduced the term *Intelligence C* to describe the sampling of Intelligence B using standardized tests. This is a very useful concept because IQ scores are often misguidedly taken as direct measures of Intelligence A or B, whereas they result from a sampling only of the latter. Much of the subsequent discussion will rest on evidence gathered using measures of Intelligence C. It is essential, therefore, to be aware of the special relationship between it and the other hypothesized origins of intelligence. The connection between Intelligence A and Intelligence C is, by definition, only fragmentary. As C samples B, and B is derived from A, we can assume a link between C and A. But it is virtually impossible to be certain of the precise relationship. Therefore we cannot regard an IQ score as a measure of innate capacity any more than we would regard it as an accurate measure of Intelligence B.

Information processing and intelligence[6]

The approach outlined above is very much in the psychometric IQ testing tradition. The last twenty years or so have seen a shift in the approach of some psychologists towards information-processing explanations of intelligent behaviour. IQ scores indicate *how much* of the quality we define as intelligence is exposed by the person doing the test, but it tells us little about *how* the individual arrived at the solution to questions in the test. Psychologists concerned with the information-processing approach to the study of intelligence would ask such questions as what rules govern the systematics of how a person arrives at a solution to a problem?; with a given knowledge base, what processing routines does a person use to arrive at a solution?; what parts do efficiency in speed and accuracy (power) of processing play?; and what aspects of the foregoing would be measured by conventional IQ tests? The aim of this approach is to examine how a person processes information to arrive at a solution and not just to look at the end product (the IQ score).

There are several kinds of process which could be examined. Amongst them are central nervous system attributes such as reaction times,[1] EEG (electroencephalograms, see Chapter 2)[1] and power tests. These have all been shown to correlate with IQ scores but the results are marginal.

Another approach postulated by Sternberg is called *componential*. A component is 'an elementary information process that operates upon internal representation of objects or symbols'.[8] There is speculation about how many components there are. The components are arrived at intuitively. For example, if one was trying to solve the problem:

glasses are to eyes as hearing aids are to ...

Sternberg suggests that one would use *encoding* and *comparison processes* – in encoding, the person is searching the long-term memory for the properties of glasses and eyes; in the comparison process he or she attempts to match the properties (cf. the eduction of relations and correlates mentioned earlier in the chapter).

This area is still speculative and readers who want to make a depth study of recent thinking in the area of intelligence should refer to the books mentioned in notes (6) and (8).

Multiple intelligences

Deciding on the specifications of intelligent behaviour has been quite a problem. Many people are still not convinced that we have succeeded in tapping all abilities. Presently

we shall look at some typical intelligence-test items which exemplify the kinds of specifications already widely accepted as demonstrating intelligent behaviour. Reasoning
tests containing analogies, synonyms, memory items and word and number series are
very common, but there may be talents which are not yet entirely susceptible to testing
in the conventional ways dictated by intelligence-test design. Creative thinking and
writing (Chapter 10), music or art, business acumen and cognitive development in the
Piagetian tradition have not all been convincingly measured, although recently some
have been incorporated into the British Ability Scale (see 'Criterion-referenced testing',
this Chapter). These activities seem, at a common-sense level, to require higher mental
processes. Also, at present we know more about *what* children can do in specified
circumstances than *how* they do it. This intractable problem of defining our terms of
reference arises because effects are more readily observed than causes; hence we have
concentrated deliberately on measuring the outward manifestations of intelligent
behaviour using test materials.

In a recent proposal by Gardner[9] a case is made for there being six independent
kinds of intelligent human behaviour. These are *linguistic, logical-mathematical,
spatial, musical, bodily-kinaesthetic* and *personal*. The first three are familiar in
contemporary test design as we have seen from the Vernon definitions, but the last
three have not been researched as thoroughly.

What evidence did Gardner use to isolate these intelligences? He looked at those
activities which (a) were affected by brain damage in different locations of the brain;
(b) were represented by exceptional people; (c) had unique core skills; (d) had distinct
developmental histories; (e) were plausible on historical and evolutionary grounds; and
(f) had support from psychological research.

The last three are more contentious. Musical ability incorporates pitch and rhythm
applied to performing and composing music. In fact, Gardner appears to define music
as 'sounds emitted at certain auditory frequencies and grouped according to a prescribed system'. Kinaesthetic ability has to do with body motion and manipulation,
including manual control. In addition to dancers and gymnasts, one might also include
surgeons and sports players. Personal intelligence includes *interpersonal* (that is understanding the moods and needs of others in such a way as to be capable of predicting
how others would behave in similar future circumstances) and *intrapersonal* – the
ability to understand one's own emotions and to harness them appropriately in one's
actions. A few people do one or more of these intelligent activities superlatively; others
seem quite unable. Gardner would maintain that there does not seem to be a correlation between them or with conventional measures of intelligence.

The next stage in the development of this theory is to show how the six intelligences
can be assessed and subsequently to verify if there is or is not a relationship between
them.

INTELLIGENCE TESTING

The work of Binet

At the turn of the century, Alfred Binet suggested that the French Ministry of Public
Instruction support him in devising a series of tests designed to pick out the mentally

defective and retarded children in state schools who were unlikely to benefit from the normal system. The idea was to segregate these children and provide them with special education more in keeping with their inabilities. This principle is still in operation today, although to a lesser extent. Binet's aim was to derive a scale of items answerable by about 75 per cent of children at given age intervals. The figure of 75 per cent was chosen because it was thought that the 'middle' 50 per cent (in ability) of an age group should be capable of solving the problems. Naturally the top 25 per cent should also have the ability, thus making 75 per cent in all. The performance of individual children was then compared with the expected performance of other age groups. If a child could answer questions for all age groups up to, say, nine years, the child's *mental age* was said to be nine years, irrespective of the actual (*chronological*) age. Sub-tests enabled the mental age to be assessed in two-monthly intervals from three years to about 13 years of age.

How did Binet decide on the sort of questions to ask the children? In the first place he used hunches from his observations of children in a variety of practical and theoretical tasks which appeared, at a common-sense level, to discriminate between their abilities. Items included naming or pointing to parts of the body, repeating digits or sentences, counting, producing rhymes for given words and defining familiar objects. For the most part the items were verbally biased. On referring back to his sample of scholastically bright, moderate and inadequate children he was able to choose items possessing the highest level of discrimination. The test has since undergone several revisions and translations, from the French as the Binet–Simon Test, the Stanford–Binet and latterly the Terman–Merrill version (1960), all used as individual tests. To avoid publishing examples of actual test items, which would give them a wide currency and therefore make them unreliable, it is better for the college or department to show sample materials from these tests.

The concept of mental age is most useful when we express it in terms of the chronological age of the child. Stern introduced the idea of *mental ratio*, which he derived by dividing the child's mental age by the actual age. The resulting ratio was thought by Stern to be constant for a given child. We now know that mental age, and in consequence the mental ratio, may have an erratic history.

The small number obtained for the mental ratio is awkward. Terman proposed, therefore, that the ratio be multiplied by 100 to give a more convenient range of numbers. The final figure obtained is known as an *intelligence quotient*, or IQ for short. If a child of 5 years 0 months has a mental age of 6 years 0 months (i.e. can answer items normally answered by six-year-olds), the mental ratio would be:

$$\text{mental ratio} = \frac{\text{mental age}}{\text{chronological age}} = \frac{6}{5} = 1.20$$

The intelligence quotient or IQ = 1.20 × 100 = 120. A child of six with a mental age of five would have an IQ of 83.33 recurring. Actually, we express IQs to the nearest whole number, in this case 83.

Binet's method is satisfactory only as long as we can produce cumulative norms for each age group. But as mental development beyond 15 or 16 years is irregular and sometimes non-existent, it is not possible to establish a continuous yardstick for comparison in the manner of Binet. Sooner or later mental development as measured by conventional tests tails off. Around 1939, David Wechsler created the Wechsler–

Bellevue tests of adult intelligence which went some way towards a scale suitable for testing beyond 15 years of age. He included 'performance' as well as verbal tests.

Modern test design

Norm-referenced testing

A method used extensively from Binet's time to the present, norm-referenced testing, employs the distribution of scores for each age group using representative samples, and they are then rescaled using a convenient mean and standard deviation (see Chapter 14). It compares the performance of an individual with that of a representative group from which 'norms' of performance have been derived. Usually the mean, no matter what value it may have in the first place, is made equal to 100. The distribution of the scores on each side of the mean is then usually manipulated so that about 70 per cent of the scores fall within the range from 85 to 115 (i.e. 15 points on either side of the newly created mean). For this method to work properly, the distribution has to be 'normal' or very near to normal (see Figure 9.1). That means the distribution of scores on either side of the mean will tail off in a regular and symmetrical fashion. If this distribution does not appear, the test is modified until it does. In other words, the normal distribution of IQ scores is not necessarily a fact of life but a feature of IQ test design. What is more, there is no direct evidence to suppose that 'intelligence' is normally distributed in society. So many factors of upbringing, inadequate sampling of intellectual skills, etc., already mentioned above, conspire against an accurate knowledge of IQ distributions. But their design is such as to impose the spread shown in the accompanying figure.

Figure 9.1 is based on the distribution with a mean of 100 and a standard deviation of 15 IQ points. There are, of course, an infinite number of means and standard deviations which are possible, but generally we adopt a mean of 100 and a standard

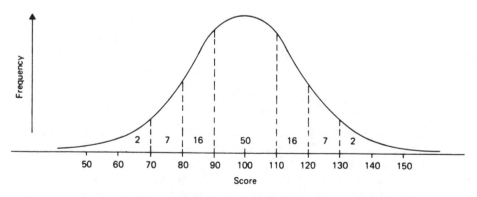

Figure 9.1 *Approximate normal distribution of people using a mean of 100 and standard deviation of 15. The figures under the curve represent the percentage of people falling within the limits indicated by the broken lines. Thus, 50 per cent fall between the scores of 90 and 110, 16 per cent between 80 and 90, or between 110 and 120, etc.*

deviation of 10, 15 or 20 points. This variation in the possible values provides the reason why we have to state the name of a test when quoting an IQ because, unless the norms are the same, the scores from different tests will not correspond. If we were comparing IQs from tests both with a mean of 100, but having, say, standard deviations of 10 and 20, an IQ of 120 on the first would be equivalent to an IQ of 140 on the second.

At one time it was common to find verbal descriptions associated with IQ ranges. For instance, those obtaining IQs greater than 140 were referred to as 'very superior' and those below an IQ of 70 (both on a scale having a mean of 100 and SD 15) as mentally deficient. In the UK these labels have fallen out of use. Later the term 'ESN' (educationally sub-normal) was used to refer to pupils who, because of mental inadequacy, were not able to benefit from conventional forms of education. The IQ of these children was used as one criterion amongst others, and a value of around 70 was regarded as critical. In the 11+ examination, a figure of 115 was often quoted as the cut-off point above which pupils were deemed suitable for a grammar school education. This amounted to roughly 16 per cent of an age group (see Figure 9.1).

Criterion-referenced testing

The comparison of a person's performance on any standardized test with that of others serves as an indicator of relative capacity and can be one of several clues in the diagnosis of, for example, actual or potential school performance. However, norm-referenced tests are not really designed to answer questions about a child's level of performance in a particular task or to help in the diagnosis of performance. To do this one would need to establish a series of criteria – hurdles which need to be cleared – in order to be able to judge whether a level or stage had been reached by an individual. In other words, we decide on criteria which we judge should have been achieved by an individual. There is no half-way house: the person either does or does not achieve a predetermined level of performance. An example from arithmetic might be to ask whether a child can subtract single digits. The criterion for successful achievement might be reached when a child can answer, say, ten consecutive problems correctly or can achieve eight correct answers in 10 problems. Note that the criterion is not necessarily based on age norms or sample norms, although teachers do operate on notional expectations of particular age groups.

There are several useful basic principles applied in the design of criterion-referenced tests.[10] First, the task or tasks to be achieved must be clearly defined at the outset. This is really an exercise in curriculum planning and analysis (see Chapter 16). Second, the purposes of the tasks must be clearly understood. For example, what is to be achieved in fulfilling a task (to identify, to describe, to calculate)? Third, the standard required from the pupils must be decided beforehand. It may be that the teacher requires answers to be 100 per cent correct (in a small, comparatively undemanding task), or some lower level of performance may be regarded as satisfactory (for example 80 per cent correct). *Mastery testing* is sometimes an alternative term for this criterion; that is, the criterion set is regarded as sufficient to conclude that, if it is reached, the individual can be said to have mastered the task. Fourth, each topic tested should be adequately sampled. One or two problems, for instance, in number or spelling may not be sufficient to test out mastery. Fifth, there must be an adequate scoring and feedback system which describes the learning tasks of the pupil.

One advantage of this approach is that judgements about progress are made in terms of a child's personal progress. Monitoring is very much geared to the differences between children, and therefore to the needs and pace of the individual child. The method is also very helpful in profiling where it is required to plot the progress of a pupil. Nevertheless, there is bound to be some norm-referencing involved. Decisions about what topics to choose, at what level to pitch the difficulty and the definition of satisfactory mastery criteria are largely based on a teacher's knowledge of what can be expected of a child at a given age or standard – and this is in a sense relying on norms built up during teaching experience.

A recent criterion-referenced test for cognitive evaluation, called the British Ability Scales (BAS), has been devised by Elliott and co-workers (1983, **R**).[11] The scales are usable between $2\frac{1}{2}$ and 17 years of age. There are 23 scales divided into tests which cover a wide range of different abilities such as speed of problem-solving, reasoning (including developmental scales), spatial imagery, perceptual matching, short-term memory, fluency and scholastic achievement (see Table 9.1). A particular kind of scaling (*Rasch* scaling) is used which allows norm-free and sample-free estimates to be made. A social reasoning scale has yet another kind of scaling, by which an estimate of developmental stages in reasoning can be made. The scales can be used in individual cases for measuring changes in abilities, drawing up profiles and calculating IQs. The versatility of the BAS makes it a most effective tool in educational psychology.

Intelligence test items

Over the years from Binet's earliest work, we have amassed many items thought to reflect reasoning ability. Let us look at some of the commonest kinds of item.[12] They have been specially compiled for the text and are not taken from existing IQ tests. It will be clear to students that we cannot use standardized items from tests because they are 'closed', that is, their content is subject to restrictions of both publication and circulation. (See reference in note (3) for more examples.) Answers appear at the end of the chapter.

Analogies

An example has already been provided to demonstrate Spearman's 'eduction of relations and correlates'. Here are a few more:

Choose the correct alternative:

1. Rein is to rain as stem is to
    (a) item (b) twig (c) seem (d) reign
2. Male is to female as dog is to
    (a) cat (b) vixen (c) canine (d) bitch
3. Author is to words as (CONDUCTOR, COMPOSER, PLAYER) is to (MUSIC, NOTES ORCHESTRA).

Table 9.1 *The British Ability Scales (from NFER-Nelson promotion pamphlet).*

		Items	Age Range
Speed of Information Processing			
1. Speed of Information Processing	4 disposable booklets of simple number exercises, differentiating between children's abilities in terms of time, not power.	40	8–17
Reasoning			
2. Formal Operational Thinking	Reasoning exercises based on illustration of pairs of boys and girls.	13	8–17
3. Matrices	Children are required to draw the correct solution in the blank square of a matrix.	28	5–17
4. Similarities	Children listen to three words (e.g. orange, strawberry, banana) and explain why they are similar.	21	5–17
5. Social Reasoning	Children evaluate stories told to them from the manual. Their responses are categorized in terms of four developmental stages.	7	5–17
Spatial Imagery			
6/7. Block Design – Level and Power	Children reconstruct two-dimensional patterns using blocks. The children can be scored in two ways: for accuracy (level) and for accuracy and speed (power).	16	4–17
8. Rotation of Letter-Like Forms	A small wooden doll is placed on the opposite side of the stimulus design from the child, who has to visualize how the design appears to the doll and then select from six alternatives.	10	8–14
9. Visualization of Cubes	Matching patterned blocks to one of four alternative pictures.	18	8–17
Perceptual Matching			
10. Copying	Children are required to copy designs and letter-like characters while the design is in front of them.	19	4–8
11. Matching Letter-Like Forms	Matching a stimulus figure to one of six representations of it viewed from different angles.	10	5–9
12. Verbal–Tactile Matching	Two bags are used from which children are asked to select: (i) objects with certain characteristics (ii) named items.	19	2½–8
Short-Term Memory			
13/14. Immediate Visual Recall/Delayed Visual Recall	A card showing 20 objects is shown for 2 minutes. The child has to recall the objects verbally at once, and then after 20 minutes.	19	5–17
15. Recall of Designs	The child draws a design from memory after being shown it for 5 seconds.	19	5–17
16. Recall of Digits	Digit strings are presented at the rate of 2 digits per second and the child is asked to repeat them in the correct sequence.	36	2½–17
17. Visual Recognition	Drawings of toys and non-representational figures are shown to children for 5 seconds. They then have to select these from a number of alternatives shown on a second card.	17	2½–8

Table 9.1 *Cont*

		Items	Age Range
Retrieval and Application of Knowledge			
18. Basic Number Skills	A new scale combining the original Basic Arithmetic and Early Number Scales, with the addition of 28 new items. It focuses on the number skills which will lead to a basic competence in arithmetical calculation.	68	2½–14½
19. Naming Vocabulary	Naming objects in the room or on picture cards.	20	2½–8
20. Verbal Comprehension	Children are asked to carry out operations using toys in response to verbal commands.	27	2½–8
21. Verbal Fluency	A creativity test comprising a variety of activities, object naming, deducing consequences from events, ink blot tests. This scale is scored solely on the number of distinct ideas the child produces.	6	4–17
22. Word Definitions		37	5–17
23. Word Reading		90	5–14

Synonyms

Choose one term in the bracket which means nearly the same as:

1. SLAKE (GROW, DRINK, QUENCH, POUR, LOOSE)
2. PREEN (TEACH, GLAND, BE ANNOYED, TRIM FEATHERS).

Antonyms

Choose one word in the first bracket which means the opposite of one word in the second bracket:

1. (TAP, TUP, TOP) (EWE, EYE, EVE)

Which one of the four words on the right bears a similar relationship to each of the words on the left:

2. EASY, SOFT (PUTTY, HARD, SIMPLE, BRITTLE).

Memory

The subject is given digits orally and is asked to repeat them. Most adults can manage to repeat around seven (telephone numbers and car registrations are about the limit). In young children, short sentences are sometimes given (Binet tests, for example).

Number and letter series (induction tests)

Fill in the missing number or letter:

1. 60, 12, 3, 1, −, −
2. JFMAM −, −
3. 2, 6, 12, 20, −, −.

Ordering and classification

Arrange the following in descending order of complexity:

1. carnivore, vertebrate, animal, domestic cats, feline animals

Which word does not belong in the list:

2. riot, subversion, turmoil, meeting, rebellion
3. bit, piece, fraction, portion, a half.

Examples of non-verbal items

1. Find the patterns for the four missing pieces:

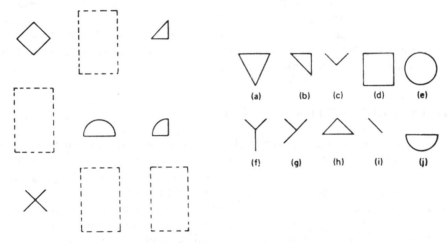

2. The two figures on the left have a feature in common. One *only* of the figures on the right has *not* the same feature. Which is it?

3.

Three examples similar to the BAS

Speed of information processing. Each item consists of a page with a block of five rows and five columns of groups of numbers. The groups have three to five digits.

The first row of a three-digit block might be:

392   574   175   589   541

The task is to cross out the largest number in each row as quickly as possible whilst being timed.

Social reasoning.   The scale is adapted from Kohlberg's analysis of the development of moral reasoning. The child is asked to evaluate a verbally presented problem and the responses are categorized qualitatively in the four developmental levels.

> You are walking past a classroom and you see a pupil by himself in the room taking something from someone else's desk. What would you do about it? Why?

The responses to the question would be scored from a predetermined classification from 0 to 3, representing the four categories of developmental level.

Perceptual matching (verbal–tactile matching).   Two bags, one green and one white, are hung round a child's neck. They contain objects of various shapes, e.g. cubes, sticks, balls, and various common materials, e.g. wool, foam. The child is shown a demonstration item and is required to feel in one of the bags for a similar shape or to pull out an object of a particular material.

SOME USES OF INTELLIGENCE TESTS

There are several ways of classifying intelligence tests. We can think of them in terms of: (a) the group for whom they are intended (children or adults, low-grade or high-grade intellect, culture fair – that is, 'free' from cultural bias which might depress or elevate scores unfairly); (b) whether they are for individual or group administration; (c) the general or special skills of those tested (verbal, spatial, performance, memory, numerical, etc.). When we talk of intelligence tests it is important to know and to specify which combination of these special features applies. It is also essential to note that intelligence test administration and interpretation is a skilled affair. Most tests require tuition and training before they can be used to the best advantage for reliable and valid results.

Verbal group tests[12]

Tests designed specifically for use with large numbers of children or adults have been widely used since their introduction as a grammar-school selection device. Their advantages are that large samples can be reliably tested in a relatively short time in the same conditions. They are particularly reliable for groups of older children and adults where it is clear that written instructions are understood and motivation is likely to be maintained throughout the testing period. Where they do not prove reliable is in testing those at the extremes of the distribution. Also, with dull children the opportunity for personal contact and for elaborating on the test instructions is vital. It is also helpful to construct separate tests of high-grade intelligence[12] to obtain a greater degree of refinement and discrimination in the score range. This follows because, where a test is intended to cover the whole range, the scores at the tail ends of the distribution cannot be sufficiently widespread to give a distinctive spectrum of scores.

Non-verbal group tests

Tests such as Raven's Progressive Matrices have been used as a supplementary and alternative measure in secondary schools. They are *not* culture fair, but they do provide additional evidence of mental competence where, for some reason, verbal opportunities in our culture have not been satisfactory. Specific group tests of number, mechanical and spatial skills are also available.

Individual tests

These are most helpful as diagnostic tools with pre-school children, infant-school children and children with special needs, where written communication, reading skills, motivation and concentration are among the particular problems which preclude group testing. The preamble to many group tests attempts to encourage continued participation during the testing session. Often the tests begin with a warming-up period to ensure that test instructions are fully understood. But even this care would not be adequate for young children. The administration of individual tests is a highly skilled and time-consuming job needing patience and a knowledge of how to extract the best from young people. They form a crucial part of the diagnostic service provided by the local education authority's psychological service, and student teachers should familiarize themselves with the functions of this service in relation to schoolchildren.

Selection tests

In the early part of the twentieth century there were several people designing group tests for use with 10- to 11-year-olds. Thomson,[13] for example, developed annual tests to help in the selection of 10- to 11-year-olds for education in grammar schools in Northumberland. Like so many at the time, he was conscious of the fact that many bright boys and girls from poor and socially deprived homes were not able to pay for grammar school education. The Northumberland tests were designed to overcome this problem. Children at 10 and 11 years of age from deprived backgrounds who passed the IQ test were offered free places by the local education authority (LEA). The idea developed into the 11 + selection system, which is still used in some LEAs today. These tests now contain verbal, non-verbal, numerical and spatial items as well as a test of English language.

Occupational selection procedures sometimes include IQ tests. The DC test[12] for entry to nurse training is one such example. The standard entry requirement to nurse training is five GCSE passes, usually in any subject. Those who have not got five GCSEs can take the DC test. It consists of verbal, non-verbal, spatial, numerical, tables and graphical items as well as a comprehension test.

Tests for babies

Tests for babies from the prenatal stage onwards have been the focus of several researches. The best-known test battery in the UK was compiled by Griffiths,[14] who derived an intelligence score from five major indices of infant behaviour skills. They are: (a) locomotor (body movement, sitting, walking); (b) personal–social (reaction to other humans); (c) hearing and speech (response to aural stimuli, vocalization skills); (d) eye and hand (response to visual stimuli, hand–eye co-ordination, use of hands); and (e) performance (broadly reaction and manipulative skills in situations conjured up by the experimenter – for example, if a baby is holding wooden blocks in both hands what will it do if a third block is presented?). The norms were obtained by observing many babies and noting the average achievement for each age in the five ways mentioned above. The reliability of the scores (how similar the performance is in several testings of the same child or group of children), particularly below two years of age, is not very high. Progress in the first year is so rapid and erratic that precise measurements are not really feasible. However, as descriptive norms for use in diagnostic cases, these measurements have proved to be of immense value.

Since the early test of Griffiths, there have been several more. The *McCarthy Scales of Children's Abilities*[14] were designed to cover the age range of two and a half to eight and a half years, giving a diagnostic profile in verbal, non-verbal, spatial, memory and motor skills. A British version has been compiled by Lynch *et al.*[14]

Gifted children[15]

What is giftedness? At first sight, one might suppose that giftedness was an easy concept to define, but it is not. Conceptions[15] ranging in explanations from social, individual, cognitive processing to developmental now abound. The individual, test-based definitions are amongst the most prominent in the history of the psychology of giftedness and the following results largely reflect this tradition.

Several methods of helping the gifted have been tried, with varying degrees of success. The commonest, often in combination, are *segregation* and grouping according to ability, *acceleration* and *enrichment*.

The separation of very able pupils is not new. Grammar and comprehensive schools use this method in preparing pupils for A and GCSE level subjects. Some introduce segregation from the first form (11-year-olds). Others start in the third year. Many readers will already know about these systems from their own schooldays and may well have been part of the 'A' band (or some other title aimed at disguising the fact that it is a bright group, although this fact is nearly always known to the pupils). In some countries (Russia, for example), special schools have been created for the gifted, particularly those gifted in maths and science.

Acceleration programmes consist of taking children out of the age group they would normally be in and providing them with a programme usually given to older children. This is done either by giving them separate lessons or by placing them with older children (vertical streaming). Vertical streaming does raise questions about the appropriateness of mixing children who could have widely different levels of physical, emotional and social competence.

Enrichment is a teaching procedure commonly used in North America. It involves giving children (singly or in small groups) a stimulating curriculum, while keeping them in the same class as their peers. The enrichment may range from a special corner with advanced books and materials to a full programme of lessons, projects and visits designed to stimulate the gifted (see Vernon *et al.*).[16] Other recent pamphlets for parents and teachers, e.g. *Spot the Gifted Child* and *Helping Children of High Intelligence*,[16] make interesting reading.

There has been growing and world-wide interest in the identification of gifted children. All human societies concerned with advancement, both humanitarian and technological, have become conscious of the need to identify and nurture those of its members who have exceptional talents. Several recent researches[16] have concentrated on the study of gifted children and have come out strongly in conveying the message that the highly gifted, the potential leaders in most walks of life, are sometimes ignored in our educational system, and the argument that they will 'make out' despite this neglect is irresponsible. Definitions of giftedness vary somewhat, but a widely accepted method is to settle for those with IQs of 140 or more on a test having a mean of 100 and standard deviation of 15. This would place them in the group representing about 0.5 per cent in the top part of the population of IQ scores.

Frequently, other kinds of evidence are used to build the picture, from the verbal reports of teachers and parents to measures of personality. The references[16] give some indication of the problems of teaching these children. Furthermore, IQ tests do not cover the full range of ways in which we might define giftedness; for example, tests of very high quality in art, writing, music, business have not been designed. As we saw in Gardner's theory[9] above, musical, personal and kinaesthetic abilities are feasible but unmeasured abilities.

In summary then, modern intelligence tests can be used as diagnostic tools and as predictors of future performance. We have seen their use with mentally defective children and their small, but continued, place in secondary selection and streaming in both primary and secondary schools. Many schools still use them as an aid to streaming or remedial teaching. Vocational selection and guidance sometimes involves an IQ measure, particularly for entry into the forces or the civil service, and occasionally into the professions and industry. Also, some universities add an IQ test to the existing selection procedures as a prognosticator of degree success.

FACTORS INFLUENCING MEASURED INTELLIGENCE

Age

We have already remarked on the complications of measuring adult intelligence. This is caused partly by the irregular development of mental ability and partly by the decline in mental ability beyond adolescence. In general, mental ability increases with chronological age up to 14 or 15 years of age in those of average ability. Naturally there are exceptions and irregularities in the development of individuals, but in the main the ratio of mental to chronological age is steady to mid-adolescence, when a slow decline sets in until old age.[17] If mental age is decreasing as chronological age increases, the mental ratio will gradually decline; hence we cannot use the method adopted by Binet and his associates for ascertaining the intelligence of adults.

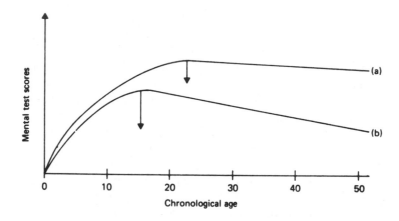

Figure 9.2 *A representative graph of mental development with chronological age.*
(a) Continued intellectual stimulus beyond mid-adolescence can lead to prolonged development and slower decline. Also more likely to be those of higher intelligence who avail themselves of the opportunity for continued intellectual work.
(b) Those who do not continue with intellectual pursuits beyond mid-adolescence experience an earlier and more rapid decline than those in (a) above.

There are, however, several limitations to be borne in mind when we are considering the results of research in this field. The particular methods and test materials we use to measure the ability of five-year-olds are conspicuously different from those for 15-year-olds or adults. Moreover, the longitudinal studies, in which the progress of an individual's mental development is plotted over a number of years, do not entirely support the evidence for this early decline in measured intelligence, as do the cross-sectional studies carried out by testing different age groups at one time. Some longitudinal studies show continued development up to 50 years of age, particularly in verbal skills, among those who continue academic studies. However, the present consensus of evidence (Figure 9.2) points to a slow decline which varies with the mental stimulation experienced by the individual. Those who continue to be mentally active after mid-adolescent schooling are more likely to have continued growth in verbal ability than others.[18] This fact has special significance at a time when more young people are staying in education, one consequence of which will be prolonged contact with verbal learning.

One thread of evidence for the decline is found in the researches of Horn,[18] who was investigating the growth of *fluid* and *crystallized* intelligence (see Cattell's theory later in the chapter). In this he was able to show that fluid intelligence, believed to be correlated with biological factors, deteriorates along with the normal physical decline of the body, and therefore rises up to early adulthood, and declines steadily thereafter (have pity on me, all you young readers!). But crystallized intelligence, associated with the accumulation of 'wisdom' and experience, rises steadily throughout life. Therefore, in measured intelligence, believed by Horn to be proportional to the sum of fluid and crystallized intelligence, there is a steady rise in performance up to middle age, followed by a steady decline thereafter.

Coaching and practice

Research into the effects of practice and coaching on ability test scores is extensive and the findings quite well established.[19] There is usually an overall improvement in scores as a result of coaching or practice.

We first need to distinguish between practice and coaching. *Practice* involves taking the same or parallel tests at intervals *without* any special instructions or rehearsal in the interval. *Coaching* involves teaching a testee (including self-help) the 'tricks' of how to take a test, of how to analyse and become familiar with the test instructions and types of items, of how to use time effectively, of working through trial items similar to those in the test to be taken and of overcoming anxiety by building confidence.

If a person sits the same test fairly soon after the first attempt, a practice effect is possible. The maximum gains are likely within a few weeks of the first test. Gains average about 5 IQ points. Gains are also possible if parallel forms are taken within a few weeks of each other. After several retakes, the scores level out – provided that the testee does not have any coaching. The score tends to level out after about five or six retakes. Practice effects are quite lasting. Gains have been recorded as long as a year after the first test. The effect is greatest when there is a wide variety of test items. The smallest gains come from verbal and comprehension tests, the largest from non-verbal and numerical tests. There appears to be little or no practice effect when there is a short practice session at the beginning of the test. For those who have never taken a test before, the practice effects are greatest.

Coaching without any practice in doing similar items to the final test is ineffective. It is usually the case that all coaching is accompanied by practice sessions. The typical gain after several hours of coaching is about 9 IQ points. In other words, coaching adds about another 4 points to practice effects. With several resits, the gains can be as much as 12 points on average. The effects of coaching reach a peak after a few hours. Further coaching leads to little improvement. Coaching gains, like practice gains, are smallest for verbal and comprehension tests and largest for non-verbal and numerical items. The effects of coaching decline more rapidly than is the case with practice.

Effects of home and school

There are striking differences in the way people from different cultures resolve their problems. Many may rarely, if ever, have used a symbolic code to solve abstract problems, as in verbal reasoning. The perceptual emphases of a culture must also have an influence on the solution of spatial tasks. For example, there is less preoccupation with linearity in some African tribes than in some western cultures, consequently the latter are more susceptible to vertical and horizontal line arrangements and to illusions.[20] It is hardly surprising, then, to find gross anomalies in the IQ measures of western and non-western cultures. The measurement of immigrant IQs is an obvious illustration. The art of devising intelligence tests which are reliable and valid for all cultures has never been accomplished satisfactorily. Some psychologists (Cattell, see later) claim to have found *culture-fair* or *culture-free* items, but the overwhelming opinion from the evidence is that there is no such thing as a culture-fair test. Whichever medium we try to communicate in – verbal, spatial, etc – it is evident that cultural differences produce variations in test results. Vernon[21] concludes that:

while western tests often worked well in other cultural groups especially when slightly adapted to increase their intelligibility and acceptability, it is generally preferable to devise new ones locally to suit the modes of perception, the language background and concepts of the particular culture.

Nearer home we find similar inadequacies of conventional tests when comparing people from different sub-cultures. Wiseman,[22] in large-scale research of 14-year-olds in the Manchester area, found, amongst other things, that an adverse environment is relatively more devastating for the intellectual development of the above-average child. His second important conclusion, which is a strong source of controversy, is that intelligence is more closely related to environmental factors (home-area circumstances such as birth- and death-rate, infantile mortality, percentage subnormal children, population density in the school catchment area) than to attainment at school. Douglas,[23] in a longitudinal study of socioeconomic, physical and intellectual variables from the prenatal stage onwards, confirms the mass of evidence showing differences between the IQs of children from different social backgrounds. Moreover, the difference widens as the children grow older. The importance of parental encouragement and enthusiasm in the academic progress of the children as a factor in improved performance at school is substantiated by his study. Other questions related to the inequality of opportunities for children from disadvantaged homes to develop their full intellectual potential, and the effect this has on their chances of succeeding in the 11 + regime or any selection system, are well documented elsewhere.[24]

Family size has been found to correlate negatively with measured intelligence, which suggests that children who belong to large families tend to have lower IQs than those of smaller families.[25] The reasons are still obscure. It could be that children with several brothers or sisters have less opportunity for adult contact and therefore are restricted in their linguistic exchanges. Or large families may be the product of less intelligent parents, thus giving less intelligent children. Also, the smaller family might enjoy greater economic and educational advantages than larger families. The influence of language opportunities is also of crucial significance in the development of verbal intellectual skills.[26]

Attempting to assess the influence of school on achievement while controlling for general ability and background factors is difficult. However, Jensen,[27] in a thorough, carefully designed project, compared the influence of the school system in California during the first eight years of schooling among black American, Mexican-American and white American children. His major conclusion was that children from different ethnic groups, by and large, made similar progress. Put another way, the schools did not depress or elevate the scholastic achievements of minority groups in comparison with majority groups. Furthermore, as time went by, there was no increase in whatever differences existed at the beginning of school life. Technically, a progressive increase in achievement differentials is known as a *cumulative deficit*, but Jensen found no evidence for such a deficit. He consequently concluded that, as far as the Californian State system of education was concerned, children from minority groups were not cheated of achievement opportunities in conventional educational settings. Implicitly, Jensen's work also points to the conclusion that children's intellectual potential has already been largely decided before formal schooling (Eysenck, 1972[28]). But the subject is still a source of heated dispute,[28] especially where the discussion involves the differences between ethnic or social groups (see also Kamin[35]).

Jensen[29] also makes the interesting proposal that environmental influences obey a 'threshold' effect. That is, below a certain range of intelligence (not specified precisely) the influence of the environment is of paramount importance, while above the range it becomes progressively less influential. The principle is said to work in the same way as the vitamin supply to the body. The latter can only assimilate so much (up to a certain threshold) beyond which further quantities are eliminated and serve no useful nutritional purposes. Also, the very bright are proportionately more able to cope with environmental disadvantages. In the next chapter we shall see that among the highly intelligent it becomes difficult to distinguish the more creative minds. Further, personality may play a vital role in the expression of intelligent behaviour.

Of particular interest to teachers is the effect, if any, of nutritional variations in the eating habits of children upon intelligence. Prominence has been given in recent years to companies claiming to have found a substance which will increase intelligence. Discovering certain food substances which could hold the key to increased problem-solving ability is likely to be a preoccupation of parents and teachers alike.

However, the research is far from conclusive and a recent series of papers in *The Psychologist*[30] (1992) shows the state of progress so far. The most optimistic conclusions by Eysenck are that:

> (1) fluid IQ can be increased significantly by dietary supplementation; (2) crystallised IQ cannot be so; (3) both conclusions may apply to certain types, amounts and times of supplementation, and should not be generalised beyond these limits; (4) duration and amount of supplementation multiply to give predicted increases; (5) increases in fluid IQ are most likely to occur in subsamples suffering from insufficient intake of vitamins and minerals . . .; (6) RDAs (Recommended Dietary Allowances) for vitamins and minerals (even American ones) may be too low and should be set at a higher level; (7) improvement of diet is the most obvious choice for producing IQ increases, but chemical supplementation is another, if inferior, choice.
>
> (note (30), p. 411)

The topic is going to develop in the coming years and readers should look at the research.[30]

Heredity and environment

The popular press and other mass media have often referred to the 'nature/nurture' controversy surrounding the subject of intelligence. The dispute centres on the dilemma of how our inherited qualities and developmental prospects interact to affect intelligent activity. The disputants seek answers to such questions as 'What is the relative influence and importance of inherited and constitutional characteristics in the growth of human ability?', 'Is intelligence really "innate general cognitive ability"?',[31] 'To what extent can social or ethnic disadvantages (whether inherited or developed) be influenced by educational programmes?' and 'Are human beings born equally endowed and therefore entirely at the mercy of the environment in creating variations in measured intelligence (Unesco, 1951), or in any case is the interaction of endowment and environment such that we cannot readily extricate their relative influence?'

The problem of the relative contributions of inherited intellectual qualities and environmental conditions in the determination of a person's measured intelligence, the well known 'nature/nurture' argument, has been obstinate and unresolved. In fact, the refined mathematical and methodological 'nit-picking' which the problem has generated would probably leave most students cold, and would be of little benefit in its detail. We shall, therefore, tread a middle way in looking briefly at the broad issues. There are very few who would ascribe all the variation in IQ to either environmental or genetic differences.

'Proof' that a particular proportion of measured intelligence is due to heredity or environment is not possible, and can only be estimated indirectly, since the two influences are interactive from the moment of conception (see Chapter 2). Teasing out the threads which are 'purely' innate or 'purely' environmental is not, as yet, within the capabilities of behavioural scientists. The main indirect lines of evidence have come from the study of intellectual genealogies, twin studies, and studies of relatives reared together and apart.

Galton's study[32] of eminent people showed that eminence seemed to be prevalent in some families more than in others – evidence of selective breeding in much the same way as producing fine racehorses. The study, unfortunately, did overlook the possibility that the home of an eminent person might have a marked effect on the children in terms of encouragement, availability of literature, the presence of a wide and varied collection of objects – enriched 'environment', 'intelligent' games and rituals, etc. At the other extreme we find the Kallikak family reported by Goddard.[33] A certain Martin Kallikak (false name) had children by two women, one feeble-minded, the other of normal intelligence. The feeble-minded mother gave rise to a high proportion of feeble-minded descendants, while the mother with normal intelligence had no feeble-minded children at all. At a pinch, we could argue that the living conditions of the feeble-minded parent would be most likely to foster dull children, although the contrast in the two sets of data is rather striking.

Twin studies form the most common line of investigation. Monozygotic twins – that is, two youngsters created from one fertilized egg which has accidentally broken apart at an early stage and given two identical eggs – have precisely the same genetic endowment. Dizygotic twins occur when two separate eggs are fertilized at roughly the same time and grow in the womb side by side. They have genetic relationships similar to those we might find among brothers and sisters (sometimes called *siblings*). A survey of the research literature on the correlations between the intelligence of people of varying degrees of family relationship reared together and apart has been conducted by Erlenmeyer-Kimling and Jarvik (**R**).[34] It shows an impressive picture of orderly decreases in the values of correlations from high for the monozygotic twins reared together to no correlation for unrelated people reared apart. Their work is reproduced in Figure 9.3, from which they conclude that the accumulated studies strongly support the opinion that 'intragroup resemblance in intellectual abilities increases in proportion to the degree of genetic relationship'. Note also the differences which can be accounted for by early environmental conditions. Take, for example, the extremes of the scale shown in Figure 9.3. The monozygotic twins with, by definition, identical inheritance, but reared apart, are not so closely related in measured intelligence as those reared together. Unrelated children reared apart give, as would be expected, a random relationship while, when unrelated children are reared together, their similar environment is sufficient to produce a positive correlation. The intervening variable in both these examples is child-rearing influences. We are left, then, in much the same dilemma as

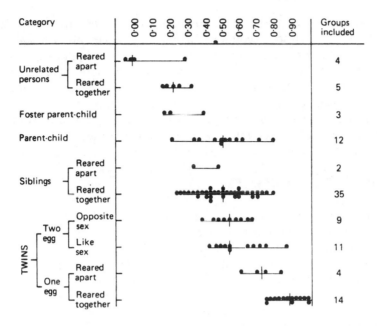

Figure 9.3 *Correlation coefficients for 'intelligence' test scores from 52 studies. Some studies reported data for more than one relationship category; some included more than one sample per category, giving a total of 99 groups. Over two-thirds of the correlation coefficients were derived from IQs, the remainder from special tests (for example, Primary Mental Abilities). Midparent–child correlation was used when available, otherwise mother–child correlation. Correlation coefficients obtained in each study are indicated by dark circles; medians are shown by vertical lines intersecting the horizontal lines which represent the ranges. Reprinted from L. Erlenmeyer-Kimling and L. F. Jarvik, 'Genetics and intelligence', Science, 142, 1478, © 1963 with permission of the American Association for the Advancement of Science.*

when we started, knowing that both nature and nurture are inextricably related in intellectual development.

The debate still rages. The contenders both accept the roles of genetic and environmental influences, but disagree about the extent of the influence of these two factors. Some, such as Eysenck,[35] have claimed that approximately 80 per cent of the variability in individual measures of intelligence can be explained by genetic factors. Others such as Kamin,[35] whilst not denying the influence of genetic factors, believe that their influence is very much less than 80 per cent. The arguments are clearly and concisely set out in a short pamphlet by Stott[35] who concludes that 'the interaction between heredity and environment is so continuous, intricate, variable, cumulative and specific that no general statement can be made about their relative contributions'.

As regards the tests of intelligence, Vernon[36] has also written an extensive book in which he concludes

> that there is no clear verdict in either direction. Genetic and environmental factors are always both involved. . . . Despite current attacks on tests in general (as well as on genetic explanations), they have much to contribute to the diagnosis of the type of education best suited to a child's needs and potentialities.

Locurto,[37] in a stimulating article, makes the suggestion that perhaps our efforts should shift in emphasis from that part of the equation which is concerned with the refined calculations of heritability (i.e. how much do we inherit), to that other part of the equation which is not accounted for by inheritance and is more likely to be susceptible to educational processes. In other words, we should be looking at the *malleability* of IQ – that is, what and how we can manipulate the environment so as to gain the maximum intellectual potential from a person. Evidence from pre-school intervention programmes, adopted siblings and within-family influences lend some support to this view. It should also be good news for teachers if, using suitable school curricula, they can enhance the intellectual prowess of children.

THE STRUCTURE OF ABILITIES

A common theme throughout the study of intelligence is the possibility that we possess a fundamental general ability which we bring to bear on all problems – a kind of general level of mental efficiency which we all possess in some degree. In the discussions above we met several kinds of items, all purporting to measure some aspect of this general intelligence. Verbal, numerical, spatial and mechanical skills were mentioned which, while displaying individual variations, nevertheless may be subsumed to give a level of ability we call 'g', general ability.

The question was first effectively examined around the turn of the century, when Spearman introduced a mathematical technique called *factor analysis*. He endeavoured to determine the extent to which all the various kinds of problems thought to reflect intelligence really did possess something in common. It is not an easy subject and the reader is advised to look at a basic text[38] for an understanding of the principles on which the method is based. For our present purpose, we will mention only enough to give the reader an idea of how the important models of the structure of human ability have appeared.

When two variables, e.g. size of house and the income of the occupant, alter together, we say they are correlated (see note (7) at the end of Chapter 14). With the variables we have chosen, it would be safe to conclude that the larger a person's income, the more likely it is that he or she will own a larger house. This relationship would give a positive, but not a perfect, correlation. Where an increase in one variable is accompanied by a decrease in a second (intelligence and family size), we have a negative correlation. Two unrelated variables (intelligence and eye colour) show zero correlation. If we obtain a systematic change in several variables it could well be that there is some common causal factor. For example, in the illustration using a person's income, we would probably find many other related variables, especially in material possessions (car, dishwasher, furniture, etc.), the common denominator being the person's salary. Applying this to human ability, suppose the scores on several tests purporting to identify intelligent behaviour were all positively intercorrelated. It could be concluded that there is a basic factor underpinning this common relationship. The mathematical procedure of factor analysis seeks to identify and isolate these common factors by using the correlations between the variables.

Spearman, using a prototype factor analysis, formulated his *Two-factor Theory*.[39] His view was rooted in the assumption that general ability – referred to for convenience as 'g' – accounted in substantial measure for differences in human performance. You will remember his belief that intelligence consisted of 'the eduction of

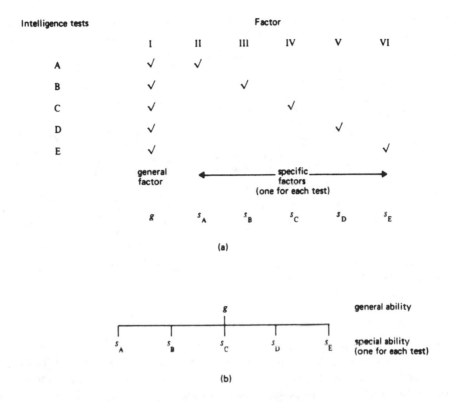

Figure 9.4 *Diagrammatic representation of Spearman's Two-factor Theory.*

relations and correlates'. Further, each test was thought to require a specific ability, '*s*', unique to each test. Specific ability accounted for the unevenness in an individual's score from one kind of test to another over and above minimum competence in all the tests (*g*). A child with high general ability, therefore, would be expected to perform well in most aspects of an intelligence test, while at the same time displaying variations in test scores arising from his or her special talents. Spearman's 'two factors', then, consisted of *g*-type and *s*-type factors.

Figure 9.4(a) shows that all the tests deemed to measure intelligence are sufficiently intercorrelated for them to appear together as factor I. Then follows a separate column for each test to indicate that certain variations in the test scores are due to the specific and unique demands made by each. A simpler diagrammatic view is given in Figure 9.4(b).

This over-simplified theory was soon superseded by the work of Sir Cyril Burt, who proposed the *Hierarchical Group-factor Theory*, widely supported in Great Britain. Spearman's choice of test material was restricted and insufficient to allow for the existence of groups of tests which reflected common skills. Many tests, for instance, require verbal ability in addition to a specific ability. Therefore Burt suggested 'group' factors as well as *g* and *s*. Group factors are illustrated in Figure 9.5, which also attempts to show the tree-like connections postulated in the hierarchical theory of Burt and developed by Vernon.[21]

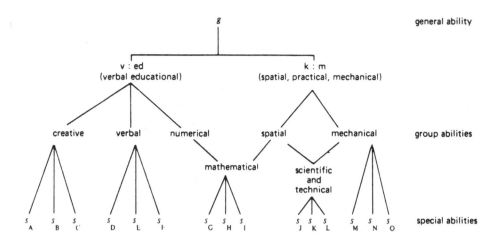

Figure 9.5 *Diagrammatic model of the hierarchical group-factor theory. These include some of the main group factors underlying tests relevant to educational and vocational achievements. Adapted from P. E. Vernon,* Intelligence and Cultural Environment, *p. 22, Methuen, London, 1969 (note (21)).*

Thurstone, an American psychologist, was not satisfied with the all-inclusive measure *g* because it revealed so little of the special talents of each person. In the 1930s he employed another factor-analytical procedure which compounded *g* and *s* to give several factors referred to as *primary mental abilities*. Examples of these are verbal comprehension (V), number ability (N), word fluency (W), perceptual flexibility and speed, inductive reasoning, rote memory (M) and deductive reasoning. They are sometimes denoted by initial letters as shown in some cases above. Thurstone, it should be noted, did not deny the possibility of a general factor, but his factor approach enabled him to isolate independent mental abilities which he regarded as more productive when applied to educational or vocational guidance. For him, it was more revealing to have a broad profile of an individual's mental abilities than an overall measure.

One approach which deserves more attention than it has received so far is formulated by Furneaux and Eysenck.[40] Most IQ tests are timed, but these researchers suggest ways in which we might also take into account accuracy of response in untimed tests. A test devised by Furneaux (the Nufferno Test) allows for both speed and accuracy of response.

Finally, we turn briefly to two contemporary, sophisticated models of human ability expounded by Cattell and Guilford. To understand the implications of these theories the reader would need to refer to more advanced texts, but the following very simple outline should serve as an introduction. Cattell (**R**)[41] has advanced a theory in which two general factors are postulated, namely fluid (g_f) and crystallized (g_c) general ability. g_f is regarded as a measure of the influence of biological factors on intellectual development and thought to be comparable to inherited ability. g_c represents the outcome of cultural experiences such as parental and educational contacts. Clearly g_f and g_c are not directly related to Hebb's Intelligence A and B respectively because, as we have already noted, the latter cannot be assessed directly, whereas Cattell has claimed to have measured both g_f and g_c.

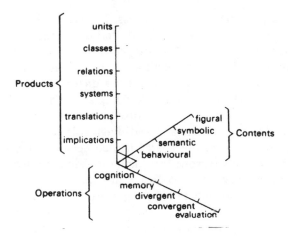

Figure 9.6 *Guilford's model of the intellect. From D. Child,* The Essentials of Factor Analysis, *Cassell, London, 1990 (2nd edn) (note (38)).*

Guilford's model of the intellect (see Figure 9.6) was first proposed in the early 1950s.[42] This ambitious model postulates no fewer than 120 mental factors, of which he claims to have isolated about 80. He derives the mental factors from three independent dimensions which he calls *operations, contents* and *products*; that is, each intelligent act requires the individual to carry out various thinking 'operations' (such as memory, convergent thinking, divergent thinking) using 'content' media (such as symbols, figures or semantics) in order to 'produce' such things as classes, relations or implications. With this three-dimensional arrangement, 5 operations × 4 contents × 6 products, we get 120 possibilities for intellectual factors.

Both theories are speculative and are the subject of criticism and controversy. Their value lies in the options which they offer in a field where there is still plenty of scope for hypothesis and experimentation. Two operations mentioned by Guilford will be central to our discussion of creative thinking in the next chapter. They are convergent and divergent thinking.

SUMMARY

The concepts of intelligence and intelligence testing have been with us for some time and are probably going to stay for a good while longer. Whilst intelligence tests are by no means perfect, they are certainly amongst the most reliable of tests so far constructed. Educators and psychologists have used them extensively and with sufficient success for us to feel justified in noting their application with children.

We started the chapter on a cautious note by defining intelligent behaviour instead of intelligence. This was done to set the record straight about intelligence not being a fixed quantity, and to show that our concern should be for the quality rather than the quantity of human behaviour. Heim's definition, that intelligence involves grasping the essentials in a situation and responding appropriately to them, was used as the basis for a discussion of the subject because it incorporated the biological and psychological view of behaviour as well as serving as an operational definition.

Inborn intellectual potential cannot be assessed directly. Similarly, the influence of the environment cannot readily be estimated. Indirect sampling of some aspects of intelligent behaviour by the use of standardized tests is the nearest we have come to judging the intellectual ability and potential of individuals. The mathematical technique of factor analysis has been used to show a differentiation between the verbal, numerical, mechanical and spatial abilities of humans. These abilities have, in turn, formed the nucleus of numerous standardized tests used with both primary and secondary school children as prognostic and diagnostic tools.

But intelligence test scores are not fixed for each person (see note (37) reference to malleability). There are many reasons for fluctuations in an individual's IQ score. The age of a person, whether he or she is coached, and the ethnic and cultural experiences of social background all contribute in differing degrees to the variability of test scores. Early childhood experiences also seem to have a marked effect on the extent to which intellectual potential finally emerges. The near abandonment of 11 + selection was partly the result of anomalous IQ measures as, for example, occurred when retesting of the same children occasionally produced conflicting scores or when a child's mental age developed more rapidly than his or her chronological age, especially in early adolescence (sometimes known as *late development*).

The unresolved nature/nurture controversy is likewise a dispute about what children bring with them into the world and the effect which particular home, community and school provisions can have upon their intellectual development. At present, most psychologists have tentatively settled for a middle-of-the-road policy in recognizing that interactive effects between inborn potential and environmental pressures culminate in an insoluble complex of behaviour characteristics. Twin studies and research using family trees have only partly answered the problem because they show equally well the effects of both inheritance and environment. In the meantime, and in the face of mounting evidence,[27] teachers must continue to be optimistic about the role of the school in developing intellectual skills.

Most educators are dedicated to the task of accommodating the individual differences displayed by children. The teacher, in the face of large classes, is set an almost impossible task not only of distinguishing the individual characteristics of the children but also of providing appropriate individual tuition to suit these characteristics. At the very least, the study and judicious application of intelligence and intelligence tests has something of value in it for teachers who wish to discover some background information about their children. IQs are not sufficient to direct the educational patterns adopted by teachers. They must be used along with other measures of scholastic variability such as the attitudes of children to work, school and teachers, motives, interests, achievement in specific subject areas and personality.

In these days of a growing conscience about the provision for the educationally underprivileged, the gifted, the backward, and the increased use of unstreamed classes, the teacher needs every available test[12] he or she can depend on. Intelligence tests, if administered satisfactorily, should provide the teacher with a valuable piece of supplementary evidence in deciding a child's educational programme.

ENQUIRY AND DISCUSSION

(a) Using whichever sources and resources are available (college or department libraries, school, tutors, etc.), discover as much as you can about the range and use of intelligence tests. It might prove helpful to invite guest speakers from the Local Education Authority Child Guidance Service to talk about psychological testing, especially about the use made of intelligence tests. Also explore the use of IQ tests in vocational guidance, diagnosis of educationally or severely sub-normal children and selection procedures for the services, schools and universities.

(b) Discuss with the group tutor how you would set about testing a group of children (or an individual) with an intelligence test. Inspect a range of test materials for this purpose and note carefully the manual of instructions and the kind of items used. Include a consideration of:
   (1) the age of the children;
   (2) the tests most appropriate for your purposes;
   (3) where one can obtain the tests and their price;
   (4) administration and scoring procedures;
   (5) how to interpret the scores and relate them to school work;
   (6) other possible achievement tests.

(c) What are the advantages and disadvantages of having and using a concept of intelligence in educational matters?

(d) Examine the possible reasons for:
   (1) the problem of defining the nature of intelligence;
   (2) the negative correlation between family size and IQ;
   (3) the decline of mental age with age (are there compensatory gains?);
   (4) the effects of coaching;
   (5) the difficulty of producing a culture-free test of intelligence;
   (6) ethnic differences in measured IQ;
   (7) the difficulty of measuring the ability of babies.

(e) What is meant by the expression 'a child has an IQ of 105'? What other information would you require when making a statement about the child's IQ in relation to other children? Explain why you need this additional information. Is intelligence normally distributed in the population?

(f) Discuss the evidence for and against the importance of heredity and environment in defining the intellectual competence of an individual.

(g) What are the strengths and weaknesses of streaming according to ability? Consider the position of the mentally gifted and mentally dull in your consideration of streaming.

(h) Examine the research literature with respect to the relationship between intelligence and academic achievement in one of the following sectors of education:
   (1) primary schools;
   (2) secondary schools;
   (3) some field of higher education.

(i) British psychologists, in the main, tend to favour the concept of general intelligence or 'g', while American psychologists prefer to regard intelligence in terms of several distinct mental abilities. Consider the pros and cons of these two points of view (you will find the books by Butcher, Kline and Richardson in 'Further Reading' a good starting point).

(j)   The gifted child, often defined in terms of intelligence rating or as having special gifts (e.g. music, dance), is considered as an exceptional case in the USA and Russia. Examine the literature to discover the nature of the provision made by these countries. What is the case for and against such provision?

NOTES AND REFERENCES

1.   A. W. Heim, *The Appraisal of Intelligence*, NFER, Slough, 1970, and *Intelligence and Personality: Their Assessment and Relationship*, Penguin, Harmondsworth, 1970.
2.   (R) T. R. Miles, 'Symposium: Contributions to intelligence testing and the theory of intelligence', *Br. J. Educ. Psychol.*, 27, 153–210 (1957).
3.   P. E. Vernon, *Intelligence and Attainment Tests*, University of London Press, London, 1960. For a more recent elaboration, see note (36), below. For a series of articles on the question: 'Can you raise IQ scores?' see C. T. Ramey and R. Haskins, *Intelligence, 5*, 5–19 and 41–48 (1981), and a critical article by A. Jensen, *Intelligence, 5*, 29–40 (1981). The question of 'fadeout' is raised – that is, the possibility that any improvement in performance on an IQ test disappears in time, i.e. *fades out*. The author also contends that an IQ test is only a partial measure of '*g*'. P. E. Vernon, 'The assessment of children', in *Studies in Education*, University of London Institute of Education, 1955, pp. 189–215.
4.   (R) D. Pidgeon, 'Intelligence: a changed view', *The Sunday Times* (1969).
5.   D. O. Hebb, *The Organisation of Behavior*, Wiley, New York, 1949, and *A Textbook of Psychology*, Saunders, Philadelphia, 1966 (2nd edn).
6.   A good recent book which makes a searching analysis of the present state of the art in the study of intelligence is K. Richardson, *Understanding Intelligence*, Open University Press, Milton Keynes, 1991. For an original view which espouses the information processing model, see R. J. Sternberg, *Beyond IQ: A Triarchic Theory of Human Intelligence*, Cambridge University Press, Cambridge, 1985 and R. J. Sternberg (ed.), *Human Abilities: An Information-Processing Approach*, Freeman, New York, 1985.
7.   H. J. Eysenck, 'Speed of information processing, reaction time and the theory of intelligence', in P. A. Vernon (ed.), *Speed of Information Processing and Intelligence*, Ablex, New York, 1987. For information on intelligence and EEG, see J. F. Stein, *Introduction to Neurophysiology*, Blackwell, Oxford, 1982.
8.   For a definitive work on R. J. Sternberg's componential theory, see *Intelligence, Information Processing, and Analogical Reasoning: The Componential Analysis of Human Abilities*, Erlbaum, Hillsdale, NJ, 1977.
9.   H. Gardner, *Frames of Mind: The Theory of Multiple Intelligences*, Heinemann, London, 1983.
10. N. E. Gronlund, *Preparing Criterion-Referenced Tests for Classroom Instruction*, Macmillan, New York, 1973.
11. (R) F. W. Warburton, 'Construction of the new British Intelligence Scale', *Bull. Br. Psychol. Soc.*, 19, 68–70 (1966), and C. D. Elliott, 'British intelligence scale takes shape', *Education, 25*, 460–461 (1975) in the Reader. C. D. Elliott, D. J. Murray and L. S. Pearson, *The British Ability Scales*, NFER–Nelson, Windsor, 1992.
12. For examples and advice on taking intelligence tests, see D. Child *et al., Taking the DC Test: A Guide for Candidates*, Nurse Selection Project, University of Leeds, 1989. There are many group tests on the market. Most can be obtained from the National Foundation for Educational Research. But there are restrictions imposed on test users to safeguard the reliability of the tests and their correct usage. NFER–Nelson supply catalogues of the tests in their stock (Educational, Clinical and Occupational). Several have been produced by the Foundation and Moray House. Two high-grade tests have been published for A. W.

Heim under the titles of AH5 and AH6. Non-verbal tests such as Raven's Progressive Matrices and Koh's Blocks are also obtainable from this source.

13. The name of Godfrey Thomson is one of the first to be associated with the IQ testing movement alongside that of Sir Cyril Burt. They were both experts in test design and wrote leading texts on the subject. Thomson was the Director of Moray House, Edinburgh, which in his time produced many standardized IQ tests, including the Northumberland and some for the 11+.

14. R. Griffiths, *The Ability of Babies*, University of London Press, London, 1954; D. McCarthy, *The McCarthy Scales of Children's Abilities*, Psychological Corporation, New York, 1972; A. Lynch, L. B. Mitchell, E. M. Vincent, M. Trueman and L. M. Macdonald, 'The McCarthy Scales of Children's Abilities: a normative study on English 4-year-olds', *Br. J. Educ. Psychol.*, **52**, 133–143 (1982).

15. R. J. Sternberg and J. E. Davidson (eds), *Conceptions of Giftedness*, Cambridge University Press, Cambridge, 1986, gives excellent contemporary views of giftedness.

16. E. M. Hitchfield, *In Search of Promise*, Longman, London, 1973, and N. R. Tempest, *Teaching Clever Children, 7–11*, Routledge and Kegan Paul, London, 1974. P. E. Vernon, G. Adamson and D. F. Vernon, *The Psychology and Education of Gifted Children*, Methuen, London, 1977. P. J. Congdon, *Spot the Gifted Child* and *Helping Children of High Intelligence*, Gifted Children's Information Centre, 941 Warwick Road, Solihull; *Gifted and Outstanding Children*, Report of City of Birmingham Education Committee Study Group, 1979.

17. For a summary of the work on age and growth of intelligence see D. B. Bromley, *The Psychology of Human Ageing*, Penguin, London, 1966, and *Human Ageing: An Introduction to Gerontology*, Penguin, London, 1988 (3rd edn).

18. (R) R. B. Burns, 'Age and mental ability: re-testing with thirty-three years' interval', *Br. J. Educ. Psychol.*, **36**, 116 (1966); J. L. Horn, 'Intelligence – why it grows, why it declines', *Trans-action*, **5**, 31 (1967). For technical detail and possible formulae for the variation of fluid and crystallized intelligence with age, see R. B. Cattell, *The Inheritance of Personality and Ability: Research Methods and Findings*, pp. 210–215, Academic Press, New York, 1982.

19. P. E. Vernon, *Intelligence and Attainment Tests*, University of London, 1960. See also L. J. Cronbach, *Essentials of Psychological Testing*, Harper and Row, New York, 1990 (5th edn).

20. S. Biesheuvel, 'Psychological tests and their application to non-European peoples', *Yearbook of Education*, Evans, London, 1949. Also see R. L. Gregory, *Eye and Brain*, Weidenfeld and Nicolson, London, 1967, for a discussion of illusions and their effect on Zulus.

21. P. E. Vernon, *Intelligence and Cultural Environment*, Methuen, London, 1969.

22. S. Wiseman, *Education and Environment*, Manchester University Press, Manchester, 1964.

23. J. W. B. Douglas, *The Home and the School*, MacGibbon and Kee, London, 1964, and J. W. B. Douglas, J. M. Ross and H. R. Simpson, *All Our Future: A Longitudinal Study of Secondary Education*, Davies, London, 1968.

24. A summary of the writing and research into social class and educational opportunity can be found in D. F. Swift, 'Social class and educational adaptation', in H. J. Butcher and H. B. Pont (eds), *Educational Research in Britain*, vol. 1, University of London Press, London, 1968.

25. A review of research into family size and intelligence can be found in J. D. Nisbet, *Family Environment*, Cassell, London, 1953.

26. D. Lawton, *Social Class, Language and Education*, Routledge and Kegan Paul, London, 1968.

27. A. R. Jensen, 'Do schools cheat minority children?', *Educ. Res.*, **14**, 3–28 (1971).

28. Comments on Jensen's paper (note (27)) made by Sir Cyril Burt, H. J. Butcher, H. J. Eysenck, J. Nisbet and P. E. Vernon can be found in *Educ. Res.*, **14**, 87–100 (1972).

29. A. R. Jensen, 'The culturally disadvantaged: psychological and educational aspects', *Educ. Res.*, **10**, 4–20 (1967).

30. A series of articles on nutrition and IQ appeared in *The Psychologist*, **15**(9), 399–413 (1992).

31. C. Burt, 'The evidence for the concept of intelligence', *Br. J. Educ. Psychol.*, **25**, 158–177 (1955).
32. F. Galton, *Hereditary Genius: An Enquiry into Its Laws and Consequences*, Horizon, New York, 1892 (2nd edn).
33. H. H. Goddard, *The Kallikak Family*, Macmillan, New York, 1921.
34. **(R)** L. Erlenmeyer-Kimling and L. F. Jarvik, 'Genetics and intelligence', *Science,* **142**, 1477–1479 (1963).
35. H. J. Eysenck and L. Kamin, *Intelligence: The Battle for the Mind*, Pan Books, London, 1981. Also see L. Kamin, *The Science and Politics of IQ*, Penguin, Harmondsworth, 1974; and D. H. Stott, *Issues in the Intelligence Debate*, NFER–Nelson, Windsor, 1983.
36. P. E. Vernon, *Intelligence: Heredity and Environment*, Freeman, San Francisco, 1979.
37. C. Locurto, 'On the malleability of IQ', *The Psychologist,* **11**, 431–435 (1988).
38. D. Child, *The Essentials of Factor Analysis*, Cassell, London, 1990 (2nd edn).
39. C. Spearman, 'General intelligence objectively determined and measured', *Am. J. Psychol.*, **15**, 202–293 (1904).
40. H. J. Eysenck, 'Intelligence assessment: a theoretical and experimental approach', *Br. J. Educ. Psychol.,* **37**, 81–98.
41. **(R)** R. B. Cattell, 'Theory of fluid and crystallized intelligence: a critical experiment', *J. Educ. Psychol.,* **54**, 1–22 (1963), and 'The theory of fluid and crystallized intelligence checked at the 5–6-year-old level', *Br. J. Educ. Psychol.,* **37**, 209–224 (1967). See also J. L. Horn, 'Intelligence – why it grows, why it declines', *Trans-action,* **5**, 23–31 (1967) in the Reader.
42. For Guilford's most recent elaboration see J. P. Guilford, 'The structure of intelligence', in D. K. Whitla (ed.), *Handbook of Measurement and Assessment in the Behavioral Sciences*, Addison-Wesley, Reading, MA, 1968.

FURTHER READING

H. J. Butcher, *Human Intelligence: Its Nature and Assessment*, Methuen, London, 1968. A clear, detailed and well-written account.

D. Child, *The Essentials of Factor Analysis*, Cassell, London, 1990 (2nd edn). An introductory text for those with a little knowledge of statistics.

D. Child, 'The growth of intelligence and creativity in young children', in D. Fontana (ed.), *The Education of the Young Child*, Blackwell, Oxford, 1984 (2nd edn).

A. W. Heim, *The Appraisal of Intelligence*, NFER, Slough, 1970. An interesting alternative view of intelligence.

P. Kline, *Psychological Testing: The Measurement of Intelligence, Ability and Personality*, Malaby, London, 1976.

D. W. Pyle, *Intelligence: An Introduction*, Routledge and Kegan Paul, London, 1979.

K. Richardson, *Understanding Intelligence*, Open University Press, Milton Keynes, 1991.

R. J. Sternberg and J. E. Davidson, *Conceptions of Giftedness*, Cambridge University Press, Cambridge, 1986.

P. E. Vernon, *Intelligence: Heredity and Environment*, Freeman, San Francisco, 1979.

ANSWERS TO INTELLIGENCE TEST ITEMS

Analogies

1. (c) seem (first one and last two letters common to both).
2. (d) bitch.
3. *Composer* is to *notes*.

Synonyms

1. Slake – quench.
2. Preen – trim feathers.

Antonyms

1. Tup – ewe.
2. Easy, soft – hard.

Number and letter series

1. 1/2, 1/2. Starting with 1/2 at the left-hand side, multiply it by 1, then multiply this answer by 2, and the next answer by 3, and so on.
2. JJ (months of the year).
3. 30, 42 (1 × 2, 2 × 3, 3 × 4, etc.).

Ordering and classification

1. Animal, vertebrate, carnivore, feline animals, domestic cats.
2. Meeting.
3. A half (word signifying a precise quantity).

Find the patterns

1.

(h)

(e)

(c)   (i)

2. (c): the others are three-sided figures.
3. A quarter to six (next but one!).

Chapter 10

Creative Thinking

There can be few students who have not encountered the concept of creative thinking in one form or another, or failed to detect the upsurge of interest in recent years. At a national level, we are told that advanced industrial societies cannot survive, develop or compete without the continued emergence of creative people in ever-increasing numbers in political, social and scientific pursuits. This has prompted many governments to sponsor research dedicated to the task of identifying, measuring, cultivating and exploiting creative talent. At a more homely level for student teachers, we find classroom practices increasingly involving such highly technical and unvalidated methods as 'creative writing', 'imaginative' work in art and drama or 'discovery methods'.

For psychologists, there are at least three factors which have contributed to the increase in enthusiasm for research in creative thinking. One is that conventional tests of intelligence have not convincingly demonstrated that they can distinguish the potentially creative from the not so creative. Teachers, incidentally, have suspected this for a long time, and the point was made in Chapter 9 that Intelligence C is but a sampling of human ability. It is just possible that the kind of items we find on an IQ test demand a particular kind of thinking strategy which may not entirely tap the creative capacities of those tested. We shall return to this point later. As Liam Hudson observes in his book *Contrary Imaginations*,[20] when you look at a class of bright boys and girls with high measures of intelligence it is virtually impossible to pick out those who will go on to be creative people from those who will not. Thus, whilst it remains true that creative individuals are amongst those with high intelligence, the relationship between creative capacity and IQ is not straightforward.

The second reason for the upsurge in enthusiasm for creative thinking is the knowledge explosion which has tended to render conventional modes of learning and teaching of limited efficiency. The teaching of science, especially in preparation for examinable subjects, has frequently taken the form of 'here are the facts; now use them'. This is not to deny the central importance of fact assimilation and recall, but where the psychologist's interests lie is in the strategies of learning and reasoning which the situation imposes on the child, and the lasting influence these might have on the way that child tackles problems. Heim's definition of intelligence in the previous chapter – the grasping of essentials in a situation and responding appropriately – goes only part of the way to an understanding of creative human behaviour because there is also the important preliminary step of exploring the situation and deciding on those essentials. Learning tactical skills of approaching a task in an open-minded fashion and selecting the important aspects in arriving at solutions may well be enhanced or inhibited by the learning methods we encourage in the classroom.

Third, we have long been interested in the interaction between cognitive and non-cognitive variables. Doubtless there are aspects of personality, motivation and decision-making (that is, qualities other than purely cognitive ones) which are involved in creativeness. The adoption of particular thinking strategies, in addition to being acquired as part of learning at home or in school, may also be a function of personality. Creative ability has long been associated with personality, and we shall return to this point later.

DEFINING CREATIVITY

You will have noticed that I have avoided using the word *creativity* up to this point.[1] It is amongst the most confused and misused concepts in the study of human behaviour and we need to understand this before using the term. Both American and British psychologists have been known to use it synonymously with 'imagination', 'originality', 'divergent thinking', 'inventiveness', 'intuition', 'venturesomeness', 'exploration', 'giftedness', and so on. The truth is we know very little about what makes a creative person and even less about the determinants of creativity. Consequently, there is no clear, unambiguous and widely accepted definition of creativity.

The reasons for this difficulty of definition are not hard to find. Consider, for example, the question of aesthetic enterprises in art, music, sculpture or writing. What objective criterion can we use to evaluate the 'amount' of creativity which has taken place in a work of art? Many would rightly say that it is a pointless question anyway because it depends too much upon value judgements within a cultural context. There is no sense in which we can arrive at a widely accepted judgement of creativeness since, in art, music or writing, one man's meat is another man's poison. For this reason, attention tends to have been directed to scientific discovery rather than to artistic creation in the study of creative thinking. There may well be a common thread running through the fabric of our artistic and scientific creativity, but at present we have no idea what it might be. Another problem is the confusion arising from our concern to describe the processes involved in creative activity from an observation of the products. We tacitly assume that particular modes of thinking have taken place when certain kinds of response appear. Later we shall discuss 'divergent' thinking, a term which implies certain kinds of mental action. But first we shall mention a theory by Wallas about the stages in a creative act which he deduced from biographies and the introspections of creative people who were deliberately analysing in detail all the conscious physical and mental states occurring simultaneously with creative activity.

There is some measure of agreement that, at its simplest, cognitive creativity (it is hard at this point in our knowledge to include aesthetic creativity as well) results in ideas which are novel, useful and relevant to the solution of problems being examined. 'Novelty' is used here in the sense of combining or rearranging established patterns of knowledge in unique fashions; of course, this can happen at many different levels, as when children constantly create new ideas which, for them, are completely original, but which within their culture are quite familiar. Originality at the highest level would have to occur in the much wider context of the world of knowledge. Nevertheless, many studies are based on the assumption that fluency, variety and novelty of ideas contrived by young people, using familiar material, signify a potentially creative mind. Perhaps one important consideration of a novel response, at present impossible to gauge with certainty, is the *quality of the process* which produced it. Even in scientific discovery where the claim is made that it has come about by serendipity, a great deal of spade work has almost invariably preceded it.

Not all novel responses reflect creative talent. False answers are novel; so are the bizarre statements and actions of the mentally ill; but we could hardly classify these as creative in the cognitive sense. Originality, then, is not enough. There must be a measure of relevance to the solution of a problem as well. Usefulness is not quite so obvious because in science we often find that an original idea has no immediate application and must wait for advances in other fields before it becomes useful.

ASSESSING CREATIVITY

Before we can focus upon the specific sense in which we shall use the term 'creativity', it is necessary to give an appraisal of the attempts made to assess it. A concept which is difficult to define is difficult to measure. Consequently, a number of approaches to the study of creativity have developed in this century. Perhaps the three most promising are: (a) studies of the lifestyles of creative people; (b) assessment, using operational definitions, of the *products* of creative activity; (c) attempts to discover the *processes* of creative activity. Of these, the first and second have been employed with somewhat greater regularity than the last, because observing people's behaviour is much less suspect and demonstrably easier than trying to discover the processes of internal mental behaviour (for a recent discussion see Alban Metcalfe[1]).

Creative people: biographical studies

The search for distinguishing characteristics and capacities of creative people has a fairly long history. In the cognitive domain it is still widely held that creative ability is largely a manifestation of the highly intelligent. Thus, in order to find creative people, you would look amongst those with high intelligence. One of the earliest and certainly the most extensive studies is that of Terman,[2] whose famous longitudinal study of gifted American children is an outstanding masterpiece. 'Gifted' in this case is defined as having an IQ greater than 140 on the Terman–Merrill Intelligence Test. In seeking out those with the highest IQs, Terman clearly believed in a linear connection between IQ and creative talent.

However, his, and subsequent, work is especially interesting for the light it sheds on the personality characteristics of highly intelligent and creative people. This group was revisited periodically from the early 1920s up to 1968 when Oden[2] retested a portion of the group. She compared the childhood of the top and bottom 100 men selected by compounding professional productivity, the extent of responsibility, influence and authority over others, honours and income. In other words, the status afforded by society to its most highly productive members was used to distinguish two groups for the research. A detailed interview with each individual revealed that the top group had less illness and greater stability in the home during childhood. Many more of the top group came from professional homes where parents had well-defined attitudes about education and gave positive encouragement to the children to do well at school. Learning tended to be valued for its own sake by their parents. There was also in the top group a higher need to achieve during early childhood.

Roe[3] and MacKinnon (**R**),[4] again in the United States, confirmed most of the characteristics suggested by Oden using short-term, intensive interviews of eminent and widely accepted experts from certain professions. MacKinnon, in fact, invited his subjects to a weekend gathering at which personal, social and biographical information was compiled. Biographical similarities in most enquiries in this area, particularly those of home background, are quite striking. For some professional groups, for instance psychologists, architects, biologists and anthropologists, it seems that a permissive, settled, middle-class home with loose, if not strained emotional ties is the prerequisite for creative thinkers. MacKinnon[5] remarks that the parents of creative architects, for example, had an 'extraordinary respect for the child and confidence in his ability to do what was appropriate'. Roe's method was to take a detailed life history from each individual in her sample, including present work, an interview, projection and IQ tests. One exception is the scientists in Roe's work, particularly physicists and mathematicians, who seem to have had the lion's share of distress in childhood. Separation of the parents, strict and conventional upbringing[6] and illness were the commonest sources of distress. Roe's explanation is that scientists might be seeking to compensate for their earlier insecurity by choosing occupations which, superficially at least, involve convergent and clear-cut procedures leading to well-defined goals. However, this provides a reason for subject choice rather than for creative talent.

Cattell,[7] using a combination of detailed literature search of biographies and measures of personality from living eminent researchers, was able to show surprising uniformity in the profiles of both groups. The tendencies, and they are only tendencies, since not all eminent scientists living or dead possess exactly the following profile, are for the researchers to be more reserved, intelligent, dominant, serious, emotionally sensitive, radical and self-sufficient than the population at large. Some of these qualities add up to an introverted personality.

Other generalizations about the personal qualities of creative men and women from these and other studies depict them as single-minded, stubborn, non-conformist and persistent in tasks which engage their imaginations. Tolerance to ambiguity[8] is high (they are not perturbed when a problem has a number of plausible solutions); they may even enjoy dilemmas and searching out problems which have diverse possibilities. Risk-taking and venturesomeness with ideas appeal to the creative mind. What we are not clear about is the evidence for distinctive qualities in the thinking styles adopted by creative people when they solve problems. The work of Harvey[9] and his colleagues on patterns of concept formation goes some way towards drawing attention to the relationship between the levels of abstraction attainable by individuals and their likelihood of producing original concepts. As one might have guessed, in general the higher the level of abstraction attainable by an individual, the more creative are his or her concepts.

What we have done in this section is to look a long way ahead to the 'finished article' and tease out some of the characteristics of creative people which may have their origins in childhood. What has not been attempted so far is a longitudinal study with these characteristics in mind to trace life histories as they unfold. Notice the importance attached to personality and the possibility that creative men and women blossom from a unique blend of both personal and intellectual qualities.

Divergent thinking

The criteria for judging an eminent person's talent in a special field are fairly obvious: he or she must create original ideas which can be clearly recognized as pushing forward the frontiers of knowledge in a chosen field. But can we devise objective tests which would predict this creative talent?

New light was thrown on this problem by Guilford in the early 1950s, when he introduced his 'model of the intellect' (see previous chapter). He postulated several cognitive operations, amongst which he included *convergent* and *divergent thinking*. The convergent thinker is distinguished by an ability to deal with problems requiring one conventional correct solution clearly obtainable from the information available. Problems of this kind can be found in all intelligence tests and in many 'objective-type' questions, in which a problem is presented with several solutions, only one of which is correct. We saw in the last chapter several examples of intelligence test items which require the testee to focus attention and reasoning to provide a single correct solution. No opportunity is given for productive thinking beyond the information supplied; in fact, items with more than one solution are discarded as unsatisfactory.

The divergent thinker, on the other hand, is adept in problems requiring the generation of several equally acceptable solutions, where the emphasis is on the quantity, variety and originality of responses. Guilford's two categories attempt to discriminate between the styles of problem-solving behaviour adopted in closed and open-ended problems. Although these are not exclusive processes (solving convergent problems might require a great deal of 'diverging' before a solution presents itself), in general the items of convergent and divergent thinking tests do encourage different approaches, and it is this aspect which has led some psychologists to correlate divergent thinking with creative thinking. As yet, the relationship has still to be verified convincingly.

Guilford[10] has defined numerous kinds of divergent test items and there is mounting evidence to support the view[11] of there being distinct *verbal* and *non-verbal* (or *figural*) factors in ideational fluency. Of the verbal kind, the 'uses of objects' test, 'consequences' test and the 'S' test are three of many in common usage. Here are some examples (for more detail see note (12)):

Uses of objects test

Write down as many *different uses* as you can for a BUCKET. Work as quickly as possible and remember that points will be given for answers which are unusual.

Consequences test

Below is given a change in the way we live. It is not likely to happen, but you are asked to pretend that it really does happen. Write down as many *different* results of the change as you can invent. Your score will depend on the number of *different* and *unusual* ideas as well as the *number* of ideas you can write.

The change is: we all have four fingers and no thumb on each hand.

'S' test

Write as many different five-letter words as you can beginning with S.

Number test

An example of a *number test* is: Given the numbers 2, 3, 4, 5 and 6, construct as many different equations as you can using only these numbers (e.g. $5 - 4 + 2 + 3 = 6$).

Of the many non-verbal tests, the commonest in Great Britain have been the 'circles', the 'squares' and the 'parallel lines' tests. A page of circles (or squares) is presented to the subject, who is told to add lines to the circles (squares) to complete a recognizable drawing. Lines can be inside the circle, outside the circle or both inside and outside the circle. The score depends on the number of objects, their variety and their originality. The 'parallel lines' test has a similar format.

The scoring techniques tell us quite a bit about the aims of the tests. There are three basic types of score obtainable. The first is a *fluency* score obtained by counting the number of responses given (but excluding those which are nonsensical or which do not answer the question as posed). In effect it is a measure of the speed with which the individual can summon up ideas. A second score can be obtained by grouping responses into categories. This score is known as *flexibility*, and in effect measures the variety of responses given. The scorer's subjectivity enters into decisions about the groupings, but this can be partly offset by assembling the opinions of several judges and using the majority consensus.[12] In Figure 10.1 five possible responses to the 'squares' test are shown. The fluency score is five, but as the first and fourth responses fall into the same category of letters of the alphabet, the flexibility score is four. A third measure is *originality* and is derived from the most infrequent responses. By counting the number of times a response occurs within the group under test, it is possible to arrive at a frequency distribution for each response and to allot scores for the least frequent. As these types of score (i.e fluency, flexibility and originality) are based on the same responses, it is not surprising to find high correlations between them.

In terms of the requirements for creativity outlined in the previous section, the divergent thinking tests leave a lot to be desired. The underlying assumption that divergent thinking scores correlate with future originality has yet to be established experimentally. Moreover, the responses are at a lower level of originality than would be required for, say, a new invention. The responses frequently serve no useful purpose and often display flights of fancy bordering on the grotesque, sadistic and trivial. What

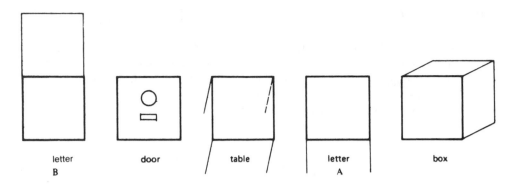

Figure 10.1   *Examples of answers to the 'squares' test of divergent thinking.*

we have are two operational definitions of short-term thinking styles: one, the divergent kind, relying on ideational fluency in open-ended problems; the other, convergent thinking, favouring those who like homing in on one solution. Much of the research on creativity has employed divergent thinking tests and we should bear in mind when reading the results of these researches the tenuous assumption that they give some clue to the creative ability or potential of individuals.

As we shall be referring to research in which divergent thinking scores have been used extensively, it would be valuable to look at other examples of their shortcomings. Perhaps their most obvious drawback lies in the administration and scoring of the tests. They are usually timed and presented as a *test*, whereas a creative act may be time-consuming[13] and require a relaxed atmosphere. Ideas frequently need to be chewed over before enlightenment occurs. The tension of a test situation may also militate against creative output. Wallach and Kogan,[14] using untimed procedures in a playful atmosphere, produced divergent thinking scores which were more unrelated to IQ scores than had been obtained hitherto. Scoring the tests requires more subjective evaluation than does the scoring of standardized tests of intelligence. We saw the difficulty posed in arriving at a flexibility score, and a similar problem arises when we have to decide on the level to be chosen in awarding a score for originality using the least frequent responses. Wallach and Kogan used only unique responses (occurring only once in their sample), but others, such as Torrance, have accepted frequencies occurring in up to 15 per cent of their samples.

As we saw above, the scoring depends to some extent on the subjective judgements of the scorers and there is doubtful uniformity amongst these about what is an acceptable response and what is not. The existence of correlation between the scoring strategies also tends to lead to unwarranted conclusions about the nature of divergent thinking in relation to convergent thinking.

We shall return to some applications of divergent thinking tests later in the chapter.

The creative process

Psychologists and teachers alike have long been intrigued by the processes of creative thought and after many years have little more than a handful of speculations. The most popular method of investigation has been the study of famous men in literature, science and mathematics, using biography and interview.

Graham Wallas,[13] after studying Helmholtz and Poincaré, recognized four stages in the creative cycle, namely preparation, incubation, inspiration (or illumination) and verification.

Preparation

The forerunner of the preparatory stage is the ability to spot a problem. The existence of a problem often excites and obsesses the creative mind so much that it becomes restless and disturbed. Preparation then takes place and involves a detailed investigation of all the possibilities surrounding the problem from reading, discussing and questioning to making notes and trying out solutions.

Incubation

Following a period of deliberate activity in search of evidence and solutions comes a time when no conscious effort is made. This incubation period may be short or very extensive. Some authors in both arts and science have remarked on the time it sometimes takes for the germ of an idea to take shape. We have no idea what goes on during this period, but speculation has it that ideas are 'worked on' at a subconscious level to re-form and evolve new combinations of ideas.

Inspiration

This is a sudden flash of insight, that penny-dropping sensation we all experience when a confusion of ideas suddenly takes shape. Sometimes it happens after sleep, during a walk or in the bath (Archimedes). Tchaikovsky, in a letter to his patron, Mme von Meck, describes his fourth symphony and makes a general comment about creative inspiration: 'As a rule the germ of a new work appears suddenly and unexpectedly. If the soul is fertile – that is to say, if the composer is suitably disposed – the seed takes root, rapidly shooting up stem, leaves and finally blossom.' We have here a classical example of the inspiration stage.

Verification

Having bright ideas is one thing; they then require confirmation. Often the creator is fairly convinced of the veracity of the solution long before he or she puts it to the test. But there follows a stage of active revision, expansion and correction.

We see from this creative cycle that creativity is rarely, if ever, an event which happens over coffee. There is usually a time-consuming, tenacious and detailed period of mental activity. The inescapable conclusion from Wallas's work is that creative output needs time and effort.

DIVERGENT THINKING AND INTELLIGENCE

Following the appearance of Guilford's model of the intellect (see chapter 9) and his views on creativity,[15] several researchers have attempted to confirm the independence of his convergent and divergent intellectual operations, the latter being taken as a measure of creativity. The earliest and most widely known research is that of Getzels and Jackson,[16] in which 12- to 16-year-olds in an American high school were given intelligence and divergent thinking tests. The scores were used to select two groups: one, the 'high creative', having high divergent and low IQ scores, and the other, the 'high IQ', having the reverse of this arrangement of scores. These groups had similar achievement levels, but they differed in several other important respects. 'High creatives' were less conformist, tended to overachieve and possessed a lively sense of humour when compared with the high IQ group. But the overall principal finding that IQ and divergent thinking scores were not significantly correlated, and therefore should be treated as separate entities, has been hotly contested largely on the grounds that Getzels and Jackson's methods of analysis left much to be desired. Moreover, the sample chosen by them was restricted to the upper ranges of intelligence (average IQ score for the sample was 132), thus rendering the results untypical of the population.

Subsequent studies have tended to use more representative samples than Getzels and Jackson. The findings, in the main, have managed to show some degree of positive relationship between divergent thinking and IQ scores. Hasan and Butcher[17] carried out a close repetition of the American study using Scottish schoolchildren, but with a much wider and more characteristic range of IQ scores. The correlations between divergent thinking and IQ scores were all positive and significant, with some as high as $+0.7$. In the few researches where no relationship has been found, the samples tend to be drawn from the upper end of the IQ range.[18]

The case for or against the distinction between divergent thinking and intelligence is a difficult one to answer. Advanced mathematical procedures, such as factor analysis, and careful monitoring of test materials and their administration do tend to show a measure of separate identity, especially where the test materials involve 'ideational fluency', that is, items designed and scored to show how quickly people can produce verbal or non-verbal responses. In this country, Sultan[17] was able to show a measure of independence using divergent tests which encouraged verbal ideational fluency. We have already mentioned the carefully constructed work of Wallach and Kogan,[14] in which, it will be remembered, a completely tension-free and friendly atmosphere was created, no time limit was imposed, each child was questioned individually and scoring for original responses was confined to unique answers.

Some evidence[19] at present points to a differentiation in the relationship between divergent test scores and IQ which depends on the level of IQ being considered. At low and moderate levels of IQ a linear relationship holds. Beyond a broad *threshold* somewhere in the region of 110–120 IQ in tests with a standard deviation of 15, the relationship of intelligence and divergent scores appears to become increasingly random; in other words, the highly intelligent are less predictable in their divergent thinking ability. This tallies with Hudson's observation that, in a class of bright children, it is difficult, if not impossible, to pick out those who will be exceptionally creative. The basic question of whether intelligence tests and divergent thinking tests are measuring different, partially related or the same human attributes is still a matter for psychological research.

In the present state of research the safest conclusion is that divergent thinking is partially dependent on intelligence and partially a function of other personality characteristics.

DIVERGENT THINKING AND SUBJECT BIAS

A recurring theme in the study of convergent and divergent thinking is the possible connection between performance on the tests and arts/science bias. Hudson[20] has been most prolific in this field. He defined a *converger* as one who obtains a relatively high score on an IQ test and at the same time a relatively lower score on a divergent thinking test compared with others in the test sample. The reverse definition was used for the *diverger*. He was able to show that science students (particularly those studying physics) tend to be convergers. Divergers, on the other hand, tend to be students of English literature, history and modern languages. The emphasis has shifted from regarding the divergent thinking tests as measures of creativity to one of looking upon them as reflecting a preferred thinking style. Hence IQ and divergent tests are more likely to distinguish science from arts specialists than to distinguish the creative from the not so creative. However, the weight of evidence from other experiments in this area[21] so far favours the convergent test as a more consistent discriminator of the science specialist, with much less support for the arts–diverger connection.

The fact that science specialists do comparatively well in convergent (IQ) tests may reflect the kind of thinking strategies in which they excel. As we have indicated above, IQ items require people to take information as given and use it to arrive at a single correct answer, a procedure not unlike the traditional demands made in science lessons.

In looking for origins, Hudson[20] sees the home (cf. the findings of Roe earlier in the chapter) as the most probable source of inspiration, and in his book *Contrary Imaginations* he has this to say:

> The convergent parent ... is probably the one who shies away from all expression of strong feeling, affectionate or otherwise. If the child demands affection, the parents do their best to provide it, but fail. In this case, either of two things may happen. The parents may guide their child into less embarrassing spheres by offering approval whenever he masters some safe, impersonal skill. Or, as a reaction to the embarrassment the child has caused them (out of shame or irritation or both), they become critical. Either way, the child realizes that security lies both in choosing an impersonal field within which to work, and in being right. Furthermore, the child latches on both to his parents' distaste for 'gush', and to their relief when the mood is once more safe. ... In every sense, therefore, impersonal work and interests become a haven: from embarrassment, from criticism, and from emotions which are disruptive and inexplicable.
>
> The diverger's mother, on the other hand, is one who binds her child to her by disregarding his practical, logical accomplishments (or even ridiculing them) and by holding out a promise of love which she may or may not be able to fulfil. The child grows up addicted to people.

Notice the importance ascribed to personality development as a feature in cognitive processes.[20] We shall refer to this point again later.

CREATIVITY AND THE CLASSROOM

This section is the least satisfactory because of the difficulty experienced in trying to define educational environments. Terms such as 'traditional' or 'progressive' give a facile black-and-white interpretation which rarely approximates to the truth. In fact these terms have never been defined satisfactorily. Our notions about effective and efficient 'creative' classroom conditions, for example, are largely intuitive. It is said by some that a tight factual syllabus delivered by authoritarian teachers (followed in some cases by an examination requiring factual reproduction) is the ideal condition for producing convergent thinkers (see previous section). And it seems common sense that the way in which knowledge is presented and acquired will affect the way in which it is subsequently used. Reasonable though this hypothesis might appear, there is very little hard evidence to support it.

Some American psychologists, notably Torrance and his associates in a long list of publications,[22] believe that at present parents and teachers actively discourage creative behaviour in the young because it is too troublesome and time-consuming. The enquiring child needs plenty of attention; questions are frequent, difficult to answer in simple language and sometimes embarrassing, while the child's unskilled hands lead to messiness and disorder. According to Getzels and Jackson,[16] precocious children are more unpopular with teachers than are the conformist and orderly children. A quotation from one of Torrance's many books should help to crystallize one aspect of his progressive philosophy:[22]

> Many social pressures stressed at home and in the community interfere with the creative process. Consider our excessive emphasis on a success-orientation – our exaggerated fear of making mistakes. Over-emphasis or misplaced emphasis on sex roles also exacts a heavy toll on the creative thinking of both boys and girls. Consider too our tendency to overrate the finished product, the great work of art, the harmonious interpersonal relationship, the well-organized behavior of a group. We fail to note the struggles through which these achievements come into being. We stress the importance of verbal skills, especially writing. We give credit frequently only for what an individual can write down, not recognizing that not all thinking expresses itself in verbal form. We place great emphasis upon what one knows rather than upon his attitude toward what he knows or what he can do with what he knows.

In a study of two informal 'progressive' and two 'formal' 'traditional' primary schools in this country, Haddon and Lytton (R)[23] demonstrated higher divergent thinking scores for the progressive schools. Lytton and Cotton (R)[23] repeated the experiment at secondary school level with no success. This was attributed to the inappropriateness of trying to classify secondary schools as 'formal' and 'informal' because the basic organization is much more complex than at primary level (pupils see several teachers, a wider range of subjects is taught, pupils come from very different primary schools in the catchment areas, and so forth).

An interesting project on the effects of streaming in this country was carried out by Barker Lunn.[24] Using a very large sample at the end of their third and again at the end of their fourth year in primary school, she was able to show that in the unstreamed schools, pupils placed with teachers who favoured 'progressive' methods showed some improvement in divergent thinking scores during the fourth year. In contrast, pupils placed with teachers who did not favour 'progressive' methods *deteriorated* in both streamed and unstreamed regimes.

Some success has been experienced where instructional methods are deliberately exploited to enhance creative abilities. Crutchfield,[25] using programmed instruction in the training of creative problem-solving, was able to improve the quality and quantity of the problems solved by an experimental group of children so that they became markedly superior to the children in a control group. The effect was still apparent several months later, although its extent had decreased. This latter observation raises the question of the permanence of any training programme dealing with this subject, and Crutchfield concludes that the 'Hawthorne' effect[26] may have intruded, although it seems to the present author to be a point worth noting that change and variety in teaching techniques bring about an increase (temporary though this may be) in creative productivity.

Long-term studies of the effect of more open-ended approaches in Nuffield Science and modern mathematics are awaited. Will methods of teaching science which emphasize possibilities rather than certainties pay off in terms of understanding or in producing more creative scientific minds? Studies comparing traditional and 'new maths' using divergent thinking tests in both secondary and primary schools in Great Britain[27] reveal that children encountering modern methods do tend to produce superior divergence scores.

Clearly there are numerous unresolved issues relating to the study of creative thinking, but there remains the practical problem of how we might stimulate and encourage such thinking in school. Osborn,[28] for example, makes a number of suggestions cast in the form of a series of questions designed to direct the children's attention towards problem-solving: 'what would happen if "it" is made larger . . .? smaller . . .? changes position . . .?' and so on. This skill of directing children's attention to a wide range of possibilities is a very potent, and not a particularly commonplace, one.

BRAINSTORMING AND LATERAL THINKING

There is a view which maintains that, as our minds become cluttered with ideas, so we become inhibited in the way we re-express them. Ideas are censored and we prejudge their value before expressing them. Osborn[28] suggests that there is a greater chance of producing original ideas when the mind is allowed to run riot in attempting to solve a problem. The ideas must come freely and without regard for their feasibility. In other words, think now, evaluate later. A technique since developed by Parnes[29] uses a group of people who concentrate on a problem, producing as many hypotheses as possible without bothering to evaluate them. The interplay of ideas apparently sparks off far more good ideas than conventional problem-solving techniques. The process is known as *brainstorming*.

The idea has been tried with children of primary-school age in America, by assembling them around a table, presenting an open-ended problem and tape-recording the ideas, which are allowed to flow uninterrupted by the teacher. At the end of the session the ideas are discussed for their feasibility. The point is to encourage ideational fluency without fear of intervention or ridicule from teachers or peers. A major task in using the method with children is the preparation needed to assemble the facts as a prerequisite to innovation (see synectics, below). What is more revealing in brainstorming sessions with children is the knowledge teachers can gain about the paths a child's roving mind will take. The central aim of the method is to produce some lasting habits of ideational fluency in the children, though this aim has never been validated. The method certainly improves the self-confidence of children in the presence of others, for they can express views without fear of rebuke or derision, but a possible limitation is that it may induce non-critical, non-factual rambling in place of reasoned judgement.

Related to brainstorming is the study of *synectics*. The word comes from the Greek and means bringing together disparate and seemingly irrelevant factors. It was first linked to creativity by the Synectics Group at Cambridge, Massachusetts.[30] The aim of synectics is extremely optimistic, for its upholders maintain that the creative process can be described and hence a teaching methodology derived for increasing creative output. By undergoing a course of training, it is thought possible to develop more efficient and creative problem-solving. Synectics is a systematic attempt at brainstorming but differs from it in that the free thinking is always preceded by a period of concentrated searching and familiarization with all aspects of the problem.

Another approach to the problem of thinking strategies which may have a lot to offer in the future has been enunciated by Edward de Bono[31] at Cambridge. Using his collection of parlour games, he argues that logical or longitudinal reasoning is not always the most effective way of arriving at a solution. Indeed, a cold, calculating, step-wise approach to problem-solving may distract a person from experimenting and may thus obscure more fruitful routes leading to a solution. How many times do we let our minds fixate on a certain way of solving a problem, convinced that we are on the right track, only to discover after much trial and error that we could never have solved the problem in that way? This process of constantly returning to 'square one' and trying a new line of approach de Bono calls *lateral thinking*. In other words, our minds should not pursue one line of thinking (longitudinal thinking) to the exclusion of all others, but should frequently return to the information provided and try another approach. The idea of the mind flirting with ideas is also embodied in brainstorming and synectics. One practical outcome has been the development of the Cambridge Cognitive Research Trust (CoRT), which is producing materials for the teaching of thinking skills (**R**).[32]

SUMMARY

The last 30 or so years has seen a marked change in the philosophy of educators about the role of children in learning environments. Inflexible, formal, syllabus-bound methods are gradually being replaced by freer, child-centred methods which place more faith in exploratory and expressive activities as ploys for improving the learning skills of children than in follow-my-leader techniques. The growth of interest in creative thinking in the United States, and more recently in Great Britain, has played some part in focusing teachers' attention on the impact of classroom procedures on the learning styles of children.

Psychologists are not yet clear about the nature of creative thinking, how to measure the quality or what can be done in the classroom to stimulate creativity in children. The efforts which have already been made are largely experimental and intuitive. Psychologists have looked at the characteristics of creative people; they have devised tests of creativity (divergent thinking tests) thought to measure ideational fluency, flexibility and originality; they have tried to analyse the creative process from a study of eminent people. But none of these methods so far has given us incontrovertible evidence or advice of value to teachers. These notes of caution are necessary in a rapidly expanding research field from which there is likely to be an avalanche of literature written with teachers in mind.

One important benefit we have reaped from the study of creative thinking is the challenge it has offered to teachers to examine the learning environments they provide in school. Do parrot-fashion methods of teaching produce different styles of problem-solving in children than discovery methods? What is the relative efficiency of directed learning and discovery methods? Does our educational system tend to produce convergers who are looking always for one right answer, and can the system produce divergers who are just as happy with open-ended or ambiguous problems? If children are always told how to solve problems, will they be less able to meet new problems?

To develop an atmosphere within which children feel sufficiently free to explore and make discoveries while being given guidance is a difficult balance for a teacher to obtain. Too much freedom might encourage anarchy; too much guidance might produce sterile conformity. Moreover, when we encourage children to be active participants in their own learning through such media as clay, bricks, paints, musical instruments, body movement, words and number symbols in speech and writing, drama, handicraft and science, we are hopefully trying to assist them in finding their particular modes of communication, which requires concentration and self-discipline. Torrance[22] believes this atmosphere can be created by teachers who learn to recognize and value their pupils' ideas and who come to believe in their pupils' capacity to be creative; teachers should give their pupils every opportunity to communicate their ideas, they should encourage 'brainstorming' – a flow of ideas without evaluation – and reward unusual questions and ideas. The balance between undirected freedom and dogged rule-learning comes when *guided discovery* prevails.[33] Here the major objective is to enable the child to acquire efficient ways of solving problems by free exploration while giving the child just sufficient framework of guidance to help in learning proficient methods of applying rules.

ENQUIRY AND DISCUSSION

(a) In your observation of children, attempt to determine those behaviours which you consider to be 'creative'. What methods are used by the teacher to create the right atmosphere?

(b) What is understood by 'discovery methods'? Are they the same for all subjects? Are there differences between primary school and secondary school methods in guided discovery?

(c) Organize a 'brainstorming' session with a small group of children by tape-recording their spontaneous responses to an open-ended problem.

(d) Distinguish between convergent and divergent thinking. Discuss the differences in terms of curriculum content, presentation and subject bias.

(e) Read and discuss the work attempting to relate divergent thinking and school achievement.

(f) Read and comment on de Bono's suggestions (note 32).

NOTES AND REFERENCES

1. Open University, *Creativity*, Educational Studies, E 281, units 3 and 4, 1971. R. J. Alban Metcalfe, *Assessment of Creativity*, Rediguide 17, TRC-Rediguides, Oxford, 1983, and 'Assessment of creativity at school and college: the state of the art', *Education Section Review*, British Psychological Society, **8**, 14–21 (1984).
2. L. M. Terman *et al.*, *Genetic Studies of Genius*, Volume 1: *Mental and Physical Traits of a Thousand Gifted Children*, Stanford University Press, CA, 1925. M. H. Oden, 'The fulfilment of promise: 40-year follow-up of the Terman gifted group', *Genet. Psychol. Monogr.*, **77**, 3–93 (1968).
3. A. Roe produced a number of monographs between 1951 and 1953. The most all-inclusive was 'A psychological study of eminent psychologists and anthropologists and a comparison with biological and physical scientists', *Psychol. Monogr.*, **67**, no. 2 (1953).
4. **(R)** D. W. MacKinnon, 'Personality and the realization of creative potential', *Am. Psychol.*, **20**, 273–281 (1963). See also 'Characteristics of the creative person: implications for the teaching–learning process', in *Current Issues in Higher Education*, National Education Association, Washington, DC, 89–92, 1961 and in the Reader.
5. D. W. MacKinnon, 'The nature and nurture of creative talent', *Am. Psychol.*, **17**, 484–495 (1962).
6. See also C. E. Schaeffer and A. Anastasi, 'A biographical inventory for identifying creativity in adolescent boys', *J. Appl. Psychol.*, **52**, 42–48 (1968).
7. R. B. Cattell, 'The personality and motivation of the researcher from measurement of contemporaries and from biography', in C. W. Taylor and F. Barron (eds), *Scientific Creativity*, Wiley, New York, 1963.
8. B. Snyder, 'Creative students in science and engineering', *Universities Q.*, **21**, 205–218 (1967).
9. O. J. Harvey, D. E. Hunt and H. M. Schroder, *Conceptual Systems and Personality Organization*, Wiley, New York, 1961.
10. J. P. Guilford, *Personality*, McGraw-Hill, New York, 1959.
11. D. L. Nuttall, 'Convergent and divergent thinking', in H. J. Butcher and H. B. Pont (eds), *Educational Research in Britain*, vol. 3, University of London Press, London, 1973.
12. A detailed analysis of test materials is given by E. P. Torrance in *Guiding Creative Talent*, Prentice-Hall, Englewood Cliffs, NJ, 1962. He has also produced a standardized test battery of items known as the *Torrance Tests of Creative Thinking*, Personnel Press, Princeton, NJ, 1966. Torrance's tests are also summarized in R. J. Goldman, 'The Minnesota Tests of Creativity', *Educ. Res.*, **7**, 3–14 (1964).
13. G. Wallas, *The Art of Thought*, Harcourt, Brace and World, New York, 1926.
14. M. A. Wallach and N. Kogan, *Modes of Thinking in Young Children*, Holt, Rinehart and Winston, New York, 1965.
15. J. P. Guilford, 'Creativity', *Am. Psychol.*, **5**, 444–454 (1950), and 'The structure of the intellect', *Psychol. Bull.*, **53**, 267–293 (1956).
16. J. W. Getzels and P. W. Jackson, *Creativity and Intelligence*, Wiley, New York, 1962.
17. P. Hasan and H. J. Butcher, 'Creativity and intelligence: a partial replication with Scottish children of Getzels and Jackson's study', *Br. J. Psychol.*, **57**, 129–135 (1966). E. E. Sultan, 'A factorial study in the domain of creative thinking', *Br. J. Educ. Psychol.*, **32**, 78–82 (1962). Other critical studies are well documented in the books suggested in Further Reading.
18. As well as Getzels and Jackson's work, see L. Hudson, *Contrary Imaginations*, Methuen, London, 1966, and D. Child and A. Smithers, 'Some cognitive and affective factors in subject choice', *Res. Educ.*, **5**, 1–9 (1971). In the first case, public-school boys were used; in the second, university students.
19. K. Yamamoto, 'Effects of restriction of range and test reliability on correlation between measures of intelligence and creative thinking', *Br. J. Educ. Psychol.* **35**, 300–305 (1965). G. P. Ginsburg and R. G. Whittemore, 'Creativity and verbal ability: a direct examination of their relationship', *Br. J. Educ. Psychol.*, **38**, 133–139 (1968). The threshold effect has

been questioned in D. Child and A. Croucher, 'Divergent thinking and ability: is there a threshold?', *Educ. Studies*, **3**, 101–110 (1977).

20. L. Hudson, *Contrary Imaginations* and *Frames of Mind*, Methuen, London, 1966 and 1968 respectively. L.Hudson and B. Jacot, 'The outsider in science: a selective review of evidence, with special reference to the Nobel Prize', in C. Bagley and G. K.Verma (eds), *Personality, Cognition and Values*, pp. 3–23, Macmillan, London, 1986.

21. See for example D. L. Nuttall, 'Convergent and divergent thinking', in H. J. Butcher and H. B. Pont (eds), *Educational Research in Britain*, vol. 3, University of London Press, London, 1973. D. Child, 'A comparative study of personality, intelligence and social class in a technological university', *Br. J. Educ. Psychol.*, **39**, 40–46 (1969) and D. Child and A. Smithers, op. cit., note (18).

22. E. P. Torrance, *Guiding Creative Talent*, Prentice-Hall, Englewood Cliffs, NJ, 1962. Also *Education and the Creative Potential*, University of Minnesota Press, Minneapolis, 1963. The quotation in the text is reprinted with permission from the latter book, pp. 54–55. Also see E. P. Torrance and L. K. Hall, 'Assessing the further reaches of creative potential', *J. Creat. Behav.* **14**, 1–19 (1980).

23. **(R)** F. A. Haddon and H. Lytton, 'Teaching approach and the development of divergent thinking abilities in primary schools', *Br. J. Educ. Psychol.*, **38**, 171–180 (1968), and 'Primary education and divergent thinking abilities – four years on', *Br. J. Educ. Psychol.*, **41**, 136–147 (1971). For the secondary-level experiment, see H. Lytton and A. C. Cotton, 'Divergent thinking abilities in secondary schools', *Br. J. Educ. Psychol.*, **39**, 188–190 (1969) in the Reader.

24. J. C. Barker Lunn, *Streaming in the Primary School*, NFER, Slough, 1970.

25. R. S. Crutchfield, 'Creative thinking in children: its teaching and testing', in O. G. Brun, R. S. Crutchfield and W. H. Holtzman (eds), *Intelligence Perspectives 1965: The Terman–Otis Memorial Lectures*, Harcourt, Brace and World, New York, 1966.

26. The 'Hawthorne' effect occurs when, as a result of introducing a novel method into a situation, part of any improvement in productivity is due to the change as much as the actual method – 'a change is as good as a rest'.

27. P. N. Richards and N. Bolton, 'Types of mathematics teaching, mathematical ability and divergent thinking in junior school children', *Br. J. Educ. Psychol.*, **41**, 32–37 (1971), and G. S. Gopal Rao, D. M. Penfold and A. P. Penfold, 'Modern and traditional mathematics teaching', *Educ. Res.*, **13**, 61–65 (1970).

28. A. F. Osborn, *Applied Imagination* (3rd rev.), Scribners, New York, 1957. See also E. P. Torrance and R. E. Myers, *Creative Learning and Teaching*, Dodd, Mead, New York, 1970.

29. S. J. Parnes and A. Meadow, in C. W. Taylor and F. Barron (eds), *Scientific Creativity: Its Recognition and Development*, Wiley, New York, 1963, Chapter 25, and S. J. Parnes, R. B. Noller and A. M. Biondi, *Guide to Creative Action*, Scribner, New York, 1977.

30. W. J. J. Gordon, *Synectics: The Development of Creative Capacity*, Harper and Row, New York, 1961.

31. E. de Bono, *The Mechanisms of Mind*, Cape, London, 1969; *Teaching Thinking*, Temple Smith, London, 1976; *Lateral Thinking: A Textbook of Creativity*. Pelican, Harmondsworth, 1977.

32. E. de Bono, *CoRT Thinking: Introductory Pack, Teachers' Notes*, Cognitive Research Trust, Cambridge, 1973. Also **(R)** G. Moore, 'Thinking for themselves', *Scot. Educ. J.*, April, 441–442 (1975).

33. B. Y. Kersh and M. C. Wittrock, 'Learning by discovery; an interpretation of recent research', *J. Teacher Educ.*, **13**, 461–468 (1962); J. A. Rowell, J. Simon and R. Wiseman, 'Verbal reception, guided discovery and the learning of schemata', *Br. J. Educ. Psychol.*, **39**, 233–244 (1969).

FURTHER READING

R. J. Alban Metcalfe, *Assessment of Creativity*, Rediguide 17, TRC-Rediguides, Oxford 1983.

P. J. Congdon, *Fostering Creative Thinking Skills: A Handbook of Practical Suggestions for Teachers*, Gifted Children's Information Centre, 941 Warwick Road, Solihull, 1980.

J. F. Feldhusen and D. J. Feldhusen, *Teaching Creative Thinking and Problem-Solving in Gifted Education*, Kendall-Hunt, Dubuque, IA, 1980.

J. Freeman, H. J. Butcher and T. Christie, *Creativity: A Selective Review of Research*, Society for Research in Higher Education, London, 1972. A technical book which summarizes the important research in this field.

G. Leytham, *Managing Creativity*, Peter Francis, Dereham, Norfolk, 1990.

M. A. Runco and R. S. Albert, *Theories of Creativity*, Sage, London, 1990.

E. P. Torrance and R. E. Myers, *Creative Learning and Teaching*, Dodd, Mead, New York, 1970. This is a guidebook for teachers experimenting with exploratory classroom techniques. A very readable text.

P. E. Vernon (ed.), *Creativity*, Penguin, Harmondsworth, 1970.

Chapter 11

Personality and Leadership

Why is it necessary for teachers to make a study of human personality? One reason is that we are daily making judgements about the affective qualities of ourselves, our pupils and our colleagues. We should, therefore, be fully conversant with the extent to which we can form a reliable assessment of personality using these judgements. Personality factors also affect learning and performance and, although we have no formula that we can apply for guiding children with diverse personal attributes, nevertheless there is every reason why we must recognize that the differences which exist in their scholastic performance may be as much a function of their personality as a function of their intellect. Recognition of the mentally disturbed and immediate recourse to professional help, especially in the earliest phases, can prevent eleventh-hour therapy. Again, our work as teachers consists of influencing attitudes and the more we know about attitude formation and change, the better are our chances of influencing others.

Much of our time is spent trying to weigh up the personalities of those around us and adjusting to them where possible. We observe the way people move, talk or react on different occasions; we watch their faces for clues to their attitudes and we listen to their prejudices; we find ourselves changing to suit the circumstances, so when people are amongst friends they are usually not the same as they are when being interviewed for a job. But the superficial observation of how others behave in particular circumstances and its use as a means of describing personality has serious drawbacks, as we shall see. The popular view of personality, where we typify others in such limited terms as 'generous', 'bad-tempered', 'morbid', 'aloof', etc., without regard for the many other qualities which go to make up an individual's overall profile, has been unfortunate. Psychologists, on the other hand, have been more concerned with a description of the total organization of a person's behaviour, and this chapter will be devoted to a discussion of some of these approaches.

The task of describing and defining the total organization of humans is very complex. Whilst we do not find any generally agreed definition of personality amongst psychologists, one which is sufficiently comprehensive for our purposes is 'the more or less stable and enduring organisation of a person's character, temperament, intellect and physique which determines his unique adjustment to the environment'.[1] Note that the definition carefully distinguishes such attributes as character and temperament as well as intelligence and physique because, as we shall show next, these terms have rather special meanings in psychology.

Temperament

This is a quality we reserve to describe the inherent disposition underlying personality. Physiological factors there from birth, such as variations in endocrine gland secretions in response to different environmental settings, distinguish our excitability, instability or placidity, so that temperament is closely allied to emotional dispositions which even at a common-sense level are seen to vary enormously from person to person. The evidence for inherited temperamental traits, as in our consideration of intelligence, is indirect. Like intelligence, temperament cannot be observed directly because the influence of environmental factors is immediate, but the study of twins, brothers and sisters and family trees gives us a clue to hereditary influence. When we compare the response patterns exhibited by newborn babies from different families, it soon becomes obvious that even in the same situation their responses are dissimilar. In research where babies' toes were dipped into icy water a whole range of responses ensued. Some babies took the whole sordid affair in their stride and placidly withdrew their limbs; at the other extreme, some screamed blue murder; others showed fear, horror and recoil.[2]

Character

This, on the other hand, is an evaluative term referring to such traits as honesty, self-control, persistence and sense of justice. It relates to qualities which we can define as socially acceptable or objectionable and incorporates the development of attitudes, and values. Environmental constraints accompany the expression of inherited temperamental qualities and lead to character development. The relationship between temperament and character described here is not unlike that between Intelligence A and B described in Chapter 9. Having certain temperamental potentialities at birth gives a blueprint for the development of character which to some extent depends on the processes of socialization to which the child is exposed. The guidelines laid down in a permissive or an authoritarian home are thought to determine the social and moral life styles (values and attitudes to race, religion, morals, etc.) within the context of the child's temperamental possibilities.

Since our definition of personality deals with 'adjustment to the environment' it is clear that intelligence must play an important role in personality. Mention was made of this in Chapters 9 and 10. Bright children do not adjust to their environment in the same way as do dull children. For one thing, the former can attain higher levels of abstraction and in consequence may face and solve life's problems in ways which contrast with the latter. *Physique* and personality will be dealt with later in the chapter.

THEORIES OF PERSONALITY

As with most unsolved problems in human experience, there are diverse theories purporting to define personality development and measurement. Not all these theories are of value to teachers, and even those which might have something to offer should be treated as possibilities and not certainties.

Interest in personality has a very long history. As long ago as the second century AD, Galen proposed a typology of personality based on the distribution of the 'body fluids' or 'humours' first suggested by Hippocrates (Greece, fifth century BC). The personality types were called the *melancholic, sanguine, phlegmatic* and *choleric*. The corresponding 'humours' and characteristics are drawn-up in Table 11.1. Notice that melancholics are opposite in nature to sanguines and phlegmatics opposite to cholerics. This particular fourfold scheme of personality types survives in a modified form in several contemporary theories (see, for example, Eysenck's work later in the chapter).

Table 11.1

Humour	Personality type	Characteristic behaviour
Black bile	Melancholic	Pessimistic, suspicious, depressed
Blood	Sanguine	Optimistic, sociable, easy-going
Phlegm	Phlegmatic	Calm, controlled, lethargic
Yellow bile	Choleric	Active, irritable, egocentric

Modern theories of personality structure are many and diverse. To assist in containing these we shall adopt as a basis the useful classification compiled by Vernon.[3] He sees three broad basic approaches to the interpretation of personality which he calls *naïve, intuitive* and *inferential*. To these may be added a fourth, the *humanist* interpretation (Cartwright).[3] An alternative method of classifying personality studies stems from the philosophy underpinning the methods of analysing human personality. One view is that human endeavour can have meaning only if studied from the point of view of the uniqueness of individuals (*idiographic*) rather than by looking for common characteristics which are thought to be possessed by all people to some extent (*nomothetic*). The intuitive and humanist traditions are idiographic, while the inferential theories are nomothetic. For a summary of these see Fontana.[3]

(a) Naïve approaches to personality

Naïve interpretations are based essentially on superficial, face-value observations and interpretations of overt behaviour without the use of standardized norms. What we see in other people is conditioned by our own dispositions, attitudes, motives, biases and interests, and we build up a rule of thumb about human nature on the grounds of previous anecdotal experience. Some have suggested that what we perceive in another person depends entirely on the intention we ascribe to that person; in other words, we project our own interpretations of behaviour to explain the intentions of others. It is very easy, for example, to invent malicious motives for the behaviour of children, which might provide one reason for child battering and abuse, when their actions are playfully and innocently disobedient. In this case we are investing their immature actions with adult motives.

There are many behavioural cues which affect people's judgement. Two important ones are *physical characteristics* and *social response* factors. Likely physical features include facial expressions, body movements, clothes, handwriting and speech. Social response factors indicate our actual or perceived social role. We try to adopt modes of behaviour and social postures in keeping with what we think are characteristic of the circumstances. Goffman[4] thinks that, even in trivial contacts, individuals try to impersonate the image they think will fit the event and possibly satisfy the expectations of others. The implication of this kind of theorizing is that there are stereotypes which we use as models for our aspirations. The doctor or headteacher might have an image of the 'typical' doctor or head teacher which he or she attempts to emulate. Children may use their fathers and mothers as models of parenthood in their approach to other people, or in solving life's problems. In short, we learn about the various roles in life by observing the important people (sometimes called 'role models') already established in these roles.

Perhaps the most extensive use made of superficial criteria for evaluating personality is in the interview. Most serious research directed towards assessing the reliability and validity of the interview as a selection procedure has been very discouraging. Vernon[5] quotes a lot of evidence against the use of interviews for selection and concludes that oral questioning and the interview are useless for assessing ability or the results of teaching. He also maintains that:

> While there is much else to be said later [in his book], particularly about clinical and coun-selling interviews, it may be stated here that the selection interview is at its best when it is used: (a) for expanding, checking and probing the information previously provided by paper qualifications and biographical data; (b) for assessing particular qualities, mainly physical, social and intellectual, that have a good chance of expression during the inter-view situation. It is at its worst when it is conceived as a means for the interviewer: (a) to intuit or infer fundamental qualities of personality and character; (b) to weigh up and synthesize the evidence from diverse sources and reach a decision in the light of his 'expe-rience' and judgement of job requirements.
>
> (note (3), pp. 70–71)

The comments were made as a result of synthesizing research findings, and they raise many doubts about traditional interview methods of selection. For example, selection for places in schools is partially dependent on interview. Career and job selection from 16 onwards nearly always uses a conventional interview. In a research by the author[6] into nurse selection, the interview was an integral part of selection procedures for admission to nurse training. However, in keeping with the findings from many similar researches, the methods used at interview were questionable. The findings showed that schools and colleges of nursing rarely had clearly stated criteria they were using in the interview in order to make judgements about suitability. Even those criteria specified like 'has a caring attitude' or 'had understanding' were not clearly defined. Indeed, some expressions were very difficult to define. One method of improving the validity of the interview was for interviewers to have a checklist of clearly definable criteria and to pose questions from this list in such a way as to expose the extent to which the interviewee meets the criteria.

Naïve interpretations of personality are doomed to failure for several reasons. These interpretations tend towards an over-simplified view of human nature, aggravated by the fact that most people create masks in order to disguise or create particular qualities at will and according to circumstances. They tend to employ rigid stereotypes, which are frequently based on limited and biased experience, to describe the behaviour observed. Naïve impressions of others are very much bound up with the interaction occurring between people. This interaction often rests on superficial contact in highly specific incidents. An added complication results from the *role play* of individuals when they are trying to put over a particular image. There is also a temptation to observe the irregular, because idiosyncratic behaviour is more conspicuous. Eccentricities such as voice intonation, twitches or an aggressive approach can disturb a balanced judgement. We also tend to undervalue those with a different point of view from our own. All in all, these shallow attempts at personality analysis are not likely to give us a stable, comprehensive picture of another's personality. In judging children it could, if carried too far, lead to quite distorted views about their actual or potential aptitudes.

(b) The humanist approaches to personality

There has undoubtedly been an upsurge of interest in humanistic psychology through the 1960s which has emphasized both the importance of the *whole being*, the person, as the centre of personality study (and not particular parts of an individual's behaviour) and the inevitable tendency of human beings to desire and actively seek to achieve life goals. These are strongly reflected in the humanists' avoidance of 'data' collection and analysis of groups to form generalizations, and their preference for whole-life case studies of individuals. The ideas of looking at the 'experiencing' person from his or her point of view and the importance attached to self-determinism of human beings is not new, for these notions come over strongly in gestalt writings. More recently, the 'ethnomethodologists' have stressed the importance of the whole-individual case and the accounts which that individual gives of the motives behind the actions.

One of the first and widely acknowledged humanist theories of personality was expounded by Maslow.[7] His hierarchy of needs appears in Chapter 3, and it forms the basis of his views on personality. The personality is shaped by the individual's reactions along the paths taken while the needs are in the process of being satisfied. As we saw in Chapter 3, the order in which the individual satisfies the needs is fundamental and those needs higher on the scale of things are more typical of adults than of children. Where deprivation occurs at a point in the hierarchy, 'stunting' of personal development involving those needs above that point occurs. Thus, if the esteem needs are deprived, development of self-actualization and cognitive understanding are distorted. Unfortunately, Maslow's work has never been thoroughly researched, largely because the concepts are very difficult to operationalize (i.e. it is hard to make and test hypotheses relating to the theory). Therefore his work has tended to remain as a descriptive rationalization of children's behaviour.

Carl Rogers[8] takes Maslow's view a stage further by suggesting that human beings perceive their experiences as reality and respond to this perceived reality in a way which helps the individual to 'self-actualization'. This term is used in the same way as in Maslow's theory (see Chapter 3) and is the central motivational concept for Rogers. The young child, for instance,[8] behaves as an organized whole (cf. gestalt theory) and is regulated in the direction of his or her behaviour by the organism's *valuing* process; that is, a process enabling the individual to evaluate the worth of experiences which might maintain and enhance the physical and social self. Hence, Rogers is referred to as a *phenomenologist* because he believes the person places emphasis on what he or she *thinks* is happening and not on what *is* happening. This is closely tied to the *self-concept*, which is, for Rogers, that part of the individual's *awareness of himself or herself* using all the perceptual means at his or her disposal. The awareness acts as a frame of reference by which an individual makes judgements about his or her well-being in relation to physical and social preservation in an effort to achieve self-actualization.

Self-concept

The notion of the self-concept has already been alluded to in Chapter 3 as an important element in motivation. Curiously, the term 'self-concept' (or synonymous expressions) is a twentieth-century one. Yet the idea has appeared in history, in one form or another, for centuries. Now only the purest behaviourist would exclude the concept of self and all those allied constructs of individual processes such as motivation, personality and human ability from any consideration of learning and teaching. Very few texts in educational psychology still persist in plugging solely a mechanical model of human learning (or teaching), with its attendant manipulable input/output devices. The concept occurs in all the areas of personality study of idiographic or nomothetic origin, from Freud through Maslow to Cattell.

The self-concept has been variously defined, but perhaps the definition offered by Burns is sufficient for our needs here. He suggests[9] that self-concept 'is the individual's percepts, concepts and evaluations about himself, including the image he feels others have of him and of the person he would like to be, nourished by a diet of personally evaluated environmental experience'. He distinguishes between self-concept and self-esteem which he takes to be the outcome of the processes of self-evaluation and self-worth. It is a 'conscious judgement regarding the significance and importance of oneself or of facets of oneself'. As Colin (not Carl) Rogers[9] remarks, 'The self-concept is what we are like, while self-esteem is the degree to which we like what we think.'

There are many and diverse influences which will tend to shape the self-concept, but the greatest impact is undoubtedly the parents, both in terms of inborn characteristics (tendencies toward being reserved, conscientious, tough-minded, self-sufficient) which might predispose us to determine, interpret and *react* to events, and in terms of the impact of external events in the child-rearing patterns. Children watch and assimilate the methods parents use in solving day-to-day problems (calmly, systematically, impatiently), which helps to create the structures of the self-concept valuing processes. Added to this is the vastly important regard which the individual builds up about his or her own competence to solve these problems as a result of interaction with significant others (whether they give one confidence, how they react to one's solutions, etc.).

The role of the self-concept in education has established a significant place in contemporary studies. Burns (**R**)[9] identifies five aspects which are of importance to education:

(a) What is the relationship between the pupil's self-concept and his or her academic performance?

(b) What roles do feedback, reinforcement and expectations play in modifying self-concept and attainment?

(c) What is the effect of different forms of school organization on pupils' self-concepts?

(d) What is the relationship between the teacher's self-concept and his or her classroom style?

(e) Can modifications of pupil and teacher self-concepts, through counselling, intensive group work, etc., be made and have these any effect on the classroom performance of pupils and teachers?

The evidence so far (discussed in Burns's book[9]) seems to show that in (a) the interaction of the self-concept and academic achievement is now well established. The surveys of Purkey[10] or Bloom[10] and researches of Brookover[10] in America, for example, give ample evidence of a relationship (correlations of between $+0.3$ and $+0.4$ are frequently obtained). The strongest link tends to exist at the low-performance end of the scale, so low attainment and low self-regard are more often found together than high attainment and high self-regard. The causal connection between these two cannot be assumed from the correlation. As Burns points out, 'At the present state of knowledge it seems reasonable to assume that the relationship between self-concept and academic attainment is reciprocal, not unidirectional.'

The role of feedback, from (b) above, is crucial. The teacher's role in providing a sounding-board by which children discover their competences is very important. The 'recognition and reinforcement of competence' theme is taken up at various places in this book, but in Chapter 3 we looked particularly at the question of self-fulfilling prophecy and attribution of success or failure. Self-esteem is enhanced by the teacher's recognition and acceptance and tactful, respectful usage of a child's strengths and limitations. A clear indication of the standards and limits of behaviour in the school and fair judgements when these are exceeded are necessary.

Controversial research findings surround the question of school organization (c) and its influence on children's self-concepts.[11] Certain school and class arrangements, such as streaming, special education, grammar, secondary modern, comprehensive, single-sex or mixed, have all been investigated inconclusively. Given the constraining effects of institutional settings, perhaps the strongest influence is related to attitudes, values and expectations of those who operate within the organization.

As we shall see later in this chapter, a teacher's personal style, the ethos this generates in negotiating with others and the response obtained from children are, of course, important in learning and teaching. However, it has to be admitted that the problems of isolating the most effective aspects of style and the extent to which one can change to adopt useful styles are largely unsolved. One could probably get by with a knowledge of the science and technology of teaching – an endless stream of reinforcement schedules – but the *act* of applying this knowledge, the skills in human relationships and what the teacher is as a person are also important conditions by means of which the art and craft of teaching influences children's learning.

(c) Intuitive theories of personality

Theories under this heading are referred to by Vernon as intuitive because the psychologists, usually those who adopt a clinical approach to their study of human personality, believe in an 'unlearned capacity for understanding others'. Clinical studies frequently depend on exploration of motivations and needs which cannot be directly observed.

Surely the most famous psychologist of all time is Sigmund Freud (1856–1939), the father of *depth psychology* (also known as *psychodynamics* or *clinical psychology*). The theory is extensive and has had a substantial following both as an instrument of research and as the basis for therapy among the mentally ill. But at present much of his theorizing has limited practical value to the teacher. For those who wish to dig deeper, note (12) contains several references, but in this chapter we shall restrict ourselves to a consideration of the basic aspects of his theory which illustrate the 'intuitive' approach to personality; 'intuitive' is also used here to emphasize the subjective, and assumed unlearned, understanding of human conduct forming the basis of Freudian psychology.

Some psychologists have little time for the theories of Freud and his followers. They claim that his view is based largely on supposition[13] and limited experimental evidence; an 'unsinkable theory', according to Hudson,[13] which can be adjusted whenever conflicting evidence is found; his methods are said to be unscientific and employed biased samples of middle-class Viennese women with sexual problems; the proportion of 'cures' of the mentally ill brought about by psychoanalysis is little better than chance, and in any case Freud exaggerated much of what he did find. These are harsh comments for a theory which has given both the layman and the psychological world a seminal framework of personality composition along with a voluminous rag-bag of terms which permeate our language (repression, ego, Oedipus complex, etc.). More important, Freud's methods have opened up new approaches to the study of human beings (for instance, Piaget used techniques of a clinical kind in his earliest work) and have given a terrific stimulus to other fields of psychology such as motivation and development. Freud's gifts to psychologists and teachers were in drawing their attention to another way of looking at childhood, to the child's affiliative relationships with parents, brothers and sisters, to the existence and potency of infantile sexuality, to the possible unconscious nature of a great deal of human motivation, to the continuum between normal and neurotic behaviour, to the ambivalence of early child–parent relationships (Oedipus and Electra complexes) and to the enduring effects of many early childhood experiences.

Basic principles relating to Freud's work

Amongst other things, Freud's theory stresses these points:

(a)   The behaviour exhibited by mentally deviant people arises from the self-same motives as the mentally normal.

(b)   In addition to a *conscious* level of mental operations, where we are fully aware of mental events, there is also the *unconscious mind* (mental traces of past experiences which were once at the conscious level). Unconscious traces can affect our behaviour without our being aware of the source. Freud considered that the unconscious was a repository consisting mainly of *repressed*, unpleasant experiences ('repression' means exclusion from the conscious level, see later) which could not be entertained at the conscious level. A *sub-conscious* or *pre-conscious* level was also postulated, consisting of traces which, though not in the conscious mind, nevertheless can be brought there by active recall of past experiences.

(c)   Unconscious motives arise from *defence mechanisms*. These we shall elaborate shortly but they are ways of behaving which enable us to protect ourselves from conflicting and intolerable situations.

(d)   Early childhood experience is the key to later behaviour patterns. For Freud, the unfolding of sexual behaviour in childhood had much to do with personality formation.

We have already said, in Chapter 3, something of Freud's views on the basic motivating forces of human action. Briefly, we noted that at the heart of our driving force are the *libidal* (sexual) and *ego* (biological) instincts. These natural forces he referred to as the *id*. Unleashed and uncontrolled, they would give rise to animal behaviour in violation of the cultural taboos of the child's society. Parental and societal pressures and constraints create in the developing child a conscience known as the *superego*, brought about by absorbing the mores of society (*introjection*). There is also a part of the personality in contact with the id, superego and the realities of the outside world. This is the *ego*, which acts as an adjuster between the raw requirements of the id and the censure of the superego.

To bring about a resolution of the demands of the id and the constraints of the superego, the ego resorts to *defence mechanisms*; these act as a shield against the otherwise intolerable conflicts between the naked demands of the human as an animal and the acquired conscience built up in childhood from the rules of society. The behaviour ensuing from defence mechanisms is, then, largely unconsciously motivated. Freud believed that simple slips of the tongue, pen or memory,[12] serious mental disarray, dreams and fantasies in waking and sleeping are all rooted in unconscious processes. Information about these processes can be teased out by devious means such as psychoanalysis, hypnosis or the use of drugs.

Let us look at a few simple illustrations of defence mechanisms which we might find in normal life:

Compensation   When an individual replaces one means of expressing a motive by some other, less direct means, compensation occurs. A married couple who are childless may treat a dog as if it were a child; parents who have missed a chance in their own education may make sacrifices to ensure success for their children.

Identification   When a person is moved to regard himself or herself as another, admired person, the result is called identification. Films or television programmes give opportunities for some to identify themselves with the people on the screen. Sometimes children try to imitate their parents as authority figures in an effort to get their own way.

Regression   Regression, is said to have occurred when an individual utilizes behaviour more characteristic of an earlier stage in life. Even amongst adults it is possible to find those who occasionally resort to stamping, weeping, overt aggression and 'going home to mother' behaviour in an effort to get their own way. The logic of this is that as children they may sometimes have been successful in getting what they wanted by stamping or weeping. As adults they regress to this earlier tactic.

Sublimation   When an original desire is unfulfilled, sublimation is the redirection of one's activities into similar activity. For example, when students who want to become doctors are unsuccessful, they often sublimate their enthusiasm in other paramedical fields (nursing, physiotherapy, pharmacy, medical social work).

Projection   When there is a tendency to project one's faults or wishes into others, projection occurs. Occasionally an adolescent girl may claim that she is constantly being watched by boys – more a wishful thought than a statement of fact. Countries often accuse each other of stockpiling troops and armaments on each other's borders whilst in fact doing it themselves.

We shall see in a moment that projection is one method used by psychotherapists and depth psychologists as a means of exposing hidden motives.

Rationalization   Also called the 'sour-grapes syndrome', rationalization is really an example of self-deception where we try to find excuses for our shortcomings – too much study ruins your eyes, if you are not fond of reading!

Repression   This is the final example – the deliberate thrusting aside, because of social inhibitions, of the libidal forces which are striving for expression. The repressed drives do not disappear; instead, they remain as traces in the unconscious and influence the actions of individuals when similar unpleasant situations arise.

All these methods of compensation occur, according to Freud, as perfectly normal reactions. Where they get out of proportion *neuroses* develop as mental conditions such as anxiety states, phobias, obsessions or hysteria. Neuroses are the outcome of an inability to find recognized ways of adjusting to life's problems. The disorders which result affect emotional and intellectual functioning, although the neurotic patient is not deprived of contact with reality. In the most serious mental illnesses, known as *psychoses* (manic-depressive conditions involving delusions and hallucinations, or schizophrenia), the sufferer is completely dissociated from reality. The neurotic, on the other hand, has the problem of living in a real world and knowing it; the psychotic lives in quite a different mental world and dissociation from the real world does not worry that person.

Freud's theory has not stood still. His two closest disciples, Adler and Jung, stressed different sources of man's motivation, such as striving for self-fulfilment and superiority (the *mastery drive* of Adler) or the desire to belong (Jung). More recently, insecurity in childhood (Horney, Fromm), social interpersonal relations (Sullivan) and creativity have attracted the attention of the 'new' or neo-Freudians.

In addition to the criticisms raised at the start of this section, we should also note the difficulty of verifying the views of depth psychologists.[14] There is also too little consideration given to human adaptability; instead, we are led to believe that our basic personalities are founded in the first few years of life and that we must live with this for the remainder of our lives. The work of social anthropologists suggests that the aggressive drive[15] is not inevitable in human nature. Only recently have neo-Freudians paid attention to the impact of social phenomena as a source of motivation. Later in the chapter we shall refer to some of the methods of depth psychology.

(d) Inferential theories of personality

Inferential theories depend on scientific, objective analysis and are the province of the *psychometrician*.[16] The psychometric movement has its origins in the belief that man's behavioural tendencies can be classified as *traits* **(R)**[22] or *factors* measurable using tests and evaluated chiefly by the use of factor analysis. The idea that humans possess personality traits is not a new one. We saw Galen's typology based on the body humours; also, Jung's extraversion–introversion typology arises from his conviction that there are stable patterns of personality characteristics. For the extravert the outer world is most important; the extravert is active rather than passive; he or she is given more to subjective feelings than to objective thoughts. Introverts resort more to the inner, personal world and are given to introspection rather than action. This is not a complete description, but it will suffice to show how Jung first conceived the concepts of introversion and extraversion. The same terms have been adopted by later psychologists, notably Eysenck, who, as we shall see, defines the traits more extensively.

Eysenck's work

In a very long list of books,[17] H. J. Eysenck has elaborated a most comprehensive objective approach to the study of personality. His theories have grown out of research with psychiatric patients at the Maudsley Hospital in London. Like the British school of thought regarding the structure of intelligence (see Chapter 9), Eysenck holds a hierarchical view of personality. At the highest point we find personality *types*, and in fact Eysenck expresses personality organization in terms of three basic types, *extraversion–introversion* (sometimes contracted to extraversion for convenience), *neuroticism–stability* (neuroticism for short) and *psychoticism–normality*.[18] He also believes that intelligence is a fourth dimension. But these dimensions are thought to be normally distributed in the population, so the majority of people possess an admixture of the qualities underlying the types and therefore would obtain scores around the mid-point of each dimension. In fact, Eysenck's starting point was the mentally ill, that is, the extremes of the dimensions, and from these extremes he devised tests and questions which defined the dimensions. He is at great pains, nevertheless, to remind us that dimensionality implies a continuum of personality possibilities and not categorical definitions. Unfortunately, the use of such black and white terms as 'introvert' and 'neurotic' give the erroneous impression that people are either one thing or the other.

Figure 11.1 illustrates the interdependence of personality characteristics and the way

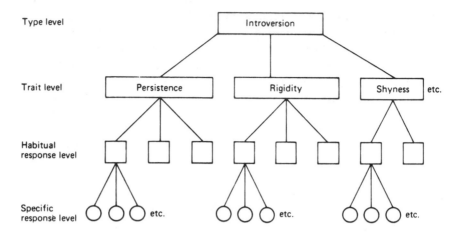

Type level

Trait level

Habitual
response level

Specific
response level

Figure 11.1   *From H. J. Eysenck,* The Structure of Human Personality, *p. 13, Methuen, London, 1953.*

in which Eysenck envisages a connection between the levels of personality organization which underpin the fundamental type. Qualities which characterize the introvert, such as persistence, rigidity, subjectivity, shyness and irritability, are known as *traits*. These in turn are associated with *habitual* ways of responding in similar conditions, so that in problem-solving or in mechanical tasks requiring vigilance we might expect the introvert to be, in general, persistent. In particular circumstances requiring vigilance we might find variations in the degree of vigilance displayed, but we would expect an introvert to be vigilant in most of his or her specific responses.

Neuroticism–stability   The term *neurosis* was first used to describe a collection of abnormal mental conditions including anxiety, obsessions and hysteria. Thus, in hysterical cases physical symptoms sometimes accompanied a mental condition (sometimes referred to as *psychosomatic* disorder). Sickness and nausea caused by apprehension before such anxiety-provoking events as examinations or interviews may be physical manifestations of a mental condition. However, the term has developed a more particular meaning in Eysenck's model because we all possess some measure of neuroticism, ranging from stability to high anxiety, worrying unduly, panicking under stress and being over-emotional.

We have already seen that anxiety, a major correlate of neuroticism, has a physiological basis. The hypothalamus was noted as the centre of control for the autonomic nervous system and endocrine secretions via the pituitary gland (Chapter 2). The extent of hypothalamic reaction depends on many factors, not least of which are inherited autonomic functioning and the extent of the crisis which initiates anxiety. We have also mentioned how severing the frontal-lobe connections of the brain has the effect of reducing the level of anxiety displayed by individuals. Arousal has also been referred to in connection with motivation. Here we saw that, in difficult tasks, high levels of anxiety could adversely affect performance, and we shall say more later about a possible application of measures of neuroticism to performance in academic work.

Extraversion–Introversion   Extraverts, in Eysenckian terms, are outgoing, relatively uninhibited, fond of activities which bring them into contact with other people, not attracted by solitary pursuits such as study, cravers after excitement, aggressive, unreliable, easy-going and optimistic. Introverts tend to possess the opposite of these qualities. Most of us, mercifully, possess most of these qualities to some degree – ambiverts. But this has been a particularly interesting personality dimension for educational psychologists. A glance at the list of traits just mentioned will soon reveal that they bear directly on a number of qualities of advantage in traditional educational settings. However, before we deal with this matter there are one or two theoretical issues to consider.

A recent theory posited by Eysenck[18] attempts to provide causal connections between physiological brain mechanisms and the personality dimensions of extraversion and neuroticism. In Chapter 2 we mentioned the ascending reticular activating system (ARAS) as the seat of arousal in response to external stimuli. Eysenck proposes that there are individual differences in the extent of arousal which can be related to extraversion–introversion. 'Arousal under identical stimulating conditions is higher in introverts than in extraverts.' The differences, therefore, can be related directly to inherited qualities in brain structure. Another part of the brain, the *visceral brain*, is thought to be responsible for individual differences in emotionality as measured using the neuroticism dimension.

The theory leads to a number of propositions which have some experimental backing. The notion that we are aroused to different levels by similar events is not new. Some people become much more 'aware' of stimulation than others. Similarly, some people take longer to 'cool off' after excitation. If Eysenck's arousal proposition is valid, introverts, by implication from our knowledge of brain functioning, are less likely to develop inhibition in a task than extraverts. Thus introverts are more likely to be able to concentrate for longer periods of time in tasks requiring vigilance, i.e. they have longer spans of attention. We shall apply this later. Again, introverts are more susceptible to conditioning than are extraverts. This could be a decided advantage in some formal educational settings, and may mean that the introvert is likely to be more readily socialized in childhood. We must not forget, however, that in using concepts such as 'introvert' and 'extravert' we are dealing with extreme cases. Most individuals are ambivert in their behaviour. For this reason, the findings we shall refer to later, in the absence of more refined measures, relate mainly to those with more extreme personality manifestations. Another complication in dealing with extraversion and neuroticism is the possibility of excessive visceral brain activity affecting the arousal mechanisms of the ARAS as well. In other words, those with high neuroticism scores are often in a state of arousal, and thus we have an interaction effect between extraversion and neuroticism.

Throughout Eysenck's arguments there is unequivocal support for the inheritance of personality characteristics. The evidence, and the debate surrounding this issue, takes on a similar form to that dealt with in Chapter 9. Evidence taken from twin studies[19] shows high correlations in adulthood using the extraversion scale. Studies of the consistency in the personality profiles of babies[2] lend further support. A thorough review of the research for and against the inheritability of personality traits is given by Eysenck.[20]

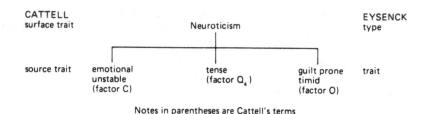

Notes in parentheses are Cattell's terms

Figure 11.2   *The relationship between the terminology of Cattell and Eysenck. Taken from D. Child,* The Essentials of Factor Analysis, *Cassell, London, 1990 (2nd edn).*

R. B. Cattell[21]

Another worker who has successfully applied psychometric methods, chiefly factor analysis, to explore personality organization is Raymond B. Cattell, in the United States. By taking the kind of analysis used by Eysenck a stage further, he has obtained 16 personality factors (sometimes known as the 16PF). Cattell distinguishes between what he calls *source traits*, which are at the root of observed behaviour, and *surface traits*, which are the superficial and detectable patterns of behaviour having their origins in source traits (**R**).[22] Neuroticism as defined by Eysenck would be a surface trait for Cattell, and the qualities which go to make up neuroticism (emotional instability, tenseness, timidity, etc.) would be source traits. Figure 11.2 demonstrates the connection between the two points of view. There are matters of detail in which the two would differ, for not all the 16 factors of Cattell will 'compress' to give the E and N dimensions of Eysenck. Nevertheless, there is a large measure of agreement between these two.

The approach of these and other psychometricians is not without its critics. The primary source of information for the detection of the dimensions is the pencil-and-paper test (see later in the chapter), which raises several questions. Do people tend to give socially desirable responses to these tests and are there universal 'yes' or 'no' responders? How total is the profile of human personality: in other words, have all the relevant questions been posed on these pencil-and-paper inventories? How stable are the factors across different groups of people or for the same person, and where variations in the scores occur are they due to unreliable test material or to genuine changes in personality from one test to the next? These and many other questions are levelled at inferential personality approaches.

Kelly's personal construct theory

One attempt at a *rapprochement* between the humanist, intuitive and inferential traditions comes in the work of Kelly.[23] A basic premise is that the theories we have regarding the world about us form the basis from which we perpetually seek to 'guess' what will happen next. In this manner we construe or reconstrue our world of experience. 'A person's processes are psychologically channelized by the ways in which he anticipates events.'[23] This view is in marked contrast to that of the inferential theorists, because Kelly's fundamental belief is that human behaviour is anticipatory rather than reactive. Thus, we react *not* to a stimulus but to what we interpret the stimulus to be. If someone digs a piece of metal out of the ground he or she may construe it as a 'thing', as a lump of metal, as a coin, as a Roman coin or as a coin of particular value from the reign of Constantine the Great, depending on his or her personal constructs. Each person's reaction to the find is different, even though the superficial sensory stimulation is the same.

The technique developed by Kelly[24] for comparing our reactions to people who are significant in our lives is referred to as the *repertory grid method*. One popular method for initiating the grid is to ask a person to name several people (six in the grid below) known to him or her. These are known as *elements* in the grid and could be objects or concepts, besides people. Next, the person is asked to group the elements into threes (the *triad* method) from the list of significant others (which might consist of mother, father, sister, brother, work friend, boss, neighbour, etc.) in such a way that two are alike but at the same time dissimilar to the third person in some specified way. The 'specified ways' are called *constructs* and are commonly expressed in bipolar form such as powerful–weak, cruel–kind, mature–immature, generous–stingy, intelligent–stupid. If the subject is now asked to place each person at one or other end of each pole (x = one end of pole, blank = the other), a grid can be constructed thus:

	Constructs	Elements					
		1	2	3	4	5	6
A	powerful–weak	x	x	x			x
B	cruel–kind	x			x	x	
C	mature–immature		x			x	

From the grid, many kinds of information are possible. By looking along each row in turn we have an idea of the individual's definition of each construct in terms of the person's acquaintances; from each column we have a personality profile of each acquaintance in terms of the constructs chosen by the individual; a 'matching score' can be obtained by counting the number of compatible elements for each pair of constructs and taking this figure from the number of pairs expected by chance. Consequently, for the constructs A and B, there is one matching pair (the first element); by chance there would be three matching pairs, and so the matching score will be $1 - 3 = - 2$. For A and C the matching score is $2 - 3 = - 1$, and for B and C it is $3 - 3 = 0$. These scores are the basis of statistical procedures too complex to mention here,[24] but by which a construct universe can be designed for an individual which Kelly claims will define the major personality variables of that individual. Hence we see the clinical technique involving a description of *individual* personalities, referred to earlier as the *idiographic* approach to personality, as compared with the *nomothetic* approach which endeavours to portray human behaviour in terms of 'average' tendencies or norms, as in the work of Eysenck and Cattell. The method has been used with schoolchildren and is attracting increasing attention **(R)**.[25]

Type A behaviour (personality)

Two American doctors, Friedman and Rosenman,[26] noticed that a larger than average number of young heart attack victims possessed particular constellations of personality characteristics. They referred to those displaying the characteristics as *Type A* personalities. It is interesting to note that some of these appear in most people, but it must not be assumed that the possession of a few of the characteristics necessarily means that the individual is a Type A personality. There must be a regular, persistent appearance of the bulk of the defining features.

There follows a list of the main characteristics. For a fuller list, the reader is advised to look at the source book by the doctors:[26]

1. tries to do or think of two or more things at once;
2. cannot sit doing nothing – feels guilty when not working;
3. develops ticks, facial movements (eyebrow raising);
4. has a 'thing' about punctuality;
5. gets impatient watching others doing a job he or she thinks can be done better;
6. plays to win – even children;
7. drums fingers impatiently;
8. does lots of arm waving when talking;
9. hurries others along who are speaking;
10. tries to steer conversation to her or his own interests;
11. tries to pack a lot of work into a little time;
12. shows no interest in aesthetic aspects of surroundings;
13. gets very cross in queues;
14. has the motto 'if you want something doing properly, do it yourself';
15. pushes other people hard at work.

With this combination of behaviours, it is not difficult to imagine Type A persons coming across as impatient, intolerant, aggressive, 'no nonsense' and fidgety. They are frequently ambitious people with a lot of self-confidence, 'pushiness' and hard work ethic. The price they sometimes pay is heart-related complaints (see the section on 'stress' in Chapter 3).

PERSONALITY AND SCHOOL ACHIEVEMENT

The definitions of neuroticism and extraversion given above have some clear implications for educational performance, especially in a system where long periods of study and concentration, both in general work and in preparation for examinations, are at a premium. Personality, then, plays an important part in learning and attainment, as well as the more obvious factors of intelligence, motivation and cognitive development. However, the *orectic* variables (variables other than the purely cognitive), especially personality, have, until recently, taken a subsidiary place in educational thinking. Yet it would be surprising if temperament and drive were not intimately involved in performance. Common experience teaches us that fear and high anxiety can play havoc with the efficiency of performance.

In Chapter 3 we mentioned that drive and performance were connected, and the Yerkes–Dodson law was one expression of this relationship. Evidence is accumulating to show that anxiety and drive are closely related. This being the case it is tempting to arrive at a picture something like this: low anxiety/low drive/poor performance; moderate anxiety/healthy drive/good performance; high anxiety/high drive/disrupted, poor performance. However, researches (Child (**R**)[22]) show neither a clear curvilinear effect nor a correlation with the level in the educational system. Anxiety is so situation-specific and the tasks we ask of students so complex that it should not surprise the reader to see no consistent pattern emerging from the research.

The case for a positive correlation between introversion as measured by Eysenck's scales and secondary school or college attainment is more substantial. When we look at the characteristics of the extravert in the definition, it is not difficult to imagine why he or she is at a disadvantage in academic pursuits. If reactive inhibition is high, then concentration in studious tasks will be marred by involuntary rest periods, and vigilance must suffer. During examination revision the extravert will have difficulty in maintaining interest in what can be a boring task. Amongst primary school children (**R**)[22,27] introversion is not of as much advantage for girls as it appears to be for boys. But in secondary education[28] and university education[29] the connection has been established more frequently. Using Cattell's personality scales, there is a tendency for academic success to be linked by age to certain introversion–extraversion traits. Younger students, while showing social interests (participating and friendly), have also introvert qualities of conformity, seriousness and self-sufficiency. Older students show all the introvert traits except aggressiveness and competitiveness (see Child (**R**)[22] for details). This age inversion between personality and achievement at around 12 to 15 years is discussed in more detail in the Reader.[22]

Thus we find a tendency for those in higher education to be more neurotic and introverted than the population at large. By definition, the introvert avoids personal situations and enjoys bookish and conceptual pursuits, all of which are rewarded by the present educational selection system. Given students with sufficient intelligence to cope with the demands of higher education, the examination system itself acts as a personality selection device which filters out the neurotic introverts. Moreover, amongst university students it appears that the science specialists are even more introverted and less neurotic than the arts specialists.[29]

In the present state of research in this field it would be unwise to make too much of the connections indicated above, especially at the primary level. Primarily, it is important to be aware that personality characteristics play a significant role both in the act of learning and in attitudes towards the act of learning. Variations in performance are not entirely a question of intellect, motivation or thinking skills, but may depend on the personal attributes which can enhance or inhibit the quality of that performance. This fact alone is sufficient to justify continued research in this field.

THE ASSESSMENT OF PERSONALITY

The approaches to the study of personality at which we have been looking have generated many methods of assessing personality and our purpose here will be to give a summary account of the better-known methods. The task facing the psychologist concerned with personality study is very complex. As we saw from the definition above, the terms of reference are broad and the intrusion of intervening variables, both personal and social, makes analysis very difficult. One of the clearest expositions of the task facing the student of personality is given by Vernon in *Personality Tests and Assessments*.[5] In this section we shall look at physique and temperament, experimental and physical measures which relate to personality, ratings made by self or others, attitude and interest inventories and the better-known methods of depth psychology, such as projection techniques.

Sheldon's typology of physique and personality

Galen's body humours mentioned earlier constitute one of the first attempts to link physiological characteristics with personality types. More recently, Kretschmer[30] drew up a body typology which was developed and refined by Sheldon.[30] The latter postulated three basic body builds having corresponding temperamental traits. The three basic body-build types are: *endomorphs*, who are round, fat and soft; *mesomorphs*, who have hard, muscular bodies; and *ectomorphs*, with a delicate, lean, linear physique. The biologists among our readers will recognize that Sheldon has taken the embryonic layers of endoderm (responsible for laying down the digestive system), mesoderm (lays down muscle, bone, heart and blood system) and ectoderm (lays down the surface structures such as the skin and sense organs, and the nervous system including the brain) as the predominant systems characterizing, respectively, the body-build types of endomorph, mesomorph and ectomorph. Each body-type dimension was rated by Sheldon using a seven-point scale. Therefore, a person with a normal physique would be rated 4 on each dimension, giving a profile of 4–4–4.

Sheldon claimed a close correspondence between these threefold measures of physique and the temperaments of an individual. Using nude photographs and detailed analytical interviews of individuals he concluded that it is possible to obtain a correspondence between physique and temperaments, portrayed in Table 11.2.

Although Sheldon has obtained some convincing correlations between physique and temperament, his work has found critics who have questioned the methods and statistics he uses. Also, there does not appear to be a satisfactory explanation for the changes in physique which often occur with age and which are not accompanied by a corresponding change in temperament. Lean individuals develop middle-age spreads without necessarily changing in temperament.

Table 11.2

Body type	Temperamental traits
Endomorph (round, fat, soft)	Viscerotonia (sociable, affectionate, lover of comfort)
Mesomorph (hard, muscular)	Somatotonia (aggressive, assertive, energetic)
Ectomorph (fragile, 'linear' physique)	Cerebrotonia (withdrawn, lover of privacy and mental activity)

Physical experiments and personality

Eysenck[31] has been particularly active in finding a series of physical tests which appear to have personality correlates. The *pursuit rotor*, which is said to discriminate between introverts and extraverts, is one such device. A disc like a gramophone record, with a metal stud near the edge, is set in motion on a turntable. The idea is to keep a metal probe, like a pencil, held on the stud for as long as possible while the disc is spinning. Concentration and persistence are obvious qualities for this task, and those in whom reactive inhibition (see note (18)) is high will be at a distinct disadvantage. Thus the extravert is rendered less efficient at this game than the introvert, so an electrical timing mechanism which can measure accurately the contact time over a given test period will show introverts as having longer contact time than extraverts. Many other experimental ploys have been used to assess persistence, dark-adaptation, reminiscence, conditionability, etc. Although Eysenck's hypotheses of excitation and inhibition are seminal in providing many plausible experiments to test the diversity of sensory, perceptual and learning functions of personality, there is still much to be done before we can apply the findings in educational settings.

Self-rating inventories of personality

Certainly the most popular means of measuring such dimensions as neuroticism–stability, introversion–extraversion, tender-minded–tough-minded, apprehensive–placid, self-concept and the like is by the use of questionnaires. These contain items by which the individual can rate himself or herself, usually by agreeing or disagreeing with the items. The following are typical examples of personality inventories:

> After each item is a space for answering 'YES' or 'NO'. Answer each item by putting a tick in the appropriate space provided at the end of each item which best expresses the way you usually act or feel.
>
> YES NO
> 1. Are you a nervy person?
> 2. Do you like playing practical jokes?
> 3. Are you frequently moody?
> 4. As a child were you afraid of the dark?
> 5. I would rather work with things than with people.
> 6. I enjoy closely reasoned argument.

Using the technique of factor analysis (see Chapter 9, note (38)), a pool of items which measure the same dimension are assembled. In the examples above, the items have been chosen to represent different personality dimensions, but normally one would find several items in an inventory which are typical of each dimension being measured. The commonest are extraversion, neuroticism and anxiety scales designed for eight-year-olds onwards to adulthood.[32] In the self-concept field many devices have appeared,[33] consisting mainly of self-appraisal scales (see also note (9), Burns's book of 1979). Test administration and interpretation require skill and training, so it would not be possible for all and sundry to obtain copies of these tests.

Much of the research we discussed under the heading of 'neuroticism, extraversion and attainment' earlier has been carried out using personality inventories of the kind described above. Students should take the opportunity to look at test materials provided by their college and explore the kinds of questions which psychologists use for assessing personality types.

The reliability obtained from testing and retesting the same group with the same or a parallel form of inventory has been encouragingly high. The closer the testing sessions in time, the higher is the reliability. Our reservations about such inventories include the problem of knowing whether changes in the score from one occasion to the next are due to the unreliability of the test material or are an accurate measure of personality change (or both). Moreover, we cannot be certain that *all* dimensions of personality have been catered for in the selection of items on existing inventories, a problem similar to that met in our discussion of intelligent behaviour.

Attitude and interest inventories

In a sense, a personality questionnaire of the kind described above is an attitude scale. However, the term 'attitude' is generally reserved for an opinion which represents a person's overall inclination towards an object, idea or institution. Interests differ from attitudes in at least three important ways:

(a)   Interests are always positive, whereas attitudes can be positive, negative or neutral.
(b)   Interests are always active, while attitudes can be dormant.
(c)   Interests are specific and functioning here and now, while attitudes are more generalized and may not function at all.

Attitude measurement has very wide currency, particularly in social psychology. Scales have been created for attitudes to almost every aspect of our lives from soap powders to school subjects. Measures attempt to detect one of three kinds: the cognitive attitude, which is what we actually *know* about an object or event; the affective attitude, which is what we *feel* about an object or event; and the behavioural attitude, indicating how we *behave* towards an object or event. Several techniques exist,[34] of which the *Likert scale* is now the most used. It consists of an attitudinal statement followed by a scale running from one extreme of opinion to the other. Between these extremes, the respondent is given a number of points which express shades of opinion. For example, here are a few statements taken from an attitude-to-school questionnaire. The respondent indicates the degree of importance he or she ascribes to each attitude by using the five-point scale of numbers after each statement:

1 – absolutely essential;
2 – important but not essential;
3 – of only moderate importance;
4 – of very little importance;
5 – of no importance at all.

For an 'ideal' school typical items might be:

(a)   plenty of opportunity for sports and athletics;   . . . . . .
(b)   informal relations with staff;   . . . . . .
(c)   has social as well as academic activities;   . . . . . .
(d)   separates the sixth formers from the rest;   . . . . . .
(e)   is concerned with preparing students for future work.   . . . . . .

Although five points have been used along the scale, it is quite possible to have seven, nine or eleven; odd numbers are chosen so that it is possible to give a central neutral response.

Interest inventories have taken four basic forms.[35] *Expressed interests* consist of extracting a direct statement of a person's liking or disliking for something. The answers tend to be very unstable, and subject to the transient moods of individuals. If you ask someone 'do you like science?', the answer could vary from one day to the next. *Manifest interest* is shown by an individual's participation in an activity. But this could be misleading, e.g. when one participates in an action for other motives, such as, companionship. *Tested interest* is ascertained using objective measures of the information known by a person. Interest in a particular field is assumed to lead to an increase in the information known in that field. Thus some believe that a measure of acquired knowledge is a partial indicator of interest. Peel's 'general information test' or Richmond's 'culture test' are examples.[36] The principle, as Peel points out, is that a child who is interested in an activity will not only feel pleasure when pursuing interests, but will amass information while participating. Two sample questions of the kind used in general information tests are:

Here are the titles of five books. Underline the one written by Robert Louis Stevenson:
    Robinson Crusoe; Dog Crusoe; Coral Island; Treasure Island; Jungle Book.

Which of the following is true of a penguin?
    A penguin is (a) a mammal, (b) a bird, (c) a fish, (d) an insect.

Inventoried tests of interest are usually constructed for the purpose of choosing occupational preferences (see later, Chapter 15). The earliest kinds required respondents to place school subjects or occupations either in rank order or as *paired comparisons* (Chapter 15).

Research into the subject interests of children using the instruments mentioned has shown in general that their choices are not particularly reliable in terms of the subjects which they choose later when specialization is possible, in vocational choice or when interest is correlated with attainment. Correlations of interest with school subjects are low and add very little in the way of predicting success at school.

Projection techniques

One of the sharp dividing lines between depth psychologists and psychometricians is in the techniques the former employ in studying human personality.[37] The clinical orientation of depth psychologists involves them in intuitive and subjective encounters with, in the main, mental patients. The purpose of these psychoanalytical techniques is to reach the recesses of the unconscious mind in an effort to expose inner, hidden motives which are said to be the cause of overt behaviour. Consequently, part of the secret is to disguise the purpose of these techniques from the patient by using indirect and veiled methods in the kind of questioning used. Then follows an interpretive session when the depth psychologist attempts to read into the findings the hidden causes of the patient's actions either with or without the presence of the patient. The psychoanalyst, therefore, is trying to break through the patient's defence mechanisms and discover their origins.

There are several projection techniques, of which *association* has proved to be an attractive one. Free word association requires a quick pairing of words from a given one; for example, given 'knife', what would its pair be? Most people would answer 'fork' to this stimulus word, but occasionally people give unusual and bizarre replies such as 'cell' or 'murder' which are thought to have hidden meaning. Continuous association requires a string of words from a given stimulus word. Incomplete sentences such as 'Other people . . .' or 'My father . . .' are also used, and the subject is required to finish the sentence. Whatever associations transpire are thought to arise from deep motives unrealized by the respondent.

Story telling is a method in which a person is asked to write a pen-picture of himself or herself. A third technique, *thematic apperception tests* (or TATs), has arisen from these. TATs demonstrate a projection device, in that they require an individual to make up a story from a picture he or she is shown and to say what might have led up to the scene in the picture, what is happening currently and what might happen in the future. By doing so one is thought to project one's own problems into the characters portrayed in the story. For an extremely clear and readable account of an application of TATs see McClelland's work.[38]

The *Rorschach ink blot test* is very well known. Again, a set of figures, originally made from symmetrical ink blots by inking a piece of paper and folding it down the middle to give a symmetrical pattern, is presented to a subject, who is asked to report on what he or she sees in the figures. The subject's responses are then analysed for deeper motives which underlie the choices. Those who favour the method have devised an extensive classification of replies from large numbers of people.

The interest of these tests to the teacher is academic. Should a child ever need the help of a psychiatrist, the teacher should immediately see that this help is given. Professional psychoanalysis has its limitations, let alone amateur psychoanalysis which could well aggravate rather than alleviate a mental condition; thus teachers should seek professional advice if they suspect that they have a mentally sick child on their hands.

CLASS MANAGEMENT

Leadership

The past twenty-five years has seen a considerable increase in the amount of research into various aspects of teaching and learning styles. This section will deal with teaching styles which have a bearing on class management and organization; the following section will look at learning, particularly cognitive, styles.

Wherever a group is formed, either formally or informally, leaders emerge. In the classroom, the teacher has a formal commitment to take the role of leader, although some activities result from democratic and shared decision-making. Leaders are those who have power to influence others. This power may be given to a person – when it goes with the job, such as service officer or foreman in industry – or it may be earned through respect from the rest of the group. Several researches have attempted to discover the characteristics of the effective leader, but no reliable generalizations have resulted from them.[39]

Several kinds of leadership descriptions have been proposed. Generally, they reduce to the twofold Model A and Model B of Hoyle.[40] These idealized models are:

Model A – a *bureaucracy* with a clearly defined hierarchy, authority being vested in a chosen person, i.e. an authoritarian system.

Model B – a *human relations* model where decision-making is shared and authority spread widely, i.e. a democratic system.

These two, plus a third referred to as *laissez-faire*, were used in one of the earliest researches on leadership patterns and their effect on performance. Lippitt and White[41] set out to describe the leadership styles of youth-club leaders. The effectiveness of the various styles was assessed using the criteria of productivity and enjoyment of the activity for members of the group (i.e. enjoyment of the relationships). The *authoritarian* system was a teacher-centred one highlighting formality, teacher-directed communication and dominance, competition and punishment. In the *democratic* system, the stress was on learner participation in decisions, on co-operation and open-ended structures in human relationships. The *laissez-faire* system was one in which the leader or teacher gave complete freedom to the group to make decisions and offered the minimum of guidance. The effectiveness of these styles was quite enlightening. The authoritarian-led group produced more in less time, but relationships were not good. The *laissez-faire* group displayed both poor productivity and interrelationships. The democratic group were a little less productive than the authoritarian group, but their relationships were the best.

In the classroom, the style of leadership will need to change with the circumstances. A lot depends on the organizational demands of a particular lesson. It is therefore not wise to limit one's leadership stance to any one of the above. Thinking of the variety of situations in a typical classroom, it seems that all three will find a place at some time in the organizational management. However, leaderless children (the *laissez-faire* régime) will quickly find their own, usually very inadequate, substitute leaders (intuitively and cleverly portrayed in William Golding's book *Lord of the Flies*). They create their own standards of performance (not strenuously high) and discipline is hard to keep.

Problems of class management

One of the earliest attempts to study classroom management techniques was by Kuonin.[42] He observed teachers' group-management techniques and by choosing the two extremes of very successful and unsuccessful managers attempted to discover the qualities which distinguished them from each other. In fact, Kuonin did not find a single consistent characteristic. They all seemed to use a similar range of strategies.[43]

However, those characteristics which did seem to count are worthy of note. The first is *anticipation*. The maxim that 'prevention is better than cure' certainly works in the classroom. The skill of being able to spot sources of trouble early on is a decided asset for a teacher. Accurate pinpointing at the start of potential trouble avoids the tedious task of having to apply disciplinary measures later. Kuonin called this ability to anticipate sources of trouble *withitness* – eyes at the back of one's head, not missing a trick. Good timing, accurate targeting and calm reaction are all characteristics of the 'with it' teacher.

Another characteristic described by Kuonin was 'smoothness'. This means passing through transitions in classroom activities as easily as possible. Where children are busy and productive or when you are starting a new activity with them try not to intrude or be abrupt. Chopping and changing (Kuonin calls these 'flip-flops') is not a good technique.

Other pieces of advice which emerged from Kuonin's research were not to stay on one topic for too long, and to be as versatile as circumstances will allow. By this latter point, he meant that the teacher should be capable of keeping tabs on all activities of all the children – no child should feel ignored or unobserved ('withitness' again). Kuonin also found a correlation between successful instructional management and behavioural classroom management. He also emphasized the importance of teacher and pupil involvement in lessons.[44]

How do teachers attempt to achieve a leader role in the classroom? Woods[45] described several survival strategies in his book *The Divided School*, which is an analysis of some aspects of life in a secondary modern school. He postulates eight 'survival strategies' in an attempt to control the classroom and thereby maintain some semblance of leadership. They are *domination, negotiation, socialization, fraternization, absence or removal, ritual and routine, occupational therapy* and *morale boosting*. These are fully defined and described by Woods; here we shall give a brief definition of each (see note (43) for applications). *Domination* involves overpowering children by physical or verbal means. At the extreme end of the scale, Woods suggests that in addition to physical violence such as knuckling, tweaking, hair-pulling and rulering there is verbal abuse and humiliation in front of other children. *Negotiation* – 'You play ball with me, and I'll play ball with you' – implies that in return for acceptable behaviour, the individual or class is rewarded. *Socialization* involves the school in laying down guidelines about the behaviour of pupils, and establishing firm rules about conduct in school; this is used by teachers as the baseline from which they take their lead. *Fraternization* goes by the saying 'If you can't beat them, join them.' Teachers, in a sense, enter the child's world and behave as young people – a somewhat immature way of solving problems! *Absence or removal* means that a teacher finds ways of being absent from the scene of trouble whenever possible – reduced timetables, easier classes, non-volunteering for extraneous jobs. *Routine and ritual* – without it, teachers would probably be driven mad. One has to know that certain aspects of classroom life are taken for granted, and some without fuss or confusion. This enables the teacher to have control over the classroom. *Occupational therapy* amounts to keeping children occupied even when the activities serve no particularly useful educational purpose. Drawing endless diagrams, maps and writing up repetitive experimental proceedings might be seen as examples of occupational therapy. *Morale boosting* – teachers display a variety of ways in which they attempt to keep their morale high. Such things as advanced work (sixth-form teaching), teasing and baiting the hierarchy (in their absence), cohesiveness of the staff and mutual support are a few of the methods which Woods identifies as being instrumental in boosting morale.

As I have indicated elsewhere,[43] some of these can be turned to good effect if done thoughtfully and with consideration for the pupil.

The use of applied behavioural methods is another strategy to enable the teacher to undertake effective class management. We have already alluded to this in some detail in Chapter 5 by reference to the work of Wheldall and Merrett (note (26) in Chapter 5).

Learning and teaching styles

The concept of *learning style* in education is important because it incorporates all those human attributes which help to determine and characterize a person's preferred approach to problem-solving. The Oxford Dictionary tells us that style is the *manner* of doing something as opposed to the *matter* in which a person is working. Therefore style has to do with personality and motivation, as well as the thinking tactics used for tackling problems. To misquote a popular song, 'it's not only what you do, but the way that you do it'. Successful patterns of behaviour most suited to our personal make-up and external constraints become established as habits of responding. These 'response sets', as they are called, become the bricks from which our personal lifestyles are built, and it is within this area that we might look for useful generalizations about achievement styles.

Cognitive style

Two crucial aspects of style are of particular concern. These are 'cognitive' and 'affective' style. *Cognitive style* involves those characteristic patterns of perceiving and thinking which an individual exhibits in problem-solving. Sometimes the patterns are referred to as 'learning' and 'thinking' styles. Cognitive (or 'thinking' style) has been defined by Messick as:

> consistent individual differences in . . . ways of organising and processing information and experience . . . These styles represent consistencies in the manner or form of cognition, as distinct from the content of cognition or the level of skill displayed in the cognitive performance. They are conceptualised as *stable attitudes, preferences or habitual strategies determining a person's typical modes of perceiving, remembering, thinking and problem solving.*[46]

A lot of speculative work has concentrated on cognitive styles and we have space only to draw attention to a few important ones. For an exceptionally good summary, students should refer to the Open University text *Learning Styles.*[47] Some have already been considered, as in the case of *convergence* and *divergence*, or Bruner's strategies of thinking, *focusing* and *scanning* in Chapter 6. Three others, which to some extent overlap, owe their origins to Witkin - *field dependence* and *field independence*; Kagan - *impulsive* and *reflective*; and Pask - *holist* and *serialist*.

In Witkin's theory[47] (and also Chapter 4), the difference established between field dependence and field independence arose from perceptual experiments. The central question 'are people able to keep the centre of interest separate from the background?' (see gestalt work on figure and ground in Chapter 4 under the heading of 'The nature of perception') led to the conclusion that some people are given to observe their surroundings *in toto* (field-dependent perceivers), whilst others are able to separate the figure from the ground (field independent). The act of faith needed here is to believe that perceptual differences will also reflect the same intellectual differences, i.e. children who perceive their environments in a field-dependent way will *think* this way as well. Vernon[48] draws together some findings relating field-independent characteristics to other attributes. Field-independent people tend to be better at spatial tasks and mathematical and scientific studies, have self-sufficiency, are assertive and encourage independence of thought. It is important, however, to keep in mind the essentially perceptual nature of Witkin's work and resist, in the absence of firm evidence, the 'halo' effect of ascribing personality characteristics as well.

Kagan's[47] concept of impulsive–reflective is more concerned with decision-making in problem-solving. The child who makes an impulsive, off-the-cuff response is contrasted with the child who is prepared to pause and reflect on the nature of a question and the accuracy of the answer. The latter has been associated with a more analytical style of problem-solving, and Kagan's findings show that reflective children make fewer errors.

The third approach is that of Pask,[49] who distinguishes between those who are good at 'seeing things as parts of a whole' (holists) and those who are good at 'stringing sub-problems into sequences' (serialists). The distinction is seen clearly in people's preferences when studying new material. Some people like to get the feel of a new area of study and skip over the whole field before embarking on the details, whilst others prefer to pursue several lines of detail before trying to form a picture.

The common element in all these styles so far is the *way* people perceive problems and the effect this might have on the paths taken to a solution. So far, these theories have only pointed in directions with which we might experiment in the classroom. Certainly the direction of research in classrooms will be towards obtaining more detailed knowledge of the strategies children adopt in problem-solving.

Affective style

The second aspect of style – affective processes – involves those motivational and temperamental characteristics which influence an individual in problem-solving. The examples of cognitive style given in the previous section all correlate with measures of intelligence and problem-solving skills. The convergent/divergent thinking tests mentioned in Chapter 10 also correlate with conventional ability measures. However, a good measure of affective style should not be related to intelligence.

Kirton[50] has introduced a dimension, *adaptors* and *innovators*, which he and others have shown to be unrelated to intelligence and yet to give some additional information about a person's preferred affective style in terms of the criteria set out in Table 11.3. He draws a clear distinction between preferred style of problem-solving and capacity or ability in problem-solving.[51] Adapting or innovating is the 'preferred mode of tackling problems at all stages. [It is] presumed to be unrelated to level or capacity, such as IQ, level of cognitive complexity or management competency.' Kirton believes the dimension is closely related to personality and should be regarded as an affective style.

The scale has been used largely in studies of organizational management, but on reading the list of characteristics in Table 11.3 it seems reasonable to assume some relevance to learning and teaching in schools.

Styles and pupil performance

Recent authors[52] have been somewhat sceptical of the applications of these various theories to education. Four questions have been raised which should occupy researchers in this field:

Table 11.3 *Characteristics of adaptors and innovators (after Kirton[50])*

The adaptor	The innovator
Characterized by precision, reliability, efficiency, methodicalness, prudence, discipline, conformity.	Seen as undisciplined, thinking tangentially, approaching tasks from unsuspected angles.
Concerned with resolving residual problems thrown up by the current paradigm.	Could be said to search for problems and alternative avenues of solution, cutting across current paradigms.
Seeks solutions to problems in tried and understood ways.	Queries problems' concomitant assumptions: manipulates problems.
Reduces problems by improvement and greater efficiency, with maximum of continuity and stability.	Is catalyst to settled groups, irreverent of their consensual views; seen as abrasive, creating dissonance.
Seen as sound, conforming, safe, dependable.	Seen as unsound, impractical; often shocks his opposite.
Liable to make goals of means.	In pursuit of goals treats accepted means with little regard.
Seems impervious to boredom, seems able to maintain high accuracy in long spells of detailed work.	Capable of detailed routine (system-maintenance) work for only short bursts.
Is an authority within given structures.	Tends to take control in unstructured situations.
Challenges rules rarely, cautiously, when assured of strong support.	Often challenges rules, has little respect for past custom.
Tends to high self-doubt. Reacts to criticism by closer outward conformity. Vulnerable to social pressure and authority; compliant.	Appears to have low self-doubt when generating ideas, not needing consensus to maintain certitude in face of opposition.
Is essential to the functioning of the institution all the time, but occasionally needs to be 'dug out' of his system.	In the institution is ideal in unscheduled crises, or better still to help avoid them, if he can be controlled.

(a)   What is the relationship between the styles, and can they be rationalized in any way?

(b)   Are cognitive style characteristics stable or capable of modification in the pupil?

(c)   How important are contexts in discussing the appearance of style characteristics in pupils?

(d)   How can a study of individual differences in cognitive styles be made so that the findings are helpful to teachers, especially in an increasingly technological era?

But the style of the learner is only part of the story. Another important part is the style of the teacher and the impact this has upon the learner's performance. Broadly, in considering teacher styles we would again be interested in the contribution of cognitive and affective aspects of the teacher's classroom tactics to the achievement of the pupils. The interaction of cognitive styles of students and teachers has been looked at by Joyce and Hudson (**R**)[53] in research using medical students. From the results, they felt there were some indications 'that teachers and students having similar styles [convergent and divergent, that is] formed the most successful combination' in terms of examination results. It would not be surprising if the style adopted by teachers did not have some effect on the learning of individuals with compatible styles, but the evidence from a large volume of American literature is not wholeheartedly supportive.

At the grosser level of classroom organization (also confusingly referred to as 'style'), Bennett[54] has shown that children's achievement in reading, mathematics and English is generally higher in the more formal, teacher-centred, subject-orientated atmosphere, than in an informal, child-centred, discovery-orientated one. When personality is considered, the insecure and less stable child appears to work harder and more successfully in a formal class setting. In writing an imaginative story no difference could be detected in 'creative' output of children in the formal or informal settings.

One important conclusion from Bennett's work was the significance of *structure* – whether the atmosphere in a classroom is formal or informal. There are, of course, dangers in unstructured, free-for-all episodes. Children whose interests have not been roused can, and do, idle away their time on projects which are not demanding. To keep things stirring in this kind of class is exhausting and requires a vigilant, grass-hopper-like creature who flits from child to child probing and directing their energies. Learning will not take place *in vacuo* and we cannot expect children to rediscover from scratch the wealth of knowledge, already assimilated by our culture. No matter how subtle we try to make the teaching–learning–thinking processes, well-founded knowledge must be transmitted so that new experiences can be set against a background of knowledge already amassed. Therefore some structure is inevitable, and it is within this structure that we establish learning strategies. 'Free discovery' sessions for children require careful premeditation on the teacher's part to ensure that children's private enterprise be full, worth while and an important means of adding to their existing knowledge.

Another important piece of research looking at the styles adopted by teachers in classroom organizational strategies is known as the ORACLE project (Observational Research and Classroom Learning Evaluation) and was conducted at Leicester University.[55] It defined four types or styles, one of which had three manifestations giving six in all. The four styles, briefly, were:

(a) *Individual monitors* – characterized by the low level of questioning and the high level of non-verbal interaction, consisting largely of monitoring the individual pupil's work (marking). The teacher using this style engages in the highest number of interactions concerned with telling pupils what to do, and to a lesser extent with marking work.

(b) *Class enquirers* place great emphasis on questioning. Most learning is teacher-managed. They begin new topics with a class, progress using the question and answer technique and walk amongst the children asking and answering questions.

(c) *Group instructors*, which the ORACLE team regard as one of the most interesting groups of teachers, tend to give a large number of factual statements compared with the number of ideas. They prefer carefully structured group work before engaging in discussion (hence the high level of information transference).

(d) *Style changers* come in three forms; i.e. *infrequent changers*, *rotating changers* and *habitual changers*. The ORACLE team found that 50 per cent of all the teachers they looked at fell into this category: 'They ask the highest number of questions relating to task supervision, make more statements of critical control and spend more time hearing pupils read than do teachers using other styles.' *Infrequent changers* were prepared, very occasionally, to change their teaching tactics to suit a change of circumstance. *Rotating changers* had groups of children working at tasks with one particular part of the syllabus being studied at any one table. The pupil groups rotated, passing from one curriculum interest to another with the whole class moving round at the same time. *Habitual changers* made frequent changes between class and individual instruction. There did not seem to be any plan to the changes.

Unlike in the Bennett study, no overall best style emerged, although class enquirers' pupils were most successful in mathematics and language skills and those of infrequent changers made the greatest progress in reading. On the other hand, the style chosen by rotating changers was the least successful.

The book on progress and performance[55] finishes with a discussion of leadership and management styles in the classroom, using some recent researches in this area, with a final consideration of the learning and teaching styles of children and teachers and their relevance to performance, particularly in the primary school.

One aspect of learning and teaching styles still under-researched is the question of *contexts*. Have we a clear idea of learning contexts? If it is reasonable to suppose there are different contexts, do they bring out of the child a range of styles? How readily can a teacher change or adapt styles, or are they too permanent to alter? These are just a few context questions in need of exploration.

SUMMARY

If the definition of personality involves a knowledge of the total organization of humans, then most avenues of educational psychology lead ultimately towards a greater understanding of personality. A classroom is not just a cognitive habitat, but consists of intricate personal interactions which deeply affect the learning and teaching processes. The pity is that psychologists are only scratching the surface of this very complex mesh of characteristic temperamental, intellectual and physical determinants of each person's adjustment.

In this chapter we noted a distinction between temperament (which refers to inherent dispositions) and character (which is an evaluative term associated with social behaviour: honesty, cruelty, self-control).

Four broad approaches to the study of personality were adopted from the writings of Vernon. These were the naïve, humanist, intuitive and inferential interpretations of personality, which can also be classified as idiographic and nomothetic. The first kind of approach relies essentially on superficial observations of other people's behaviour. All the idiosyncratic, as well as the 'normal', experiences in our lives are compounded to give us thumb-nail sketches of how people 'tick', and from these we establish a theory of human personality. The humanist emphasizes the whole being striving towards self-fulfilment. Intuitive theories, 'intuitive' because they are dependent on subjective assessments of human conduct, are led by the psychoanalytical school of psychology. Freud and his followers constitute the mainstay of this movement. Although psychoanalytical theories were outlined, it was suggested that there were few direct applications in classroom practice. Nevertheless, the particular contribution of this line of thinking was to increase our awareness of the importance to be attached to the lasting influences of childhood experiences as a source of adult motivation.

Inferential theories were illustrated using the psychometric analyses of Eysenck and Cattell. In particular, the dimensions of extraversion–introversion and neuroticism–

stability described by Eysenck were discussed in some detail and their bearing on academic achievement explored. The idea was mooted of a connection between the emphases and appeal of particular educational methods and corresponding personality characteristics. Introverts, for instance, tend to prefer their own company and tend not to be as inhibited by routine tasks (study, for example) as extraverts. Clearly, these are advantageous qualities for students.

The problem facing the psychologist who attempts to quantify personality characteristics was put into perspective by describing some of the assessment methods now in use. These included Sheldon's typology of physique, physical experiments, rating scales and inventories, and projection techniques.

The chapter concludes with a consideration of leadership, classroom organization, cognitive and affective styles and pupil performance by reference to several recent researches.

ENQUIRY AND DISCUSSION

(a) Look at school record cards and decide on the validity and reliability of the personality characteristics reported. While observing children, which personality qualities would you consider to be the really important ones from the point of view of (a) learning behaviour; (b) conduct in class? What dangers exist in this kind of observation?

(b) As a background to the study of conduct and personality deviance, read J. S. Kuonin, W. Freisen and A. Norton, 'Managing emotionally disturbed children in regular classrooms', *J. Educ. Psychol.*, **57**, 1–3 (1966), and for the role of the school in the important task of minimizing deviance see M. Power *et al.*, 'Delinquent schools?', *New Society*, **264**, 542–543 (1967). Other useful texts are M. Hoghughi, *The Delinquent: Directions for Social Control*, Burnett Books, London, 1983, and M. Rutter and H. Giller, *Juvenile Delinquency: Trends and Perspectives*, Penguin, Harmondsworth, 1983.

(c) Get your tutor to show the group some sample personality questionnaires, including projection tests. Inspect these in terms of: (1) the traits they purport to measure; (2) their fallibility – whether the responses are superficial, whether the respondent can falsify answers, how these problems have been countered by the test designer (lie detection, duplication of items, parallel forms of the tests, etc.); (3) their particular use (age range, intelligence, verbal skills); (4) the use to which teachers can put the results of such tests when applied to children.

(d) Debate the various roles of leadership by teachers in the classroom.

(e) Using the research from Bennett[54] and the ORACLE project,[55] examine the critical aspects of styles which teachers appear to adopt in primary classrooms. Are they likely to be the same in secondary schools? Does the adaptor/innovator theory of Kirton add anything to our knowledge of affective styles?

NOTES AND REFERENCES

1. The definition is taken from H. J. Eysenck, *The Structure of Human Personality*, Methuen, London, 1953.

2. A. Thomas, S. Chess, H. G. Birch, M. E. Hertzig and S. Korn, *Behaviour Individuality in Early Childhood*, University of London Press, London, 1964.

3. P. E. Vernon, *Personality Assessment: A Critical Survey*, Methuen, London, 1969. D. S. Cartwright, *Introduction to Personality*, Rand McNally, 1974. D. Fontana, *Personality and Education*, Open Books, London, 1977.

4. E. Goffman, *The Presentation of Self in Everyday Life*, Monograph 2, Social Science Research Centre, University of Edinburgh, 1956.

5. P. E. Vernon, *Personality Tests and Assessments*, Methuen, London, 1953, and the reference in note (3) above. Also see 'The use of tests in student selection', in H. J. Eysenck, *Uses and Abuses of Psychology*, Penguin, London, 1953.

6. D. Child, C. Borrill, J. Boydon Jagger and D. Bygrave, *Selection for Nurse Training: Making Decisions*, Nurse Selection Project, University of Leeds, 1988.

7. A. H. Maslow, *Motivation and Personality*, Harper, New York, 1954.

8. Carl Rogers, 'A theory of therapy, personality and interpersonal relationships, as developed in the client-centred framework', in S. Koch (ed.), *Psychology: A Study of Science*, vol. 3, McGraw-Hill, New York, 1959.

9. (R) R. B. Burns, 'The self-concept and its relevance to academic achievement' in the Reader. Also see his book, *The Self-concept: Theory, Measurement, Development and Behaviour*, Longman, London, 1979. Colin Rogers, *A Social Psychology of Schooling*, Routledge and Kegan Paul, London 1982, Chapter 7.

10. W. Purkey, *Self-concept and School Achievement*, Prentice-Hall, Englewood Cliffs, NJ, 1970. W. B. Brookover, E. L. Erikson and L. M. Joiner, *Self-concept in Ability and School Achievement*, US Office of Education, Co-operative Research Project No. 2831, Michigan State University, East Lansing. B. S. Bloom, *Human Characteristics and School Learning*, McGraw-Hill, New York, 1976.

11. M. Rutter, B. Maughan, P. Mortimore and J. Ouston, *Fifteen Thousand Hours*, Open Books, London, 1979.

12. J. A. C. Brown, *Freud and the Post-Freudians*, Penguin, London, 1961; C. S. Hall, *A Primer of Freudian Psychology*, World Publishing, Ohio, 1954. Another interesting text written by Freud himself attempts to explain the little accidents and slips of pen and memory occurring in our daily lives in terms of his psychoanalytical theory. S. Freud, *The Psychopathology of Everyday Life*, Penguin, London, 1914.

13. L. Hudson, *Contrary Imaginations*, Methuen, London, 1966.

14. P. Kline, in a book entitled *Fact and Fantasy in Freudian Theory*, Methuen, London, 1972 (2nd edn 1981), attempts to survey the research in support of Freud's theory. But see H. J. Eysenck and G. D. Wilson, *The Experimental Study of Freudian Theories*, Methuen, London, 1973 for a critical comment on Kline's book.

15. R. Benedict, *Patterns of Culture*, Routledge and Kegan Paul, London, 1935.

16. P. Kline, *Personality Theories and Dimensions*, Open University E 201 Block 2, gives a splendid summary of psychometric and Freudian theories. Also *Personality: Measurement and Theory*, Hutchinson, London, 1983.

17. It is difficult to recommend just one text of H. J. Eysenck's which examines his point of view because they are rather technical for the beginner. The earliest fundamental texts were *The Dimensions of Personality*, Routledge and Kegan Paul, London, 1947; *The Scientific Study of Personality*, Routledge and Kegan Paul, London, 1952; and *The Biological Basis of Personality*, Thomas, Springfield, IL, 1967.

18. H. J. Eysenck and S. B. G. Eysenck, *Psychoticism as a Dimension of Personality*, Routledge and Kegan Paul, London, 1976. H. J. Eysenck, *The Structure of Human Personality*, Methuen, London, 1970 (3rd edn). In this book, Eysenck outlines a new approach which overlaps and partly supersedes a previous view of his in which Hull's theory of learning played a large part. Because this latter theory still appears in the literature and still finds a place in contemporary educational journals, it is briefly mentioned here. There are two basic postulates which involve the use of the concepts of *excitatory potential* (that is, the tendency to make a response to a given stimulus) and *reactive inhibition* (that is, the tendency not to repeat a response which has just been made). The two postulates are:
    (a) Human beings differ in the speed and strength with which excitation and inhibition are produced and the speed with which inhibition is dissipated.

(b) Individuals in whom excitatory potential is generated slowly and relatively weakly and in whom reactive inhibition is developed quickly and strongly, but dissipated slowly, are thereby predisposed to extravert patterns of behaviour. The reverse is true of the introvert.

The notion expressed in (a), that we are aroused to different levels by similar events, is widely accepted. Some people become much more excited by certain pleasant or unpleasant events than others. Similarly, some people take longer to 'cool off' after arousal than others. What Eysenck has done in (b) is to relate these differential levels of excitation and inhibition to the extravert and introvert personality. The extravert experiences far more involuntary rest pauses than the introvert. Because excitatory potential is generated slowly and weakly while inhibition is quick and strong, the actual excitation will not be high unless the driving force which is motivating the activity is very high. The important point to remember from Eysenck's work is that extraverts possess high levels of reactive inhibition, and this tends to make them less able to concentrate for any length of time on tasks requiring prolonged concentration. They require more lapses, or *involuntary rest pauses*, in carrying out a task, although these breaks are fractions of a second. The longer the task, the greater is the inhibition which accumulates.

By a similar argument, introverts are more readily conditioned than extraverts. The reason is that the involuntary rest pauses which extraverts experience more frequently than introverts interfere with the concentration necessary for conditioning to occur.

19. J. Partanen, K. Brunn and T. Markkanen, 'Inheritance of drinking behaviour', *Finnish Foundation for Alcohol Study*, **14** (1966); J. Shields, *Monozygotic Twins*, Oxford University Press, Oxford, 1962.

20. H. J. Eysenck, *The Biological Basis of Personality*, Thomas, Springfield, IL, 1967.

21. R. B. Cattell, *The Technical Handbook to the 16PF*, Institute for Personality and Achievement Tests, Illinois, 1970. R. B. Cattell and P. Kline, *The Scientific Analysis of Personality and Motivation*, Academic Press, London, 1977.

22. (R) D. Child, *Personality and Achievement*, in the Reader. There are other summaries of this work in N. J. Entwistle, 'Personality and academic attainment', in H. J. Butcher and H. B. Pont (eds), *Educational Research in Britain*, vol. 3, University of London Press, London, 1972; and D. Child, 'Affective influences on academic performance', in P. Gordon (ed.), *The Study of Education*, vol. 2, The Woburn Press, London, 1980.

23. D. Bannister and J. M. M. Mair, *The Evaluation of Personal Constructs*, Academic Press, London, 1968. Also, D. Bannister and F. Fransella, *Inquiring Man: The Theory of Personal Constructs*, Penguin, Harmondsworth, 1971.

24. D. Bannister and M. Bolt, 'Evaluating the person', in P. Kline (ed.), *New Approaches in Psychological Measurement*, Wiley, London, 1973.

25. (R) A. T. Ravenette, 'Grid techniques for children', *J. Child Psychol. Psychiat.*, **16**, 79–83.

26. M. Friedman and R. H. Rosenman, *Type A Behavior and Your Heart*, Knopf, New York, 1974.

27. N. J. Entwistle and S. Cunningham, 'Neuroticism and school attainment – a linear relationship?', *Br. J. Educ. Psychol.*, **38**, 123–132 (1968).

28. For example, M. P. Callard and C. I. Goodfellow, 'Neuroticism and extraversion in school children as measured by the Junior Maudsley Personality Inventory', *Br. J. Educ. Psychol.*, **32**, 241–250 (1962).

29. D. Child, 'A comparative study of personality, intelligence and social class in a technological university', *Br. J. Educ. Psychol.*, **39**, 40–46 (1969). D. Child and A. Smithers, 'Some cognitive and affective factors in subject choice', *Res. Educ.*, **5**, 1–9 (1971).

30. E. Kretschmer, *Physique and Character*, Harcourt, Brace, New York, 1925; W. H. Sheldon and S. S. Stevens, *The Varieties of Temperament: A Psychology of Constitutional Differences*, Harper, New York, 1942. An extract from this book appears in B. Semeonoff (ed.), *Personality Assessment*, Penguin, London, 1966.

31. Most of Eysenck's books contain examples of apparatus designed to measure physical correlates of personality such as persistence, endurance and conditionability. Look at H. J. Eysenck, *The Scientific Study of Personality*, Routledge and Kegan Paul, London, 1952.

32. Amongst the commonest inventories are Eysenck's personality inventories of extraversion and neuroticism, Cattell's 16PF or 16 personality factors and his anxiety scale for adults. A children's form has been devised by W. D. Furneaux and H. B. Gibson under the title of *The New Junior Maudsley Inventory*, suitable for mental ages of 11 to 16 years. Eysenck and his wife have also prepared a junior form. Both these junior inventories measure extraversion and neuroticism.

33. L. Cohen, *Educational Research in Classrooms and Schools: A Manual of Materials and Methods*, Harper and Row, London, 1976.

34. Three good introductory texts are A. L. Edwards, *Techniques of Attitude Scale Construction*, Appleton-Century-Crofts, New York, 1957; A. N. Oppenheim, *Questionnaire Design and Attitude Measurement*, Heinemann, London, 1966; and M. E. Shaw and J. M. Wright, *Scales for the Measurement of Attitudes*, McGraw-Hill, New York, 1967.

35. D. E. Super, *The Psychology of Careers*, Harper and Row, New York, 1957.

36. Several psychologists in the 1940s set out to discover predictors of success in school subjects in the form of information tests. E. A. Peel, 'Assessment of interest in practical topics'. *Br. J. Educ. Psychol.*, **18**, 41–48 (1948), and T. F. Fitzpatrick and S. Wiseman, 'An interest test for use in selection for technical education', *Br. J. Educ. Psychol.*, **24**, 99–105 (1954), were amongst the earliest to devise 11+ examinations to assist in the selection of pupils for technical and grammar schools. As it happens, these tests were never adopted throughout the country.

37. Eysenck has little time for depth psychology. He feels that psychoanalytical sessions give an opportunity for the mind of the analyst to run riot in seeking to make sense out of the mumbo-jumbo of semi-consciousness. A. R. Jensen, 'Personality', *Ann. Rev. Psychol.*, **9**, 295–322 (1958) found little by way of validation for projection techniques and Eysenck doubts whether they are any better than chance in helping to cure the mentally ill. See also note (14) above.

38. D. C. McClelland and R. S. Steele, *Motivation Workshops: A Student's Workbook for Experimental Learning in Human Motivation*, General Learning Corporation, New York, 1972.

39. R. A. Schmuck and P. A. Schmuck, *Group Processes in the Classroom*, Brown, Dubuque, IA, 1971. For a discussion of motivation and personality patterns in learners see Chapter 10 of R. B. Cattell and D. Child, *Motivation and Dynamic Structure*, Holt, Rinehart and Winston, Eastbourne, 1975.

40. E. Hoyle, 'Leadership and decision-making in education', in M. G. Hughes (ed.), *Administering Education: The International Challenge*, Athlone Press, London, 1975.

41. R. Lippitt and R. K. White, 'An experimental study of leadership and group life', in E. E. Maccoby, T. M. Newcomb and E. E. Hartley, *Readings in Social Psychology*, Holt, Rinehart and Winston, New York, 1970.

42. J. S. Kuonin, *Discipline and Group Management in Classrooms*, Holt, Rinehart and Winston, New York, 1970.

43. For a practical analysis of Kuonin's observations the student might look at D. Child, *Applications of Psychology for the Teacher*, Holt, Rinehart and Winston, Eastbourne, 1986.

44. For confirmation of the importance of pupil and teacher involvement see E. C. Wragg (ed.), *Classroom Teaching Skills*, Croom Helm, London, 1984.

45. P. Woods, *The Divided School*, Routledge and Kegan Paul, London, 1979.

46. S. Messick and associates, *Individuality in Learning*, Jossey-Bass, San Francisco, 1976.

47. Open University, *Learning Styles*, E 281, Units 1 and 2, 1971. Also see K. M. Goldstein and S. Blackman, *Cognitive Style*, Wiley, New York, 1978.

48. P. E. Vernon, *Intelligence and Cultural Environment*, Methuen, London, 1969.

49. For a translation of Pask's work, see N. J. Entwistle, 'Knowledge structures and styles of learning: a summary of Pask's recent research', *Br. J. Educ. Psychol.*, **48**, 255–265 (1978).

50. M. J. Kirton, 'Adaptors and innovators: a description and measure', *J. App. Psychol.*, **61**(5), 622–629 (1976).

51. For a recent comment on the theory and some research using the test, see M. J. Kirton

(ed.), *Adaptors and Innovators: Styles of Creativity and Problem-Solving*, Routledge, London, 1989.

52.   D. Child, 'Cognitive styles: some recent ideas of relevance to teachers', in C. Bagley and G. Verma, *Personality, Cognition and Values*, Macmillan, London, 1985.

53.   **(R)** C. R. B. Joyce and L. Hudson, 'Student style and teaching style: an experimental study', *Br. J. Med. Educ.*, **2**, 28–32 (1968).

54.   N. Bennett, *Teaching Styles and Pupil Progress*, Open Books, London, 1976. But see M. Aitkin, N. Bennett and J. Hesketh 'Teaching styles and pupil progress: a reanalysis', *Br. J. Educ. Psychol.*, **51**, 170–186 (1981).

55.   M. Galton, B. Simon and P. Croll, *Inside the Primary School*, 1980, and M. Galton and B. Simon (eds) *Progress and Performance in the Primary Classroom*, 1980, both published by Routledge & Kegan Paul, London.

FURTHER READING

D. S. Cartwright, *Introduction to Personality*, Rand McNally, Chicago, 1974.

M. Cook, *Levels of Personality*, Holt, Rinehart and Winston, Eastbourne, 1984.

D. Fontana, *Personality and Education*, Open Books, London, 1977.

P. Kline, *Personality: Measurement and Theory*, Hutchinson, London, 1983.

P. E. Vernon, *Personality Assessment: A Critical Survey*, Methuen, London, 1966 and *Personality Tests and Assessments*, Methuen, London, 1953. Both these texts provide a thorough examination of the problems of personality assessment.

Chapter 12

Education for Special Needs

The title of this chapter used to be 'Educational handicap', but this term is no longer used because it tended to perpetuate and perhaps exaggerate the distinction between 'those that have and those that have not'. The classification categories of handicap have also disappeared. The Education Act of 1981,[1] formally introduced in 1983 and based very much on certain recommendations made in the Warnock Report (1978),[1] introduced a much broader concept of *special educational needs* (SEN) involving some 20 per cent of the school population. This was in stark contrast to the 2 per cent of 'handicapped' children thought to require a specialist form of educational provision. The broader term covers children who have varying degrees of difficulty in learning than the majority of children of a similar age, and those with disabilities which prevent them from using the normal educational facilities usually provided in schools. The change in terminology was intended to shift the emphasis from the disability to the particular educational provision needed. Nevertheless, it is recognized that the disabilities have to be identified and these now tend to be grouped in terms of general areas of development. These include physical, motor, cognitive, language, social, behavioural and emotional development.

None of us, of course, is completely equipped for all eventualities in life, yet most of us manage to survive either because some of our assets can be used to compensate for our inabilities or because we are able to avoid situations in which our weaknesses are exposed. Of the 20 per cent, however, there is likely to be around 2 per cent of children whose disabilities are so extreme that they are unable to benefit from our normal state educational facilities and therefore must receive special provision. The new Act endeavoured to place the remaining 18 per cent of children with special educational needs in the ordinary primary and secondary system. It will thus be impossible to go through one's professional life without meeting several children with serious learning difficulties. With these percentages, in every classroom of 30 children, a teacher is likely to have six children at some time with SEN and at least four at any one time.

THE WARNOCK REPORT[1]

Probably one of the most publicized reports on special education has been the Warnock Report (1978) on children with special educational needs (see Further Reading). Several of its conclusions were incorporated into the 1981 Education Act. A summary of the important conclusions follows. The central aims of special education should be to help children towards understanding and independence within the limits of their capacities. The reader will recognize these aims as the same as those of education in general. The Committee abandoned the notion of a distinct definition of handicapped and non-handicapped and preferred the idea of a continuum of severity, the most serious of which would require a particular form of educational provision (possibly 2 per cent school-aged children), but included in the brief of the Committee would be a further 18 per cent or so requiring special provision in normal schools.

> The form of the child's need is not necessarily determined by the nature of his disability or disorder. At present children are categorized according to their disabilities and *not* according to their educational needs. But the Committee recommended that *statutory categorization of handicapped pupils should be abolished*. The basis for this decision about the type of educational provision required should not be a single label, but rather a detailed description of the special need in question.
>
> (*Meeting Special Educational Needs*, HMSO, 1979)

However, they agreed that in the case of severe, complex or long-term disabilities there would have to be special provision. It was important to start special education as early as possible and finish late. The under-5s and over-16s were coped with least satisfactorily.

Thus special schools would still be needed for severe cases, but integration was crucial wherever feasible. With the passing of categories, the method of assessment would require rethinking. Teachers in the normal state system should be able to recognize children in special need. Along with efficient record-keeping there would have to be five stages. First, the head teacher is informed by the class teacher, and the former collects information about school performance, medical and social background and any information from the parents. Second, the case is discussed with the specialist teacher of children with special needs. If the advice is to take the matter further, then stage three is entered, and a professional is invited in by the head teacher. This professional might be an educational psychologist, a teacher for the deaf (peripatetic), a health service visitor, etc. The decision would then be made either to arrange a special programme within the resources of the school or to carry the case outside the school for multi-professional help. These professionals might be a medical officer, a health visitor, an educational psychologist, a social worker or a special educational advisory teacher. At stage five the specialists would be widened or narrowed according to the findings at stage four, and would form a *district handicap team*. Whatever stage is reached, an educational programme must ensue which is in keeping with the nature and severity of the problem.

This report has had a substantial impact on the view taken of special educational provision. An increase in the training of specialists by means of in-service courses, attempts at improving the resources necessary if normal schools are to cope, the introduction of some elements on the teaching of children with special needs in courses of initial teacher-training and a revised system of assessment are just some of the directions it is now taking.

THE AIMS OF SPECIAL EDUCATIONAL PROVISION

All teachers are concerned with the mental progress of children by promoting intellectual skills in the acquisition of knowledge. Further, they attempt to encourage individual children in their efforts to adjust both personally, in preparation for adult life, and socially, as a member of a community. The same aims are true of special educational provision, except that the order of priority must take into account the exceptional disadvantages of each child. The key to special educational provision is to help each needy child to adjust and compensate for his or her disability as well as to fulfil the broader aims suggested above. The mentally retarded will grow up, find work, run a home and have many exacting responsibilities for which they must be prepared. Work which is other than skilled is becoming harder to find and the business of budgeting for a family taxes the ingenuity of most people, let alone those with mental backwardness. Sometimes the physically disabled are prone to emotional and social side-effects because they have difficulty in coming to terms with the inadequacy they feel in comparison with others. Problems of this kind require different emphases and careful handling which only special, individual education can provide.

The Warnock Report and by implication the 1981 Act,[1] clearly interpreted for teachers by Solity and Raybould[2] (for a legal interpretation see Cox[2]), defined a child with *learning difficulties* as one who 'has a significantly greater difficulty in learning than the majority of children of his age', or 'has a disability which either prevents or hinders him from making use of educational facilities of a kind generally provided in schools, within the area of the local authority concerned, for children of his age'. It is important to notice that classifications of children with special needs were avoided in an effort to prevent stereotyping and labelling of children. However, without some qualification of the somewhat circular definitions offered by the Warnock Report, it was thought difficult to begin the process of identification. Four terms were suggested which described degrees of learning difficulty, placing emphasis on the curricular and organizational problems as much as the child's difficulties. The four degrees are *mild*, *moderate*, *severe* and *specific*.

Mild learning difficulties cover those children who would receive mainstream teaching with support from ancillary help and special facilities in the normal classroom. The children would have the normal curriculum with some additional help. Moderate learning difficulties require a 'modified curriculum similar to that provided in ordinary schools but, while not restricted in its expectations, has objectives more appropriate to children with moderate learning difficulties'. Children with severe learning difficulties require individually worked out curricula with 'a range of educational experience but more selectively and sharply focused on the development of personal autonomy and social skills'. Many of these children are multiply handicapped and will require special educational and physical resources. They will constitute the 2 per cent referred to above. Specific learning difficulties refers to particular problems which a child may experience without it affecting other aspects of the curriculum. Specific reading difficulties (see the references to Clay's work in Chapter 6) might be one such example.

One major shift in emphasis has accompanied both the 1981 Education Act[1] and the 1988 Education Reform Act[1] and that is from child-focused assessments to a curriculum focus. Traditionally, the approach has been child-focused which places importance upon identifying the intellectual deficiencies of a child using norm-referenced tests such as ability (Chapter 9) or personality (Chapter 11) tests. These are needed to show the potential of a child, but they are insufficient in providing solutions. Consequently, more curriculum-related assessment is needed to establish those areas where the child is having difficulty, for example in literacy or numeracy, and shaping the subsequent work in order to monitor and improve performance. Careful thought is given to the provision of suitable programmes necessary to compensate for the particular problems experienced by the child.

The testing process moves from norm-referencing to criterion-referencing (see Chapter 9 for definitions), although it should be understood that all criterion-referencing of this kind is based on a notion of what would be a 'normal' expectation for a child of a given age. Once this has been decided, there follows an examination of the curriculum, organization, resources and teaching methods in the school to meet the wide range of SEN of the children.[3]

IDENTIFYING AND ASSESSING CHILDREN WITH SEN

Procedures and assessment

Accompanying the Act was a requirement that local education authorities (LEAs) should adopt a statutory procedure for identifying and assessing those children for whom a *statement* of SEN was required. These children, the 2 per cent mentioned above, were to receive special educational provision.

Before a statement is made about a child's needs, several steps are required. Procedures have to be followed, the first of which is to inform the parents (i) that an assessment is to be made, (ii) the procedures to be followed in making the assessment and (iii) of the rights of the parent. After a fixed period of time (a few weeks) in which an appeal and further evidence can be presented, the LEA can begin the assessment.

To make the assessment, the four sources of advice used are educational, medical, psychological and any other advice which might be helpful in making an assessment. The sources of advice are of significance. The help of teachers is sought for educational advice – usually all those who have taught the child and the headteachers of the schools attended by the child. It is also possible to bring in persons who are qualified to teach children with special needs, including specialists in the education of deaf and blind people.

Medical advice is obtained from a medical practitioner chosen by the district health authority. Psychological advice is obtained from a qualified educational psychologist appointed by the LEA. Either one or both school-based curriculum assessment and standardized tests of the kind described in Chapters 13 and 14 can be used to make the psychological assessment.

Statementing

The Education (Special Educational Needs) Regulations of 1989[4] give advice on the form which a statement should take when submitting comments about a child's problems and the proposed special educational provision most suitable for that child. The 'prescribed Form' contains several headings under which the LEA is required to set out the special needs and provision required, any additional non-school provision and the various reports and advice given by the educational, medical and psychological specialists involved as well as the parents' view. Another useful document is a DES circular 22/89[4] which gives a checklist of points which specialists are advised to consider when assessing a child. This is shown in Table 12.1 on pp. 294–295. Discussion about a number of elements in the list will be found in other chapters of this book (e.g. emotional states, cognitive functioning, educational attainments).

INTELLECTUAL DISABILITY (INCLUDING LANGUAGE)

In the following pages we shall consider various kinds of disability, of interest to psychologists, which need special educational provision. They are intellectual (including cognitive and language difficulties), emotional, social (including behavioural), and physical (including motor impairment). It should, however, be made clear from the outset that it is now unfashionable to attach too much importance to this separation into different types of disability, since the symptoms and remedies are so often interrelated and the provision is frequently geared to the particular problems of each child. Although there are still institutions where specialist attention is provided (schools for the educationally subnormal, partially sighted, profoundly deaf, etc.), they all recognize that a stereotyped pattern of educational facilities would be totally inadequate for the range of problems one can find within each kind of institution. Frequently those with one major disability suffer in other ways. A physically disabled child may also be mentally backward, have language difficulties or suffer from emotional and social problems; the emotionally disturbed, in addition to faltering in their school work, sometimes display socially deviant behaviour.

Most of the cases we are likely to consider in this chapter, whether they be physically disabled, emotionally disturbed or culturally deprived, exhibit some degree of intellectual or mental disability where scholastic performance is below the average expected of a child's age group.[5] Most teachers who deal with average and below-average pupils, especially in infant and primary schools, meet children who do not seem to profit from the usual educational methods and content provided. Intellectual disability in the present context is being reserved for those who are *slow learners*. Where children are not coping with the work normally expected of their age group, they are said to be slow learners.[6]

Although the sources of intellectual disabilities are many, complex and diverse, it is possible to perceive two broad distinctions. There are children who by nature or as a result of brain damage have limited intellectual capacity and who would not be expected to become bright adults after receiving specialized education. These have, in the past, been referred to as *mentally dull* children. But there are also children whose achievements are depressed by causes other than low mental ability and who could in fact, with careful handling and remedial aid, be expected to do better (quite remarkably in some cases). These have been referred to as *retarded* children. We need to give dull children special education either within the normal school setting or in special schools. Retarded children most frequently require remedial education to discover their

Table 12.1   *Advice on Special Educational Needs: suggested checklist.*

(a) DESCRIPTION OF THE CHILD'S FUNCTIONING

1. *Description of the child's strengths and weaknesses*

    Physical state and functioning
    (physical health, developmental function, mobility, hearing, vision)
    Emotional state
    (link between stress, emotions and physical state)

    Cognitive functioning

    Communication skills
    (verbal comprehension, expressive language, speech)

    Perceptual and motor skills

    Adaptive skills

    Personal and social skills

    Approaches and attitudes to learning

    Educational attainments

    Self-image and Interests

    Behaviour

2. *Factors in the child's environment which lessen or contribute to his or her needs*

    In the home and family, and including the language of the home

    At school

    Elsewhere

3. *Relevant aspects of the child's history*

    Personal

    Medical

    Educational

(b) AIMS OF PROVISION

1. *General areas of development (reference should be made to the relevant attainment targets of the National Curriculum where possible)*

    Physical development
    (e.g. to develop self-care skills)

    Motor development
    (e.g. to improve co-ordination of hand and fingers, to achieve hand–eye co-ordination)

    Cognitive development
    (e.g. to develop the ability to classify)

    Language development
    (e.g. to improve expressive language skills)

    Social development
    (e.g. to stimulate social contact with peers)

2. *Any specific areas of weaknesses or gaps in skills acquisition which impede the child's progress*

    (e.g. short-term memory deficits)

3. *Suggested methods and approaches*

    Implications of the child's medical condition
    (e.g. advice on the side-effects of medication for epilepsy)

Teaching and learning approaches
(e.g. teaching methods for the blind or deaf, or teaching through other specialized methods)

Emotional climate and social regime
(e.g. type of regime, size of class or school, need for individual attention)

(c) FACILITIES AND RESOURCES

1. *Special equipment*

    (e.g. physical aids, auditory aids, visual aids)

2. *Specialist facilities*

    (e.g. for incontinence, for medical examination, treatment and drug administration)

3. *Special educational resources*

    (e.g. specialist equipment for teaching children with physical or sensory disabilities, non-teaching aids)

4. *Other specialist resources*

    (e.g. Nursing, Social Work and Welfare Support, Speech Therapy, Occupational Therapy, Physiotherapy, Psychotherapy, Audiology, Orthoptics)

5. *Physical environment*

    (e.g. access and facilities for non-ambulant pupils, attention to lighting environment, attention to acoustic environment, attention to thermal environment, health care accommodation, privacy of continence care)

6. *School organization and attendance*

    (e.g. day attendance, weekly boarding, termly boarding, relief hostel accommodation)

7. *Transport*

Source: Annex 1 of DES Circular 22/89.

particular problems and provide additional educational support to normal schooling.

Detecting cases of learning difficulty is usually left to the teacher. Children with severe subnormality, disability, blindness or deafness are usually, but not always, noted and reported by parents, but mental backwardness is not always notice by them. The first intimations come either from medical services – doctors, clinics, social workers – or from teachers in the first few months at school. Often the parents of slower-achieving children, particularly those who have not helped their children in language, number or play prior to school, are blissfully unaware of their children's standing (largely because they have little or no yardstick for judging their child's ability in relation to other children) and it is left to the reception-class teacher to spot intellectual underfunctioning or dullness. All these sources provide invaluable information for statements in severe cases.

When suspicions are aroused the headteacher is informed and the procedure then involves the parents, the local education authority, the School Psychological Service and whatever previous medical evidence is available. As well as medical evidence, intelligence tests and performance in basic school subjects, simple manipulative skills, language usage and social adjustments are other variables which are considered (see Table 12.1).

The distinction between mentally dull and retarded children is generally confirmed using intelligence tests. A clue to the degree of dullness can also be obtained from the IQ score, although we should remember that IQ scores are not constant and retesting is an advisable part of the programme. We saw in Chapter 9 that IQs are distributed 'normally' in the population. There are a few very bright and a few very dull individuals – some so intellectually disadvantaged that mental testing is impossible. When a mean of 100 and standard deviation of 15 have been used in test design, something approaching 70 per cent of the population would obtain an IQ between 85 and 115 (standard deviation is dealt with later). Dull children are usually found to have IQs lower than 85–90. Retarded children, on the other hand, may in fact be quite bright, and their IQ scores could be much higher than 90.

Slow learners with low intellectual ability

The majority of intellectually dull children have mild and moderate learning difficulties and find their way into primary and non-selective secondary schools. As stated before, they form about 18 per cent of schoolchildren, and consequently demand a substantial investment of teachers' time and effort. The special education offered endeavours to find and provide ways by which the children can fulfil whatever limited potential they possess. Sometimes they are placed in a separate group or class, but it is often possible, especially in unstreamed class groups, to find them with brighter children. Provided the class is small enough, individual help from a sympathetic and adequately trained teacher can be effective in unstreamed classes. Where circumstances permit or when class sizes are too large, remedial education using part-time or visiting teachers often becomes an additional source of educational provision. Intellectually dull children's involvement in the normal school setting, where this is at all possible, is to be encouraged.[8] Most of them grow up to be useful members of the community consisting of people from all walks of life and of varying intellectual skills; therefore segregation early in life could militate against the slow learner's taking a responsible part in the community.

Children with low intellectual ability need tactful, resourceful and skilful teaching of basic language and number skills together with a programme of *activities*, with the emphasis on children doing things in craft, art, drama, movement and communication.[8] The curriculum is very much concerned with the concrete and practical aspects of scholastic work rather than with abstract thinking. Both from our definitions of intelligent behaviour and from Piaget's view of concept formation it follows that mentally limited children are operating intellectually at a level well below their actual age. Some children may rarely, if ever, operate abstractly in the sense used by Piaget in concept formation. Nevertheless, they still have to grow to adulthood, facing similar problems of earning a living, providing for a family and taking leisure. Clearly the examination system is quite unsuited to the needs and abilities of these pupils, and the raised school-leaving age must be used to provide children with competence to meet the demands of an age in which unskilled and semi-skilled work is rapidly disappearing.

Evidence (Hegarty *et al.*[7]) has been accumulating in recent years to show that children can benefit from integration in the normal system. Warnock[1] distinguished between *social* integration (children mixing for leisure), *locational* integration (where a special unit or separate building is incorporated on a normal school site) and *functional* integration (where children are mixed socially and intellectually).

Teachers have, understandably, been worried about their abilities to cope with any form of special need as their training and experience have largely been devoted to normal school settings. Despite this, the evidence shows that children do benefit from integration. The NFER,[7] for example, showed improvement not only in the performance of the handicapped children but also in the facilities available to them.

Slow learners who are retarded

Some children are backward in school work not because they lack intellectual potential, but because their ability has been depressed by some environmental cause. These children are most likely to be found in mild and moderate cases of learning difficulty. Implicit in remedial education is the notion that there is going to be an improvement after a short-term or medium-term remedial programme intended to remove or counteract the source of trouble and recover lost ground in the scholastic attainment of the child to a point more in keeping with his or her potential ability. It is quite possible to find children with IQs of well over 100 in need of remedial teaching.

The conditions which accompany retardation tend to resolve into physical–personal (other than mental dullness, as we have noted above), environmental and emotional difficulties. Personal factors include long illness or absence from school, undetected physical defects such as partial sight and hearing, and mild aphasias (see Chapter 2); environmental variables range from poor home facilities for learning speech and reading skills, low quality and quantity of food, shortage of sleep and adverse parental attitudes towards education, to poor or inappropriate opportunities at school, such as large classes, poor teaching of basic skills (going too quickly, choosing inadequate or advanced material), incompatibility between home and school, repeated changes of school and consequent changes in teaching styles and content (changing from i.t.a. to traditional orthography or from 'new maths' to conventional number teaching). Emotional states will be dealt with later, but here we should mention dislike of teacher through clashes of personality, negative parental attitudes to school, creating in the child similar adverse attitudes, failure in school snowballing into feelings of inadequacy and subsequently depressing the child's confidence and need to achieve, and extreme timidity and anxiety, giving rise to poor levels of attainment.

Remedial education for the retarded generally takes the form of individual or small-group tuition by skilled teachers or educational psychologists from the School Psychological Service. The commonest subject is reading, but speech therapy, number and writing also figure.

Severe learning difficulties

Following Warnock and the 1981 Act, categories such as ESN(M) and ESN(S) (Educationally Subnormal (Moderate or Severe)) have gone out of use. As mentioned above, the emphasis is now on learning difficulties and their degree, i.e. mild, moderate or severe.

Whilst we might all agree with Circular 276 of the Department of Education and Science (1954) that 'no handicapped child should be sent to a special school who can be satisfactorily educated in an ordinary school', it is sometimes in the best interests of the severely incapable child to attend a special school which can cater for individual needs using skilled and specially trained staff and low staff–pupil ratios, as few state schools are able to provide at the moment. Where possible, children with severe learning difficulties attend the day special school, but when (a) home conditions adversely affect the child's development; (b) special services such as medical or psychological treatment are necessary; (c) rural children have no local day special facilities; and (d) there are emotional complications aggravated by home circumstances, the children are sent to a residential special school. These children cannot fully profit from the same educational provision found in classes in normal schools. Small classes (ideally containing no more than 12 pupils) are in evidence and the school size is rarely more than 200. The curriculum is less verbal and more practical. The three Rs are taught with a view to helping children in the difficult task of adjusting to a normal life in society.

Children whose intellectual competence is very low (often associated with an IQ of less than 50) and who are not capable of taking advantage of the type of education found in state schools are now under the jurisdiction of the Department for Education through the local education authority. The special schools, along with hospitals for the subnormal (children with physical complications as well, who cannot care for themselves), cater for children who would get no benefit from academic kinds of schooling. (For a DES pamphlet refer to note (9R).)

Until recently these children were considered to be ineducable, but it has been shown that some of the more able can learn simple reading and writing skills. The priority is to help them in motor, perceptual and simple language skills so that they can gain some personal competence in looking after themselves (feeding, dressing, toilet, homely routines), social competence in communicating with others and possibly engaging in some kind of manual work. There are some unfortunates who are hospitalized and never attain even these basic human competences, and who must depend on others for their daily routines.

There are organic disorders which lead to low mental competence. During pregnancy the brain may be damaged, or diseases of both mother or foetus can lead to degeneration of brain tissues. These are congenital disorders of mental functioning. Injury during birth is also a possible, but a comparatively rare, cause nowadays. These give spastic and cerebral palsied conditions. Diseases in early childhood can leave a permanent mental scar if they are serious and remain untreated (measles, scarlet fever and several others). Children with Down's syndrome usually have low IQ scores too, although one can find wide variations[10] (see also Chapter 2).

EMOTIONAL PROBLEMS

Emotional disturbance is commonplace. All of us at some time have experienced symptoms of emotional stress and disturbance without their unduly affecting our daily lives. Temporary effects such as lack of concentration, quick arousal to anger or tears, temperamental fickleness or fecklessness are soon overcome. There is a small group of children and adults who are unable to overcome their emotional problems. In a submission from the Plowden Committee[1] it seems that more than 15 per cent of schoolchildren in primary schools experience strong debilitating influences from their emotional stresses.

When emotional handicaps reach the stage of being so grave as to affect social development leading to behaviour disorders (and frequently influencing school work), we term this *maladjustment*. The definition enunciated by the Handicapped Pupils' and School Health Service regulations of 1945 suggests that maladjustment is exemplified by 'pupils who show evidence of emotional instability or psychological disturbance and require special educational treatment in order to effect their personal, social and educational readjustment'. Definitions of maladjustment also imply that behaviour is judged in terms of a society's existing standards. Thus, what is commonly acceptable to a society at one time (take our own at present, compared with the beginning of this century) might be thought of as quite unacceptable at another time. Young children talking about sex might have been regarded as promiscuous or precocious 50 years ago; today it would be tolerated, if not encouraged as being forthright, honest and frank. Again, changes in attitude as a result of the processes of maturity should not be taken as signs of maladjustment. Adolescents in search of adult standards, values and privileges may appear to some parents to be suffering from behaviour disorders, whereas, in fact, the onset of these attitudes is a healthy developmental sign.

The Underwood Committee[11] looked at the whole question of maladjustment and educational provision. They set out six groups of symptoms commonly associated with maladjustment. The appearance of any of these symptoms does not of itself signify maladjustment. Nor are these symptoms necessarily permanent. They range from mild to severe, and many cases can be dealt with in the normal school setting by teachers aware of the problems and possible solutions. Examples of the six groups of disorders are:

(a) *Nervous disorders:* fears and anxiety; marked solitariness and timidity; depression and obsession; excitability–apathy; hysteria and amnesia.
(b) *Habit disorders:* speech defects and stammering (other than those caused by physical defect); excessive daydreaming, sleeplessness and nightmares; facial and body tics, nail-biting, rocking; bed-wetting and general incontinence; physical symptoms such as asthma and allergies.
(c) *Behaviour disorders:* temper tantrums; destructive, defiant or cruel; stealing, lying, truancy; sex aberrations.
(d) *Organic disorders:* neurological dysfunctioning – head injuries; brain tumours; epilepsy.
(e) *Psychotic disorders:* hallucinations; delusions; bizarre behaviour.
(f) *Educational and vocational difficulties:* lacking concentration; unable to hold down a job; irregular response to school discipline; slow learning – retarded in reading particularly.

Looking around a class of children (or just contemplating one's own earlier characteristics) will soon reveal the presence of some of the symptoms without its necessarily signifying maladjustment. Many children have an eye or facial twitch, bite their nails or have sleep problems. But when these symptoms accumulate we normally have a maladjusted case on our hands. Some symptoms, such as psychotic and organic disorders, are quite conclusive in their effects.

Apart from the obvious organic disorders mentioned above, the origins of maladjusted behaviour are not understood. It might be, as we noted in Chapter 11, that some individuals are predisposed to maladjustment, given the right conditions. Consequently, it is important to examine the environment in which maladjusted behaviour is exhibited. Home and school, therefore, could present problematic situations which might provoke emotional discord. Frustration and strained relationships between parent and child, between teacher and child or between the children will influence some children more than others. Withholding affection or generating feelings of insecurity are likely to precipitate maladjustment in some children. Inability to cope with school work or teachers whose approach is too demanding or intimidating are also likely causes of maladjustment.

Maladjustment is frequently dealt with while the child is attending a primary or secondary school.[11] Close liaison between the school and home to discover the background to the child's problems and the involvement of social psychiatric workers, psychiatrists and psychologists from the School Psychological Service are necessary in determining possible causes and, in some cases, preventing the situation from worsening. School attainment often shows a marked improvement as a consequence of detecting and tackling the cause. This is sometimes accomplished by visits to the home and school from the School Psychological workers. At school or the clinic the child receives lessons and treatment in keeping with the causes. Where the home is clearly not suitable in its influence on the emotional development of the child, the child is sent to a special residential school for the maladjusted designed to provide a therapeutic environment. Cases of retarded mental development are given remedial help.[12]

Autistic children [13]

Autism (from the Greek *autos*, which means *self*) has only relatively recently, though controversially, been isolated as a specific handicap (Kanner in 1943). Many views about its nature and causes have been suggested, of which the most recent is that autism is caused by a disability in interpreting sensory experiences, particularly hearing and seeing. Symbol interpretation is especially difficult. Autistic children seem to lack the ability to symbolize and therefore have great difficulty acquiring language. Other causes which have been proposed are brain damage and inherent emotional bleakness, but the evidence is not convincing.

To an outsider the most conspicuous symptom of autism is the lack of contact, either with eyes or in speech, between the child and others (even parents). Speech, where it appears, is grossly retarded and unusual (e.g. 'echolalia', where the child repeats something which has just been said). Excessive and persistent movement such as rocking in a chair and banging the head against the back of it or flapping hands with or without a piece of string are characteristic. Some perceptual experiences are ignored (sights and sounds and even heat and pain) whilst other perceptual experiences seem to become hypnotic (music and regular beats). For other symptoms see Creak *et al.*[13]

The special provision for autistic children has not been clear cut. The numbers involved are about 3000 throughout the UK. They receive attention in hospitals for the subnormal and in special schools, and a few are in normal day schools. A few special schools have been established by the National Society for Autistic Children. This haphazard organization is partly the result of uncertainty about the assistance which can be fruitfully afforded to these children. If the supposition that autism involves impaired perceptual interpretation in mainly the visual and hearing modalities is correct, it would seem appropriate to explore the other senses – touch, movement, olfaction. A stable environment, where a close watch can be kept on each child to capitalize on those sensory channels which can be appreciated, is also recommended (Furneaux[13]).

SOCIAL AND BEHAVIOURAL PROBLEMS

Social and behavioural problems are a vast topic which is an important province of the sociologist and social psychologist and should be fully dealt with in these areas. We shall content ourselves with a summary of the major factors in educational backwardness which have psychological significance in a social context.

The potent influence of cultural background on scholastic performance, social and emotional development and competence in adult life is not a new discovery. A number of psychologists and teachers in the 1920s, highlighted by Burt,[14] recognized the place of home circumstances as a causal factor in educational backwardness and behaviour problems which sometimes culminated in delinquency. However, it is really only since the Second World War that a systematic assault on the origins of, and possible compensations for, cultural deprivation has been launched (Mortimore and Blackstone[14]). Most of the major reports in education have presented evidence and suggestions relating to the life-chances of children. The Crowther Report and *Early Leaving*[15] point to several cultural differences which have led to a shortfall in the numbers of children from working-class homes who go on to higher education compared with those from middle-class homes. Furthermore, the former seem to be losing ground in their attainment as they move through the school.[16] The Plowden Report on primary schools[1] devotes a whole chapter, well worth reading, to *educational priority areas* (e.p.a.), where some children (not necessarily all children) are handicapped by home and neighbourhood conditions (both physical and mental), where schools are starved of amenities and high turnover of staff is disturbing to the stability of the children; where, in a nutshell, educational handicaps are reinforced by social handicaps.

To cope with the social and cultural casualties, a series of programmes has been devised which emphasizes strategies in the presentation of content designed within a conducive atmosphere and aimed at counteracting the disadvantages of the child's social background. These programmes are referred to as *compensatory education*, about which more will be said later.

Some social disadvantages

From the earliest work of Burt to the present time, a lot has been written about the social factors thought to conspire against successful progress in and beyond school.

While there will undoubtedly be those of low intellectual ability among children from deprived backgrounds, there is strong evidence for believing that many are under-functioning, as in the case of those receiving remedial education. However, remedial education is not enough to compensate for the many overlapping cultural factors at work, and a total education programme is required from the earliest possible moment in a child's life.

Several summaries of the characteristics of disadvantaged children have been compiled,[17] from which the following has been freely adapted.

(a) Poverty and inadequate care often mean cramped and impoverished living conditions, overcrowding, low income (and pressure on children to start earning) and feelings of insecurity.

(b) Restrictions in language experience (see Chapter 8) often disable the child from a working-class home when it comes to forming abstract concepts. The character and content of the language are obvious barriers to scholastic success as we know it. There are few books around in the home and conversation is neither informative nor extensive. Immigrant children in some cases have the added problem of living with the language of their parents (sometimes called L1, pronounced 'L one') and trying to learn a second language (L2) which is the language of transmission of knowledge in the school.

(c) Sensory deprivation is often the case in homes with little in the way of sensory stimulation. There is often a shortage or absence of toys or surrounding objects offering some variety of stimulation (see Chapter 4).

(d) A hedonistic outlook, 'don't put off to tomorrow what you can spend today', is very common. There is little medium-term or long-term planning and this reappears in the secondary school when decisions have to be made about whether the pupil will stay on for several years to obtain a qualification (perhaps until 21 or 22 years of age) or whether he or she will leave and earn a living.[15] Deprived children often succumb and leave school. The signs are also seen in a lack of perseverance in school work.

(e) Parental attitude to school and a clash of values between children and their schools often give rise to disillusionment and reduced motivation to do school work.

(f) Performance at school, especially in standardized tests, tends to deteriorate as children proceed through school life.[16]

(g) Emotional deprivation arising from inconsistent and inconsequential parents, broken families or loss of a parent can give rise to maladjustment, as we have seen.

(h) Large families sometimes produce a greater possibility of poverty and language deprivation (parents have less opportunity to converse with their children and there will be more communication between less verbally mature siblings). IQ is also negatively correlated with family size[18] – as the family size increases the average intelligence decreases.

(i) Children from socially deprived homes tend to develop poor self-images. The 'self-fulfilling prophecy' in Chapter 3 is an example of the way in which a poor self-image can soon be nourished in children who have little in their backgrounds to be confident about, by teachers who are insensitive to children's potential.

Compensatory programmes[19]

Research into approaches to the teaching of disadvantaged children is a fairly recent feature, and far more has been done in America than in this country. Some programmes emphasize language remediation[20] and use drill methods in order to create a firm foundation for symbolic reasoning. Another approach adopts the developmental stages postulated by Piaget, with the emphasis on cognitive development to ensure that the child's progress is paced and punctuated with active participation in learning. Early intervention has been shown to have advantages (Tough, 1975[20]).

All the programmes seem to have certain objectives in common. Enrichment is provided in language, perceptual and social skills. Plenty of talk about stimulating objects and events, tape-recordings, films, visits to places of interest to children (zoos, parks, famous places) and abundance of reading materials are the order of the day. School must offer a stable and secure atmosphere, a place where children want to be and to work. An adequate self-image needs to be fostered through encouragement and the feel of success. Personal standards and development in terms of cleanliness and social behaviour are frequently the subject of compensatory programmes. But this sphere is still the subject of a lively research effort.

Chapter 8 on language also contains useful references to programmes including the Head Start for disadvantaged children mounted in the United States in the 1960s. Neither this nor the follow-through programmes have yet proved to be as successful as had been hoped, although the programmes are not yet complete. Improvements that appeared in the early stages of the research seem to have evaporated with time. This is not uncommon in acceleration programmes – that is, initial gains are lost.

Delinquency

> Our youth now loves luxury. It has bad manners, contempt for authority, disrespect for older people. Children nowadays are tyrants. They contradict their parents, chatter before company, gobble their food and tyrannise their teachers.

In the broadest terms, a delinquent act is any behaviour on the part of a juvenile (under 18 years of age) to which the more senior members of a society object. Couched in these terms, we have all been delinquents at one time or another. Judging from the quotation at the beginning of this section, it would seem that things were not much different in the days of Socrates, who wrote it in 329 BC. The kinds of non-indictable offences for which young people can be brought to justice as delinquents are truancy, taking and driving a car, vandalism, stealing, trespassing, sex misdemeanours (e.g. rape, prostitution) and youths who are beyond parental control. The testimony of Burt[14] in *The Young Delinquent*, and other research since (R),[21] shows that most delinquents are not mentally unbalanced or completely devoid of moral standards. Many do not persist in crime and a high proportion are never caught.

The causes are as yet little understood (Wilkins (R)[21]). One school of thought lays stress on the punitive, poverty-stricken or broken home giving a bad example to children. Another school of thought feels that a permissive home with spoilt and lonely children could be a cause. Others lay the blame on personality deviance. These views have been summarized according to the emphasis on underlying psychological assumptions. The three important approaches are: (a) family influences; (b) personality delinquency; and (c) 'sociological' or situational delinquency.

In the familial kind of delinquency, the significant determinant of antisocial behaviour is thought to be family conflict (Burt;[14] Bowlby (R)[21]). Such factors as defective home management, immorality, drunkenness, criminality, broken homes, poverty and the child-rearing practices and experiences during the first five years of life are thought likely to precipitate delinquent behaviour. There are a small number of delinquents who have personality deviances. Psychopathic conditions and character disorders through excessive emotional stress, chiefly at home, are seen as causes (Stott (R)[21]). Finally, situational delinquency (Cohen (R)[21]) lays great stress on the influence of the environment in city sub-cultures and the formation of gangs where the individual is able to create an identity which is respected and gives that individual status. There is also a negative correlation between delinquency and social class (although the statistics are not very convincing because middle-class parents are usually in a better position to get their children 'off the hook'). All the culture theorists of delinquency, however, give pride of place to lifestyles either in the home or in the surrounding sub-culture.

Disruption and delinquency in the classroom take many forms and are, unfortunately, on the increase. In Chapter 5 we looked at the applied behavioural methods used for classroom management to avoid or control disruption. This topic was also dealt with in Chapter 11 under the headings of 'Leadership' and 'Problems of class management'.

Where special facilities are required, such as at Aycliffe School[22] which deals with the most severe cases of delinquency in Great Britain, a variety of methods have been used. One particularly interesting technique involves a *token economy* (Chapter 5) with a small number of youngsters living in an isolated environment (one level of a three-storey building with most of the essential facilities available). If readers would like to see how a token economy operates in such extreme conditions there is a useful article by the principal of the school which is helpfully detailed about the shortfalls as well as the advantages of this method. Token systems are used in normal day schools (house rewards, points, cups), but not, of course, with the same control as would be possible in a boarding situation.

EDUCATION OF THE PHYSICALLY AND MOTOR IMPAIRED[23]

There are many forms of physical disability which are classified as handicaps. Children with loss of limb functioning, causing them to be chair-bound or bed-bound, profound deafness, blindness, spasticism, spina bifida, polio, cerebral palsy, delicacy and other disabling malfunctions generally need to attend special schools which can cater medically as well as provide educational services. There are cases, and we have probably all met some, of children with physical handicaps who are still able to attend normal day school, but these cases are rare. Special schools for the blind, deaf and physically handicapped used to cope with some 25 000 children between 5 and 16 years of age. Now, many more children are within or attached to normal schools in special units.

The ability range is wide because there are many cases of physical disability which are not accompanied by mental handicap. Team work in special schools is necessary. The paramedical staff (nurses, physiotherapists, occupational and speech therapists) work alongside the teaching staff to give individual help to the child. Where children are able to go on to more academic work every encouragement is given. There is now greater concern to ensure that blind, deaf and chair-bound adults who have found a place in higher education and in work demanding high intellectual skills will have relevant facilities.

In the USA, for example, there are institutions (Gallaudet University and Rochester National Institute for the Deaf) which specialize in education for all levels of deafness through to degree standard. The advances made in deaf education and the integration of the profoundly deaf into society is progressing remarkably because of these institutions. Durham University in the UK now has facilities for deaf students.

Some children have complications arising from their physical handicaps which make communication difficult – for example, speech organ deformities or hand paralysis which prevents writing. Emotional and social problems can soon arise from the frustrations of immobility unless carefully handled. Where possible, family life is encouraged, for parents can do a great deal in providing a secure and stable background for their children. Central to all their efforts is an attempt to give children as much self-assurance and independence as they are capable of and, where possible, to draw on the children's capacities to enable them to take some part in community life.

SUMMARY

There is now a substantial investment of time and effort in our educational system devoted to the task of providing for those with special needs. Strictly speaking, children who, by virtue of disablement in physical, mental, emotional or social attributes, are not always able to benefit from conventional state day schools are included in the official definition of the educationally handicapped. We meet children in need of special education in our daily work, however, partly because some can benefit more from the companionship of normally endowed children both in work and play, and partly because special educational facilities are not always available for those who are in need of them. We will all have to deal with slow learners, the partially disabled, on occasion, the gifted, epileptics, delinquents and the emotionally disturbed within the State school.

The Warnock Report[1] and subsequent Education Acts[1] have had a marked influence on the direction of special education in the UK. The main reason is in the change of philosophy regarding the recognition and assessment of children with special needs and the strategies recommended for suitable educational programmes.

Categorization has been replaced with an informal description which relies more on the degree of learning difficulty than the source of the difficulty. Mild, moderate, severe and specific learning difficulties are identified. This, in turn, has led to more pupils being educated in the normal school setting and to revisions in the content, resources and delivery of the curriculum.

Revised procedures for assessment of the most severe cases, referred to as *statementing* were introduced in 1983 and revised in 1990. These involve seeking advice from educational, medical, psychological and other relevant specialists in order for an education authority to recommend the most appropriate provision for the child's particular educational needs.

Children with severe learning difficulties tend to be catered for in special units attached to the normal state schools or in special schools.

Physical disadvantages such as blindness, severe physical handicap, severe learning difficulties and severe maladjustment often require the expert attention of professionals in medicine, clinical psychology and special education. Remedial education is most often a part-time, short-term affair for those with particular problems in scholastic or mechanical skills. Reading and speech difficulties are among the commonest subjects for remedial education. Outside help from a child guidance unit is frequently necessary. Compensatory education is most needed when the environmental circumstances have to be compensated for by the use of enrichment programmes aimed at giving disadvantaged children the right kind of conditions. The socially disadvantaged are fast becoming the subject of new programmes of compensatory education. The help available often takes place in part of a school in the form of special classes, or the whole school is involved in providing an atmosphere intended to enhance social and communication skills.

Slow learners – those children who are not coping with the work normally expected of their age group – are generally either low in intellectual endowment compared with their contemporaries or, through impoverished educational opportunities, emotional hazards at home or other mentally disabling circumstances, have fallen behind their peers (retarded). It would be futile to take the same syllabus for a given age group and to give it to these children at a slower pace. Adjustment in presentation methods and curriculum content is frequently necessary. The emphasis is 'local', active and practical, although the curriculum must include language and those abilities which enable an individual to cope sufficiently with the concrete problems of daily life. Children who are not mentally endowed need to be weaned from isolation to taking a useful place in the community. Those whose capacities have been artificially depressed by circumstances require remedial help intended to recover lost ground in the basic skills of reading and communicating.

Children who display emotional instability or psychological disturbance sufficient to warrant professional treatment are said to be maladjusted. Teachers who suspect that they have an emotionally disturbed child on their hands must be in a position to decide on the seriousness of the problem and whether they can deal with it or will need to obtain the help of the School Psychological Service.

Delinquency amongst children has been with us for centuries. Delinquent children are in a somewhat unfortunate position in that their 'disabilities' are also a source of anti-social behaviour. Fortunately their plight is rarely permanent and our job must be to make sure that the passage of young people through difficult times of behavioural deviance is quick and complete. Offering trusted ears and gradually re-educating delinquents in terms of moral and social values are often arduous and thankless jobs in which the community, the school and the teacher have a stake. The ultimate aim is to create conditions in which our youth find delinquency an irrelevance. In particular, the school must look at the motivational problems which currently beset us in the secondary sector, especially in these days of extended education.

ENQUIRY AND DISCUSSION

(a) Whilst on school visits or practice try to meet and observe children in some of the following categories. Also discover whether there is any special provision for the children.

(1) Those with severe learning difficulties.

(2) Gifted.

(3) Maladjusted.

(4) Culturally disadvantaged.

(5) Retarded.

(6) Low intellectual endowment.

How were they assessed? When? Are there record cards? How is the Education Authority involved?

(b) Try to arrange visits to the relevant institutions or invite speakers who can give specialist information about the identification and education of children provided by the following:

(1) Special schools.

(2) Branches of the School Psychological Service.

(3) Services related to delinquency.

(4) Schools and homes for the physically handicapped.

(c) Consult the Warnock Report, the 1981 Education Act, the 1988 Education Reform Act and Circular 22/89,[1] for comments and suggestions relating to children with special needs.

(d) What are the arguments for and against the segregation of educationally handicapped children?

(e) Read about and discuss the psychological and sociological theories associated with delinquency.

NOTES AND REFERENCES

1. *Special Educational Needs*, The Warnock Report in the Education of Handicapped Children and Young People, Cmnd 7212, HMSO, 1978. *Education Act, 1981* (Chapter 60), HMSO. Department of Education and Science, Circular 22/89, *Assessments and Statements of Special Educational Needs*, HMSO, 1989. *Children and Their Primary Schools*, The Plowden Report, vol. I, HMSO, 1967. *The Education Reform Act, 1988*, HMSO.
2. B. Cox, *The Law of Special Educational Needs: A Guide to the Education Act 1981*, Croom Helm, London, 1985. See also J. Solity and E. Raybould, *A Teacher's Guide to Special Needs: A Positive Response to the 1981 Education Act*, Open University Press, Milton Keynes, 1988.
3. Read J. Solity, *Special Education*, Cassell, London, 1992, for a critical appraisal.
4. DES Circular 22/89, *Assessments and Statements of Special Needs*, HMSO, 1989. *The Education (Special Educational Needs) Regulations*, HMSO, 1983.
5. For an exceptionally good introduction to the subject of mental handicap, see B. Kirman, *Mental Handicap: A Brief Guide*, Crosby Lockwood Staples, London, 1975. See also J. Hogg and N. V. Raynes (eds), *Assessment in Mental Handicap*, Croom Helm, London, 1987.
6. C. Burt defined a backward child as one unable to cope with work normally expected of average children in the year below the child's age. But in the less formalized settings existing in our infant and primary schools, the definition is not as meaningful as it used to be.

The definition appears in *The Backward Child*, University of London Press, London, 1937.

7.   S. Hegarty, K. Pocklington and D. Lucas, *Educating Pupils with Special Needs in the Ordinary School*, 1981, and *Integration in Action*, 1982, both published by NFER–Nelson, Windsor. W. K. Brennan, *Curriculum for Special Needs*, Open University, Milton Keynes, 1985.

8.   There are many books written in the last ten or so years which bear on the issues and problems facing pupils and teachers in normal schools who are attempting to introduce programmes for children with special needs. For a good introduction to the problems, read S. Hegarty, *Meeting Special Needs in Ordinary Schools*, Cassell, London, 1987, and S. Wolfendale, *Primary Schools and Special Needs: Policy, Planning and Provision*, Cassell, London, 1987. A DES document, *A Survey of Pupils with Special Needs in Ordinary Schools*, HMSO, London, 1989, is also worth looking at.

9.   (R) *Educating Mentally Handicapped Children*, Education pamphlet No. 60, HMSO, London, 1975.

10. Down's syndrome is thought to be the result of chromosome excess. In the normal human cell we find 46 chromosomes, but when 47 chromosomes appear, 'mongoloid' characteristics result. These characteristics include stunted size, flattened bridge on the nose, slanting eyes, dry, open lips, a squarish flat face and short neck. They occur in about one in every thousand births. Children with Down's syndrome are more often born to older women.

11. *Maladjusted Children*, a report by the Underwood Committee on maladjustment, HMSO, London, 1955. *The Education of Maladjusted Children*, DES, Education pamphlet No. 47, HMSO, London, 1965.

12. M. Chazan, A. F. Laing, J. E. Jones, G. Harper and J. Bolton, *Helping Young Children with Behaviour Difficulties*, Croom Helm, London, 1983.

13. B. Furneaux, *The Special Child*, Penguin, London, 1969, Chapter 9, and B. Furneaux and B. Roberts, *Autistic Children – Teaching, Community and Research Proposals*, Routledge and Kegan Paul, London, 1977. S. Elgar and L. Wing, *Teaching Autistic Children*, College of Special Education, 1969. See also *Aspects of Autism* by P. J. Mittler, British Psychological Society Publication, London, 1968. M. Creak *et al.*, 'Schizophrenic syndrome in children', *Br. Med. J.*, **2**, 889–890 (1961). See also M. Rutter's paper, 'Autism: concepts, consequences and educational issues', *Special Education*, **59**(2), 20–24 and **59**(3), 6–10 (1970).

14. C. Burt, *The Causes and Treatment of Backwardness*, University of London Press, London, 1957 (4th edn). Also see *The Young Delinquent*, University of London Press, London, 1925, as evidence of some early thinking about the effects of social deprivation on educational performance and behaviour. J. Mortimore and T. Blackstone, *Disadvantage and Education*, Heinemann, London, 1982.

15. *Early Leaving*, HMSO, London, 1954. The Crowther Report: *15 to 18*, HMSO, London, 1959.

16. J. W. B. Douglas, *The Home and the School*, MacGibbon and Kee, London, 1964.

17. A thorough elaboration of social deprivation appears in M. Chazan, *Compensatory Education: Defining the Problem*, Occasional Publication No. 1, The Schools Council, London, 1968. A useful summary also appears in a chapter by G. Williams, 'Compensatory education', in H. J. Butcher and H. B. Pont (eds) *Educational Research in Britain*, vol. 2 University of London Press, London, 1970. See also Mortimore and Blackstone in note (14).

18. J. D. Nisbet, 'Family environment: a direct effect of family size on intelligence', *Eugenics*, Occasional Paper No. 8, Eugenics Society, London, 1953.

19. For a summary of compensatory programmes see A. F. Laing, *Compensatory Education for Young Children*, Occasional Publication No. 1, The Schools Council, London, 1968.

20. C. Bereiter and S. Englemann, *Teaching Disadvantaged Children in the Pre-School*, Prentice-Hall, Englewood Cliffs, NJ, 1966. J. Tough, *Listening to Children Talking*, Ward Lock, London, 1975.

21. (R) M. Willmott, *Adolescent Boys of East London*, Penguin, London, 1969; J. Bowlby, *Forty-four Juvenile Thieves*, Baillière, Tindall and Cox, London, 1946; D. H. Stott,

Studies of Troublesome Children, Tavistock Publications, London, 1966; A. K. Cohen, *Delinquent Boys*, Routledge and Kegan Paul, London, 1956. See in the Reader, L. T. Wilkins, 'Juvenile delinquency – a critical review of research and theory', *Educ. Res.*, **5**, 104–119 (1963).
22. M. Hoghughi, 'The Aycliffe token economy', *Br. J. Criminology*, 384–399 (1979). For a summary of the area of delinquency, see M. Hoghughi, *Treating Problem Children: Issues, Methods and Practices*, Sage, London, 1988.
23. M. Craft, B. Bicknall and S. Hollins (eds), *A Multidisciplinary Approach to Mental Handicap*, Baillière Tindall, London, 1985.

FURTHER READING

M. Chazan, A. F. Laing and D. Davies, *Helping Five- to Eight-Year-Olds with Special Educational Needs*, Blackwell, Oxford, 1991. DES Circular 22/89, *Assessments and Statements of Special Educational Needs*, HMSO, 1989.
Education Act (Chapter 60), HMSO, 1981.
Education Reform Act (relevant chapters), HMSO, 1988.
P. Evans and V. Varma, *Special Education: Past, Present and Future*, Falmer Press, London, 1990.
R. Gulliford and G. Upton (eds), *Special Educational Needs*, Routledge, London, 1992, and *Teaching Children with Learning Difficulties*, NFER–Nelson, London, 1985.
Special Educational Needs, the Warnock Report, HMSO, 1978.
L. Stow and L. Selfe, *Understanding Children with Special Needs*, Unwin Hyman, London, 1989.

Chapter 13

Educational Assessment

Attempting to assess the quality and quantity of learning has been, and probably always will be, a regular feature of classroom practice. While experts argue the toss about the efficiency or desirability of examinations, teachers will continue in their own way to establish whether their pupils have been learning. There are many ways in which teachers might try to assess progress, ranging from simple observation or conversation to standardized testing. It will not be possible to touch on all the multitude of methods which could be adopted. Instead, this chapter will tend to draw on the more acknowledged methods of assessment employed by examining bodies and teachers, although many of the arguments can be applied equally well to less formal classroom procedures.

The public examination system continues to grow in size and importance year by year.[1] Prior to the late 1960s the vast majority of the country's 11-year-olds sat the 11+ entry examination to grammar schools. Now, with the evolution of the General Certificate of Secondary Education (GCSE) and the raising of the school-leaving age, the emphasis has shifted from 11+ to 16+, when ever-increasing numbers of young people are becoming involved in public examinations. In 1967, for instance, no fewer than half a million pupils in the age range from 15 to 17 years sat some form of public examination, usually GCE O and A levels, CSE and various technical exams. This figure is about a third of the age group. As the GCSE is made available to more and more pupils, and both higher education and many industries continue to be geared to an examination system, it is inevitable that numbers will swell over the next few years. A 1979 survey by HM Inspectors of Schools[2] showed from a representative sample of schools that 83 per cent of fifth-formers were sitting O level or CSE maths and 90 per cent of fourth-formers were in O level or CSE English classes. With these and other factors in mind, we need to stress the importance of knowing the pitfalls and limitations which accompany examinations. The turn of the century will also see a marked increase in the number of students moving into higher education. The intention is to see approximately 30–35 per cent of the 18–19 age group in some form of higher education.

SOME PURPOSES OF EXAMINATIONS

A system which is used so extensively should have substantial justification. Let us look, therefore, at the important purposes which the protagonists of conventional examinations would claim.[3] Later it will be necessary to re-examine some of these points to assess the extent to which these purposes are achieved.

Attainment

One of the teacher's objectives, amongst others, is to stimulate the acquisition, understanding and application of knowledge. It therefore seems perfectly reasonable and desirable that the teacher should also want to explore the extent to which these objectives have been achieved. Indeed, in any walk of life, a time comes when we have to expose our knowledge and have it evaluated. This evaluation of attainment at a given time is one of the central aims of examinations.

Beyond the classroom there are employers and professions who require some assurances about the level of competence reached by prospective entrants. These assurances must be expressed as accurately as possible and in terms which are readily understood by all concerned. Examination marks in secondary and higher education are thought to provide one such criterion, although, as we shall see, marks can just as readily be misunderstood. When an organization external to the school is engaged, it adds a measure of objectivity and credibility to the marks obtained.

Diagnosis

The pupil

By comparing the attainments of a group of people who have taken the same examination, it is possible to draw some conclusions about the strengths and weaknesses of individuals. Of course, we have only measured the effects and not the causes of success or failure in the exam. Detecting the origins of failure is no easy task, particularly if the exam is not all that it should be. Essay-type papers, for example, are less useful when we want to see how extensively a pupil has covered the syllabus. An objective-type test which endeavours to cover a good portion of the syllabus is more likely to be of value in this kind of diagnosis, Also, the failure of a large number of pupils to give an adequate answer to particular questions could arise from inadequate teaching.

The teacher and the topic

It is part of the process of curriculum design for teachers to evaluate the effectiveness and efficiency of their methods and the suitability of the content. Care is clearly needed in making these judgements because so many variables, apart from considerations of the teacher's competence, impinge on pupil performance. Nevertheless, the methods of presentation and communication, the suitability and level of content, in fact all the learning experiences offered by the teacher will be reflected to some extent in the results of any evaluative programme.

The teacher's task of using examination scores as one source of pupil analysis and self-analysis, known as *feedback*, is very important and requires careful scrutiny of the scripts. Insufficient attention is given to the feedback made possible by this kind of analysis. In school examinations pupils should be allowed to see their scripts after they have been marked. The opportunity for pupils to see where they have gone wrong, to evaluate their competence and to set realistic goals is a most important function of well-designed examinations.

Prediction

Success in public examinations opens the door to a number of careers. Whether or not we agree with the validity of this process, most external exams are used to assess the potential of the examinee. If a student obtains so many O-level or GCSE passes he or she is deemed suitable for A-level studies; A-level successes are taken as the basis for choosing an academic or professional course; authority and professional status are placed in the hands of those who succeed in conventional examinations.[4] The tacit assumption in all these cases is that examination results are valid predictors. The 11+ entrance examination was probably the most widespread prognostic device ever used in British educational history. Success in standardized tests of numerical, verbal and spatial ability was said to indicate those children who would benefit most from an academic schooling.

Providing and maintaining standards

A carefully devised examination can be set at whatever level one chooses. Attempts used to be made to arrange that, for example, O-level chemistry exams were of the same standard from one year to the next or from one examining board to the next, although that claim was hotly contested.[5] Establishing standards of attainment is inevitable in a society which demands minimum levels of competence as a prerequisite for certain qualifications. How would we find our next generation of teachers if the last generation of teachers abandoned the idea of distinguishing between the qualities of their pupils? A public exam system is also an admission that we cannot trust each other. Its presence gives an air of impartiality and respectability to whatever standards are obtained.

Motivation

Learning is not easy. It requires self-discipline and hard work. Interest is obviously a good starting point, but this often comes as a product of becoming competent in a subject.[6] One major source of motivation is the long-term prospect of obtaining a qualification and a good job.[7] It was thought by some teachers that the CSE injected new life and purpose into the work of moderately able secondary pupils who at one time would have impatiently played out their last school years longing to be wage earners at the end of the fourth form. The motivational qualities of exams need hardly be mentioned to student teachers, who have all experienced the annual retreat into studies and libraries (around Easter time, usually) and the feverish activity which preceded the exams.

Development

Examinations have been said to bring out qualities of perseverance and industriousness. They are thought to give practice in expressing ideas lucidly, fluently and quickly. They compel students to organize their ideas and develop systems of study and concentration which may be adapted for service in later life.

Social (and administrative) engineering

By making examinations available to anyone who feels capable of sitting them, it is possible for social mobility to take place. At one time, favouritism and patronage played a large part in the life-chances of young people entering schools, universities or business. Now nepotism (favouring relatives irrespective of their qualities) no longer has any significant effect. The 11+ was seen by many as promoting social justice and enabling the children from less fortunate home backgrounds to enter grammar schools. Robbins,[8] in a report on higher education, foresaw the existence of 'pools of ability' largely consisting of able youngsters leaving school before attempting to get into higher education. Government policy is now set to increase the numbers entering higher and further education from its present figure of about 18 per cent to 33 per cent by the turn of the century.

These aims should not be regarded in isolation from each other. They are complex and interrelated. The student should question these assumptions in the light of his or her experience and reading and make some decision as to whether there are more suitable alternatives. The following sections should help to pinpoint some of the limitations imposed by exams.

LIMITATIONS

There are many problems associated with conventional examinations, tests and assessments. Much research money and energy has been spent in discovering the problems and trying out or suggesting solutions. Government bodies such as the Schools Council, which produced a stream of *Examinations Bulletins* (still relevant and readable),[9] and the successor bodies (the National Curriculum Council and the School Examinations and Assessment Council) have researched this area. So too has the National Foundation for Educational Research (NFER).[9] A recent report by a task group for the DfE called Task Group on Assessment and Testing (TGAT) has set the pattern for the present National Curriculum assessments[9] (see later in this chapter and Chapter 16).

First amongst the limitations are fundamental requirements of any test or assessment which is going to be used to make judgements about how much a person has learned, how performance compares for a person from one testing occasion to the next, how a person's performance compares with that of comparable people and whether the test measures what it was designed to measure. There are three statistical criteria which play a particularly important part in defining the adequacy of examinations. They are *reliability*, *validity* and *comparability*. For a sound introduction to these concepts see Satterly's book in note (1).

Reliability

Let us first define this term as applied to examinations. A reliable exam is one which will give a consistent score from one occasion to the next for the same individual or group irrespective of the person who marks it. We are dealing here with the adequacy of the measurement, and not the content. A simple example should suffice. If a teacher gives a primary-school class a home-made arithmetic test on two separate occasions and the two scores for individuals are irregular, the teacher would be justified in suspecting that the test was unreliable. If most of the scores increase on the second testing, it may mean that the children have had some practice in the meantime or that they have remembered some answers and left more time for the solution of other questions. If, on the other hand, the scores for some children are higher and those for others lower, then it could mean that the questions are poor or the marking inconsistent, and these are the kinds of inconsistency which give rise to unreliability of tests.

First, there are inconsistencies arising in one examiner's marks for a particular paper when it is marked on different occasions. This occurs primarily because of fatigue, mood, time of day and inadvertent changes in interpretation of an answer from one script to the next. Therefore, on marking the same batch of scripts on two occasions, two different sets of scores for each candidate or variations between candidates who have given similar answers could result.

Second, different examiners often have different interpretations and expectations of the candidates' answers. An essay-type answer is especially prone to varied interpretations because examiners can look for so many differing qualities. Some might be influenced by a fluent and witty style even when the content is thin; others might reward grammatical structure. An 'impression' mark is also decidedly open to criticism because of the high degree of subjective judgement involved.

As evidence of the fluctuations in essay marks which happen when a panel of markers is used, the famous research in the 1930s by Hartog and Rhodes[10] will be quoted. Satterly[1] gives a useful table (p. 229) of the results of studies into the reliability of essay tests. For subjects like French, English essays, history and mathematics at levels from junior school to university, Hartog and Rhodes invited panels of expert examiners to mark sets of papers. Table 13.1 shows the marks awarded to six candidates in the Entrance Scholarship Examination to university by five examiners. These have been chosen from a larger table given by the authors because the range of discrepancy, 25 marks, is the same for each candidate. Often one finds in a panel of examiners consistently generous or mean individuals. But notice the irregularity with which the highest (ringed) and lowest (boxed) marks have been awarded, although

Table 13.1 *Disparity in examiners' marks in an essay question*

Candidate no.	Examiner					Discrepancy range
	a	b	c	d	e	
9	48	30	55	55	40	25
13	67	50	45	42	52	25
23	42	35	60	58	47	25
34	65	52	40	60	55	25
47	32	36	35	55	30	25
25	60	32	65	50	68	36
Mean score	52.3	39.2	50.0	53.3	48.7	

Extracted from Table 96, p. 143 of *The Marks of Examiners* (1936) by P. Hartog and E. C. Rhodes. Reprinted with the kind permission of the publishers, Macmillan, London and Basingstoke.

examiner (b) appears to be heavy-handed. The maximum discrepancy for a candidate was 36, as shown in the last line of the table. These results speak for themselves, by exposing enormous differences in the marks allotted to candidates by different examiners for the same essay, particularly where there was no co-ordination between examiners. However, these findings from the mid-1930s have only partial relevance today. A great deal has been done by examining bodies to overcome unreliability by making improvements in marking procedures. For example, it is now common practice for examiners in a subject to meet and co-ordinate a marking scheme. Decisions are made about the allocation of marks and the range of answers which the panel will accept, and these are adhered to by them all. Marked scripts are sampled and re-marked by a second examiner, usually the leader of the team. Borderline candidates' scripts are always re-examined. Nothing is now knowingly left to chance in public examinations.

The idea of re-marking, particularly essay-type answers, has the support of research. Wiseman[11] suggested from his work that several examiners should mark each paper, thus diluting the idiosyncrasies of individual examiners. Work published by the Schools Council[12] on *multiple* marking in English composition at O level, using a combination of marks for impression (three independent assessors) and mechanical accuracy (one assessor) reveals an improvement in reliability over the official mark awarded by an examining board. There was also closer agreement with a continuous assessment given by the schools of the candidates.

Mathematics can also be subject to variation from one sitting to the next. Dale[13] found several disconcerting movements in the marks obtained by candidates at O level in successive June and September (resit) examinations. He gives four examples of increased marks which seem to go far beyond what one might reasonably expect as a result of concentrated effort in the time between the two exams. Table 13.2 is a reproduction of his findings.

This kind of unreliability is of particular interest, for it calls into question the comparability of test papers which, superficially at least, are thought to be similar. In mathematics there is an additional problem: candidates may spend disproportionate amounts of time on a few questions without necessarily being successful in solving them.

Apart from a stricter control of marking schemes and increasing the number of

Table 13.2 *Differences in mathematics marks between June and September (resit)*

Candidate	June	September	Range
	Marks as percentages		
A	27	58	31
B	25	63	38
C	32	59	27
D	36	76	40

Reproduced from *From School to University*, 1954, by R. R. Dale, p. 141, with the kind permission of the publishers, Routledge and Kegan Paul, London.

examiners, it is also possible to improve the reliability by increasing the length of the examination paper. This is usually the case in multiple-choice tests, as we shall see.

Validity

If a test achieves what the originators intended it to achieve, it is a valid test. There are several kinds of validity,[14] but we shall be concerned here with *content* and *predictive* validity. Before describing these, it ought to be noted that there is a connection between the validity and the reliability of a test or examination paper. If a test is unreliable, then plainly it cannot be valid for any purpose. On the other hand, if it is highly reliable it need not necessarily be valid; in other words, it might be highly reliable at measuring something which the designers never intended! Briefly, tests can be reliable and invalid, but they cannot be unreliable and valid.

Content validity

For an examination to have content validity it must contain qualitative and quantitative representation in the sampling of the whole syllabus. This rests upon the judgement of the examiner in completing questions from the syllabus. Essay-type papers often fall short of this requirement. It is very difficult to cover a significant portion of a syllabus using only ten or so questions. Multiple-choice designs overcome this difficulty to some extent by setting a large number of short questions covering a major part of a syllabus. However, there is more to content validity than merely making sure the syllabus content has been sampled adequately. We also need to know whether the questions are set in such a way as to fulfil the purposes and aims of the course. The teaching has been geared to certain objectives (see Chapter 16). Have these objectives been realized in the choice of questions and the answers given? Unfortunately, there are no formulae for finding content validity. The teacher must make up his or her mind about it from experience with the material and by using, where possible, a second opinion, because this is a qualitative rather than a quantitative activity. Deciding on objectives and setting appropriate questions is a difficult business. In this respect, Bloom's *Taxonomy of Educational Objectives*[15] is quite helpful in defining the scope and extent of the purposes we ascribe to educational procedures and in providing the kinds of questions appropriate for them.

Predictive validity

We saw earlier that one function of many public examinations is to enable us to select people for certain occupational or scholastic pursuits. The predictive validity of an examination is characterized by its ability to forecast those who might succeed in these pursuits. For example, A level results are used by universities and colleges as a major source of evidence of a student's capacity for coping with the course requirements. A degree is often taken as evidence that a person has the ability to cope in industry.

The results of research into the predictive value of examinations have not been encouraging. Investigations into the prognostic use of the 11+, O and A levels, teachers' certificates and degree results[16] have all, at one time or another, provided conflicting results. The reasons for this confused picture are complex, but one fairly obvious cause of low correlations is that some occupations demand qualities which are not disclosed by traditional written examination papers, and some qualities required in the preparation and competition of examinations are of little use in certain jobs.

Comparability

Comparability is closely linked with reliability, but it is so often neglected that a separate discussion is needed. Basically, if we want to compare the results of an individual on two or more tests or the results of several groups using the same test, we have to make sure that the comparisons are legitimate. For example, given two parallel forms of a French or arithmetic paper, are we justified in comparing the raw scores obtained by an individual on the two parts? This depends on a number of factors. Have the tests similar content? Do the scores for each group have similar means? Are the scores spread out in a similar fashion in both tests? The GCSE results in 1992 were the subject of criticism from the Inspectorate[5] for their lack of comparability across the examining bodies operating in England and Wales. Again, a number of worries have been expressed (Nuttall[17]) about the comparability of Standard Assessment Tasks (SATs) now in operation with the National Curriculum at ages 7, 11, 14 and 16.

Up to this point the emphasis has been on the suitability of the measuring device and the problems encountered in scoring. However, there are other criticisms which have been levelled at examinations, and we shall now consider some of the important ones.

The examinee

There are many intellectual, personal and social reasons which impose limitations on the performance of students but which have little or nothing to do with the setting or marking of the papers. Whether we could in some way allow for these variables is an extremely difficult and unresolved matter. They exist, and we should at least be aware of them. There are several obvious reasons which need little comment. Some people are over-optimistic about their talents and do not really have the necessary skills. Choosing the wrong subject is at the root of some students' problems. Few people are entirely consistent in their mood from one examination to another. The physical and mental condition of a candidate can affect performance, and in some cases candidates do not do themselves justice. Others are capable, but do not work, often through lack of motivation or over-confidence. Poor study strategies, lack of guidance about the requirements or faulty examination technique, all of which can be remedied, are common sources of trouble. Sometimes a teacher has a style of presentation which is incompatible with the style of learning of the pupil (cognitive style). Student teachers out on school practice will have experienced those blank looks on a child's face when something is being described, even when the student is convinced that the presentation was simple and logical. The art of simplification, using metaphor and analogy, and discovering the modes of thinking of pupils are skills which every teacher has to cultivate.

Some have argued that examinations engender an unnecessary spirit of competition between pupils. However, in most public examinations where an external paper and examiner are employed, the pupil and the teacher are, in some respects, in partnership. They co-operate in an attempt to meet the external demands of the examination system.

Research[18] suggests that those who succeed in conventional written examinations may have particular personality predispositions. It would be surprising if this were not the case. Characteristics such as persistence, a theoretical turn of mind, fondness for books, solitude and reflection are clearly beneficial to a student. These characteristics have been associated with the introverted personality, and research has shown that introverts abound in higher education, where theoretical, solitary study is at a premium.

Another influence arises from the fact that British exam systems tend to over-emphasize the written word. Recently an effort has been made to introduce other means by which students can communicate their skills and knowledge, besides the two-hour or three-hour written paper. Practicals, vivas, project work and orals (some of which have been in use for a long time) are amongst the commonest methods.[1]

Curriculum

To what extent are syllabuses determined and restricted by the existence of an examination? How are teaching methods affected by syllabus demands? Are there important educational needs (social, moral and intellectual) which are not examinable and which have to be sacrificed in favour of examinable themes? It has been suggested by many teachers that both they and their pupils have to make many omissions in their work because they get caught up in the frenzied scramble towards GCSE exams or the Standard Assessment Tasks (SATs)[20] set at 7, 11, 14 and 16 years of age (Nuttall[17]). For many years the teaching of mathematics and science was designed to provide routine strategies for problem-solving without arousing much exploratory interest in these subjects. The phenomenon of the examination dictating the content of the curriculum and methods of teaching is known as the 'backwash' effect. It is a subject with which every teacher should be familiar.

Question 'spotting' (guessing in advance the content of the exam questions) is commonly practised by pupils and teachers. Some teachers have developed the art to a high degree by juggling the questions on back papers with great dexterity. Unfortunately, it makes nonsense of a syllabus intended to give a comprehensive grounding in a subject.

KINDS OF ASSESSMENT IN USE

There has been a marked growth in recent years[1] of alternative forms of academic assessment to *conventional written examinations*. The most important of these has been the *objective-type test*, of which the now familiar multiple-choice item is an example. Other forms in use are *continuous* (or, more accurately, *intermittent*) *assessment*, *orals* and *practicals*. (See extract from the Schools Council's *Examinations Bulletin No. 3* in the Reader (**R**).[19] The most recent innovations to be introduced with the new General Certificate of Secondary Education (GCSE) have *grade-related* criteria[19] and the Standard Assessment Tasks (SATs),[20] which include *rating scales* and *checklists*.[1]

Conventional written examinations

It is hardly necessary to remind readers of the design of traditional exam papers. We are all too familiar with the rubric 'Answer 3 from 7 in 3 hours: careless and untidy work will be penalized'. But a number of interesting variations have been tried. Some universities, for instance, are experimenting with 'open-book' methods where the candidate is allowed to take specified texts into the exam room (if time is found to use them). Some candidates have been given the actual questions in advance or have been allowed to set their own papers. Naturally, the tendency is to set questions which make greater demands on the students if they are being given the advantage of a preview. The questions require answers which are less factual, more analytical and not unlike essays.

Objective-type examinations (R)[19]

In essay questions students are free to plan their own answers using whatever knowledge can be recalled, usually without any clues from the question. In objective questions the information given (or 'stem' of the question) is posed in such a way that there is only one acceptable answer, which either can be recalled from memory or recognized from a collection of probable answers. They are called 'objective' because the questions and answers are carefully predetermined, rendering the responses free from the personal biases of the examiner. Designing items is a skilled job,[21] as we shall see in the next chapter. Item analysis is required to provide a measure of the difficulty of each item for a given ability group, and to determine the discriminative qualities of the item.

In the UK the use of objective tests has been gathering momentum. Examination papers now contain many items of this kind. The Schools Council has been most prolific in the researches it has sponsored, and its publications relating to many important aspects of the whole field of educational assessment make important reading for both students and teachers.[9]

Several examples are given below (answers at the end of the chapter) to give the student some idea of the scope of objective-test items now available. They by no means cover all the variations in use, but represent the commonest. For convenience, we might make a broad distinction between items requiring straightforward *recall* and those requiring the *recognition* (or choice response) of an answer, although some designs require both these mental activities.

Recall items

As stated above, these require the candidate to remember a simple correct answer without its appearing on the answer sheet. Some factual essay questions require just this, except that the answers are buried in continuous prose. There are three basic kinds of recall item.

Simple recall. Here the candidate must recall a single fact (or series of facts), as in the following example taken from a CSE paper:

(a)   'Here am I; send me.'
(b)   'I do not know how to speak, for I am only a youth.'

Each of these sentences was spoken by a prophet when God called him. Name the prophets.

(a)   (b)

(West Yorkshire and Lindsey Regional Examining Board for the Certificate of Secondary Education, Religious Knowledge, 1970.)

Open (or sentence) completion. The candidate fills in an incomplete phrase or sentence. For example:

Jeremiah said that the Lord 'Will give all Judah into the Hand of . . .'
Complete the sentence.
(From the same paper as the example for simple recall.)

The unlabelled diagram. This is used extensively in science, particularly biology, where candidates are asked to recall parts of an organ or apparatus. For example:

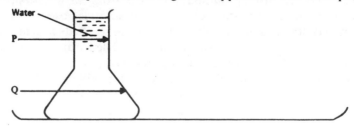

The diagram shows a conical vessel full of water. Show, on the diagram, the jets of water which occur when small holes are made in the vessel at the points marked P and Q; assume that air resistance is negligible.
(University of Cambridge Local Examinations Syndicate, GCE O-level Physics, 1970.)

Recognition items

Recognition items require the candidate to choose a correct answer from two or more possible answers which are given. There are several ways of presenting this kind of item, and four will be illustrated below.

True/false items. The candidate is given a stem and is required to say whether it is true or false. For example:

Place a tick in either the 'True' or 'False' column after each statement depending on which you think is the appropriate answer.

True   False

1. Intelligence may be defined as inborn all-round mental efficiency.
2. Intelligence is largely a product of the culture in which a child is reared, and the stimulation he receives.
3. Intelligence is entirely distinct from attainments or acquired information, and education received.
4. The IQ (if tested by a reliable test) remains constant to within about 5 points either way throughout school life.

(Taken from a questionnaire by P. E. Vernon in *The Bearings of Recent Advances in Psychology on Educational Problems*, Evans, London, 1955.)

Multiple-choice responses. These are the commonest form of objective test. Usually there are about five alternative answers provided for each item. It is possible to have more than one acceptable answer in some cases. The following are examples having one correct response:

You are asked to underline the appropriate item in each case.

1. The chief danger from FALL-OUT comes from   Cosmic dust, fission fragments, fusion fragments, cosmic rays, disturbance of the atmosphere, any of these, none of these.

2. ALTAMIRA attracts visitors for the same reason as   Palmyra, Nimes, Alicante, Bonn, Lisieux, Lascaux, Arles, none of these.

3. Which of these has the most complex MOLECULAR STRUCTURE?   Salt, sugar, starch, protein, petroleum, potassium permanganate, nitrous oxide.

4. One of these Shakespearean characters is out of keeping with the others.   Iago, Macbeth, Cassius, Claudius, Feste, Richard III, Timon.

(Taken from a 'culture test' by W. K. Richmond, in *Culture and General Education*, Methuen, London, 1963.)

Example having several correct responses:

Place tick in the box opposite each correct response.
Plaster of Paris is often used to immobilize fractures because of the following advantages
(a) It is relatively cheap ☐
(b) It is unaffected by water ☐
(c) It is relatively light ☐
(d) It is non-toxic and non-inflammable ☐
(e) It is easily moulded to fit the part ☐
(Trial multiple-choice question for physiotherapy students. With the kind permission of J. L. Low, St Thomas's Hospital, London.)

Example using the 'best reason' method:

Answer the question implied in the following statement by selecting the answer A, B, C, D or E which best completes the sentence.
A metaphorical expression

A. is allowable in poetry but not in prose
B. is never used except for rhetorical ornament
C. falsely likens one thing to another
D. is always in the form 'A is B'
E. implies a comparison
(Joint Matriculation Board, GCE A-level General Studies – Paper I, 1968.)

Matching items and rearrangement. These are self-evident from the examples below. The following is an example of matching items:

The names of some composers are given below. Which of these composed the operas named in question a to e?

A. Berg	a. *La Bohème*
B. Beethoven	b. *La Traviata*
C. Britten	c. *Peter Grimes*
D. Gounod	d. *The Magic Flute*
E. Mozart	e. *The Mastersingers*
F. Puccini	
G. Rossini	
H. Verdi	
I. Wagner	

(Joint Matriculation Board, GCE A-level General Studies – Paper I, 1968.)

Example of rearrangement:

Write in the box alongside the statement in the second column the letter which is given to the structures in the first column which is best related to that statement.
Also write in the name of the structure that has been omitted from the first column in the question.
(a) DNA   Carries information from nucleus to cytoplasm   ☐
(b) Chloroplast   Combines loosely with oxygen   ☐

(c)   Haemoglobin   Every plant and animal has a fixed number of these
                    structures in the nucleus   ☐
(d)   RNA   Contains 'coded information' from parents   ☐
(e)   ——————   Absorbs light energy for photosynthesis   ☐
(West Yorkshire and Lindsey Regional Examining Board for the Certificate of
Secondary Education, Biology, 1970.)

The unlabelled diagram with labels provided is another form of this method.

Continuous (intermittent) assessment

Continuous assessment is now the most popular method of assessment in colleges of
education (particularly in the subject of Education) and has slowly found a place in
other areas of education, from CSE **(R)**[22] to university level.[22] It involves mainly
essays, projects and perhaps some formal examination, but may include seminar
papers marked for presentation and content. The actual assessment process most frequently adopted is a five-point literal grading system (A to E), judged largely by
impression marking. It is possible to have in mind specific qualities such as facts,
ability to write fluently or the extent of the literature covered, but these matters of
detail often become submerged in the overall mark. The reliability of marking can be
improved by operating a ranking system in which the points on the scale in use are
first established using essays chosen so as to obtain one at each point on the grading
system. The consequent marking is based upon these. But judging the quality of
extended written work is arduous if it is properly done with the criteria clearly stated
and weighted before marking commences. Anyone marking essays should be in a
position to include what is being assessed and how much emphasis is being placed on
different aspects of the answers.

The snares of intermittent assessment are legion,[1] but not insurmountable. Marking is more subjective than in multiple-choice questions and attempts the very difficult
task of measuring complex, ill-defined skills ('analytical' qualities, creativity, coher-
ence, etc.) from what is usually a combined effort between the essay writer and his
or her reference sources. Where a marker knows the writer, there can be tendencies
towards self-fulfilling prophecy (see Chapter 3). This occurs when a general impression
of the pupil's competence is allowed to colour *all* the work he or she does. Other
qualities which have nothing to do with essay writing may intrude ('a nice person
deserves a nice mark' – the halo effect). Lack of refinement in the marking scale or
several markers, as mentioned above, causes the grades to cluster in the middle of the
range. There tend to be fewer 'A's and 'E's than in conventional written exams.
Further, when the marks for a course are compiled, the central tendency is exaggerated
even more, particularly if several people have been responsible for the marking (either
as moderators re-marking an essay or in separate essays). The pressures on pupils or
students can be quite heavy. Therefore the setting of questions has to be worked out
most carefully between all the teachers concerned to avoid log-jams of work at certain
times in the course. Essays hurriedly put together often contain ideas which pass from
a reference source to the essay without being considered by the writer. In fact this
aspect of essay writing, that is, how much of the reference material is assimilated by

the student and can be recalled or recognized at some future date, has not been researched thoroughly. It is also very important to choose suitable essay titles. Without care, it is easy to give essays which are unmanageable.

Nevertheless, with the sting of the three-hour unseen exam paper drawn, it is felt by some that learning is more effective and less anxiety-provoking. Essays allow us to expose our ability to produce, organize and express ideas, to integrate information from several sources, to pose and solve problems and evaluate ideas.

Oral and practical examinations

Oral and practical assessment methods have been with us for many years. In the GCSE and A levels we have orals in language, and practical work and assessment in the sciences. The marking of orals depends on a variety of criteria hinging on pronunciation, understanding of conversation and the accuracy of response. Some subjective judgement is needed, but the criteria of student performance are generally stated clearly. Similarly, in the science practicals, the expectations in student performance should be clearly mapped out (and generally are with all the public examining boards). Some students find the face-to-face aspect of orals intimidating, and it is probable that a few do not do themselves justice.

In higher education these methods are used extensively. In teacher education the student has to carry out a school practice, under observation; in medicine and professions supplementary to medicine (physiotherapy, nursing) the student is observed in a variety of practical settings relating to professional skills in either real or simulated circumstances. Other kinds of practical experience are found in technological courses ('sandwich' experience), dentistry and the law. The need for practical professional experience is regarded by most as crucial, but the accuracy of assessment of performance during this experience is still a matter of contention and research.

Case history and interpretive questions

These questions have particular relevance in examinations for applied fields such as medicine, teaching and management. The case-history technique provides the candidate with sufficient information about a case to enable diagnosis, indicate complications and offer treatment or decisions. Hubbard and Clemans,[23] in a book about multiple-choice examining in medicine, give a number of examples of this approach. The A-level General Studies papers have also adopted a similar procedure. The questions are usually long-winded because a thorough exposition of all the symptoms or observations must be given in order for the student to select answers. Very complex and searching questions are possible using this design, chiefly when the candidate is required to recall and evaluate rather than recognize the answer.

A great deal of evidence is still required before we are able to evaluate the various kinds of assessment now being adopted. Several questions still need to be answered. Are all these methods measuring more or less the same qualities, thus obviating the need for such an elaborate array of methods, or do they inspire different modes of learning and thinking? Do continuous assessment methods have an inhibiting effect on students in fear of prejudicing their assessment? Nisbet[24] makes the point that:

> The advantages of a prescribed examination over informal or continuous assessment are that the examination is, to some extent, a public occasion, revealing at least some of the bases of assessment; and that the examination identifies the occasions when the student is on trial and thus gives him freedom at other times. Examinations impose on students occasions of submission, but they also define areas of freedom.

Again, we might ask whether continuous methods are less reliable because they are more susceptible to manipulation than formal examinations. These and many other problems are the focus of research at present.

Standardized tests

There are now many standardized tests of ability and attainment in a wide variety of subjects designed for use with children from 4 to 16 years of age. Several of these tests are compiled with teachers in mind, so that the tests can be administered by the teacher in his or her own class, either individually or as group tests. For obvious reasons, the tests are available only to registered persons who have a need for them and who are able to use them properly. Of the publishing firms and organizations in this country, the National Foundation for Educational Research undoubtedly has built up a tradition as a designer and supplier of well-standardized test material. Its publications cover clinical, educational and psychometric materials (NFER–Nelson catalogues). They contain a comprehensive selection of ability and attainment tests covering reading, comprehension, word recognition, number, arithmetic or mathematics, verbal and non-verbal reasoning, interest and practical-skill tests. We shall deal more extensively with the concept of standardization in the next chapter.

Ability tests

Ability tests have already been mentioned in Chapter 9. They attempt to measure the all-round mental efficiency of a person, without necessarily indicating specific subject skills. Verbal and non-verbal reasoning tests are amongst those ability tests most used in schools. As we have seen, they have been used to define broad classifications of pupils for streaming or selection purposes in the belief that pupils so classified should, in general, be capable of coping with academic work of a given standard. But they do not tell us *in particular* if a child is better at physics than at history. They are most efficient when it comes to showing the extremes of mental functioning; that is, the very dull or the gifted.

Attainment tests

While they correlate to some extent with ability tests, attainment tests are designed principally to sample achievement in specific school subjects, having first been tested out on a large representative group of children. The sampling usually occurs over a fairly small age range (three or four years at the most) to enable a reasonably accurate estimate of attainment to be made. In the next chapter, on standardization, we shall look more closely at the method of standardizing the age norms. These are commonly used in primary schools as a means of estimating progress in specific basic subjects such as reading, arithmetic and word recognition. *Aptitude tests* are designed to predict success in future academic work and are said *not* to depend on the effects of instruction, i.e. they are said to predict future learning despite previous learning.

Diagnostic tests

Constructed in a similar way to attainment tests, they are intended to give a more detailed picture of the weaknesses in a school subject. They are common in basic subjects such as reading and arithmetic, where they usually consist of several sub-tests constructed to show the finer details of the difficulties experienced by children. Their application is particularly helpful in cases of retarded development.

Grade-related criterion tests

In Chapter 9 criterion-referenced testing was discussed. This method of testing was introduced under the heading of grade-related criterion testing to replace O-level and CSE examinations by the GCSE (General Certificate of Secondary Education), but it has been discontinued.[25] The Secondary Examinations Councils (SEC, replaced part of the activities of the Schools Council) established working parties to look in detail at the 10 examination subjects with the largest entries. They were to identify six 'domains' to be assessed, specifying the skills and competence which must be demonstrated by the candidates in order to obtain grades at specified levels on a seven-point scale from A to G. This means that the examiners would work from a set of statements about the level of performance required for the award of a grade within each of the six domains. As indicated in Chapter 9, candidates would have to demonstrate 'mastery' by reaching a predetermined level of skill or competence. Mastery would vary from topic to topic, but success rates of 70 per cent to 80 per cent have been suggested. Their criteria for achievement must be expressed in positive terms, i.e. what the candidates know or can do, and not in negative terms based on what candidates do *not* know. The starting point for building up these criteria is taken to be the bottom two grades, F and G, so that the importance of positive knowledge and skill acquisition can be emphasized.

Rating scales and checklists

Rating scales and checklists[1] are very much dependent on personal feelings and opinions. They are used chiefly by teachers as they observe their children in the performance of a task.

Rating scales most often consist of an odd number of points, such as five or seven, where each point is a gradation of opinion ranging from, say, 'very much', 'much', 'average', 'little', 'very little'. The respondent is required to choose one point on the scale which she or he thinks is most appropriate. The kinds of items which could be used are 'How well does a child concentrate on a task'? or 'To what extent does a child become involved in practical work?' These scales are not reliable and careful consideration should be given as to whether they should be employed.

Checklists are similar to rating scales, except that the scoring system is usually briefer; indeed, more often than not a two-point scale is used with 'yes' or 'no' as the scale points to be ticked. Occasionally, there may only be one point indicating whether a child can or cannot carry out a given task. For example, a teacher may require a quick check on a child's reading performance. A list of crucial criteria would be compiled, such as 'can recognize . . .', 'can read fluently . . .', 'can say . . .' certain words appropriate for a given age group. The teacher would run through the list ticking the appropriate boxes. The overall score would give a general impression of performance level.

ADVANTAGES AND LIMITATIONS OF OBJECTIVE EXAMINATIONS

Advantages

Many more questions can be set in a given time than is possible in essay examinations. Some writers[19] have suggested that about 100 items per hour, without a choice, is a reasonable pace. As a consequence, more extensive sampling of syllabus content is practicable, and this gives a corresponding increase in the reliability of the score. Marking is made easier because responses are short, to the point and systematically arranged on the answer sheet. Clearly there is complete impartiality in the marking, although mistakes are still possible, e.g. when adding is incorrect, two pages are turned by mistake or accidents occur in the marking. Some American test agencies are now able to automate the marking and totalling.[26]

Less time is spent by candidates in writing out their answers. This, one hopes, leaves more time for thinking! There is little opportunity for padding or writing long, elaborate answers to questions which the examiner has not set.

As we shall see in the next chapter, the construction of objective tests enables a careful control of the difficulty levels associated with each item. In this way we can decide in advance the spread and frequency of each level of difficulty. With essay answers the level of difficulty experienced by candidates is discovered in retrospect once the marks have been awarded. Much time and skill are required to accumulate an 'item bank' containing questions of known difficulty for a given ability range.

By taking a large number of items covering small sections of a syllabus it is easier to detect and counsel a pupil's (or teacher's) weaknesses. This has an added advantage, in that students have not only knowledge of results but a detailed analysis of the shortcomings. Essays are not easy to analyse in this way.

Limitations

Although scoring is made easy, setting the questions is a difficult business. Badly constructed tests can have a disastrous effect on the study and morale of students. Poor design often reflects the subjective element which enters into the choice of questions. So we see that the position in 'objective' questions is the reverse of that in essay-type questions: the former require subjective judgement in the setting, the latter in the marking. Panels of judges for question-setting will overcome this problem to some extent.

There is something deceptively comforting about a paper which provides the answers as well as the questions. It is certainly easier to recognize an answer than to recall it from memory (see Chapter 6). But not all questions need be of this kind. In medical questions, for example, and presumably in any applied field, the student can be given information from which he or she must provide evidence of not only knowledge but also reasoning and judgement. Advanced level General Studies papers contain many examples of questions requiring comprehension, interpretation and application of knowledge. Nevertheless, there is limited opportunity for disciplined expression.

The short, sharp question and answer requires a particular kind of behaviour which can be developed. Sophistication in answering these questions is also a criticism levelled at the IQ test, where concentrated practice can give increased scores. A corollary of this is the influence that practice may have on the whole pattern of study. There could be serious distortions if only this kind of question is used.

Little opportunity is afforded for imaginative and creative work. The emphasis is on fact rather than fancy and little, if any, account is taken of the *quality* of thought which has led to the answer. Consequently, only certain subjects, chiefly factual areas of mathematics, the sciences, history, geography etc., lend themselves to objective assessment. Skills such as organizing and presenting knowledge in a lucid, concise and fluent manner are not in evidence. In fact, the examinee spends rather more time reading than writing. The obvious way round this criticism is to ensure that essays are included somewhere in the examination.

Guessing is quite possible in multiple-choice answers, but it is not as great a problem as some people have supposed. It must first be made quite clear to the candidates that they must not attempt a question which they cannot answer and that guessing will be penalized. A formula can then be used to counteract guesswork. It is derived in the following way. Suppose a test consists of 10 questions, each having five alternative answers, of which only one is correct. A candidate who can answer five correctly would obtain only five marks if the instructions were followed. However, with guesses at the remaining five answers the candidate would, by chance, obtain one more mark, because in a five-way choice with one correct choice there would be a one-in-five chance of being correct. The total, therefore, would be six. The formula devised to overcome guessing should give a total of five, because this extra mark was a guess.

$$\text{Total mark} = \text{number of correct items} - \frac{\text{number of incorrect items}}{\text{number of choices in an item} - 1}$$

In our example, number correct = 6
number incorrect = 4
number of choices in each item is 5

$$\therefore \text{Total mark} = 6 - \frac{4}{5 - 1} = 6 - 1 = 5$$

which is exactly the mark deserved.

Finally, a word about *anxiety* and *stress* aroused by the tensions which accompany an examination system. Whenever there is a fear of failure[27] and a threat to one's self-esteem, anxiety is inevitable. In turn, anxiety states will have some influence on learning and performance. Intellectual and personal factors interact in a complex fashion not yet understood by psychologists, and the direction in influence is still not predictable. In some circumstances a moderate level of stress may provide drive energy which can be harnessed to good effect. In other cases, the level of stress may be so high as to be disruptive (driving tests have a habit of being this!). This deleterious influence has been shown, for example, in higher education,[28] where increasing numbers of referrals for temporary mental disorganization are a testimony to the growing problem. Malleson,[29] at university level, managed to reduce examination panic by carefully designed interviews in order to gain a thorough knowledge of the individuals concerned and the specific source of their disturbance.

Most teachers soon discover those pupils who have a nervous disposition. It is up to teachers to put pupils at ease by showing sympathy and a willingness to talk through the problems. The anxiety generated by examinations, especially public exams on which one's future career might hinge, is a regular source of trouble. Similarly, younger children get worked up about standardized tests. Teachers should do all in their power to allay excessive tension. Where possible, the test or examination should be held in familiar surroundings in the school, with familiar faces as invigilators; also, the examination should be fitted into the normal school routines if possible. The atmosphere in an examination room should not be unduly tense and distant, but relaxed, quiet and conducive to concentration. Pupils should have a clear idea of what is expected of them, and this can frequently be achieved by making sure they understand the rubric of their papers, without unduly prolonging the period of preparation before the exam.

PROFILES AND RECORDS OF ACHIEVEMENT IN SCHOOLS[30]

Following the DES policy document on records of achievement in 1984,[31] there has been considerable research into the most effective modes of presenting a pupil's progress. The issues and problems, not surprisingly, have not yet been resolved. Finding ways of showing a pupil's achievements which are relevant, accurate and carry some conviction that they are usable by teachers, parents and employers has not been easy. At present, it appears that the first pupils to have complete school records will be those leaving school in 1995.

There are many technical issues relating to records (see Satterly[1] for a good chapter on profiles and records). For example, what forms of presentation are available in showing profiles? Should the content be honest in presenting weaknesses as well as strengths? Should profiles be confidential or open? How credible will reports be where personal judgement has played a large part in the assessment? Can the profiles of, say, different children in the same class or school be compared with other children, classes or schools?

Most existing records contain the following information: (a) biographical details – name, age, sex, birth date, address and general information about schools attended; (b) health and home conditions such as illness or handicaps which may affect a child's progress or require regular treatment; (c) attainments in general ability, verbal reasoning, word recognition, reading, comprehension and arithmetic taken at various ages in school along with the name of the test; (d) interests such as music, drama, sport, social activities or practical skills; (e) attendance; (f) behaviour and personality, including deviant behaviour (delinquency, truancy) and emotional disturbance; (g) other general comments by the teachers or headteacher. To the new style profiles would be added the assessments from SATs at ages 7, 11, 14 and 16. The attainment targets for each subject are to be arranged in groups called profile components. An example of a profile component might be taken from English (5–11) in which one would find three such as speaking and listening, reading, writing. Not only will the results be available to parents, but class profiles are to be made public.

In secondary schools, subject reports are also sent to the child's parents. These very familiar school reports containing (frequently unstandardized) exam marks with teachers' comments have uncertain utility. Research into the value of school reports, both from the school's and the parents' points of view, has been scant up to now (but see note (30)). At the least, they are intended to convey to the parents a measure of their child's progress and standing in particular subjects and to indicate any strengths or weaknesses. Whether parents interpret the marks and comments in quite this way is open to question. However, reports, coupled with personal contact between the teacher and the parent, can often resolve some of the instrumental questions ('Will he get a decent job?', 'Has she a chance of passing O levels?') running through the minds of parents.

The National Curriculum Council has adopted the assessment system proposed by TGAT[20] in which there are 10 levels of achievement covering the period a pupil is at school. Table 13.3 shows some typical attainment targets at the Key Stages.

Sometimes Table 13.3 is expressed as a graph. However, the question of stress both for teachers and pupils has been raised by the spectre of endless testing. No matter how hard one tries to 'sugar the pill', most teachers and pupils feel they are under the microscope. The assessments which will attract the most attention will be the *high stakes* ones, i.e. SATs and any others which form an obvious part of any assessment likely to be transformed into pupil, teacher, class or school bench-marks. Other kinds of assessment such as those for which subjective rating scales, checklists and self-assessment profiles by the pupils are in evidence are *low-stake* assessments with less chance of getting the attention thought, by some, to be due to them.

Table 13.3 *Attainment targets for Key Stages*

Key Stage	Expected range for most pupils	Typical achievement at end of Key Stage
1	1–3	2
2	2–6	4
3	3–8	5/6
4	4–10	6/7

The Assessment of Performance Unit[31]

There has been a growing belief that we do not know enough about the formulation, measurement and monitoring of educational standards in the educational system. Prior to the introduction of the National Curriculum and apart from nationally organized exams such as GCE and the new GCSE, there was little by way of common core agreement about the curriculum in schools or what is a reasonable expectation of content and standards. In 1975 the Department of Education and Science set up the Assessment of Performance Unit charged with the task of promoting the development of methods of assessing and monitoring the achievement of children at school and seeking to identify the incidence of underachievement. To do this, the Unit was to look at existing instruments and methods of assessment, to consider new ones and to co-operate with LEAs in assessing and identifying underachievement. There are six areas of interest to the Unit:

(a) Language: Communication through reading, writing, listening and speaking in a wide range of modes to suit the occasion, the purpose and the subject; performance in the first foreign languages most commonly taught in British schools: French, German and Spanish.

(b) Mathematics: Communication through numbers, graphs, models and diagrams.

(c) Science: Observation, selection, evaluation and the use of evidence, the testing of hypotheses, the use of experiments and the drawing of conclusions.

(d) Personal and social development: The pupil's understanding of himself or herself, development as a responsible person and moral response to the social and physical environment.

(e) Aesthetic development: The pupil's appreciation of form, colour, texture, sound and material, emotional response to the environment, feeling for quality, and capacity to harness imagination in creative activity.

(f) Physical development: The pupil's developing co-ordination, the ability to use his or her body expressively and effectively. This involves a range of physical skills, from those needed by the child when he or she first starts to use a pencil to the sensitive handling of tools and instruments and the use of movement and dance in communication.

The idea is not without its critics. Will the monitoring create a syllabus to which teachers and pupils will direct a disproportionate amount of their time? Is this the beginning of a rigid-core curriculum? How will the information gathered about children's performance in a particular school or authority be used by the DfE? Can these six areas really be monitored effectively with the measuring devices at present at our disposal? These and many other problems will be a source of contentious discussion over the coming years.

SUMMARY

Evaluating pupils' learning is a necessary step in any formalized educational system. We need to have some valid and reliable assessment of a child's personal progress, potential and standing relative to the peer group. At the same time, the assessment should be in a form which is readily understood by pupils, teachers, parents and, where necessary, employers. Examinations provide, with varying degrees of success, an estimate of attainment and a means of diagnosing weaknesses and misdirections in the pupils' studies. They are used with the intention of predicting aptitude for further study or entry to work. Examinations provide an opportunity for upward mobility for the successful, but they can produce feelings of inadequacy in the unsuccessful as an unfortunate spin-off. They are used, too, as a gauge in predetermining and maintaining standards as well as measuring the efficiency of the content of a teacher's work and methods used. Revision for examinations acts as a means of reinforcing the learning of the content.

These ambitious suggestions about the purposes of examinations must be considered along with two important criteria. Any evaluation must measure what it is supposedly designed to measure – it must be valid; and if it is valid, the evaluation must be consistent when used with the same or similar pupils – it must be reliable. But the potency of examinations also depends on conditions external to the design of the test material. Among these, the psychological condition of the pupil is paramount. Too little is known about the interaction of personality attributes and performance, although we are well aware that excessive anxiety can adversely affect a pupil's achievement. The presence of unfamiliar people or conditions, lack of understanding of what is required and undue pressure from parents or teachers to perform well can all take their toll. Faulty learning strategies are also effective in depressing performance.

The range of evaluative instruments and methods is now quite extensive. Among these are the essay-type tests, projects, vivas, practicals, rating scales, checklists, attainment tests and objective tests, of which the last mentioned are becoming very significant alternatives to the well-established unseen essay paper. The method does compensate for several criticisms levelled against essay-type questions, but the preparation of objective-type questions must be a highly technical and time-consuming job for the outcome to be of value. Assessment is used largely as a means of communication between pupil, teacher and parent. Therefore we should endeavour to give a pupil every opportunity of using as many communication media as possible. The emphasis in our system has been on the written word produced over a timed period. It seems equally important to encourage children to communicate their knowledge in oral or practical ways where this is feasible.

Often assessments have to be formalized so that we can convey to others the level of attainment and progress made in particular school subjects. Other teachers, parents, local education authorities and employers need to know this information. School reports are the commonest method of conveying the information to parents. Many authorities also provide a cumulative school record card on which attainments, amongst other helpful details, are recorded by the child's teacher. Regular insertions on these records enable an extremely useful profile to be compiled for each child.

ENQUIRY AND DISCUSSION

(a)   On school practice or school visits, investigate the following:
   (1) School and local education authority (LEA) records and profiles of achievement. What are they for? How are they compiled? What use do teachers, LEAs and employers make of them?
   (2) Discuss with teachers their methods of assessing children, both in term time as part of continuous assessment and in end-of-term tests. What difficulties do they experience? What use do they make of these assessments? Are they reliable and valid? How does assessment vary with the subject?

(3) School reports and parents' day are routine features in most schools. How do teachers overcome the tricky task of telling parents about their children's shortcomings? How do parents respond? Do parents have difficulty in evaluating how their children are developing or how they are progressing in relation to others? (See note (30) for some useful references.)

(4) Discover pupils' views of the public examination system and continuous assessment.

(5) Inspect and compare intelligence, attainment and diagnostic tests. Look also at some examples of objective-type tests. If at all possible, try to become involved in the administration of a test programme. Have a look at the administration manuals of these tests.

(b) Examine the place of assessment in (1) junior or (2) secondary or (3) higher education. What forms might it take? What are the purposes served by such assessment? Are the purposes achieved? How might we overcome the difficulties mentioned in this chapter?

(c) Read the TGAT Report (full reference in note (20). What are the problems in fixing attainment targets? Is it possible to combine 'levels of achievement' to obtain overall profiles?

(d) Read, then write about or discuss the following:
(1) the effects of anxiety or fear of failure in examinations;
(2) the role of ambition in examination motivation;
(3) validity and reliability of 'home-made' examinations in primary or secondary schools;
(4) the evaluation of project work or 'creative writing';
(5) the distinction between ability and attainment tests;
(6) the work of the Assessment of Performance Unit (APU).

(e) Obtain as much information as you can from the examining Boards and relevant publications, ready for discussion in tutorials.

NOTES AND REFERENCES

1. D. Satterly, *Assessment in Schools*, Blackwell, Oxford, 1989 (2nd edn).
2. *Aspects of Secondary Education in England*, a survey by HM Inspectors of Schools, HMSO, 1979.
3. C. B. Cox, 'Examinations: seven questions', in C. B. Cox and Rhodes Boyson, *Black Paper 1975*, The Critical Quarterly Society London, 1975. See also D. Satterly, op. cit.
4. For a thought-provoking fantasy about where present trends are leading us, have a look at M. Young, *The Rise of the Meritocracy 1870–2033: An Essay on Education and Equality*, Penguin, London, 1961.
5. HMI Report, GCSE Examinations: Quality and Standards, HMSO, 1992.
6. Some researches have shown little or no correlation between interest and attainment. Interest, by its very nature, is subject to change and does not always depend on competence. The work of R. G. Rowlands, 'Some differences between prospective scientists, non-scientists and early leavers in a representative sample of English grammar school boys', *Br. J. Educ. Psychol.*, **31**, 21–32 (1961), is an example. L. Cronbach in *Essentials of Psychological Testing*, Harper International, New York, 1984 (4th edn), an extensive summary of this field of investigation, concludes that:

> Interests are poor academic predictors. . . . Out of 21 correlations of course mark with interest in that subject matter (expressed prior to the course), 17 were below + 0.3. (p. 431).

For a discussion of this topic see B. S. Bloom, *Human Characteristics and School Learning*, McGraw-Hill, New York, 1976.

7. We are told by sociologists that this ability to postpone an immediate gratification for a long-term goal such as a qualification is more characteristic of children from middle-class homes than from working-class homes. This is one of many social reasons why early leavers come largely from working-class backgrounds.

8. The Robbins Report: *Higher Education*, HMSO, London, 1963.

9. The Schools Council produced many working papers and examinations bulletins in its time (published by HMSO). They were written by teachers with teachers in mind and are exceptionally readable and still useful. Try, for example, *Examinations Bulletin 32*, Evans/ Methuen, 1975, or *18+ Research Programme Studies Based on the N and F Proposals*, 1977. The National Foundation for Educational Research (NFER) has initiated many projects which are reported from time to time and advertised in their catalogue *Books for Education* published by NFER–Nelson each year. A recent DES report, *National Curriculum: Task Group on Assessment and Testing*, HMSO, 1988, is helpful in giving the rationale behind the present assessment and SATs system.

10. P. Hartog and E. C. Rhodes, *The Marks of Examiners*, Macmillan, London, 1936.

11. S. Wiseman, 'The marking of English compositions in grammar school selection', *Br. J. Educ. Psychol.*, **19**, 200–209 (1949) and 'The use of essays in selection at 11+. Reliability and validity', *Br. J. Educ. Psychol.*, **26**, 172–79 (1956).

12. Schools Council Examinations Bulletin No. 12, *Multiple Marking of English Compositions*, HMSO, London, 1966.

13. R. R. Dale, *From School to University*, Routledge and Kegan Paul, London, 1954.

14. Satterly, op. cit., includes thorough chapters on reliability and validity.

15. B. S. Bloom (ed.), *Taxonomy of Educational Objectives. Handbook I: Cognitive Domain*, Longman, London, 1956.

16. For a summary of American work, see D. E. Lavin, *The Prediction of Academic Performance*, Wiley, New York, 1967. In this country, a paper by L. Cohen and D. Child entitled 'Some sociological and psychological factors in university failure', *Durham Res. Rev.*, **22**, 365–372 (1969), points to researches in higher education. Comments about the 11+ are numerous and both the Newsom Report: *Half Our Future*, HMSO, London, 1963, and the Plowden Report: *Children and Their Primary Schools*, HMSO, London, 1967, have something to say on this subject. More critical views appear in J. E. Floud, A. H. Halsey and F. M. Martin, *Social Class and Educational Opportunity*, Heinemann, London, 1956, and B. Jackson and D. Marsden, *Education and the Working Class*, Routledge and Kegan Paul, London, 1962.

17. D. L. Nuttall, 'National assessment – will reality match aspirations?', *Educ. Section Rev.*, British Psychological Society, **13**, (1–2) (1989).

18. D. Child, 'Affective influences on academic performance', in P. Gordon (ed.), *The Study of Education*, vol. 2, The Woburn Press, London, 1980.

19. (R) For a splendid introduction to the problems of objective testing, the reader is recommended to read the Schools Council's Examinations Bulletins 3 and 4. Bulletin No. 3 is *An Introduction to Some Techniques of Examining*, HMSO, London, 1964 and Bulletin No. 4 is *An Introduction to Objective-type Examinations*, HMSO, London, 1964.

20. DES report, *National Curriculum: Task Group on Assessment and Testing*, HMSO, 1988, and three supplementary reports, 1988. There is also a very useful DES summary of the main contents of TGAT in *National Curriculum: Task Group on Assessment and Testing Report – A Digest for Schools*, HMSO, London, 1988.

21. See Satterly, op. cit., Chapter 4, on constructing tests.

22. (R) D. Boyall, 'CSE Mode III In English', *Dialogue*, **11**, 8–9 (1972). J. W. Starr, 'Final examination versus cumulative assessment in a postgraduate education course: a comparative study', *Durham Res. Rev.*, **5**, 239–243 (1968).

23. J. P. Hubbard and W. V. Clemans, *Multiple-choice Examinations in Medicine: A Guide for Examiner and Examinee*, Kimpton, London, 1961.

24. J. D. Nisbet, 'The need for universities to measure achievement', in *Assessment of Undergraduate Performance*, which was a report of a conference convened by the Com-

mittee of Vice-Chancellors and Principals and the Association of University Teachers, 1969, pp. 15–18.

25. 'Problems of the GCE Advanced level grading system', Joint Matriculation Board, Manchester, 1983.
26. P. D. Groves, 'Marking and evaluating class tests and exams by computer', *Computer J.*, **10**, 365–367 (1968).
27. R. C. Birney, H. Burdick and R. C. Teevan, *Fear of Failure*, Van Nostrand Reinhold, New York, 1969.
28. F. Zweig, *The Student in the Age of Anxiety*, Heinemann, London, 1963.
29. N. Malleson, 'Treatment of pre-examination strain', *Br. Med. J.*, **2**, 551 (1957) and 'Panic and phobia', *Lancet*, **1**, 225 (1959).
30. Considerable research has been devoted in recent years to the problems of record keeping and school reports. The Schools Council and NFER carried out a study of profiling and school reporting. An indication of their findings can be found in J. Balogh, *Profile Reports for School-leavers*, Schools Council Programme 5, Longman, 1982; B. Goacher, *Recording Achievement at 16+*, Longman, 1983 for the Schools Council; P. Broadfoot (ed.), *Profiles and Records of Achievement*, Holt, Rinehart and Winston, London, 1986. B. Goacher and M. I. Reid, *School Reports to Parents*, NFER–Nelson, Windsor, 1983.
31. There is now a considerable literature on the Assessment of Performance Unit. Perhaps the most basic and accurate statements have been written by members of the APU. See the APU leaflets such as *Introduction, Language Performance, Monitoring Mathematics, Reporting on Performance and Assessment – Why, What and How*. The APU has also brought out interim documents such as *Foreign Language, Science Progress Report 1977–78* and *Assessment of Scientific Development* available from the Publications Department of the Department for Education, Elizabeth House, York Road, London SE1 7PH. Other publications of value include the APU occasional paper 1 *Learning Mathematics* (1983) and paper 3 *Standards of Performance – Expectations and Reliability* (1984). The various reports on the DES are also full of valuable material for specialists in English Language, Science, Mathematics and Modern Languages.
32. **(R)** T. Fawthrop, *Education or Examination*, published by the Radical Student Alliance, 1968.

FURTHER READING

A. Anastasi, *Psychological Testing*, Collier Macmillan, New York, 1982 (5th edn).

P. Broadfoot (ed.), *Profiles and Records of Achievement*, Holt, Rinehart and Winston, London, 1986.

D. G. Lewis, *Assessment in Education*, Unibooks, University of London Press, London, 1974.

D. Satterly, *Assessment in Schools*, Blackwell, Oxford, 1989 (2nd edn).

J. M. Thyne: *Principles of Examining*, University of London Press, London, 1974.

ANSWERS TO TEST ITEMS

Recall:

Simple recall. (a) Isaiah (Chapter 6); (b) Jeremiah (Chapter 1).
Open completion. 'the king of Babylon' (Chapter 20).

The unlabelled diagram

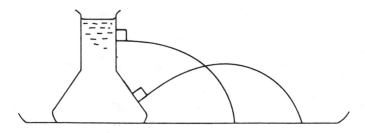

Recognition:

True/false. (1) False; (2) True; (3) False; (4) False.

Multiple-choice: one correct. (1) Fission fragments; (2) Lascaux; (3) Protein; (4) Feste.

Multiple-choice: several correct. Responses (a), (d) and (e).

Multiple-choice: best reason. Response E.

Matching items. (a) *La Bohème* – Puccini; (b) *La Traviata* – Verdi; (c) *Peter Grimes* – Britten; (d) *The Magic Flute* – Mozart; (e) *The Mastersingers* – Wagner.

Rearrangement. (a) d; (b) c; (c) no response; (d) a; (e) Chromosomes and b.

Chapter 14

Standardization and Item Analysis

This chapter is offered as an optional extra for those who wish to know more about the statistics of standardizing test scores and the fundamentals of item analysis. It is not an attempt to introduce students to statistics. That would require a whole textbook, and some are recommended in note (1) and the Further Reading list at the end of the chapter. Even so, students without any mathematical background or with a phobia about mathematical concepts are likely to find this chapter somewhat intimidating. The author, nevertheless, believes that students should at least attempt to fathom basic statistical concepts in order to make their reading of the research literature more meaningful, as well as helping to expose for them some of the dangers inherent in the design and use of standardized tests. In this respect, colleges and departments have an important role to play in providing suitable introductory courses in statistics for students in educational studies.

STANDARDIZATION OF EXAMINATION MARKS

Teachers are often faced with the task of pooling several sets of marks, sometimes for the same school subject, sometimes between different subjects. But there are good reasons why it is not always justified simply to add all the marks together and use the total, or average, as a measure of the relative competence of pupils. The standard of marking varies for an individual from one occasion to the next. Standards also vary between teachers and between subjects. Often the marks are widely spread in subjects such as science and mathematics with well-defined expectations in the answers, whereas essay marks tend to bunch round the average mark. The average itself is also affected by the leniency or severity of the marker or the content of the examination questions. Even when the standards for each subject are the same, one may question the sense of adding the marks of such disparate subjects as French, arithmetic and needlework. What we shall do in this section is demonstrate a method for adjusting the marks in two subjects to make them comparable. This process of converting the raw marks to a common scale is known as *standardization*.

Table 14.1 *Marks for arithmetic and English (N = 50). (Maximum score = 10)*

Pupil	Arithmetic	English	Pupil	Arithmetic	English
1	9	3	26	4	8
2	1	9	27	4	6
3	4	8	28	3	7
4	8	4	29	7	7
5	7	5	30	2	7
6	4	7	31	5	5
7	2	2	32	3	4
8	4	8	33	5	8
9	6	6	34	4	8
10	5	7	35	6	7
11	3	5	36	0	6
12	4	6	37	1	3
13	8	7	38	5	8
14	7	6	39	6	7
15	10	3	40	5	8
16	4	7	41	2	7
17	3	8	42	5	4
18	2	7	43	4	9
19	5	9	44	5	8
20	4	6	45	6	2
21	3	6	46	1	6
22	6	7	47	3	5
23	4	4	48	2	4
24	3	5	49	7	7
25	4	5	50	6	9

Tabulation

Suppose a form teacher has received two sets of marks (variously referred to in the following text as raw marks and scores), one for arithmetic, the other for English. When the marks for each pupil are assembled, the list will have the chaotic appearance of Table 14.1. Gathering systemic information would be impossible from the confusion of figures as they appear in this table.

The first task is to rearrange the scores to provide us with a concise picture of the *distribution*, that is, the frequency with which successive scores occur. The best and most easily interpreted arrangement is a *tabulation* obtained by writing down all the possible scores in ascending or descending order. By working through the list of marks we *tally* each one against the appropriate mark to build up a tabulation looking something like Table 14.2. The fifth tally mark is drawn through the first four, like a gate, and a second set is started with the sixth occurrence of the mark. This has the advantage of breaking the scoring into convenient units of five, thus giving easy addition at the completion of the tally.

Where the range of marks involved is extensive, as would most likely be the case for a percentage scale, the tabulation of single numbers is not sufficiently compressed to give a clear picture of the frequency distribution; nor is it convenient for the calculation of statistical quantities. In this case, we group the marks in useful *class intervals*. For a percentage scale the interval might be five consecutive marks such as 0 to 4,

Table 14.2 *Tabulation of arithmetic and English marks*

Mark	Arithmetic Tally	Frequency	English Tally	Frequency
0	I	1		0
1	I I I	3		0
2	LHI	5	I I	2
3	LHI II	7	III	3
4	LHI LHI II	12	LHI	5
5	LHI III	8	LHI I	6
6	LHI I	6	LHI III	8
7	IIII	4	LHI LHI III	13
8	II	2	LHI IIII	9
9	I	1	IIII	4
10	I	1		0
		Total 50		Total 50

5 to 9, 10 to 14 and so on. A score of 8 would be tallied in the class interval 5 to 9. In subsequent calculations the mid-point of the interval is then used to represent the interval. For example, the mid-points of 0 to 4 and 5 to 9 are 2 and 7 respectively, convenient whole numbers which result from taking class intervals containing an odd number of scale points such as five.

Graphical representation

Although we can now see some semblance of order, there is an even more graphic way of presenting the information. If the frequencies of Table 14.2 are plotted against the corresponding marks in the form of bars we have a *histogram*, as portrayed in Figure 14.1(a). For each mark along the horizontal axis of the graph we erect a block whose height represents the frequency of the mark. Figure 14.1(a) is the histogram for the arithmetic distribution. At a glance we can see that the frequencies for arithmetic accumulate around a mark of 4; for English the most frequent mark is 7.

An alternative method of presenting the frequencies is the *frequency polygon*. If, instead of drawing bars, we join up the mid-points at the top of each bar, as in Figure 14.1(b), a frequency polygon is generated. In the histogram the base of the bar is one mark unit wide, with the actual mark value at the centre of this base, while in the frequency polygon the points to be joined correspond to the centre of the base at the mark value. The lines joining the points are straight. However, with large numbers and a good spread of marks the lines joining the points take on the appearance of a continuous *curve*. For ease of presentation the subsequent illustrations will be smoothed; readers should appreciate that the curve will have been derived from a less regular distribution.

Distributions

The shape of the curve tells us a lot about irregularities in the distributions. Many statistical formulae rely on the fact that the distribution of data is *normal*. A normal

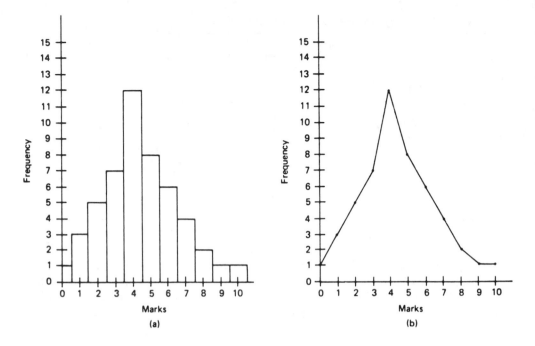

Figure 14.1   *(a) Histogram and (b) frequency polygon for arithmetic.*

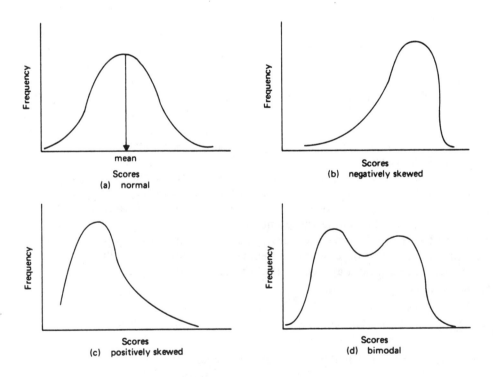

Figure 14.2   *Different kinds of distribution.*

curve has a symmetrical appearance of frequencies regularly diminishing on either side of the most frequent score. Figure 14.2(a) is a normal distribution; our distributions in arithmetic and English are close to normal. Intelligence tests are designed to give normal distributions when administered to a random sample of a population. Test items are chosen so as to give this kind of distribution. Consequently, it is meaningless to suppose that intelligence tests can 'prove' intelligence to be normally distributed in a population because the tests are manipulated to make normality inevitable.

The English marks tend to fall towards the high end of the distribution, and where this becomes exaggerated, as shown in Figure 14.2(b), it is known as a *negative skew*. A preponderance of scores towards the low end of the scale gives a *positive skew*, as in Figure 14.2(c). When two obvious maxima occur in a distribution, as would result if we plotted 1, 3, 7, 10, 17, 14, 14, 17, 11, 5, 1, a *bimodal* distribution is said to exist. Bimodal distributions are common where there are two clearly defined groups in the sample chosen – clearly defined because they give rise to conspicuously different maximum frequencies. The figures chosen above are in fact the totals of frequencies for the marks between 0 and 10 in arithmetic and English. As we saw in Table 14.2, the maxima for these subjects are different, and this is reflected in the overall distribution of the totals shown in Figure 14.2(d). Heights or weights of men and women, if combined, would also tend to give bimodal curves, one maximum connected with the men and the other with the women.

Means

The difference in the distributions and maxima for arithmetic and English makes it highly improbable that we can make direct comparisons of the raw marks for each pupil. If we wanted an overall mark we could not simply add the raw scores. We must first convert the distributions to some common standard – a technique known as standardization and used, for example, in the 11 + examination where verbal, numerical and general ability scores were first adjusted before being added to get a grand total. Occasionally, it is achieved by altering one distribution to comply with the second (see the discussion of cumulative frequencies later) or, as in the following case, by converting the two scales to a third common scale. To do this, we need to know two things about the marks: we need (a) the *mean* or average of each distribution, sometimes known as a measure of central tendency along with *mode* and *median*[2] and (b) the spread or *standard deviation* of the marks in a distribution, sometimes known as a measure of dispersion. These two important statistics are closely connected to the distribution and provide an accurate way of describing it. Where the scores give a small standard deviation, the curve is steep and high, whereas a large spread would give a flat curve; both are illustrated in Figure 14.3.

The popular way of finding a mean is to add all the figures and divide by the total number of figures involved. Unfortunately, this is a laborious job if there are numerous figures to contend with. One short cut is demonstrated in Table 14.3.

The weird and wonderful symbols employed are in very common usage. X represents the raw mark, $\bar{X}$ (pronounced 'ex bar') is the mean, $\bar{X}_A$ (pronounced 'ex bar sub A') is the particular mean for arithmetic, Σ means 'the sum of', so Σf is the 'sum of all the frequencies', which is bound to equal the sample size, N. $\Sigma f X$ means 'the sum of

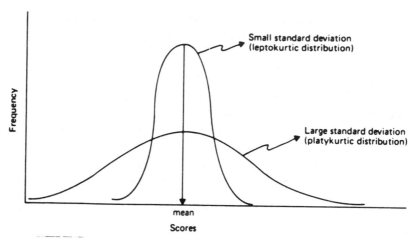

Figure 14.3   *Extreme kinds of normal distribution.*

Table 14.3   *Finding the mean for arithmetic*

Mark (X)	Frequency (f)	fX
0	1	0
1	3	3
2	5	10
3	7	21
4	12	48
5	8	40
6	6	36
7	4	28
8	2	16
9	1	9
10	1	10
	$\Sigma f = N = 50$	$\Sigma fX = 221$

The mean $\bar{X}_A = \Sigma fX/N = 221/50 = 4.42$

all the separate *frequencies times the marks*'. If one inspects the table it will become clear that each fX saves the trouble of having to add all the separate marks together, that is, instead of adding twelve lots of the mark 4, one has $12 \times 4 = 48$. With our simple example not much saving is apparent, but if the numbers were larger there would be considerable economy of effort. The reader might like to calculate the mean for the English marks using the same technique as shown in Table 14.3. The value $\bar{X}_E$ should be 6.20.

Note that if a class interval system had been used, the mid-point of the interval would have been taken to represent the range of marks falling within the interval. Thus the interval 0 to 4 is represented by 2, 5 to 9 is represented by 7, and so on. The term fX would then be found by multiplying the frequency of marks within a given interval by the mid-interval score. For any one interval this procedure may be slightly inaccurate, as we see in Table 14.4.

Table 14.4 *Calculating a mean using class intervals for arithmetic marks*

Range	Mid-point	f	fX	(actual totals of fX)
0–4	2	28	56	82
5–9	7	21	147	129
10	10	1	10	10
			$\Sigma fX = 213$	221

One would never dream of calculating a mean using the very small range in our example, but it does illustrate the effect on fX of taking the mid-interval point. For the range 0–4, mid-point 2, the product fX would be 56. In fact, it should be 82 if we consider the marks separately as in Table 14.3. The inaccuracy is lessened by the second range, and the total for fX comes very close to the true value. With a greater number of class intervals the minor variations in fX tend to cancel each other out.

Standard deviation

The second important statistic we need to know is the standard deviation. A knowledge of the central tendency of the marks, the mean for instance, tells us nothing about the way in which the marks are distributed on each side of the mean and the next stage will be devoted to finding the dispersion of the marks. In the following, we will concentrate on the *method* of finding a standard deviation rather than the reasons for the procedures we adopt – in a similar manner to using a cookery book! As was observed above, one would really need a course in statistics to understand the reasoning behind the mathematical manoeuvres.

The stages necessary for the calculation are: (a) find the mean; (b) find the difference between the mean and each mark; (c) square the difference obtained in (b); (d) multiply the square from (c) by the frequency f if this applies; (e) find the sum of the results from (d); (f) divide the answer from (e) by the number of pupils in the sample; (g) find the square root of the answer in (f). This gives the standard deviation of the marks. Using symbols again, let the mean be $\bar{X}$ let the raw mark be X, then (a) to (g) would be represented by:

(a) $\bar{X}$;

(b) $\bar{X} - X$;

(c) $(\bar{X} - X)^2$;

(d) $f(\bar{X} - X)^2$;

(e) $\Sigma f(\bar{X} - X)^2$;

(f) $\Sigma f(\bar{X} - X)^2 / N$;

(g) $\sqrt{\Sigma f(\bar{X} - X)^2 / N}$.

The headings and calculations in Table 14.5 follow this pattern. Stage (f) is $\Sigma f(\bar{X} - X)^2 / N = 222.36/50 = 4.447$ and the standard deviation σ (sigma) $= \sqrt{4.447} = 2.11$. Notice that we include the correct sign in the column $(\bar{X} - X)$ and when this is squared in the next column the sign becomes positive. Squaring, therefore, overcomes the problems of a negative sign. Readers may like to try a similar calculation for the standard deviation of the English marks. The answer should be $\sigma = 1.82$ using a mean, $\bar{X}_E$, of 6.20.

Table 14.5 *Finding the standard deviation for arithmetic ($\bar{X} = 4.42$).*

Mark (X)	Frequency (f)	$\bar{X} - X$	$(\bar{X} - X)^2$	$f(\bar{X} - X)^2$
0	1	4.42	19.54	19.54
1	3	3.42	11.70	35.10
2	5	2.42	5.86	29.30
3	7	1.42	2.02	14.14
4	12	0.42	0.18	2.16
5	8	−0.58	0.34	2.72
6	6	−1.58	2.50	15.00
7	4	−2.58	6.66	26.64
8	2	−3.58	12.82	25.64
9	1	−4.58	20.98	20.98
10	1	−5.58	31.14	31.14
	$\Sigma f = N = 50$			$\Sigma f(\bar{X} - X)^2 = 222.36$

One interesting fact about standard deviations for distributions approaching nor-mality is that the percentage of the sample falling within one standard deviation on both sides of the mean is approximately 68 per cent of the total sample. Figure 14.4 is a diagrammatical expression of this fact. The mean for arithmetic was 4.42 and one standard deviation of 2.11 above and below this value gives a range from 2.31 to 6.53. We were operating with whole numbers and this range would include values between 3 and 6. Reference to Table 14.2 shows that, for arithmetic, 33 pupils obtained scores between these limits, that is, 68 per cent of the sample. Two standard deviations on both sides of the mean would enclose about 95 per cent of the sample. Three standard deviations on both sides encloses almost the whole sample (99.7 per cent), as shown in Figure 14.4.

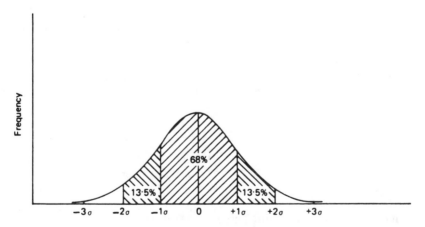

Figure 14.4 *Standard deviation related to percentage of cases in a normal distribution. σ is the symbol for standard deviation. In the area between −1σ and +1σ there will be about 68 per cent of the cases.*

Standardization

Armed with the means and standard deviations of the two subjects, we are now in a position to equate the two sets of marks. But what standard are we going to choose for the third scale? To make life easy in the transformation calculations, it is usual to take whole numbers for the new mean and standard deviation. A convenient mean would be 5, with standard deviation of 2. The common quantity which links all the scales together is the *standard score (z)*. This is obtained by dividing $(\bar{X} - X)$ by the standard deviation (σ). For the arithmetic marks

$$\frac{\bar{X}_A - X_A}{\sigma_A} = \frac{\bar{X}_S - X_S}{\sigma_S}$$

where $\bar{X}_S$, X_S and σ_S are the mean, new standardized mark and standard deviation for the new scale. The only unknown quantity in this equation is X_S the new set of standardized scores. Rearranging the equation we get:

$$X_S = \bar{X}_S - \frac{(\bar{X}_A - X_A)\sigma_S}{\sigma_A}$$

Suppose we want to standardize a score of 9/10 in arithmetic, then substituting in the formula above for $\bar{X}_S = 5$, $\sigma_s = 2$, $\bar{X}_A = 4.42$, $X_A = 9$ and $\sigma_A = 2.11$, we obtain:

$$X_S = 5 - \frac{(4.42 - 9)2}{2.11} = 5 + 4.34 = 9.34$$

Referring to Table 14.1 will reveal that pupil 1 obtained 9/10 for arithmetic. He also managed 3/10 in English, which converts to 1.48 when standardized using $\bar{X}_E = 6.20$ and $\sigma_E = 1.82$. In fact, pupils 1, 4, 5, 9 and 10 have all obtained a raw score total of 12 when arithmetic and English are added. Yet on standardizing their marks, a rank order is created as shown in Table 14.6. Wider variations in the means and particularly the standard deviations than those cited here can produce conspicuous changes when scores are adjusted.

Table 14.6 *Marks before and after standardization*

Pupil	Raw marks Arithmetic	English	Total	Standardized marks Arithmetic	English	Total
1	9	3	12	9.34	1.48	10.82
4	8	4	12	8.40	2.58	10.98
5	7	5	12	7.45	3.68	11.13
9	6	6	12	6.50	4.78	11.28
10	5	7	12	5.55	5.88	11.43

Cumulative frequency

Short-cut methods of finding an estimate of standardized scores are available. Students are recommended to read a pamphlet by J. C. Daniels entitled *The Standardisation*

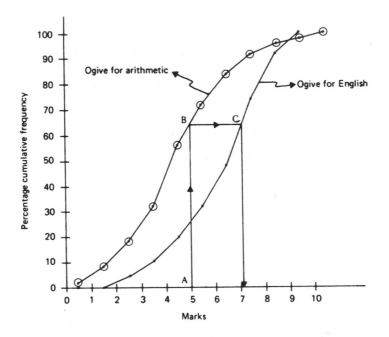

Figure 14.5 *Standardizing scores using a cumulative frequency method.*

of School Marks (University of Nottingham, Institute of Education), in which these are described. Where there is some doubt regarding the normality of a distribution, it is possible to employ a *cumulative frequency graph* or *ogive* (usually pronounced 'ohjive'). For this solution the frequencies are arranged as in Table 14.2, but with the lowest score or mark at the bottom of the column. The frequencies are then added in succession, starting at the lowest score. For arithmetic the cumulative frequency (*cf*) is given in Table 14.7. The highest *cf* should equal the sample size, giving 50 in the present case. To construct a cumulative frequency graph, plot the marks along the horizontal axis against the *cf* along the vertical axis. For our purposes a percentage cumulative frequency graph is required. To convert *cf* into percentage *cf*, simply divide the value of *cf* by the sample size and multiply the result by 100. At a mark of 5 in arithmetic the *cf* is 36. Hence the percentage *cf* to this point in the distribution is 36/50 × 100 which gives 72. The graph of percentage *cf* against marks from Table 14.7 has the appearance of Figure 14.5. Note the characteristic shallow S-shaped curve of the ogive.

To produce a conversion graph, first draw percentage cumulative frequency curves for arithmetic and English on the same graph (Figure 14.5). In this case we are going to convert marks on one subject to a comparable scale in the other subject. To convert 5/10 in arithmetic so that it has a comparable mark in English, first draw a vertical line from 5 on the mark scale until it reaches the curve for arithmetic, marked B on the graph. Then draw a line horizontally from B until it meets the curve for English, marked C. Drop a line from C on to the mark scale and this reading gives the corresponding mark, which in English is 7.1. Notice that both these marks occur at the 64th percentile, as indicated on the percentage cumulative frequency axis.

Table 14.7 *Cumulative frequency of arithmetic marks*

Mark	Frequency (f)	Cumulative frequency (cf)	Percentage (cf)
10	1	50	100
9	1	49	98
8	2	48	96
7	4	46	92
6	6	42	84
5	8	36	72
4	12	28	56
3	7	16	32
2	5 ← plus — gives → 9		18
1	3 ← — gives → 4		8
0	1 — plus — 1		2

Standard scores and percentage of a population

Whenever we have a normal distribution of ten scores it is possible to calculate the percentage of cases (number of people, for instance) falling between given scores on the scale. This is a very useful piece of information, particularly when we want to discover the number of people who, for example, might have IQ scores greater or less than given values. Figures 14.4 and 9.1 were both calculated using this knowledge.

The first stage involves the calculation of the standard score corresponding to the range of scores required and using this standard score to determine the percentage for the range chosen. Table 14.8 gives a series of standard scores and the corresponding percentages of the population falling in the range *between the mean and a point along the scale of scores* which would give the standard score.

Table 14.8 *Percentage of cases under a normal curve using standard scores from the mean*

Standard score	0.5	1.0	1.5	2.0	2.5	3.0	3.5
Percentage of cases	19.15	34.13	43.32	47.72	49.38	49.87	49.98

Let us suppose we wanted to know how many in a population of children would obtain IQ scores between 100 and 115 on a test which has a mean of 100 and a standard deviation of 15. The standard score for 115 is:

$$\frac{100 - 115}{15} = -1$$

Ignoring the negative sign, which merely tells us which side of the mean we are operating on, the percentage of cases falling between the mean of 100 and one standard score higher (115), according to Table 14.8, is 34.13. From the mean to the far end of the distribution on either one side or the other would incorporate half or 50 per cent of the population. Thus, if we wanted to know the percentage from a point along the scale to the end, let us say 115 and greater, we could subtract the percentage obtained in the method just described from 50 per cent. Hence we would find 50.00 − 34.13 = 15.87 per cent above 115 IQ points on a scale with a mean of 100 and a standard deviation of 15.

ITEM ANALYSIS

Several references have already been made to item design and analysis as the starting point in the production of multiple-choice test papers. In the next few pages we cannot do more than suggest some important considerations which are taken into account when these tests are required. It is not anticipated that students will be able to construct their own items after reading this brief description. For details the reader is referred to the Schools Council's publications and other references made at the end of this chapter. One particularly relevant description appears in the work of a research unit at the University of London which investigated test materials for the Nuffield Science Teaching Project. We shall draw on the team's work in O-level chemistry to introduce the student to item design and analysis.[3]

Test blueprint[4]

Before we can design a set of items we must have a clear idea of the aims, objectives and scope of the subject matter (see Chapter 16) as well as making explicit the kinds of student ability and behaviour we wish to exploit. Rather than pulling topics out of a hat or dreaming up essay titles while watching television, it is essential to make a detailed map of the nature and content of the whole paper, with regard to the activities and abilities being tapped. We have to decide if our pupils are required to use comprehension or evaluative techniques in the questions posed. Are they to apply knowledge to novel problems? What proportions of these skills do we hope to represent in the questions? In a nutshell, we have created a syllabus to bring about the growth and development of behavioural skills in our pupils; the examination should aim at testing these skills.

Once these skills and the subject matter through which they are expressed have been defined, a *blueprint* which incorporates all the essential features of test design is required. The blueprint consists of a grid which must include all the attributes so defined. For the purposes of building this grid, the Nuffield Project team decided to use some of the educational objectives proposed by Bloom[5] as a workable classification of student behaviour.

The categories chosen were knowledge (recalling facts), comprehension (calculating, translating, interpreting and making deductions to solve problems with familiar solutions), application (applying knowledge to unfamiliar situations) and analysis/ evaluation (analysing information for the purpose of making value judgements). These skills represent one important dimension to be accounted for in item design.

A second dimension is, obviously, the content of the syllabus, and this should be divided into conveniently discrete areas of similar material. A third possibility results when the content is classified according to the operations of 'activities' required by the wording of the problem. In Nuffield chemistry the activities postulated were: composition and change in materials; practical techniques; patterns in the behaviour of materials; essential measurements; and concepts. These can be seen as broader groupings of the syllabus content.

If we consider the 'activities' and 'abilities' dimensions as shown in Figure 14.6 a grid is generated. The cells of the grid are used to guide us in accounting for whichever

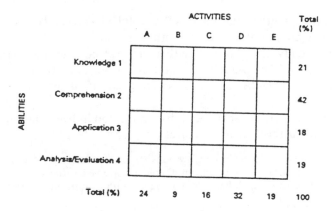

Figure 14.6 *Grid taken from Nuffield Chemistry Project (page 4).*

combinations of the categories we desire. Not all cells will necessarily be represented. It may transpire that some topics cannot be expressed in all forms of activity. The important point to remember is that we can scrutinize in detail the distribution of the syllabus content and the behaviour we wish to evoke from the questions. Sorting out the proportion of items to appear in each cell is complex and rests on value judgements made by the test designer. Weighting of specific categories along the two-way table is a starting point, and these have been inserted along the sides of the grid. By judicious manipulation of these marginal proportions we obtain the individual proportions to be assigned to each cell, according to the emphases we wish to observe. If nothing else, blueprint design is a most effective way of getting a teacher to examine and define his or her purposes in providing a particular course.

Test item design

Having created a ground plan of the skills, topics and activities we wish to examine in a predetermined proportion we must devise appropriate items. There are two important indices which help in forecasting the suitability of test items. These are the *facility index*, which shows whether the candidates have found an item easy or difficult, and the *discrimination index*, which shows how far an item distinguishes the high-scoring from the low-scoring candidates. In all that follows we are assuming that large samples are involved, certainly more than 30 individuals.

Facility (or difficulty) index

It is plainly important to know the level of difficulty experienced by a group of candidates in answering each item. In setting traditional examination questions chance plays a major part in the choice of easy or difficult questions. What appears easy to a teacher in the setting may be very difficult for the pupil in the execution. The teacher's comprehension of a subject often makes it difficult for him or her to assess, before the fact, the quality of the answers that will be received. To overcome this problem, the questions are initially tried out with a similar group of pupils, referred to as a *pilot sample*. Usually a teacher has neither the time nor the resources to embark on this kind of venture. Consequently, research has been done to test the feasibility of creating 'libraries' or 'banks' of items covering specified ability levels and school subjects.[4]

For an examination of the facility and discrimination indices, the following example has been taken from the Nuffield Project.[3]

Directions: the group of questions below consists of five lettered headings followed by a list of numbered phrases. For each numbered phrase select the one heading which is most closely related to it. Each heading may be used once, more than once, or not at all.

Classify the following changes into one of the categories, A–E
A Radioactive decay
B Catalysis
C Hydrolysis
D Cracking
E Oxidation

1. The conversion by heat alone of an organic liquid consisting of one compound only, into a mixture of compounds which are gaseous at room temperature.
2. The production of thermal energy from the fossil fuels.
3. Changes in the nuclei of atoms.

The originators of this item are testing comprehension, their argument being that the questions require not just simple recall but an understanding of the chemistry in the example and the terms used for sorting out the type of change involved. Note also that the activity involved in questions 1 and 2 is 'composition and changes in materials'; for question 3 it is 'concepts'.

To deal only with question 1, 348 candidates took the paper and eight did not respond to this question. The remaining candidates gave one of the alternatives A to E as set out in Table 14.9.

The step before this table was built required the pupils to be arranged in rank order according to the total mark obtained on the whole paper. The order was then divided into five equal, or almost equal, groups shown as fifths in the table.

Look first of all at the column totals. Not surprisingly, alternative D attracted the highest proportion of respondents because it was the correct answer. Expressed as a

Table 14.9 *Distribution of responses to question 1 (N = 348)*

Students classified by total test score	Alternative A	B	C	D[a]	E	Omits[b]	Total
Lowest fifth	5	17	11	13	21	3	70
Next lowest fifth	4	7	7	33	16	3	70
Middle fifth		8	8	37	15	2	70
Next highest fifth	2	3	7	47	11		70
Highest fifth	1	2	4	56	5		68
Total	12	37	37	186	68	8	348

[a] Correct answer.
[b] Number of students who reached question but did not answer it (i.e. omitted the question).

percentage, 53 per cent of the total sample (186 × 100/348) got the question right. The proportion (0.53) of respondents giving the correct solution is known as the *facility index* (*F* or *p*). If only 20 per cent had managed to get the right answer, the question would clearly be a difficult one. Higher percentages or *F* values would signify easy questions. The inverse of the facility index is known as the *difficulty index*. Whether items are included which give a wide distribution of facility levels depends on the purposes of the test. Nevertheless, indices which are lower than 0.10 or higher than 0.90 are often caused by badly worded questions or, as we shall see, because alternative answers may distract the respondent. The inclusion of a few easy items may help the less confident to settle down or the less able to gain some benefit from the test; difficult items, which are frequently analytical or evaluative, may reveal the 'high fliers' in a group. But most papers possess a substantial proportion of items with near to average facility levels (ranging from roughly 0.30 to 0.70).

The totals for the alternative answers are also very important. An incorrect answer which attracts a large proportion of respondents is known as a *distracter* and should be treated with caution. In multiple-choice items it is common practice to select alternatives which give the appearance of being plausible. If the alternatives were superficial and ridiculous, the candidate could arrive at the correct solution by a process of elimination. On the other hand, the inaccurate answers should not readily draw the candidate off the scent. There is a very real danger that distracters arise through poor and inaccurate teaching or ambiguity in the wording of the question. In our example, alternative E has the largest response rate, apart from the correct answer, and claims some 20 per cent of answers. There are no hard and fast rules governing the limits set for distracters, and test designers create their own standards from experience. If distracters are appealing to better candidates they should certainly be replaced. Ideally, in the multiple-choice item we are looking for alternatives which would be equally attractive to someone with little knowledge of the subject being tested. Thus if the brighter candidates are being fooled by distracters it is wiser to discard and replace them.

Discrimination index (D)

It seems obvious that an item should be answered correctly most often by those with the highest overall mark. It would be a curious question indeed if it were answered correctly by poorer candidates and incorrectly by the better ones. The *discrimination index* gives us a measure of how far an item distinguishes between high-scoring and low-scoring candidates. A formidable collection of methods now exists for estimating discrimination. Of these, it will suffice to mention two and to direct the student to Anastasi's book in Further Reading for a thorough exposition of the subject.

The simplest measure, and one adopted in researches sponsored by the Schools Council, can be used when the numbers involved are high (certainly not less than 30 and preferably over 100) and when the high-scoring and low-scoring groups contain the same number of individuals. The formula is simply $p_1 - p_2$, where p_1 is the proportion of high scorers getting the question correct and p_2 the proportion of low scorers getting the question right. The number of high and low scorers must be the same. So we could find p_1 from the highest 2/5 and p_2 from the lowest 2/5. Extracting the values from Table 14.9:

$$p_1 = \frac{\text{number getting questions right in highest 2/5}}{\text{total in the highest 2/5}}$$

thus $p_1 = 103/138 = 0.747$

and $p_2 = 46/140 = 0.328$

then $p_1 - p_2 = 0.747 - 0.328 = 0.419$

The closer this D value is to 0.5, the better is the discriminative power of the item. Again no statistical rule about limits exists, but many test constructors avoid D values outside 0.3 to 0.7.[6]

A second, more sophisticated measure of discrimination can be obtained by correlating an individual's correct or incorrect response to an item with his or her total score. When this is performed for the whole sample, a high correlation means that, generally speaking, those who obtained the correct answer to the item also obtained a high overall score (and vice versa for the low scorers). For a discussion of correlation see note (7). The value obtained from Table 14.9 is $+0.54$. Interpreting the significance of the correlation coefficient depends on the size of the sample. For $N = 100$ or more a value of at least 0.20 is needed, although most item users would look for somewhat higher values than this if at all possible. With a D value of 0.419 by the first method and 0.54 by the second, question 1 appears to discriminate satisfactorily whichever method is applied.

The final decisions in fabricating a test paper depend largely on the pool of items available. It pays to start with a large number of well-formulated questions in order to create a store of items with adequate facility and discrimination levels. The final test can be assembled with an eye to satisfying the blueprint and at the same time introducing questions with known standards of difficulty. But there are many pitfalls which confront the would-be test designer. These are discussed in the books recommended for further reading at the end of the chapter.

SUMMARY

In order to make school marks meaningful and to justify the comparison of marks from different subjects it is necessary to standardize them. The technique of standardization is also used in the design of objective and intelligence tests (see Chapter 9). In this chapter we have touched lightly on some of the basic statistics involved in standardization processes to help students in their interpretation of marks and scores obtained from examination and test material. Such fundamental concepts as tabulation, distribution, mean and standard deviation are mentioned. Item analysis is also mentioned in the hope that it will serve as an aid in the understanding of objective test construction and as a preliminary to our further discussions of curriculum design in Chapter 16.

ENQUIRY AND DISCUSSION

(a) On school practice or school visits, investigate the following:
  (1) Does the school use a system of mark standardization? Explore the reasons for its presence or absence. How do the teachers view the prospect of standardizing the marks for the terminal or annual reports?
  (2) How do teachers *actually* devise examination questions? What attempts are made to sample the syllabus and the skills required in answering questions?

(b) Investigate:
  (1) The work of the School Examinations and Assessment Council (SEAC).
  (2) Other current research into question design and item analysis.
  (3) A blueprint analysis of a recent college examination paper. What, roughly, is the percentage of the syllabus covered by the paper? What student skills are being tapped by the questions?
  (4) The contrast between the histogram and frequency polygon for the arithmetic and English marks in this chapter. Also check on the mean and standard deviation of the English marks. You should get $\bar{X}_E = 6.20$ and $\sigma_E = 1.82$.

(c) It has been suggested that children with IQs less than 70 on a scale having a mean of 100 and SD of 15 would usually require some special form of education. What percentage of the population of children would this involve? Using the same scale, and taking 145 IQ and above as the criterion of giftedness, what percentage of children would you expect to be gifted, assuming always that intelligence is normally distributed? Again with the same scale, what percentage of the population would you find between IQ 85 and 115? Compare your answer with the value quoted in Figure 14.4. You should now be in a position to check the other values in this figure.

(*Answers*: number of cases less than 70 IQ = 2.28 per cent;
number of cases greater than 145 IQ = 0.13 per cent;
number of cases between 85 and 115 IQ = 68.26 per cent.)

NOTES AND REFERENCES

1. It is not an easy matter to advise students on the best books to read in statistics without knowing their previous experience in mathematics and availability and quality of the guidance they might receive at college. D. Satterly, *Assessment in Schools*, Blackwell, Oxford, 1989 (2nd edn), and A. C. Crocker, *Statistics for the Teacher*, NFER, Windsor, London, 1974, are probably the best for students still 'cutting teeth' in educational assessment. More adventurous students might like to look at the other, more advanced, texts suggested in Further Reading.

2. Mode and median are alternative ways of describing central tendency. The mode is the value along a scale or set of marks which has the maximum frequency. The mode for marks in arithmetic (Table 14.2) occurs at mark 4, where the frequency, 12, is higher than at any other point. Likewise, the mode for English is at mark 7, it having a maximum frequency of 13. Hence we can trace the origin of the term bimodal, which refers to a distribution with 'two maxima'. The median is the point along a scale with exactly half the number of cases above it and half the cases below it. In arithmetic the median can be found directly from the cumulative frequency curve in Figure 14.5 by reading off the value of the mark corresponding to the 50th percentile. The value is 4.25 in arithmetic and 6.60 in English. Where the distributions are normal the mean, mode and median occur at the same point

along the scale. In the present case, the mean for arithmetic is 4.42 and that for English is 6.20. These values are at odds with those obtained for the modes and medians, thus showing some variation from normal distribution.

3.   Pamphlets have been prepared for teachers and candidates by the Research Unit of the School Examinations Department, University of London, as a result of their research into the Nuffield Science Teaching Project in Chemistry at O level, 1967.

4.   See, for example, the use of test blueprint techniques adopted by R. Wood and L. S. Skurnik in *Item Banking*, NFER, Slough, 1969.

5.   B. S. Bloom (ed.), *Taxonomy of Educational Objectives. Handbook I: Cognitive Domain*, Longman, London, 1956.

6.   S. Henrysson, 'Gathering, analyzing and using data on test items', in R. L. Thorndike (ed.), *Educational Measurement*, American Council on Education, Washington, DC, 1971.

7.   Correlation is undoubtedly the most widely used statistical concept. It has even crept into common usage in a great variety of forms. Fundamentally, it tells us in a numerical form known as the *correlation coefficient* the extent to which two sets of measures for the same group of people are related. If we take as an illustration the length of people's legs compared with the length of their arms, we would expect tall people to have long limbs and small people to have short limbs. In other words, there is a direct connection between the two measures. If this relationship were perfect, that is, for each slight variation in arm length there is an exact corresponding variation in leg length as we pass from one person to another, the numerical value obtained would be a 'positive correlation' of $+1$. With two measures in which one increases while the other decreases in exact steps we obtain a 'negative correlation' of -1. But things are never that perfect. We will always find the 'sports' with long arms and short legs (or vice versa), tending to give a correlation somewhat less than $+1$. In fact the numerical value can be anything between $+1$ through 0 to -1. A value of 0 or thereabouts represents 'zero correlation', the sort of value we might obtain if we compared the size of shoe which a person takes with that person's hair colour.

To give some idea of typical values, if we gave a group intelligence test to a class of 100 pupils and retested them a week later, the correlation for a good test between the scores obtained on the first and second occasions by each person would be about $+0.90$ to $+0.98$, a very good value. If now we compared the marks obtained in a school physics examination with intelligence test scores we might get a value in the region of $+0.50$. In a study by the author the correlation between IQ and biology came to $+0.14$, which, as we shall see below, is not much different from zero. In the chapter on personality a correlation of $+0.30$ was typical between self-concept and academic attainment. Negative correlations are less common in behavioural studies than in natural sciences, but one often-quoted example is the relationship between intelligence test scores and the number of children in a family. The value is around -0.25 and is taken to mean that the larger the family the lower the measured intelligence. Another topical negative correlation occurs between the cost of living (rising) and a person's spending power (falling), given a constant wage.

It is most important when interpreting a correlation coefficient to take the sample size into account. This is obvious, because if we obtained a correlation of $+0.20$ for a sample of five people we would not view it with the same confidence as for a sample of 500. In fact $+0.20$ for five sets of data is *not significant*; that means the correlation is no better than zero. For a sample of five we would have to obtain a correlation coefficient of $+$ or -0.88 for us to place any reliance on its being a significant positive or negative correlation, i.e. significantly different from zero. For 500 the value need only reach ±0.12 for it to be significantly better than zero. The value of $+0.14$ between IQ and biology quoted above proved to be insignificant once the sample size was taken into account.

Another important point to watch is the interpretation we place on the underlying causes of the correlation. All the correlation tells us is the extent and direction of a relationship, and not the reason for it. As an example, just think of the many reasons for the negative correlation of -0.25 between family size and measured intelligence; it would be impossible to arrive at a single causal relationship from this information alone.

For a short and readable account of correlation, look at the book by Satterly in Further Reading.

FURTHER READING

A. Anastasi, *Psychological Testing*, Collier Macmillan, New York, 1982 (5th edn).

L. J. Cronbach, *Essentials of Psychological Testing*, Harper and Row, New York, 1990 (5th edn).

J. P. Guilford and B. Fruchter, *Fundamental Statistics in Psychology and Education*, McGraw-Hill, New York, 1977 (6th edn).

D. Satterly, *Assessment in Schools*, Blackwell, Oxford, 1989 (2nd edn).

Chapter 15

Vocational Development and Guidance

Almost everyone has to find employment at some time. For the majority, this happens immediately after secondary or higher education. But the important role of our educational system in forming and directing occupational preferences has not, until recently, been fully appreciated in Great Britain. The many psychological and sociological influences brought to bear on young people by the family, the school and society helping to shape their career life-chances tend to have been ignored in our educational arrangements. In the USA,[1] career and personal counselling have become well established as necessary elements in the educational system, and there is no doubt that their value has at last been recognized in this country. The coming years[2] will see a growth in vocational guidance in our schools, with teachers playing a conscious part. In this respect there will be growing dependence on psychological material and its evaluation.

Perhaps the most striking feature of occupational choice in the past, if 'choice' is really the appropriate term in this context, was the apparent haphazard or coincidental way in which young people ended up in jobs. Talent-matching, either cognitive or affective, between individuals and the work they undertook was more a matter of chance than choice. Work choice was, and still is to some extent, governed far more by availability in circumstances such as geographical distribution of industries,[3] regional manpower needs or the financial position of the family and its willingness to be mobile in pursuit of work than by medium-term or long-term analysis of talent.[3] The emergence of guidance and counselling in our schools is, of course, in response to a great many related factors. Craft,[4] for example, believes that change in political ideology towards an egalitarian system, which attempts to provide for the underprivileged and adds a measure of security in employment, is one reason. Again, the growth of our economy requires employees who are more adaptable to work situations and more highly skilled than previous generations. With fewer unskilled and semi-skilled jobs available, it becomes important to seek out the talents of people to avoid wastage. But the really crucial point is for individuals to find work which is personally satisfying whilst being useful to the community.

This chapter can do no more than introduce students to some elementary theories of occupational development and their bearing on vocational guidance in schools. In addition, we shall look at the systematic attempts to discover useful psychological factors in vocational choice.

THEORIES OF VOCATIONAL DEVELOPMENT

Prior to the 1950s, no thoroughgoing theory describing occupational development had been formulated. No one had drawn together the rapidly accumulating results of research, chiefly in the USA, to provide a working model. To this time, three broad approaches had been suggested, based more on speculation than on empirical research. These are known as 'accident', 'impulse' and 'talent-matching' methods of occupational choice. Some people are convinced that their entry into a career results from some unexpected incident thought to be beyond their control. 'I was watching my teacher one day and suddenly thought that I wanted to do a similar job.' This accident hypothesis takes no account of personal and social factors which in unperceived ways might have rendered one range of jobs more appealing than others. Impulse theories stress the unconscious drives laid down in childhood and their pervading influence on the pattern of occupational choice. In later life, particular occupations will gratify particular personality needs. Galinski[5] was able to show that discipline in the early lives of physicists was rigid, stressed obedience and was consistent and predictable while, for clinical psychologists, childhood discipline had been flexible, unpredictable and appealed more to 'feelings'. Impulse theory shifts the emphasis to internal factors and early influences. Both this and the accident viewpoint place the individual in a somewhat passive role, helplessly drifting in the currents of chance or the irrevocable influence of infantile experience. The third approach, talent-matching, attempted to fit a person's expressed occupational interests with previously determined interest profiles of people already established in occupations. Strong,[6] who produced a vocational-interest questionnaire, was a pioneer in this field, and we mention the application of these questionnaires later in the chapter. Their weakness is the limited information they afford. It is not possible to evaluate from the responses why or how a person arrives at a choice of job, so vital when we want to know the effect of educational or home circumstances. The information they provide is very much 'after the fact'. Again, interests tend to be unstable in early life, hence one cannot be certain about the lasting appeal of a choice. However, interest inventories certainly have a place as part of the picture we build up about an individual's occupational possibilities.

Ginzberg's theory

It is to Ginzberg and his associates[7] that we owe the earliest detailed formulations. Their main interest was to elucidate a sequence of developmental stages leading to entry into an occupation. The model was based on three postulates which they regarded as basic conditions in the process of vocational choice. These were: occupational choice is a development process consisting of three periods covering 15 or so years from early childhood; the process is largely irreversible; compromise is an essential aspect of every choice.

Occupational choice as a developmental process

Occupational choice as a developmental process is seen to last from four or five years of age to early adulthood. This time span embodies three periods: *fantasy choices* (thought to coincide with the Freudian latency period from 6 to 11 years of age); *tentative choices* (between 11 and 17 years of age); and *realistic choices* (between 17 and the early 20s). The timing of these periods depends to some extent upon other aspects of development (e.g. intellectual), cultural variations such as school-leaving age and the availability and complexity of work, to mention but a few.

During the period of *fantasy choices* little Johnny, for example, believes that he can become anything he desires. If you ask a young child what he wants to be when he grows up, his answer will probably be based on recent experience of watching someone at work or hearing a description of work, and his preference will have no regard for the skill or qualification necessary. Johnny can think himself into any role without having to bother about such grown-up complications as training or physical strength. His dream world of play does much to obscure the realities of working life. Frank and Hetzer[8] discerned two stages of this period. Younger children were more concerned with satisfying some specific pleasure they might experience in a job. Brick-laying might appeal because of the enjoyment the child can have in mixing up and splashing around in the cement and water and sticking the bricks together; shopkeeping might appeal because the child could rifle sweets or cakes at will. Frank and Hetzer referred to this earliest kind of motivation as 'functional pleasure' and noted that pleasure was based on superficial observation of the enjoyable aspects of work. The later stage was thought to be motivated by more socially orientated notions of doing work which gave self-satisfaction derived from helping or pleasing others. Nursing would enable the child to help other people (notably parents) back to health; bus drivers could carry people where they wanted to go.

The essential features of this period are the lack of regard for medium-term or long-term outcomes of the choices made and an almost complete disregard for the skills or qualifications required. There is no connection in the child's mind between means and ends. Often children centre on pleasant or simple, beneficial aspects of a job while being able to ignore the less pleasant, complicated or routine nature of the work. The child fantasizes about work in the same way he or she would any other activity he or she sees taking place.

The period of *tentative choices* coincides roughly with the period of adolescence, from 11 to 17 years of age. The onset of a transition from the fantasy period varies according to the experiences and personal maturity of the individual. It is charac-terized, like many other features of adolescent life, by uncertainty, exploration and self-conscious analysis. Wisely, the young adolescent makes few firm commitments about occupational choices, although exceptionally one meets a very determined youngster who has an occupation in mind, often conditioned by parents, and sticks to it. The period sees the gradual awareness of the need for criteria by which the adolescent can make reasoned choices. It is, nevertheless, a most difficult time because often many decisions have to be made from the flimsiest evidence; our educational provisions demand it. Secondary school pupils often have to choose between several subjects at 13 or 14; they may have to decide whether to stay on at school and take certificate examinations or whether to make an early start in an apprenticeship.

Directions chosen at this time are often irrevocable in a system which values the specialist.

Ginzberg divides the period into four stages: interest, capacity, values and transition. Taking them in order, at the *interest* stage, around 11 and 12 years of age, children begin to realize that they will be required to make a decision about their future jobs. Their outlook is not too serious and their choices are based primarily on interests and hobbies. New subjects at school often act as a temporary spur to choosing a job; starting technical drawing or science usually produces a short-term rash of potential draughtsmen and scientists. Parents' occupations also intrude at this age, and the influence of parents' suggestions about future employment is beginning to take effect.

Soon the adolescent realizes that interest is not enough. Enthusiasm for an interest or hobby does not guarantee success. Consequently what one sees of the skills required in occupations directs one's attention to one's own *capacities* and a career pattern becomes oriented toward those things one is good at. Teachers, as well as parents, now become influential, because they are the means by which one can discover one's capabilities, chiefly from feedback in school subjects. The adolescent also begins to recognize more clearly that education has a role to play in helping future career decisions.

At the *values* stage, around 15 to 16 years, the adolescent begins to relate capacities and skills to the satisfaction that might be realized from the range of occupations suited to his or her abilities. Value complexes, which have built up in childhood and adolescence from personal and social influences, make their appearance and help to guide the adolescent in choosing which capacities and skills to apply. Such questions as the personal satisfaction offered, prospects (in very sketchy terms), income and scientific orientation become important. However, questions of status or leadership opportunities do not appear voluntarily at this stage. The need for indirect satisfaction is also in evidence. The desire to be a doctor for its own sake becomes an intrinsic desire, thought by Ginzberg to satisfy an emotional need and a desire to do something constructive. This is in contrast with earlier stages of development where a boy or girl might say, 'I want to do so-and-so because I am interested in (or good at) it.' Now he or she would say, 'I want to do so-and-so because I think I might like to do it – it has value for me and others.'

The final stage in the tentative period of occupational choices is known as the *transition* stage because it is at this time that the realities of impending work prospects, opportunities and demands begin to assert themselves. A consideration of values, interests and capabilities alongside the hard facts of work conditions tends to complicate rather than simplify the decision-making process; a period of consolidation and adjustment is therefore needed. The age at which transition occurs is determined largely by the school-leaving age. Ginzberg's analysis was carried out using evidence from the USA, where large numbers of 17-year-olds are still at school and many will move on to some form of higher education. The transition stage, whenever it might appear, is clearly a time in which realistic goal-setting in relation to achievement becomes increasingly important. At the same time, these older and more stable adolescents have to realize that they will have to wait until they have sampled work before an intelligent decision can be made. For those leaving for work there is a preoccupation with what is in store. Likewise, those going into higher education are waiting in anticipation, having made a tentative choice to enter on a degree or profession. Ginzberg calls this a time of 'restrained suspense about the future'. Concern about work conditions, length and nature of preparation and the financial returns are uppermost in their minds. In a word, youth becomes more 'instrumental' in outlook.

The stages briefly outlined above are cumulative and not mutually exclusive. The point has been made of a gradual build-up in the realization of personal strengths and limitations and a growth of self-knowledge, all of which help the adolescent in occupational decision-making. A burning interest in an occupational task at 12 soon begins to die when the child realizes that certain abilities are required to carry out the task adequately. Also, the ability to perform a task is no guarantee that the child would want to do it for the rest of his or her life. Routine work probably would not appeal to most bright adolescents. They are likely to aspire to more mentally exacting work for personal satisfaction and reward. Here we see values operating. We can readily discern how home and school play a critical part in the development of values. Contrast the short-term hedonistic philosophy in some working-class homes with the long-term, cold, calculating, almost ruthless view of occupational preparation prevalent in middle-class homes.[3] This has often been demonstrated in the past by the early school-leavers who are disproportionately represented from working-class backgrounds, while many who stay on from middle-class homes, a number with modest intellectual means, succeed and go to college or university. The way in which a boy or a girl handles occupational choice is a measure of his or her level of maturity; Super called it *vocational maturity*.[9]

The period of *realistic choices* during early adulthood marks the final stage in Ginzberg's developmental hypotheses. It is important to note that he derived these later stages using students in higher education, and this accounts, in part, for the examples he chooses. The period is divided into three stages: exploration, crystallization and specification.

The individual passes from the uncertainty inherent in the transition stage, while changing from school to work or to another educational institution, through an experimental stage in which a person explores in some detail the occupational horizons open to him or her. During the *exploration* stage, the individual gains experience by looking closely at the intellectual or physical requirements within the band of jobs available. The focus has narrowed because one has chosen a job or subject area with specific demands. But one will still search within the narrow band of possibilities for those aspects which are likely to give greatest satisfaction and prospects.

When the individual becomes increasingly conscious of the attractions of particular aspects or studies he or she is said to have reached the stage of *crystallization*. For students in higher education, Ginzberg found this stage at around 20 to 22 years of age. It may happen at a different, and probably earlier, time for young working men. It is a time when, rightly or wrongly, an individual feels in possession of sufficient information about his or her potentialities to make a firm decision about entering a career. The distinguishing feature from earlier stages is the firm commitment, a series of compromises having culminated in an unswerving choice.

Having crystallized their views in broad terms, the individuals in Ginzberg's sample now select a *specific* occupation which calls for particular requirements. Having settled for history, they might choose to teach the subject or enter politics or become an archaeologist. The characteristics of this last stage are a willingness to state a speciality and to possess a determined dedication to the idea of a specific occupation. Obviously, many students are still in need of guidance, which in Great Britain is conducted by appointments services within the universities. Appointments officers are kept busy with clients who need help in finding work in keeping with their specific aspirations. Some clients may not have reached the stage of crystallization, while others may even want to change direction. Moreover, Ginzberg observed a greater degree of variation in the *pattern* of development during the period of realistic choices than in other periods.

It appears[7] (pp. 133–159) that a similar pattern existed in the tentative period for young people who were not going into higher education. However, there were fundamental differences in the expectations and values held by school-leavers. They tended to be looking for work which offered more money than their fathers were earning, steady employment, skilled work so that in time they could become their own bosses, and a job free from serious accident risk. Ginzberg says little of the realistic period for normal school-leavers. He did, however, show that this final period was (at the time) somewhat different for women.[7] To quote:

> the general theory of occupational choice developed on the basis of our study of the men seems to require no major change for interpreting the behavior of the girls throughout the tentative period.... From that point on, the strategic influences on the girls are decidedly different from those on the men by reason of one major consideration: the girls are thinking of and planning for their future primarily in terms of marriage: everything else falls into a subsidiary position. Because of this they are not deeply concerned about an occupation.

As with most developmental theories, it is not claimed that these periods and stages are rigid in their emergence. We only need recall our own experience in occupational terms to be aware that variations and omissions in the pattern outlined above are quite feasible. Ginzberg showed a number of variations in his own researches. Some young people had a clear idea of the work they wanted to do from an early age, and not only stuck to it but reached a high level of accomplishment. Others with special aptitudes such as musical, mathematical or mechanical skills also displayed single-mindedness in their desire to achieve an occupational aim once they had recognized their talents. For teachers, a major concern must be vocational *immaturity*; that is, where young people have arrested or omitted essential stages in occupational development, giving rise to inappropriate choices later on. A person who 'gels' at an early stage in development or who is inadequately informed about aptitudes or work availability is at a serious disadvantage. As Super suggests, work is a way of life, and if one has to live with it for so many years it is imperative to have made a decision which is likely to give some lasting satisfaction.

The irreversibility of occupational choice

This is a second postulate of Ginzberg. The longer one is engaged in the preparation or execution of a career the harder it is to see one's way of changing it. The dilemma of a second-year college of education student affords a good illustration of this statement. Having entered college by the conventional academic route of O and A level successes of a moderate standard, and having discovered that teaching is not what had been anticipated, what can a student do? Does he or she leave college with a possible feeling of failure at having got two-thirds of the way towards a professional qualification and with the prospect of starting afresh in some other area, or should the student stay on in the knowledge that the next 40 years or so may have to be played out in an occupation which does not appeal? It becomes increasingly difficult to reverse the investment in time and effort as one continues along a given occupational route. Psychologically, feelings of failure can have a devastating effect on self-esteem and security.

The prospect of irreversibility is notably acute in a system where specialization is at a premium. Industry and higher education entry requirements are often translated in very narrow terms, leaving the less successful in very insecure positions. The more we can do to help schoolchildren in becoming informed about their potentials, intellectual, practical and occupational, the better. As we shall see later in the chapter, the work of vocational counsellors involves this kind of service.

Occupational choice: the outcome of compromise

The main point here is that the vast majority of young people are engaged in decision-making and risk-taking as a product of assembling what information they can muster. Each step usually requires a compromise between two or more possibilities, as when interests have to be balanced against talents, or later, when one must contemplate the subjects needed in order to enter a profession, even though it may involve one in the study of subjects not necessarily to one's liking. Medical students need to have sciences other than the biological sciences. The greater an individual's vocational maturity in terms of using the information available, the more enlightened the compromise decision is likely to be.

Super's view of occupational development

One of the best-known names in the field of occupational choice is that of Super (**R**).[10] His researches have partly been incorporated in the theory proposed by Ginzberg, although he has several points of criticism. He felt that the Ginzberg theory did not take into account all the relevant research which had preceded it, particularly in the use and value of occupational interest inventories. The use and interpretation of the word 'choice' left much to be desired. In some cases it was used to signify *preference* for an occupation in the absence of any urgency to enter that occupation, as when a 12-year-old boy says he would like to be a plumber without having the obligation to stand by his decision. This hypothetical kind of choice has a different implication and meaning from that made by someone seeking a job who, having made a choice, must act on it and *enter* on a career. Another drawback of Ginzberg's formulation was the absence of a detailed analysis of the compromise process. For the purposes of guidance and counselling, Super rightly claims that we need an elaboration of the variables and the routes by which people arrive at, and enter, an occupation.

Super was also responsible for a life-stages model of occupational development, details of which can be found in the references.[11] The time spans are compared with Ginzberg's in Figure 15.1. Super regards the whole of life in five major states: growth, exploration, establishment, maintenance and decline of occupational choice. Further,

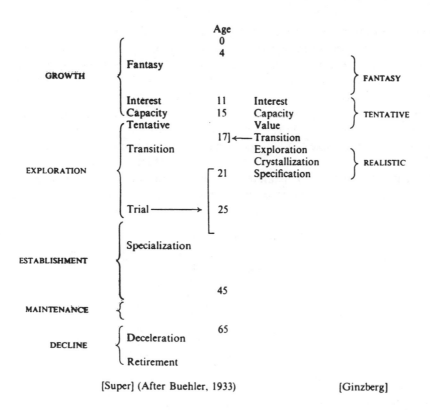

Figure 15.1 *The main stages of vocational development described by Super and Ginzberg. Reprinted with permission from B. Hopson and J. Hayes,* The Theory and Practice of Vocational Guidance, *Pergamon, Oxford, 1968.*

he makes ten propositions which he feels are central to any enlightened theory of vocational development. They are considered here very briefly. Students will notice that they are incorporated in one form or another into later models.[12]

(a) Individual differences such as abilities (both general and specific), interests and personality should be considered.

(b) There exists in all of us 'multipotentiality' by which the attributes mentioned in (a) above qualify us for a number of occupations by which we can succeed and gain satisfaction. These can be discerned using occupational-interest inventories.

(c) Occupational ability patterns are present in us all. A characteristic pattern of abilities, interests and personality is more appropriate for some occupations than for others.

(d) Vocational preferences and competencies change with time and experience, thus making choice and adjustment a *continuous* process.

(e) This process can be expressed as a series of life stages, outlined in Figure 15.1.[11]

(f) A career pattern, that is, the level, sequence, frequency and duration of trial and stable jobs, is determined by external factors such as socioeconomic background and work opportunities, and internal factors such as mental abilities, achievements and personality.

(g)   Progress through life stages can be guided by counselling in which self-knowledge of abilities and interests, aptitudes and career prospects is encouraged.
(h)   The process of vocational development is essentially that of developing and implementing a self-concept; it is a compromise process in which the self-concept is a product of interaction of inherited aptitudes, neural and endocrine make-up, opportunity to play various roles, and evaluations of the extent to which the results of role playing meet with the approval of superiors and fellows.
(i)   The role playing suggested in (h) above is a process of compromise between one's self-concept and the realities of external social factors.
(j)   Work is a way of life. Adequate vocational and personal adjustment are most likely when both the nature of work and the way of life that goes with it are congenial to the aptitudes, interests and values of an individual.

Super stresses the interaction effects of personal and social factors and the part they play in forming a self-concept. The latter has a crucial influence on the choice of, entry into, maintenance of and satisfaction gained from work. Another point is his emphasis on development as a continuous process following a sequence of characteristic stages only loosely connected with chronological age. For the counsellor, awareness of the level of developmental maturity attained by a client is important, for it is only when the client's vocational maturity is known that steps can be taken to decide on a course of guidance.

Holland's theory

A number of developmental theories have appeared since these earlier ideas of Ginzberg and Super (see Zytowski).[1,38] But there are other approaches worth noting for their attempts to go beyond a developmental paradigm to a detailed consideration of causal influences in vocational decision-making. The work of Holland[13] and Blau *et al.*[14] is of particular interest.

Holland's is a very useful model because it demonstrates a convenient link between the theoretical formulations already described and the practical issues of defining occupational interest profiles for the benefit of counsellors. His theory

assumes that at the time of vocational choice the person is the product of the interaction of his particular heredity with a variety of cultural and personal forces including peers, parents and significant adults, his social class, American culture, and the physical environment.

Holland postulates six *occupational environments* (Table 15.1) or major kinds of work situations typical of western cultures. Others have attempted to define occupational categories, and some will be discussed later in the chapter.

Each person has a lifestyle compounded from values, interests, aptitudes, personality factors, intelligence and self-concept which helps to orientate him or her in differing degrees towards the six occupational environments. In fact, for everyone, we can arrive at a rank order of these orientations by using measures of occupational interests, personality, values, needs, etc. The orientations are given the same names as the occupational environments and the rank order of these orientations is referred to as the *developmental hierarchy*. Figure 15.2 should help clarify the description. The

Table 15.1 *Holland's occupational environments*

Environment	Illustrative occupation
Motoric	Labourer, machine operator, truck driver
Intellectual	Physicist, anthropologist, biologist
Supportive	Social worker, teacher, vocational counsellor
Conforming	Secretary, book-keeper, clerk
Persuasive	Salesman, politician, publicity officer
Aesthetic	Musician, poet, writer, photographer

occupational environments are illustrated at the top of the diagram and the developmental hierarchy shows the person's particular rank order of occupational preferences. Of the six possible orientations, the person exemplified has chosen a motoric field as the first priority. According to Holland, he or she would enjoy work involving the use of physical strength, motor co-ordination and skill; those with a motoric orientation 'prefer dealing with concrete, well-defined problems as opposed to abstract, intangible ones'.

Within each vocational field there are several possible levels of entry, partly determined by the ability and self-evaluation of the individual. In the motoric orientation

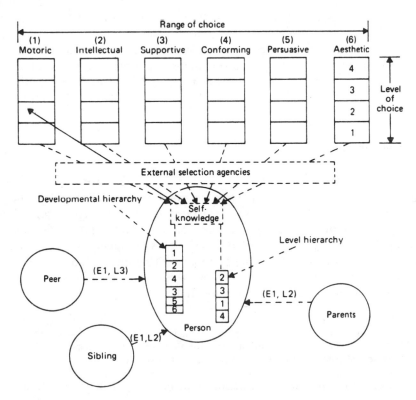

Figure 15.2 *Constructs and dimensions for the prediction of vocational choice. Reprinted from J. C. Holland, 'A theory of vocational choice', J. Counsel. Psychol., 6, 35–43 (1959), with the permission of the American Psychological Association and the author.*

we find jobs ranging from civil engineer to motor mechanic or welder. Both ability and self-evaluation can be found using tests of intelligence and status scales. The latter measures a person's perception of competence and the worth he or she attributes to him or herself with respect to others. The two internal factors of ability and self-evaluation are supposed by Holland to interact in a manner which has not yet been worked out, but he derives a crude formula to represent the interaction: occupational level = (intelligence + self-evaluation), where self-evaluation includes socioeconomic origins, need for status, education and self-concept. Four levels are postulated (arbitrarily chosen) and these he calls the *level hierarchy*, as shown in Figure 15.2.

The picture as it stands is grossly over-simplified. The reader should not be put off by the appearance of precise numbers of levels. They are not intended to impose limitations on the general structure of Holland's model, but simply to bring home the fact that there are different occupational expectations, some of which are beyond the capacities of some people.

There are many other mediating factors which affect the ultimate direction and level of entry. One important internal process is *self-knowledge*, or the amount of information a person possesses about self. Figure 15.2 shows how ability and self-evaluation are seen as the contributory elements of self-knowledge. From without, environmental influences like the social pressures from family, friends and school, the economic position and work availability also intrude on the final choice. Holland shows in his diagram the social pressures of peers, siblings and parents directed towards the person. The picture might have been more accurate if another intermediate process had appeared between the person and the occupational areas, representing the fact that self-knowledge is not enough when external manpower demands and work opportunities have to be considered. This has been shown in Figure 15.2 in the dotted line marked 'external selection agencies'.

Blau's conceptual model

Throughout the previous discussion the emphasis of the theorists has been on the development and *processes of choice and entry* to an occupation. Blau and his colleagues[14] rightly point to a second major determinant in the *process of selection* by external agents (employers, university and college authorities) in response to the demands of the economy or the availability of places in higher education. These decisions are somewhat out of the hands of those seeking entry. Blau, in his model, is concerned with showing the equally dominant role of social agencies in shaping a person's hierarchy of preferences. He notes that:

> the social structure – the more or less institutionalized patterns of activities, interactions, and ideas among various groups – has a dual significance for occupational choice. On the one hand, it influences the personality development of the choosers; on the other, it defines the socio-economic conditions in which selection takes place.

The overall effect of this dual interaction is demonstrated in Figure 15.3.

The most useful feature of this conceptualization is its regard for the details of factors which affect the 'how' and 'why' of career choice. It adds body to the framework proposed by Holland, particularly with regard to the effect of environmental

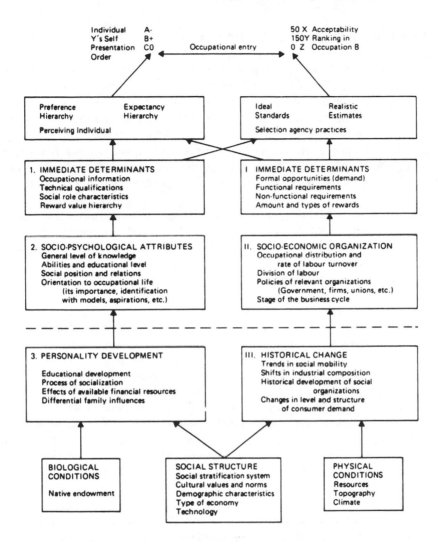

Figure 15.3 *Schema of the process of occupational choice and selection. Reprinted from P. M. Blau, J. W. Gustad, R. Jessor, H. S. Parnes and R. C. Wilcock, 'Occupational choice: a conceptual framework',* Industrial and Labor Relations Review, **9**, *No. 4 (1956), copyright © New York State School of Industrial and Labor Relations.*

agencies. It also raises the important issue of socioeconomic and labour requirements which mediate in the selection process.

The theories outlined above are presented as a pattern of increasing complexity starting with a developmental description and ending with a scheme which attempts to pinpoint causal influences in job choice. There are several other approaches: some emphasize self-expression and self-concepts;[15] some lay great stress on childhood experiences of a direct[16] or psychoanalytic nature;[17] others have approached the problem using decision-making theory.[18] But enough has already been said to indicate the primary considerations facing those who are responsible for guiding and counselling young people in their career decisions.

CAREERS EDUCATION AND GUIDANCE

The last twenty years have seen a marked advance in the importance attributed to careers education and guidance in local education authorities and schools. This applies to primary as well as secondary education. Government education and training initiatives such as the Technical and Vocational Education Initiative (TVEI) and a number of documents such as *Working Together – Education and Training*[19] and *Careers Education and Guidance from 5 to 16*[19] have sprung up in the last few years. The National Curriculum Council[20] has circulated documentation about careers guidance syllabuses in an attempt to ensure that this topic permeates the curriculum of state schools.

Despite this stimulus and the availability of training programmes, careers education and guidance in our schools is still an amateur affair. Well-meaning teachers with full teaching programmes take on additional career advice duties and are approached by pupils and parents bewildered by the job market. Therefore, greater emphasis is now placed on the training of teachers willing to become specialist careers teachers and co-ordinators.

The curriculum guidance documents from the National Curriculum Council, of which *Careers Education and Guidance* (Number 6) is a pamphlet,[20] set out in some detail the contemporary thinking. There are several psychological principles elaborated in the recommendations. Broadly, career education should help pupils to get to know themselves better, become aware of the training and career opportunities available, be capable of making reasoned choices about further education, training and career pathways and to be capable of making the transition into new work roles and situations. These aims are thought to be met by assisting pupils in five areas of concern. These are: *self* (knowledge of self – qualities, attitudes, values, abilities, strengths, limitations, potential and needs); *roles* (position and expectations in relation to family, community and employment); *work* (application of productive effort, including paid employment and unpaid work in the community and at home); *career* (sequence of roles undertaken through life and the personal success, rewards and enjoyment it brings); *transition* (development of qualities and skills which enable pupils to adjust to and cope with change – e.g. self-reliance, adaptability, flexibility, decision-making, problem-solving).[20] An important aspect of the curriculum planning is that the aims should run through subject areas and ages from 5 to 16.

Guidance in schools requires two kinds of counsellor who have specialist interests in *careers* and behavioural or *therapeutic counselling*.

Careers teachers/co-ordinators

Planning for a career is now seen as a long-term and wide-reaching function of schools from reception onwards. But specialist input from a teacher is generally left to the secondary stage. As we saw in the formulations of Ginzberg and Super, vocational development and choice are cumulative processes and these require regular tracking and guidance.

Careers teachers have an exacting responsibility for which specialist training is imperative. Initial teacher-training courses do not, at present, provide this specialist training. Careers teachers should at least have a knowledge of occupational development and guidance theory and be capable of relating this knowledge to the practical needs of adolescents. As their planning runs across the curriculum, they will have to know which aspects of the curriculum are related to working life and opportunities. To ensure co-ordination requires skilful negotiation between staff and careers teachers. They will also have to acquire skills in careers counselling and have a wide and detailed knowledge of the educational, employment and training opportunities available in the area.

There is now a wealth of information aimed especially at the secondary age group about work chances. Several have been computerized, of which CASCAID and JIIG-CAL are best known.[21] But the teacher also needs to have a firm idea about economic and occupational trends and how these relate to local circumstances.

Links with important outside agencies are essential. The Careers Service, employers and parents are part of this network, and understanding how the Service and industry operate is necessary. Experience of work and the workplace is essential. Arranging visits by pupils to local workplaces, work and interview simulations, projects about industrial problems and the community give some idea of what might be achieved.

The Careers Service is a crucial part of the partnership with schools. Careers officers need to be involved with schools in their area in order to help in planning those parts of the curriculum relevant to occupational interests. They should contribute to the school programme and keep the careers teachers informed of job opportunities in the locality. They will also be knowledgeable about guidance and the use of computers in providing job information checklists. Careers officers also have strong links with industry and this should be used by the schools.

The National Curriculum Council[20] places great importance on career guidance and it concludes that:

> Careers education and guidance is an essential part of every pupil's curriculum. In promoting self-awareness, it is a prerequisite to pupils making well-informed educational, vocational and training choices and to managing the transition from education to new roles, including employment . . . This process of personal and social development begins in the home and continues through adult life.

Therapeutic (personal) counsellors

No mention has been made so far of how we might deal with pupils who show signs of stress and mental disturbance. A whole range of problems, such as truancy, withdrawn behaviour, underachievement, exam nerves and delinquency, come under this heading. Whoever takes on this work must have acquired psychological training and skill in distinguishing the symptoms of different disturbed conditions both in nature and intensity. Mild cases, where a usually normal child experiences mental distress, would be dealt with by the therapeutic counsellor. Severe morbidity would have to be referred to the School Psychological Service for psychiatric treatment. Clearly this work requires a highly competent and well-qualified person.

There are very few counsellors of this kind in Great Britain, basically because the School Psychological Service, with its attendant Child Guidance and Psychiatric Units, has dealt with the situation. It is in the milder forms of mental deviance that a school-based counsellor would have an important function. A major task is to prevent the development of serious cases from mild beginnings, rather than to provide cures. The small-scale pressures which beset young people and occasionally assume undue proportions can often be contained by well-timed treatment and understanding. In this respect the parents are frequently an important element in the treatment, and sometimes in the cause, of disturbances. This requires skill on the part of the therapeutic counsellor in handling other significant people as well as the client. It is vital to repeat that this role, apart from demanding particular personal qualities, requires people qualified in psychiatry.

Some determinants used in vocational counselling

Returning to the work of the educational and vocational counsellor, there now exists a growing number of devices by which a client's capabilities, values and aspirations can be assessed and knowledge of work opportunities and demands widened. A formal or informal discussion with a client is rarely, if ever, the only means used and would not be sufficient for an appraisal of career profiles and possibilities. Many schools, in addition to providing literature, computer-based information and talks about regional employment or higher education, have schemes for industrial visits, together with the help of the Careers Service officer.

But a systematic exploration of a client's occupational potentialities is also a necessary prerequisite. One fruitful format has been devised by Rodger (R)[22] (see also McKenzie in the same note) for assembling and classifying information about the career patterns of clients, under the title of *The Seven Point Plan*. The resulting profile can be matched against the profiles of people already in work and against the special intellectual, physical or social challenges of the work itself. This is not the only format, but it is sufficiently comprehensive to overlap with all the others. Its particular merit is in directing our attention to some really essential factors which affect occupational choice and performance. Rodger's seven points, although examined separately, should ultimately be considered together. The results also represent a poorly focused snapshot in the life of the client at a time when, as Ginzberg observed, the choices are still only tentative and partially informed. Let us look at Rodger's seven points – physical make-up, attainments, general intelligence, special aptitudes, interests, disposition and circumstances – in some detail. A book by Kline[23] gives further helpful information on exploring these determinants.

Physical make-up

It is self-evident that certain physical attributes are essential for some jobs. Small stature bars a man or woman from entering some police forces, although a person must be small in order to work as a jockey! Physical handicaps place limitations on the kind of work people can attempt. The loss of limbs or senses imposes some restrictions. Physical stamina obviously plays a part in fitting boys or girls for jobs requiring tough constitutions. A knowledge of physical prowess is more likely to operate in a negative sense in excluding people with deficiencies or disabilities from certain jobs rather than in deeming them suitable. Physical or personal attractiveness and an ability to handle people are useful qualities for work involving contact with others, as in the case of shop assistants and social work.

Attainments

Bearing in mind the limitations referred to in Chapter 13, scholastic achievement is one source of information. To begin with, the level of education and success at school are widely used by employers as measures of potential competence. Certification, amount and quality of schooling and progress through the school are most commonly used as evidence for suitability and entry level to industry or higher education. Whatever might be said about the unreliability of public examinations as an indicator of occupational competence, employers continue to use exam results, such as the GCSE and degree classifications, as one of the first criteria for reducing the application list. This is particularly true in times of massive unemployment when there may be many applicants for few jobs. Often the first sifting of application forms consists of selecting those with the highest formal qualifications.

The counsellor needs a well-documented record card of clients' achievements, together with background information from teachers and parents. Knowledge of weaknesses is just as valuable as knowledge of strengths: clients who have great difficulty with, say, number skills might be discouraged from entering certain occupations such as accountancy.

General intelligence

Our educational system has for many years used general ability as one of several criteria, for choosing children for, or excluding them from, certain kinds of educational opportunity, at least in the early stages of secondary education. An up-to-date assessment of a client's *general* level of ability can give a clue to broad occupational horizons which may satisfy his or her intellectual powers. Obviously a pupil with low general ability would never obtain the level of attainment needed for a career in medicine. A bright boy or girl *might* be dissatisfied with a job requiring little use of the intellect, particularly if it involved routine concrete operations. Research[24] has shown broad ranges of general ability within occupational areas and minor differences in the averages between these occupational areas. But this could *not* be used as a precise indication of a client's suitability, only as a guide to potential.

There are many reasons which have nothing to do with intelligence for underperformance in public examinations. A pupil may dislike a subject or the teacher. There may be no motivation to perform well or little encouragement from home. A pupil may have been tempted to leave at 16 in order to earn money rather than staying on at school or college for several years with little more than a grant. Intelligence tests can often give a more objective estimate of a person's abilities than school marks, exam results or teachers' estimates.

An example of this is afforded by a recent ability measure known as the *DC test*.[25] Part of the selection process for nursing requires candidates to have at least five GCSE passes in order to enter nurse training, but there are many people of all ages who would have liked to have entered nursing but have not managed to achieve five passes. The DC test was designed to overcome this problem for those with the necessary ability. About a third of those who take or retake the test succeed, increasing the potential entrants to nursing.

Special aptitudes

As we saw in the chapter on human ability, there are a number of specific capacities, such as memory, spatial perception, number manipulation, manual dexterity, artistic ability and verbal fluency, which may be present to a greater or lesser extent in individuals in spite of a modest overall general intelligence. Combinations of these aptitudes can give composites such as clerical and musical talent. Possession of a special aptitude can compensate to some extent for a deficiency in general intelligence, provided, of course, that the deficiency is not marked. The aptitude may be pressed into service in certain kinds of work.[26] For example, even moderate intellectual power together with numerical aptitude can be an advantage in work requiring manipulation of numbers, as in accountancy, but not necessarily in higher mathematics, which requires a high general intelligence.

Interests

The exploration of occupational interests and dispositions (see the next section) has become an important industrial enterprise in the last 10 years.[27] A number of companies now offer expertise in job selection, evaluation of employees and training in the use of psychometric tests. These tests consist of ability, aptitude and interest inventories, personality tests and occupational inventories.

The design of occupational inventories remains a matter for research[28] and their administration and interpretation are the subject of several courses. Super[29] has given a handy classification of interests in terms of the methods applied to their assessment. He suggests four categories: expressed, inventoried, tested and manifest interest. Of these, we are concerned with inventoried interest tests.

Commonly, the client is required to make a choice between two or three occupations or activities involved in an occupation, over a wide range of vocations (sometimes known as the method of *paired comparisons* for two-way choices).[30] The same occupation turns up in combination with all the others so that an order of preference can be obtained. We saw an example of occupational categories in Holland's model. The most comprehensive is given by Miller,[31] consisting of 12 'stereotype categories and representative occupations'. Examples are given in note (31). In this inventory a ranking method is used between the 12 categories.

The evidence for a marked positive connection between success in an occupational pursuit and a stated interest, using an inventory, is by no means conclusive. In general, it seems[32] that interest patterns of young people of 14 years are beginning to look like those of adults (compare Ginzberg). Thus the inventories can be used to identify the general direction of vocational aspiration (and assumed concomitant success). In addition, the inventory profile points to wider occupational horizons than would be the case if the client simply stated a job preference.

Disposition

The use of well-designed personality inventories as part of the occupational selection and monitoring process has become widespread. The most frequently used is Cattell's 16PF (16 Personality Factors).[33] There are versions for primary age (CPQ – Children's Personality Questionnaire) and secondary age (HSPQ – High School Personality Questionnaire). The scores from these tests have been used as the basis for occupational profiles relating to specific jobs.[34]

There are some indications from research[35] that those who are actually engaged in scientific work in laboratories or in higher education tend to be oriented towards things rather than people, do significantly better on intelligence tests when compared with 'arts' specialists (especially in spatial tests) and tend towards 'convergent' rather than 'divergent' thinking strategies. Hudson[36] notes that science specialists in sixth forms, as contrasted with arts specialists, tend to be conformist, less emotional, interested in practical hobbies and outdoor pursuits, somewhat humourless, pacifist and careful. But these studies relate specifically to the extensive categories of arts or science orientation. We know little about dispositions in particular occupational categories.

Tests of general and occupational values have been devised. Rosenberg,[37] using a large sample of American college students, found three major value orientations. First, he found a 'people-oriented' value complex preferred by those who view work in terms of pleasure derived from personal contacts. Ideally, they like a job which offers an opportunity to work with, and be helpful to, other people. The second is an 'extrinsic reward-oriented' value complex appealing to those who emphasize rewards obtained for work done. They prefer a job to offer a chance to earn a lot of money and to give prestige and status. The third value complex Rosenberg called 'intrinsic reward-oriented'. Those responding to this value viewed work as an opportunity to be creative and self-expressive. They looked upon work as a chance to permit them to use special abilities and be original.

Clearly, the direction of a client's values and beliefs in terms of social and personal relationships, need for status, leadership, scholarship, aesthetic experience or autonomy is central to an understanding of the kind of work which might appeal to the client.

Circumstances

The home background of a client is a most important determinant in career choices. The ambitions, values and actual employment of parents will have had some effect on the client. The economic position of the family, whether they are willing to forgo another wage packet and encourage their children are important considerations. As Rodger (R)[22] declares, it is only by looking at the social and economic conditions in which a client has been raised that we can evaluate past performance and forecast his or her future prospects.

An elaborate speculation about childhood experiences as occupational determinants has been suggested by Roe.[38] Broadly, she relates the child-centred and over-protective or over-demanding upbringing to ultimate choice of person-oriented work such as social service, persuasive, cultural and aesthetic occupations. Those from rejecting, neglecting and casual backgrounds tend not to be oriented towards people and choose scientific, outdoor or technological fields. The evidence in support of this claim is not altogether convincing.[38]

SUMMARY

If we took work and leisure away from adult life there would not be much left. Our life-chances are so closely tied to the nature and demands of our work that we cannot escape from the need to consider, as scientifically as we can, the adequacy and influence of our educational provisions on career choice. Whilst many teachers may feel that their influence on, and opportunity to assist, children in selecting a career is marginal, an awareness of the effects of school life and school work on career choice is most important. This is not to suppose that each teacher should feel obliged to act in the capacity of a citizens' advice bureau, but one must at least be alive to the relevance of one's contribution in the career structure of one's children. There is no doubt about the increasing importance which will become attached to those aspects of the curriculum dealing with career prospects in these days of prolonged schooling at adolescence.

We have seen in this chapter some of the important psychological and social factors which profoundly influence, or which are profoundly influenced by, the work we choose. Ginzberg and his colleagues pointed to some valuable conditions present in the process of vocational development and choice which have since been elaborated by Super. Basically, occupational choice is preceded by a gradual developmental process from childhood through adolescence. The process is largely irreversible and the final choice is essentially a compromise between several possibilities available at the moment of choice. As well as having an understanding of the part played by home and school, we need to know something about individual abilities, interests, personality, occupational interests, self-concepts and self-knowledge in order to ascertain whether a choice is realistic and appropriate for a particular person. The question of irreversibility is a constant source of concern to most people. Because work possesses our lives so substantially, it might make better sense if we reorganized the time devoted to educational and career matters so that we dispersed them during a lifetime, rather than having a 'grand slam' of education in childhood, thus having to commit ourselves so early in life. With the system as it exists at present, Ginzberg and Super have provided a theoretical framework which must be set against a background of such practical problems as manpower demands, geographical distribution of work, guidance facilities available and other external agencies.

Counselling in schools can take many forms. We pass from the informal, 'over coffee' chat to a full-blooded analysis of educational and occupational potential. Where counselling is taken seriously, it appears to have at least six objectives. Counselling is a long-term and continuous process from primary school onwards; it is wide in its concern about social as well as personal characteristics; it is the pupil who must ultimately make the decision and must, therefore, be led to a position of independence in order to make such a decision adequately; counsellors should be specialists and not necessarily teachers; there should be no room for last-minute decisions; counsellors should be able to call on all the resources of the school and community in helping each child. It must be remembered that counselling school-leavers is a very small part of the task: the work extends well beyond the boundaries of finding jobs for the boys and girls. Advice on curriculum choice, achievement and motivation are but a few additional concerns of the educational and vocational counsellor. There are also behaviour problems and anxieties which require specialist therapeutic counsellors who have undergone training in psychology. Behaviour deviance in the delinquent, minor neurotic or anxiety states prior to examinations or as a result of social relationships in class, truancy and under-achievement are the kinds of difficulties with which a therapeutic counsellor might be faced.

There is still much to be done in this relatively new and complex area of vocational guidance and counselling before we can place it on a firm scientific footing. We have at our disposal a number of psychological tools which can give us information about physical make-up, attainment, intelligence, special aptitudes, interests, temperamental and cognitive dispositions. The coming years should see an increase in the refinement and use of these instruments.

ENQUIRY AND DISCUSSION

(a)   By using visits and/or inviting speakers, become familiar with the structure and functions of:
  (1) the Careers Service;
  (2) the School Psychological Service, including the Child Guidance and Psychiatric Unit;
  (3) JIIG–CAL and/or CASCAID (or other local computer-based service);
  (4) the Child Care and Probationary Service.
  What links are usually forged between these services and the schools? See as much of the test materials in (1), (2) and (3) as you can.

(b)   Ask children from a range of ages what they would like to be when they grow up and why they chose those occupations. Do the answers fit into Ginzberg's sequence of developmental stages?

(c)   Discuss the possible terms of reference of a careers education and guidance service within the school framework (include work experience, industrial visits, social studies about the trade union movement, work communities, the European Community, economic issues).

(d)   Investigate:
  (1) Occupational interest inventories and their uses.
  (2) Personality and various occupational groups. Are there generalizations about certain jobs suiting certain kinds of personality profile (see notes (27), (28) and (35)–(38))?
  (3) The reaction of teachers to career education and guidance.

(e)   As a group, discuss how each of you came to decide on your present career choice. You will probably have some difficulty recalling the precise details or the precise moment of decision, but try to discover *who* or *what* influenced you most in arriving at the decision. Now that you are 'on course', what information would you have liked prior to coming on a course of teacher-training? How might this information have been conveyed to you while in the sixth form (or whenever you had to make the decision)?

NOTES AND REFERENCES

1. There is a growing technical and research literature, largely in the United States. See summaries in D. G. Zytowski, *Vocational Behavior: Readings in Theory and Research*, Holt, Rinehart and Winston, New York, 1968; B. Hopson and J. Hayes, *The Theory and Practice of Vocational Guidance*, Pergamon, Oxford, 1968; J. O. Crites, 'Career counselling: a review of major approaches', in J. M. Whiteley and A. Resnikoff, *Career Counselling*, Brooks/Cole, Monterey, CA, 1978.
2. Several counselling courses have been established in British universities. Keele, Exeter and Reading are among the first. See H. Lytton and M. Craft, *Guidance and Counselling in British Schools*, Arnold, Leeds, 1969; B. M. Moore, *Guidance in Comprehensive Schools*, NFER, Slough, 1971; Schools Council Working Paper No. 15, *Counselling in Schools*, HMSO, London, 1967; Special Issue on Guidance and Counselling, *Journal of Education Section of British Psychological Society*, 7(2), 5–61 (1983).
3. A recent research by L. Raby and G. Walford, 'Job status aspirations and their determinants for middle and lower stream pupils in an urban, multi-racial comprehensive school', *Br. Educ. Res. J.*, 7, 173–181 (1981), shows quite strongly that children's career aspirations are limited largely to the work possibilities available in their local environment. This applies specifically to the school-leavers who were not examination candidates. See also *Early Leaving*, HMSO, London, 1954; The Crowther Report: *15 to 18*, HMSO, London, 1959.
4. H. Lytton and M. Craft, *Guidance and Counselling in British Schools*, Arnold, Leeds, 1969.
5. M. D. Galinski, 'Personality development and vocational choice of clinical psychologists and physicists', *J. Counsel. Psychol.*, 9, 229–305 (1962). See also B. Vachmann, 'Childhood experiences in vocational choice in law, dentistry and social work', *J. Counsel. Psychol.*, 7, 243–250 (1960).
6. E. K. Strong, *Vocational Interests in Men and Women*, Stanford University Press, CA, 1948.
7. E. Ginzberg, S. W. Ginsburg, S. Axelrad and J. L. Herma, *Occupational Choice: An Approach to a General Theory*, Columbia University Press, New York, 1951.
8   M. Frank and H. Hetzer – a reference given by E. Ginzberg *et al.* on p. 61 in their book mentioned in note (7).
9. D. E. Super, 'Dimensions and measurement of vocational maturity', *Teachers College Record*, 57, 151–163 (1955).
10. (R) Over the years D. E. Super has written extensively on the subject of occupational psychology. See, for instance, *Vocational Development: A Framework for Research*, Teachers College Press, Columbia University, New York, 1957; *The Psychology of Careers*, Harper, New York, 1957; 'A theory of vocational development', *Am. Psychol.*, 8, 185–190 (1953) and in the Reader.
11. The model is elaborated in reference (10) (*Vocational Development: A Framework for Research*). Apparently, the five stages are taken from a pattern described by Buehler as the five possible socioeconomic expectations of an individual, in C. Buehler, *Der menschliche Lebenslauf als psychologisches Problem*, Hirzel, Leipzig, 1933.
12. See reference (10) ('A theory of vocational development').
13. J. L. Holland, 'A theory of vocational choice', *J. Counsel. Psychol.*, 6, 35–43 (1959); *The Psychology of Vocational Choice: A Theory of Personality Types and Environmental Models*, Ginn, New York, 1966.

14. P. M. Blau, J. W. Gustad, R. Jessor, H. S. Parnes and R. C. Wilcock, 'Occupational choice: a conceptual framework', *Industrial and Labor Relations Rev.*, **9**, 531–543 (1956).
15. D. E. Super, R. Starishevsky, N. Matlin and J. P. Jordaan, *Career Development: Self-concept Theory*, College Entrance Examination Board, New York, 1963.
16. A. Roe, *The Psychology of Occupations*, Wiley, New York, 1956.
17. S. J. Segal, 'A psychoanalytic analysis of personality factors in vocational choice', *J. Counsel. Psychol.*, **8**, 202–210 (1961).
18. T. L. Hilton, 'Career decision making', *J. Counsel. Psychol.*, **9** 291–298 (1962); D. B. Hershenson and R. M. Roth, 'A decisional process model of vocational development', *J. Counsel. Psychol.*, **13**, 368–370 (1966).
19. *Working Together for a Better Future*, DES/DoE, 1987; *Working Together – Education and Training*, HMSO, 1986. A very useful guide to government thinking about careers guidance, with further references, can be found in *Careers Education and Guidance from 5 to 16*, Curriculum Matters No. 10, which is an HMI series, HMSO, 1988.
20. *Careers Education and Guidance*, National Curriculum Council, 1990. This is a curriculum guidance pamphlet (No. 6).
21. There is an increasing reliance on computer-based job information and analysis of a pupil's occupational interests, guidance on suitable job areas and subjects to take at school for particular occupations. Some examples of computer aids are JIIG-CAL (Jobs Ideas and Information Generator–Computer Assisted Learning, based at Edinburgh University), CASCAID (Careers Advisory Service Computer Aid) and JOBWISE. These systems are for adult as well as young clients.

    For example, the JIIG-CAL system claims to be the most comprehensive careers guidance system in the UK, providing job ideas, careers education, career plans, job information, subject choice advice and adult guidance. It is suitable for all ages from school pupils through FE and HE students to adults. It consists of a three-year programme offering career work materials, computing facilities and career support for classrooms. The programme is administered by those trained in the use of JIIG-CAL materials. Many local education authorities are registered users.
22. (**R**) A. Rodger, *The Seven Point Plan*, Paper No. 1, National Institute of Industrial Psychology, London, 1970 (3rd edn). See also a paper in the Reader by R. M. McKenzie, 'An occupational classification for use in vocational guidance', *Occup. Psychol.*, **28**, 108–117 (1954).
23. P. Kline, *Psychology of Vocational Guidance*, Batsford, London, 1975.
24. P. E. Vernon, 'Occupational norms for the 20-minute Progressive Matrices Test', *Occup. Psychol.*, **23**, 58–59 (1949). Also P. E. Vernon and J. B. Parry, *Personnel Selection in the British Forces*, University of London Press, London, 1949.
25. There is a guide to the DC test which gives a clear indication of the kinds of items found in this kind of test. There are four sections covering verbal, spatial, number, non-verbal and comprehension skills. See *Taking the DC Test: A Guide for Candidates*, Nurse Selection Project, University of Leeds, 1989.
26. P. E. Vernon offers some evidence from his researches relating to aptitudes and the differentiation of jobs in *The Structure of Human Abilities*, Methuen, London, 1950.
27. Several companies have sprung into being in the last ten years which provide expertise in occupational selection, management and job evaluation – in effect, the efficient use of human resources in the workplace. *Team Focus* and *SHL* are examples of such companies.
28. Research to produce such inventories continues unabated. The older ones, such as the Strong Vocational Interest Blank, the Kuder Preference Record and the Thurstone Interest Schedule in the USA, and the Rothwell–Miller Interest Blank, the Connolly Occupational Interests Questionnaire, the Factual Interest Blank and more recently the APU Occupational Interests Guide developed by the Applied Psychology Unit, University of Edinburgh in this country, are rarely used now, although the recent ones have built on the shoulders of the earlier versions. They have been replaced by those produced by, for example, the JIIG-CAL system mentioned above, the SHL occupational interest inventories or Team Focus's Office Systems Battery to measure the skills required within an office environment. The Careers Research and Advisory Centre in Cambridge (CRAC) and

the Careers and Occupational Information Centre in Sheffield (COIC) are active in producing courses and information about tests in use.

29. D. E. Super, *The Psychology of Careers: An Introduction to Vocational Development*, Harper, New York, 1957. 'Expressed' interests are disclosed by asking a person to name his or her choice directly. In younger children these choices are subject to change and therefore are not reliable, although exceptions exist where, for example, family pressure leaves little to chance in career expectations for the children. Ranking and rating methods fall into this category; in these, pupils are presented with a list of school subjects or occupations and are asked to re-assemble them in order of preference. 'Inventoried' interests are examined using questionnaires endeavouring to discover preferences by objective methods. The vocational-interest inventories of Strong, Kuder and Thurstone are based on this principle and make the assumption that a person with interest patterns similar to those of people already committed to, and successful in, an occupation is most likely to follow that occupation. 'Tested' interest relies on the assumption that an interested person will learn more about a topic than one who is not motivated. By sampling a person's knowledge it may be possible to assess the ultimate preference. 'Information' and 'culture' tests are examples which seek to discover the level of accumulated knowledge as a measure of interest. Finally 'manifest' interest is revealed by a person's strength of participation in activities, such as an interest in sport which leads a child to playing that sport. But this method of assessment can be highly unreliable, in that the centres of this kind of interest often show marked changes.

30. As a sample of how *paired comparisons* works, let us imagine that we give a client three occupations in every possible combination of pairs presented in the following way:

Place a tick against the one of each pair of occupations you would probably prefer:

doctor ☐	bricklayer ☐	commercial traveller ☑
commercial traveller ☑	doctor ☑	bricklayer ☐

Preferences fall into an order, with commercial traveller = 2, doctor = 1, bricklayer = 0. Straightforward counts of the number of times each activity is given preference are used for a profile. Note that calculating such quantities as a mean is pointless where the scores obtained are interrelated. Apart from anything else, the scores are *relative* to each other: as 'commercial traveller' has two endorsements, it would be impossible for either 'doctor' or 'bricklayer' to have the maximum of two. Therefore the profile must be viewed as a whole and not in isolated parts.

31. K. M. Miller, *Manual for the Rothwell–Miller Interest Blank*, NFER, Slough, 1968. Illustrations from this inventory are given here to demonstrate the categories in use. The 12 categories are: 'outdoor' (e.g. farmer, surveyor, physical education teacher); mechanical (civil engineer, motor mechanic, petrol-pump attendant, weaver); computational (auditor, cashier, income-tax clerk); scientific (industrial chemist, laboratory assistant, geologist); persuasive (sales manager, insurance salesman, radio announcer); aesthetic (artist, photographer, window dresser); literary (journalist, librarian, book reviewer); musical (music teacher, pianist, music-shop assistant); social service (teacher (primary), social worker, missionary); clerical (bank manager, office worker, town clerk); practical (carpenter, house decorator, cook); medical (doctor, physiotherapist, pharmacist).

32. E. K. Strong, *Vocational Interests in Men and Women*, Stanford University Press, California, 1952, and 'Nineteen-year follow-up of engineer interests', *J. Appl. Psychol.*, **36**, 64–74 (1952).

33. For details of occupational profiles from the 16PF, see R. B. Cattell, H. W. Eber and M. M. Tatsuoka, *Handbook of the 16PF*, IPAT, Illinois, 1970 Edition (1988 reprint). Two other books giving details of profiles for various activities and clinical cases are H. Birkett Cattell, *The 16PF: Personality in Depth*, IPAT, Illinois, 1989, and S. Karson and J. W. O'Dell, *A Guide to the Clinical Use of the 16PF*, IPAT, Illinois, 1976.

34. Interpretation of 16PF profiles is a skilled and technical task. S. E. Krug, *Interpreting 16PF Profile Patterns*, IPAT, Illinois, 1981, gives a good introduction.

35. Some confirmation can be found in A. Roe, 'A psychological study of eminent psychologists and anthropologists and a comparison with biological and physical scientists',

Psychol. Monogr., **67**, No. 352 (1953); D. W. MacKinnon, 'The personality correlates of creativity: a study of American architects', *Proc. XIVth Int. Congress Appl. Psychol.*, Munksgaard, Copenhagen; D. C. McClelland, 'On the psychodynamics of creative physical scientists', in H. E. Gruber *et al.* (eds), *Contemporary Approaches to Creative Thinking*, Atherton, New York, 1962; C. Bereiter and M. B. Freedman, 'Fields of study and the people in them', in N. Sanford (ed.), *The American College*, Wiley, New York, 1967; L. Hudson, *Contrary Imaginations*, Methuen, London, 1966, and *Frames of Mind*, Methuen, London, 1968.

36. L. Hudson, 'Personality and scientific aptitude', *Nature*, **198**, 913–914 (1963). See also D. Child and A. G. Smithers, 'Some cognitive and affective factors in subject choice', *Res. Educ.*, **5**, 1–9 (1971).

37. M. Rosenberg, *Occupations and Values*, The Free Press, Glencoe, IL, 1957.

38. A. Roe, 'Early determinants of vocational choice', *J. Counsel. Psychol.*, **4**, 212–217 (1957), *The Psychology of Occupations*, Wiley, New York, 1956. Research using the theory does not strongly support it. See D. G. Zytowski, *Vocational Behavior*, Holt, Rinehart and Winston, New York, 1968, pp. 240–255 for papers relating to Roe's theory.

FURTHER READING

B. Ball, *Careers Counselling in Practice*, Falmer, Basingstoke, 1984.

Careers Education and Guidance from 5 to 16, Curriculum Matters No. 10 in HMI series, HMSO, 1988.

R. Holdsworth (ed.), *Psychology for Careers Counselling*, British Psychological Society and Macmillan, London, 1982.

B. Hopson and J. Hayes, *The Theory and Practice of Vocational Guidance*, Pergamon, Oxford, 1968. A thorough textbook. Intended for all those who want to study the subject in depth.

R. Jackson and D. F. Juniper, *A Manual of Educational Guidance*, Holt, Rinehart and Winston, London, 1971. Another full text which also deals with some of the bread-and-butter problems facing the teacher–counsellor in school.

P. Kline, *Psychology of Vocational Guidance*, Batsford, London, 1975.

National Curriculum Council, *Careers Education and Guidance*, pamphlet No. 6, 1990.

Chapter 16

The Curriculum Process

In Great Britain, we have evolved a tradition in our primary schools and non-examination classes in secondary schools of being the masters of our own curricula, chiefly in having considerable freedom to choose what we do and how we do it. This freedom to sell wares in whichever way takes our fancy places a great responsibility on the shoulders of teachers. But as public interest in education increases, as qualifications become ever more important as a passport to work, as our mode of living increases in complexity and the knowledge explosion imposes increases in both the quantity and levels of abstraction, we must recognize the need for a systematic appraisal of school curricula. Assumptions about what is worth teaching, priorities in subject matter, order of presentation, how a subject might be presented, what forms the evaluation of learning experiences for the children or teaching methods of the teachers might take are but a few major considerations. It should come as no surprise to student teachers that this book includes a chapter on some factors bearing on curriculum development. One of the first and inescapable jobs of a teacher is to design a curriculum. Students on teaching practice also have to devote many hours to the preparation of their lessons.

For most teachers the main concern has almost inevitably been what to teach and how to teach it,[1] with some, though diminished, regard for evaluating the effectiveness of content and method. In effect, teachers have broken into their curriculum planning at the 'knowledge' or 'contents' stage (see Figure 16.1), taking for granted that the material chosen is justified and relevant. In secondary education, the state of affairs is largely a legacy of an exam-oriented system. In a regime where external, public examinations are compiled and tested by long-established agencies external to teachers and their schools, there is little wonder that teachers have taken most syllabuses as read. Mode III of the Certificate of Secondary Education attempts to overcome this tendency by placing the responsibility of syllabus design and evaluation in the hands of teachers (see Chapter 13 of the Reader, reference (23R)). Apart from this novel idea, which has not caught on at the rate originally envisaged (presumably because it is very much harder than allowing someone else to do it), the secondary schools are tied to a system of external curriculum design and assessment.

Even at the primary level, the long-standing traditions of what and how to teach, the folk-lore of primary education, are sometimes devoid of a rationale defining the reasons for choosing a particular content area or method. Yet clarity in the aims and objectives of an educational programme would seem to be an obvious starting point if we are to justify a public educational system.

THE MEANING OF CURRICULUM PROCESS

What do we mean by curriculum process? Is it that timetable pinned to the staffroom notice-board or in the back of the diary, looking for all the world like a bookie's price list of runners with the times of each race? Is it the syllabus or the lesson notes? In fact, the curriculum is more than these. Neagley and Evans[2] propose that the curriculum process is *all of the planned experiences provided by the school to assist pupils in attaining the designated learning outcomes to the best of their abilities.* Hirst[3] puts it another way: programmes of activities designed so that pupils will attain, so far as possible, educational ends or objectives. This conscious, planned aspect of the curriculum process is sometimes referred to as the *intentional* curriculum, but we need to bear in mind that some of our influences are not planned and are by-products of the main purposes. These are *unintentional* curriculum processes,[3] or the *hidden curriculum.*

Implicit in most definitions of the curriculum process are at least four important elements. The order is not fortuitous, although, as we shall see, there is a very necessary interplay between the elements in the construction of a curriculum. Tyler[4] expresses these elements in the form of questions:

(a)   What educational purposes should the school seek to attain?
(b)   What educational experiences can be provided that are likely to attain these purposes?
(c)   How can these educational experiences be effectively organized?
(d)   How can we determine whether these purposes are being attained?

These four questions often appear in contracted form as:

$$\text{objectives} \rightarrow \text{course content} \rightarrow \text{methods} \rightarrow \text{evaluation}$$

Note that Tyler prefers to talk about 'educational experiences' in preference to course content, because experience involves not only the substance of what is taught but the processes by which the pupil learns. In other words, educational experience involves content *and* what the pupil does.

As was hinted above, before deciding what to teach, we have to settle the matter of the reasons for its being taught in the first place and the outcomes we anticipate. Why teach reading to children? What purposes are served by studying art in secondary schools? It is also necessary to make a regular appraisal of whether the purposes of a curriculum are being fulfilled.

The simple linear representation of Tyler's questions gives an over-simplified view of the interaction of these components of curriculum design. It gives the impression that evaluation is the end of the line, but as Richmond remarks,[5] 'Death is the only terminal behaviour'! A more comprehensive and dynamic demonstration of curriculum

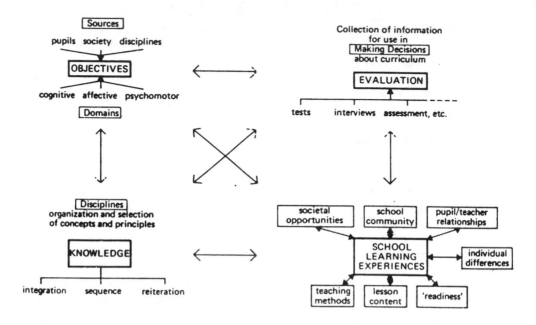

Figure 16.1 *A model for curriculum theory. Reprinted from Professor Kerr's inaugural lecture, 'The problem of curriculum reform', University of Leicester, 1967, with kind permission of the author.*

theory can be gained from Kerr's model,[6] containing components similar to Tyler's but presented in a cyclical pattern. This is shown in Figure 16.1. Note the interrelationships between the components demonstrated by the arrows. There are, of course, dangers in selecting just one model *if* we forget that it is only representative of complex processes. Also, we get no idea from the model of the relative importance attached to each component.

The impact of psychology on curriculum processes has been significant. Considerations such as Piaget's scheme of cognitive development (especially influential in the junior-school curriculum), the concept of readiness, learning theory (for example, activity rather than passivity programmes, aids in mathematics teaching, programmed learning in the broadest sense), language and concept formation, studies in skills, aptitudes, attitudes and values, and the contribution of psychologists to the question of evaluation in education are just a sample of psychological influences on curriculum processes. This contribution has been well summarized by Taylor **(R)**,[7] who sees psychology as having been used for three purposes:

(a) as a guide to the structuring of the subject matter for learning and teaching;
(b) as a source of empirical methodologies for studying how the curricular materials are transacted in teaching;
(c) similarly, as a source of methodologies, of instrumentation for the evaluation of outcomes.

OBJECTIVES

When we specify the behavioural changes we anticipate as a result of learning experiences, the specifications are said to be *objectives*. They usually begin with a verb, thus emphasizing that certain behaviours are hoped for; 'to recognize . . .', 'to acquire . . .', 'to apply . . .', 'to understand . . .' are examples. Returning to a question posed in the previous section, what are the objectives of teaching children to read? There are several possible objectives; for example, children learn to read to gain knowledge and understanding, to reap satisfaction from being able to read, to assist their work and leisure, and so on. Some activities are more specific, as when we teach Newton's laws of motion to help in an understanding of the generalizations applying to bodies which move on earth with low or moderate velocities. There could be other objectives subsumed under the ones suggested above and applying to each of Newton's three laws of motion. But, clearly, defining objectives is a skilled occupation requiring a careful consideration of the knowledge we wish to transmit to our children and the impact this knowledge will have on them.

The term 'aim' is sometimes used as an alternative to objective. However, it is more accurate to distinguish between the two. Aims are much more general and frequently refer to philosophical issues in the wider context of education. They also tend to refer to the end-product of the system. We might find expressions of the aims of a course couched in more general terms such as 'to produce technologists' or 'to educate for leisure'. Objectives relate to the route as well as the goal, whereas aims usually relate only to the goal.

How do we decide on the skills, attitudes and activities we wish to promote in our pupils when we are trying to specify objectives? Some curriculum planners start with a consideration of human needs (see Chapter 3) which encompass both personal and social needs.[8] Moreover, these decisions, especially where aims are involved, are made within a very wide context of opinion. Goodlad[9] sees three levels of decision-making in curriculum design. These are: (a) societal, largely through central government and local education authority decisions, sometimes based on government reports (Robbins, Newsom, Plowden); (b) institutional, representing school, college or university; and (c) instructional, at 'shop floor' level in the classroom, culminating in the teacher's decisions. The reorganization of secondary education, for instance, leaves local education authorities with the freedom to decide on the system to adopt, whether it be comprehensive, three-tier or whatever. In the short term, these decisions have an effect on curriculum design. For example, middle schools inherited from a primary-school tradition may give rise to a different scheme of objectives than a middle school inherited from a secondary-school tradition. In the latter, one might see a specialist programme including science, mathematics, handicraft and domestic science for the nine-year-olds, which is not at present typical of primary schools. In the former one might find greater use made of the integrated day or non-streaming. Our existing curricula also bear the marks of our history, and we shall return to this point later in the chapter.

Bloom's taxonomy[10]

Nowadays it would not be possible to write about objectives without making some reference to the major psychological contribution to curriculum development of Bloom and his associates on a taxonomy of education objectives and their influence on examining techniques. Broadly, he classified objectives into three major domains: (a) *cognitive objectives*, placing the greatest emphasis on remembering, reasoning, concept formation and creative thinking; (b) *affective objectives*, emphasizing emotive qualities expressed in attitudes, interests, values and emotional biases; (c) the *psychomotor objectives*, emphasizing muscle and motor skills and manipulation in all kinds of activities such as handwriting, speech, physical education, etc. The latter domain has not yet been fully developed by Bloom (see note (11), however). A brief gallop through the full list of objectives in the cognitive or affective domain would do very little to assist the student in understanding Bloom's intentions. The only way of really getting to grips with his views would be to refer to his books. However, one illustration will be given to show how the taxonomy operates.

Bloom and his associates organized their taxonomy (or classification) of cognitive factors under six major headings. The six are arranged hierarchically to demonstrate that the objectives are cumulative, so higher classes are built on the skills involved in lower classes. Briefly, the six classes involve *knowledge* which emphasizes those processes which require recall of such things as specific facts, terminology, conventions and generalizations. Clearly, if one has no fund of knowledge, one cannot operate cognitively. *Comprehension* represents a low level of understanding sufficient to grasp the translation and meaning of mathematical or verbal material for the purposes of interpretation or extrapolation. *Application* employs remembering and combining material to give generalizations for use in concrete situations. *Analysis* means the breakdown of material into its constituents in order to find the relationship between them. Note that all the previous classes are required before analysis is possible. *Synthesis* necessitates the putting together of the constituents by rearranging and combining them to give an arrangement not apparent before. Lastly, *evaluation* requires value judgements about materials, ideas, methods, etc. All the skills of knowledge, comprehension, application, analysis and synthesis are necessary to perform this operation satisfactorily and for a valid judgement to be made possible.

Task analysis

In Chapter 6 we met with the theories of Gagné,[10] which provide an alternative approach. In his book on the conditions of learning he postulates that when a learning task is decided upon in order to arrive at a particular learning outcome, it should be possible to construct a *learning task analysis*. It is clearly a behaviourist approach which relies on a carefully planned sequence of steps drawn up as a flow chart of activities necessary for the satisfactory completion of the learning event. In Chapter 6 we referred briefly to learning outcomes or 'human capabilities', as Gagné calls them. A corresponding verb is used to signify unambiguously the type of task implied in the learning outcome. Table 16.1 illustrates how his human capabilities can be phased. Examples are also included. Once a task has been categorized using the table, Gagné

Table 16.1 *Illustrations from some of Gagné's learning outcomes with corresponding verbs and examples.*

Capability	Verb	Example
Intellectual skill		
Discrimination	Discriminates	Discriminates, by comparing outlines, the difference between oak and chestnut leaves
Concrete concept	Identifies	Identifies, by pointing, named countries on a map
Defined concept	Classifies	Classifies, by writing lists, the phyla of a given number of animal species
Rule	Demonstrates	Demonstrates, by writing down the arrangement of 'i' and 'e' after 'c'
Higher-order rule (problem-solving)	Generates	Generates, by building up the steps in the argument, the solution to a quadratic problem
Motor skill	Executes	Executes a hand stand
Attitude	Chooses	Chooses, on leaving school, a job which does not involve manual labour

then proposes a task analysis of prerequisites for the achievement of the learning. Put simply, each step in a learning event requires some previous kind of accomplishment. Successful task analysis consists of accurate judgements of the size and hierarchical arrangement of the steps.

The flow chart created by such hierarchical choices looks something like the example shown in Figure 16.2 (p. 386). This is a much more detailed and painstaking approach than the one suggested by Bloom. It has a salutary effect on the person planning the lesson. The detailed knowledge required of a teacher to make this kind of analysis is quite appreciable. In addition the teacher must have a sound knowledge of the logical sequence and developmental capabilities of pupils in an age group. Such cold-blooded, detailed tactics are very time-consuming, but repay dividends, especially where the teacher is dealing with a topic for the first time.

The term *spiral curriculum* has been coined by Bruner to demonstrate a species of task analysis in which the same material is reintroduced at different levels in school, with increasing conceptual difficulty.

Devising curriculum objectives

Designing a curriculum has a salutary effect on teaching, provided the job is done properly. It is all too easy to end up with a somewhat vague and amorphous list of statements having little operational value. It should be possible in most cases for the objectives to be stated in such a way as to lend themselves to systematic evaluation. One cannot measure what one cannot define. Plainly there are occasions when we wish to 'pilot' or try out a new method in a spirit of 'let's see what happens' (scientists employ this method in addition to conventional scientific inquiry). But, apart from occasional pilot runs, we ought to know precisely where we are going and what we hope to achieve on the way.

As an illustration of curriculum design in action, a study of curriculum objectives in teacher-training by a team in the Leeds area will be used.[8] A panel of representatives

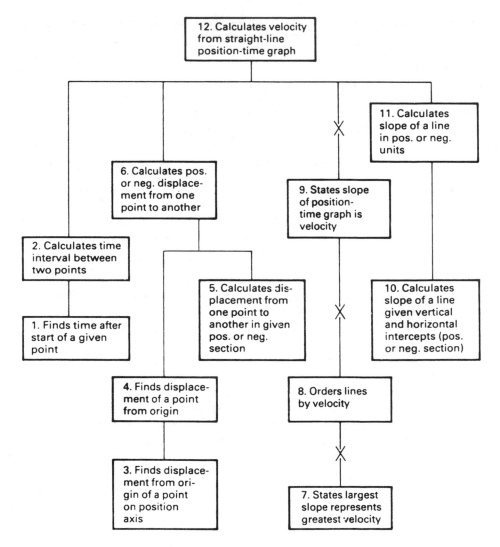

Figure 16.2 *A learning hierarchy showing relationships of prerequisite skills to the task: Calculating velocity from a straight-line graph of position (vertical axis) and time (horizontal axis). X = relationships found invalid. (Based on a description in R. T. White and R. M. Gagné, 'Formative evaluation applied to a learning hierarchy', Cont. Educ. Psychol. (1978), 3, 87–94.)*

from schools, colleges of education and universities was assembled, as experienced informants from the teaching profession. Their first task was to compile a provisional working definition of the teacher's role and to work back from this definition to the learning experiences provided in colleges of education. It was decided that, to be effective, teachers must command:

(a)   a range of *professional skills and techniques* which are directly related to the day-to-day work of a teacher;

(b) *knowledge and understanding* of subject matter and the appropriate methods of teaching it to children;

(c) *personal qualities.*

A closer examination of these professional qualities should prove to be beneficial in providing a rationale for college work as showing how these objectives are related to classroom practices.

Professional skills and techniques

Taking their cue from research in the area of the probationary year in teaching and teachers' opinions of college courses, the team drew up a list of skills and techniques along with corresponding reasons for choosing the list. As suggested earlier, one way of breaking into this ground is by looking at children's needs, particularly those they must acquire (to be found in Chapter 3) in order to cope with their environment. Four particular kinds of experience were defined in terms of curriculum subject areas; these were *language skills, human studies, science studies* and *expressive arts.* For example, language skills would include subject studies in English, foreign languages and mathematics (regarding this subject as a form of symbolic language). Children were also considered in three groups following roughly the pattern of the three-tier system, with children in early years (3 to 9), middle years (9 to 12) and later years (12 onwards). Each group had representative members of the panel. The total picture would look like Table 16.2.

Table 16.2

		Curriculum elements			
		Language skills	Human studies	Science studies	Expressive arts
Age range	Early (3–9) Middle (9–12) Late (12–)				

Within each curriculum element for each age range would be an elaboration of children's needs and some corresponding professional skills required by the teacher. Table 16.3 is a selection from the entries for the early age range in human studies set out with children's needs opposite the teacher's professional skills.

These are just a few of the recommended needs to give readers a clue to the findings. Students and teachers might have something to gain from looking at the full list[8] and analysing them in terms of their own work.

Teacher's knowledge

What areas of knowledge should teachers possess in addition to personal subject knowledge as part of their own education? For those teaching children in the early

Table 16.3 *Human Studies*

The needs of children	The professional needs of the teachers
Opportunity for play, which helps to fulfil the needs for:	Knowledge of the use of play in this context and skill in exploring its possibilities
adventure co-operation knowledge of one's own and other people's reactions experience in accepting responsibility for one's own actions	Knowledge of the social development of children and skill in applying this knowledge in the classroom Knowledge of the customs, etc., of people from cultures different from our own
learning to accept others and be accepted by them an awareness of one's own ability in relation to the ability of others the control of one's own feelings, etc.	Knowledge of different cultures within our own community: their clothes, food, religions, etc. Skill in the use of materials and resources in the classroom
Opportunity to learn about people and to satisfy curiosity about them: within one's own family within one's own class at school within one's own neighbourhood	Skills in writing, printing and drawing on the blackboard, etc. Skills in assessing children's work and progress in Human Studies
And about: people and where they live people in other lands people in the past	Knowledge of children's work (particularly in Human Studies) in the next stage of their education at school
By means of: stories, films, television, books, pictures, etc.	

years at school, the panel postulated six areas of knowledge. These were knowledge of: (a) philosophical considerations; (b) the four curriculum areas in sufficient depth for teaching purposes; (c) human development and other psychological issues relevant to teaching; (d) the formation of human relationships; (e) the country's system of education past and present; and (f) the various welfare services. The middle and later school years are similar except that later school years should include a knowledge of the work conditions which prevail for children leaving school.

Teachers' personal qualities

For many years research into those qualities which distinguish 'good' teachers from others has attracted great interest. The findings are frequently disappointing and unhelpful because the characteristics which appear to be popular might equally well describe a secretary or a bank manager. Taylor[12] found with primary-school and secondary-school children that cheerfulness, even temper and a sense of humour were especially important qualities for teachers to possess. In the United States, Ryans[13] carried out a massive study of teacher characteristics and their relationship to teacher effectiveness in junior and high schools. Three patterns of teacher behaviour stood out from all others: (a) friendly (warm, understanding, friendly v. aloof, egocentric, restricted); (b) organized (responsible, business-like, systematic v. evading, unplanned, slipshod); and (c) stimulating (imaginative, surgent v. dull, routine). According to Start,[14] high general intelligence, dominance, relaxed security, introversion and conservatism are the hallmarks of a superior teacher. From this rag-bag of qualities, the Leeds team chose the following:

(a) *professional attitudes*, including a sense of responsibility, strong moral sense, punctuality and appropriate standards of dress;
(b) *flexibility and adaptability*, involving appropriate attitudes to learning, enthusiasm, motivation, imagination, resilience, vitality, courage, a sense of humour, curiosity;
(c) *confidence*.

Unfortunately, lists of qualities of the kind described here are not very useful unless we know more about the particular combinations which prove to be effective. It would be rare for a teacher to possess all these qualities. They tend to read like a reference for the post of Archangel!

We have spent some time looking at an analysis of objectives partly to see the way in which this analysis was approached and also because the findings are of value to intending and serving teachers. Note that implicit in some of the objectives of teacher education is a view of what is important in the education of children.

Defining objectives

Several authors have laid down guidelines which will assist curriculum planners during their attempts to establish curriculum objectives.[15, 16] When we are planning a course, the objectives must be:

(a) Realistic, appropriate and capable of being translated into learning experiences in the classroom. Plans are laid after we have borne in mind the limitations imposed, by, for example, the intellectual development of children, their home circumstances and school background. There is no point in specifying objectives which cannot be defined operationally. For instance, the term 'creativity' is sometimes used in primary and secondary curricula without any clear indication of its meaning in this context, or of the processes by which it can be achieved, or for that matter precisely how or when it *has* been achieved.
(b) Specified in terms of behaviour which is recognizable. Aims as we have defined them above are often not capable of being recognized in the short term. 'To educate a child so as to enable him to play a useful part in a community' would require some very careful defining of terms such as 'useful' and 'community' so that we could pin down the learning experiences necessary in the curriculum. Bloom's taxonomy of educational objectives is useful in providing recognizable behaviours.
(c) Capable of being evaluated. Needless to say, if it is intended to bring about behavioural change in learners, we ought to be able to assess the quality and quantity of this change.

Criticisms of behavioural objectives

There have been several critics of the rigid, detailed approach to lesson planning. Nobody would argue against planning lessons, but some people consider very detailed planning of the kind required by the Bloom taxonomy[10] by Tyler[4] as not always helpful.[15]

The critics argue that broad criteria are sometimes more helpful than narrow ones. Narrow criteria seem to relate to simple factual recall, and do not allow for the broader aims of the teacher, such as 'understanding'. Teachers often have these broader goals for which the short, step-by-step breakdown of behavioural objectives is not appropriate; they also require a lot of time. Eisner[17] reckons that the number of objectives for a primary curriculum is well over 25 000. In some cases this preoccupation with behavioural objectives could well mean an uneconomic use of a teacher's time. Where a pupil's contribution, particularly in exploratory activity, is extensive, behavioural objectives are difficult to define precisely. Some of the outcomes of exploratory learning are not always predictable, and many teachers use incidental findings by children as a source of material for their lessons. Rigid objectives seem more suited to knowledge which is to be recollected (i.e. straight learning), and this does not necessarily mean that the learner 'understands' what has been assimilated. Methods of learning vary according to the aspects of knowledge or experience being dealt with. It is necessary for the teacher to match his or her teaching with what the children are expected to be doing, e.g. creative and expressive activities, and this frequently extends beyond the narrow confines of the acceptable behavioural terms found in, for example, Bloom's taxonomy.

When applying the above ideas to lesson planning, readers are advised to refer to *Applications of Psychology for the Teacher* (Chapter 3), by the present author.[17]

KNOWLEDGE OR SUBJECT CONTENT

Deciding what to select from the whole spectrum of content in a discipline in order to achieve our stated objectives is the central concern in this stage of curriculum planning. But what do we hope will be the essential influence of the content? Taba[15] supposes there are two schools of thought which we might term *structure-oriented* and *task-oriented*. There are those who see each subject as having its own brand of mental discipline quite apart from the teaching methods employed. Physics, for example, demands a different mental attitude and cognitive style from literary criticism. Expectations in art are not the same as those in history. With this in mind, the proponents of structure orientation tend to concentrate on the theoretical aspects of the subject to illustrate the characteristic way of thinking afforded by the nature of the subject itself.

Task-oriented teachers view the subject matter as a means of acquiring learning skills such as memorizing (historical dates, chemical formulae, poems) or developing manual skills (play with material which is manipulated, physical education, handicraft). There is a good deal of faith placed in the concept of transfer of training.

However, most curriculum planners steer a course between these extremes, allowing that some subjects demand specialized cognitive strategies while recognizing certain similar cognitive demands which cut across subject disciplines. In fact there is a decided move towards more integrated syllabuses, although there is little research of any kind to show the advantages or disadvantages of combined courses. Teaching number skills to a junior class, quite apart from the basic numeracy of the children or their developmental level, presents special problems which contrast sharply with, say, the teaching of reading. Yet both these subjects involve memorization or relational thinking.

Decisions about the content of the school curriculum are as much a matter of philosophical and political debate as psychological. Views[18] have focused on seven or eight areas (historically accumulated 'forms' of knowledge – Hirst,[18] 'a selection from the culture' – Lawton[18]).

These are not necessarily equivalent.

Hirst

1. Mathematical knowledge
2. Empirical knowledge in the physical and social sciences
3. Aesthetic knowledge
4. Moral knowledge
5. Mental and personal knowledge involving explanations of human behaviour
6. Religious knowledge
7. Philosophical knowledge.

Lawton

1. Mathematics
2. The physical and biological sciences
3. The expressive and creative arts
4. Moral education
5. Humanities and social sciences (including explanations of human behaviour history, geography, classical studies, literature, film, TV, religious studies)
6. Interdisciplinary work.

(See Barnes[17] for a discussion of these points.)

A document from the DES[18] roots the curriculum in educational aims and suggests the following as desirable:

(a)   to help pupils to develop lively, enquiring minds, the ability to question and argue rationally and to apply themselves to tasks, and physical skills;
(b)   to help pupils to acquire knowledge and skills relevant to adult life and employment in a fast-changing world;
(c)   to help pupils to use language and number effectively;
(d)   to instil respect for religious and moral values, and tolerance of other races, religions, and ways of life;
(e)   to help pupils to understand the world in which they live, and the interdependence of individuals, groups and nations;
(f)   to help pupils to appreciate human achievements and aspirations.

There is some interesting discussion in the DES document about how these aims might be achieved in terms of the subjects in primary and secondary curricula.

LEARNING EXPERIENCES

Few would now deny the importance of purposeful activity by the learner as an aid to learning. We pay a good deal of attention to methods of presenting material, so much so that we often forgo the content. Vast methodological researches and school programmes have been mounted – Nuffield Science, integrated day methods, 'free activity' methods – all testifying to the enthusiasm generated. Less emphasis is now placed on transmission of knowledge and more on the processes of assimilation by developing skills in understanding.

Psychology has much to offer in this respect. Considerations of learning, individual capacities, motivation, personality, the growth of skills and 'readiness' are all major issues in devising learning experiences for pupils. In one sense this aspect of curriculum planning draws together many threads in the syllabus of educational psychology.

Our view of childhood has altered and has in turn affected the teacher's approach to structuring learning situations in the classroom. A greater recognition of individual worth and differences has brought a corresponding recognition that individual help is a vital alternative to class teaching. Our knowledge of child development and our changed attitudes towards the young have revitalized learning procedures. They have converted us from regarding the child as a passive receptacle to seeing him or her as an active participant in learning.

Theories of instruction, already mentioned in Chapter 6, have grown in response to the need for 'prescriptions' of learning and teaching instead of the 'descriptions' so prevalent in learning theories. The work of Bruner[19] is well known, although Skinner[20] and Gagné[20] have also made considerable contributions. As we saw, Bruner pays attention to the most effective 'sequence' in which materials should be presented and goes on to argue that optimal sequences need to be judged in terms of an individual's speed and power to learn, transfer possibilities, economy of learning in keeping with the 'cognitive strain' imposed and the ability of the material thus learned to help in generating new ideas.

The impact of social psychology has rapidly made us aware that children's learning processes are markedly influenced by social factors and group dynamics. Studies of home background, the school community and teacher–pupil interaction are leaving their mark on the methods we are adopting. Experiments with open-plan schools, unstreamed classes, sixth-form colleges and schools where the local community is being drawn into the life of the school are but a few recent examples.

EVALUATION

Curriculum evaluation is the servant by which we clarify and substantiate the effectiveness of our objectives, learning experiences and content. The idea of evaluation as an ongoing process is conveyed in Kerr's model (Figure 16.1) by the dotted arrows leading from the evaluation component to all the other components. Evaluations should be seen as a tool to assist in refining learning processes as well as in measuring the acquisition of knowledge.

Thus evaluative techniques should do more than examine a pupil's knowledge. They should also help in locating the factors which influence performance, such as the conditions and procedures in the classroom. Two kinds of evaluation which draw attention to this dual function have been defined.[16] *Formative evaluation* takes place during the developmental stages of a curriculum and is seen as a continuous process, whilst *summative evaluation* occurs when the curriculum is established and we are measuring the achievement of those on the course as well as the effectiveness of the course. Even with established courses, formative evaluation would still be an essential aspect for reappraising the curriculum.

Mention has already been made of evaluation techniques in Chapter 13. In most instances teachers have to devise their own instruments. There are a few standardized tests in mathematics, English, reading and spelling for a wide age range,[21] but these have a special function and, like all standardized material, require very careful handling.

A necessary first step in evaluation is to prepare a blueprint (see Chapter 14). This is a carefully designed breakdown plan of the content areas and objectives showing their relative importance in terms of hours (or units of time) allotted to each section. A blueprint should be assembled *before* the course commences. As we saw in Chapter 13, multiple-choice items are particularly favoured for evaluation, although orals, written essays and practical work may be used provided they can be validated and made reliable. Other forms of evaluation have been tried with limited success; custom-made attitude and interest scales and interviews are amongst those currently being tried.

It is important to remember that our primary aim in using evaluative methods is concerned with the value of the course using group performance of the pupils in knowing, understanding and applying the skills specified. We would not necessarily be concerned with diagnosing pupils for selection or with finding their rank order of achievement.

CURRICULUM PLANNING AND THE TEACHER

Establishing a new curriculum is really a combined effort requiring expert advice in the aspects we have discussed above. However, there is also the task of keeping a close watch on our existing programmes and modifying or changing parts of them as the need arises. In the light of what has been said above, we might apply one method suggested by Taylor,[1] who recommends that the teacher should keep a double-page 'ledger' account of the syllabus topics with a column for answers to each of the following questions:

(a)   What am I expected to teach, and in what order? (CONTENT)
(b)   What educational purposes is my teaching to serve? (AIMS)
(c)   What teaching methods are known to achieve these purposes? (METHODS)
(d)   What standard of achievement am I expected to aim at? (OBJECTIVES)
(e)   How will I discover whether the course I've been teaching has been successful or not? (EVALUATION)
(f)   What can I usefully be told about the abilities, interests and attitudes of the pupils I am to teach? (PUPILS)
(g)   COMMENTS about alternative possibilities.

As Taylor comments, the purpose of the ledger is 'to help the teacher understand the nature and purpose of the course, not to determine the form and style of his teaching'.

CURRICULUM TRENDS

The present state of affairs in curriculum design is part of a chain of events in the development of educational practices in this country. Looking back over the history of our present curriculum, there seem to be at least two major strands in the development of educational practices in Great Britain. One strand arises from the public-school system of the past, which permeated the grammar-school system. The other strand arises from legislation relating to the elementary-school system of education for all.

The classical tradition of Latin and Greek, with a little geography, history and mathematics, prevailed through many centuries. Latin, in the first instance, was very important because most of the literature, including law, medicine and theology, was written in that tongue. In time, however, it became symbolic of a particular way of life serving to distinguish the gentry, leaders with 'cultivated' minds, from the serving classes. Where the latter were able to receive an education it consisted of an iron ration of the three Rs, just sufficient to enable children to serve God and the factory owners. Later, the 1902 Act insisted that children should be fitted to meet the practical as well as the basic intellectual demands of a working life. In this century we have seen rapid and extensive changes in elementary education, emerging as the present-day primary and secondary systems.

As the students' work in the History of Education will show, a long train of Education Acts and government reports (Plowden and Newsom, for example) has had a marked effect on the direction of curriculum designs. Consider the effect of the Spens and Norwood Reports on the 1944 Act. The Reports saw children as falling into three categories, academic, technical and practical, for which the secondary-grammar, secondary-technical and secondary-modern schools were created. Curriculum designers attempted to build into their schemes a style of teaching and a special emphasis on content design to satisfy the supposed characteristics of 'academic', 'technical' and 'practical' children.

During the past 25 or so years we have experienced a phenomenal period of experimentation without finding, regrettably, a corresponding rigour in the evaluation of these innovations. In the content areas, we have seen 'modern maths', French and science (other than 'nature study') in the junior schools, together with Nuffield, the Schools Council programmes (R),[22] STEP (Science Teacher Education Project) and so on at all ages. Greater and diverse use of technological aids have been evident (TV, radio, programmed learning, computer-assisted learning, microprocessors, etc.). Classroom organization has, in some cases, veered towards informal arrangements, vertical grouping, team teaching, open plan, mixed-ability grouping and the integrated day.

Since the 1944 Act we have seen the gradual evolution of a system dedicated to giving pupils an equal chance to benefit from whatever education would be satisfying and serviceable. Theoretically, there also seems to be a strong desire to extend the syllabus to give more attention to moral and social education: the behavioural sciences at secondary level (psychology, sociology and anthropology) and what might be termed the 'survival sciences', such as demography, pollution and conservation, race relations, peace studies, contraception, sexually transmitted diseases, and health studies. In practice, the emphasis, as seen by teachers, has been largely on intellectual and moral development. Musgrove and Taylor (**R**)[23] asked primary, secondary modern and grammar school teachers to rate the relative educational relevance of moral training, social training, intellectual training (instruction in subjects), education for family life, social advancement and education for citizenship. Grammar school teachers had a more confined outlook than secondary modern teachers and viewed their role as limited to intellectual and moral education ('character training'), with indifferent regard for social training. Surprisingly, primary school teachers likewise seemed to place less emphasis on social than on intellectual and moral training.

Parents of university students also have some clear ideas about the roles which universities should serve through their curricula. Child (**R**)[24] showed three aspects of university life which were uppermost in the minds of parents: (a) students should be worked hard in a few specialized subjects with a supporting cast of academic counsellors; (b) the university should be primarily concerned with preparing and guiding students for a career; (c) the university should help in developing students' skills in dealing with other people. The study of knowledge 'for its own sake' and without regard for its practical application was placed right at the bottom of the list of priorities. Here we see an important dilemma between the teachers' cognitive outlook and the parents' highly businesslike vocational and instrumental order of priorities.

THE NATIONAL CURRICULUM

As mentioned earlier in the chapter, one of the most persistent criticisms of curriculum planning in schools has been aimed at the vagueness with which the content has been chosen, apparently sometimes without regard as to whether the content is justified and relevant. An attempt to give purpose as well as direction to school curricula has been enshrined in the new National Curriculum which came into force in England and Wales in 1989. The Education Reform Act of 1988[25] stated that the National Curriculum was to give a 'balanced and broadly based curriculum which . . . promotes the spiritual, moral, cultural, mental and physical development of pupils at school and of society and prepares pupils for the opportunities and experiences of adult life'.

There are three *core subjects*, namely, mathematics, English and science (plus Welsh in schools where it is the language of instruction). Religious education must also be provided. Other subjects are termed *foundation subjects* and consist of history, geography, technology (including design), music, art, PE, modern foreign languages (including Welsh).

Four landmarks in a pupil's school life are defined as *Key Stages*. School age from 5 to 16 is correspondingly broken into ranges giving Stage 1 covering 5–7 years of age, Stage 2 covering 8–11, Stage 3 covering 12–14 and Stage 4 covering 15–16. As we saw in Chapter 13 attainment targets have been set to occur at the end of each Key Stage.

Statements of attainment are detailed objectives to be achieved for a particular age group and performance level. Assessments, both internal and national, are derived and used to judge the quality of the child, the teacher and the school. Attainment targets are clearly defined for all the core and foundation subjects mentioned above. *Levels of attainment* are defined (see Chapter 13) in terms of a continuum for the school age range from 5 to 16. The national assessment aspect referred to above, the standard assessment tasks (SATs), is used alongside the internal assessment to give the level of attainment. From these are obtained the *profiles of attainment* and *records* for the benefit of other teachers, parents and employers.

All schools are provided with detailed information about the National Curriculum and the methods of assessment to be used. HMSO documents are available. There is a short, but useful, package entitled *An Introduction to the National Curriculum* produced by the National Curriculum Council (1989), and supplementary material from the same source which students will find helpful.

SUMMARY

One of the most important jobs for any teacher is to plan what to teach, how to teach it and how to evaluate the outcome of teaching. But it is no accident that a chapter on the curriculum appears at the end rather than at the beginning of the book. Curriculum design is a difficult task requiring a profound knowledge of psychological principles apart from content knowledge. So, although it is one of the first things to confront a student on school practice or fresh out of training, curriculum planning is most effectively done as a consequence of accumulated information and skills in handling children and the subject area.

The curriculum is erroneously thought of by many as the subject matter of a course. This is a very limited view. In fact, the curriculum represents the interaction of all the activities aimed at assisting pupils in reaching specified educational objectives. In short, curriculum planning involves specifying objectives, devising appropriate content, arranging educational experiences for presenting the content, and evaluating the processes of learning which have taken place, along with testing the suitability of the content in relation to the stated objectives.

This is a tall order. To begin with, we have to know a lot about children in terms of their interests, motives, intellectual competence or what they have done already in school in addition to making judgements about what is most suited to their skills and needs at a particular stage in their development. Hence it is clear that objectives can be specified only against this background of information in order to make them realistic, appropriate and capable of being expressed in terms which can be transposed into learning behaviour. Vague, all-inclusive statements are not appropriate when they cannot be converted into activities. Again, objectives must ultimately be put to the test: they must be capable of evaluation because all educational objectives lead to learning, and we must be in a position to assess whether learning has taken place.

Evaluation is an ongoing process. It enables us to review the objectives and modify them if they prove to be inappropriate. Mention was made in Chapter 13 of methods of evaluation. Selecting content demands both a knowledge of particular cognitive structures inherent in a subject area and a knowledge of general learning tactics common to all disciplines.

Needless to say, much of the earlier part of the book concentrated on the individual qualities and learning habits of children most likely to influence learning. Such factors as motivation, attention, retention, recall, language skills, cognitive developmental stage, intellectual abilities and personality are frequently the source of variability and interaction in the learning experiences of the individual child.

The next few years will see greater demands being made of teachers to examine their curricula. Innovation is now almost routine in education and teachers should be in a strong position to examine the worth of the many new ideas which will flood into their working life.

ENQUIRY AND DISCUSSION

(a) Take a close look at the topics you have been asked to teach on school practice in terms of objectives, content, methods of teaching and learning and evaluation. Enquire of teachers their reasons for giving particular topics.

(b) What do you consider to be the important criteria when deciding on the methods or 'educational experiences' you would offer a specified group of children in a given topic? (You may have to think out a solution to this problem for a mixed-ability group or in an integrated subject area.)

(c) The Plowden and Newsom Reports contain a section entitled 'recommendations' giving many suggestions for a curriculum reform. Examine the psychological assumptions implicitly or explicitly connected with recommendations in one or both of these reports.

(d) Read *An Introduction to the National Curriculum*.[25] Note the implications in terms of classroom practice.

(e) Using the recommended texts, particularly D. Barnes, *Practical Curriculum Study* (see note (17)), produce sets of objectives and subject skills which justify the inclusion of your main subject in the school timetable.

(f) Engage your tutor in a group discussion on the objectives of various aspects of the education course, e.g. philosophy, 'methods' of education (if such a course exists), sociology, psychology, history, comparative education.

NOTES AND REFERENCES

1. The conclusion that teachers tend to lay greatest stress on content and method is demonstrated in a research report by P. H. Taylor, *How Teachers Plan Their Courses*, NFER, Slough, 1970.

2. R. L. Neagley and N. D. Evans, *Handbook for Effective Curriculum Development*, Prentice-Hall, Englewood Cliffs, NJ, 1967.

3. P. H. Hirst, 'The contribution of philosophy to the study of the curriculum', in J. F. Kerr (ed.), *Changing the Curriculum*, University of London Press, London, 1968. This is a very useful and readable book of individual papers.

4. R. W. Tyler, *Basic Principles of Curriculum and Instruction*, University of Chicago Press, Chicago, 1949.

5. W. K. Richmond, *The School Curriculum*, Methuen, London, 1971. A thought-provoking book, in part light-hearted, in part serious.

6. J. F. Kerr, in *Changing the Curriculum*, gives a model which has much to commend it. The diagram appears in his chapter 'The problem of curriculum reform' (op. cit., note (3)). See also P. H. Taylor's chapter, 'The contribution of psychology to the study of the curriculum', in Kerr's book.

7. (R) P. H. Taylor, 'Purpose and structure in the curriculum', in P. Gordon (ed.), *The Study of Education*, vol. 2, Woburn, London, 1980.

8. The University of Leeds Institute of Education embarked on a curriculum project relating

to colleges of education. Stage I, which considers the objectives of teacher-training, uses as its starting point a model of individual needs (material and experiential) by which to isolate the professional skills needed by teachers and thus to indicate the appropriate curriculum in colleges. *Report Number 1: The Objectives of Teacher-Training*, The Institute of Education, University of Leeds, May 1971.

9. J. I. Goodlad, in *Curriculum Innovation in Practice*, The Schools Council, HMSO, London, 1968. See also S. Wiseman and D. Pidgeon, *Curriculum Evaluation*, NFER, Slough, 1970.

10. B. S. Bloom *et al.*, *Taxonomy of Educational Objectives. Handbook I: Cognitive Domain*, Longman, London, 1956, and *Handbook II: Affective Domain*, 1964. For a task analysis reference see R. M. Gagné, *The Conditions of Learning*, Holt-Saunders, New York, 1985 (4th edn).

11. E. J. Simpson, *Vocational-Technical Education*, US Department of Health, University of Illinois, 1966.

12. P. H. Taylor, 'Children's evaluations of the characteristics of the good teacher', *Br. J. Educ. Psychol.*, **32**, 258–266 (1962).

13. D. G. Ryans, *Characteristics of Teachers: Their Descriptions, Comparison and Appraisal*, American Council of Education, Washington, DC, 1960.

14. K. B. Start, 'The relation of teaching ability to measures of personality', *Br. J. Educ. Psychol.*, **36**, 158–165 (1966).

15. H. Taba, *Curriculum Development: Theory and Practice*, Harcourt, Brace and World, New York, 1962.

16. S. Wiseman and D. Pidgeon, *Curriculum Evaluation*, NFER, Slough, 1970.

17. E. W. Eisner, 'Instructional and expressive educational objectives: their formulation and use in curriculum', in W. J. Popham *et al.*, *Instructional Objectives*, Rand McNally, Chicago, 1969. L. Stenhouse, *An Introduction to Curriculum Research and Development*, Heinemann, London, 1975. D. Barnes, *Practical Curriculum Study*, Routledge and Kegan Paul, London, 1982. D. Child, *Applications of Psychology for the Teacher*, Holt, Rinehart and Winston, Eastbourne, 1986.

18. P. H. Hirst, *Knowledge and the Curriculum*, Routledge and Kegan Paul, London, 1974. D. Lawton, *Class Culture and the Curriculum*, Routledge and Kegan Paul, London, 1975. DES, *The School Curriculum*, HMSO 1981.

19. J. S. Bruner, *Toward a Theory of Instruction*, Norton, New York, 1966. See also *The Relevance of Education*, Norton, New York, 1971.

20. B. F. Skinner, 'The science of learning and the art of teaching', in A. A. Lumsdaine and R. Glaser (eds), *Teaching Machines and Programmed Learning*, National Educational Association (USA), Washington, DC, 1960; R. M. Gagné, *Essentials of Learning for Instruction*, The Dryden Press, Hinsdale, IL, 1974. For research on discovery methods see J. A. Rowell, J. Simon and R. Wiseman, 'Verbal reception, guided discovery and the learning of schemata', *Br. J. Educ. Psychol.*, **39**, 233–244 (1969).

21. The National Foundation for Educational Research has designed several standardized tests suitable for use in primary and secondary schools. The Educational Guidance and Assessment Catalogue and the ASE catalogue published by NFER–Nelson give details of their function and availability to teachers.

22. (R) A. M. Ross, A. G. Razzell and E. H. Badcock, *The Curriculum in the Middle Years*, Schools Council Working Paper No. 55, Evans/Methuen Educational, London, 1976.

23. (R) F. Musgrove and P. H. Taylor, 'Teachers' and parents' conception of the teacher's role', *Br. J. Educ. Psychol.*, **35**, 171–179 (1965).

24. (R) D. Child *et al.*, 'Parents' expectations of a university', *Universities Q.*, **25**, 484–490 (1971).

25. Education Reform Act, HMSO, London, 1988. National Curriculum Council, *An Introduction to the National Curriculum*, 1989.

FURTHER READING

D. Barnes, *Practical Curriculum Study*, Routledge and Kegan Paul, London, 1982.
A. V. Kelly, *The Curriculum: Theory and Practice*, Chapman, London, 1989 (3rd edn).
W. K. Richmond, *The School Curriculum*, Methuen, London, 1971.
M. Skilbeck, *School-based Curriculum Development*, Harper and Row, London, 1984.
P. H. Taylor, *How Teachers Plan Their Courses*, NFER, Slough, 1970.

Many useful publications about the National Curriculum have been produced by the National Curriculum Council, HMSO. Your tutors will have access to them all.

Chapter 17

Psychological Research and Education

The strongest tradition adopted by the majority of workers in the psychology of education is that which employs the methods and assumptions of the sciences. The bulk of the experimental evidence offered in this textbook has its origins in scientific method. As we have seen in previous chapters, the limitations imposed are such that answers to the kinds of questions of significance to practising teachers are not clear cut. In fact some psychologists in education have questioned the suitability of scientific method in its purest form as the appropriate technique at this stage in our hazy knowledge of human behaviour. They ask, 'Are the highly sophisticated methods of science too refined for the uncharted realms of complex human conduct?' However, the alternatives, inspired (and uninspired) guesswork, speculation or teaching folklore, whilst they may assist in formulations, are hardly likely to provide us with the foundations from which decisions in the classroom are made possible.

Of course there are differences of approach even within the bounds of scientific method. Some psychologists are concerned with the study of the mind, whilst others concentrate on the observable products of man–environment interaction. Some restrict their observations to description, classification and generalization, whilst others venture to suggest causal relations from which prediction and control are envisaged. Some make a point of individual 'eyeball-to-eyeball' analysis (idiographic studies), whilst others prefer elaborate statistical designs for group analysis from which to derive norms of behaviour (nomothetic studies). In all these cases, we meet the problem of research design and the applicability of the results to classroom procedures. The increasing criticism of traditional research methods in educational psychology stems from the difficulty of bridging the gap between theoretical findings and the practical 'nitty-gritty'. We shall return to this dilemma later in the chapter. At this point we shall look briefly at the methods and intentions of scientific method as applied in the behavioural sciences (psychology, sociology, political science, anthropology, economics) and at some of the cautions necessary when interpreting and appraising the findings. For a sound introduction to this topic, students should see one of the books recommended in note (1).

Generally speaking, then, researchers in the behavioural sciences have adopted the methods of the natural sciences. Dewey[2] has speculated about the main stages of this 'scientific method' as follows:

(a)   the recognition of a problem which has not been solved before;
(b)   an experiment is designed in such a way as to define the problem clearly, then information is accumulated through careful observations;
(c)   the information is organized to see whether regularities exist;
(d)   explanations for such regularities are suggested – this is known as setting up hypotheses (that is, tentative theories);
(e)   experiments are designed to test the hypotheses;
(f)   the hypotheses are used to predict new effects which in turn are put to the test.

Probably very few experiments take this precise form. Nevertheless, broadly speaking, the method has been used as the basis for many research findings which are quoted in the textbook. Where the psychologist has a special difficulty is in setting up hypotheses and experiments in which there is control of all the variables operating. It will repay us, therefore, to look at some of the important methods used for gathering information. One useful way of classifying the assembly of information (suggested by Kerlinger[3]) is: (a) *experimental*; (b) *ex post facto*; and (c) *survey*. In all three we are dealing with *variables*. These are qualities or attributes which can have differing values. In psychology and education we meet with variables such as type of school, motivation, sex of pupil, aptitude, extraversion, achievement and a host of others dealt with in this textbook. Some are referred to as *independent variables*; for example, systems or methods used in education, the sex of a person or coaching using the initial teaching alphabet (i.t.a), which are presumed to be causal variables. *Dependent variables* consist of measures which fluctuate and 'depend' for their value on the independent variables. The latter are of special interest to the teacher, for they include the methods employed in the classroom. The most common dependent variable in education is achievement, or the amount of learning that has taken place as a consequence of given methods.

In the experimental set-up we deliberately hold constant, or *control*, most of the independent variables and vary just one or two. For example, if we wanted to test the efficiency of the i.t.a. as a means of teaching children how to read as compared with a more traditional method, the independent variables would be the i.t.a. and the traditional orthographical method of teaching reading. The relevant dependent variable – that is, the children's reading ability – would have to be tested for both groups, either after or both before and after a trial experiment, whilst all other independent variables on which the children's reading performance might also depend, such as intelligence, home background and school experience, would have to be the same for both groups. However, strict experimental control is rarely possible in educational research. The difficulty of controlling and experimenting when we are dealing with people and situations of great complexity is not easily surmounted without raising ethical questions.

Moreover, the activities of concern to us in the classroom rarely, if ever, occur in isolation from real-life events, and the manipulative experiments of traditional psychology, in which variables are taken a few at a time, have limited value because the interactive effect between the crucial variables is central to an understanding of behaviour. Several researchers are now looking to *multivariate* techniques in which large numbers of interrelated activities are measured in natural settings on several occasions, thus allowing for nature to carry out the spontaneous manipulations in behaviour to be captured in the data. The ethnomethod of participant observation, for instance, may have much to offer us in helping to provide clearer classifications of the important classroom behaviours so necessary if we are to define the conditions of learning and teaching. Such detailed plotting of life in classrooms will inevitably provide some fundamental data from which multivariate methods of analysis will derive information.

Animals are frequently the subjects of strict laboratory approaches. But there are obvious dangers in transferring the results of animal experiments to human situations. The presence of different levels of psychological organization, intellect and motivation, amongst other things, is certain to give rise to difficulties when interpreting human in terms of animal behaviour.

Ex post facto research involves an examination of events which have already occurred in the hope that such examination will reveal significant generalities. We cannot manipulate the independent variables because they have already happened. Take as an illustration a field study of juvenile delinquency (dependent variable). The starting point has been to take a group of attested delinquents and look at their life histories (presumed independent variables) in terms of family background, friendship networks, relationship with parents, personal and intellectual characteristics, and compare these with a group of non-delinquents. The independent variables of delinquency have already occurred and we must inspect these to see which might have a bearing on the problem.[4] Clearly, in some cases it is no easy task to determine which of the possible independent variables are relevant. Research in education relies extensively on this method of analysis because of its convenience in cases where we cannot carry out controlled experiments with people as subjects.

There are two main forms of field studies relying on *ex post facto* techniques, which, along with survey methods (to be described next), are sometimes referred to as *descriptive research*. These are *case* and *developmental* studies. In case studies, 'clients', either as individuals or in small, well-defined groups such as the family, are examined in great detail. Background information about home, school and community is gathered, together with interviews and, in some cases, standardized test scores. The method is popular in clinical settings and social work. Developmental studies involve a detailed description of selected variables at different stages in the lives of children and adults. We may look at the same group of people at intervals in their lives; this is a *longitudinal study*. Or we may take samples at different ages covering the range with which we are concerned and test each sample on one occasion; this is a *cross-sectional* study. Developmental studies have been of great service in theories of the growth of thinking skills and vocational choice, both of which have been discussed.

In the survey technique, the results of which are now used extensively in educational policy-making at government level, the object is to collect information about readily obtainable facts from a total population or a representative sample of the population. A national census affords a well-known example of a fact-finding survey of existing conditions. Most of the data consist of 'head counting' or frequency determination. A statement of the number of boys and girls in primary education between the ages of 5 and 11 years on the first day of July 1970 would be a fact obtainable by survey techniques. Successive governments have increasingly employed survey reports such as those of the Crowther, Robbins, Plowden and Warnock Committees.[5]

Action-based research has become a popular method with those teachers anxious to try out a new method of teaching. The results of such research, most frequently based on a teacher's own class, are not generalizable, but for a particular teacher they may be of considerable help in decision-making in subsequent similar circumstances. Most teachers try out schemes of work; when these are done with the care of a research project, the outcome is action research.

LIMITATIONS OF RESEARCH IN PSYCHOLOGY OF EDUCATION

Behavioural research is still a long way from reaching the level of experimental sophistication of the natural sciences. Some believe it will never do so. Medawar (**R**),[6] in summarizing some of the problems facing scientists, put his finger on many shortcomings of 'scientific method' which apply equally well to behavioural sciences. According to him, the formulation of theories purporting to be scientific starts with, one assumes, the 'unvarnished and unembroidered' evidence of the senses. Initial observations should be simple, unbiased, unprejudiced, naïve and innocent. From evidence through the senses we should end up with simple declarations which express, in an orderly fashion, the laws of nature. The ornithologist unobtrusively watches nature in the raw without disturbing the facts as they exist. In the same dispassionate way, the behavioural scientist would like to be regarded as a 'man watcher'.

These high aims are bedevilled by many setbacks which the cautious teacher should bear in mind when studying research and its implications for teaching. Some of the questions posed in education are as large as life itself. Sociological themes sometimes have this awkward habit of depending on so many independent variables as to render controlled research impossible. The terms of reference are never as clear cut as those found in physics or chemistry. Our subject matter is cumbersome with variables; our methods are messy rather than elegant and clean; our results are tentative and rarely capable of direct application to classroom practice. Nevertheless, such small steps forward are essential if we are to put the psychology of education on a firm, reliable footing.

How unbiased can research be? The act of choosing a subject for research nearly always reflects a bias. Fashions come and go in educational research as the climate of opinion about values in education changes. With limited resources, this means that some topics have to be ignored. Selecting methods of measurement, analysis and interpretation requires decisions which often call for biased judgement. The experimenter brings to a research a lifetime of prejudices and predispositions about human nature, thus making it difficult to be objective about research design and interpretation.

In educational research there is a marked dependence on introspection. When questions of attitude or opinion are asked, the responses depend entirely on the selective memory of the person being asked. Some of our behaviour is moderated by attitudes of which we may not even be aware. The way in which the questions are posed may influence the answers given. The answers also depend on the communication skills of individuals, and this is particularly difficult with children.

Ex post facto methods necessarily lead to an emphasis on the products of our behaviour. We look at the outcome of a perceptual task or examination results and make assumptions in retrospect about what might have been taking place in the process of perceiving or studying for the examination. On the other hand, many of the teacher's problems focus on processes, assumptions about which can be used to modify and make efficient the learning behaviour of children.

THE NATURE OF EDUCATIONAL RESEARCH

Education is an applied science and as such it must draw inspiration and knowledge from theories which are serviceable. Ausubel (**R**)[7] draws attention to three ways in which we have attempted to use knowledge from research in educational decision-making. In the first, *basic science research*, the experimenter is concerned with discovering general principles as ends in themselves. In the case of education, the fundamental principles derived in psychology, sociology or philosophy would be the source of information. One problem here is that the principles are commonly discovered using controlled experimental designs which bear only a marginal, if any, similarity to the situation which exists in a classroom. The level of complexity in a classroom frequently militates against the direct application of fundamental findings using animal or controlled human experiments. Again, the researcher is often not particularly concerned to find laws or generalities which have predetermined applications. In fact, where attempts are made to take the findings and apply them directly to classroom settings, they sometimes fail because the level of generality is at a much higher point than is required in a classroom, where knowledge of individual differences is crucial. The real contribution made by basic research findings is in directing our attention to what is possible in the way of generalizations about behaviour, and in generating possible hypotheses for the direction of behaviour. For example, the Yerkes–Dodson law mentioned in Chapter 11 is an example of a basic science research finding. It shows that there is a predictable relationship between performance and drive, provided we can specify the conditions under which a task is being conducted. All manner of conclusions are possible which, from a knowledge of the law, are particularly relevant to classroom practices, but we still have some way to go in determining the details of the conditions which influence the relationship.

A second approach defined by Ausubel is the *extrapolated basic science research* in which the experimenter sets out with a specific practical problem in mind and designs an analogous basic science research from which general principles can be extracted. The original research is rarely carried out in the applied setting for which it is being used and suffers from much the same shortcomings as in applying basic research. We draw on studies from the psychology of language acquisition and apply these to the classroom. Operant conditioning, for example, can be used in language learning in the junior school (see Bijou, however[8]). The fault is in the tendency to extrapolate from basic research and apply the results to pedagogical problems without first finding out the extent to which this link is valid.

The third suggestion Ausubel calls *research at an applied level*, by which he means performing research *in situ* and in the conditions which normally pertain in schools. Action research in the classroom involves the identification and exploration of learning environments *as they exist* in terms of such variables as motivation, facilities, personal relationships, etc. Naturally, this approach presents far more difficulties because of the complex nature of the task than would be the case in classical controlled researches.

However, Ausubel believes that the pay-off for teachers would be much greater than that which exists at present.

There are the beginnings of a shift in emphasis from the study of individual differences to the study of learning environments in education.[9] Shulman[10] makes the point that 'the language of education and the behavioural sciences is in great need of a set of terms for describing environments that is as articulated, specific and functional as those already possessed for characterizing individuals'. We need to know far more about the characteristics by which we can describe educational environments and the significance of these to the processes of behaviour change and the job of teaching. To some extent, the social psychologist in education has been concerned with detecting the influence of these environmental variables on individuals, but rarely has this occurred with the classroom as the environment. It is not just the content of lessons which the teacher manipulates, but the whole background of the classroom. We need to discover how these manipulations influence performance in different environmental structures and how this might be evaluated (**R**).[11,12] The detailed scientific study of life in classrooms[13] is a growth point about which we are going to hear more. But before we get carried away with enthusiasm for the future of educational research, let us reflect on the fact that we are already standing on the ground laid down by the psychologists alluded to in this book.

SUMMARY

In this final chapter we have looked at some of the basic attitudes and problems which beset the researcher in education. Psychology is still in its infancy as a scientific enterprise and its contribution to our understanding of children as cognitive and social creatures must be viewed with cautious optimism. The teacher's role remains that of diagnostician, both in the sense in which the findings of others are treated and in the way evidence is assimilated and interpreted regarding the classroom. Psychological research has gone only so far, within the limitations discussed in the chapter, in providing generalizations about human nature. It still remains for the teacher to keep abreast of new knowledge and to devise courses of action from all the sources of evidence available.

ENQUIRY AND DISCUSSION

(a)   Read the papers by D. P. Ausubel (**R**)[7] and M. Parlett (**R**)[11] and note in particular their suggestions for alternative methods of researching classroom behaviour. What are the snags in these approaches? Why have they not been adopted before now?

(b)   Observe the psychological assumptions of teachers on school practice. Are they based on psychological theory or on teaching folklore?

(c)   Initiate a group discussion with a tutor on the applicability of educational psychology emanating from (1) basic science research; (2) extrapolated basic science research; and (3) research at an applied level. In what ways will the 'learning environments' approach take us nearer to an understanding of the teacher's role?

NOTES AND REFERENCES

1. W. R. Borg and M. D. Gall, *Educational Research: An Introduction*, Longman, New York, 1989 (5th edn); J. D. Nisbet and N. J. Entwistle, *Educational Research Methods*, University of London Press, London, 1970; L. Cohen, *Educational Research in Classrooms and Schools*, Harper and Row, London, 1976.
2. J. Dewey, *How We Think*, Heath, Boston, 1933.
3. For those who want detail, F. N. Kerlinger, *Foundations of Behavioral Research: Educational and Psychological Inquiry*, Holt, Rinehart and Winston, London, 1969, is an excellent text.
4. Another topical example of independent variables is provided by the increase in lung cancer (dependent variable) and the possibility that smoking (independent variable) is the cause. This is a very good case of *ex post facto* analysis. We cannot (ethically) manipulate the independent variable before cancer has appeared; we can only look in retrospect at the possibilities which might distinguish cancer from non-cancer sufferers. Kerlinger, mentioned in note (3), devotes a whole chapter to *ex post facto* research.
5. The Plowden Report: Children and Their Primary Schools, HMSO, London, 1967; The Crowther Report: *15 to 18*, HMSO, London, 1959; The Robbins Report: *Committee on Higher Education*, HMSO, London, 1963; The Warnock Report: *Special Educational Needs*, HMSO, London, 1978. National Curriculum, *Task Group in Assessment and Testing*, Final and Supplementary Reports, DES and Welsh Office, London, 1987.
6. (R) P. B. Medawar, 'Is the scientific paper a fraud?', *The Listener*, 1963, and *Induction and Intuition in Scientific Thought*, Methuen, London, 1969.
7. (R) D. P. Ausubel, 'The nature of educational research', *Educational Theory*, 3, 314–320 (1953).
8. S. W. Bijou, 'What psychology has to offer education – now', *J. Appl. Behav. Anal.*, 3, 65–71 (1970).
9. K. Marjoribanks, 'Social theories of education', in K. Marjoribanks (ed.), *The Foundations of Students' Learning*, Pergamon, Oxford, 1991.
10. L. S. Shulman, 'Reconstruction of educational research', *Rev. Educ. Res.*, 40, 371–396 (1970).
11. (R) M. Parlett, 'The new evaluation', *Trends in Education*, 34, 13–18 (1974).
12. W. B. Dockrell and D. Hamilton (eds), *Rethinking Educational Research*, Hodder and Stoughton, Sevenoaks, 1980.
13. P. W. Jackson, *Life in Classrooms*, Holt, Rinehart and Winston, New York, 1968. See also the references in Chapter 11: note (45) (Woods), note (54) (Bennett) and note (55) (Galton *et al.*).

FURTHER READING

W. R. Borg and and M. D. Gall, *Educational Research: An Introduction*, Longman, New York, 1989 (5th edn).

G. Brown, D. H. Cherrington and L. Cohen, *Experiments in the Social Sciences*, Harper and Row, London, 1975.

L. Cohen, *Educational Research in Classrooms and Schools*, Harper and Row, London, 1976.

L. Cohen and L. Manion, *Research Methods in Education*, Routledge, London, 1989 (3rd edn).

F. N. Kerlinger, *Foundations of Behavioral Research: Educational and Psychological Inquiry*, Holt, Rinehart and Winston, London, 1969. An advanced text for the strong in heart!

Name Index

Subject Index

Page numbers in *italics* refer to illustrations or tables.